At All Costs

The British Army on the Western Front 1916

Wolverhampton Military Studies No. 30

Edited by Spencer Jones

 Helion & Company

To my great-grandfathers:
Edward Carless, Royal Field Artillery
&
Rice Davies, 7th South Staffordshire Regiment

Helion & Company Limited
Unit 8 Amherst Business Centre
Budbrooke Road
Warwick
CV34 5WE
England
Tel. 01926 499 619
Fax 0121 711 4075
Email: info@helion.co.uk
Website: www.helion.co.uk
Twitter: @helionbooks
Visit our blog http://blog.helion.co.uk/

Published by Helion & Company 2018
Designed and typeset by Mach 3 Solutions (www.mach3solutions.co.uk)
Cover designed by Paul Hewitt, Battlefield Design (www.battlefield-design.co.uk)
Printed by Gutenberg Press Ltd, Tarxien, Malta

Text © Spencer Jones and contributors 2018
Images open sources unless otherwise credited
Maps drawn by and © Barbara Taylor 2018

Every reasonable effort has been made to trace copyright holders and to obtain their permission for the use of copyright material. The author and publisher apologize for any errors or omissions in this work, and would be grateful if notified of any corrections that should be incorporated in future reprints or editions of this book.

ISBN 978-1-912174-88-1

British Library Cataloguing-in-Publication Data
A catalogue record for this book is available from the British Library.

All rights reserved. No part of this publication may be reproduced, stored in a retrieval system, or transmitted, in any form, or by any means, electronic, mechanical, photocopying, recording or otherwise, without the express written consent of Helion & Company Limited.

For details of other military history titles published by Helion & Company Limited contact the above address, or visit our website: http://www.helion.co.uk.

We always welcome receipt of book proposals from prospective authors.

Contents

List of Illustrations		v
List of Maps		ix
Abbreviations		x
Notes on Contributors		xii
Series Editor's Preface		xvii
Foreword by Professor Peter Simkins		xix
Acknowledgements		xxiii
Introduction: The Endless Battle		xxv
1	The Battle of the Somme and British War Plans 1916 *Stephen Badsey*	33
2	The Puppetmaster: Sir William Robertson as CIGS in 1916 *John Spencer*	53
3	Douglas Haig and the Somme *Andrew Wiest*	71
4	British Intelligence and the Battle of Verdun *Jim Beach*	93
5	The Changing Nature of Supply: Transportation in the BEF during the Battle of the Somme *Christopher Phillips*	117
6	Lessons Unlearned: The Somme Preparatory Bombardment, 24 June-1 July 1916 *Bill MacCormick*	139
7	"The Battle in Miniature": The BEF and the Art of Trench Raiding 1916 *John Pratt*	164
8	"I shall hope to try an officer and at least one corporal for cowardice": The German Trench Raid at La Boisselle, 11 April 1916 and the British Response *Michael LoCicero*	194

9	Henry Horne as Corps Commander on the Somme *Simon Innes-Robbins*	252
10	XIII Corps and the Attack at Montauban, 1 July 1916 *Spencer Jones*	270
11	French XX Corps and Preparations for the Somme Offensive *Tim Gale*	292
12	Learning from Defeat: 32nd Division and 1 July 1916 *Stuart Mitchell*	324
13	Cooperation on the Somme: The Application of Firepower on Pozières Ridge *Meleah Hampton*	354
14	Lessons and Legacy: Notes on 1st Canadian Division Attack, Regina Trench, 8 October 1916 *Kenneth Radley*	370
15	Early Tank Tactical Doctrine and Training *Philip Ventham*	394
16	"A Ragged Business": Officer Training Corps, Public Schools and the Recruitment of the Junior Officers Corps of 1916 *Timothy Halstead*	414
17	Infantry Battalion Command on the Somme 1 July-18 November 1916 *Peter Hodgkinson*	430
18	Muddy grave? The German army at the end of 1916 *Tony Cowan*	451
19	Ripples of the Somme: Commemorating and Remembering the Battle, 1919-2016 *Mark Connelly*	474
20	The Somme: War Memoirs and Personal Memories *Brian Bond*	497
Index		510

List of Illustrations

German cartoon lampooning Allied strategic decision-making during early 1916: "They each keep their own wise counsel, but no one is asking for an appointment [to hear it]!" (*Kladderadatsch*, 5 March 1916)	34
Prime Minister Herbert Asquith (centre) disembarks at Queenstown Quay, Ireland to assess the situation in the immediate aftermath of the Easter Rising, 12 May 1916.	43
Field Marshal Lord Kitchener arrives at an Allied conference, Paris 27 March 1916. (Private collection)	47
General Sir William Robertson.	54
Robertson (fourth from left) inspects French troops at Blaincourt with King George V, Edward Prince of Wales and General Joseph Joffre, 26 October 1915. (Private collection)	61
Haig and Joffre at Chantilly, 23 December 1915.	75
Dismissive German cartoon commentary on the introduction of the tank: Hannibal and Haig (A Historical Parallel): I. Hannibal once succeeded when he sent the elephants in! II. Thus Haig, that renowned warrior, built his "Tank" for this purpose. III. Bravely the beast stormed to the front – until it was no longer able to continue. IV. Thus the meaning of this tale, "Haig, you are no Hannibal!" Furthermore, "The elephant had more wisdom than the tank!" (*Kladderadatsch*, 5 November 1916)	86
Detail from Alan d'Egville, *Our Agents*, 1917. (Military Intelligence Museum)	96
German rail movements as reported by agents in GHQ intelligence summary, 16 February 1916 (17N 308, SHD(T))	103
German concentration at Verdun as depicted in a GHQ intelligence summary, 22 February 1916. (17N 308, SHD(T))	106
Detail from Alan d'Egville, GHQ Intelligence Christmas card, 1916. (Military Intelligence Museum)	115
British horse transport traversing the devastated Somme battlefield, autumn 1916. (Private collection)	123
British and French troops labour to free a stalled locomotive, Maricourt September 1916.	125
Sir Eric Geddes.	129
British 6-inch gun.	141

British 8-inch howitzers of 135th Siege Battery at La Houssoye on the Somme, 1916.	141
French *Canon de 75 Mle 1897* battery.	147
French *Canon de 155 Long mle 1877* battery.	147
British 18-pdr field gun. (Private collection)	149
British 4.5-inch howitzer.	149
Major-General J.F.N. Birch. (John Bourne)	161
Armed with rifles, revolvers and Mills bombs, a British raiding party poses during training, summer 1916.	170
17th Highland Light Infantry trench raid on the night of 22/23 April 1916 as reported by the battalion's newspaper. This article demonstrates how raiding could bolster a battalion's morale. (Royal Highland Fusiliers Museum)	173
Lurid artist's impression of a trench club wielded with effect during a raid.	177
Second Lieutenant E.F. Baxter VC.	188
Well-known photograph of 1/8th King's Liverpool Regiment raiders following the enterprise launched on the night of 17/18 April 1916. Second Lieutenant E.F. Baxter was the sole fatality.	189
Private A.H. Procter VC.	191
Lieutenant-General Sir William Pulteney, GOC III Corps (National Portrait Gallery)	197
Major-General Havelock Hudson, GOC 8th Division 1915-16.	197
Trench raid spoils: German officers and men pose with captured British booty spring 1916. Regiment unknown, but more than likely a unit of *26th Reserve Division*. (Private collection)	204
German M1915 *Gummimaske*.	209
Brigadier-General James Pollard, GOC 25th Brigade 1916-17. (John Bourne)	215
British PH (phenate-hexamine) gas helmet.	221
Photograph purported to be 1st Royal Irish Rifles prisoners, 11 April 1916. Attired in the first pattern Australian tunic, this image appears to have been taken during the following summer when I Anzac Corps was engaged at Pozières and Mouquet Farm. (Greiner & Vulpius, *Reserve-Infanterie-Regiment Nr. 110 im Weltkrieg 1914-1918*)	229
2nd Lieutenant Percival Maxwell Harte-Maxwell, the only 1st Royal Irish Rifles officer fatality sustained during the 11 April 1916 trench raid. (Hennessey (ed.), *The Great War 1914-1918: Bank of Ireland Staff Service Record*)	239
La Boisselle, *Schwaben-Höhe* and vicinity from the air, 21 April 1916. (Landesarchiv, Baden-Württemberg)	241
Approximate 11 April 1916 trench raid jumping-off site, Bécourt Wood in the left distance. (Author)	250
Lieutenant-General Sir Henry Horne.	254
Major-General Herbert Watts.	263
Major-General Ivor Philipps.	264
Major-General Thomas Pilcher.	266

Lieutenant-General Walter Congreve. (Author)	275
General Sir Henry Rawlinson.	277
Major-General Ivor Maxse.	279
Major-General John Shea. (Author)	280
General Maurice Balfourier (centre).	285
A "monstrous heap of rubble": Montauban after capture.	287
Eyewitness artist's depiction of the attack on Montauban. (*Illustrated London News*, 22 July 1916)	289
General Émile Fayolle.	297
Mle 1877-1916 155L Gun unlimbered. Captain Leroy, *Cours de l'artillerie – Historique et Organisation de l'Artillerie* (École Militaire de l'Artillerie, 1922)	300
XX Corps: *Groupement Anglade* heavy artillery emplacements, June 1916. (22N1364)	306
M. 220 Heavy Mortar. This weapon could be mounted on a wooden or metal platform. (Captain Leroy, *Cours de l'artillerie – Historique et Organisation de l'Artillerie* (École Militaire de l'Artillerie, 1922)	309
C–270 de Côte coastal heavy mortar. (Captain Leroy, *Cours de l'artillerie – Historique et Organisation de l'Artillerie* (École Militaire de l'Artillerie, 1922)	309
XX Corps bombardment zones 4-12 (Hardecourt to Maurepas). Artillery map abstract, 17 June 1916. (22N1364)	313
XX Corps bombardment zones 13-15 (Curlu to Frise). Artillery map abstract, 17 June 1916. (22N1364)	313
British 2-inch Medium Trench Mortar. (Private collection)	331
Major-General W.H. Rycroft. (John Bourne)	335
Leipzig Salient from the air, 1 June 1916.	341
Contemporary diagrammatic illustration depicting German barbed wire entanglement arrangements, observation posts and mined dugouts of the kind constructed by the Thiepval defenders during the period 1914-16.	343
Ruins of Thiepval Château, July 1916. (Anon., *Die 26. Reserve Division 1914-1918*)	347
Thiepval Château Park, July 1916. (Anon., *Die 26. Reserve Division 1914-1918*)	347
General Sir Hubert Gough.	355
Lieutenant-General Sir William Birdwood.	357
Australian 18-pdr field gun in action, July 1916.	363
Pozières sector bombardment, August 1916.	364
Lieutenant-General Sir Julian Byng.	371
Canadian dead near Courcelette, September 1916.	373
Major-General Arthur Currie.	375
Brigadier-General Garnett Hughes.	377
Brigadier-General George Tuxford.	382
Regina Trench from the air, 21 October 1916. (Private collection)	390
Lieutenant-Colonel Ernst Swinton.	396
Albert Stern.	399
"Mother" prototype tank undergoing trials.	400

HSMGC officer and NCO in 1916 issue leather tank helmet.	407
Mark I 'Female' tank, September 1916. This photograph provides a clear impression of its camouflage paint scheme.	412
Dulwich College OTC camp inspection 1913.	418
Cranleigh School OTC summer camp postcard 1914.	418
OTC cadets, Hare Hall Camp, Romford, Essex 1915.	422
Dulwich College OTC 1915.	422
Lieutenant-Colonel Godfrey Davenport Goodman.	435
Lieutenant-Colonel Francis Aylmer Maxwell VC.	442
Lieutenant-Colonel Percy Wilfrid Machell.	449
Memorial card commemorating one of 1.2 million German casualties sustained during 1916. (Private collection)	455
Crown Prince Rupprecht of Bavaria.	458
General Fritz von Below.	461
Shattered German trench near Combles. (Private collection)	465
British prisoners with armed escort, August 1916. (Private collection)	468
Men of the *185th Infanterie Regiment*, *208th Division*, November 1916. This wartime-raised unit entered the line north of the Ancre on the 18th of that month. (Private collection)	469
Ruins of La Boisselle, 1919.	478
Newfoundland Memorial dedication, June 1925.	482
Locally-produced Thiepval Memorial to the Missing postcard c. 1930.	484
Max Plowman.	488
David Jones.	491
The Somme: From Defeat to Victory (2006) production still. (Taff Gillingham)	495
MA group at the Welsh Dragon Memorial, Mametz Wood, 1 November 1996. Rear row: Brian Bond, Simon Doughty, Mark Williams. Front row: Sam Clark, Ryan Walsh and Alan Jeffreys. Photograph taken by Michael Piercy. (Author)	501
MA group at the Burma Star café, Poziéres, 28 February 1990. John Lee is second from the left and Brian Bond third from the left respectively; Peter Robinson is third from the right. Standing: Café proprietor Madame Brihier. Notebooks on table; shell cases and rum jar in window. (Author)	504

List of Figures

1	Total German Army Wastage, January-December 1916.	456
2	Total German Army Wastage by front, January-December 1916.	472

List of Maps

In colour plate section

1	Western Front 1916.	ii
2	German trench raid at La Boisselle, 11 April 1916.	iii
3	Plan and reality, 1 July 1916.	iv
4	Battle of the Somme, July to November 1916.	v
5	XV Corps, 1 July 1916.	vi
6	XIII Corps, 1 July 1916.	vii
7	French XX Corps, 1 July 1916.	viii
8	Thiepval, 1 July 1916.	ix
9	Bazentin Ridge, 14 July 1916.	x
10	Pozières and vicinity, 23 July-4 September 1916.	xi
11	Mouquet Farm and vicinity.	xii
12	The Battle of Flers-Courcelette, 15-22 September 1916.	xiii
13	Thiepval Ridge, 26-30 September 1916.	xiv
14	Regina Trench, 8 October 1916.	xv
15	Battle of the Ancre, 13-19 November 1916.	xvi

Abbreviations

AA	Assistant Adjutant
ADC	Aide de Camp
AG	Adjutant General
AQMG	Assistant Quarter-Master General
BEF	British Expeditionary Force
BM	Brigade Major
CAS	Chief of the Air Staff
CB	Companion of the Order of the Bath
CFS	Central Flying School
CID	Committee of Imperial Defence
CIGS	Chief of the Imperial General Staff
CinC	Commander in Chief
CO	Commanding Officer
CoS	Chief of Staff
CRA	Commander, Royal Artillery
CRE	Commander, Royal Engineers
DAAG	Deputy-Assistant Adjutant General
DGMA	Director General of Military Aeronautics
DMA	Director of Military Aeronautics
DMO	Director of Military Operations
DMT	Director of Military Training
DQMG	Deputy Quartermaster General
DSO	Distinguished Service Order
EEF	Egyptian Expeditionary Force
GHQ	General Headquarters
GOC	General Officer Commanding
GQG	Grand Quartier Général (General Headquarters French Army)
GS	General Staff
GSO	General Staff Officer [numerical designation indicates grade, e.g. GSO1]
IGC	Inspector General of Communications
IGS	Imperial General Staff
IWGC	Imperial War Graves Commission

IWT	Inland Water Transport
KCMG	Knight Commander of the Order of St. Michael & St. George
LoC	Line of Communication MGGS Major-General General Staff
MW	Military Wing (of Royal Flying Corps)
NER	North-Eastern Railway
NCO	Non Commissioned Officer
OH	(British) Official History
QF	Quick Firing (Artillery gun)
QMG	Quarter-Master General
RA	Royal Artillery
RAMC	Royal Army Medical Corps
RE	Royal Engineers
RFA	Royal Field Artillery
RFC	Royal Flying Corps
RGA	Royal Garrison Artillery
RHA	Royal Horse Artillery
TF	Territorial Force
VC	Victoria Cross
WO	War Office

Notes on Contributors

Professor Stephen Badsey PhD MA (Cantab.) is Professor of Conflict Studies and Co-Director of the First World War Research Group at the University of Wolverhampton UK, and a Fellow of the Royal Historical Society. An internationally recognised authority n military history and military-media issues, he has written and edited more than 25 books and 80 articles, and his writings have been translated into seven languages. He appears and advises frequently for television and other media, and he is also the series editor of the *Wolverhampton Military Studies Series* for Helion publishers.

Dr Jim Beach is Senior Lecturer in Twentieth Century History at the University of Northampton. His research focuses upon British military intelligence during the First World War. He is the author of *Haig's Intelligence: GHQ and the German Army, 1916-1918* (2013).

Professor Brian Bond is a professor emeritus at King's College, London. In an academic career which spans more than fifty years he has published many books and articles on the First World War. Key works include *Liddell Hart: A Study of His Military Thought* (1977); *Look to Your Front: Studies in the First World War* (1999); *The Unquiet Western Front: Britain's Role in Literature and History* (2002) and *Survivors of a Kind: Memoirs of the Western Front* (2008). His most recent work is *Britain's Two World Wars Against Germany: Myth, Memory and the Distortions of Hindsight* (2014).

Professor Mark Connelly is Professor of Modern British History at the University of Kent. His main research interests are on the memory of war, the image of the armed forces in popular culture and aspects of operational military history. His publications include *Steady the Buffs! A Regiment, a Region and the Great War* (2006); *Celluloid War Memorials: British Instructional Films Company and the Memory of the First World War* (2015) and, with Ian Beckett & Timothy Bowman, *The British Army and the First World War* (2017).

Dr Tony Cowan is a retired British diplomat and was awarded his PhD by King's College London. His thesis, 'Genius for War? German Operational Command on the Western Front in Early 1917' analyses German higher-level command in the First

World War through a case study covering the Entente offensive of spring 1917. Tony is a member of the British Commission for Military History and was one of the historians supporting the British Army's major staff ride to the Somme in 2016. He is currently editing a translation of the German official monograph for the Battle of Amiens.

Dr Tim Gale was awarded his PhD by the Department of War Studies, King's College London for his work on French tank development and operations in the First World War and he is now one of the leading experts on this aspect of armoured warfare. His book *The French Army's Tank Force and the Development of Armoured Warfare in the Great War* (Ashgate/Routledge) was published in 2013 and was followed by *French Tanks in the Great War* (2016). He is currently researching books on the Battle of Cambrai and the career of General Charles Mangin.

Timothy Halstead was educated at Uppingham and for studied for an MA in British First World War Studies at the University of Birmingham. His MA dissertation examined public school ethos in the Great War using Uppingham as a case study. He has published on Uppingham in *War and Society* and on the Junior OTC before the Great War in the *British Journal of Military* History. His most recent publication is A *School in Arms: Uppingham and the Great War* (2017). He is a member of the British Commission of Military History and Treasurer of the Army Records Society.

Dr Meleah Hampton is an historian in the Military History Section of the Australian War Memorial. She is the author of *Attack on the Somme: 1st Anzac Corps and the Battle of Pozières Ridge 1916* (Helion & Co, 2016) and is a graduate of the University of Adelaide. Her primary interest is in the operational conduct of the First World War on the Western Front. She is a member of the editorial staff of the Australian War Memorial's magazine, *Wartime*, and continues to research and write biographies for the Memorial's Last Post Ceremony project.

Dr Peter Hodgkinson trained as a clinical psychologist. He is the author of *Coping with Catastrophe: A Handbook of Post-Disaster Psychosocial Aftercare* (1998). He obtained an MA in British First World War Studies and his PhD in the Department of War Studies, Birmingham University. His military history volumes include: *British Battalion Commanders in the First World War* (2015); *Glum Heroes: Hardship, Fear and Death – Resilience and Coping in the British Army on the Western Front 1914-1918* (2016) and *The Battle of the Selle: Fourth Army Operations on the Western Front 9-24 October 1918* (2017).

Dr Simon Innes-Robbins is Senior Curator, Department of Narrative and Content, at the Imperial War Museum. He is the author of *British Generalship on the Western Front, 1914-18: Defeat Into Victory* (runner-up, 2004 Templer Medal), *The First World War Letters of General Lord Horne* (2009), and *British Generalship during the Great War:*

The Military Career of Sir Henry Horne 1861-1929 (2010) and has contributed chapters to Ian Beckett & Steven J. Corvi (eds.) *Haig's Generals* (2006); Spencer Jones (ed.), *Stemming the Tide: Officers and Leadership in the British Expeditionary Force 1914* (2013) and Spencer Jones (ed.), *Courage Without Glory: The British Army on the Western Front 1915*. His next volume is *British Army Training on the Western Front 1914-1918*.

Dr Spencer Jones is Senior Lecturer in Armed Forces and War Studies at the University of Wolverhampton and serves as the Regimental Historian for the Royal Regiment of Artillery. His key works include *From Boer War to World War: Tactical Reform of the British Army 1902-1914* (2012) *Stemming the Tide: Officers and Leadership in the British Expeditionary Force 1914*, which was runner-up for the 2013 Templer Medal and *Courage without Glory: The British Army on the Western Front 1915*.

Dr Michael LoCicero earned his PhD from the University of Birmingham in 2011 and is a Helion & Company commissioning editor and independent scholar. His publications include a contributory chapter on Brigadier-General Edward Bulfin in the highly regarded Spencer Jones (ed.), *Stemming the Tide: Officers and Leadership in the British Expeditionary Force 1914*; *A Moonlight Massacre: The Night Operation on the Passchendaele Ridge, 2 December 1917* (2014), which was nominated for the Templer Medal; a chapter chronicling the forgotten battle of International Trench in Spencer Jones (ed.), *Courage Without Glory: The British Army on the Western Front 1915*; the co-edited *We Are All Flourishing: The Letters and Diary of Captain Walter J.J. Coats 1914-1919* (2016) and the forthcoming co-edited *Gallipoli: New Perspectives on the Mediterranean Expeditionary Force, 1915-16* (Helion 2018).

Bill MacCormick was born in 1951 and educated at Dulwich College. He spent the 1970s playing bass in various progressive rock bands before moving into politics in the 1980s. He was the London Agent for the Liberal Party then Elections Co-ordinator of the Liberal Democrats. In the 1990s, he conducted their market research before ill-health brought about early retirement. Under the pen name Alan MacDonald he has written three books on the Battle of the Somme: *Pro Patria Mori*: *A Lack of Offensive Spirit?* (2008) and *Z Day: The VIII Corps at Beaumont Hamel* (2014). He is currently working on a book on the planning of the Battle of the Somme.

Dr Stuart Mitchell is Senior Lecturer in War Studies at the Royal Military Academy Sandhurst where he specialises in operational performance, learning and leadership in the British Army. He is an editor of the *British Journal of Military History* and a member of the British Commission for Military History. He has published on a variety of topics including the battle of the Somme, the campaign in German East Africa and learning in the British military since the Napoleonic Wars.

Dr Christopher Phillips was awarded a PhD by the University of Leeds in 2015. His thesis, entitled 'Managing Armageddon: the science of transportation and the

British Expeditionary Force, 1900-1918', won the Association of Business Historians' Donald Coleman Prize in May 2016. Christopher is currently writing a monograph, *Britain's Transport Experts and the First World War*, which will be published by the Institute for Historical Research/Royal Historical Society. He is also the co-lead of the Arts and Humanities Research Council-funded First World War Network, an international hub linking postgraduate and early career researchers with an interest in all aspects of the conflict.

John Pratt completed the MA in British First World War Studies at Birmingham University in 2013 and an MSc in Battlespace Technology at Cranfield University in 2014. In May 2014, he retired from the British Army after a 34-year military career in the Royal Electrical and Mechanical Engineers and is now employed as a systems engineer. His research focuses on the Battle of the Somme and armoured warfare. He is also a keen battlefield guide and accredited member of the International Guild of Battlefield Guides, having been awarded Badge Number 68 by Professor Gary Sheffield in 2014.

Lieutenant Colonel (Retired) **Kenneth Radley** is a former officer of The Queen's Own Rifles of Canada. He holds a doctorate in Canadian History from Carleton University, Ottawa, and is a graduate of the Canadian Forces Command and Staff College, Toronto. He is the author of *Rebel Watchdog: The Confederate States Army Provost Guard* (1989) and paperback edition 1997), *We Lead Others Follow: First Canadian Division 1914-1918* (2006) and *Get Tough, Stay Tough: Shaping the Canadian Corps, 1914-1918* (2014) which was nominated for the Templer Medal. He is also a contributor to the *Encyclopedia of the Confederacy* (1993). At present, he is working on another unexplored aspect of the Canadian Army's effort and accomplishments during the Great War.

Dr John Spencer spent 35 years as a journalist before concentrating on the study of military history. He has an MA in Great War Studies from the University of Birmingham and completed his doctorate, on the wartime career of Field Marshal Sir Henry Wilson, at the University of Wolverhampton. He contributed chapters on 'Wully' Robertson to Spencer Jones (ed.), *Stemming the Tide: Officers and Leadership in the British Expeditionary Force 1914* and Spencer Jones (ed.), *Courage without Glory: The British Army on the Western Front 1915*.

Philip Ventham served as both a Regular and Territorial Army officer in the Royal Artillery and attended the Armour Course at the Armour Centre at Bovington. In retirement he completed the MA course in First World War studies at Birmingham University under Dr Spencer Jones and Professor Gary Sheffield. He has recently completed a MPhil thesis on the operational doctrine and training of the First World War Tank Corps. His previous published work was on the mechanisation of the Royal Artillery between the wars. He has an interest in all aspects of the Great War and regularly attends and conducts battlefield tours. He lives in Dorset within sight and sound of the Tank Corps' successors.

Dr Andrew Wiest is University Distinguished Professor of History and the Founding Director of the Dale Center for the Study of War and Society at the University of Southern Mississippi history department. He has written widely on the First World War and Vietnam War. His publications include *Passchendaele and the Royal Navy* (1995); *Haig: The Evolution of a Commander* (2005); *Vietnam's Forgotten Army: Heroism and Betrayal in the ARVN* (2009) and *The Boys of '67: Charlie Company's War in Vietnam* (2012).

The Wolverhampton Military Studies Series
Series Editor's Preface

As series editor, it is my great pleasure to introduce the *Wolverhampton Military Studies Series* to you. Our intention is that in this series of books you will find military history that is new and innovative, and academically rigorous with a strong basis in fact and in analytical research, but also is the kind of military history that is for all readers, whatever their particular interests, or their level of interest in the subject. To paraphrase an old aphorism: a military history book is not less important just because it is popular, and it is not more scholarly just because it is dull. With every one of our publications we want to bring you the kind of military history that you will want to read simply because it is a good and well-written book, as well as bringing new light, new perspectives, and new factual evidence to its subject.

In devising the *Wolverhampton Military Studies Series*, we gave much thought to the series title: this is a *military* series. We take the view that history is everything except the things that have not happened yet, and even then a good book about the military aspects of the future would find its way into this series. We are not bound to any particular time period or cut-off date. Writing military history often divides quite sharply into eras, from the modern through the early modern to the mediaeval and ancient; and into regions or continents, with a division between western military history and the military history of other countries and cultures being particularly marked. Inevitably, we have had to start somewhere, and the first books of the series deal with British military topics and events of the twentieth century and later nineteenth century. But this series is open to any book that challenges received and accepted ideas about any aspect of military history, and does so in a way that encourages its readers to enjoy the discovery.

In the same way, this series is not limited to being about wars, or about grand strategy, or wider defence matters, or the sociology of armed forces as institutions, or civilian society and culture at war. None of these are specifically excluded, and in some cases they play an important part in the books that comprise our series. But there are already many books in existence, some of them of the highest scholarly standards, which cater to these particular approaches. The main theme of the *Wolverhampton Military Studies Series* is the military aspects of wars, the preparation for wars or their prevention, and their aftermath. This includes some books whose main theme is the technical details of how armed forces have worked, some books on wars and battles, and some books that re-examine the evidence about the existing stories, to show in a different light what everyone thought they already knew and understood.

As series editor, together with my fellow editorial board members, and our publisher Duncan Rogers of Helion, I have found that we have known immediately and almost by instinct the kind of books that fit within this series. They are very much the kind of well-written and challenging books that my students at the University of Wolverhampton would want to read. They are books which enhance knowledge, and offer new perspectives. Also, they are books for anyone with an interest in military history and events, from expert scholars to occasional readers. One of the great benefits of the study of military history is that it includes a large and often committed section of the wider population, who want to read the best military history that they can find; our aim for this series is to provide it.

Stephen Badsey
University of Wolverhampton

Foreword

As the Great War continued to widen in 1916, momentous events were taking place in many different areas of the world – on land, at sea and in the air – often far beyond the relatively narrow confines of the British zone of operations in France and Belgium. During the year, forces from Britain and the Empire were on active service in Salonika, Mesopotamia, Egypt and German East Africa. On the Eastern Front, in June, Russia launched the Brusilov offensive which, although initially successful, was finally halted in September and called off in October. Romania entered the war against the Central Powers on 27 August only to suffer punishing reverses leading to the fall of Bucharest on 6 December. Italy was the scene of the ongoing see-saw struggle on the Isonzo as well as heavy fighting on the Trentino front. In the Middle East, Sherif Hussein, with British support, initiated the Arab revolt on 5 June, declaring the Hejaz independent of Ottoman rule. At sea, the British Grand Fleet and the German High Seas Fleet at last met in a massive and long-awaited naval action at Jutland on 31 May-1 June. On the Western Front itself, the German and French armies were locked in a titanic battle of attrition at Verdun from February to December. Even at home in Britain civilians, where conscription was introduced in January and extended in May, civilians were not immune from danger. The Easter Rising in Dublin posed a serious internal threat which, though quickly suppressed, had important longer-term implications, and bombing raids by German airships – mainly on London, East Anglia and the Home Counties- killed hundreds.

All these events notwithstanding, the reality was that, from mid-June, the attention of the British people was primarily focused on the struggle on the Somme. This was hardly surprising, given that, for Britain, this was a battle on an unprecedented scale and was being fought by the nation's first-ever mass citizen army. In total, 44 British infantry divisions were involved in the battle at various times from 1 July onwards, along with the New Zealand Division, all four Canadian divisions and three Australian divisions. Twenty-five, or more than half, of the British formations were Kitchener 'New Army' divisions; the 63rd (Royal Naval) Division also fought on the Somme ; and a further nine of the British divisions involved were drawn from the Territorial Force. The remaining nine were Regular divisions. Most of the constituent infantry battalions of these divisions had been locally-raised and therefore had close ties with particular cities, towns, recruiting districts or social and occupational groups at home. The BEF's losses too were on a hitherto unprecedented scale and were numerically the highest it incurred in any single offensive or defensive campaign during the war. By the end of the Somme battle in November 1916, Britain and the Dominions had suffered a staggering total of 419,654 casualties. These figures, in turn, represented a daily casualty rate on the Somme of 2,953 officers and men, which meant that the BEF, with its Dominion contingents, lost the equivalent of three infantry battalions every twenty-four hours. Such attrition necessitated the constant reinforcement, regeneration and reorganisation of units. Moreover, because the BEF of 1916 retained a highly-localised character, the impact of the above casualties on individual communities at home was, at times, especially severe. If one also considers the large numbers of men and women working in the munitions industry to satisfy the gargantuan appetite of the guns, it can be claimed that most families in Britain were affected, in one way or another, by the fighting in Picardy. This was, in essence, the *core experience* of the British nation in the First World War.

The suffering, sacrifice and human tragedies which coloured this whole experience on the Somme in 1916 left a deep, raw and persistent scar on the nation's psyche and have contributed to a somewhat bleak and critical view of the battle. Our collective folk memory and popular perceptions of it remain, to this day, largely dominated, at a superficial level, by an amalgam of ill-digested facts, half-truths and media clichés, encompassing the war poets, Pals battalions on 1 July, doomed youth, the death of innocence, the shattering of Edwardian illusions, 'butchers and bunglers', 'lions led by donkeys' and *Blackadder*. Indeed, such perceptions of the war in general and the Somme in particular have proved remarkably stubborn and difficult to dispel or shift.

Over the last two or three decades, however, a growing number of 'revisionist' historians (Including myself) have, as a result of detailed and dedicated archival research, revealed and described a distinct process of learning, improvement and 'reskilling' in the BEF which gathered pace on the Somme in 1916 and culminated in the successful all-arms battles of August-November 1918. Various elements of this process have been clearly identified. For example, parties of British and Dominion officers visited Chalons and Verdun in November 1916 and January 1917 to learn from current French army practice which, in some key respects, was more advanced than that of the BEF. The January 1917 party included various influential senior officers such as Major-General J.F.N. 'Curly' Birch (Haig' chief artillery advisor at GHQ), Herbert Uniacke (MGRA, Fifth Army), Major-General Cyril Deverell (GOC 3rd Division) and Major-General Arthur Currie (GOC 1st Canadian Division, together with promising junior officers such as Major Alan Brooke. The presence of men like Deverell, Currie and Brooke suggests a degree of 'talent spotting' by GHQ and Haig's Army Commanders. Earlier, in November 1916, the Chalons party had included Brigadier-General Arthur Solly-Flood, who had worked under Haig on the preparation of *Field Service Regulations* and would soon be appointed Director-General of Training at GHQ. There is strong evidence that, having observed what the French had done in this area, Solly-Flood recommended and oversaw crucial changes in the structure of the BEF's infantry platoons from four rifle sections to specialist rifle, bombing, Lewis gun and rifle grenade sections. This facilitated more flexible small-unit tactics than hitherto, with the platoon now becoming a miniature all-arms team , capable of providing its own integral fire support and of maintaining the impetus of an advance for longer periods. Solly-Flood also played an important role in the associated attempt to standardise and co-ordinate training based on the new tactical principles, to increase the number of schools of instruction at all levels of the BEF, and to disseminate these operational and tactical reforms through the issue of pamphlets such as *SS143: Instructions for the Training of Platoons for Offensive Action* and *SS144: The Normal Formation for the Attack*. In addition, it seems likely that the Verdun visit was linked to improvements in the BEF's counter-battery organisation and the publication of the pamphlet *SS139/3: Counter-Battery Fire*.

These were not the only measures and reforms instituted in and by the BEF during and immediately after the Somme battle. The creeping barrage had become standard and was being more successfully applied ; the introduction of the 106 fuse helped the artillery to achieve more effective wire-cutting ; better flash-spotting and sound-ranging underpinned the improvements in counter-battery fire ; overhead machine-gun barrages were now more common ; and the creation, in late 1916, of Army Field Artillery (AFA) brigades provided a flexible artillery reserve which could reinforce divisional gunners when required and also reduce the volume of calls on the latter to help other formations, thus giving them more rest between actions. In a different sphere, the appointment of the civilian railway expert, Sir Eric Geddes, as Director-General of Transportation in the autumn of 1916, led to the rationalisation and streamlining of the BEF's transport and supply system and eventually to a vast improvement in the BEF's logistical support. In view of the extent of these changes, it is surely beyond reasonable doubt that various aspects of the BEF's command, organisation, training and tactics showed marked progress during or as a direct result of, the Somme. In spite of its costly and painful failures in 1916, the measures outlined above scarcely indicate that the BEF was totally in the grip of command paralysis, intellectual stagnation or stifling tradition.

Almost inevitably, this interpretation has been challenged in recent years by a number of able historians who might loosely be described as 'counter-revisionists'. Some scholars have tended to stress the BEF's shortcomings and failures as well as its achievements, rightly pointing out that the process of improvement was far from uniform, was subject to periodic setbacks and, with these ups and downs, often resembled a roller-coaster rather than appearing as a smooth learning curve. Indeed, a few of the contributors to this impressive collection of essays hold a somewhat negative view of the BEF's performance on the Somme, comparing it unfavourably, in several respects, to that of the French and German armies. Whatever one's own stance may be, this is a sign of healthy, lively and well- informed debate – itself a reflection of substantial, and growing, scholarly research in this field. Equally, one should possibly beware of taking the 'counter-revisionist' argument too far. What its advocates sometimes neglect to acknowledge sufficiently is the fact that the BEF of 1916, unlike its French and German counterparts, had been created virtually from scratch, making its achievements all the more noteworthy. In this situation, growing pains were only to be expected. Similarly, one might remark that it was the Germans, not the British, who felt it necessary to fall back to the Hindenburg Line and to adopt the ultimately suicidal policy of unrestricted submarine warfare in 1917. And it was the French army, not the BEF, which suffered a wave of mutinies the same year.

This excellent collection of essays by distinguished scholars from Britain and the Commonwealth has been splendidly edited – like its predecessors in this series – by Dr Spencer Jones, one of the very best and brightest young historians of the British army in the early twentieth century. Both collectively and individually, these essays demonstrate that Great War scholarship rests on increasingly secure foundations and is manifesting ever-greater depth and width. It is hugely encouraging to note that several of the contributors to this volumes in this series are graduates of the MA courses in British First World War studies at the Universities of Birmingham and Wolverhampton – programmes which I am proud to have helped to teach in some small way since 2005. Some of these graduates, indeed, have gone on to produce impressive doctoral theses and to publish the fruits of their research.

Even so, it has to be admitted that, for all the admirable progress in Great War studies at an academic level, deep-rooted public and media perceptions of the conflict remain deeply entrenched. To counter such views, perhaps it would be wise for the scholarly community to settle in for a long battle of attrition, and to adopt a policy of 'bite and hold' or a step-by-step approach rather than strive for an early breakthrough. So, to borrow a rallying-cry from Ferdinand Foch; *'Tout le monde à la bataille'*!

Professor Peter Simkins
University of Wolverhampton

Acknowledgements

Following on from *Stemming the Tide: Officers and Leadership in the British Expeditionary Force 1914* and *Courage Without Glory: The British Army on the Western Front 1915*, the current volume is the third in a series that is intended to cover the British Army's experiences for each year of the war on the Western Front. Reflecting the immense historical importance of 1916, this volume is the largest yet. Positive reader feedback on *Stemming the Tide* and *Courage Without Glory* has been inspiring but has also set very high standards for the current work. I trust that this edition meets expectations.

As with previous editions, the first and foremost acknowledgement must always go to the contributing authors. Their excellent scholarship is the cornerstone of every book in this series. The contributors for *At All Costs* were especially diligent and, without exception, a pleasure to work with. I also owe a debt to Duncan Rogers, owner of Helion & Co., for his unstinting support for this book and the series and to Michael LoCicero for his editing support and assistance in acquiring many of the images in this volume. Special thanks are due to Barbara Taylor for providing yet another series of excellent maps.

The development of this book was greatly aided by my participation on the British Army Somme 16 Staff Ride in September 2016. Touring the ground in the company of eminent academics and serving soldiers produced sparks of imagination and furthered my understanding of the battle.

Many individuals have contributed to the book through sharing their knowledge and research. I am particularly grateful to Rodney Atwood (who kindly shared the fruits of his as then unpublished research on the career of Henry Rawlinson), Bob Foley, James Cook, John Bourne, Paul Fantom, the late Colin Hardy, Victoria Kingston, William Philpott, Gary Sheffield and Peter Simkins. I am grateful to my colleagues at the University of Wolverhampton for their encouragement, particularly Stephen Badsey, John Buckley, Howard Fuller and Gary Sheffield. I am also sincerely grateful for the encouragement provided by the alumni of the First World War MA course at the University of Birmingham and the past and present students of the First World War MA at the University of Wolverhampton.

My friends remain a bedrock of support for all my writing endeavours and I am very grateful to Andy, Jon, Martyn, Deb, Jake and Helen. They shared my joy during the highs and lifted my morale during the lows. I could not ask for a better set of friends. I owe a very special thank you to Mia, who has listened to my grumbles, tolerated my unsociable hours, and done everything she can to support the creation of the book. Her kindness is far more appreciated than she realises.

Finally, and as in all previous volumes, I must extend my heartfelt thanks to my parents once more. None of my books would have been possible without them and I am forever grateful for their love and encouragement.

Introduction: The Endless Battle

A.J.P. Taylor once wrote that the First World War was too big for statesmen and generals.[1] After more than a century of controversy, reflection and analysis, it is tempting to suggest that the Battle of the Somme is too big for historians. Both the physical scale of the battle and its cultural legacy are vast.[2] Even describing it as a "battle" poses problems of definition, for in magnitude and duration it was a battle quite unlike any which Britain had ever fought. Prior to the Somme, Britain's longest offensive on the Western Front had been the Battle of Loos, which lasted for almost three weeks in September and October 1915. In contrast, the Battle of the Somme raged for months with almost continuous fighting from July to November 1916. This truly industrial battle was an unprecedented experience for soldiers, statesmen and the public.

Grasping the scale of the Somme strains the limits of imagination. It is thus little surprise that the memory of the battle often crystallises upon a single moment: its terrible first day. Writing in the 1930s, James Edmonds captured the eve of the attack in an uncharacteristically poetic paragraph in the *Official History:*

> Under a cloudless blue sky which gave full promise of the hot mid-summer day which was ahead, wave after wave of British infantry rose and, with bayonets glistening, moved forward into a blanket of smoke and mist as the barrage lifted from the enemy's front trench… No braver or more determined men ever faced an enemy than those sons of the British Empire who 'went over the top' on the 1st July 1916. Never before had the ranks of a British Army on the field of battle contained the finest of all classes of the nation in physique, brains and education. And they were volunteers not conscripts. If ever a decisive victory was to be won it was to be expected now.[3]

---

1 A.J.P. Taylor, *The First World War: An Illustrated History* (London: Hamish Hamilton, 1963), pp. 68-71.
2 For a useful summary of the cultural legacy of the Somme see Mungo Melvin, 'The Long Shadows of the Somme' in Matthias Strohn, (ed.), *The Battle of the Somme* (Oxford: Osprey, 2016).
3 James Edmonds, *Military Operations: France and Belgium 1916*, Vol.1 (London: Macmillan, 1932), p. 315.

Edmonds chose to end a chapter with this paragraph, leaving it as a tantalising cliff hanger before plunging into the carnage of the first twenty-four hours. In doing so, Edmonds reflected a popular sense that Britain had changed forever on 1 July 1916. The hopeful volunteers had been promised a famous victory and advanced in weather conditions redolent of the Edwardian summers that had characterised the last years of peace. But as the attack began on 1 July the sun was blotted out by smoke and the brave soldiers of the New Army would fall in their thousands. The spirit of optimism died with them. The image of this loss of innocence on 1 July 1916 is not entirely without basis but it is simplistic and coloured by nostalgia for a half-remembered Edwardian world.[4] Nevertheless, the picture retains remarkable power. The events of the first day and the imagery surrounding them have proved irresistibly fascinating to successive generations. The Somme is revisited time and time again until the media threatens to portray not the battle itself but rather the *memory* of the battle. No British battle of the First World War has attracted such attention from so many quarters.

The interest is understandable. The 1 July 1916 was, in terms of casualties, the worst day in the history of the British Army, a gruesome fact which gives it a uniquely awful status. But the battle did not end with this reverse. The offensive continued unabated and the battle would go on to become the bloodiest ever fought by British soldiers. It did not end with a clear victory. The German line, although shaken, was far from broken, and it would take two further years of bloodshed before Germany was finally defeated. In the disillusioned atmosphere of the 1920s and 1930s some commentators saw the sacrifice on the Somme as being in vain and condemned the battle as useless slaughter.[5] These critics were in turn challenged by authors who regarded the Somme as an essential step towards the eventual victory in 1918. In this interpretation the fighting of 1916, dreadful as it was, was necessary to harden the inexperienced New Army and to grind down the strength of their German opponents. Douglas Haig came to view it as the opening act of a "long and continuous engagement" that culminated in victory in 1918.[6] These diametrically opposed views set the terms of the debate. The arguments which began in the 1920s continue unabated a century later.

It is against the background of this contentious debate that military historians have studied the battle. The scale of the engagement has provided a rich field for research.[7]

---

4   Peter Simkins, *From the Somme to Victory: The British Army's Experience on the Western Front 1916-1918* (Barnsley: Praetorian Press, 2014), p. 59 notes that the "unique character" of the BEF of 1916 was lost forever on 1 July.
5   The best summary of the historiography surrounding the Battle of the Somme can be found in Simkins, *From the Somme to Victory*, pp. 12-59.
6   J.H. Broaston, (ed.), *Sir Douglas Haig's Despatches: December 1915-April 1919* (London: J.M. Dent, 1919), p. 319.
7   A number of important single volume studies of the battle have been produced including Gary Sheffield, *The Somme* (London: Cassell, 2004), William Philpott, *Bloody Victory: The Sacrifice on the Somme* (London: Abacus, 2014), Robin Prior & Trevor Wilson, *The Somme* (London: Yale University Press, Original 2008; second edition 2016).

Much recent scholarship has revisited the arguments of the earliest defenders of operations on the Somme by considering its place within the British Army's learning process. Driven by the pioneering work of historians such as John Terraine, Peter Simkins, John Bourne, Paddy Griffith and John Lee, scholars have examined the mechanics of military learning in great detail.[8] New studies have conducted in-depth examinations of how information was disseminated between units, armies and even theatres, and how the culture of the British Army contributed to the process.[9] Interest in the British learning process has been mirrored by work examining the development of the French and German armies.[10]

Learning amidst a bitterly fought war was no easy matter. Lessons were paid for in blood and precious expertise was lost as veterans fell in combat. The British Army of 1915 had suffered greatly in this regard and too often perpetuated its inexperience by throwing its dwindling stock of Regular soldiers into unwinnable battles.[11] On the eve of the Somme the comparative lack of experience in the British Expeditionary Force relative to the war-hardened French and German armies was marked. The Somme would prove a brutal school for the novice British Army and was its true introduction to modern warfare on a mass scale. Although recent scholarship has noted the importance of the first eighteen months of the British war effort there is no denying the scale

---

8   For example: John Terraine, *White Heat: The New Warfare 1914-18* (London: Sidgwick & Jackson, 1982); Simkins, *Somme to Victory*; J.M. Bourne 'British Generals in the First World War' in G.D. Sheffield (ed.), *Leadership and Command: The Anglo-American Military Experience Since 1861* (London: Brassey's, 1997); Paddy Griffith (ed.), *British Fighting Methods in the Great War* (London: Frank Cass, 1998); John Lee, 'Some Lessons of the Somme: The British Infantry in 1917' in Brian Bond (ed.), *Look to Your Front: Studies in the First World War* (Staplehurst: Spellmount, 1999).

9   Robert T. Foley, 'Dumb Donkeys or Cunning Foxes? Learning in the British and German Armies during the Great War' in *International Affairs*, Vol. 90, No.2, pp. 279-298; Jim Beach, 'Issued by the General Staff: Doctrine Writing at British GHQ, 1917-18' in *War in History*, Vol 19, No.4, 2012; Stuart Mitchell, 'An inter-disciplinary study of learning in the 32nd Division on the Western Front, 1916-1918', Unpublished PhD Thesis, University of Birmingham, 2015; Aimée Fox, *Learning to Fight: Military Innovation and Change in the British Army 1914-1918* (Cambridge: Cambridge University Press 2017).

10 For the French army, see Jonathan Krause, *Early Trench Tactics in the French Army: The Second Battle of Artois, May-June 1915* (Farnham: Ashgate, 2013) and Elizabeth Greenhalgh, *The French Army and the First World War* (Cambridge: Cambridge University Press, 2014). For the German army, see Robert T. Foley, 'Learning War's Lessons: The German Army and the Battle of the Somme', *Journal of Modern History*, Vol.75, 2011, pp. 471-504; Christopher Duffy, *Through German Eyes: The British and the Somme 1916* (London: Phoenix, 2007) and Jack Sheldon, *Fighting the Somme: German Challenges, Dilemmas and Solutions* (Barnsley: Pen & Sword, 2017).

11 On the battles of 1915, see Nick Lloyd, *Loos 1915* (Stroud: Tempus, 2006) and Spencer Jones (ed.), *Courage without Glory: The British Army on the Western Front 1915* (Solihull: Helion & Co., 2015).

and intensity of the Battle of the Somme made it a pivotal moment for the BEF.[12] The disaster of the opening day gave way to a prolonged struggle that would become the longest, bloodiest battle in British history.[13] Reflecting on the battle beyond the 1 July, John Bourne offered an apt summary:

> In some ways, the most important day of the war was 2 July 1916. The British had suffered an appalling reverse, but it was apparent that they were not going away, that their operational method was bound to improve and that the resources available to them from the mobilisation of British industry would make them what they eventually became, a formidable enemy.[14]

The bloodshed of the Somme can make dispassionate analysis difficult. The battle continues to inspire strong emotions. Yet the importance of the battle and its enduring legacy demand scholarly inspection. The search for context has allowed the Somme to be viewed through a wide lens and the battle is no longer seen as a purely British experience. Important works have explored the role of Australian, Canadian and South African forces at the Somme.[15] Recent scholarship has emphasised the importance of French involvement and valuable studies have examined the battle from a German perspective.[16]

Our understanding of the battle is greater than ever before, yet it continues to inspire passionate, and sometimes ill-tempered, debate.[17] It is difficult to identify a clear consensus on the outcome of the fighting, but recent academic work has inclined towards the view that the Somme was a bloody victory for the Allies.[18] Although

---

12 For the influence of the first eighteen months of the war, see Spencer Jones (ed.), *Stemming the Tide: Officers and Leadership in the British Expeditionary Force 1914* (Solihull: Helion & Co., 2013) and Jones (ed.), *Courage Without Glory*.
13 Casualty figures for the Battle of the Somme are much disputed. See Prior & Wilson, *Somme*, pp. 300-309, for a useful discussion.
14 John Bourne, 'A Personal Reflection on 1 July 1916' in *Firestep: The Magazine of the London Branch of the Western Front Association*, Vol.5, No.2, November 2004, p. 27.
15 Tim Cook, *At the Sharp End: Canadians Fighting the Great War 1914-1916* (Toronto: Penguin, 2009); Kenneth Radley, *Get Tough Stay Tough!: Shaping the Canadian Corps 1914-1918* (Solihull: Helion & Co., 2014); Meleah Hampton, *Attack on the Somme: 1st Anzac Corps and the Battle of Pozières Ridge, 1916* (Solihull: Helion & Co., 2016). For a useful summary of Dominion operations, see Christopher Pugsley, 'Trial and Error: The Dominion Forces on the Somme in 1916' in Strohn (ed.), *Battle of the Somme*.
16 For the importance of the French see Philpott, *Bloody Victory* and Greenhalgh, *French Army*. For German perspectives see Ralph Whitehead, *The Other Side of the Wire: With the German XIV Reserve Corps on the Somme,* Vol.1 (2013) and Vol. 2 (2017) (Solihull: Helion & Co.,); Duffy, *Through German Eyes;* Sheldon, *Fighting the Somme*.
17 Proof that the debate retains its heat is given by Prior & Wilson's caustic criticism of other historians in the introduction to the revised edition of *The Somme*, pp. xvii-xx.
18 Philpott, *Bloody Victory*, is clear on this point. Other authors have offered similar assessments, albeit tinged with reservation. Duffy, *Through German Eyes*, pp. 324-328.

it cost the Allies a terrible price in lives it was one which, in the cold economics of world war, they could afford to pay. The same was not true for Germany. Estimates of total German casualties vary wildly but there is no doubt that her army had suffered heavy losses in men and material that could not be easily replaced.[19] Furthermore, the mental strain of battle and the revelation of British material superiority corroded German confidence.[20]

The controversies surrounding the Battle of the Somme and continued interest in the subject encourages fresh research. This collection contributes to the historiography through a series of thematic studies. The Somme looms large in these chapters but, reflecting the tremendous legacy of the battle, the work also considers elements beyond the front line. Furthermore, in contrast to earlier volumes in this series, this book includes chapters which address the French and the German armies as a way of offering valuable comparisons to the British experience.

To begin the collection, Stephen Badsey examines how strategic decisions made in 1915 brought the British Army to the Somme a year later. John Spencer continues the exploration of strategy with a study of William Robertson's influence as Chief of the Imperial General Staff, whilst Andrew Wiest tackles the perennial controversy of Douglas Haig's command performance at the Somme. Jim Beach offers an insight into the intelligence available to the British and addresses the claim that the Battle of the Somme was fought primarily to assist the French at Verdun. Christopher Phillips explores the remarkable overhaul of logistics that allowed the BEF to conduct large scale and prolonged operations, whilst Bill MacCormick considers the problems of the preliminary bombardment and argues that the planners had misunderstood lessons from Verdun. The second half of the book examines the operational and tactical conduct of the battle. John Pratt studies the development of trench raiding and places it within the context of British strategy on the Western Front. Michael LoCicero builds upon the theme of trench raiding through a forensic examination of the German trench raid at La Boisselle in April 1916 and the reaction it prompted from the British Army. The importance of command emerges in the following chapters: Simon Robbins explores Lieutenant-General Henry Horne's performance as a corps commander and my own chapter examines XIII Corps with a focus upon the commanders Lieutenant-General Walter Congreve VC, Major-General Ivor Maxse and Major-General John Shea. As a useful comparison to the study of British corps, Tim Gale examines French XX Corps and reveals how their battle-forged doctrine resulted into thorough preparation and planning. The debate surrounding the so-called 'learning process' is explored

---

argues that it was a "costly strategic success" for the Allies. Sheldon, *Fighting the Somme*, p. 203, suggests it was a German tactical success but a strategic defeat. This view is not universal, however. See Prior & Wilson, *The Somme*, pp. 300-315 for a view of the Somme as a British strategic and operational defeat.

19   Duffy, *Through German Eyes*, p. 324,
20   Ibid., pp. 324-326; Alexander Watson, *Ring of Steel: Germany and Austria-Hungary at War, 1914-1918* (London: Allen Lane, 2014), pp. 326-327.

in depth in by Stuart Mitchell in his study of 32nd Division. Learning – or indeed lack of it – is a feature of the two chapters examining the performance of Dominion forces which follow. Meleah Hampton offers a stark critique of Australian operations on the Pozières Ridge whilst Kenneth Radley studies Canadian efforts to capture Regina Trench. Learning without the benefit of experience is the theme of Philip Ventham's essay on tank doctrine prior to their battlefield deployment in September 1916. Turning to officers at the sharp end of battle, Timothy Halstead studies the creation of the Junior Officer Corps and casts light on how the New Armies were officered, whilst Peter Hodgkinson presents a series of insightful case studies which explore how infantry battalion commanders operated in action in 1916. Closing the examination of the conduct of the Battle of the Somme is the work of Tony Cowan, who discusses the consequences of the fighting for the German army and addresses some of the myths that have arisen on this subject. The collection is concluded by two chapters exploring the complex legacy of the battle. Mark Connelly shows how the Somme was memorialised after the war and examines its rich literary history. Finally, Brian Bond considers the memoirs of the Somme and how they have shaped the subsequent historiography.

Several themes emerge from the chapters, including the difficulties of Allied strategy in 1916, the importance of individual decision making in planning and upon the battlefield, and the sheer complexity of First World War operations. The latter point is especially important given the inexperience of the British Army on the eve of the battle. By 1916 the BEF had grown to an army of continental proportions and its limited pool of experienced officers and men were spread too thinly to have anything more than local influence. Whereas the French could draw upon a practical doctrine born from the battles of 1915, the British Army was still grappling with the difficulties of trench warfare and relied upon individual officers and commanders to solve problems. This threw a great burden onto inexperienced corps and divisional officers who in turn commanded novice formations. The consequence was that unrealistic orders were carried out without question. As Ivor Maxse noted, all too often "companies are directed to 'take the place at all costs', and this order has been obeyed quite literally."[21] Given such universal inexperience it is not surprising that many commanders were unable to adapt to the intensity of modern warfare. The difficulty of absorbing the lessons of combat and the uneven learning process is a recurring theme. This inconsistency is understandable. Although there were common lessons to be learned, the confusion and chaos of battle made identification and application difficult. Different units digested their lessons in different ways and with varying degrees of success. Nevertheless, as many chapters show, adaptation was essential. Failure to do so could result in defeat and needless casualties.

The consequences of the Battle of the Somme remain open to debate. The picture that emerges from these essays is that the offensive, although not a clear victory for

---

21 Imperial War Museum, Maxse Papers, 17/2, Maxse to Montgomery, 31 July 1916.

either side, marked a turning point for the British Army and for the war itself. The armies that fought on the Somme were changed forever. The courageous yet inexperienced New Army of 1 July 1916 was lost amidst the storm of steel, but the same crucible of battle forged the well-equipped and hard fighting British Expeditionary Force of 1917. This army would prove to be Germany's most dangerous battlefield foe throughout 1917 and arguably into 1918. As the British grew in strength, so the Germans declined. The German army had fought admirably on the Somme but its casualties, and consequent loss of confidence, began an irreversible decline in fighting power.[22] Stunned by the battles of 1916, Germany would turn to its navy to defeat Britain in 1917. The disastrous consequences of this decision would only become fully apparent in 1918. To borrow a phrase used by Winston Churchill to describe the Battle of El Alamein in 1942, the Battle of the Somme was not the beginning of the end, but it was "the end of the beginning."[23]

---

22 Sheldon, *Fighting the Somme*, p. 203.
23 For a discussion of contemporary opinions on how the battle was a turning point, see Philpott, *Bloody Victory*, pp. 433-436.

1

The Battle of the Somme and British War Plans 1916

Stephen Badsey

Before 1916, the Western Front was one of several critically important areas of British strategy for the First World War, one of the areas of decision-making in which the war might be won or lost. But from the start of 1916, and in the course of fighting the Battle of the Somme from July to November, the Western Front increased in importance to become the central focus of the British war effort. Already, for most British people the Western Front had held this central place since the German invasion of Belgium in August 1914; and with the deployment of the majority of the New Army volunteers to the Western Front over winter 1915-16 its importance in popular consciousness had grown even greater. But the rise in importance of the Western Front during 1916 was also linked to national and international affairs mostly beyond the awareness of ordinary British citizens. The eventual dominance of the Western Front in British strategy was closely linked to the failure of British attempts to win the war by any other means, and led those directing Britain's war effort to undertake the costly and desperate offensives on the Western Front of 1916-17. Despite an attempt by Prime Minister David Lloyd George over winter 1917-18 to place greater emphasis on the war against the Ottoman Empire, the Western Front stayed in this position of chief importance for the British until the end of the war. Other areas including the war at sea and the war on the Home Front remained critical to the British, but from 1916 onwards these were seen and understood in terms of their relationship with the Western Front.

The decisions which shaped British strategy for 1916 and produced the Battle of the Somme were taken principally at the Chantilly Conference of 6-8 December 1915, held at the Grande Condé hotel in Chantilly just north of Paris, part of GQG (*Grand Quartier General*), the headquarters of General Joseph Joffre, Commander-in-Chief of the French Army. Building on previous discussions that had taken place both within and between the principal Allies, the Chantilly Conference decided that the French, the British, the Italians and the Russians would each make a major attack with their land forces against those of the Central Powers

German cartoon lampooning Allied strategic decision-making during early 1916: "They each keep their own wise counsel, but no one is asking for an appointment [to hear it]!" (*Kladderadatsch*, 5 March 1916)

in June-July 1916.[1] The French plan to make their attack alongside the British in the Somme region were to be pre-empted by the German offensive at Verdun starting on 21 February, and as a result the Battle of the Somme became largely a British affair; but the Battle of Verdun did not change the strategy agreed at Chantilly in any fundamental way. One of the factors that made the Battle of the Somme unique was that up to the end of 1915 the British had fought their battles on the Western Front separately from the French, and they would do so again

1   W. Philpott, *Attrition: Fighting the First World War* (London: Abacus, 2014), pp. 215-18; E. Greenhalgh, *Victory Through Coalition: Britain and France During the First World War* (Cambridge: Cambridge University Press, 2005), pp. 42-6.

in 1917 (other than the isolated case of French *First Army* fighting under British command in the Third Battle of Ypres). In 1918 in contrast, Allied forces often fought intermingled or in very close co-operation, with General Ferdinand Foch as their supreme commander. Only in 1916 on the Somme did British and French armies fight side by side as equals, co-ordinating their plans.[2] The Italian contribution to the strategy agreed at Chantilly was also pre-empted by the Battle of Asiago, an Austro-Hungarian offensive which began on 15 May. But after blunting this attack, the Italians opened the Sixth Battle of the Isonzo on 5 August, their most successful battle of the war up to that date. On 4 June (22 May by the Russian calendar) a Russian attack against the Austro-Hungarian Army, known as the Brusilov Offensive from its commander, General A.A. Brusilov, resulted in the greatest Russian success of the war thus far.[3] Even the much smaller French and British forces at Salonika (modern Thessaloniki) in northern Greece made a brief advance at the end of September.

The idea behind all these offensives taking place within weeks of each other was to over-strain and break the German and Austro-Hungarian armies. One of the major strategic features of the First World War was that rail transport enabled the Central Powers to switch considerable forces from one major front – their Western, Eastern and Italian fronts – to another in a matter of days or weeks, operating on what were militarily known as interior lines, while there was no way for the Allies to mount a sustained attack on these strategic railways and interdict the movement of these forces. Attacking simultaneously was meant to thwart this strategy, leaving the Central Powers without the reserve divisions to block every Allied attack, and it came very close to success. On 21 August, the Chief of the Great General Staff, General Erich von Falkenhayn, informed Chancellor Theobald von Bethmann Hollweg that "Given the terrible pressures upon us we have no forces to spare. Every redeployment in one direction leads inevitably to a dangerous weakening in other places, which – if even the slightest error is made with regard to our assessment of the enemy's next moves – could mean our destruction."[4] At one of the most critical periods of the Battle of the Somme, during the Battle of Morval of 25-28 September, *Armee Gruppe Rupprecht*, fighting against both the British and French, had to put all its available troops into the line leaving it with no reserves at all, and reinforcing divisions had to be thrown straight into the battle as they arrived.[5] Whatever he may have thought

---

2 This point is made by Greenhalgh, *Victory Through Coalition*, p. 42.
3 T. C. Dowling, *The Brusilov Offensive* (Bloomington: Indiana University Press, 2008), pp. 1-2.
4 Quoted in M. Stibbe, *German Anglophobia and the Great War 1914-1918* (Cambridge: Cambridge University Press, 2001), p. 135.
5 W. Miles (ed. J. Edmonds), *History of the Great War Based on Official Documents: Military Operations France and Belgium, 1916*, Vol. 2 (London: HMSO, 1938), pp. 423-5 and pp. 554-5; G. C. Wynne, (ed. R. T. Foley), *If Germany Attacks: The Battle in Depth in the West* (Brighton: Tom Donovan, 2008). p. 86; H. Herwig, *The First World War: Germany and*

about the immediate conduct of the war on the Western Front, on 28 September Lloyd George as Secretary of State for War gave (without the approval of his cabinet colleagues) his famous "Knock-out Blow" interview with the United Press of America (UP). Deliberately using terms familiar to American readers, Lloyd George asserted that the war was turning in the Allies' favour, that "the fight must be to a finish – to a knock-out", and that "We have no delusion that the war is nearing an end. We have not the slightest doubt as to *how* it is to end."[6]

The Allies also hoped that their successes in summer 1916 would prompt other European countries to enter the war on their side. Following the initial success of the Brusilov offensive, Romania declared war on Germany and Austria-Hungary on 17 August, starting with an offensive of its own into Austro-Hungarian territory. In Germany this was the last straw for opponents of General Falkenhayn, and led directly to his dismissal. Falkenhayn's critics, including Chancellor Bethmann Hollweg, believed that Falkenhayn's strategy of aiming for a limited victory and a negotiated peace in 1916 had produced only a series of mistakes and defeats. Falkenhayn was replaced as Chief of the Great General Staff by Field Marshal Paul von Hindenburg with Erich Ludendorff as his deputy, both of whom were appalled at the state of crisis in which they found the German Army on the Western Front.[7] If the British would never forget the disaster of 1 July that opened the Battle of the Somme, by early September the Germans were facing the prospect of fighting not only the French Army on the Western Front, but a British Army that was emerging against all predictions as an additional first-class enemy, with a growing superiority in artillery that would soon become overwhelming. Hindenburg ordered the construction of new deep defensive positions to the rear of the Somme battlefield, later to be known by the British as the Hindenburg Line, to which the Germans retired in March 1917. As the Battle of the Somme came to an end, the outspoken Sir Henry Wilson (at that date commanding IV Corps which had not been involved in the battle), was advising influential figures that fighting "two Sommes at once" in 1917 would bring victory.[8]

Austria-Hungary 1914-1918 (London: Arnold, 1997), p. 198. For more on the problems of German reserves, see Tony Cowan's chapter elsewhere in this volume.

6   Mutually consistent versions of this interview appear as 'Never Again: Battle-Cry of the Allies,' *The Times*, 29 September 1916, and 'Lloyd George Calls All Peace Talk Unfriendly,' *New York Times*, 29 September 1916; for Lloyd George's own version of this episode see his own (D. Lloyd George,) *The War Memoirs of David Lloyd George* (London: Odhams, [1935]), Vol. I, pp. 508-13.

7   M. Kitchen, *The Silent Dictatorship: The Politics of German High Command under Hindenburg and Ludendorff, 1916-1918* (London: Croom Helm, 1976), pp. 25-44; R. T. Foley, *German Strategy and the Path to Verdun: Erich von Falkenhayn and the Development of Attrition, 1870-1916* (Cambridge: Cambridge University Press, 2005), pp. 237-268.

8   Quoted in K. Jeffery, *Field Marshal Sir Henry Wilson: A Political Soldier* (Oxford: Oxford University Press, 2006), p. 171; see also Philpott, *Attrition*, p. 249.

In the event, the fighting at Verdun and on the Somme did not prevent the Germans from moving an estimated 20 divisions to the Eastern Front, 15 from the Western Front and five from Germany itself, and also moving six divisions from the Eastern Front to the Western Front; although 18 of the 20 divisions sent to the Eastern Front had either taken heavy losses on the Somme or at Verdun, or were new divisions created by stripping other formations.[9] The initial Romanian attacks were held and defeated, and a German-led counter-offensive involving Austro-Hungarian and Bulgarian forces over-ran Romania by the end of 1916. The imminent collapse of Romania in late September also drew off considerable reserves from Brusilov's South-Western Front (a 'Front' was a Russian military unit), ending the chance of even greater Russian successes.[10] Although Romania as a neutral had already been trading with Germany and Austria-Hungary, the seizure of Romanian grain and oil supplies was vital to the economic survival of the Central Powers into 1917. However close the Chantilly strategy came to success in 1916, neither the German nor the Austro-Hungarian armies collapsed that year.

When this strategy was agreed at Chantilly, senior Allied politicians and generals held differing opinions and judgements on whether it could produce a breakthrough and a complete Allied victory in 1916, or would be part of a longer wearing-out process calculated against the ability of the German Army to replace its losses, or a combination of limited breakthroughs leading to further attacks and victory perhaps in 1917. General Sir William Robertson as Chief of the Imperial General Staff (CIGS) believed more in the wearing-out fight and attrition, while General Sir Douglas Haig as the Commander-in-Chief of the BEF envisaged limited breakthroughs on the Somme and some gains in territory, but also saw this as part of a longer wearing-out strategy. Haig's plans for fighting the Battle of the Somme have been subject to extensive examination and debate, particularly his plan for the first catastrophic British attack on 1 July. The resulting loss of life can never be ignored or underplayed, even in a battle that lasted for another 140 days. Some historians have argued very strongly that Haig envisaged a large-scale breakthrough on 1 July alone, and that this unrealistic belief compromised a plan that should have been based from the start on a less ambitious, attritional approach favoured by General Sir Henry Rawlinson commanding Fourth Army.[11] These views

---

9 The figure of 15 divisions is in A. Watson, *Ring of Steel: Germany and Austria-Hungary at War, 1914-1918* (London: Allen Lane, 2014), p. 323; the other figures are in tables in Miles, *France and Belgium, 1916*, Vol. 2, pp. 554-5.
10 Dowling, *The Brusilov Offensive*, pp. 160-1.
11 That Haig's plan was in fundamental contrast to Rawlinson's superior plan was first proposed in the seminal work by R. Prior and T. Wilson, *Command on the Western Front: The Military Career of Sir Henry Rawlinson 1914-1918* (Oxford: Blackwell, 1992), pp. 137-170, and taken further in their book R. Prior & T. Wilson, *The Somme* (New Haven: Yale University Press, 2005), pp. 35-118, and still further in J.P. Harris, *Douglas Haig and the First World War* (Cambridge: Cambridge University Press, 2008), pp. 204-7. For other assessments see G. Sheffield, *The Chief: Douglas Haig and the British Army* (London: Aurum, 2011) pp. 159-169; Greenhalgh, *Victory Through Coalition*, pp. 55-63; W. Philpott,

do not reflect the discussions that took place at the highest levels between British politicians and generals from the Chantilly Conference onwards about the future course of the war. Haig hoped for and expected greater territorial gains from the British attack on the Somme than either Robertson or Rawlinson, but all senior British Army commanders were united in their view that the battle would be long and hard, and that victory was more likely to come in 1917 than in 1916. Similarly, calculations based on projected enemy attrition rates showed that Germany would face severe problems in keeping its army up to strength well before the end of 1916, but although Asquith and his government hoped for victory in 1916, they did not automatically expect or demand it.[12] The basic idea for a strategy of simultaneous offensives had already been presented to the British government before December 1915. But one of the marked features of the Chantilly Conference was the relative lack of political oversight of its decisions; political leaders were expected to examine and approve the military plans after they had been made, but not to overturn them. Instead, political leaders decided to place their confidence in the hands of their military professionals, which in the case of the British Cabinet meant the General Staff in Whitehall under Robertson as CIGS, very much as a reaction to what was seen as the amateurism and political interference which had damaged the Allied war effort up to that point.[13] Just as this was the only occasion on which the British and French would fight side by side as equals, so the Chantilly Conference marked the first and only occasion on which the main Allies co-ordinated their strategy on a continental scale in this way. There was no equivalent co-ordination in 1916 between Germany and Austria-Hungary; nor did either of these two empires co-ordinate their plans with either Bulgaria or Ottoman Turkey.[14]

The British path to the Battle of the Somme was not a direct one. In the dramatic first few months of the war in 1914 the British had fought chiefly not to lose. In terms of grand strategy, the most important event of 1914 for the British, other than the German defeat in the Battle of the Marne, was the Pact of London of 5 September, which at Russian insistence turned the three Entente powers of Russia, France and Great Britain into a formal alliance against Germany. This tied the British into supporting France and Russia as the two major land powers of the alliance, something which caused the British much trouble throughout the war as Russia teetered on the brink of collapse, before finally doing so in October-November 1917. The next most

---

Bloody Victory: The Sacrifice on the Somme and the Making of the Twentieth Century (London: Little, Brown, 2009), pp. 144-175 and pp. 434-6; and S. Badsey, *Doctrine and Reform in the British Cavalry 1880-1918* (Farnham: Ashgate, 2008), pp. 268-73.

12 There is also debate on this point; for assessments of Asquith's position and understanding of strategy see G.H. Cassar, *Asquith as War Leader* (London: Hambledon Press, 1994), pp. 171-210, and D. French, *British Strategy and War Aims 1914-1916* (London: Allen & Unwin, 1986), pp. 158-199.

13 See J. Gooch, *The Plans of War: The General Staff and British Military Strategy c.1900-1916* (London: Routledge & Kegan Paul, 1974), p. 530.

14 Herwig, *The First World War*, p. 197.

important grand strategic event of 1914 for the British was the entry of the Ottoman Turkish Empire into the war against Russia in October, with Britain declaring war on Ottoman Turkey on 5 November. This together with the German military successes in Western Europe in August-September, which led to their occupying almost all of Belgium and important industrial areas of northern France, gave the rest of the First World War its strategic geographical shape. The dominance of Allied seapower, and particularly the strength of the Royal Navy, meant that even before the end of 1914 the main theatres of the war had been confined to Europe and its adjacent seas and oceans. But strategic communications between the British and French to the west of the Central Powers and the Russians to their east had been cut by the Ottoman entry into the war. The critical element in British grand strategy up to and including 1916 was the risk of either Russia or even France being defeated or making a separate peace before the new mass armies that the British had committed themselves to creating could be deployed effectively.

Because of this, the British war effort throughout 1915 combined military and industrial preparation with political frustration, as they found themselves committed to military actions controlled or dictated by their allies and their enemies, rather than holding the initiative themselves. In terms of military achievement 1915 was almost entirely a disaster for the British. In February 1915, British, Indian and ANZAC troops defeated an Ottoman Turkish attack on the Suez Canal, the temporary loss of which would have been a minor strategic defeat. Otherwise, the British did not win a single battle of strategic importance in 1915, on land or at sea. For the small British Army, which had to fight principally on the Western Front whilst simultaneously undergoing an unprecedented expansion and reorganisation, this outcome was disappointing, but not very surprising. The battles of 1915 at least convinced General Joffre and GQG that the British were capable of fighting, although both the French and the Germans continued to see the British Army as tactically inept. With memories of the poor performance of the British volunteer forces in the Anglo-Boer War of 1899-1902 still fresh in the memories of all sides, it seemed unlikely that even the British with their global Empire and considerable resources could turn themselves into a first-class land power in less than three years. At the start of the war, much more had been expected of the Royal Navy, and it had in fact delivered on establishing virtually total control of the seas, with the swift elimination of Germany's surface raiding cruisers, and a naval blockade of the Central Powers. But despite some ambitious hopes, by the end of 1915 there was still no sign of the blockade playing any major role in bringing about victory. Naval engagements in the North Sea had been inconclusive, usually with both sides claiming success. A German attempt at conducting unrestricted submarine warfare in February-September 1915, including the sinking without warning of the passenger liner RMS *Lusitania* on 7 May, had been defeated by a combination of naval and diplomatic pressure, but again the results fell short of British expectations. Above all, the United States resisted British diplomatic and propaganda efforts to bring it into the war on the Allied side. In 1916, with an American presidential election due in November, this seemed even less likely.

The outstanding failure of British strategy for 1915 had been the Dardanelles campaign, with its attempt to re-open strategic communications with Russia, starting with the naval bombardment of the Gallipoli peninsula in February, followed by two amphibious landings in April and August, all of which had led only to stalemate. The central problem for the British was that in 1915 they had mounted two major offensive campaigns in two widely separated theatres of war, one on the Western Front and one at Gallipoli, at a time when they did not have the troops, resources, training or experience to mount and sustain even one of them properly. A breakthrough at the Dardanelles in August 1915 would have solved a number of interlocking strategic problems for the British, and for a brief period in mid-1915 consideration was given to a major change in strategy that would have made Ottoman Turkey the principal British theatre of war, reducing the Western Front to a secondary status.[15] But all these possibilities had come to nothing, and by the end of 1915 a chastened Cabinet had agreed that the only effective way to support Russia, like France, was by attacking the Germans on the Western Front.

In terms of international politics, 1915 had also been a year mostly of failure and at best of partial successes for the British. From the start of the war, the principal target for British diplomacy and propaganda had been the policies and ultimately the neutrality of the United States. Policy and public opinion in the United States remained generally favourable towards the Allies in the first part of the war, although rather more towards the French than the British, and much less so towards the Russians. This included the substantial financial links and commitments created by Allied orders with American firms for munitions and military equipment, and American toleration of the problems and restrictions caused for them by the Allied naval blockade. But even the sinking of the *Lusitania* with the death of 128 American citizens, the most prominent of a number of German violations of international law in 1915, was not enough to bring the United States into the war. Other than the three principal Allies and their empires, together with Serbia, Montenegro and Belgium, the only countries that had entered the war on Britain's side in August 1914 had been Japan and Liberia. 1915 saw a British search for further allies among the smaller powers of Europe, most of which had pre-war conscript armies that were larger and in some cases better trained than the newly-forming British armies. In this, the only British success was the entry of Italy into the war on the Allied side on 23 May, declaring war against Austria-Hungary but not against Germany, nor against the Ottoman Empire until 21 August. Although having the Italians as yet another enemy on a new front was a major threat to Austria-Hungary, it ultimately produced only another military stalemate along the frontier of the River Isonzo. The British had also hoped to use their landings at Gallipoli as an incentive to prompt the formation of a coalition of Balkan countries, including Greece, Romania and even Bulgaria, that would enter the war on

---

15 S. Badsey, 'The August Offensives in British Imperial Grand Strategy,' in A. Ekins (ed.), *Gallipoli: A Ridge Too Far* (Wollombi: Exsile, 2013), pp. 56-75.

the Allied side accompanied by a Russian offensive across the Black Sea. Instead, the French-led landing at Salonika on 5 October 1915 failed to provide additional help for Serbia, and was more than counterbalanced when Bulgaria entered the war on the side of the Central Powers on 14 October. There was nothing that the British could do to prevent German and Austro-Hungarian forces over-running Serbia during the winter, except to evacuate the last of the Serbian government and army by sea in February 1916. The British also remained inherently suspicious of the commitment to Salonika, mostly seeing it as a waste of men and resources linked to French political ambitions in the Balkans rather than to any likely military victory, although at the Chantilly Conference they did agree to their troops remaining there.

The absence throughout 1915 of any notable British success, or even of a major British military effort on the scale of those made by France or Russia, caused such disquiet and anxiety that as part of the wider attempt to explain Britain's war effort their leading official propaganda organisation, the War Propaganda Bureau at Wellington House, went to the lengths of sponsoring a film over an hour in length (monochrome and silent like almost all films of the time) to be shown all over the world, titled *Britain Prepared*. This was at a time that most commercial films lasted only a few minutes, and cinema was regarded in political circles as a rather disreputable form of mass entertainment that had only just replaced the music hall. First shown in London in January 1916, *Britain Prepared* featured the might of the Royal Navy's warships at sea, along with munitions production, and troops training in Britain, but no actual fighting. Although the British propagandists could reasonably have claimed to have invented the full-length documentary film, both the need to make *Britain Prepared*, setting aside long-held military and naval prejudices over security, and its undramatic content were reflections of how little the British had actually achieved for the war effort in 1915, and of their promise to themselves and the allies that 1916 would be different.[16]

One of the most positive British achievements in winning the war up to the end of 1915 had been largely invisible to the wider world, and in most cases to the British public. The British financial system and the City of London had survived the shock of the outbreak of war, with the London Stock Exchange re-opening in January 1915 following its closure in August 1914. This financial strength and stability enabled the British to continue as the chief paymaster for the other Allies (although not the French on any large scale), obtaining financial credit on the international money markets, chiefly from New York, making substantial loans to both Russia and Italy, and supporting the war effort of the wider British Empire. Although this British financial strength would be critical to the eventual Allied victory, it was both linked to and potentially in conflict with another major British achievement that depended

---

16   M.L. Sanders, 'British Film Propaganda in Russia 1916-1918,' *Historical Journal of Film, Radio and Television*, 1 (2) (1983), pp. 117-130; N. Reeves, *Official British Film Propaganda during the First World War* (London: Croom Helm, 1986), pp. 142-5 and 225-240.

entirely on the public and their response. Lord Kitchener's call for volunteers as Secretary of State for War in August 1914 had exceeded all expectations, resulting in some two and a half million men coming forward, and the expansion of the British Army from six to over sixty infantry divisions with their supporting troops and equipment. This marked the peak of Kitchener's achievement as Secretary of State for War, and in gross terms the expansion of the British Army had been accomplished by mid-1915. But the formation of the Asquith coalition in May 1915 had been a consequence both of the constitutional necessity either for a new government or for a general election to take place, and of dissatisfaction over the British strategic direction of the war, with the double failure of the first British attacks on the Western Front in March and the first Gallipoli landing in April. In the new coalition government, Winston Churchill was demoted from First Lord of the Admiralty to Chancellor of the Duchy of Lancaster, being replaced by the Conservative Arthur Balfour, and Kitchener's powers at the War Office were reduced by the creation of the Ministry of Munitions under Lloyd George. For the remainder of 1915 and on into early 1916, the Asquith coalition's ministers responsible for finance, Walter Runciman as President of the Board of Trade and Reginald McKenna as Chancellor of the Exchequer, argued against the cost of raising and equipping a first-class mass land army while at the same time Britain subsidised its allies through war loans. The financial orthodoxy of the time was that governments should not run a deficit, and that spending should be linked to a country's gold reserves. At its existing rate of spending, Britain was technically facing bankruptcy by the end of 1916, although in the context of war finance this had little real meaning.[17]

The view of the mass of the British people on the Home Front, insofar as this can be measured, was that they remained supportive of the war effort. Until 1916, dissent was chiefly limited to a few political or ideological opponents, or those reacting against the idea of the war almost on aesthetic grounds as an unendurable tragedy regardless of any other circumstances. There was little sign of any mass movement against the war, and volunteers to serve in the British Army far outnumbered dissenters.[18] However, the decline in volunteers after mid-1915, and some minor political episodes including the loss of two parliamentary by-elections in early 1916, helped convince some members of the British government that public support for the war might be fading. In consequence, the argument over whether Britain should limit its war effort in order to preserve its post-war fiscal strength became closely linked to the major political debate of the time: the need for conscription. The National Registration Act in August 1915,

---

17 French, *British Strategy and War Aims 1914-1916*, pp. 116-136 and pp. 158-9; H. Strachan, *Financing the First World War* (Oxford: Oxford University Press, 2004), pp. 57-60.
18 For valuable discussions of dissent in 1916, see S. Hynes, *A War Imagined: The First World War and English Culture* (London: Bodley Head, 1990), pp. 145-167, and A. Gregory, *The Last Great War: British Society and the First World War* (Cambridge: Cambridge University Press, 2008), especially pp. 131-6.

Prime Minister Herbert Asquith (centre) disembarks at Queenstown Quay, Ireland to assess the situation in the immediate aftermath of the Easter Rising, 12 May 1916.

which required all men and women to register their identity including address and place of employment, led to a government estimate that up to 1,400,000 men were 'shirkers' who, although not debarred from military service for reasons ranging from physical incapacity to essential war work, had still failed to volunteer.

The idea of conscription was anathema to many Liberals, and the Asquith coalition nearly fell apart over the issue, especially after an initial compromise, the Derby Scheme of 23 October to 12 December 1915 in which men were invited to attest their willingness to volunteer, produced only 249,238 new soldiers.[19] The Military Service Act introducing conscription was passed on 27 January 1916, although when the Battle of the Somme began on 1 July there were still no conscripts among the troops who made the first attacks. This introduction of conscription came some three months before the British government formally agreed on 7 April to the BEF participating in the Battle of the Somme, but the passing of the act guaranteed that Haig would have the front-line troops and reserves with which to fight a protracted campaign. Once the principle of conscription had been established, a second and much wider

---

19 D. Silbey, *The British Working Class and Enthusiasm for War, 1914-1916* (London: Frank Cass, 2005), pp. 34-7.

Military Service Act became law on 25 May. This act extended conscription to include all men aged 18-41 regardless of their marital status, causing a minor political revolt with 41 Liberal MPs voting against it. In the event, the imagined pool of shirkers turned out to be non-existent, the product of a substantial statistical miscalculation. Almost all of those who had failed to volunteer by 1916 were either medically unfit, or debarred from military service overseas, or required for essential war work, or the sole supporters of their families. This had major implications for the way that the Battle of the Somme would be fought. The recruits produced by conscription from January 1916 onwards were usually sufficient to keep the British Army on the Western Front up to strength, but no more than that, and the politics of military manpower became a major concern for the rest of the war.[20] But the absence of any large-scale opposition to conscription except in Ireland, and the willingness of each new class of 18 year olds to serve as they came of age, both suggest that British popular support for the war effort remained strong throughout the rest of the war. In contrast, the Easter Rising in Dublin in April 1916 was seen as a protest against conscription as well as against British rule, and in practice conscription was not applied to Ireland. The Easter Rising itself had surprisingly little impact on Irish troops on the Western Front, or any immediate impact on wider British war plans, although it did point to longer term problems.[21] As the countdown to the Battle of the Somme began, the gloomy and pessimistic belief of the British government was that they were facing the choice between on the one hand bankruptcy if they carried through their strategy of full mobilisation and conscription (including for industry) while still borrowing overseas and supporting their allies, and on the other hand a crushing military defeat if they failed to take these actions to the full.

The military response of the British Empire up to 1916 had also exceeded pre-war expectations. The Indian Army was already making a major contribution to the war effort, chiefly in Mesopotamia and Egypt. The two Indian Army infantry divisions sent to the Western Front in September 1914 were withdrawn in December 1915, but two Indian cavalry divisions remained, and even when these were transferred to the Egyptian Expeditionary Force in early 1918, this still left over 15,000 Indian troops serving on the Western Front in various capacities until the end of the war.[22] The first Canadian troops had fought on the Western Front in 1915, and in 1916 they were joined by Australian, New Zealand and South African contingents, plus others from around the Empire, including famously the single battalion of the Newfoundland Regiment, which was the only dominion unit to take part in the attack on the Somme

20 The best study of this remains K. Grieves, *The Politics of Manpower 1914-18* (Manchester: Manchester University Press, 1988), pp. 19-62.
21 For the perspective of Irish soldiers taken prisoner on the Western Front see C. Duffy, *Through German Eyes: the British and the Somme 1916* (London: Weidenfeld & Nicolson, 2006), pp. 98-103.
22 Anon., *Statistics of the Military Effort of the British Empire during the Great War 1914-1920* (London: HMSO, 1920), p. 62.

on 1 July. At this stage of the war the Empire was still strongly committed to supporting Britain's war effort. From the perspective of London, the most important aspect of the failure at Gallipoli in 1915 was its potentially negative effect on the Muslim population of the British Empire, especially in India and Egypt. But although this Muslim response existed, it did not manifest itself strongly during 1916; rather, like the Easter Rising in Dublin, the defeat at Gallipoli pointed the way to resistance against British rule after the war. Gallipoli was rapidly followed by another disastrous British defeat against the Ottoman Army in Mesopotamia. In August 1915 it had seemed possible that a British advance of about 100 miles from Kut-el-Amara could capture Baghdad. But after reaching the limit of his advance at the Battle of Ctesiphon on 25 November, Major General Charles Townshend with his chiefly Indian Army force retreated back to Kut, which they reached on 3 December. A protracted siege and the failure of a relief force led Townshend to surrender with 13,000 men on 29 April 1916, exactly coinciding with the Easter Rising in Dublin 24-29 April. At the same time, the Ottomans scored a further small victory over the British on 23 April at the Battle of Katia, an assault along the Sinai coastal route towards the Suez Canal. A further Ottoman attack towards the Suez Canal in August was defeated at the Battle of Bir Romani, but the Egyptian Expeditionary Force did not start its main advance across the Sinai desert until December. Instead, the main British military effort against the Ottoman Empire went into giving support and armaments to the Arab Revolt against Ottoman rule, which increased substantially in scale during 1916.[23]

The combination of the defeats at Gallipoli and Kut contributed to a British re-evaluation of the war against the Ottoman Empire in the first half of 1916, of which the most important strategic decision was that the War Office in London took over the direction of the campaign in Mesopotamia from the government of India. Even so, it was only a month after the surrender of Kut, and after encouraging the Arab Revolt, that the British and French concluded the Sykes-Picot agreement of 16 May on the post-war partition of the Ottoman Empire, an agreement which was compatible with previous British promises of Constantinople to Russia, but less so with the understanding under which Italy had entered the war in 1915, or with British promises to the Arab leaders. As the basis of their plans, the British continued to assume that they could defeat any substantial attack by the Ottoman Army, and that since the eventual dismemberment of the Ottoman Empire was an inevitability, it could wait while the defeat of Germany was accomplished.

The most significant change for the BEF on the Western Front at the end of 1915 was the replacement of Field Marshal Sir John French as Commander-in-Chief in December by General Sir Douglas Haig. This was part of even more significant changes in British command at a high level, prompted by an awareness of the failures of 1915 and a growing sense of inadequate leadership. Under Asquith, the main political body for decision-making about the war had been known as the War

---

23 E.J. Erickson, *Gallipoli and the Middle East 1914-1918* (London: Amber, 2008), pp. 162-7.

Council, an inner circle of the Cabinet which first met in 1914. In May 1915 with the creation of the Asquith coalition, essentially the same body had been re-formed as the Dardanelles Committee. In October 1915 Asquith changed this again to become the War Committee, which after some political dealings came to consist of six members, rising to eleven by the end of 1916. Winston Churchill, who was left out of the War Committee, resigned his Cabinet position as Chancellor of the Duchy of Lancaster in the expectation of being given an important military staff post at BEF GHQ by Sir John French. Instead, with French's replacement by Haig, Churchill spent January to May 1916 commanding 6th Royal Scots Fusiliers on the Western Front, before returning to Parliament as a back bencher. Surprisingly, the higher command of the Royal Navy was left unchanged over winter 1915-16, with Admiral Sir Henry Jackson remaining as First Sea Lord, and Admiral Sir John Jellicoe remaining in command of the Grand Fleet at Scapa Flow. But the War Office and the high command of the Army went through almost revolutionary changes over the same period, prompted in part by the desire of Kitchener's Cabinet colleagues and critics to limit his authority still further. These changes began quietly, when in September the ineffectual Lieutenant-General Sir James Wolfe Murray was replaced as CIGS by the temporary appointment of General Sir Archibald Murray. On 2 October, Murray presented a plan advocating scaling back the war against the Ottoman Empire and concentrating on the Western Front, an early indicator of what would become the Chantilly strategy. The major change, accompanied by much political manoeuvring, was the appointment as CIGS on 23 December of Sir William Robertson.[24] Robertson had already been consulted by the War Committee, and on 15 November he also advised them to consider supporting a plan for multiple Allied attacks in 1916, as another forerunner of the Chantilly strategy. Murray, understandably aggrieved to find himself replaced by Roberson, was given command of the Egyptian Expeditionary Force.[25] As a consequence of Robertson's appointment, coupled with Haig's succession to French in command of the BEF, over winter 1915-16 several senior staff officers who had joined the BEF on the outbreak of war and were serving with GHQ moved back to the War Office to serve under Robertson. These included Brigadier General Robert Wigham, who moved from Sub-Chief of Staff at GHQ to become Deputy CIGS, Sir Nevil Macready who moved from being Adjutant-General at GHQ to the same post at the War Office, Sir George Macdonogh who moved from chief of Intelligence at GHQ to become Director of Military Intelligence, and Brigadier-General Frederick Maurice, who moved from GHQ Operations to become Director of Military Operations. These moves allowed Haig to bring into GHQ staff officers with whom he had already served when commanding First Army, but they also deprived GHQ of some very

---

24 Robertson's path to CIGS is examined by John Spencer elsewhere in this volume.
25 These changes are well described in French, *British Strategy and War Aims 1914-1916*, pp. 161-3.

Field Marshal Lord Kitchener arrives at an Allied conference, Paris 27 March 1916. (Private collection)

able and experienced officers, who might have been more independent of Haig in their thinking.

Robertson's main condition for taking over as CIGS was that the War Committee alone should decide British strategy for the war, and that he alone as CIGS should act as its adviser on military matters and issue operational orders, rather than the Secretary of State for War. In November 1915, while these changes were starting to take place, Asquith, caught between Kitchener's immense public popularity and the political pressure to sack him, sent him on a fact-finding trip to the Dardanelles and the eastern Mediterranean. Kitchener, who had been consul-general for Egypt when the war broke out, was already tired of the War Office and may have been thinking of his next appointment. The rumour went round Whitehall that he would not return to London, but would take up a new post connected with the war against the Ottoman Empire. Haig, still at that date commanding First Army, was worried that this might happen, since "by his masterful action he will give that sphere of the operations an undue prominence in the strategical picture", detracting from the emphasis on the Western Front.[26] When Kitchener learned of the new command arrangements that

---

26   Haig's diary for 14 November 1915, in G. Sheffield, and J. Bourne (eds.), *Douglas Haig: War Diaries and Letters 1914-1918* (London: Weidenfeld & Nicolson, 2005), p. 170; see

came with Robertson's appointment he considered resigning his post, but after discussion with Asquith he accepted the situation, and having reached an accommodation he and Robertson surprised and impressed their critics by working well together, going some way to rehabilitate Kitchener's political reputation. His last important act before leaving on a high-level mission to Russia was to address a confidential meeting in the House of Commons on 2 June, with Robertson alongside him, and again he impressed his invited audience of MPs with a speech which in the event became his last political testament on his role in the war.[27] It cannot be certain, but it is very probable that only Kitchener's death in the sinking of the armoured cruiser HMS *Hampshire* just off the Orkney Islands on 5 June put an end to his taking up some further important role in the British war effort on his return from Russia.

If Robertson does not seem to have faced much difficulty with Kitchener, the same cannot be said for his relationship with Sir John French, who was made Viscount French of Ypres in February 1916. French had been given the appointment of Commander-in-Chief of Home Forces, partly to create a post for him, partly because of his high reputation as a trainer and organiser of troops, and partly so that the CIGS could deal with one man rather than with several district commanders. But Robertson was also anxious that French should not become "C-in-C on the old lines", by which he meant something close to the post of Commander-in-Chief of the Army, which had been abolished in 1904, and that French must not have a seat on the War Committee.[28] Until early 1914 French had himself been CIGS, and despite his removal from command of the BEF he remained an influential political and military figure. There was a sense in early 1916 that French's headquarters at Horse Guards was becoming a focus for opposition to both Robertson and Haig, including his contacts with Churchill and Sir Henry Wilson. Haig was equally concerned when in October 1916 French visited GQG and other French Army headquarters and reported back to Lloyd George as Secretary of State for War, rather than to Robertson as CIGS. In short, the higher command relationships that existed during the Battle of the Somme, and the focus of British strategy on the Western Front, were not as settled in mid-1916 as they were later made to appear. These political aspects of the Battle of the Somme remain relatively unexplored in discussions about its military conduct and outcome.

At sea, Britain's position against Germany had strengthened by the end of 1915. The final naval evacuation from the Gallipoli peninsula in January 1916 worked well, and fears that there might be a massacre of the troops as they withdrew proved groundless. One further unexpected consequence of the naval war was that Germany's continued

---

also Viscount O. Esher (ed.), *Journals and Letters of Reginald Viscount Esher, Vol. 3 1910-1915* (London: Ivor Nicholson, 1938), p. 281.

27 For this and Kitchener's speech in full see G. Arthur, *Life of Lord Kitchener*, Vol. 3 (London: MacMillan, 1920), pp. 326-43; see also H. Cassar, *Kitchener's War: British Strategy from 1914 to 1916* (Washington: Brassey's, 2004), pp. 284-8.

28 Robertson quoted in R. Holmes, *The Little Field-Marshal: Sir John French* (London: Jonathan Cape, 1981), p. 315.

use of ports and territory in Portuguese Mozambique to support its forces in East Africa led the British to demand that Portugal seize all German ships sheltering in Portuguese harbours. Portugal agreed in return for British financial support, and Germany responded to this by declaring war on Portugal on 9 March. Two Portuguese infantry divisions would serve on the Western Front from early 1917 onwards. There was also a sustained British attempt to improve the naval blockade. In December 1915 the Trading with the Enemy Act was passed in an attempt to prevent British firms trading indirectly with the Central Powers. In February 1916 a Ministry of Blockade was established under Lord Robert Cecil at the Foreign Office, which was the principal ministry for organising the blockade in co-ordination with the Admiralty. This brought some improvement to Britain' strategy of the Royal Navy stopping ships at sea to inspect their cargoes, in combination with bringing political and economic pressure against neutral countries, such as the Netherlands or Denmark, which were acting as conduits for goods actually intended for Germany, and also against British firms still engaged in this trade. In July the British formally repudiated the Declaration of London of 1909, which had never been ratified by Parliament, but which had rejected the inclusion of food among banned or blockaded goods and had so far had some influence on the blockade policy.[29] The blockade was much tighter in the second half of 1916 than it had been at the start of the year; by September 1916 the Royal Navy was routinely stopping and checking an average of 135 ships a week.[30] As well as being deprived of critical metals and other resources, Germany was heading for the *Steckrübenwinter* ('turnip winter') of 1916-17.

The further British redeployment of some of their warships that followed the entry of Italy with its own battlefleet into the war in 1915, together with the decision to close down the Gallipoli campaign, meant that in early 1916 the Grand Fleet at Scapa Flow was significantly stronger when compared to the German High Seas Fleet than it had been a year before. The success of the naval code breakers of Room 40 Old Admiralty Building (or OB40) also gave the British a further, important advantage. A month before the start of the Battle of the Somme, and only days before Kitchener's death at sea, the German High Seas Fleet's repeated tactics of making sorties into the North Sea in the hope of drawing the British battlecruisers or part of the Grand Fleet's battleships into a battle at unfavourable odds finally produced the war's only major fleet action at the Battle of Jutland 31 May-1 June, when the battlefleets of both sides finally met. The British lost three battle cruisers, three armoured cruisers, eight destroyers, and 6,094 men; the Germans lost one battle cruiser, a pre-dreadnought battleship, four light cruisers, five torpedo boats, and 2,551 men. Both sides claimed victory, the Germans because of heavier British losses, the British more convincingly

---

29 F. W. Osborne, *Britain's Economic Blockade of Germany 1914-1919* (Abingdon: Frank Cass, 2004), pp. 120-143.
30 C. P. Vincent, *The Politics of Hunger* (Anthens, Ohio: Ohio University Press, 1985), pp. 44-5.

because the Germans had not damaged the Grand Fleet enough to affect the strategic circumstances, meaning that the blockade would continue. On 4 July, Admiral Reinhard Scheer commanding the High Seas Fleet wrote gloomily but realistically that for the future "There can be no doubt that the best possible outcome [for Germany] of any sea battle would not force England to make peace in this war."[31] The High Seas Fleet came out into the North Sea again in August and in October 1916 and finally in April 1918, but it never again engaged the Grand Fleet. Short of the Germans somehow annihilating the Grand Fleet, the blockade and the war would continue as they were, unaffected by German surface sea power.

It was a reflection of the nature of the First World War at sea, including the vulnerability of warships to coastal defences, mines and submarines that even had the British sunk far more German battleships at Jutland than they did, this also would not have changed either side's war plans significantly. The possibility of a British amphibious assault into the Baltic to open up another route through to Russia, in defiance of Danish neutrality, was discussed at various times in the war but never appeared practical in either political or operational terms. Nevertheless, the failure of the Grand Fleet to deliver a decisive victory on the scale of the Battle of Trafalgar in 1805 caused disappointment both among British politicians and the wider public, with Kitchener's death soon adding to the public gloom. Lloyd George's move from the Ministry of Munitions to take over the War Office also marked an intensification of his struggle against the control of strategy that had been established by Robertson and Haig. The Royal Navy, with its pre-war role in protecting trade and stimulating heavy industry, had always been preferred by the Liberal Party, which regarded the Army and its upper ranks – correctly – as too closely associated with the Conservatives. In December 1916, just as Asquith was about to lose office, in response to an apparent German peace offer his wife Margot recorded in her diary (perhaps not remembering her husband's exact words) his assessment that "It's our navy that has done this. We have throttled them slowly but surely by our Blockade. No one can say that they have been beaten on land: except for the Somme offensive they have had no failures. Haig's success on the Somme has three great values: It relieved Russia in the East; France at Verdun; and our Gen[eral] Staff think the French and ourselves have killed more Germans than we have had killed."[32] All three of these assertions have been disputed by historians. In reality, although the blockade had been strengthened by the creation of the new Ministry of Blockade and the victory at Jutland, it was not a war-winner in 1916. The tentative German peace offer which had excited Asquith also turned out to be unacceptable to the Allies. As with the failures against the Ottoman Empire,

---

31 Quoted in Stibbe, *German Anglophobia and the Great War 1914-1918*, p. 135.
32 M. Brock & E. Brock (eds.), *Margot Asquith's Great War Diary 1914-1916* (Oxford: Oxford University Press, 2014), p. 304; Margot Asquith compiled her diary at irregular intervals of some days, working from notes.

the lack of decisive victories at sea meant that British options for success in 1916 were narrowing down to the hope of a victory by the Army on the Western Front.

Back in July 1915, Kitchener had estimated that the British Army would have 70 infantry divisions in the field by April 1916, but that they would not be fully equipped with the necessary artillery until the end of the year. Haig expressed a similar view to Kitchener on 29 March 1916, "I have not got an Army in France really, but a collection of divisions untrained for the field."[33] With the decision to abandon the Gallipoli campaign and to scale back the war against the Ottoman Empire, most of the last of the infantry divisions created since 1914 were sent to the Western Front over winter 1915-16. These New Army or "Kitchener" divisions had been raised in five intakes (originally six had been planned) of six divisions each. The first three of these intakes, designated K1 to K3, had already been mostly sent to the Western Front before September 1915, along with most of the first-line Territorial divisions, to join the Regular divisions, all together forming the First, Second and Third Armies of the BEF. Between November 1915 and June 1916 most of the K4 and K5 divisions also crossed to France, as did the remaining dominion divisions (chiefly Canadian and Australian), resulting in the creation of the Fourth Army under General Sir Henry Rawlinson, and the Reserve Army – later named Fifth Army – under Lieutenant General Sir Hubert Gough. It is notable that both these armies, which would make the British contribution to the Battle of the Somme, combined regular, territorial, new army and dominion divisions. By the end of 1916 any distinction between these divisions would exist mostly on paper only, with high quality divisions belonging to any of the original types.

Whatever their respective shortcomings, or later criticisms made of them, by 1 July the Allies had agreed a Europe-wide strategy for 1916 from which they were not to be deflected. It was unthinkable in terms of alliance strategy that the British should not attack while their other Allies did so. The British had a command structure in place to implement this strategy, the reinforced BEF was in place on the Western Front to fight the Battle of the Somme, and all other strategic possibilities had been exhausted or excluded. The result would always remain controversial. Haig's uncompromising view in his final despatch as Commander-in-Chief, published in March 1919, was that "the long succession of battles commenced on the Somme in 1916 and ended in November of last year [1918] must be viewed as forming part of one great and continuous battle", and that the Battle of the Somme was the necessary beginning of an eventual victory.[34] Arguments can also be made for the Battle of the Somme, as part of the wider Chantilly Conference strategy, having forced the German govern-

---

33   Haig's diary for 29 March 1916 in Sheffield & Bourne (eds.), *Douglas Haig: War Diaries and Letters 1914-1918*, p. 183; Haig added to the typed version of this entry 'The actual fighting Army will be evolved from them'. See also French, *British Strategy and War Aims 1914-1916*, p. 158.
34   J.H. Boraston (ed.), *Sir Douglas Haig's Despatches (December 1915–April 1919)* (London: J.M. Dent & Sons, 1919), p. 319.

ment into the position of either conceding defeat in late 1916 or adopting unrestricted submarine warfare, which was the chief factor in bringing the United States into the war on 6 April 1917. But at the end of 1916 the Central Powers, having over-run Romania, were actually in control of more enemy territory than they had held at the start of the year. The continuing lack of a decisive victory in 1916 led to the fall of Asquith, who was replaced on 7 December by Lloyd George at the head of a principally Conservative coalition government, with much of the Liberal Party following Asquith into opposition. After the experience of the Battle of the Somme, Lloyd George's principal objectives for 1917 would be to regain civilian control of British strategy from Robertson and Haig, and to look for an alternative to fighting on the Western Front. Meanwhile, the war would go on.

2

The Puppetmaster: Sir William Robertson as CIGS in 1916

John Spencer

When Lieutenant-General Sir William 'Wully' Robertson walked into the War Office in late December 1915, the new Chief of the Imperial General Staff found things in an even "greater state of chaos and muddle than I had feared". Three days after his Boxing Day appointment, Robertson predicted that he would "get properly going" in a week or so.[1] Fortunately for Britain's war effort the "ambulating refrigerator", as one admirer described him, did exactly that.[2]

'Getting going' were Robertson's watchwords. He peppered his correspondence and, it is safe to assume, his conversation with them. Now he was ensconced as the government's principal military adviser he was determined to ensure the British Army on the Western Front got going. There was much to do. In 1915 the British Expeditionary Force (BEF) in France and Flanders had played second fiddle to their French ally. The offensive operations it had conducted had suffered from every form of shortage, from high explosive shells and grenades to properly trained officers and men. As far as Wully and many of his fellow senior officers were concerned, what was also lacking was clearly expressed political direction upon which considered military strategy could be built. In 1915 Robertson had been clear that this could only be achieved if the politicians received consistent, resolute and professional advice from their military experts. The "chaos" Robertson found in Whitehall was symptomatic of the fact that such advice had, so far, been unavailable.

This chapter considers how Robertson brought order to the chaos, "revitalized"[3] and emboldened the moribund General Staff, and dominated British military strategy

---

1   Liddell Hart Centre for Military Archives (hereafter LHCMA), Robertson papers, Robertson to Douglas Haig, 26 December 1915 (7/6/3).
2   Brigadier-General E.L. Spears, *Prelude to Victory* (London: Cape, 1939), p. 33
3   Hew Strachan, *The Politics of the British Army* (Oxford: Oxford University Press, 1997), p. 132.

for much of 1916. This strategy was Western Front focused, with considerable energy exerted to avoid extensions of what he considered to be "sideshows", especially in the Balkans. The chapter also considers the many pressures on both senior soldiers and politicians, and a nation coming to terms with industrial warfare. These included the ever-present demands of fighting as part of a coalition in several disparate theatres with an inexperienced citizen army.[4]

To appreciate the impact Wully had at the War Office it is important to understand the background and character of the institution he inherited. The British Army's shambolic and costly performance in the Boer War (1899-1902) had forced Britain's political leadership to reform the institution's governance and make it fit for the twentieth century. Reginald Brett, the Second Viscount Esher, oversaw the process. His reforms included the creation of an overarching General Staff with the duty of planning for potential conflicts and ensuring that the army was trained, equipped and ready for any future campaign. He also established the Army Council, intended as an administrative body to assist the Secretary of State for War and comprised of both military and civilian members.[5] These changes, formalised in 1906 by Lord Haldane as Secretary of State, undoubtedly modernized the army's administration. Nonetheless, as with any new and evolving structure, the choice of Chief of the General Staff (CGS), renamed Chief of the Imperial General Staff (CIGS) in 1907, was key. In the two years immediately before the Great War the CIGS was Sir John French, a brave leader of men but not an intellectual or administrative titan. In a lecture to Staff College students, he told them their role was largely subservient to their regimental colleagues; hardly the kind of talk to be expected from the man

General Sir William Robertson.

---

4 The BEF grew from just under 270,000 officers and men at the end of 1914 to slightly under one million on 1 January 1916, *Statistics of the Military Effort of the British Empire during the Great War 1914-1920* (London: HMSO, 1922), p. 64 (iii).
5 John Gooch, *The Plans of War: The General Staff and British Military Strategy c.1900 – 1914* (London: Routledge, 1974) esp. pp. 50-55 and 97-130.

leading the staff.[6] French was forced to resign the post over the Curragh Incident in March 1914 and was succeeded by General Sir Charles Douglas.[7] Brigadier-General Sir James Edmonds considered Douglas had the "talents of an orderly room clerk".[8] Robertson more generously thought of him as "a very conscientious officer who would insist upon working more hours a day than his state of health justified".[9] On 25 October 1914 Douglas died, his colleagues believed, of overwork.[10]

In the first week of the war two fundamental events shaped the future of the General Staff for the next 18 months and served to create the "chaos" Wully discovered on his appointment. Firstly, all the senior and most of the junior members of the small but competent team of staff officers serving in the War Office left their desks and rushed to serve at the front. They were replaced by older officers, many of whom had not studied at the Staff College at Camberley, who were "dug out" of retirement.[11] Secondly, Prime Minister Herbert Henry Asquith persuaded Britain's greatest soldier-hero to become Secretary of State for War. Lord Herbert Horatio Kitchener of Khartoum, or "K of K" as he was sometimes known, was a hugely popular choice with the public but a disaster for the independence of the General Staff. Kitchener's distinguished career, during which he had operated "practically as an Oriental autocrat", was not the ideal background for a person entering Cabinet government.[12] The domineering Kitchener paid no heed to the views of either Douglas or his successor as CIGS, the "notoriously incompetent" Lieutenant-General Sir James Wolfe-Murray.[13] The latter's inability to stand up to Kitchener saw him nicknamed "Sheep" Murray by Winston Churchill.[14] Kitchener was a supremely self-confident figure at this time and, very importantly for a junior partner in a coalition war, popular with Britain's French ally.[15] Kitchener treated the CIGS and his staff as little more than clerks, doing both their work and his

---

6   Richard Holmes, *The Little Field Marshal: A Life of Sir John French* (London: Cassell, 2005 [1981]), p. 136.
7   Ian F.W. Beckett, *The Army and the Curragh Incident 1914* (London: The Bodley Head for the Army Records Society, 1985).
8   Ian Beckett (ed.), *The Memoirs of Sir James Edmonds* (Brighton: Tom Donovan Editions, 2013), p. 287.
9   Field-Marshal Sir William Robertson, *From Private to Field-Marshal* (London: Constable, 1921), p. 195.
10 The official cause of death was 'renal colic, bronchitis and pulmonary congestion'. Edward M. Spiers, 'Sir Charles Douglas', *Oxford Dictionary of National Biography*, online edition <http://www.oxforddnb.com/view/article/32870?docPos=3>
11 Gooch, *Plans of War*, p. 302.
12 Lord Hankey, *The Supreme Command*, 2 Vols. (London: George Allen & Unwin, 1961), [Vol. 1], p. 186.
13 Gooch, *Plans of War*, p. 303.
14 Churchill Archive Centre (hereafter CAC), Hankey diary, (HNKY 1/1), 23 September 1914.
15 For Kitchener's character see George H. Cassar, *Kitchener: Architect of Victory* (London: William Kimber, 1977) and George H. Cassar, *Kitchener's War* (Washington DC: Potomac Books, 2004).

own as Secretary of State.[16] This was clearly untenable and yet it continued until the end of 1915. Winston Churchill, never a shrinking violet himself, offered an evocative description of Kitchener:

> The sole mouthpiece of War Office opinion in the War Council …When he gave a decision it was invariably accepted as final. He was never, to my belief, overruled by the War Council or the Cabinet in any military matter, great or small… Scarcely anyone ever ventured to argue with him in council … All-powerful, imperturbable, reserved, he dominated absolutely our counsels at this time.

Wolfe Murray said Kitchener acted as his own Chief of Staff and never asked him, the CIGS, to express any opinion.[17]

The result of the dearth of advice from experienced staff officers was a strategic "policy vacuum".[18] This vacuum was filled by "strategic entrepreneurs" such as Churchill, David Lloyd George and the Cabinet Secretary Maurice Hankey.[19] None of these men had any relevant military command experience and yet their conviction that there was more to be gained fighting in theatres other than the Western Front became a major feature of British war policy in 1915. Their task was made easier by the Prime Minister. Asquith had been a successful premier before the war, adept in the arts of parliamentary deal-making, but his "wait and see" style meant his administration never got a grip on the numerous wartime problems facing the country. His approach was much criticised by Conservatives, many senior military figures, and his Liberal Party colleague Lloyd George.[20] As Chief of Staff to Field Marshal Sir John French, Commander-in-Chief (C-in-C) of the BEF in 1915, Sir William Robertson looked upon these events with a mixture of horror and disdain. He spent the year lobbying colleagues in the War Office, hoping they would be able to convince the politicians that Germany was Britain's principal enemy and could only be defeated on the principal, i.e. Western, front.[21] The failure of the "frocks" to see what he believed to be blindingly obvious was the fault, he rightly deduced, of an impotent General Staff.[22] He chided colleagues in the War Office, including his friend Charles Callwell

---

16   J.M. Bourne, *Britain and the Great War 1914-1918* (London: Arnold, 1989), pp. 139-145.
17   The National Archives (TNA), CAB 19/1, Dardanelles Commission: First Report, pp. 3-4, 6.
18   Ian Beckett, 'King George V and His Generals' in Brian Bond, *The First World War and British Military History* (Oxford: Oxford University Press, 1991), p. 257.
19   Gooch, *Plans of War*, p. 299.
20   See Roy Jenkins, *Asquith* (London: Collins, 1964), pp. 367-386, and George H. Cassar, *Asquith as War Leader* (London: Hambledon Press, 1994), pp. 111-124.
21   John Spencer, 'Friends Disunited: Johnnie French, "K of K" and Wully Robertson in 1915' in Spencer Jones (ed.), *Courage Without Glory: The British Army on the Western Front 1915* (Solihull: Helion, 2015), pp. 80-102.
22   'Frocks', used pejoratively by senior soldiers when referring to politicians and alluding to the frock coats they usually wore in Parliament.

the Director of Military Operations and Intelligence (DMO&I), to get matters "in hand".[23] Wully noted that Sir Archibald "Archie" Murray, who succeeded the hapless Wolfe-Murray in September 1915, agreed with him about the primacy of the Western Front but it was "no use laying down these excellent principles and expressing such entire conviction of their soundness, unless we are prepared to carry them to their logical conclusion and stand or fall by them".[24] It was clear that Murray, although an able enough administrator, was never going to prevail against Kitchener.

Ultimately, Britain's 1915 strategic model was unsustainable. The disastrous failure of the Gallipoli campaign, which dragged on throughout the year, was very damaging to the government and the "strategic entrepreneurs" who had championed it. Disappointing and costly offensives on the Western Front in support of the French diminished both Kitchener's prestige and that of the C-in-C.[25] By the end of the year French was relieved of his command and Kitchener politically emasculated. Robertson, along with Haig, and even King George V, had a hand in both events but the final blows were struck by the politicians who made the appointments in the first place. It was ever thus.[26]

In December 1915 Kitchener, exhausted by a workload he refused or was unable to share, and haunted by the Dardanelles stalemate, accepted the inevitable and asked Robertson to become CIGS. Wully stuck to the line he had pursued throughout the year: for the General Staff to exert real authority by giving advice to the government directly.[27] He refused to take on the role unless he and the Secretary of State came to a "definite understanding in writing" about how the appointment would work.[28] "Our Bargain", as Robertson called the final agreement, had a fundamental impact on British military policy for the rest of the war. It bestowed powers on Robertson as CIGS which were "unprecedented in British history" and ensured that, despite the almost constant urgings of Lloyd George and others, that the Western Front remained the principal theatre for British operations until the end of the conflict.[29] For Robertson the focus when he became CIGS was "not on personalities but on systems".[30] The key points of the Robertson-Kitchener agreement may be summarised[31] as follows:

23 LHCMA, Robertson papers, Robertson to Callwell, 26 October 1915, (7/2/33).
24 Ibid., Robertson to Murray, 23 October 1915, (7/3/1).
25 The BEF's main offensive battles of 1915: Neuve Chapelle, 10-13 March; Aubers Ridge, 9-10 May; Festubert, 15-25 May; Loos, 25 September-16 October.
26 Holmes, *The Little Field Marshal*, pp. 303-307; see also George H. Cassar, *The Tragedy of Sir John French* (Newark: University of Delaware Press, 1985).
27 CAC, Hankey papers, Hankey diary, 8 December 1915, (HNKY 1/1).
28 Robertson, *Private to Field Marshal*, p. 237.
29 David R. Woodward, *Field Marshal Sir William Robertson: Chief of the Imperial General Staff in the Great War* (Westport: Praeger, 1998), p. 25.
30 Strachan, *Politics*, p. 145.
31 LHCMA, Robertson papers, 5 December 1915, memorandum from Robertson to Kitchener (4/3/27); a slightly revised version appears in Robertson, *Private to Field-Marshal*, pp. 239-243.

i. The establishment of a "supreme directing authority", with "real executive power" to formulate war policy, decide on the theatres of military operations and to make decisions when required. It should not have to refer every decision to the full Cabinet because "the absence of a decision may be little less than criminal because of the loss of life which may be entailed". Robertson called this body the "War Council" in his proposal but in fact these responsibilities fell to the recently established War Committee.[32]

ii. It was "essential" that the new body "should receive *all* advice concerning military operations through one authoritative channel only. With us that must be the Chief of the Imperial General Staff". To reduce time wasted in Cabinet discussion Robertson effectively ruled out the possibility of them receiving advice from elsewhere. Once they had been briefed by the CIGS it was for the politicians to accept or reject his advice. Robertson was quite specific. He, and not the aforementioned "strategic entrepreneurs", would be the fount of all military knowledge. Any suggestions from civilians should be "sifted, examined, and presented, if necessary with reasoned conclusions", to the War Committee by the CIGS and *his* General Staff.

iii. Robertson's original proposal to Kitchener included the sticking point that all orders to the British armies in the field should be issued by him as CIGS and not through the Army Council of which the Secretary of State was president. The result, as Kitchener pointed out, was that the only responsibilities left to him would be to feed and clothe the army, an unacceptable humiliation that would force him to resign.[33] Robertson wanted Kitchener to stay in post and the two settled on the face-saving formula that Robertson would issue orders to armies in the field but "under the authority" of the Secretary of State. This was formalised by a special Order in Council on 27 January 1916.[34]

iv. In future all correspondence regarding military operations would come into and leave the War Office under Robertson's control. This would improve confidentiality, he argued, and in return ministers would receive "at all times full information of all that they should know". What it meant in practice was that theatre C-in-Cs and their staffs communicated with Robertson alone and received their instructions from him. But this also sowed the seeds

---

32 Asquith formed the War Committee on 11 November 1915 while Kitchener was inspecting the Dardanelles theatre. It consisted originally of the First Lord of the Admiralty, Arthur Balfour, the Minister of Munitions, Lloyd George, the Conservative and Unionist Party leader Andrew Bonar Law, the Chancellor of the Exchequer, Reginald McKenna, the Prime Minister and Kitchener; Paul Guinn, *British Strategy and Politics: 1914 to 1918* (Oxford: Clarendon Press, 1965), pp. 109-10.
33 Sir William Robertson, *Soldiers and Statesmen* (London: Cassell, 1926), pp. 165-166.
34 Robertson, *Private to Field-Marshal*, p. 243.

of future discord as politicians, especially those critical of British strategy, tired of Wully being the fount of all they were told about military policy.

Robertson took over at the War Office on 23 December 1915 and immediately commenced reorganisaton. The first job for Robertson's Aide-De-Camp (ADC), Major C.C. Lucas was to sort out the Chief's office.[35] Wully spent just one day in the first room he was given and it was:

> [Q]uite the most exasperating day of my life. The telephone, which I have always detested, rang incessantly and a constant stream of people of both sexes and all grades – girl typists, wives of officers, members of parliament, boy-scout messengers, general officers – entered the room, one after another, unannounced, either to see me on some trivial matter or someone else whose room they thought it was.[36]

Lucas found a new office, "expelled" the phone and guarded his chief's door with all the tenacity deserving of his nickname of "the Monument". Accommodation crisis resolved, Robertson got on with the establishment of his own team of officers to run the organisation. As his deputy (DCIGS) Robertson chose Robert "Bob" Whigham. The two men knew each other well. Whigham had been Wully's Sub-Chief of Staff at GHQ and was an instructor at the Staff College when Robertson was Commandant there in the years before the outbreak of war. An important change to the working of the General Staff organisation was Robertson's decision to split the directorship of military operations and intelligence into two, as he had done as Chief of Staff to French at GHQ. As a result, another Camberley colleague of Robertson's, Frederick "Freddie" Maurice moved from GHQ to the War Office as Director of Military Operations (DMO). Charles Callwell, DMO&I, lost the operations remit of his brief and became Director of Military Intelligence, albeit for only a matter of days.[37] During 1915 Robertson had kept up a regular correspondence with Callwell, usually urging him to help assert the independence and strategic views of the General Staff. Despite paying Callwell credit in his memoirs, Wully was ruthless in replacing the self-confessed "Dug-Out".[38] On 3 January 1916 Callwell was replaced by

---

35 Major C.C. Lucas had been a pupil of Robertson's at Camberley. Nicknamed 'the Monument' for his steadfast support of his CO, he served as Robertson's ADC from his time as Chief of Staff of the BEF in early 1915 and for the rest of the war, David R. Woodward, *The Military Correspondence of Field-Marshal Sir William Robertson, Chief of the Imperial General Staff, December 1915-February 1918* (hereafter *MCWR*) (London: Army Records Society, 1989), p. 339.
36 Robertson, *Private to Field-Marshal*, p. 249.
37 Ibid., pp. 250-251.
38 Ibid., p. 251; C.E. Callwell, *Experiences of a Dug-Out, 1914-1918* (London: Constable, 1920).

Major-General George Macdonogh who had headed up the Intelligence operation at GHQ under Robertson's command. Macdonogh was an able and experienced officer and one of Robertson's mainstays while he was CIGS. His intelligence briefings were less relentlessly optimistic than those of his successor at GHQ, John Charteris. One of Macdonogh's protégés Edgar Cox, went with him to London. Cox was another supremely talented officer and succeeded Charteris as head of intelligence at GHQ in 1918.[39] Another figure in the Robertson initiated "brain drain" from GHQ which, as Wully's most recent biographer observed, had "serious consequences for the future of BEF operations" was acting Lieutenant-General Sir Neville Macready.[40] Macready, or "Make-Ready" as he was known due to the correct pronunciation of his name, had been Adjutant-General with the BEF and joined Robertson at the War Office as Adjutant-General to the Forces in February 1916. It is important to stress that Macready held his office independently of the CIGS. Nonetheless, he was a "helpful colleague to do business with" according to Robertson, who worked alongside him throughout the war.[41] The same was true of the Quartermaster-General (QMG), Lieutenant-General Sir John Cowans. Robertson began the war as the BEF's QMG and worked closely and effectively with his opposite number at the War Office.[42]

A crucial element in Robertson's assumption of control of the General Staff was his domination of the Army Council. This body had, until the Robertson-Kitchener "bargain", been the mechanism through which orders were issued to the army on behalf of the government. Headed by the Secretary of State for War it was endowed with a broad range of administrative powers, including the appointment of officers to their respective units. When the Army Council was set up by the 1904 reforms, precedence amongst the military members was by their appointments. This meant that the CGS was "First Military Member", followed by Adjutant-General, Quartermaster-General then Master-General of the Ordnance. During the war this had altered to give precedence to rank. Wully would have none of this and said so to Kitchener, who overcame the issue by promoting him to temporary general.[43] The issue was not one of arcane pedantry. With his new powers, Robertson controlled both the information on the progress of the war and the strategic advice senior government ministers received. He also ensured the DCIGS, his loyal deputy Whigham, joined the Council.[44] By

39 Jim Beach, *Haig's Intelligence: GHQ and the German Army, 1916-1918* (Cambridge: Cambridge University Press, 2015 [2013]), pp. 24, 44-48, 56-60.
40 Woodward, *Robertson*, p. 29.
41 Robertson, *Private to Field-Marshal*, p. 198.
42 For Robertson's performance in the first months of the war see John Spencer, "'The big brain in the army": Sir William Robertson as Quartermaster-General', in Spencer Jones, (ed.), *Stemming the Tide: Officers and Leadership in the British Expeditionary Force 1914* (Solihull: Helion, 2013), pp. 89-108.
43 Robertson, *Private to Field Marshal*, p. 230.
44 In January 1916 the Army Council was made up of civilian and military members. The civil group comprised the Secretary of State for War as President of the Council, the Parliamentary Under-Secretary of State for War and the Financial Secretary. The military

Robertson (fourth from left) inspects French troops at Blaincourt with King George V, Edward Prince of Wales and General Joseph Joffre, 26 October 1915. (Private collection)

becoming "first amongst equals" on the Army Council, Robertson's influence was enhanced.[45]

Before being offered the role of CIGS, Robertson had produced a detailed strategy document setting out his views on the priorities for Britain's future war policy.[46] These priorities remained unchanged for the entirety of Wully's time at the General Staff and the memorandum is therefore worthy of examination. Kitchener had asked for Wully's opinion, urging him to "hold nothing back". Because Kitchener was on his way to the Dardanelles Robertson penned a covering note to Asquith, who was standing in as War Secretary, acknowledging that he was trespassing on Archie Murray's terri-

---

    members were the CIGS, DCIGS (added 23 December 1915), Adjutant General to the Forces, Quartermaster-General to the Forces, and Master-General of the Ordnance. As the demands on the machinery of war expanded a Director-General of Military Aeronautics was added in February 1916, a Director-General of Movements and Railways (February 1917), and a Surveyor-General of Supply (May 1917); Major A.F. Becke, *History of the Great War Based on Official Documents: Order of Battle of Divisions, Part 4, The Army Council, GHQs, Armies and Corps 1914-18* (London: HMSO, 1945), pp. 2-3.

45 Robertson, *Private to Field Marshal*, p. 250-251.

46 'Memorandum on the Conduct of the War, 5 November 1915,' reproduced in full in Robertson, *Soldiers and Statesmen*, vol. 1, pp. 196-206; a printed copy of the same document, for the Committee of Imperial Defence, dated 8 November 1915, can be found at LHCMA, Robertson papers, (3/2/25).

tory and "you should receive advice from the responsible officer only", adding that he believed Murray would agree with it.[47] In essence this was a closely argued plea for two things: the restoration of the authority of the CIGS, supported by the General Staff, as the government's principal military adviser; and the primacy of the Western Front. On the former issue, Robertson pointed out that Britain was now fighting on four fronts. It was essential that the government had one military authority to advise it on all these theatres. The current system was not working:

> Experience has shown that in a war of the magnitude of the present one it is undesirable to combine in one person the functions of supreme military adviser and of War Minister. In our case it is especially undesirable to combine these functions, because we are engaged in the stupendous task of raising large armies during the progress of the war…It is not possible to carry on war in an efficient manner if each of a considerable number of men has authority to make plans, to endeavor to convince his fellow members of the of his views, and to search for those who are prepared to carry out his plans.

As for the government itself, the Cabinet should establish a small body delegated to make prompt decisions and take equally prompt action. On the matter of strategic priorities, the aim of the Entente, said Robertson's memorandum, was to defeat the Central Powers. This could only be achieved by the defeat or exhaustion of Germany, the predominant party in the enemy alliance.[48] The key question for the politicians was, could Germany be defeated by "direct means"? If this was considered impossible, or more difficult to achieve than by "indirect means", then the latter course was a valid option. He then reviewed the four theatres in which the British Army was engaged: France and Flanders, Mesopotamia, the Dardanelles, and at Salonika in the Balkans. Robertson, mistakenly as it turned out, was sanguine about the Mesopotamia campaign, believing the possible capture of Baghdad to be helpful to the Allied cause with little impact on men and resources for the Western Front.[49] Britain had embarked upon the Dardanelles campaign, said Robertson, due to impatience at home for a victory which had not yet been achieved in the west. The effort had failed "and the force in the Peninsula has no longer any prospect of contributing, directly or indirectly, to the defeat of Germany". Robertson therefore recommended withdrawal and opposed any intermediate transfer of more troops from Europe. As for Salonika, the French-led operation could "only assist us to our end and in the most favourable circumstances, and only then very indirectly". Robertson was against any further extension of the

---

47 LHCMA, Robertson Papers, Robertson to Asquith, covering note with Robertson's 'Memorandum on the Conduct of the War', 6 November 1915, (4/3/14).
48 LHCMA, Robertson papers, (3/2/25).
49 In fact, the Mesopotamian campaign was to divert men and resources for much of the war.

enterprise and urged that all forces which were not essential to holding the current position be redeployed to the Western Front.

Unsurprisingly, Robertson's memorandum was clear that it was only in France and Flanders where the allies would achieve their aim of defeating Germany. He pointed out that Britain was still building its citizen army and learning the techniques needed to win. Germany, on the other hand, was condemned to the defensive in the west and was beginning to suffer in terms of shortage of men and materiel. He counselled against the expectation that individual battles, no matter how carefully planned, would lead to speedy and overwhelming victory. Time and patience was needed. This was to become a familiar Robertson refrain and one which contrasted with Sir Douglas Haig's more ambitious plans. Admonishing, by implication, those politicians who had favoured the illusory "short cuts" proffered by the Salonika and Gallipoli theatres he summarised his argument thus: "France and Flanders must continue to be the principal theatre of war, and on it our main efforts must be concentrated." As for Britain's relations with its French ally it was necessary "to take a hold of the war as a whole to a much greater extent than we have done in the past". In future, French plans needed to pay more attention to British views because "we have now a great Army in the field, our Navy is all-powerful, financially we are the dominant party". Perhaps unsurprisingly Callwell noted that Robertson "undoubtedly has impressed the politician people, and I do not know that Murray has; they think he is too much under K's thumb – as indeed he is".[50]

On the day he became CIGS Robertson asked the War Committee to confirm that France and Flanders was the "main theatre of operations", that Gallipoli should be evacuated, an attempt made to persuade France to leave Salonika, and a defensive policy adopted in Mesopotamia: "If the War Committee does not approve of the above policy it is necessary that an alternative policy (regarding which I have no recommendation) should be formulated."[51] The Committee had no "alternative policy" to suggest and Robertson now found himself architect of British military strategy. Nonetheless, "his powers were far from absolute, and unless he had the confidence of the political leadership, he would ultimately fail".[52] The dominating issues in Robertson's "in-tray" at the War Office in January 1916 were, therefore, largely of his own making. The Gallipoli Peninsula had to be evacuated and Britain's commitment in the Balkans curtailed, or at least minimised. The Cabinet had accepted that the Western Front was the principal front, with the growing British armies playing a leading role. The challenge for Robertson and the General Staff was to ensure that Haig as C-in-C had the tools, and the men, with which to do the job.

50 Imperial War Museum (IWM), Callwell papers, (2/75/74), Callwell to Sir Henry Wilson, 13 December 1915.
51 Guinn, *British Strategy*, p. 115; LHCMA, Robertson papers, Robertson to the War Committee, printed note, 23 December 1915, (4/1/3).
52 Woodward, *Robertson*, p. 30.

The extraction of British forces from Gallipoli was completed on 9 January 1916. It was the most successful operation of a disastrous campaign.[53] Much more complicated was Britain's entanglement in the Balkans. This had begun in October 1915 when British forces were sent to the port of Salonika in Macedonia (Thessaloniki in modern Greece). The enterprise, initiated and led by the French, failed in its first objective to protect Serbia against the Central Powers. Allied forces found themselves defending an enclave which, by the end of March 1916, required five British divisions. Domestic politics, and concerns for its post-war role in the Middle East, meant that France placed much more importance on the campaign than Britain.[54] It also had considerable support from Russia. Lloyd George saw it as an opportunity to put pressure on Austria, one of the "props" supporting the German war effort, but there was little enthusiasm for the venture amongst other British statesmen, and still less amongst the soldiers.[55] The War Committee was prepared, in a gesture aimed at protecting the Entente, to allow British forces to remain if they took on a defensive role. Opponent-in-chief was Robertson who wanted the entire theatre abandoned. Throughout 1916 the French favoured an offensive posture. Wully did all he could to frustrate such initiatives. In February, he complained to Haig that the French intended to add another 100,00 men to their 200,000-strong force at Salonika. Marshal Joseph Joffre, the French C-in-C "sprung a bomb" on Robertson by saying he had told his government he was unable to find the men in France but that the British might find them from their force in Egypt. Robertson was "very straight" with Joffre but repeated his view that "we are not taking nearly sufficient lead in the conduct of the war, considering the great amount we are contributing towards it…We [General Staff] must take charge of the thing in politics in the same way as we are gradually beginning to do in military affairs."[56]

A few weeks later Lieutenant-General Sir Brian Mahon, the C-in-C British Salonika Force (BSF) informed Robertson that General Maurice Sarrail, commanding the French forces in Greece, had been ordered by his government to begin offensive operations. The CIGS replied:

> Until you hear from me you can take it that I am not out for any offensive operations in the Balkans. Such operations would be unsound from every point of view, and the day they are sanctioned I shall leave the War Office. I know the Balkans pretty well, I also know the Germans, and I know where a decision will be got, and that certainly will not be in the Balkans., I do not intend to have

---

53   For recent scholarship on the Dardanelles campaign see Les Carlyon, *Gallipoli* (London: Pan MacMillan, 2002 [2001]) and Peter Hart, *Gallipoli* (London: Profile Books, 2011).
54   Elizabeth Greenhalgh, *The French Army and the First World War* (Cambridge: Cambridge University Press, 2014), pp. 106-110
55   Keith Neilson, *Strategy and Supply: The Anglo-Russian Alliance, 1914-17* (London: Routledge, 2014 [1984]), pp. 110, 114-116.
56   Woodward, *MCWR*, Robertson to Haig, 17 February 1916, pp. 36-37.

anything to do with British soldiers being engaged in killing Bulgars and getting killed themselves in return.

PS: Always let me know if I can help you. Sarrail is a wrong 'un I should say. Too much of the politician about him.[57]

No such offensive, if one had ever been intended, took place, but the above neatly summed up Robertson's attitude to the Salonika campaign, Britain's French allies, and politicians. He continued to fret about the Balkan front, telling Archie Murray "I hope Mahon will be careful and not lose any more British lives than possible in foolhardy enterprises".[58] Robertson clearly had his doubts about his colleague's judgement and acted decisively. As the dominating figure on the Army Council in 1916 he replaced Mahon in early May because "he is not at all up to Sarrail and in any case he is not the kind of man we want there. Sarrail is trying to get us committed to an offensive by indirect means and I want them to be scotched."[59] As outlined already, one of the Army Council's powers was its ability to make and break military careers. Even General (later Field Marshal) Sir Douglas Haig, while entitled to express a view, was unable to choose his own generals. At the close of 1917 it was Robertson and the Army Council which decreed that the C-in-C should reorganise his senior team at GHQ. This led to the removal of both Charteris and, in early 1918 of Haig's CoS Launcelot Kiggell.[60] As for Macedonia, Robertson replaced Mahon with Lieutenant-General George Milne who had been one of his contemporaries at the Staff College and who had also worked under Robertson when the latter headed the Foreign Military Intelligence Section at the War Office after the Boer War.[61] Robertson's first communication with Milne as C-in-C of the BSF was much more measured in tone, perhaps illustrating the trust he had in the new man. Wully urged Milne keep him informed of any French offensive plans and accepted the need to "co-operate with our Allies to the full extent possible but this would not justify our undertaking futile and costly operations".[62] The issue continued to rankle for the rest of the year and into 1917, with Robertson fighting a rearguard action, avoiding French entreaties to send more men; men Haig needed for the Western Front.[63]

Towards the end of 1915 the Allies had agreed to a programme of coordinated offensives on the Russian, Italian and Western fronts.[64] In the latter theatre, of course,

---

57 Woodward, *MCWR*, Robertson to Mahon, 6 March 1916, p. 38.
58 Ibid., Robertson to Murray, 5 April 1916, p. 45; after making way for Robertson at the War Office Murray had been made C-in-C of British forces in Egypt.
59 Woodward, *MCWR*, Robertson to Murray, 18 May 1916, p. 49;
60 Gary Sheffield, *The Chief: Douglas Haig and the British Army* (London: Aurum Press, 2011), p. 258-259.
61 Robertson, *Private to Field Marshal*, pp. 88-89, 132.
62 Woodward, *MCWR*, Robertson to Milne, 8 May 1916, pp. 47-48.
63 Neilson, *Strategy and Supply*, pp. 150-154.
64 Guinn, *British Strategy*, p. 133.

this resulted in the Somme offensive. For Robertson and Haig this was reason enough to resist the relentless political pressure to expend resources elsewhere, either on what they saw as domestic political whim, or an over-anxiety to please allies. Robertson's "bargain" with Kitchener had serious repercussions for civil-military relations after the latter's death in early June 1916. As Robertson wrote in his memoirs, throughout 1916 "the General Staff were accorded suitable freedom of action in all matters lying within their sphere … Unfortunately…the same mutually helpful relations were not forthcoming in 1917."[65] This was because Kitchener's successor, David Lloyd George, did not believe the relationship to be "mutually helpful". He resented having to abide by rules which, he later wrote, would see him as "a mere ornamental figurehead in Whitehall".[66] He took the War Secretary portfolio, but bridled at the powers Robertson had secured in the fraught days of December 1915. Unlike most of his War Committee colleagues, Lloyd George had not accepted the generals' belief in the offensive in early 1916.[67] He continued to believe there were other fronts where greater successes could be achieved at lower cost to Britain. The Gallipoli operation had damaged the reputation of the "Easterners" in government, but the new War Secretary, having favoured the Balkans as an alternative to France and Flanders, was consequently in astronger position. As soon as he entered the War Office he challenged the Robertson-Haig orthodoxy. His task was made easier by the disappointments following the start of the Somme offensive. Optimistic promises from GHQ about the potential for significant advances had raised the expectations of politicians and public. Lloyd George's position was that the War Committee had failed to support his belief in a large-scale Balkan offensive because of their faith in great success in the west. By the end of July 1916 it was clear that an overwhelming victory had not been achieved and that an attritional battle would grind on.

For Robertson and the General Staff, events in the summer of 1916 sowed the seeds of problems which would continue for the next eighteen months. Significantly, Robertson and Haig disagreed about the best method for the Somme campaign. A few days after the initial and largely disastrous assault on the German defences, Robertson wrote to Kiggell, Haig's CoS, that he was "convinced" that "the road to success lies through deliberation". In other words, unlike Haig, Wully did not expect a rapid transition from breaking in to the enemy defences, breaking through them and then breaking out. He wanted limits to how far troops could advance:

> The thing is to advance along a wide front step by step to very limited and moderate objectives, and to forbid going beyond these objectives until all have

---

65 Robertson, *Soldiers and Statesmen*, vol 1., p. 286.
66 David Lloyd George, *War Memoirs of David Lloyd George*, 2 Vols., (London: Oldhams, 1938), [Vol. 1], p. 456.
67 David R. Woodward, *Lloyd George and the Generals* (Newark, Delaware: University of Delaware Press, 1983), p. 82.

been reached by the troops engaged…Once we get into the open country we can make our numbers tell. Until we get there it is on no use crowding in more men.[68]

Despite this fundamental difference of view, Robertson made it clear to Kiggell that he did not want his letter shown to Haig, or anyone else. In his dealings with politicians Robertson's loyalty to Haig never wavered; the C-in-C's policy was the General Staff's policy. Nonetheless, Robertson quickly learned that Lloyd George wanted a much more 'hands-on' role in the way the war was being fought. Robertson's life was made more difficult by Haig's failure to keep him informed of the ongoing developments in the campaign. Lloyd George and his senior colleagues wanted information:

> I hope you will keep me informed of what you think as to your future prospects. This is really essential because of the many theatres and Allies which we here have to deal with. Our vast and complicated foreign policy necessitates the War Committee being kept full informed of our prospects and doings in ever theatre. I am not referring to detailed plans but to the General situation…If you could send me a short letter which I could read to the War Committee I am sure it would be to the General interest and to *your* interest in particular.

The deferential tone Robertson adopted says much about the relationship between the two men, and the pressure he was under to keep the government informed. Haig, focusing on his own continuing offensive, could not be expected to concern himself with the other theatres to which Robertson referred. In addition, neither he nor Robertson were keen to oversupply their political masters with detail that some of them might then use to debate strategy. In the same vein, the politicians would have been negating their responsibilities if they had not attempted to keep abreast of events. Kitchener had been a secretive and overbearing Secretary of State who had been worn down over time by the burden of his responsibilities. He had passed much of that burden on to a CIGS who had a similar aversion to telling politicians any more than he thought essential. Lloyd George was a different character altogether, a War Secretary with clear views on military policy and a desire to know as much as possible about the progress of events. As a result, Wully remained under pressure to say more to the War Committee. The paucity of Haig's briefing notes left him exposed: "I don't want your plans and you can rely upon me acting discreetly. But if I have to depend almost entirely upon press communiqués, my opinion is regarded as not much more valuable than that of anyone else, and indeed it is almost impossible to give an opinion." Unhelpfully Haig responded that he did not think a weekly paper would be of any use because it would ordinarily "only amount to 'views unchanged since last report'!" He did condescend, however, to provide a weekly summary for Robertson's

---

68   Woodward, *MCWR*, Robertson to Kiggell, 5 July 1916, pp. 65-66 (original emphasis).

information.[69] A few days later Robertson, with Lloyd George's support, managed to blackball Haig's chances of being promoted to Field Marshal. The King, with whom both Haig and Robertson had a good relationship, was behind the initiative but Wully argued that "the battle of the Somme is not nearly finished yet". It might have been that Robertson was exacting a little revenge.[70]

Despite this rare example of collaboration, Lloyd George's antipathy towards Robertson, and to a lesser extent Haig, and their Western Front strategy as whole was exacerbated at this time. Relations never recovered. During the late summer and autumn of 1916 Lloyd George continued to urge British initiatives in the Balkans and the Middle East. The friction between the two men reached a peak in October when Robertson threatened to resign over what he saw as Lloyd George's interference in his responsibilities. The CIGS had long opposed sending more Allied forces to the Salonika front, despite the impending collapse of Britain's new Romanian ally in the face of a devastating Central Power's offensive.[71] Lloyd George persuaded the War Committee to instruct Robertson to ask Joffre for his opinion. Wully was angered again when, after advising the politicians not to send a force to protect the Muslim holy city of Medina from the Ottoman Turks, Lloyd George went behind his back and suggested "certain commanders subordinate to me", should be consulted. As result, he wrote to the Secretary of State for War:

> You will I think agree with me that it is essential to the proper conduct of the war that that the CIGS should be able to count upon the support of the Secretary of State for War in regard to the military plans which he puts forward for the consideration of the War Committee. If this support is not forthcoming but conflicting views are presented to the Committee the general cause must suffer.

Wully forwarded a copy to Prime Minister Asquith and fired off letters of complaint to Lord Northcliffe, the proprietor of both *The Times* and the *Daily Mail*, and to Lieutenant-Colonel Clive Wigram, the King's deputy private secretary. Undaunted, Lloyd George responded by upbraiding Robertson for taking his concerns to the press. Although he did not accuse the CIGS directly, referring instead to "some one [sic] in your close confidence", he put it to Robertson that:

---

69 Woodward, *MCWR*, Robertson to Haig, 1 August 1916, pp. 76-77 and Haig to Robertson, 3 August 1916, pp. 77-78.
70 Woodward, *MCWR*, Robertson to Stamfordham, 10 August 1916, p. 81; Lord Stamfordham was King George V's private secretary; Haig was appointed Field Marshal on 1 January 1917.
71 Romania entered the war on the side of the Allies in August 1916, only to be overrun by a German and Austro-Hungarian offensive which captured Bucharest by December. Fragments of the Romanian army continued to operate with Russian armies in Moldova and Ukraine until late 1917 when the Bolshevik Revolution forced Romania to sign an armistice with the Central Powers.

> I feel confident you must agree with me that this state of things is an outrage on all the best traditions of the service & must tend to impair discipline in all ranks of the Army & I am certain that I will receive your assistance & that of the Army Council in putting an end to these injurious practices. Privates have recently been court-martialed for complaining direct to their MPs & to the Secretary of State & the Army Council have asked me to enforce discipline against MP officers who ventilate their grievances in Parliament. How can I do so when such an example of indiscipline is set by men in high places.

As to Robertson's specific complaint, Lloyd George asked whether he should participate in debate in the War Committee or "choose between the position of a dummy or a pure advocate of all opinions expressed by my military advisers." The soon-to-be Prime Minister defended his pro-Balkan views, stressed his admiration for Robertson's "great gifts" but concluded ominously "[Y]ou must not ask me to play the part of a mere dummy. I am not in the least suited for the part."[72] Robertson liked to give the outward impression that he was a simple soldier, unconcerned with and opposed to the "intrigue" and "politicking" of the "frocks". In fact, he was extremely adept at using his contacts outside the military to support his position. Robertson, in his capacity of CIGS, cultivated newspaper editors, particularly Geoffrey Dawson of *The Times* and H.A. Gwynne of the right-wing *Morning Post*. This was not a new departure for Wully. Throughout the later months of 1915, when he became convinced of Sir John French's unsuitability to remain as BEF C-in-C, he conspired with colleagues, and the King, to have him removed.[73] Robertson and Lloyd George continued to spar for the rest of the year; friction only increased at the turn of 1916 when Lloyd George moved into 10 Downing Street.

When Robertson assumed the role of Chief of the Imperial Staff at the end of 1915 that office, and the General Staff which supported it, were devalued and moribund. A series of ineffectual predecessors had allowed what was already a relatively new and evolving institution to wither to the state of mere appendage to the Secretary of State for War, Lord Kitchener. Robertson succeeded in not only restoring the authority of his own appointment, but enhancing it, securing powers never since equaled in the history of the British Army. His "bargain" with Kitchener allowed him to dominate British military policy in 1916 and restore the strategic initiative to the soldiers. He achieved this not only through sheer force of personality, although this was undoubtedly a factor, but by rebuilding the General Staff as an expert body, competent to both administer the army machine and give clear and definitive advice on war policy. Robertson ensured the revived General Staff was populated by his own nominees. Those officers both at home and overseas with whom he disagreed were replaced. The

---

72 Woodward, *MCWR*, Robertson to Lloyd George, Lord Northcliffe, Clive Wigram, and Lloyd George to Robertson, all 11 October 1916, pp. 90-96.
73 Spencer, 'Friends Disunited', pp. 90-93.

result was that for the rest of the war the Western Front dominated British military policy, even if as CIGS Robertson spent a considerable amount of his time fending off those politicians who thought other theatres offered better strategic opportunities. Inevitably, Robertson's style and views made him enemies, none greater than David Lloyd George. The latter was convinced that Britain's losses could be curbed by pursuing the fight away from the Western Front; Robertson was not. The two positions would never be reconciled. Once Prime Minister Lloyd George did all he could to rein Robertson in, eventually removing him as CIGS. Significantly enough the new CIGS, General Sir Henry Wilson, accepted the role with the same pre-Robertson powers. Thus the politicians had finally regained control of military policy.

3

Douglas Haig and the Somme

Andrew Wiest

Words change their meaning over time. At one point the words "the Somme" simply denoted a river in France. After 1916, however, these words were imbued with multifaceted power and emotion. They meant battle. They meant futility. They meant the death of a generation. And they were representative of Britain's experience in the Great War. Any study of the Great War must grapple with the complex meaning of the Somme. A full investigation of the Somme campaign leads down several intellectual tracks, from the trenches, to logistics, to technology, to the impact of war on the psyches of the soldiers and their nation. But inexorably those tracks of inquiry all lead back to a single source – the person of the British commander in chief.

The words Douglas Haig are no less charged with meaning than those of the Somme – the first great battle under his full command. Haig's role at the Somme has been characterized as that of a butcher, perhaps best portrayed in the satirical British television series *Blackadder Goes Forth*. Serious histories of the Somme and of its commander are less hyperbolic, but within Great War scholarship a "traditional school" has quite successfully portrayed Haig as a chronically mistaken, overly ambitious man who, surrounded by sycophants, consistently believed that God was leading his hand. The frightening combination of these personal traits led to unmitigated disaster at the Somme. A "revisionist school," however, has contended that Haig was a perceptive commander, perhaps even a great one, and that he oversaw a transformation of the British Expeditionary Force (BEF) that was revolutionary in nature – a transformation of which the Somme was an indispensable part.[1]

---

1 For treatments of Haig and his place in history see, J.M. Bourne, 'Haig and the Historians', in Brian Bond & Nigel Cave (eds.) *Haig: A Reappraisal 70 Years On* (London: Leo Cooper, 1999), and Keith Simpson, 'The Reputation of Sir Douglas Haig' in Brian Bond (ed.), *The First World War and British Military History* (London: Clarendon, 1991).

Even after the passing of a century, the debate over Haig's command, and especially his role in the Somme, shows no signs of slowing. In recent years two major new works on Haig's career have appeared – J. P. Harris's *Douglas Haig and the First World War* and Gary Sheffield's *The Chief: Douglas Haig and the British Army*. Both works are based on mountains of primary source evidence; both works are invaluable additions to the library of any Great War scholar. But Harris and Sheffield come to vastly different conclusions regarding Douglas Haig in general and his command at the Somme in particular. Harris's conclusions regarding Haig can, in part, be seen in his summation of the first day on the Somme:

> The holocaust of British infantry on 1 July 1916 was not a natural disaster or an act of God. It was a product of human error. Haig proceeded with an approach that practically all of the sources of advice available to him indicated to be dangerously overambitious. It is, therefore, difficult to avoid the conclusion that the error was primarily his.[2]

Sheffield, however, sees the same situation quite differently. Haig, in his view, was not simply "overambitious," but instead had hit on a hard reality of the Great War that would eventually grind the German army to dust.

> During the Somme, and arguably until the end of the war, the BEF was incapable of conducting any sort of offensive operations that were economical in human lives ... Attrition was the key: wearing down the enemy's army by destroying its morale. Haig never deviated from that basic understanding.[3]

That two monumental studies of Haig, based on the same primary sources, can reach such different conclusions regarding the efficacy and meaning of his command at the Somme is indicative of the continued vibrancy of the field of Great War studies and of the deep importance of the Somme to British history.[4]

---

2   J. P. Harris, *Douglas Haig and the First World War* (Cambridge: Cambridge University Press, 2008), pp. 539-540.
3   Gary Sheffield, *The Chief: Douglas Haig and the British Army* (London: Aurum Press, 2012), p. 373.
4   The author has also investigated the mountain of available primary evidence regarding the career of Douglas Haig, including the quintessential source of Haig's voluminous wartime diary. Other rich sources include the war diaries of the many units under his command and the personal papers of many of his subordinate commanders, especially General Sir Henry Rawlinson, Haig's chief subordinate at the Somme. The author's research in these sources has been presented in his own publications, notably *Passchendaele and the Royal Navy* (Westport, Connecticut: Greenwood Press, 1995) and *Haig: The Evolution of a Commander* (New York: Potomac Press, 2005). The latter contains a chapter on Haig's Somme command, and as such still stands as representative of the author's conclusions regarding Haig and his command style at the Somme. The research for that chapter and

Even a brief assessment of Haig's command at the Somme must take into account the unique circumstances faced by the BEF in 1916. Never before in its history had Britain attempted something so militarily massive as it did in the Great War. Historically reliant on the strength of the Royal Navy and a small but often highly trained army, in the Great War Britain undertook a radical change in policy and trained and shipped millions of men to the Western Front. The result was the creation of Britain's second largest gathering of humans (with the sole exception of London) and its deployment to France. These millions of young men and women required a logistic effort unmatched in British history, requiring everything from shipping, railway networks, constant training, medical aid, artillery shells, beer, fodder for horses, road work, mail, tanks, to uniforms. Haig, thus, not only commanded a military force unmatched before or since in British history but one which was sustained by a cobbled together logistic effort of nearly infinite complexity.[5] Although the BEF certainly made mistakes in its logistical prosecution of the Great War, levels of supply remained consistently high, even during the resource intense fighting at the Somme, which stands as a clear success of Haig's command.

Of greater tactical concern for Haig in 1916 was the simple reality that the rank and file of the BEF had until only recently been civilians. Men had flocked to the colours in 1914 and 1915, and pushing them to the Western Front so quickly meant that their training had often been rudimentary. Even as the battles of 1914 and 1915 raged, and whittled away at the BEF's veteran core, training for the "Kitchener Army" continued in France. But in March 1916, as planning for the Somme got underway in earnest, Haig remained concerned regarding the tactical limitations of his new army. In March, in a letter to Kitchener discussing his planning for the year, Haig wrote:

> I am strengthening the long line which I have recently taken over, and training the troops. I have not got an Army in France really, but a collection of divisions untrained for the Field. The actual fighting Army will be evolved from them.[6]

The rapid expansion of the BEF had also placed great stress on Britain's limited number of experienced officers. Haig's five army commanders at the time of the Somme had only been at best divisional commanders in 1914. Most of the BEF's corps commanders had only led brigades in 1914, and divisional commanders had

---

its conclusions form the basis of the present chapter, but has been updated to include new sources – especially the work of Gary Sheffield and John Harris. The brevity of this chapter forces footnotes to be kept to a minimum, but interested readers can consult the above works for more detailed information on source material.

5 John Hussey, 'Portrait of a Commander-in-Chief', in Brian Bond & Nigel Cave, *Haig: A Re-appraisal 80 Years On* (Barnsley: Pen & Sword, 2009). For further details of BEF logistics, see Christopher Phillips's chapter elsewhere in this volume.
6 Robert Blake (ed.), *The Private Papers of Douglas Haig* (London: Eyre & Spottiswoode, 1952), p. 137.

started the war commanding battalions.[7] In essence, then, the leadership of the BEF at the Somme, with the exceptions of Haig and General Henry Rawlinson, had never before led a unit larger than a division into battle. From the highest to the lowest level the BEF was an untried, amateur force that required "on the job" training. At the command level some officers would rise to the challenge and prove consummate professionals; others would be found badly wanting. This unevenness in command helped to lead to some of the successes of the Somme, as well as to some of the battle's most notable failures. Issues of command experience also influenced the development of Haig's battle planning and command style throughout the campaign. Most notably, though, battlefield experience was crucial to Haig's single most important decision of the Somme – the choice of the battle's tactical commander. Haig had considerable differences with Rawlinson of Fourth Army – differences that would play a paramount role in the failures of the first day of the Somme. Rawlinson, though, was arguably Haig's most experienced subordinate, having played a leading role in the battles of 1915, most notably at Neuve Chapelle. It was this experience that led Haig to choose Rawlinson as his battlefield commander at the Somme.[8]

The deep roots of the Battle of the Somme lie beyond the scope of this chapter. However, Haig was a comparatively recent convert to the idea of an offensive by the BEF in the region, preferring an assault in Flanders, which he argued would garner Britain a more direct strategic benefit by liberating the Belgian coast. The French commander Joseph Joffre, though, placed constant pressure on Haig in favor of joint Allied operations in the neighborhood of the Somme – entreaties that became all the more serious in the wake of the onset of the German offensive at Verdun. Finally convinced of the Allied need for an offensive at the Somme, Haig first had to come to grips with the strategic goals for the greatest military effort to date in British history.

Haig is often accused of being wildly over optimistic in both his tactical planning and strategic vision of the stalemated Western Front – an over-optimism that falls into its starkest focus in the planning for the Somme. There was an intellectual background to Haig's tendency toward optimism, based in part on his command experience in 1915 when he believed that the battles of Neuve Chapelle and Loos had very nearly achieved overwhelming success. Haig, though, consistently balanced a hope for a breakthrough attack against the strategic need to "wear down" the Germans on the Western Front, which would necessarily precede any opportunity to achieve great gains in a single offensive. With German troops so heavily engaged at Verdun, and with a steady stream of intelligence reports that indicated a drop in German morale, Haig had reason to hope that the "wearing out" had been accomplished. Therefore, the British effort at the Somme might even break the German lines and restore a war

---

7   Robin Prior & Trevor Wilson, *Command on the Western Front: The Military Career of Sir Henry Rawlinson* (Oxford: Blackwell, 1992), p. 138.
8   Sheffield, *The Chief*, p. 168.

Haig and Joffre at Chantilly, 23 December 1915.

of movement, which could conceivably lead to peace as early as the coming winter.[9] Haig's Great War planning constantly rested in balance between the need for attrition based on limited gains on one hand, and the temptation to seek decisive breakthrough on the other. His initial Somme planning tended uncomfortably toward the latter.

Having received orders from Haig to draw up an initial plan for a BEF attack at the Somme, by March 1916 Rawlinson had discovered that the German defenses in the area were formidable, consisting of two main trench systems and incorporating several fortified villages including Fricourt, Thiepval and Beaumont Hamel. To breach these defences, Rawlinson and his Chief of Staff Brigadier-General Archibald Montgomery, advocated a methodical, "bite and hold" offensive scheme. Their initial plan proposed that after a 5-day bombardment the infantry would advance on an attack frontage of 20,000 yards to seize only the German front line trench system. After a delay of three days the attack would be renewed to seize the German second line of defenses. In considering the possibility of a further advance, Rawlinson opined:

> It does not appear to me that the gain of 2 or 3 more kilometers of ground is of much consequence ... Our object rather seems to be to kill as many Germans as possible with the least loss to ourselves ... [by seizing] points of tactical importance which will provide us with good observation and which we may feel quite certain the Germans will counterattack.

9   Haig Diary, 7 June 1916. On the subject of intelligence and the influence of Verdun, see Jim Beach's chapter in this volume.

Rawlinson suspected that his advocacy of a methodical advance went against Haig's thinking and he wrote in his diary: "I daresay I shall have a tussle with him over the limited objective for I hear he is inclined to favour the unlimited with the chance of breaking the German line."[10] Indeed, Rawlinson's draft plan did not receive the support of G.H.Q. Haig, favoring a shorter bombardment, instructed Rawlinson to amend his plan and to aim for greater goals, namely the seizure of both German lines of defense in one operation followed by a push eastward toward Combles. In addition Haig instructed Rawlinson to extend the front of the attack southward to the junction with the French army, and to have the cavalry on hand to exploit any favorable development. Though not without misgivings, Rawlinson conformed to Haig's new design, and the goals for the Somme came to include an overthrow of both the German first and much of the second line trench systems and an advance toward a newly discovered third line of defenses. Rawlinson did, however, persevere regarding the nature of the bombardment, which remained scheduled for five days' duration. Most importantly, though, the alteration to the plan added considerable depth to the area under attack, from an advance of roughly 1,250 yards under Rawlinson's original plan to an advance of 2,500 yards under the new scheme.[11]

Most histories conclude that Haig simply overruled Rawlinson's sensible scheme based on an almost senseless optimism that the German lines could be overthrown in a great rush forward. However, a thorough reading of Haig's diaries and letters shows a commander in search of strategic balance – a search that would continue well beyond the Battle of the Somme. Throughout 1916 and 1917 Haig would continue to understand the need for attrition of German military might, and the place that step-by-step attacks would play in that attrition.[12] But he also continually hoped that attrition was near its end and that offensives might achieve great results. Haig's dual strategic vision, and the tension inherent within it, was best expressed by his statement to a meeting of his army commanders two weeks before the launch of the Somme attacks:

> As regards the objective of the Fourth Army attack, it was, *Firstly*, to gain the line of the Pozières heights, organise good observation posts, and consolidate a strong position. Then, secondly, (a) If enemy's defence broke down, occupy enemy's third line … (b) *If enemy's defence is strong* and fighting continues for many days, as soon as Pozières heights are gained, the position should be

10 Prior & Wilson, *Command on the Western Front*, pp. 144 and 141.
11 Harris, *Douglas Haig*, pp. 220-222.
12 Although Haig seemingly understood the efficacy of the step-by-step approach, his understanding of the mechanics of that approach was in a state of flux throughout the Battle of the Somme and even Third Ypres. Depth of assaults and weight of artillery bombardments, the stock in trade of step-by-step advances, remained in question for an inordinate length of time as Haig and the BEF stumbled toward a winning offensive formula.

consolidated and improved, while arrangements will be made to start an attack on Second Army front.[13]

What Haig and Rawlinson adopted for the first day of the Somme, then, was not a limited bite and hold offensive. Neither was it a blind attempt at breakthrough. Instead it was an uncomfortable compromise; a hybrid offensive born of Haig's difficulties in coming to grips with the tactical and strategic realities imposed by the Western Front.

The unevenness of command at the Somme had deadly practical realities. Although Haig had, on the one hand, reached into Rawlinson's tactical level planning to extend the scope and depth of the Somme operation, in the actual implementation of the plan Haig left Rawlinson a great amount of latitude. Within the broad outline of the operation, Haig let Rawlinson proceed essentially unsupervised. It was a trend that Rawlinson continued. Neither Haig nor Rawlinson, with some 17 infantry divisions at their disposal, imposed a standard upon their subordinates, and thus in some cases the infantry advanced across no-man's-land in rushes, while in others the infantry infamously received specific orders to advance only at a walk. Additionally there was no uniformity in the use of the greatest weapon at the BEF's disposal – artillery.[14]

In its Somme offensive the BEF had amassed an awesome array of weaponry including over 1,000 field guns and howitzers, and more than 400 heavy pieces of various calibers. The absolute numbers, though, are misleading. Given the ineffectiveness of infantry against trench systems, the lion's share of the work at the Somme fell to the artillery, which was called on to destroy barbed wire, silence enemy artillery and crush the entire German defensive network. The field guns dealt with enemy barbed wire, but often failed in their task due to faulty ordinance and inaccurate fire. Though there had been advances in locating enemy artillery, the counter battery guns frequently failed to subdue the carefully concealed German artillery. Finally, the main task of the offensive, destroying the German defenders themselves, fell to a comparatively small number of field and heavy howitzers. Making matters worse, the German defences in the area were very strong, including deep dugouts that were impervious to everything but a direct hit from a heavy calibre shell.

Even against such defenses, a heavy weight of artillery fire, similar to that utilized at Neuve Chapelle, would have made seizure of the German front line trench possible. Critically, though, Haig's decision to attack the German defenses in depth had the effect of diluting the overall effectiveness of the bombardment. Thus the fault for the impending disaster must fall to Haig, for it was as a consequence of his decision that, "the British command decided to send its infantry against some of the strongest defenses on the Western Front in the wake of a preliminary bombardment

13 Sheffield, *The Chief*, 165; Haig Diary, 15 June 1916.
14 For a full discussion of the artillery preparations prior to the Somme, see Bill McCormick's chapter in this volume.

approximately half as intense as that employed against the much sketchier German defenses at Neuve Chapelle."[15]

The night before commencement of the Somme offensive, Haig wrote in his diary before bed:

> With God's help; I feel hopeful. The men are in splendid spirits. Several have said that they have never before been so instructed and informed of the nature of the operation before them. The wire has never been so well cut, nor the Artillery preparation so thorough. I have seen personally all the Corps Commanders and one and all are full of confidence.[16]

The first day on the Somme is perhaps the blackest mark against Haig's command. While other chapters in this volume discuss the ebb and flow of the battle more completely, it is necessary here to include a summary of some of the tactical details as they related to the command relationship between Haig and Rawlinson. North of the Albert-Bapaume Road, the story of the British attack was one of almost unremitting failure – poor coordination, an ineffective artillery barrage, and command gaffes at the intermediate levels represented Haig's planning and command implementation at their worst. South of the Bapaume Road, though, was a different matter. XV Corps, and XIII Corps achieved nearly all of their initial goals including the overthrow of the German first line trenches in the area and the seizure of the defended villages of Mametz, Montauban and Fricourt.[17] The first major British use of the "creeping barrage," as well as coordination with the French on the southern flank of the British attack, helped to represent Haig's plan at its best.

Leading historians now view the successes in the south as a great missed opportunity. The British advance here left the Germans in sketchy defenses with few local reserves. Haig's plan had called for reinforcements, including cavalry, to sustain the advance in that area. Here the flawed relationship between Haig and Rawlinson, though, became clear. Haig had not ensured that his plan was followed. For his part Rawlinson had believed the German defences to have been too strong, and, expecting little success, had not placed his reserve formations far enough forward to take advantage of the fast developing situation. The reserve attacks, which were central to Haig's plan, thus never materialized. If reinforcements had been committed in strength, Rawlinson's biographers Robin Prior and Trevor Wilson argue that British forces could have at least taken the important areas around Trones and Mametz woods, which would be the scene of much bitter fighting in following months.[18] Gary Sheffield takes

---

15   Prior & Wilson, *Command on the Western Front*, 169.
16   Haig Diary, 30 June 1916.
17   Fricourt actually fell the next day. This was primarily due to advances on its flanks which made the defensive works there untenable.
18   Prior & Wilson, *Command*, p. 184.

the case a step further contending that an advance of three miles, taking the strong point of Thiepval, was very possible. Perhaps even a further advance of over 10 miles, achieving a truly strategic result, was not out of the question.[19] Whether the possible results were more tactical or strategic, Haig's plan in the south verged on success. But it was another failure of Haig's command, the flawed relationship between Haig and his principal subordinate Rawlinson, that left that success begging. In the words of Gary Sheffield:

> We know that by failing to capitalize on the success in the south the British commanders let an opportunity for a substantial advance go begging. Rawlinson never believed in Haig's plan for a breakthrough, and this probably influenced his reaction to events on XIII Corps' front. To lack any form of immediately deployable operational reserve was a mistake.[20]

Perhaps the local mistake was Rawlinson's, but to allow such a mistake was the fault of Haig.

At the cost of approximately 57,000 casualties killed, wounded and missing, the first day of the Battle of the Somme had fallen far short of Haig's considerable goals. The scale of the setback only slowly dawned upon Haig, who two days later still believed that the casualties only numbered 40,000. Regardless of the losses and the failures, especially in the north, Haig never seriously considered calling a halt to the Somme. Firstly, the strategic rationale for the battle remained in place – it represented the British contribution to the Allied "General Offensive" and would take pressure from Verdun and the embattled French. Secondly, Haig had always understood the Somme within the context of an attritional battle – wearing down of the German forces being a necessary precursor of any potential breakthrough. The pressure on the Western Front needed to continue, whether a breakthrough beckoned or not.

In a meeting on 3 July, Joffre made his opinion clear by pressing the BEF to continue the offensive with the entreaty that the British should attack in the north of the battle sector toward Thiepval. Haig, though, believed that it was in the south, toward Longueval, that opportunity best beckoned. The result is indicative of another important part of Haig's command. Relations between the British and French were always strategically strained in the Great War. As the junior partner in the war the British in general, and Haig in particular, had to acquiesce to the French lead in planning. However, Haig was also the commander of his own national force and as such jealously guarded Britain's military best interests. There existed a constant tension between being a good ally and being an independent commander. The July 3 meeting revealed that tension, with Haig recording in his diary on his suggestion of attacking in the south:

---

19 Sheffield, *The Chief*, p. 173.
20 Gary Sheffield, *The Somme* (London: Cassell, 2003), p. 68.

At this Joffre exploded in a fit of rage. '*He* could not approve of it.' He '*ordered* me to attack Thiepval and Pozières.' If I attacked Longueval, I would be beaten, etc., etc. I waited calmly until he had finished. His breast heaved and his face flushed! … When Joffre got out of breath, I quietly explained what my position is relatively to him as the 'Generalissimo.' *I am solely responsible to the British Government for the action of the British Army*; and I had approved the plan.[21]

Having decided to attack south of the Bapaume Road after a delay to prepare, Haig stipulated that, preparatory to the attack, Rawlinson's forces had to reach a proper jumping off point for the offensive. Rawlinson, in turn assigned the complex task of line straightening to subordinate corps commanders. The result was some 46 uncoordinated attacks against various German strong points in the area and approximately 25,000 additional casualties. Again, the losses represent a failure for the command team of Haig and Rawlinson, for more sizable assaults with better artillery preparation could have achieved the same results at far less cost.[22]

As these subsidiary operations continued, Rawlinson got down to the planning for the second main offensive at the Somme. Since the distance to the German trenches in the area of the attack was a deadly 1,500 yards, Rawlinson's scheme called for British troops to move into no-man's-land at night. After a shorter and more intense bombardment British troops would aim, in the main, only to seize the German front line trench system. Rawlinson's plan, often lauded for its limited scope, also called on the cavalry to be ready for action in case of the rupture of German defenses in the area of Delville Wood, which he hoped would initiate a drive to Flers.[23]

When presented with Rawlinson's plan, Haig responded with many objections. Believing that a night assembly in no-man's-land was beyond the tactical ability of the men of Kitchener's Army, Haig advocated a more traditional assault involving a complicated turning maneuver toward Longueval.[24] Haig also questioned the cavalry exploitation portion of Rawlinson's plan, counseling caution. In his discussion of Rawlinson's plan with his advisors at GHQ, Haig posed four questions that were indicative of having learned important lessons in the wake of the opening day of the Somme:

> 1. Can we take the position in the manner proposed? 2. Can we hold it after capture? 3. What will be the results in case of failure? 4. What are the advantages, or otherwise, of proceeding methodically, viz. extending our front and sapping forward to take the position by assault?[25]

---

21 Haig Diary, 3 July 1916; emphasis in the original.
22 Prior & Wilson, *Command*, pp. 187-190.
23 Ibid,, p. 192.
24 Harris, *Douglas Haig*, p. 247.
25 Sheffield, *The Chief*, p. 181.

After meeting with his corps commanders, Rawlinson reported back to Haig that both he and they remained certain that the original plan, with only slight modifications, was the best alternative. In the face of the united opinion of his subordinates, Haig relented and allowed Rawlinson's plan to move forward. The moment was an important one in Haig's command. The planning for the 14 July offensive represented a give and take, rather than the dictatorial approach usually ascribed to Haig, indicating that the commander-in-chief was also learning his role in modern combat. Sometimes, as before the first day on the Somme, he intervened in the planning of his subordinates, on other occasions he stood aside. In a very important sense, then, Haig's command style remained uneven and unpredictable, reflecting his confidence or lack thereof in the abilities of his subordinates. On occasion Haig would meddle, involving himself in tactical minutiae. At other times he would give only the broadest of orders, allowing his army commanders wide latitude. It was Haig's unpredictability of command, rather than a dictatorial bent, that was perhaps his greatest command failure.

As in any Great War battle though, artillery remained the key. Although Haig was still far from a scientific solution to artillery preparation, he and Rawlinson did much to rectify the critical artillery deficiencies that had doomed the first day of the Somme offensive. For the attack of 14 July, Fourth Army's artillery support came from 1,000 artillery pieces, of which 311 were heavy howitzers. Although these raw numbers account for almost 500 fewer artillery pieces than on the first day of the Somme, the artillery was called upon to do much less. The attack frontage was only 6,000 yards as opposed to over 20,000 yards on the first day of the battle. The more limited nature of the proposed advance added only 12,000 additional yards of trenches to the area under bombardment, where there had been 300,000 additional yards of trenches on the first day of the battle. Thus the artillery fire accompanying the assault was five times more intense than that on 1 July, leading to a far greater level of destruction in the German defensive system.[26]

There had been no lasting alteration in doctrine or any scientific application of the ratio of shell weight to yardage of trench under assault. Changes of such a revolutionary nature were arguably still over a year away. But in the space of just two weeks Haig and Rawlinson had made significant alterations to their style of attack. Though communication would remain a nagging problem, both artillery and infantry tactics were much improved as the results of the battle would indicate. No army in any war revolutionizes itself in mere weeks – especially an army like the BEF that is new, inexperienced and led by commanders facing something unprecedented. The transformation towards professionalism was inevitably slow. But what is seen in the shift from 1 July to 14 July is a BEF and a commander that were intellectually supple and capable of learning – instead of the hidebound commander of popular legend. There would

---

26 Prior & Wilson, *Command*, pp. 187-193

be regression. The overly optimistic Haig would certainly make a return. His style of command would remain frustratingly uneven. But Haig did learn. Haig did adapt.

On 14 July at 3:25 a.m., the British attack moved forward after a whirlwind bombardment. Everywhere the attackers met with great success, and along the entire front the III, XV and XIII Corps reached their final objectives and overthrew what had been the German second line of defense, seizing Bazentin le Petit and Trones Wood, although communications difficulties and command hesitancy at the lower levels led to a missed opportunity to capture High Wood. For both Haig and Rawlinson the success of the attack was reason for great optimism. Through the proper use of artillery in limited steps the BEF could achieve its goals in battle against the Germans.

At the same time the strategic nature of the war on the Western Front began to change, with the Germans suspending major offensive operations at Verdun in favor of shifting effort to the embattled Somme. Although pressure on the French had eased, and political angst regarding the plodding nature of the British advance was rising at home, Haig never really considered calling the Somme to a halt. The successes of 14 July, coupled with intelligence reports indicating dwindling German morale, conspired to convince Haig that maintaining the pressure on the Germans at the Somme was more important than ever. As July drew to a close Haig outlined his goals for the future of the Somme offensive in a document that revealed the conflict between his expectations of only limited, attritional battlefield gains against his ongoing hope of a strategic victory:

> We have inflicted very heavy losses on the enemy. In one month, 30 of his Divns. have been used up, as against 25 at Verdun in 5 months. In another 6 weeks, the enemy should be hard put to it to find men. The maintenance of a steady offensive pressure will result eventually in his complete overthrow.
>
> Principle on which we should act. *Maintain our offensive*. Our losses in July's fighting totaled about 120,000 more than they would have been had we not attacked. They cannot be regarded as sufficient to justify any anxiety as to our ability to continue the offensive. It is my intention:
>
> a) To maintain a steady pressure on Somme Battle.
> b) To push my attack strongly whenever and wherever the state of my preparations and the general situation make success sufficiently probable to justify me in doing so, but not otherwise.
> c) To secure against counter-attack each advantage gained and prepare thoroughly for each fresh advance.
>
> Proceeding thus, I expect to be able to maintain the offensive well into the Autumn. It would not be justifiable to calculate on the enemy's resistance being completely broken without another campaign next year.[27]

---

27   Blake, *Private Papers*, pp. 157-158. Note on letter received from C.I.G.S. dated 29 July 1916; emphasis in the original.

The next "big push" would not take place until September, but required preparatory offensives by Rawlinson's Fourth Army, and the Reserve Army of General Hubert Gough to seize German defensive works in the areas near High Wood, Delville Wood, and Guillemont. The result was a series of small and all too often uncoordinated assaults during which Fourth Army alone mounted some 90 operations, only four of which were launched across its entire front. In all during this period of "line straightening" Fourth Army suffered 82,000 casualties while advancing only 1,000 yards on a 5-mile front. Thus, while capturing less than the area seized on the infamous first day of the Somme, Fourth Army suffered 40 per cent more casualties.[28]

During this period of "forgotten battles," Rawlinson's tendency was to set general objectives and simply delegate them, and the planning involved, to subordinates. After the significant failure of a combined French and British attack of 18 August, Haig expressed displeasure to Rawlinson. Haig's memorandum was actually indicative of the struggle the commander-in-chief himself faced in attempting to balance initiative with control:

> In actual *execution* of plans, when control by higher Commanders is impossible, subordinates on the spot must act on their own initiative, and they must be trained to do so ... [but] in *preparation*... close supervision by higher commanders is not only possible, but is their duty ... This close supervision is especially necessary in the case of a comparatively new army.[29]

Although the fighting on the Somme during July and August was indecisive, Haig's characteristic optimism remained. German General Erich von Falkenhayn had been sacked and reports came in that German morale was low and that artillery and ammunition were in increasingly short supply. The French also strongly advocated launching another major offensive on the scale of 1 July, at the nexus of the French and British armies. While there was considerable allied disagreement about the timing and goals of the coming effort, eventually the attack was set for mid September as a major advance in the neighborhood of Flers-Courcelette. Most of the planning again fell to Rawlinson. The Fourth Army commander understood that the German defenses in the area of the offensive remained quite strong, with 3,000 yards between the first and second line defenses and a third line of defenses that was out of range of most of the British artillery. As a result, Rawlinson proposed to advance step by step, with separate attacks made on each of the German lines with about 24 hours between each operation.[30]

---

28 Prior & Wilson, *Command*, pp. 203-205.
29 GHQ Memorandum to Fourth Army, 24 August 1916 quoted in Harris, *Douglas Haig*, p. 257; emphasis in the original.
30 Prior & Wilson, *Command*, pp. 227-228.

Haig, however, had reason to hope that the attrition of the previous months had provided the prerequisites for a more strategic result. With regard to Rawlinson's plan, he observed:

> In my opinion he is not making enough of the situation with the deterioration and all-round loss of morale of the enemy troops. I think we should make an attack as strong and as violent as possible, and plan to go as far as possible.[31]

Thus Haig overruled Rawlinson in favor of an attack designed to breach all three German lines in a single attack, with the hope of cavalry exploitation to follow. Once again Haig's alteration of Rawlinson's plan had the effect of diluting the all-important covering artillery barrage, which now included creeping barrages as a matter of course, to a level of one-half of the intensity of the barrage accompanying the successful 14 July attack. That the commander-in-chief of the BEF was still struggling to come to terms with the optimum formula for weight of artillery fire in the offensive is sadly obvious. It was not an abundance of artillery fire, though, that made Haig confident of success. Instead it was a stubborn and continuing belief that attrition had taken its toll and that the Germans were nearing the end of their capability to resist.

There was, however, an additional reason for optimism in this particular attack – the use of a new battlefield weapon; the tank. Haig had first heard of the tank in 1915 and immediately supported the new weapons system, placing an order for 150 tanks to accompany the initial Somme offensive.[32] Far from being a technophobe, then, Haig was actually one of the first and leading proponents of the tank. But production of the new weapon proved slow, with the new tanks being dogged by a well-deserved reputation for mechanical difficulties and breakdowns. Nevertheless, Haig was impressed by the prototypes he had seen in action and remained convinced that the weapon had utility on the modern battlefield. As the Somme continued, Haig received word from Colonel E. D. Swinton, principally responsible for the later stages of the development of the tank, that at least seventy-five of the vehicles would be ready for the mid-September push. Swinton had earlier warned Haig not to use the tanks in "driblets," but to keep their existence secret until they could be utilized in large numbers in a great offensive.[33] Given his perceptions regarding the weakened nature of the German army on the Somme, Haig judged that seventy-five tanks would be sufficient to meet Swinton's requirements.

However, even the estimation of seventy-five tanks proved over optimistic, and only forty-nine tanks reached France in time for the September offensive, with only thirty-two reaching their eventual starting points for the assault. Shortly thereafter,

---

31   Haig Diary, 29 August 1916.
32   J.P. Harris, 'Haig and The Tank', in Bond & Cave, *Haig*, pp. 146-147.
33   Gerard De Groot, *DouglasHaig, 1861-1928* (London: Unwin Hyman, 1989), pp. 265-266.

nine tanks broke down, and five became ditched, leaving just eighteen in action,[34] meaning that tanks were indeed used in "driblets" as Swinton feared. The story of the use, or misuse, of the tank has become a central part of judging Haig's command at the Somme.[35] The most damning blow was struck by wartime Prime Minister David Lloyd George who remarked in his *War Memoirs*:

> But the decision to launch the first handful of these machines ... has always appeared to me to have been a foolish blunder ... We made the same error as the Germans committed in April, 1915, when by their initial use of poison gas on a small sector alone, they gave away the secret of a new and deadly form of attack, which, had it been used for the first time on a grand scale, might have produced results of a decisive character ... So the great secret was sold for the battered ruin of a little hamlet on the Somme, which was not worth capturing.[36]

Most recent historical accounts, though, tend to vindicate Haig for his early use of the tank. He had tried to amass as many of the machines as possible and hoped that their addition to the battle would result in a favorable decision. Neither he nor Rawlinson saw the tank as a decisive weapon, but merely as another important piece to the puzzle of breaking the deadlock of trench warfare. Understanding their unreliability Haig and Rawlinson planned to use tanks in shallow advances, especially to trample barbed wire entanglements – for which there was still no real tactical solution – and to help subdue strong points in the German first line defensive network. That the tank had no "results of a decisive character" to give away became clear in the later, groundbreaking use of armour at Cambrai and Amiens. Haig, taking account of its limited deployment on the Somme, saw enough in the tank to support its continued development and production, even while many in the British military remained in great doubt concerning the value of armour. Following the decidedly mixed debut of the tank at the Somme, Haig placed an order for 1,000 more machines and encouraged the growth of a new branch of the army to operate the new weapons system. With regard to armour, Haig was far ahead of his time, hoping to add large and more independent tank formations to his offensive plans for the coming year.[37]

The general offensive of 15 September produced mixed results, achieving much more than had the first day on the Somme, but far less than Haig's renewed optimism had hoped. In most areas an advance of 2,500 yards had been achieved, and in some

---

34 John Terraine, *Douglas Haig: The Educated Soldier* (London: Hutchinson, 1963), p. 222.
35 The preparation and training of the Heavy Branch is considered in Philip Ventham's chapter in this volume.
36 David Lloyd George, *War Memoirs* (London: Odhams, 1938), p. 385.
37 Harris, 'Haig and the Tank', pp. 148-149. One of the best accounts of the tank's development and use can be found in J.P. Harris, *Men Ideas and Tanks* (Manchester: Manchester University Press, 1995).

Dismissive German cartoon commentary on the introduction of the tank: Hannibal and Haig (A Historical Parallel): I. Hannibal once succeeded when he sent the elephants in! II. Thus Haig, that renowned warrior, built his "Tank" for this purpose. III. Bravely the beast stormed to the front – until it was no longer able to continue. IV. Thus the meaning of this tale, "Haig, you are no Hannibal!" Furthermore, "The elephant had more wisdom than the tank!" (*Kladderadatsch*, 5 November 1916)

areas even the German second line of defenses had fallen, representing more than twice the ground taken on 1 July at half the cost. The performance of the tanks had, though, been spotty. In some areas they had broken down or had been outpaced by the infantry, achieving little. However, in the center of the British line, under the cover of a punishing barrage and accompanied by twelve tanks, British troops made notable advances, seizing the village of Flers and breaking the German second line of defences.

It is at this point in the battle that the two most recent and authoritative studies of Haig make clear the stark differences in historical perception regarding his strategic thinking at the Somme. J. P. Harris contends that the limited success of 15 September meant that Haig had been wrong to eschew Rawlinson's more limited step-by-step approach. Similar gains could have been made under Rawlinson's plan, which would have left British forces "less depleted and exhausted and thus in a position to assault the third line rather sooner."[38] Gary Sheffield, however, argues that greater successes beckoned, especially in the neighborhood of Flers – and that it was Rawlinson's failure to adhere to Haig's strategic vision that led to a failure to exploit success contending:

> The situation seems tailor-made for Haig's original all-arms concept, or even cavalry alone. But this is ultimately fruitless speculation, since the disposition of troops as a consequence of Rawlinson's plan effectively neutered the cavalry.[39]

One thing is certain: if after the passing of a century the two leading scholars on Haig's command can reach such different conclusions about his role at this point in the Somme, it is safe to say that the argument over Haig's command legacy will neither conclude in this short chapter nor indeed in the near future. What is certain, though, is that the BEF's efforts at the Somme had improved dramatically. Even on occasions in which optimism might have led to operational overreach, artillery was better, planning was more professional, and gains were achieved with greater frequency and at less cost. Haig, Rawlinson, and the entire BEF were learning and becoming more professional at their craft. The learning, though, was by no means uniform, especially at the command level – which is evident in the arguments posed by Harris and Sheffield. Either Haig was not yet listening to the cogent advice of his subordinates and pushing for overly distant objectives or Haig was correct in his combined arms ideas but failed adequately to control his subordinates. Either eventuality represents a command failure on Haig's part.

September would mark the last "big push" but the battle lingered on into November – a postscript of sorts that is central to the criticism of Haig's command in 1916. The question is why did Haig choose to persist in fighting, as weather worsened and as hope for a major victory dimmed? Part of the answer lies in the fact that Haig

---

38 Harris, *Douglas Haig*, p. 263.
39 Sheffield, *The Chief*, p. 190.

was undertaking the Somme as part of an alliance. Joffre and the French remained convinced that pressure needed to be kept on the Germans and that the attritional victories of Verdun and the Somme had weakened the Germans to a point where success was possible. In October Joffre wrote to Haig imploring him to continue to launch ambitious operations. Haig replied:

> Meanwhile to the utmost extent of the means at my disposal, and so far as weather conditions render possible, I will continue to co-operate with you in exploiting to the full the successes already gained. But I must remind you that it lies with me to judge what I can undertake and when I can undertake it.[40]

There was, of course, another reason that Haig chose to continue the Battle of the Somme – his inherent optimism. In late September, though, Haig's natural optimism was grounded in hard facts. The Germans, at the point where the British next planned to attack, were holding the lines with only six understrength and exhausted divisions, and their local reinforcements were few. Their trench lines in the area were weak, often without barbed wire entanglements, and with few dugouts.[41] Indeed historian J. P. Harris, who often argues that Haig was overly optimistic, contends that by the end of September the Germans "were, perhaps, closer to collapse than they would be again before 1918."[42]

But the onset of bad weather slowed the preparations for continued British offensive actions. During the first two weeks of October the Germans were quick to take advantage of the relative respite, replacing their frontline troops between Le Transloy and the Ancre with seven fresh divisions taken from the general reserve and increasing their artillery in the area with 23 new heavy batteries. The Germans also switched to a new method of defence, removing more of their machine gun firepower out of range of the increasingly effective creeping barrages that habitually accompanied BEF advances.[43] The opportunity that had beckoned had arguably passed.

Although the chance for a strategic gain had slipped away, the tactical need for continuing the offensive remained. Previous advances had left British troops in a valley near Le Transloy, a difficult and unsuitable position in which to spend the coming winter. As a result there were three more late October attacks on the Le Transloy line, which achieved very little. The situation deteriorated so far that Lord Cavan, in command of XIV Corps, wrote to Rawlinson:

> With a full and complete sense of my responsibility I feel it my bounden duty to put in writing my considered opinion as to the attack ordered to take place on Nov 5th ... An advance from my present position with the troops at my disposal

---

40 Haig Diary, 23 October 1916 quoted in Sheffield, *The Chief*, p. 193.
41 Prior & Wilson, *Command*, p. 252.
42 Harris, *Douglas Haig*, p. 266.
43 Prior & Wilson, *Command*, p. 252.

has practically no chance of success … I perfectly acknowledge the necessity of not leaving the French left in the air … but I feel bound to ask if this is the intention, for a sacrifice it must be … No one who has not visited the front trenches can really know the state of exhaustion to which the men are reduced.[44]

Both Rawlinson and Haig were aware of Cavan's entreaty, but Haig argued that supporting the French flank took precedence. Perhaps of greatest concern, though, was the accusation that both Rawlinson and Haig did not understand the deteriorating battlefield conditions because they had failed to visit the front. Indeed, Haig had not visited the front lines, believing that the presence of the commander-in-chief wandering the trenches would be a senseless circus in times of battle. Haig's diary, though, indicates that he did regularly visit the headquarters of his subsidiary commands and enquired about the conditions of the battlefields and of the morale of the men under his command. Haig was a man of his time, an Edwardian gentleman. Expecting him to wander the front lines clapping soldiers on the shoulder and playing the jovial, approachable commander is to misunderstand both the man and his era.

Regardless of motivation, the attack of 5 November proceeded as planned, with predictably poor results. Rawlinson now joined Cavan in advocating an end to the offensive. There remained, though, a final postscript to the Battle of the Somme. In mid-November Gough's Fifth Army attacked in the north in what became known as the Battle of the Ancre. The limited, set piece battle was a success, resulting in the seizure of the village of Beaumont Hamel – one of the objectives for the first day of the offensive – on November 14, and the capture of 4,000 German prisoners. The Battle of the Somme had come to an end.

The 1916 Battle of the Somme was quite possibly the most important battle ever in British military history. In simple terms of stark numbers it is easy to view the campaign as a futile struggle designed by a butcher of a commander – a view made famous by war poets and subsequent popular accounts of the war. At a cost of an estimated 420,000 casualties, in roughly six months of fighting the BEF had only made a dent in the German lines some 30 miles long and 7 miles deep at its deepest point – failing even to reach all of the goals slated for the *first day* of the attack. Surely these paltry gains at such a dear cost must completely damn the reputations of the men responsible for the offensive? A closer look, though, at the nature of Haig's command at the Somme results in a more complex assessment. Haig was leading a vast, new and untested army into a battle of unprecedented scale, with the nature of the fighting peculiar to this particular time period of the Great War. The task was mammoth, the job new, the tactical situation unique, and Haig's position as an alliance commander was uneasy. Expecting Haig to command in the manner of a Napoleon or a Patton is unrealistic. He was not going to ride the front lines

---

44 Lord Cavan to Rawlinson, 11 November 1916 quoted in Prior & Wilson, *Command*, pp. 256-257.

cheering his men on. He was not able to find a silver bullet solution to the war. In that way Haig was comparable to the other commanders of the First World War, from Ludendorff, to Petain, to Foch, to Pershing, They too failed to find answers to the tactical riddles of trench warfare. They also did not fire their men with charismatic leadership. In fact, Haig proved more forward looking than these other commanders in the case of technology, specifically the support and use of the tank. But these other commanders do not come in for the same historical opprobrium as does Haig – in large part because they did not command on the Somme, which is Haig's particular albatross.

Historical hyperbole aside, Haig's command at the Somme was a very mixed affair. One central question with which historians and students of the battle have to grapple is the issue of Haig's planned objectives. Again, on the surface, it is very easy to damn Haig for setting goals for the first day of the offensive that were not completely met during six months of fighting. Here Haig did indeed make a critical error in eschewing Rawlinson's scheme for a more limited advance, which had the effect of critically weakening the effectiveness of the all important artillery barrage. But even the claim that Haig hoped to break through the German lines in one fell swoop on the first day of the Somme must be tempered. On 1 July, and through the remainder of the battle, Haig sought a balance between the understood need for attrition of German strength and the hope for a decisive victory. Here we perhaps see the truest criticism of Haig at the Somme and even through the remainder of the war until 1918 – the balance between attrition and breakthrough was always a shifting target. Throughout the six months of the campaign, the target shifted wildly, with some assaults aimed at local tactical gains, whilst others aimed for much greater results.

Even when his optimism had waned, Haig made one of his greatest mistakes in his Somme period of command by allowing the battle to linger on even as the tactical situation had swung in favor of the Germans and weather dashed nearly all hopes of a meaningful advance. Here we see a Haig not overawed by hopes of a breakthrough, but a calculating commander who hoped to continue to pulverize the German army and its morale. Although he pressed his attritional hopes too far and too long at the Somme, Haig had struck on what was to be the winning formula for the war. No matter how intellectually unsatisfactory and pyrrhic, the tactical reality of the Great War meant that Germany had to be ground down before significant victory could be won. That Haig and the Allies were on the right strategic track at the Somme was borne out by Ludendorff's summation of the year for the political leaders in Berlin:

> The enemy's great superiority in men and material would be even more painfully felt in 1917 than in 1916. They had to face the danger that 'Somme fighting' would soon break out at various points on our fronts, and that even our troops

would not be able to withstand such attacks indefinitely, especially if the enemy gave us no time to rest and for the accumulation of material.[45]

Another criticism of Haig's command concerns its variable personal style. Serving under Haig were men of limited experience, who had often been promoted quickly and beyond their effective rank. If the BEF was untried, so was much of its officer class. Haig's dealings with his subordinates were quite uneven. Instead of being the dictatorial commander surrounded by sycophants of popular lore, Haig regularly consulted with his subordinate officers. Often Haig only set general goals for his subordinates, allowing them great latitude in planning and execution of battles, resulting in spotty effectiveness in some of the most important engagements of the war. On other occasions, though, as on 1 July, Haig involved himself deeply in elements of tactical planning even to the point of overruling subordinates. Haig's variable command style would persist through 1917, contributing to similar difficulties during the Third Battle of Ypres.[46]

Most disturbing, perhaps, is that neither Haig nor Rawlinson came to fully grasp the importance of artillery fire at the Somme. Both men understood that artillery would be the key to victory, and both men came to a general realization that the artillery fire accompanying the 1 July advance had been woefully inadequate. A concentration of fire on more limited objectives was a major contributor to the unquestioned success of the 14 July attack, which certainly stood as a learning moment. However, there were great periods in the battle (especially in the run up to 14 July and in the "forgotten battles" of August and September) where inadequate artillery support continued to cost the infantry greatly. The mid-September offensive also represented something of a step backward in terms of artillery support. While the tactics of artillery, ranging from the increased professionalism and accuracy of individual batteries to the use of advanced techniques such as the creeping barrage, clearly improved, command at the highest levels struggled to come to terms with a comprehensive understanding of how artillery was best utilized in offensive actions both great and small.

The Douglas Haig of the Somme, then, was not a dull-witted butcher leading the brave men of the BEF to needless slaughter. Nor was he a great captain in the mold of a Napoleon or Robert E. Lee. Instead he was a man of his time wrestling with some of the most difficult military challenges ever faced by a commander at any level. At the Somme we can see a Haig who was struggling toward true military modernity, in terms ranging from logistic control, to alliance relationships, to command style, to striking a strategic balance between attrition and breakthrough, to a full understanding of artillery's functional role on the battlefields of the Great War. In some

---

45 E. Ludendorff, *My War Memories 1914-1918* (London: Hutchinson, 1919), p. 307.
46 For further information on Haig's command at Third Ypres see Andrew Wiest, 'Haig, Gough, and Passchendaele', in G.D. Sheffield (ed.), *Leadership & Command: The Anglo-American Military Experience Since 1861* (London: Brassey's, 1997).

areas, notably his early support of the tank, Haig was ahead of his peers. In other areas Haig learned the lessons of the Great War more slowly. But learn he did. While the remainder of his command experience was by no means free of mistakes, Haig took the lessons of the Somme and used them to help create a BEF that was, by 1918, the best fighting force in the field.

4

British Intelligence and the Battle of Verdun[1]

Jim Beach

Just before Christmas 1915 John Charteris learned that he would be appointed head of intelligence at the General Headquarters (GHQ) of the British Expeditionary Force (BEF) in France. He wrote candidly to his wife, telling her that:

> The army at large is inclined to criticise my appointment with a good deal of venom on the grounds of my extreme youth!! […] It is natural enough that they should criticise, but I am very sorry, for their criticism is naturally directed against Sir Douglas [Haig, the new commander-in-chief] more than against me. He makes the appointments not me […] I shall not mind and you must not.[2]

On 8 January 1916, a week after assuming his new appointment, Charteris reached his thirty-ninth birthday. By coincidence, that day the German high command ordered their Sixth Army to prepare for a major offensive operation against the BEF.[3] This was one element of a strategy developed by Erich von Falkenhayn, the chief of the German General Staff. He envisaged an attack against the fortress of Verdun that would prompt costly French counter-attacks in the face of heavy German artillery fire. Then, once the French army had been "bled white" and the British had exhausted

---

1 For permissions to quote from the Charteris, Haig, Kirke, and Robertson papers, thanks are offered to Charles Kirke, the Trustees of the Liddell Hart Centre for Military Archives (LHCMA), the Trustees of the National Library of Scotland (NLS), and the Robertson family.
2 LHCMA, Charteris Papers 2/2, Letter to wife, 22 December 1915. For additional context on Charteris, see Jim Beach, *Haig's Intelligence: GHQ and the German Army, 1916-1918* (Cambridge: Cambridge University Press, 2013), pp. 48-56.
3 Robert Foley, *German Strategy and the Path to Verdun: Erich von Falkenhayn and the Development of Attrition, 1870-1916* (Cambridge: Cambridge University Press, 2005), p. 198.

themselves in a relief offensive, a German offensive would deliver a decisive blow to the Allies.[4] This meant that, with a relatively inexperienced new head, the intelligence staff at GHQ now faced their most significant analytical challenge since 1914. To what extent, if at all, could they uncover Falkenhayn's intentions?

But the first half of 1916 is not just significant for British anticipation of a German offensive that did not eventually happen. It is also important to understand their intelligence perception of the attack that did take place; the one against the French at Verdun. This dimension has been overlooked within the historiography, so it is hoped that a thorough examination may be useful. In particular, it is hoped that it will contribute to the discussion about the relationship between the Battle of Verdun and British intentions before the Somme offensive. There has been a lively debate surrounding this issue, with William Philpott and Elizabeth Greenhalgh acting as champions for divergent perspectives. Central to their debate has been the question of whether relieving pressure on Verdun was truly Britain's "strategic priority".[5] Philpott adopted a traditionalist line – first articulated in Haig's post-battle despatch – that by 1 July relief had become central to the offensive's rationale.[6] Conversely Greenhalgh has taken a revisionist path, arguing that it was a *post-facto* rationalisation. At the core of her thesis is a re-interpretation of the Anglo-French meeting at Saleux on 31 May. She suggests that Haig only then began stressing the significance of Verdun relief; his reason being a desire to assist Joseph Joffre, the French commander-in-chief, who was then under significant domestic political pressure.[7]

Examining British intelligence material should therefore provide fresh insight into GHQ's contemporaneous perception of the military situation on the Western Front. The surviving operational documentation has featured prominently in the Somme/Verdun historiography, but intelligence assessments and summaries can reveal hitherto hidden assumptions underpinning British decisions. Through to the start of the Somme offensive, some key questions need to be addressed. First, what was British

---

4   Foley, *German Strategy*, 189, pp. 192-3.
5   Phrase used in: William Philpott, *Anglo-French Relations and Strategy on the Western Front* (Basingstoke: MacMillan, 1996), p. 85.
6   William Philpott, "Why the British were really on the Somme in 1916: A Reply to Elizabeth Greenhalgh", *War in History*, 9(4), 2002, p. 459; William Philpott, *Bloody Victory: The Sacrifice on the Somme and the Making of the Twentieth Century* (London: Little Brown, 2009), pp. 83, 95. Haig's Despatch stated that before the offensive "the Germans were continuing to press their attacks at Verdun", that the German movement of troops to the Eastern Front in June had "not lessen[ed] the pressure", and the primary objective of the offensive was "to relieve the pressure on Verdun": *London Gazette*, 29 December 1916, pp. 12719-20.
7   Elizabeth Greenhalgh, "Why the British were on the Somme in 1916", *War in History*, 6 (2), 1999, 149, 171-172; Elizabeth Greenhalgh, "Flames over the Somme: A Retort to William Philpott", *War in History*, 10(3), 2003, p. 338; Elizabeth Greenhalgh, *Victory through Coalition: Britain and France in the First World War* (Cambridge: Cambridge University Press, 2005), pp. 49-51.

intelligence's contribution to Allied understanding of German intentions before the German assault on Verdun's defences? Essentially, how many pieces of the jigsaw did Britain provide and how successfully did their analysts predict events? Second, once the Battle of Verdun was underway, how did the British interpret German intentions and how did this influence their choices about assisting the French? And, third, how did the British evaluate the effects of the Verdun fighting upon their enemy?

Anticipating Verdun

The British Secret Service, through an agent in Maastricht, heard that a substantive attack on Verdun was imminent; they informed the French ambassador in London who immediately warned the War Ministry in Paris.[8] But this occurred in April 1915 and so, for the purposes of this chapter, the incident serves only to illustrate the vagaries of agent reports and the close intelligence relationship between the British and French. In establishing a baseline, it should also be noted that in the field of espionage Britain had done rather well in 1915.[9] The Secret Service and the I(b) sub-section of GHQ France had both recruited extensive networks of agents across occupied Belgium. Indeed, by the end of that year they had full coverage of the Belgian railway network with the exception of some of the north-south routes across the Ardennes. Therefore, until their sudden collapse in mid-1916, these networks made a very significant contribution to the Allied intelligence picture. As will be seen, the agents were able to report – albeit with a slight delay – most of Germany's major movements in the west. This capability was crucial because tangible reporting on the transit of troop trains could cut through the constant stream of vague reports regarding German intentions; especially when the Germans themselves were deliberately seeking to disseminate false information.[10]

In mid-November 1915 Falkenhayn initially instructed his subordinates to draw up plans for three limited offensives, against Belfort, Verdun, and in the Vosges.[11] A week later the British reported, from Greek and Spanish sources, that the Germans were planning simultaneous attacks on the Meuse at St Mihiel, in the Champagne sector, and also in Flanders.[12] The partial congruence of German planning and these

---

8   Service historique de la défense, Département Terre (SHD(T)), 7N 1275, French ambassador London to War Ministry, 7 April 1915.
9   For additional context regarding British espionage, see Beach, *Haig's Intelligence*, pp. 115-142.
10 For German deception work in early 1917 and 1918, see Beach, *Haig's Intelligence*, pp. 224-5, 277-8
11 Foley, *German Strategy*, pp. 188-9.
12 One report claimed the Kaiser had informed the Greek King of Germany's intentions: SHD(T), 7N 1275, Undated notes on War Office paper [report dated 23 and 25 November 1915], French Military Attaché London to GQG, 25 November 1915.

Detail from Alan d'Egville, *Our Agents*, 1917. (Military Intelligence Museum)

agent reports is interesting. Both indicate three target areas but there is perhaps misdirection as to the specific locations, implying German deception. Perhaps more interesting are two reports regarding Germany's wider strategic intent. The first came from Switzerland. Agent *Lynx* provided information from "military men of position in Berlin" suggesting the German high command considered "a decisive issue can only be reached on the Western Front". Although this general statement was correct, the report then went on to claim the Germans had already made "great preparations [...] for an advance in the direction of Paris".[13] Therefore, betrayed by its lack of specific detail, this may have been imaginative prose in pursuit of a cash payment. During the same period the British espionage authorities in Switzerland were also duped by Agent *Bernard*, who falsified numerous reports supposedly from Germany.[14] More credible was an early December report from the Secret Service's Rotterdam station derived from "a very good military source". Because only part of it has hitherto been cited in the Verdun historiography, it warrants quotation in full:

> The German General Staff is said to have delivered itself as follows regarding the present position of affairs on the Western Front:
>
> In order to carry through successfully a really energetic break-through, we lack unfortunately the necessary numbers, seeing that our resources in men are commencing to give out; but all the same it is and will remain our firmly uttered oath that England shall be punished. Therefore our one and only way of forcing

13 SHD(T), 7N 1018, MH044, 'Miscellaneous', Berne, 8 December 1915.
14 Beach, *Haig's Intelligence*, 133. For examples of his reports in this period, see SHD(T), 7N 1018 & 1020, 'Miscellaneous', Lausanne, 28 November, 12 December, 13 January 1915. The periodicity of the reports and their numbering indicates that *Bernard* had been deceiving the British since the spring of 1915.

a decision is to adopt an enormous artillery offensive and thus destroy by our tremendous fire all the enemy's hopes.

In order to obtain the necessary quantities of ammunition for such a task, the number of ammunition workers must be doubled, and even so, a very long period will be required for the output of such a gigantic amount of munitions as would be necessary to achieve our purpose. The proper time for this will not arrive till next year when we can once more attack the enemy in the west with another million fresh troops – and this million we can provide from the Class 1916 now in course of being called up and trained.

On the Eastern front all danger has vanished, as Russia's strength is broken, and furthermore our own forces in that quarter are sufficient to counter any possible offensive of the enemy.[15]

Guessing the provenance of anonymous agent reports is a hazardous activity, but in this case some speculation is possible. The British Secret Service in the Netherlands had a close relationship with the Dutch military who in turn had significant interactions with the German army.[16] Therefore the originating station and the attribution to a military source would be consistent with information passed on by the Dutch or, alternatively, another neutral source such as a military attaché with access to the German high command. What is clear, with the benefit of hindsight, is that the report is fairly accurate with regard to the general contours of German strategy. As Robert Foley has noted, the first part "outlined well Falkenhayn's thinking".[17] Similarly, the final section distilled German perception of the situation on the Eastern Front. The middle sections are also intriguing because they imply some delay in Germany's offensive intentions while resources were built up. But, overall, the existence of this information in Allied hands at the end of 1915 is symptomatic of at least limited espionage success.[18]

On 15 December, a week after the British had received this interesting intelligence, the Germans narrowed their focus to a single offensive at Verdun. As Foley explains, Falkenhayn anticipated that an attack here would cause the French to "send all their

---

15   SHD(T) 7N 1018 & The National Archives (TNA), MUN4/3586, R293/253(d), 'Miscellaneous', Rotterdam, 9 December 1915.
16   Beach, *Haig's Intelligence*, pp. 128-9. For Dutch military contact with the Germans in 1915, see Maartje Abbenhuis, *The Art of Staying Neutral: The Netherlands in the First World War, 1914–1918* (Amsterdam: Amsterdam University Press, 2006), 182. For a recent unpacking, from local sources, of the Netherlands as an espionage hub, see Edwin Ruis, *Spynest: British and German Espionage from Neutral Holland, 1914-1918* (Stroud: History Press, 2016). For Dutch intelligence gathering and sharing, see Wim Klinkert, *Defending Neutrality: The Netherlands Prepares for War, 1900-1925* (Leiden: Brill, 2013), pp. 165-182, 216-228.
17   Foley, *German Strategy*, p. 192.
18   For general difficulties with agents penetrating Germany, see Beach, *Haig's Intelligence*, pp. 127-8.

reserves [...] to support Verdun. Thus, by seizing or by threatening to seize such a vital point in the French line [... the French] would exhaust themselves in fruitless attacks against [...] German positions supported by powerful artillery".[19] A few days later Haig assumed command of the BEF and, as part of his induction, was briefed on GHQ's intelligence arrangements. He judged them to be "wonderfully well organised", with the espionage dimension being "particularly good, better than the French in many respects". At this point the outgoing head of GHQ Intelligence, George Macdonogh, assessed that the Germans had twenty-five divisions "out of line" and therefore available for an offensive.[20] Over Christmas and New Year, British espionage reporting was unremarkable. Reporting from Switzerland suggested a German offensive against Ypres, while Agent *Church* stated that August von Mackensen, the recent conqueror of Serbia, was to lead an attack against the British front.[21] On 3 January GHQ noted that the French were concerned about "a possible offensive by the Germans in the direction of Roye-Montdidier", but the French official history tells us that a day later the French War Ministry received warning that Verdun was to be the target of a German attack.[22]

On 6 January German Fifth Army submitted to Falkenhayn their attack plan for Verdun. He then ordered German Sixth Army to make preparations for the downstream and decisive offensive against the British front.[23] From this point German strategy for early 1916 was set and over the next six weeks its core element – an offensive against Verdun – would become clear to the Allies. Their difficulty came in understanding what the Germans were trying to achieve at Verdun and whether it was a main effort or a diversion. Additionally, throughout January British threat perceptions were further complicated by intelligence regarding German activities in Flanders. In early January reports suggested a concentration of heavy artillery in central Belgium and, at the end of the month, "continuous rumours" and railway activity around Béthune led to warnings being issued to the BEF in case a "small effort" was made around Ypres or Loos to mark the Kaiser's birthday.[24] This would develop into genuine diversionary operations in the Ypres Salient during February and, from an intelligence perspective, they achieved their purpose of partly clouding the picture in advance of the Verdun attack.[25] British attention was perhaps also accentuated by Haig's exploration of his

19 Foley, *German Strategy*, pp. 192, 204.
20 NLS, Haig Papers, Diary, 21, 26 December 1915.
21 SHD(T), 7N 1019-20, Ib/01530, 'Miscellaneous', Lausanne, 31 December 1915; 'Miscellaneous', London, 5 January 1916.
22 LHCMA, Robertson Papers, 7/6/6, Haig to Robertson, 3 January 1916; Ministère de la Guerre, *Les Armées Françaises dans la Grande Guerre*, Tome 4, Vol.1 (Paris, 1926), p. 137.
23 Foley, *German Strategy*, pp. 193, 197-8.
24 TNA WO157/4, GHQ intelligence summary, 11 January 1916, WO158/185, GHQ to Armies, 26 January 1916; NLS, Haig Papers, Diary, 25-26 January 1916, For 15 January indications of an attack against the British front, see *Armées Françaises*, Tome 4, Vol.1, p. 140.
25 Bombardments and limited German attacks occurred 8-19 February: James Edmonds, *Military Operations: France & Belgium: 1916*, Vol. 1 (London: HMSO, 1932), pp. 163-167.

own attacking options in that area.[26] According to Pierre des Vallières, the French liaison officer at GHQ, the net result was that on the eve of Verdun Haig was "definitely preoccupied" by German activities in Flanders.[27]

With regard to Verdun, during the first half of January indications began to accumulate but they were far from conclusive.[28] Initially British agents reported significant movements of ammunition by rail within Belgium, with the main focus being towards the Ardennes.[29] This was followed, on 9 January, by clear indications that a German corps had been moved by train to the area north of Verdun.[30] Concentrations of heavy artillery and troops transferred from Serbia were also reported there.[31] This all coincided with a recent upsurge in railway movement in that area. But, with similar rail movements also occurring behind the Champagne sector, French Grand Quartier Général (GQG) concluded that the Germans were moving individual replacements rather than formed units. However, these new developments led GQG to adjust its overall assessment. Having previously thought that any German offensive would be focused much further west, towards Compiègne, they now concluded that the point of main effort could not yet be determined.[32] A few days later, on 15 January, the British Secret Service gave the French a lengthy report from their supposedly "reliable" Agent *Church*. Drawing upon testimony from three separate informants, *Church* stated that the Germans intended an offensive on the Western Front and assessed that it would be directed against Verdun.[33] The evidence for that conclusion came from two "travelling agents" who had both visited Cologne and a French evacuee from the region to the north-east of Verdun.[34] Both travellers had seen many troop trains moving west, with one stating that he had met a soldier heading specifically for Verdun, while the other reported a soldier telling him that the Germans were about to

---

This imitated German behaviour before the Gorlice-Tarnow offensive on the Eastern Front in May 1915: Foley, *German Strategy*, p. 203.

26 NLS, Haig Papers, Diary, 10, 18 January 1916. For further discussion of these plans, see JP Harris, *Douglas Haig and the First World War* (Cambridge: Cambridge University Press, 2008), pp. 206-7.
27 Vallières to Joffre, 20 February 1916, Elizabeth Greenhalgh (ed.), *Liaison: General Pierre des Vallières at British General Headquarters, January 1916 to May 1917* (Stroud: History Press for the Army Records Society, 2016), p. 66.
28 For a succinct summary of indicators received by the French in early January, see Robert Doughty, *Pyrrhic Victory: French Strategy and Operations in the Great War* (Cambridge: Belknap, 2005), p. 262.
29 TNA WO157/4, GHQ intelligence summary, 4 January 1916.
30 VIII Reserve Corps. TNA WO157/4, GHQ intelligence summary, 9 January 1916.
31 SHD(T), 7N 1276, War Ministry to Lebrun, 11 June 1917. In response to parliamentary interest, this document summarised intelligence indicators received by the French before the Verdun attack.
32 *Armées Françaises*, Tome 4, Vol.1, pp. 138-9.
33 SHD(T), 7N 1019, 'Miscellaneous', London, 15 January 1916,
34 Agent *Church* had previously provided information from western Germany: SHD (T), 7N 1020, 'Miscellaneous', London, 5, 11 January 1916.

attack in the Argonne, to the west of Verdun. The evacuee was more vague; she stated that before Christmas "an important personage" had made a speech telling German troops that Verdun "must be taken" before the Kaiser's birthday. But she also reported an early January arrival of large numbers of German troops from the Eastern Front. During the second half of January another significant troop movement was reported by the British agent networks in Belgium.[35] From 17 January they began monitoring a southward transit across the Ardennes which, by the end of the month, was assessed as being the equivalent of one German corps. However, initial certainty about its identity was undermined by conflicting information indicating some units were still in their original location. Additionally, another corps was provisionally identified in the western Ardennes.[36] Both of these corps would participate in the initial attack at Verdun, but at this stage their probable positioning was not conclusive because they could just have easily been committed to another sector, such as the nearby Champagne. That said, German activity in the Verdun area became more noticeable in late January, causing unease for the local French commander.[37] Rather ominously, the Germans had recently destroyed church steeples and other landmarks north-east of Verdun, presumably to hinder French artillery targeting.[38]

In the first week of February indications of German activity continued to mount up. At this point Franco-British consultation on their meaning occurred with the visit to GHQ of Charles Dupont, head of intelligence at GQG.[39] At this stage he did not seem to have been too alarmed. Haig recorded that Dupont thought the Germans were "likely to attack the Russians in early spring and probably towards the south-east with a view to isolating Roumania".[40] This opinion reflected, in part, a recent Russian report that suggested the Germans would seek "a decision" in France, followed by an attack on the south-eastern part of the Eastern Front. But the British had not given any weight to the Russian report.[41] On the Western Front, the indicators were still mixed. Artillery had been noted passing west through Cologne and troop trains had been seen passing through Luxembourg towards Verdun.[42] In that area a concentration of troops and the digging of new tunnels had also been noted, but this also coincided with similar concentrations in Champagne.[43] With regard to the latter, there

---

35 XV Corps. TNA WO157/4 & SHD(T), 17N 308, GHQ intelligence summaries, pp. 21, 26-27, 30 January, 4 February 1916.
36 III Corps. TNA WO157/4, GHQ intelligence summaries, 25 January 1916.
37 Doughty, *Pyrrhic Victory*, p. 262.
38 *Armées Françaises*, Tome 4, Vol.1, p. 140
39 LHCMA, Charteris Papers 2/2, Letter to wife, 3 February 1916.
40 NLS, Haig Papers, Diary, 4 February 1916. This contrasts somewhat with Dupont's subsequent assertion that he had already divined German offensive intentions towards Verdun: Charles Dupont, *Mémoires du chef des services secrets de la Grande Guerre* (Paris: Histoire & Collections, 2014), p. 143.
41 NLS, Haig Papers, Diary, 1 February 1916.
42 SHD (T), 7N 1276, War Ministry to Lebrun, 11 June 1917.
43 *Armées Françaises*, Tome 4, Vol.1, p. 145.

were indications that a German corps – another of the ones that would be used in the initial Verdun attack – had perhaps moved from reserve to the west of that sector.[44] A few days later the French noted "above normal" rail activity behind enemy lines in Champagne,[45] while reporting from a source in Alsace suggested imminent German concentrations in both the Verdun and Champagne sectors.[46] Over the following fortnight the threat to Verdun crystallised and brought with it tension within the alliance over what should be the appropriate British response. In part, this can be explained by ongoing uncertainties about the scale of the likely offensive and difficulties in understanding the strategic logic of Germany attacking there.

A key milestone was reached on 10 February when GQG issued a warning to their troops at Verdun and started taking steps to reinforce the sector.[47] This development was prompted by fresh and credible intelligence.[48] First, deserters helped to identify near Verdun the presence of a fresh corps from the German reserve.[49] Second, a "reliable" source provided a detailed summary of German intentions for a major offensive against Verdun. The source pointed to the presence of an additional corps from the German reserve,[50] a concentration of heavy artillery, the arrival of the Crown Prince to command the operation, and a plan for a heavy bombardment to open the attack. However, the source also stated the Germans were preparing two other offensives; one against Arras and the other in Champagne. The same day Charteris briefed Haig on an agent report saying that "attacks [would] be launched at three different points" on the Western Front. The timing and similarity suggest it was the same French report, but Haig also noted the agent's assertion that the "German General Staff look upon a breakthrough on the Western Front as feasible and likely to succeed".[51] The latter point is interesting because an assumption that German strategy was seeking a breakthrough would remain an important feature of GHQ's perspective. This can be seen immediately. On 11 February Haig acknowledged French expectations of a Verdun offensive but noted that, with only seven divisions available, the Germans did not have "enough to achieve a decision". He therefore concluded that the attack might be a diversion to "cover a movement of troops" to the Eastern Front.[52] But GHQ was certainly taking a keen interest in developments, causing Charteris to cancel his planned leave because he was "very, very busy".[53]

44 XVIII Corps: SHD(T), 17N 308, GHQ intelligence summary, 3 February 1916.
45 SHD(T), 17N 308, GHQ intelligence summary, 8, 11 February 1916.
46 SHD(T), 7N 1276, War Ministry to Lebrun, 11 June 1917.
47 *Armées Françaises*, Tome 4, Vol.1, pp. 146-7.
48 Précis of this material available in: Doughty, *Pyrrhic Victory*, pp. 262-3.
49 III Corps: SHD(T), 17N 308, GHQ intelligence summary, 9 February 1916; 7N 1276, War Ministry to Lebrun, 11 June 1917.
50 XV Corps: *Armées Françaises*, Tome 4, Vol.1, p. 146.
51 NLS, Haig Papers, Diary, 10 February 1916.
52 NLS, Haig Papers, Diary, 11 February 1916.
53 LHCMA, Charteris Papers 2/2, Letter to wife, ['Thursday', so probably 10 February 1916].

The Germans had intended to launch their offensive on 12 February, but poor weather led to a nine-day postponement.[54] This gave the Allies additional warning time and allowed the French to reinforce Verdun with three divisions, but the British remained untroubled by the impeding attack. On 13 February Charteris briefed a meeting of the BEF's Army commanders. He told them that "the French fear an attack on Verdun, but the enemy is in no great force".[55] One of his subordinates went further. As head of the I(b) sub-section, Walter Kirke was responsible for running GHQ's agent networks and in his diary he reflected upon the impending "German offensive". He wrote that the "French [were] jibbering – which is curious as a German attack suits us above everything and therefore seems improbable except to [a] strictly limited extent". He then suggested that the Germans would switch their attention to the Eastern Front in the spring because "they can hardly hope to get a decision [in the west], having an inferiority of some twenty divisions".[56] Therefore, at this juncture, the apparent consensus at GHQ was that the Germans had committed insufficient forces to their putative Verdun attack and so it could not achieve a decisive outcome, such as a breakthrough. The next day Haig and Charteris visited GQG to discuss the Franco-British summer offensive.[57] During the meeting Dupont apparently told Charteris that he was now convinced "that the German concentration was towards [Verdun]".[58] However, according to Haig, at this point Joffre "was firmly convinced that the Germans meant to attack Russia".[59] Over the next few days, more deserters, abnormal rail movements, and additional information on heavy artillery positions all confirmed German offensive preparations at Verdun.[60] But GQG remained unsure as to whether it was to be a main effort or diversion.[61] And at this stage another agent report repeated the suggestion that Verdun would be just one of three German offensives.[62]

From a British perspective, matters came to a head on 18 February when Haig was visited by the Vicomte de Castelnau, Joffre's chief of staff. Because Verdun was about to be attacked, he asked that the BEF extend its frontage to relieve at least part of the French Tenth Army. Haig agreed that there were "many signs of an impending attack" but questioned its potential seriousness. Because the Germans had only concentrated nine additional divisions at Verdun, he argued this was "not sufficient to enable a

54 Foley, *German Strategy*, pp. 216-7.
55 NLS, Haig Papers, Diary, 13 February 1916.
56 Imperial War Museum (IWM), Kirke Papers, Diary, 13 February 1916.
57 Philpott, *Anglo-French Relations*, p. 120.
58 Edmonds, *Military Operations, 1916*, Vol. 1, p. 30.
59 Reference to Joffre's opinion three days earlier in: NLS, Haig Papers, Diary, 19 February 1916.
60 GHQ intelligence summary, 15 February 1916, 17N 308; SHD(T), 7N 1276, War Ministry to Lebrun, 11 June 1917,
61 *Armées Françaises*, Tome 4, Vol.1, pp. 148-9.
62 SHD(T), 7N 1276, War Ministry to Lebrun, 11 June 1917.

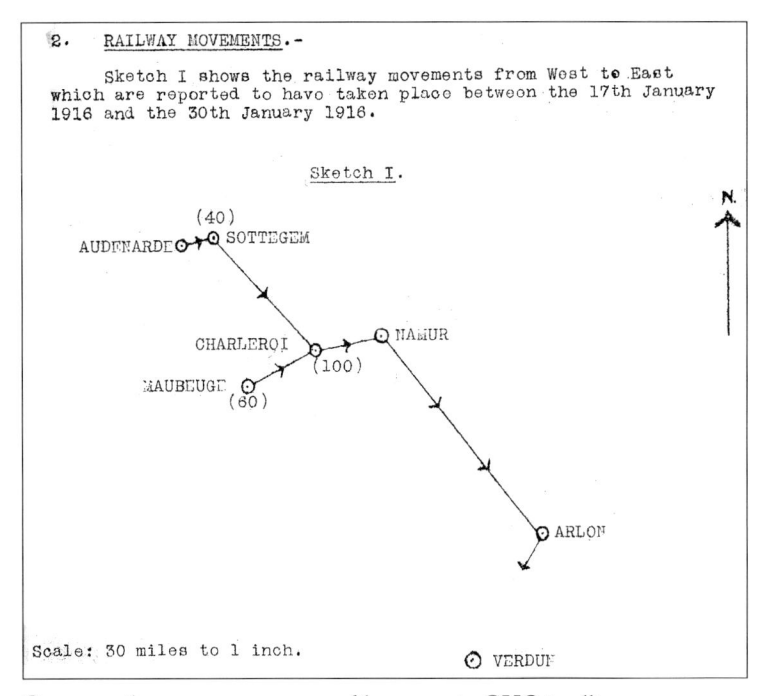

British Intelligence and the Battle of Verdun 103

```
2.    RAILWAY MOVEMENTS.-
       Sketch I shows the railway movements from West to East
       which are reported to have taken place between the 17th January
       1916 and the 30th January 1916.

                            Sketch I.
                                                                    N.
              (40)
      AUDENARDE○─→○ SOTTEGEM


            CHARLEROI      ○ NAMUR
                    ○─→
         MAUBEUGE  (100)
               ○
              (60)



                                      ○ ARLON



    Scale: 30 miles to 1 inch.       ○ VERDUN
```

German rail movements as reported by agents in GHQ intelligence summary,
16 February 1916 (17N 308, SHD(T))

decisive result to be obtained by the enemy" and so a German attack on the British front "was more than likely".[63] Haig wrote afterwards to William Robertson, the Chief of the Imperial General Staff in London. He said that Castelnau had "returned" to an earlier request to relieve Tenth Army and that "his excuse now is that they are to be attacked at Verdun! Funny creatures are they not?" Robertson replied that "the French are most tiresome […] I fear they are fumbling this Verdun thing".[64] On 19 February Charteris again briefed the Army commanders, telling them the Germans had now concentrated ten divisions at Verdun. Haig followed up, telling them that:

> Although the French feared an enemy attack at Verdun, we [know] German strategy sufficiently well to feel certain that, at the same time as they attack Verdun, another attack would be made on the British front. This latter might eventually turn out to be their main attack![65]

63 NLS, Haig Papers, Diary, 19 February 1916.
64 LHCMA, Robertson Papers, 7/6/24 & 26, Haig to Robertson, 18 February; Robertson to Haig, 20 February 1916.
65 NLS, Haig Papers, Diary, 19 February 1916.

Writing to Joffre the following day, Haig summarised his perspective which, to some extent, deserves credit for correctly guessing Falkenhayn's broad strategic intent. After noting that they had not discussed a German offensive when the two of them had met on 14 February, Haig argued:

> The indications so far do not establish anything approaching to certainty as to where the German attack [...] would fall. Although we know of a considerable concentration towards Verdun, we have also definite information of German movements into Belgium, and it is still quite possible that the German plan may be to draw reserves down towards Verdun and then, shifting their centre of gravity northwards, to make their great effort against some part of our front between the sea and the Somme.[66]

Haig therefore thought it necessary to maintain his reserves against such a contingency. But he conceded that if the Germans made their "main effort" against the French, he would relieve Tenth Army and offer additional assistance. With regard to the latter, he pointed out his own preparations for an offensive.

Joffre was also sent a report by des Vallières. Although concerned primarily with operational matters, it also provides an excellent insight into British intelligence perceptions just before Verdun:

> Charteris does not believe that the enemy concentration taking place at the moment north of Verdun means that the Germans have chosen this area for their decisive action: the multiplication of Verdun's defences, the river Meuse, the Argonne [Forest] appear to him to be insurmountable obstacles to the movement of great masses with their vehicles. There will only be a large demonstration before Verdun, with the aim of drawing in our reserves and affecting French public opinion. The Germans will attempt their breakthrough in an area where the rapid deployment of troops, masses of artillery and supply convoys is easier, such as Champagne.[67]

This is interesting because it shows the British struggling to find a conventional military rationale for the Germans attacking a supposedly strong part of the French line. This underlying sense that the enemy was making a strategic mistake would carry forward into subsequent British perceptions of the battle. But this passage also illustrates a more important assumption in British thinking; that the Germans were seeking to break through the French lines rather than engage in a deliberately attritional battle. Again, this assumption would persist and, over the following four months, it helps to explain the framing of British commitments to 'relieve' the French

---

66 TNA WO158/14, OAD444, Haig to Joffre, 20 February 1916.
67 Vallières to Joffre, 20 February 1916, Greenhalgh, *Vallières*, p. 66.

under certain circumstances. Finally, it must be noted that on the eve of the Verdun offensive GQG was itself rather hesitant about German intentions. On the Verdun front itself, the local commander was expecting an attack east of the Meuse by four German corps supported by gas. But, as Robert Doughty has stressed, Joffre – like Charteris – "could perceive no strategic result to be gained by the Germans" at Verdun and thus considered it to be a diversion.[68] Meanwhile at GHQ Haig noted, with more than a hint of vindication, that: "the French today seem to be less certain that the main German blow will fall on Verdun!"[69]

Evaluating Verdun

On 22 February, GHQ's intelligence summary noted the start of the German infantry attack at Verdun:

> The bombardment continued and the Germans attacked yesterday evening the French positions […] They gained a footing in some of the French advanced and support trenches, but were driven out of the latter. The French captured about fifty prisoners.[70]

The positive tone is unsurprising as these snippets were usually recycled communiqués. But the content is also symptomatic of the lack of alarm on the part of the British given that the attack had not come as a surprise and no great threat was perceived. As Kirke later noted, "we had one month's notice of this attack, first by agents reports, vague – then by [railway] watchers, definite – then by deserters".[71] But over the following month, as the situation on the Meuse became clearer and the fighting heavier, a re-evaluation occurred. Almost immediately prisoners revealed that the Allies had correctly estimated the scale of the German effort at Verdun. Before the attack they had added nine divisions to the ten previously in the sector.[72] On 23 February GHQ also noted the testimony of a deserter who had told his French interrogators that the offensive had been delayed by poor weather and that "his officers [had] told him that the objective of the attack was to capture Verdun and force France to a separate peace".[73] The same day Joffre sent a telegram to Robertson suggesting that the German attack at Verdun was a "violent offensive that could be the beginning

---

68 Doughty, *Pyrrhic Victory*, 263. For French expectation of additional attacks, see also: *Armées Françaises*, Tome 4, Vol.1, p. 150.
69 NLS, Haig Papers, Diary, 20 February 1916.
70 SHD(T), 17N 308, GHQ intelligence summary, 22 February 1916.
71 IWM, Kirke Papers, Diary, 26 February 1916.
72 III, VII Reserve, XV, XVIII Corps; 21 Reserve, 22 Reserve Divisions: SHD(T), 17N 308, GHQ intelligence summary, 22 February 1916.
73 SHD(T), 17N 308, GHQ intelligence summary, 23 February 1916.

```
4.    GERMAN CONCENTRATION AT VERDUN.-

       The capture of prisoners of the XVIII Corps in the VERDUN
area now shows a concentration of 19 divisions between the MEUSE
at CONSENVOYE and ST. MIHIEL.
       In December there were 10 divisions in the same sector; since
that time the following units have moved into the area:-

       VII R. Corps (13th and 14th Res. Divs.)  from CHARLEROI -
                                                     MAUBEUGE area.
       III Corps    (5th Division      -         from SEDAN.
                    (6th Division      -         from HIRSON.
       21st Reserve Division (XVIII R. Corps)  from West of the MEUSE.
       XV Corps (30th and 39th Divisions)      from COURTRAI area.
       XVIII Corps (21st and 25th Divisions)   from ST. QUENTIN.
       also 22nd Reserve Division to MALANCOURT area from CHAMPAGNE.

                   (Signed)     J. CHARTERIS,

                                     Brigadier-General,
"I".                                 General Staff.
```

German concentration at Verdun as depicted in a GHQ intelligence summary, 22 February 1916. (17N 308, SHD(T))

of an action of a decisive character"; he therefore reiterated his request that the British relieve the French Tenth Army. Robertson deferred to Haig's judgement on this matter, but noted that the War Office had no indications of the Germans concentrating troops beyond Verdun.[74] On 24 February Robertson told Joffre that the BEF was preparing to relieve part of Tenth Army's front, but he was untroubled by the German decision to attack:

> It seems to me that we can desire nothing better than that the enemy should continue his attacks, as they will use up his troops to a much greater extent than the operations of "usure" [attrition] which you had proposed that we should employ against him. I am strongly of the opinion that, by attacking, the enemy is playing our game. This is the first time he has attempted to attack us in force since our lines have been as strong as they are now and our reserves have been so plentiful.[75]

Over the next three days the British policy response was discussed in London. First across the Channel was des Vallières. He met with Robertson and Lord Kitchener, the Secretary of State for War, both of whom:

---

74   TNA WO158/21, War Office to GHQ, 23 February 1916.
75   TNA WO158/21, Robertson to Joffre, 24 February 1916.

Refused to believe that a highly significant battle had begun before Verdun. They persist in seeing only a local action in which the French, thanks to their excellent defensive works and large number of guns and munitions, are going to inflict heavy losses on the enemy. By attacking the enemy is playing the coalition's game: it is the wearing down fight that the French high command was advising the British army to carry out in the spring so as to weaken the German resources.[76]

At this stage GHQ's position was also unchanged. Haig wrote to Joffre restating his belief that "the attack now being made towards Verdun may prove to be merely preliminary to greater [German] efforts to be made elsewhere later on".[77]

Accompanied by Charteris, Haig reached London shortly after des Vallières. Haig met initially with Kitchener and briefed him on the situation. He envisaged three potential outcomes; a "stalemate" at Verdun, in which case the offensive on the Somme should proceed as planned; a French "success" that would permit an early British offensive; or a "disaster" which would require an immediate British counter-offensive.[78] Then, on 26 February, a noticeable British policy shift took place. The catalyst was probably the German capture, the previous day, of Fort Douaumont, the lynchpin of Verdun's outer defences.[79] Kirke's diary gives us some hint of the British reaction to this development, with him observing that the "Germans [had] done very well considering the small number of men employed" in the offensive. But he still believed that "they cannot hope to get any decisive result unless they can make another and surprise attack somewhere else".[80] The operations staff at GHQ were told by their French liaison officers that the Verdun situation was "serious" but, in a telegram to Haig, noted that it was "impossible to ascertain" whether that was true.[81] At this point the British also reviewed Germany's commitment to Verdun. They concluded that the Germans had committed twenty-one divisions and nearly 400 heavy guns.[82] Haig, Robertson, Charteris, and Macdonogh met at the War Office; the latter having become the Director of Military Intelligence after leaving GHQ. Macdonogh outlined his assessment of the situation, arguing the "main offensive" would occur "in Champagne close to the Verdun Salient". To support this fresh operation, he estimated the Germans could commit up to 2,000 artillery

---

76 Vallières to Joffre, 26 February 1916, Greenhalgh, *Vallières*, p. 73.
77 TNA WO158/14, OAD459/1, Haig to Joffre, 25 February 1916.
78 Diary, 25 February 1916: Gary Sheffield & John Bourne (eds.), *Douglas Haig: War Diaries and Letters, 1914-1918* (London: Weidenfeld & Nicolson, 2005), pp. 181-182.
79 "Naturally, the German press made a great propaganda victory out of the fort's capture": Elizabeth Greenhalgh, *The French Army and the First World* War (Cambridge: Cambridge University Press, 2014), p. 136.
80 IWM, Kirke Papers, Diary, 26 February 1916.
81 TNA WO158/21, GHQ to War Office, 26 February 1916.
82 SHD(T), 17N 308, GHQ intelligence summary, 25 February 1916.

pieces.[83] Macdonogh's exposition is interesting for two reasons; first, it reconciled the Verdun situation with the previous accumulation of indicators suggesting an attack in Champagne. In this imagined scenario, the danger was presumably that the French would commit their forces to the Verdun salient only to find them enveloped by a breakthrough further west. Second, we see Macdonogh, the more experienced intelligence officer, taking the lead in assessment. This reminds us that both Haig and Charteris were new to their roles and so close consultation with London was, at this stage, an important part of any decision-making process.

Haig returned to GHQ and arranged for the BEF to relieve the French Tenth Army.[84] During his absence Joffre had communicated his assessment of the situation following the fall of Douaumont. He noted the increased intensity of the Verdun fighting and argued that the Germans had committed a significant part of their reserves in an attempt to break through the French front.[85] Haig also met with des Vallières who told him that the French had done "badly" at Verdun and that the German artillery fire had been "terrific".[86] But at this point there was a relative lull in German operations; they had completed their first phase and on 29 February, after an evaluation of its results, decided to extend their offensive to the west bank of the Meuse.[87] That day Haig reported to Robertson that he had "spent an hour with Joffre [...] He does not think that the attack [...] against Verdun is the German main attack. He expects attacks elsewhere and has made preparations to meet them".[88] He also noted that Joffre thought the "troops which are at present around Verdun can cope with the situation" and the French had "ample reserves to meet all contingencies".[89] Similarly, at GHQ des Vallières suggested to the British that if the French army could hold the east bank of the Meuse for another couple of days the Germans would then be unable to dislodge them.[90] Therefore the initial crisis had passed and at this point the Allies still anticipated the next German move to be an attack somewhere other

---

83 NLS, Haig Papers, Diary, 26 February 1916. The entry reads as follows: "[Macdonogh] thought that the attack against Verdun would prove to be their main effort. Some 8 or 7 Divns still remained available for attack. He thought that the main offensive would be in Champagne close to the Verdun Salient. As regards heavy guns 2000 still remained unaccounted for out of a total of 4,700". From the content of the second sentence, it would appear that Haig omitted a "not" in the first. Alternatively, he did not err and Macdonogh envisaged the Champagne operations as a broadening of the attack.
84 TNA WO158/184, GHQ to Armies, 27 February 1916; NLS, Haig Papers, Diary, 27 February 1916.
85 TNA WO158/14, [Telegram & letter] Joffre to Haig, 26 February 1916.
86 Diary, 27 February: Robert Blake (ed.), *The Private Papers of Douglas Haig, 1914-1919* (London: Eyre & Spottiswoode, 1952), p. 134.
87 Foley, *German Strategy*, pp. 219, 224.
88 LHCMA, Robertson Papers, 7/6/28, Haig to Robertson, 29 February 1916.
89 TNA WO158/21, British Mission GQG to War Office, 29 February 1916.
90 TNA WO158/21, GHQ to War Office, 29 February 1916.

than Verdun. Indeed, when commenting on agent reports of German heavy artillery moving by rail, Haig anticipated their employment either at Arras or in Champagne.[91]

On 3 March Joffre sent an analysis of the strategic situation to Haig.[92] Although GQG's letter has been highlighted within the historiography,[93] the internal response within GHQ is worth unpacking because it highlights some British assumptions. The French began by arguing that the Verdun offensive was increasingly important because the Germans had committed twenty divisions and much of their reserves of manpower and ammunition. They assessed that they retained another ten to twelve divisions in their western reserve, but these could be augmented by a similar number from the east within six weeks. Therefore the worst case scenario would be the Germans committing over twenty divisions to the Verdun offensive or a fresh attack against another part of the French line. On arrival at GHQ, the letter was passed to the intelligence section for comment. Charteris was absent in Paris, so a response was prepared by Basil Bowdler, the head of the I(a) sub-section, which was responsible for analysis. Bowdler agreed with French estimates of the German force levels at Verdun and also the size of their Western Front reserve. On the question of additional transfers from the east, he pointed to the fact that the agent reporting was unreliable but suggested at least three divisions had been transferred from the Balkans to Belgium. Therefore Bowdler saw "no reason to disagree" with Joffre's overall conclusion.[94] Shortly afterwards Haig was told by his intelligence staff that seven divisions may have been sent from Germany and, if this was correct, "we must expect that the Germans will bring every available man [to the west] in the hope of gaining a decisive success".[95] A few days later Charteris returned to GHQ and immediately issued a correction to his subordinate's earlier assessment.[96] Although he concurred with the number of divisions at Verdun and estimated the Western Front reserve at ten divisions, he strongly disagreed with the projection of an additional dozen divisions being brought from the east. Although it was theoretically possible for the Germans to transfer such a force, there was "no evidence" that the process had begun and even if it did occur, it would take the Germans two months to make it happen. Charteris also noted that during his recent visit to GQG the French had agreed with much of his analysis. Therefore, as the Battle of Verdun entered its next stage, the British still saw no reason for any great alarm. Their general attitude was perhaps best summed up, rather uncharitably, by Robertson, who told another theatre commander that:

> The Verdun business has been magnified unduly by the French. They were caught napping as usual and with few or no trenches, they lost their heads and

91 NLS, Haig Papers, Diary, 28 February 1916.
92 TNA WO159/14, Joffre to Haig, 3 March 1916.
93 Edmonds, *Military Operations 1916*, Vol. I, p. 39.
94 TNA WO159/14, GHQ Intelligence to CGS, 5 March 1916.
95 NLS, Haig Papers, Diary, 7 March 1916.
96 TNA WO159/14, BGI to CGS, 8 March 1916.

began to chatter and in general behaved as the French always do. No doubt the Germans tried to see what they could do, but they ought not to have been able to do anything like what they did had the French taken reasonable precautions. I should imagine that the German losses are no greater than the French.[97]

The last sentence is particularly interesting; the notion that the Germans were helpfully wearing themselves out at Verdun would remain a basic British assumption.

On 6 March, the Germans attacked again at Verdun; extending their offensive to the west bank of the Meuse. This was a significant change to the scale of the battle and the following day Joffre told his government that the German offensive was deliberately targeting French morale.[98] The British response to this new phase was to communicate to GQG their admiration for the "gallant Frenchmen in the great battle still raging" while observing that Germany had "chosen to break her strength in vain" at Verdun.[99] This general attitude caused deep concern to des Vallières who was "worried at the attitude of Haig and Robertson over Verdun […] They [are very] glad at Boches being killed but don't consider the [French] losses".[100] In a letter to Joffre, des Vallières expanded upon this basic point. He felt that the British, encouraged by French resistance at Verdun, had:

> Returned to the state of mind they had during the opening days of the battle […] which amounted to […] the enemy is playing into our hands by attacking, because he is carrying out the wearing down fight that the French high command wanted the British army to begin in the spring; and […] French casualties are light; German losses considerable; the enemy is exhausting his strategic reserves by this operation, and will be ripe in the summer for the great general offensive of the [Allied] coalition.[101]

He added that the British remained 'obstinately' focused on their own front because the "very tendentious" GHQ Intelligence staff, under Charteris, was playing up the German threat to their own front. Following an Allied offensive planning conference at GQG on 12 March, a key turning point was reached three days later. At Verdun the fighting had intensified with the Germans attacking vigorously, particularly on the western side of the Meuse.[102] At GHQ Haig decided to press ahead with British

---

97 Robertson to Murray, 6 March 1916, David Woodward, *The Military Correspondence of Field Marshal Sir William Robertson, Chief of the Imperial General Staff, December 1915 – February 1918* (London: Bodley Head for the Army Records Society, 1989), 39.
98 Doughty, *Pyrrhic Victory*, pp. 263-4.
99 TNA WO159/14, CGS to French Mission, 10 March 1916.
100 Churchill Archives Centre, Spears Papers, SPRS 5/13, Diary, 9 March 1916, cited in Greenhalgh, *Vallières*, p. 76.
101 Vallières to Joffre, 10 March 1916, Greenhalgh, *Vallières*, p. 78.
102 Foley, *German Strategy*, pp. 224-227.

offensive preparations because "the Germans seem to be still massing troops towards Verdun. If they continue to press the French hard it might be necessary for us to attack somewhere to relieve the pressure on the French". He also noted a slight reduction in the threat to the British front and, because the Germans had "suffered so much at Verdun", there was no longer a requirement for preparatory attacks before the main British offensive.[103] Therefore, at this juncture, the British appear to have recognised the gravity of the situation at Verdun, but they continued to believe the battle was also inflicting significant damage upon the Germans. Unfortunately, Haig did not specify what sort of additional German pressure would warrant the sudden launching of his relief offensive but, working from previously held assumptions, a German breakthrough at Verdun was probably his primary fear.

From this second point of crisis in mid-March through to the opening of the Anglo-French offensive on the Somme in late June, Verdun features less prominently in the British intelligence documentation. When it did appear, the focus was upon the effects of the fighting upon the German army. Three analytical aspects can be identified; coverage of the fighting in the enemy press, the number of casualties, and the size of the German reserve on the Western Front. GHQ regularly surveyed the German press.[104] Because of a time delay in receiving the newspapers, it was late March before coverage of the Battle of Verdun began to appear in their analyses.[105] Initially they detected a "reticence about the Verdun operations", with "great care […] taken not to discuss the prospects of the so far successful fighting and not to disclose the aim of the offensive".[106] In early April the British interpreted German coverage as arguing that their successes had spoiled Allied plans for an offensive.[107] This argument was reiterated in later articles with, for example, the *Frankfurter Zeitung* of 8 April saying that German actions at Verdun "forestalled [the Allies] and have overthrown their carefully worked out plans".[108] Perhaps reflecting a declining British interest in the subject, subsequent press summaries made no mention of Verdun.[109]

GHQ was more consistent in its analysis of German casualties at Verdun and, as the Somme offensive got closer, the picture became more encouraging for the Allies. Using the published lists of killed and wounded, they could gauge the German army's

---

103 NLS, Haig Papers, Diary, 15-16 March 1916.
104 For additional context, see Beach, *Haig's Intelligence*, p. 173.
105 TNA WO157/5, Summary of German Press, 26 February to 3 March 1916, GHQ intelligence summary, 4 March 1916.
106 TNA WO157/5, Summary of German Press, 3-11 March 1916, GHQ intelligence summary, 22 March 1916.
107 TNA WO157/6, Summary of German Press, 19-25 March 1916, GHQ intelligence summary, 3 April 1916.
108 TNA WO157/6, Summary of German Press, 4-10 April 1916, GHQ intelligence summary, 22 April 1916.
109 TNA WO157/6-7, Summaries of German Press, 10 April to 8 May 1916, GHQ intelligence summaries, 29 April, 2, 4, 18 May 1916.

112   At All Costs

losses.¹¹⁰ Because they knew from other sources which units had been engaged at Verdun, they could also estimate the human cost of the battle by examining individual battalions. The Germans had actually lost 80,000 casualties at Verdun when, at the end of March, the first lists were published.¹¹¹ GHQ immediately highlighted an infantry battalion that had lost 500 men.¹¹² A week later they disseminated an analysis of eight battalions from five different corps to illustrate the "heavy losses among units engaged at Verdun". In this case the average loss was over 300 men per battalion, with one regiment sustaining over 450 casualties in each of its battalions.¹¹³ These battalion analyses caught Haig's eye; he recorded in his diary that one had lost over 1,000 men at Verdun.¹¹⁴ At the end of April GHQ conducted "a careful estimate" of German losses and assessed them as being 278,000 in total.¹¹⁵ They also highlighted one German corps that had lost 11,000 men, with the spaces being filled by recent conscripts of the 1916 Class.¹¹⁶ A month later GHQ updated its estimates. This time they collated 83 battalions from four different corps and from this data suggested an average loss of over 500 men per battalion.¹¹⁷ At this point Haig noted the French had estimated overall German losses to be 300,000 to 350,000.¹¹⁸ This was an over-estimate as the real figure was around 250,000 casualties at Verdun.¹¹⁹ Finally, at the end of June an analysis of 133 battalions indicated average losses had reached over 600 men.¹²⁰ This growing cost of operations at Verdun had forced Falkenhayn to commit additional units to the battle and, by the end of April, he had already used most of his reserve divisions.¹²¹ Conscious of the potential threat to their own front, the British continued to monitor the rail movements of these units through their agent networks.¹²² And by the end of May the British assessed that over thirty German divisions had been engaged at Verdun; up from twenty in mid-March.¹²³

110 For additional context, see Beach, *Haig's Intelligence*, pp. 176-8.
111 Foley, *German Strategy*, p. 227.
112 2/116 Regiment, 18 Division: TNA WO157/5, GHQ intelligence summary, 28 March 1916.
113 12 Grenadier, 28 Ersatz, 38 Reserve, 81, 105 Regiments (Bavarian Ersatz, III, VI Reserve, XV, XVIII Corps): TNA WO157/6, GHQ intelligence summary, 8 April 1916.
114 3 Jäger Battalion (III Corps): NLS, Haig Papers, Diary, 12 April 1916.
115 TNA WO157/6, GHQ intelligence summary, 27 April 1916.
116 III Corps: TNA WO157/6, GHQ intelligence summaries, 27, 30 April 1916. For British monitoring of German conscription, see Beach, *Haig's Intelligence*, p. 175.
117 III, VI Reserve, XV, XVIII Corps; 22 Reserve Division: TNA WO157/7, GHQ intelligence summary, 30 May 1916.
118 NLS, Haig Papers, Diary, 30 May 1916.
119 Foley, *German Strategy*, p. 235.
120 TNA WO157/10, GHQ intelligence summary, 26 June 1916.
121 Foley, *German Strategy*, p. 235.
122 TNA WO157/5-7, 10, GHQ intelligence summaries, 20 March, 21-22, 24 April, 5-6, 11, 14, 17-18, 24 May, 5 June 1916; NLS, Haig Papers, Diary, 20 March, 8, 17-18, 28 May 1916. For German rail movements in June following the Brusilov offensive, see Beach, *Haig's Intelligence*, p. 198.
123 TNA WO157/5, 7, GHQ intelligence summaries, 22 March, 31 May 1916.

Overall, the flow of intelligence from the middle of March did suggest that the Germans were indeed weakening themselves by continuing to prosecute an offensive at Verdun. For GHQ this was most encouraging in light of the planned Somme offensive, but the fighting on the Meuse was also damaging their French ally. From a British perspective, in late May we can therefore discern another moment of crisis regarding Verdun. Although less serious than the previous instances, it did reinforce the importance of gauging the likelihood of a sudden German success. From late March through to mid-May there are very few indications that the German threat to Verdun had much impact upon GHQ. For example, on 27 March Joffre wrote to Haig to stress that German attacks at Verdun should not detract from their offensive intentions.[124] In this context it is difficult to disagree with Robin Prior and Trevor Wilson who have argued that the British government's 7 April decision to participate in the summer offensive "was not forced upon [them …] by the circumstances of the French at Verdun".[125] A few days later the apparently favourable situation was summed by Haig. He told Joffre that no preliminary attacks would be needed before the Somme because the Germans would have "used up" their reserves in "unsuccessful efforts at Verdun".[126] This benign strategic environment persisted, with Haig recording a week later that Verdun seemed "quieter", although the French anticipated continued attacks.[127] On 4 May, a couple of days after visiting Joffre to discuss the start date of their joint offensive, Haig discussed the military situation with a French politician. He told Georges Clemenceau that he was preparing to attack in case "a catastrophe were to happen at Verdun. But such a situation seems most unlikely to arise now".[128] This perception would, presumably, have been reinforced by a Secret Service report a few days later. It came from a source who, as a guest of the German high command, had spent "several days at Verdun". He stated that the Germans had been disappointed initially by the inability of their 420mm howitzers to "smash" the French defences and that they no longer intended to capture Verdun. Instead the extension of the offensive to the west bank of the Meuse had been "to compel the French to concentrate their men […] and spoil […] their plans for an [Allied] offensive".[129] Around this time Robertson told the British government that the

---

124 TNA WO158/14, Joffre to Haig, 27 March 1916.
125 Robin Prior & Trevor Wilson, *The Somme* (New Haven: Yale University Press, 2005), p. 28.
126 TNA WO158/14, Haig to Joffre, 10 April 1916.
127 Diary, 17 April 1916, Haig Papers, NLS.
128 Diary, 4 May 1916, Sheffield & Bourne, *Douglas Haig*, p. 186. Clemenceau was then President of the Senate Army Commission.
129 TNA FO371/2678/338-342, "Internal Conditions (Enemy Countries)", Rotterdam, 10 May 1916. The source is described as a "casual contributor" who had also visited the German army on the Eastern Front after "being a guest at the German Headquarters, to view the attack on Verdun, and was there several days watching operations against Douaumont and Fort Vaux". When he was at Verdun is not indicated in the report, but such a travel profile would be consistent with that of a neutral military attaché or journalist. The source also reported that the Germans' initial intent had been to take Verdun and then stand on the defensive. Assuming he had been a guest at an Army or Army Group HQ rather than *OHL*, this

French had lost 115,000 casualties at Verdun.[130] As noted above, this compared favourably with the quarter million casualties the Germans were thought to have sustained. But des Vallières was concerned; he believed Haig did "not have true picture of the severe efforts made by the French army" at Verdun.[131]

A shift in British perceptions can be detected in mid-May. While corresponding over his suggestion that the Somme attack could be delayed to allow additional training and preparations, on 15 May Haig noted that Joffre pressed him not to delay because "the continuance of the German attacks at Verdun are causing the French considerable loss".[132] Similarly, a couple of days later Kitchener told the government that the Germans were succeeding in wearing out the French forces, with the net effect being a significant reduction in the French contribution to the Somme.[133] On 27 May Haig told his Army commanders that the French were "losing severely at Verdun".[134] The source of this assessment seems to have been des Vallières who, three days earlier, had told him that French losses were approaching 200,000.[135] This was a considerable jump from the figure Robertson had briefed two weeks earlier and, on 30 May, it was clarified when Haig was informed the French losses then stood at just under 150,000.[136] Therefore when Haig attended the historiographically significant Saleux meeting on 31 May, his understanding of French casualties had just been revised downwards. He had also just been informed of "reports from Berlin" indicating that the Germans had already expended 7.5 million shells at Verdun and had been forced to divert ammunition from the Eastern Front. This report, presumably from an agent or intercepted neutral cable, also suggested that the Verdun offensive would "be continued at all costs".[137]

Conclusion

Reflecting upon this examination of British perceptions, it must be stressed that the evidence presented in this chapter is not wholly conclusive. Unfortunately, an understanding of the intelligence dimension cannot resolve decisively the debate about the relationship between Verdun and the Somme in Anglo-French relations. However, it

would be consistent with the thesis of a strategic disconnect between Falkenhayn and his subordinates in the early stages of the battle: Foley, *German Strategy*, pp. 193-7
130 Prior & Wilson, *Somme*, p. 29.
131 Vallières to Renouard, 11 May 1916, Greenhalgh, *Vallières*, p. 93.
132 NLS, Haig Papers, Diary, 15 May 1916.
133 From forty divisions down to twenty-five: Prior & Wilson, *Somme*, p. 29.
134 TNA WO158/185, GHQ to Armies, 30 May 1916.
135 Diary, 24 May 1916, Blake, *Haig*, p. 144.
136 NLS, Haig Papers, Diary, 30 May 1916.
137 NLS, Haig Papers, Diary, 30 May 1916. For high-level signals intelligence, see Beach, *Haig's Intelligence*, pp. 155-6.

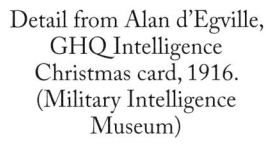

Detail from Alan d'Egville, GHQ Intelligence Christmas card, 1916. (Military Intelligence Museum)

has provided insight that answers important questions and thereby lends weight to one side of the argument.

The core truth is that the British perceived the Battle of Verdun as significantly degrading the German army on the Western Front. The intelligence documentation is certainly conclusive in that regard. Even before the Germans had launched their offensive, the British saw it as a strategic error; insufficient forces attacking a strong point on the French front which would wear down the German army. Although there were occasional scares – especially early on – about their ally's ability to hold against these attacks, there was a consistent perception that the Germans were being damaged just as severely, or even more so, than the French. Put simply, the British struggled to foresee the Germans 'winning' at Verdun, either by breakthrough or attrition.

This chapter therefore finds no underlying intelligence rationale for the belated appearance and subsequent prominence of "relieving Verdun" within British preparations for the Somme. As would be the case in subsequent autumns, in June 1916 British policy decisions on the Western Front, and their justifications, were at odds with the intelligence feed.[138] So if perceptions derived from intelligence sources were not driving decisions then different explanations, such as inter-allied politics and civil-military relations, come to the fore. Having refuted one plausible explanation, this chapter has cleared a better path for Greenhalgh's alternative suggestion that, prior to 1 July, British statements about the primacy of relieving Verdun were probably a politicised confection.

Finally, it is worth revisiting Falkenhayn's overall plan for 1916. His original strategy relied upon retention of some forces for a decisive blow, probably against the British. But, as this chapter has shown, the British were acutely conscious of this threat and through their agent networks were able to closely monitor the movement of the German reserves.[139] So regardless of how well operations might have proceeded against the French at Verdun, an offensive against the BEF would probably have foundered against the British ability to 'see' their enemy's intended moves. GHQ Intelligence would face a similar scenario in early 1918, but with a much improved and better practiced intelligence system.[140] In first half of 1916 this apparatus only performed adequately, but with regard to anticipating and evaluating the Germans at Verdun, it was good enough.

---

138 Beach, *Haig's Intelligence*, pp. 216-7, 260.
139 The collapse of the networks in the summer of 1916 degraded rather than destroyed the capability. Coverage shrank, but the core routes across central Belgium remained under surveillance: Beach, *Haig's Intelligence*, pp. 133, 140.
140 Beach, *Haig's Intelligence*, pp. 274-302.

5

The Changing Nature of Supply: Transportation in the BEF during the Battle of the Somme

Christopher Phillips

The preparations for, and conduct of, the Battle of the Somme have remained a point of controversy ever since the battle began.[1] Within the strategic labyrinth of inter-allied politics,[2] and the ongoing debate over the existence of a 'learning curve' after 1 July 1916, the logistical foundations of the Somme, have been largely overlooked.[3] An examination of the supply preparations for the Somme and the British response to the evolving nature of the fighting as the battle unfolded, reveals that a lack of appreciation for the importance of the transport factor exerted a critical influence over events in France during 1916. This chapter will demonstrate how the logistical challenges of the Battle of the Somme compelled the British Expeditionary Force (BEF) to acknowledge the inapplicability of its extant supply arrangements in 1916, and led to the creation of a new, civilian-led directorate that coordinated military transportation for the remainder of the conflict.

The Directorate-General of Transportation, created by the Deputy General Manager of the North-Eastern Railway (NER), Sir Eric Geddes, engendered a change in policy within the BEF from reactive adjustments and short-term tinkering towards the emergence of an integrated, multi-modal transport network founded on the latest managerial tools from the railway industry and populated by a "large number of skilled and experienced civilians … drawn from the railway companies

---

1 W. Philpott, *Anglo-French Relations and Strategy on the Western Front, 1914-18* (Basingstoke: Macmillan, 1996), pp. 112–28.
2 W. Philpott, *Bloody Victory: The Sacrifice on the Somme* (London: Little, Brown, 2009), p. 56.
3 H. Strachan, 'The Battle of the Somme and British Strategy', *Journal of Strategic Studies*, 21 (1) (1998), pp. 79–95; Philpott, *Bloody Victory*, p. 158 provide brief but notable exceptions to the rule.

117

of Great Britain and the Dominions."[4] The directorate established by Geddes in the autumn of 1916 supplied the men, materials, and coordination required to sustain the BEF during the *Materialschlacht* of the second half of the war. From October 1916 onwards until the Armistice, through Arras, Passchendaele, Amiens and the final Hundred Days, the BEF was reinforced and equipped by a logistics network organised by some of Britain's most experienced transport professionals. As one post-war commentator noted, it took the "railway crisis of 1916" to "open our eyes" to the fundamental importance of supply on the Western Front.[5] Geddes "showed what *transportation* meant,"[6] fused the best in civilian and military expertise, and ensured that the BEF did not face an emergency to match that experienced on the Somme for the remainder of the conflict.

Preparing the largest battle in British military history

As discussed elsewhere in this volume, the Battle of the Somme was not a purely 'British' battle. From its conception at the Chantilly conference in December 1915, through to its culmination eleven months later, it was planned and undertaken as part of a coordinated, all-front strategy designed to eliminate the Central Powers' advantage of interior lines of communication.[7] The location of the offensive to which the BEF was committed was chosen by the French commander, Joseph Joffre, rather than either Sir John French or his successor, Sir Douglas Haig. An attack at the meeting place of the French and British armies offered a number of advantages in 1916. The soil was well drained in comparison to that in Flanders, and there were no "industrial wildernesses" to aid the defence as had been the case at Loos.[8] To Fourth Army's commander, Henry Rawlinson, Picardy offered "capital country in which to undertake an offensive."[9] However, Rawlinson's gaze was fixed on the view to the east of the British trenches. To the south and west, in the area which would be asked to supply the battle, it was a different story. According to the official historian, "the railways were inadequate, [and] the roads in the area behind the front ... were few and indifferent."

4   J.H. Boraston (ed.), *Sir Douglas Haig's Despatches (December 1915-April 1919)* (London: J.M. Dent & Sons, 1919), p. 351.
5   M.G. Taylor, 'Land Transportation in the Late War', *Royal United Services Institution. Journal*, 66 (464) (1921), p. 711.
6   Taylor, 'Land Transportation', p. 705; emphasis in original.
7   E. Greenhalgh, *Victory Through Coalition: Britain and France during the First World War* (Cambridge: Cambridge University Press, 2005), p. 42; W. Philpott, 'Why the British Were Really on the Somme: A Reply to Elizabeth Greenhalgh', *War in History*, 9 (4) (2002), pp. 460–1.
8   R. Prior & T. Wilson, *The Somme* (New Haven, Connecticut: Yale University Press, 2005), p. 37.
9   Rawlinson to Wigram, 27 February 1916. Quoted in D. Winter, *Haig's Command: A Reassessment* (Barnsley: Pen & Sword, 2004), p. 45.

In 1916, "almost any part of the Arras–Ypres front was better furnished with villages, railways and roads."[10] Even in the more understated words of Colonel Henniker, "the railways serving [the Somme] … were not good."[11] Two single-lines to Arras and the double-line between Amiens and Albert (which was itself within range of the German artillery) were the only pre-war main line rail communications available in the 23 miles between Arras and the river. Furthermore, the undulating countryside was impractical for the construction of reliable railways. In order to sustain a fighting force of unprecedented size and appetite the BEF had to create the infrastructure of a major city virtually from scratch.[12]

The absolute necessity for construction around the Somme had been recognised in the early months of the war. French engineers began work on improving and doubling lines in October 1914, and as soon as the Somme had been settled upon as the location for the offensive in 1916, further construction had been commenced. One such line, a 17-mile section linking Fienvillers, Candas, and Acheux, was completed in April 1916 and handed over to the Railway Operating Division to run.[13] However, the major infrastructure developments took place further south, around the key railway junction of Amiens. The extension of a gun-spur near Dernancourt, to supply ammunition to the artillery located on the high ground south-east of Albert, was particularly important. It was envisaged that this extension would only be responsible for the carriage of a relatively small tonnage during the battle, and in some places on the line a gradient of 1-in-45 was adopted.[14] This decision had profound consequences when the offensive began.

Construction could not alleviate all of the potential problems behind the front. A major bottleneck existed near Amiens, a one mile-long section of track heading east from St Roch that was situated in tunnels or cuttings which made the laying of extra track alongside the existing route an impossibility. This section of line comprised: the main rail connection between Amiens and the BEF's southernmost Channel ports; the only inland line which ran north-south between the French coal mines and Paris; a heavily worked civilian traffic route; and the vital junction for any strategic troop movements that might be required during the battle. At the Camon–Longeau interchange east of Amiens, all of the traffic heading to and from Rawlinson's Fourth Army would meet, and be forced to intersect the route of, the vast majority of traffic for the French Sixth Army operating on the BEF's right flank.[15] The implications of such a voluminous traffic flow were recognised, and engendered both a series of inter-allied

---

10 J.E. Edmonds, *History of the Great War. Military Operations, France and Belgium, 1916*, Vol. I (London: Macmillan, 1932), p. 271.
11 A.M. Henniker, *History of the Great War: Transportation on the Western Front, 1914-1918* (London: HMSO, 1937), p. 120.
12 Strachan, 'The Battle of the Somme', p. 86.
13 Edmonds, *1916*, I, p. 273.
14 Henniker, *Transportation*, pp. 120–121.
15 I.M. Brown, *British Logistics on the Western Front, 1914-1919* (London: Praeger, 1998), p. 184; Henniker, *Transportation*, pp. 136–137.

120   At All Costs

discussions and preparations within Fourth Army. Initial projections made in April were unpromising: only through the use of every available station, worked to the utmost of their capacity, could the armies in the field be maintained.[16] Furthermore, this conclusion depended upon the completion of substantial pre-battle construction, undertaken by both British and French engineers. The pressure applied to the latter to ensure their tasks were finished on time was severe. The Chief Road Engineer was reported as having received fifteen days' arrest for not opening a road "in the specified time."[17] Ironically, given the subsequent importance placed upon the early commencement of the battle to relieve pressure on Verdun, the BEF's liaison officer noted in mid-June that the progress of building work at the Somme meant that "unless … absolutely unavoidable" the French should not be asked to attack before 1 July.[18]

This short-term desire to ensure readiness for zero hour eclipsed long-term considerations. The effect of a prolonged, intense battle on the existing infrastructure was given virtually no thought. The Deputy Quartermaster-General (DQMG), Colonel Woodroffe, embodied the prevalent attitude within the BEF on the eve of the battle: "It seems quite clear that in view of the operations now going on, every effort should be made to get *as much as possible as far forward as possible*, even if the roads in rear do suffer a bit for the time being."[19] As far as the BEF's administrative departments were concerned, their primary mission before the battle was to send forward items required by the *fighting* troops. Other stores, such as engineering materials and road building equipment, had to wait. The problems which arose from this practice were already visible in the week before zero. Woodroffe noted during inspections on 28 and 29 June that the roads near Corbie and in the III Corps area were "in a terrible condition" and "a bad state" respectively.[20] Although the surviving war diary records that at least one meeting took place between representatives of Fourth Army and the Directorate of Inland Water Transport (IWT) with regards to the establishment of a barge service to supply road stone, arrangements had not been finalised nor a service initiated prior to 1 July 1916.[21] The decision to suspend deliveries of road stone, taken in order to ensure

16   The war diary of Fourth Army's Deputy Adjutant and Quartermaster-General records several meetings at which "various problems in connection with … railheads and roads" took place, emphasizing the numerous administrative questions which had to be addressed prior to the commencement of the offensive. Unfortunately, the details of these discussions is not elaborated upon within the surviving records. See The National Archives (TNA): WO 95/441, Fourth Army Deputy Adjutant and Quartermaster-General, diary entries, 10 March to 30 June 1916; Edmonds, *1916*, I, p. 272.
17   Liddell Hart Centre for Military Archives (LHCMA): Major-General Sir Edward Spears Papers, 1/7/9, Spears to Kiggell, 17 June 1916.
18   LHCMA: Spears Papers, 1/7/15, Spears to Elles, 18 June 1916.
19   Imperial War Museum (IWM): Brigadier-General C.R. Woodroffe Papers, 3/38/1/2, Unofficial notes, 30 June 1916. Emphasis in original.
20   IWM: Woodroffe Papers, 3/38/1/2, Unofficial notes, 28 and 29 June 1916.
21   TNA: WO 95/441, Fourth Army Deputy Adjutant and Quartermaster-General, diary entry, 1 May 1916.

the delivery of food to the troops and to maintain a schedule of seven-to-ten ammunition trains per day on the Fourth Army front, exposes the lack of logistical foresight in the preparations for the Somme.[22] By cutting the supply of road stone, the BEF solved one supply problem but created another, one which would only increase as the battle wore on and the roads behind the army were placed under unprecedented pressure.[23]

Collapse of the transport network

The opening weeks of the battle exacerbated the transport problems which the reactive policies of the previous months had generated. The poor weather of late June that contributed to the postponement of zero hour, continued into July. Lieutenant-Colonel Whitty, a Quartermaster with the 25th Division, noted several days of "heavy rain" in July which made movement "very difficult."[24] In periods of poor weather, horse transport which would normally travel by the open ground next to the roads was forced to share road space with the BEF's lorries.[25] The inevitable result of this extra traffic was congestion and, as the roads themselves had not been designed to withstand much more than their pre-war traffic of farmers' carts and bicycles, degradation of the road surface. During the opening days of the offensive, the sheer volume of traffic drew comment from even the most experienced of campaigners. Henry Wilson's brother-in-law, Brigadier-General Llewellyn Price-Davies VC, a Boer War veteran, remarked on 4 July that "there was a *great deal* of traffic all over the country."[26] Within the first fortnight of the battle, the French and British units in the battle zone were forced to make arrangements to minimize the use of particularly damaged roads,[27] and the volume of traffic was carefully monitored by Fourth Army. Traffic censuses taken by Rawlinson's force demonstrate the scale and intensity of the traffic required to keep an industrial army fed. In the 24 hours which ended at 9am on 22 July, the numbers which passed Fricourt Cemetery were recorded as: 26,516 troops; 568 cars; 1,244 lorries and ambulances; 3,832 horse-drawn vehicles; 1,660 motorcycles and cycles; and 5,404 horses. All this was on a day described by the Provost Marshal as "one of the quietest we have had." In just six hours the following day over

22 H.L. Pritchard (ed.), *History of the Corps of Royal Engineers* (Chatham: Institute of Royal Engineers, 1952), V, pp. 255–6; Brown, *British Logistics*, p. 120; Edmonds, *1916*, I, p. 280.
23 TNA: WO 95/441, Fourth Army Deputy Adjutant and Quartermaster-General, diary entry, 15 July 1916.
24 E. Astill (ed.), *A Quartermaster at the Front: The Diary of Lieutenant-Colonel Allen Whitty, Worcestershire Regiment, 1914-1919* (Eastbourne: Reveille Press, 2011), pp. 110–17.
25 Lieutenant-Colonel H. Osborne Mance. Quoted in discussion of Taylor, 'Land Transportation', p. 715.
26 IWM: Field-Marshal Sir Henry Wilson Papers, HHW 2/83/61 Price-Davies to Wilson, 4 July 1916. Emphasis in original.
27 LHCMA: Spears Papers, 1/7/58, Interview between Generals Fayolle and Sir Henry Rawlinson at 11:15am, 9 July 1916.

2,500 vehicles rumbled along the Amiens–Albert road.[28] Under the combination of wet weather and the pounding of poorly-sprung, solid-tyred lorries, "a chalky ooze" appeared on the road surface before "the granite setts [worked] loose, and the whole road [began] to disintegrate."[29] The "deplorable state of the roads" soon became the chief source of anxiety for the Chief Engineer of Fourth Army,[30] a development which was catalogued by an equally concerned DQMG in a series of notes.[31]

As noted above, the delivery of road stone by rail had been suspended at the outset of the battle in order to prioritise the limited capacity of the railway network for the provision of food and ammunition. However, the alternative to rail, France's considerable river and canal network, was inadequately exploited for the provision of road stone. Although the IWT directorate had grown substantially over the previous 18 months,[32] it had not been effectively integrated into the BEF's transport mix. As its commander, Brigadier-General Gerald Holland, later revealed, during the opening phase of the battle he was forced to return barges requisitioned from the local population for want of cargo to carry on them.[33] Ludicrously, given the concerns of Fourth Army's engineers about the lack of roadmaking materials available to them and the effect this would have upon the BEF's ability to sustain operations, British barges were being used for the conveyance of road stone along the River Somme at the request, and for the use of, the French Army![34] The lack of a centralizing transport authority to coordinate and prioritize transport requests, combined with a preoccupation with the maintenance of frontline troops to the detriment of all other considerations, led to an incomplete use of the entire range of transport methods open to the BEF in 1916.[35]

---

28   TNA: WO 95/441, Fourth Army Deputy Adjutant and Quartermaster-General, Census of Traffic at Fricourt Cemetery, 24 July 1916; Amiens-Albert Road, Census of Traffic, 24 July 1916. Further south, a traffic census reported that the Amiens-Proyart road, which was responsible for supplying French *Sixth* and *Tenth* armies, carried 38,000 men and 3,700 tons of material on 30 September, "twice as much as passed along the road to Verdun on its busiest day." See Philpott, *Bloody Victory*, p. 389.
29   Pritchard, *Royal Engineers*, V, p. 293. See also G.D. Clarke, 'Supplying the Battlefront. British Frontline Transport in Mobile Warfare, 1918' (unpublished Masters dissertation, University of Birmingham, 2006), p. 14.
30   R.U.H. Buckland, 'Experiences at Fourth Army Headquarters: Organization and Work of the R.E.', *Royal Engineers Journal*, 41 (3) (1927), pp. 391–2.
31   IWM: Woodroffe Papers, 3/38/1/2, Notes and Reports (forwarded to QMG), June to November 1916.
32   C. Phillips, 'Logistics and the BEF: The Development of Waterborne Transport on the Western Front, 1914-1916', *British Journal for Military History*, 2 (2) (2016), pp. 42–58.
33   University of Warwick Modern Records Centre (MRC): Papers of Sir William Guy Granet, MSS.191/3/3/4 Geddes to Lloyd George, 15 September 1916, p. 2.
34   TNA: WO 95/56, Director of Inland Water Transport, Memorandum number 3, 3 December 1916, p. 3.
35   Geddes reinforced this point after the battle, writing of IWT that "a great carrying capacity has been provided and no adequate use found for it." See MRC: Granet Papers, MSS.191/3/3/102, Memorandum by Sir Eric Geddes, 26 November 1916, p. 23.

British horse transport traversing the devastated Somme battlefield, autumn 1916.
(Private collection)

A similar story of inefficiency unfolded on the railways. Following the success of the French and the BEF's southernmost units on 1 July, Fourth Army requested that the gun-spur at Dernancourt be extended towards Maricourt on what became known as the Plateau Line.[36] When further progress was made in the southern sector of the British front during the first fortnight of the battle, it soon became clear that the traffic on the Plateau Line would be far heavier (in terms of both the weight and number of trains) than had been envisaged. A conference at Fourth Army Headquarters on 15 July projected the requirements of the forces in the area at 35 trains per day in each direction.[37] In contrast to the strained relationship between Haig and Joffre over the strategic direction of the battle as it progressed, the enlargement and improvement of the Dernancourt line was amicably discussed at an inter-allied conference of railway authorities on 18 July and work began almost immediately. By 1 August the line was carrying heavy goods trains weighing between 600 and 800 tons. Simply moving trains on the steep, winding line required great skill on the part of the locomotive crews involved, combined with significant motive power: "to take such a train up … required two engines in front and three behind."[38] The time-consuming process of

---

36 TNA: WO 95/441, Fourth Army Deputy Adjutant and Quartermaster-General, diary entries, 5 and 7 July 1916.
37 Henniker, *Transportation*, pp. 129–31.
38 W.A.T. Aves, *The Railway Operating Division on the Western Front: The Royal Engineers in France and Belgium, 1915-1919* (Donington: Shaun Tyas, 2009), p. 56.

attaching extra engines to cope with the gradient also dislocated movement on the network. Despite the rigorous enforcement of a five miles-per-hour speed limit and the installation of catch points to trap runaway trains, derailments and accidents were a frequent occurrence. The French constructed a single line with an easier gradient to the west of the existing line. However, the location of the new line meant that all trains going up the hill had to cross the track of those descending. On one occasion, a runaway train on the downhill line crashed into a train which had just begun its ascent, interrupting all traffic on the line for 24 hours.[39]

Thanks to ongoing congestion at the ports which made loading times unpredictable, the goods trains of the BEF were not despatched according to a set timetable but instead moved off when they were ready. This meant that trains arrived at the Amiens bottleneck from three different directions at largely random intervals. Each day, 240 trains were scheduled to pass through Camon junction, intersecting one another's routes at a rate of one train every six minutes. When several trains arrived at the bottom of the Plateau line in quick succession, the delay caused by the attachment of extra engines meant that those trains at the rear of the queue could do nothing but block the main Amiens–Albert line. Serious congestion was inevitable, and not helped by what was perceived by British observers as "local mismanagement" of the railway traffic by the French engineers responsible for the operation of the line.[40] At Amiens, "eighteen miles of trains under load stood end-to-end waiting to get to railheads."[41] The effects of this paralysis spread through the transport network on the Western Front. With so many trains held up on their way to or from the front line, too few locomotives and too little rolling stock were available at the base ports to help clear the ever increasing quantities of material arriving in France. With the railways unable to clear imports from the docks, the wharves on the Channel coast became overcrowded with goods and the unloading of ships became more difficult and less efficient. Urgently required items were buried beneath "mountains" of stores not yet required at the front, such as the warm clothing which was stockpiled for issue in the winter months.[42] Further delays were created thanks to the constant stacking and restacking which was required in order to unearth the desired goods and load them into the limited number of wagons whilst retaining some semblance of order in the warehouses. At the same time, responding to the sustained calls for ammunition continued to take precedence over the delivery of road metal, which meant that fewer new railheads could be completed nor the existing ones maintained. The consequences were increased delays at the railheads which were operational, the continued sluggish unloading of trains, and further degradation of the

---

39 Henniker, *Transportation*, p. 134.
40 TNA: WO 95/441, Fourth Army Deputy Adjutant and Quartermaster-General, diary entry, 3 August 1916.
41 J.C. Harding-Newman, *Modern Military Administration, Organization and Transportation* (Aldershot: Gale & Polden, 1933), p. 16.
42 MRC: Granet Papers, MSS.191/3/3/51, Memorandum to Sir Guy Granet, 19 October 1916, p. 8.

British and French troops labour to free a stalled locomotive, Maricourt September 1916.

already worn-out road network.[43] Such was the character of the war of material, with its absolute reliance on items such as food, ammunition, petrol, road metal, sandbags, and myriad other pieces of kit that were produced away from the fighting zone and had no means of self-propulsion to the battlefield, that it was impossible for an army to "tear loose" from their railheads and penetrate deep into enemy territory for an extended period of time. In the first two years of the war, the amount of supplies consumed by each front-line division rose from 55 tons per day to around 150 tons.[44] Therefore, regular and efficient contact with the supply bases and ports was a prerequisite for sustaining an advance. Although the average number of loaded wagons which were moved over the Nord Railway for the BEF actually increased over each full month that the Battle of the Somme raged (see Table 1), the figures for August and September would have been substantially higher but for "the lack of rolling stock to meet demands and congestion in the Somme area which limited despatches."[45] According to Sidney

---

43   Taylor, 'Land Transportation', pp. 704-5; Harding-Newman, *Modern Military Administration*, p. 47; Brown, *British Logistics*, pp. 126–7; W.J.K. Davies, *Light Railways of the First World War: A History of Tactical Rail Communications on the British Fronts, 1914-18* (Newton Abbot: David & Charles, 1967), pp. 34–5.
44   M. Van Creveld, 'World War I and the Revolution in Logistics', in R. Chickering and S. Förster (eds.) *Great War, Total War: Combat and Mobilization on the Western Front, 1914-18* (Cambridge: Cambridge University Press, 2005), pp. 66–7.
45   Henniker, *Transportation*, p. 179.

Crookshank, who served as a Chief Royal Engineer at both divisional and corps level during 1916 and ended the war as Director-General of Transportation, "on the Somme the British Army was practically immobile ... Had the Germans fallen back after the big British attack in September 1916, as they did in the early part of 1917, effective battle pursuit could not have been given."[46]

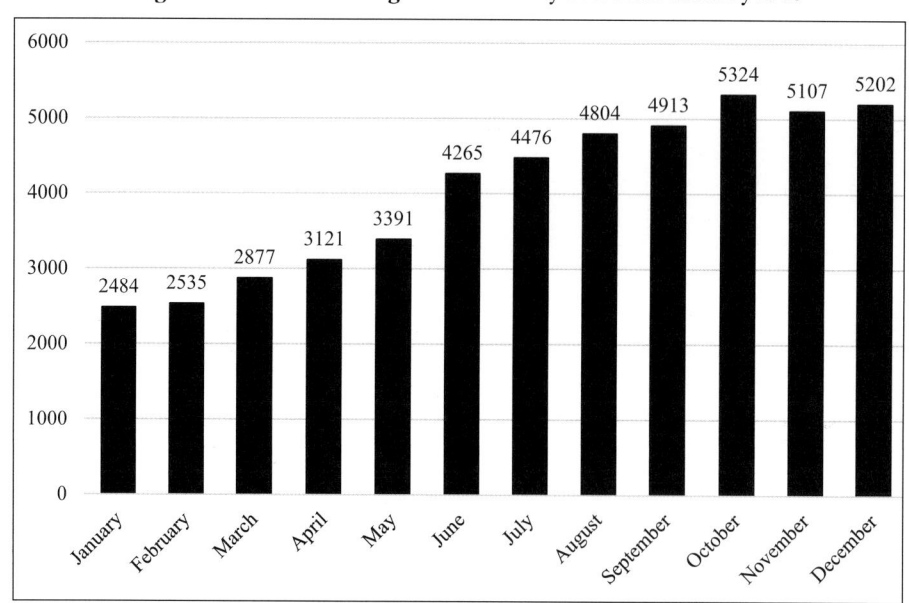

Table 1. Average number of loaded wagons moved daily over Nord Railway 1916

Month	Wagons
January	2484
February	2535
March	2877
April	3121
May	3391
June	4265
July	4476
August	4804
September	4913
October	5324
November	5107
December	5202

Furthermore, the Germans had not been idle bystanders during the battle. In response to the artillery barrages of the Allies, German tactics had been modified with further negative implications for the BEF's supply network. Rather than remain located in their trenches, which presented an obvious and static target for bombardments, the German machine-gunners who had inflicted such heavy losses on the advancing troops on 1 July began to deploy in shell holes well clear of the trench lines. This meant that the BEF's artillery commanders could no longer concentrate their fire only upon the known and easily located trenches, but instead had to "batter down a whole area of ground, using an immense quantity of ammunition to ensure the destruction of the German defenders."[47] However, despite the priority which had been afforded to it, even the supply of ammunition was severely affected by the

---

46   S.D'A. Crookshank, 'Transportation with the B.E.F.', *Royal Engineers Journal*, 32 (5) (1920), pp. 194–5.
47   Prior and Wilson, *The Somme*, p. 150.

deterioration of the BEF's transport situation. As early as 2 July, the supply of ammunition was viewed at General Headquarters (GHQ) as the "limiting factor on the battlefield,"[48] and Haig was keen to use it to illustrate the BEF's inability to cooperate with Joffre's strategic vision for the continuation of the offensive.[49] Despite attempts by the two commanders to "thrash out" the logistical difficulties engendered by the course of the offensive (in addition to the conferences which took place at the army level of command),[50] by early August it appeared that another shells shortage was imminent on the Western Front.[51]

For David Lloyd George, who had been a vocal critic of previous attempts to match the supply of shells to the demands of the army, a scandal reminiscent of that which had arisen in 1915 would have been a source of acute personal embarrassment.[52] However, Lloyd George was fully aware of the increases in shell production which had taken place since the establishment of the Ministry of Munitions. He also understood the importance of the transport network in France as a key component of the production and distribution system upon which Britain's mass army depended. As early as September 1915 he had written to Lord Kitchener to question whether the French rail network would be able to handle the enormous volume of warlike stores which would be thrown upon it in the following year.[53] Despite having received reassurances at the time (produced by a military that was at best sceptical of Lloyd George's claim that the munitions deliveries would amount to 5,000 tons per day),[54] events on the Somme had proven unequivocally that it could not. Too much had been asked of a location bereft of, and ill-suited to the establishment of, an integrated, multi-modal transport network, and of an organisation created by 'ad hoc' reaction to events rather than thorough forward planning and careful analysis of Britain's increasing burden on the European mainland. Lloyd George laid out the transport problem in plain terms:

48 National Library of Scotland (NLS): Papers of Field-Marshal Sir Douglas Haig, Acc.3155/107, Note of Interview at Fourth Army HQ, Quierrieu, at mid-day, 2 July 1916, p. 2; Kiggell to Rawlinson, 2 July 1916.
49 NLS: Haig Papers, Acc.3155/107, diary entry, 3 July 1916; Note of Interview between Sir Douglas Haig and General Joffre on 3 July 1916 re: direction of the British attack, 4 July 1916.
50 NLS: Haig Papers, Acc.3155/107, Haig to Robertson, 8 July 1916.
51 K. Grieves, 'The Transportation Mission to GHQ, 1916', in B. Bond et al (eds.), *'Look to Your Front!' Studies in the First World War by the British Commission for Military History* (Staplehurst: Spellmount, 1999), p. 63.
52 Strachan, 'The Battle of the Somme', p. 83.
53 TNA: WO 107/15, Inspector-General of Communications, General Correspondence, Cowans to Maxwell, 10 September 1915.
54 TNA: WO 107/15, Inspector-General of Communications, General Correspondence, Cowans to Maxwell, 10 September 1915; Maxwell to Cowans, 12 September 1915. Maxwell stated confidently that "we have no fear of being unable to cope with all situations that can arise as regards railway transport up to the point that the railways are workable."

The output at home of munitions has now so greatly increased that we can meet with comparative ease the higher demands which you quite properly make on us, but I doubt whether, without careful preparation, the powers of absorption of the ports and lines of communication can expand to a commensurate degree. What I have specifically in mind is the desirability of ensuring such an expansion as will next year, and the year after if necessary, enable us to cope with the ever increasing volume of munitions and stores which will be needed for the services of your force.[55]

If the transport network in France could not cope with the offensive requirements of the Somme, how could that same network be expected to deal with the ever growing quantities of material in the process of being manufactured for the consumption of an even larger BEF in 1917 and beyond?[56] Lloyd George believed that there had to be a comprehensive re-evaluation of the available transport facilities in France. The goal was to assess what resources were available, what they would be required to carry in forthcoming battles, and what improvements would be necessary in order to ensure that the carriage of such quantities would be possible. To tackle this imposing challenge, Lloyd George turned to a civilian. Sir Eric Geddes' transportation mission was received at GHQ on 24 August, and began work the following day.[57]

Sir Eric Geddes and the transportation mission

The terms of reference for Geddes' mission were as follows: to review the existing capacity of the transport network in France and ascertain if it was able to deal with the "very considerably increased quantity of ammunition and other stores" scheduled for delivery over the coming year; to identify the repairs, extensions and operational improvements required at the ports, on the railways, and on both the canal and road networks in order to render them capable of sustaining an advance;[58] and, in Lloyd George's words, doubtless chosen to ingratiate himself to the BEF's hosts, to learn

---

55 TNA: WO 32/5163, Appointment of Sir E. Geddes and others to investigate transport arrangements in connection with the British Expeditionary Force at home and overseas, Lloyd George to Haig, 1 August 1916.
56 K. Grieves, *Sir Eric Geddes: Business and Government in War and Peace* (Manchester: Manchester University Press, 1989), p. 27 highlights that this question had pre-occupied Lloyd George and Geddes prior to the opening of the Somme campaign.
57 For further detail on those, both civilian and military, who joined Geddes on the transportation mission, see Grieves, 'The Transportation Mission'; C. Phillips, 'Managing Armageddon: The Science of Transportation and the British Expeditionary Force, 1900-1918' (unpublished doctoral thesis, University of Leeds, 2015), pp. 189–99.
58 TNA: WO 32/5164, Facilities and arrangements for Sir E. Geddes in conducting his investigation on transport arrangements in connection with the British Expeditionary Force at home and overseas, Lloyd George to Haig, 16 August 1916.

"all that is possible from the very excellent transport arrangements of the French Army."⁵⁹ After a period of investigation, Geddes was to produce a series of statistical breakdowns detailing the quantities of materials required by the BEF for the conduct of future operations. Accompanied by Colonel Woodroffe, Geddes was given a two-day tour of ammunition railheads, newly constructed sidings and stations, and given the opportunity to discuss the existing supply system with officers on the ground, most notably those in charge of artillery batteries in action along the Mametz–Carnoy valley.⁶⁰ Although Grieves states that the tour was "largely uninformative" due to the "model" nature of the sites visited,⁶¹ Woodroffe's record of the trip illustrates that it was actually the chrysalis for many of Geddes' subsequent recommendations to Haig. The tour impressed upon Geddes the immediate need for action to be taken in order to alleviate congestion and increase efficiency in the BEF's transportation services, and provided the lines of enquiry upon which the wider investigation rested. The points which impressed themselves most upon Geddes were: the enormous quantity of labour required for road maintenance and the construction of station yards; the urgent need for "some form of light railway to take the traffic off the roads"; the waste of manpower inherent in the transhipping practices which took place at the intersection points of the various modes of transport in use; and the significant quantities of expended material (such as ammunition cases) which had congregated in the British rear and become obstructive to the supply services.⁶²

At the conclusion of Geddes' tour, Haig asked the railwayman for his opinion on what he had seen. "His reply was guarded – to the effect that he had seen plenty to think about but as yet did not know what to think."⁶³ There was good reason for Geddes'

Sir Eric Geddes.

---

59 TNA: WO 32/5164, Facilities and arrangements for Sir E. Geddes in conducting his investigation on transport arrangements in connection with the British Expeditionary Force at home and overseas, Lloyd George to Roques, 23 August 1916.
60 IWM: Woodroffe Papers, 3/38/1/2, Notes, 25 August 1916.
61 Grieves, *Sir Eric Geddes*, p. 29.
62 IWM: Woodroffe Papers, 3/38/1/2, Notes, 25 August 1916.
63 A.C. Geddes, *The Forging of a Family. A Family Story Studied in Its Genetical, Cultural and Spiritual Aspects and a Testament of Personal Belief Founded Thereon* (London: Faber & Faber, 1952), p. 232.

reluctance to cast judgment on a supply system which Haig himself had adjudged to be both "methodical" and "very remarkable" upon his becoming commander-in-chief.[64] Geddes' mission had been foreshadowed by a visit to GHQ from Lord Derby, who had taken with him an initial memorandum on the subject of a new transport organisation in France.[65] Haig, understandably, had referred the memorandum to his Quartermaster General (QMG), Sir Ronald Maxwell, for his comments. Maxwell's reaction was icy, and claimed that the proposal (which bore a striking resemblance to the arrangements ultimately settled upon by Geddes, lending credence to Haig's assumption that it had been written by one of "Lloyd George's men") was "quite impracticable." In a demonstration of his inability to foresee the necessity for strong forward planning as the BEF continued to expand, Maxwell responded that "it is not stated why the time has arrived to strengthen the transport arrangements of the BEF. So far as the work in France is concerned these arrangements have worked perfectly smoothly and efficiently: 1. in the ports; 2. on the railways and canals; 3. on the roads."[66] Maxwell's attitude was replicated by Haig's other senior supply officer, the Inspector-General of Communications (IGC), Sir Frederick Clayton.

Earlier in the summer, the shipping magnate Sir Thomas Royden had led a commission into the ongoing problem of congestion at the ports used by the BEF. It was the latest in a long line of civilian and military-led investigations into aspects of the BEF's operations, but its goals had clearly not been understood by Clayton. He took the existence of the commission as a personal slight. Geddes, who had read Clayton's remarks on the Royden report, was fully aware that his mission had to contend with a mind-set that stated:

> The only conclusion one can come to after reading [Royden report] is, that it is impossible for the ordinary business civilian to understand what are the conditions under which we have to work and that it is a mistake to allow them to interfere with an army business that most of us have studied all our lives ... *when we fail in any way to keep the army supplied it will be time for criticism.*[67]

---

64 NLS: Haig Papers, Acc.3155/104, diary entry, 30 December 1915.
65 Grieves claims that Derby was sent to perform this role, instead of Lloyd George himself, as Derby "posed no threat to GHQ's autonomy." Certainly, Haig's diary illustrates that Derby was well-liked at GHQ, as he was "so straightforward as compared with the usual politicians." If Grieves' contention is accurate, the ploy did not work, as a handwritten note from Haig to Maxwell on the memorandum itself shows that Haig believed the document to be the work of the man who would seek to run the directorate outlined in 'Derby's' paper. See Grieves, *Sir Eric Geddes*, p. 29; NLS: Haig Papers, Acc.3155/105, diary entry, 11 March 1916; Acc.3155/215Q, Memorandum (received from Lord Derby), 11 July 1916.
66 NLS: Haig Papers, Acc.3155/215Q, Memorandum (by Maxwell), 17 July 1916.
67 MRC: Granet Papers, MSS.191/3/3/14, Remarks on the Report of the Commission sent out by the Shipping Control Committee, 30 July 1916. Emphasis added.

Even Sir William Robertson, whose understanding of logistical issues early in the war had helped to sustain the BEF as a fighting force,[68] believed that criticisms of congestion at the ports, bad storage practices, neglect of the French canal network, and the failure to develop railway traffic prior to the Somme were "misinformed."[69]

Such responses exemplified the reactionary portion of the military establishment whose influence Lloyd George sought to eradicate. Until the supply line had *actually* broken down, Clayton believed it was unfair for the War Office to continue bombarding the BEF with "constant attacks" from civilians bent on interfering with the prosecution of the war.[70] The evidence suggests that, at the very least, Clayton was unwilling to countenance the potential problems awaiting the BEF should the transport network be suffocated under the weight of goods being despatched from Britain. Nothing within Clayton's remarks implied that he appreciated how investigations such as Royden's were undertaken precisely to ensure that catastrophic failure did not occur as the British war effort continued to grow.

Despite the successful working relationship fostered between civilian and military figures both prior to and during the early stages of the war, there remained a clear and palpable sense of mistrust between the soldiers of the BEF and the politicians charged with managing the war effort. Suspicion and reservation over the motives of outsiders, particularly those with close connections to Lloyd George,[71] to do anything other than meddle with pre-existing structures and erode the jurisdiction of the army, were matched by wariness and doubts over the competence of those tasked with overseeing the operation of the BEF's umbilical cord. Lord Derby described Clayton as "very stupid, conceited and narrow-minded."[72] Maxwell, it was feared, would also not be the "sort of man who would favourably impress Lloyd George" on account of his "hide-bound manner."[73] These were the BEF's two senior supply officers, and it was their working methods and procedures which Geddes examined. Fortunately for the sake of the mission, their hostility towards civilian investigations was not replicated by their chief. When Geddes asked for a 'free run' of the BEF's lines of communication, Haig acquiesced. Haig had become increasingly concerned by the blockage around Amiens, and notified Maxwell of the impending investigation alongside issuing an instruction to all armies and administrative departments which ordered that "all

---

68 J. Spencer, "'The Big Brain in the Army': Sir William Robertson as Quartermaster-General' in S. Jones (ed.) *Stemming the Tide: Officers and Leadership in the British Expeditionary Force 1914* (Solihull: Helion, 2013), pp. 89–107.
69 LHCMA: Field-Marshal Sir William Robertson Papers, 7/6/60, Robertson to Haig, 28 July 1916.
70 TNA: WO 95/3969, Headquarters Branches and Services. Inspector-General, Clayton to Maxwell, 14 June 1916.
71 NLS: Haig Papers, Acc.3155, Robertson to Haig, 24 January 1916.
72 Houses of Parliament: David Lloyd George Papers, LG/E/1/1/3, Derby to Lloyd George, 30 August 1916. Conversely, Derby was "much impressed by Geddes."
73 LHCMA: Robertson Papers, 7/6/60, Robertson to Haig, 28 July 1916.

necessary information and any statistics required will be placed at the disposal of Sir Eric Geddes … and the C-in-C desires that every facility will be afforded [Geddes] in the conduct of [his] enquiries."[74] Geddes' team split upon their return from London. Part of the team went to the coast with the task of discovering the capacity of the Channel ports based on the nature of the traffic to be dealt with, whilst Geddes and the others surveyed the rest of the network in order to "build up a complete statement of the weight of traffic" required to support the BEF.[75]

Within a fortnight Geddes felt sufficiently informed to offer a preliminary view of the situation to Lloyd George. Geddes implored Lloyd George not to reveal its contents to anyone in the War Office or at GHQ, demonstrating that he remained sensitive to the fragility of relations between his mission and the BEF. Geddes feared that the criticisms the letter contained could severely jeopardise the remainder of the investigation were they to have been leaked. His primary observation, produced before the bulk of the necessary data had been collected, let alone analysed, was an unequivocal condemnation of the BEF's logistical foundations and the innate reactivity of the administrative echelons. "This is a war of Armies backed by machinery and 'movement'," Geddes wrote, "and I do not think that 'movement' has received sufficient attention in anticipation of the advance. I judge this by the total absence of light railway or road organisation, or policy for the use of waterways."[76] The fact that even as the railways continued to be clogged up by ever-increasing quantities of material, canal barges were being returned to civilian work, exemplified the problem. Rather than being viewed as an essential part of the transport mix, canals were only used when rail conveyance was not available. Whilst the commander of IWT, Lieutenant-Colonel Holland, believed IWT to be capable of moving a great deal more than had been requested of it, "neither [in Great Britain] nor in France" could Geddes "ascertain what the policy of canal use is. I doubt if one exists."

The problem facing the BEF was one of insufficient forward planning and coordination, a result of the policy of decentralisation instigated as soon as the BEF began to expand early in 1915. Whilst Robertson had noted at the time that "the force is now assuming too great a strength to admit of matters being centralised at GHQ to the extent they are now,"[77] the corollary was that the departments responsible for supply became heavily compartmentalised; officers were capable only of making adjustments to their own sections, with no oversight in place to ensure such modifications did not adversely affect other departments whose work was necessarily interconnected. The geographical barrier between Maxwell at GHQ, and Clayton, whose offices were

---

74 TNA: WO 95/31, Branches and Services: Quartermaster-General, Circular to All Armies, Inspector-General of Communications and Engineer-in-Chief, 3 September 1916.
75 MRC: Granet Papers, MSS.191/3/3/102, Memorandum by Sir Eric Geddes, 26 November 1916, pp. 2–3.
76 MRC: Granet Papers, MSS.191/3/3/4, Geddes to Lloyd George, 15 September 1916. Unless otherwise stated, all quotations in this passage come from this source.
77 LHCMA: Robertson Papers, 2/2/63, Robertson to Cowans, 8 January 1915.

at Abbeville some 25 miles away, was a physical manifestation of an organisational problem. As J.C. Harding-Newman, employed on Maxwell's staff during the battle, wrote later: "the IGC seldom, if ever, saw the QMG. There seemed to be little administrative influence on the decisions arrived at. In fact, those responsible for the plan of action were never given the benefit of expert or technical knowledge on the transportation situation. They certainly had none themselves."[78] No internal structure existed for the regular review of the BEF's supply systems. Forward planning had hitherto been conducted in "pennyworths," and was liable to be subordinated to short-term exigencies at times of heavy demand such as immediately prior to the opening of the Somme offensive. Transport facilities had been improved "here and there" as the movement of the front and the battle plans of the senior commanders had dictated, but the system was a "hand-to-mouth" one.[79]

Nowhere was this lack of leadership and direction more apparent than in the question of light railways. As early as January 1916, Haig had written in his diary that light railways could be constructed in order "to save the roads" from excess wear through the winter.[80] Where units had acquired light railway systems from the French Army as the share of the line had changed, individual formations had requested equipment over the spring. However, the constant redeployment of formations negated the chance for a coherent, methodically planned light railway policy to develop within the BEF. By 1 July there were less than half a dozen tractors employed on the BEF's small, dispersed light railway systems, a number which led Haig to order that a comprehensive policy for the employment of light railways – as used by the French and German armies – had to be adopted by the BEF.[81] Yet discussions between the armies led nowhere. A lack of strong central control from GHQ (Haig placed the Director of Railways, based at Abbeville, in charge) and the absence of a sufficiently senior team to ensure priority was afforded the scheme, against the backdrop of Britain's largest ever military offensive, meant an inevitable stagnation between the 'stakeholders' in each army. For the army commanders, the appearance of the light railways question was yet another intrusion upon the day-to-day business of running their armies. A month after he had received Haig's orders, the Director of Railways reported to Geddes that he had made no progress on the matter.[82]

Haig was not alone in recognising the potential utility of light railways. Whilst accompanying Geddes on a tour of the French Sixth Army's supply system, Woodroffe wrote that it was "necessary to apply all our efforts to developing a 60cm system at the greatest possible speed in order to ensure that as much of the front area as possible is served by this means before winter sets in." However, although some construction

78 Harding-Newman, *Modern Military Administration*, p. 16.
79 Grieves, *Sir Eric Geddes*, p. 32; Henniker, *Transportation*, p. 184.
80 NLS: Haig Papers, Acc.3155/104, diary entry, 4 January 1916.
81 Davies, *Light Railways*, pp. 24–6.
82 MRC: Granet Papers, MSS.191/3/3/4, Geddes to Lloyd George, 15 September 1916.

had begun on new lines in the area about La Boisselle and the Sausage Valley, "owing to a lack of materials," no others could be commenced in September 1916.[83] Geddes had gained experience in the operation and management of a light railway system in the Himalayas prior to his employment with the NER,[84] and was equally convinced of the possibilities which surrounded the extended use of the medium. A light railways department, he wrote to Lloyd George, would be a great success provided the "right men" were appointed to run it. "If they are not," he warned, "it will be a dismal failure."[85]

Light railways were not the only department in need of the "right men" either. As Geddes concluded in his letter to Lloyd George:

> It is beyond argument that there is today no one who controls the continuous transit from this country to the front. There is no one who can tell you throughout where his weak places are, or coordinate the policy and resources, present and future, of the various means of transit. It is not possible for the C-in-C or QMG in France to do it; it is alone a big job for the best man you can find. If the C-in-C is not satisfied with his transport arrangements and desires someone to go into them in anticipation of the spring, he must, I think, appoint a man for the job, put him in charge of it, and back him strongly.

Lloyd George agreed wholeheartedly with Geddes' assessment that "executive action is called for both on this side [of the Channel] and in France." He was also convinced that the "man for the job" was Geddes. Crucially, so did Haig. The common ground between the two was used as a platform for the restructuring of the BEF's logistical organisation, and for the appointment of some of Britain's leading transport experts into the higher ranks of the military within the newly created Directorate-General of Transportation.[86] As Haig recorded in his diary, the process was not smooth. Maxwell tendered his resignation over the "position and responsibilities of the new Director-General." Haig had to convince his QMG that Geddes had not "been sent out by L[loyd] G[eorge] to take over the duties which I had assigned to him," and requested that Maxwell instruct his directors to cease their criticisms of Geddes.[87] That such an instruction was necessary in the first place indicates the level of hostility displayed

---

83 Quotations from IWM: Woodroffe Papers, 3/38/1/2, 60cm railways, 9 September 1916. See also Notes on a visit to the 60cm Railway System of the French Sixth Army south of the Somme, 6 September 1916.
84 Grieves, *Sir Eric Geddes*, p. 3.
85 MRC: Granet Papers, MSS.191/3/3/4, Geddes to Lloyd George, 15 September 1916. Unless otherwise stated, all quotations in this passage come from this source.
86 On the process by which Geddes populated the Directorate-General of Transportation, see Grieves, 'The Transportation Mission'; Phillips, 'Managing Armageddon', pp. 205–15.
87 NLS: Haig Papers, Acc.3155/108, diary entry, 30 October 1916. See also Grieves, 'The Transportation Mission', pp. 70–1; Brown, *British Logistics*, p. 141.

within some sections towards the encroachment of a civilian into such a prominent military position.

The abolition of the post of IGC and subsequent removal of Sir Frederick Clayton did nothing to alleviate the fears of the soldiers who perceived Geddes as a civilian usurper;[88] nor did Haig's sacking of Brigadier-General Twiss as Director of Railways on Geddes' advice in November 1916. According to Geddes, Twiss had failed to supply the required quantities of rails and locomotives to satisfy the BEF's needs, and had proven himself unequal to the challenges of the department.[89] Although Haig acknowledged the concerns within the BEF as to Geddes' unprecedented position, he recognised the importance of employing those best suited to the task at hand regardless of their background:

> There is a good deal of criticism apparently being made at the appointment of a civilian like Geddes to an important post on the Headquarters of an Army in the Field. These critics seem to fail to realise the size of this Army, and the amount of work which the Army requires of a civilian nature. The working of the railways, the upkeep of the roads, even the baking of bread and 1000 other industries go on in peace as well as in war. So with the whole nation at war, our object should be to *employ men on the same work in war as they are accustomed to do in peace*.[90]

In the context of an industrialised war in which the resources of entire nations were required to be mobilised and coordinated, Haig recognised that the inefficient use of the British Empire's human and material resources just to placate the sensibilities of the professional soldier was unacceptable. A far more logical approach to the growing problem of supplying an expanding army was to employ a "civilian who was unafraid of large-scale planning and had access to the necessary resources" as opposed to officers who were handed the work "merely because they are generals and colonels." Although Haig's reflection ignores the contribution of other 'non-generals and colonels' to the development of the BEF's logistics capacity prior to Geddes' intervention,[91] it emphasises the hitherto subordinate position of transportation within the army on the Western Front and the escalating contribution the British Army was being required to make to the fighting. What had been since 1914 a "never ceasing struggle … to make

---

88 Brown, *British Logistics*, p. 146. However, as Brown notes (p. 141), Clayton did conceded to Haig that the new system "would work well" prior to his departure.
89 NLS: Haig Papers, Acc.3155/109, diary entry, 9 November 1916.
90 NLS: Haig Papers, Acc.3155/108, diary entry, 27 October 1916. Emphasis in original. Unless otherwise stated, all quotations in this passage come from this source.
91 C. Phillips, 'Early Experiments in Civil–Military Cooperation: The South-Eastern and Chatham Railway and the Port of Boulogne, 1914–15', *War & Society*, 34 (2) (2015), pp. 90–104; Phillips, 'Logistics and the BEF'.

an unsuitable machine carry out vital work,"[92] succumbed to the stresses of industrial warfare in 1916 and engendered a new approach to supplying Britain's largest ever, and still expanding, military force. However, that new approach could not be employed immediately. On 7 November, Haig recorded in his diary that "owing to the soft state of the roads," it was "impossible to carry forward ammunition for the 15-inch howitzers – only two of these big shells go into a lorry!"[93] The following day, he reflected that the BEF was "fighting under the same conditions as in October 1914, i.e. with rifle and machine guns only, because bombs and mortar ammunition cannot be carried forward as the roads are so bad."[94] And finally, after the offensive had ground to a halt, Haig's appreciation of the situation on 22 November stated that:

> Existing conditions render it impossible to continue the offensive on our front at present, on any considerable scale, with sufficient prospects of success. The ground, sodden with rain and broken up everywhere by innumerable shell holes, can only be described as a morass, almost bottomless in places: between the lines and for many thousands of yards behind them it is almost – and in some localities quite – impassable. The supply of food and ammunition is carried out with the greatest difficulty and immense labour, and the men are so much worn out by this and by the maintenance and construction of trenches that frequent reliefs – carried out under exhausting conditions – are unavoidable.[95]

Clearly, the limitations of transportation continued to exert a critical influence over the BEF's operations in Picardy until the end of the campaign and beyond.

Conclusion

The year of the Somme was a transformative one for the BEF, the culmination of what Martin van Creveld described as "the logistic revolution" which took place between 1914 and 1916.[96] Those charged with managing the BEF's lines of communication prior to 1916 had, it is true, correctly identified the challenges to be faced in the establishment, expansion, and maintenance of a mass army on foreign soil. They had also engaged with and accepted the advice of technical experts from some of Britain's largest companies. However, as the existence of the Amiens bottleneck demonstrated, the supply echelon of the BEF had proven unable to design and sustain a logistics system capable of responding to the unprecedented demands placed upon it. Instead,

---

92 Taylor, 'Land Transportation', p. 702.
93 NLS: Haig Papers, Acc.3155/109, diary entry, 7 November 1916.
94 NLS: Haig Papers, Acc.3155/109, diary entry, 8 November 1916.
95 NLS: Haig Papers, Acc.3155/109, Appreciation of situation, 21 November 1916, p. 5.
96 Van Creveld, 'World War I', p. 72.

it was reactive amendments and adjustments to an inadequate system, rather than the establishment of an integrated, multi-modal transport network based on a holistic consideration of priorities and capacities, which characterised the BEF's approach. The magnitude of operations on the Somme overloaded a transport system created through short-term amendments over the previous two years; adjustments which had been made in the absence of any comprehensive, centrally directed policy taking account of the myriad questions of coordination, resourcing, staffing, and expansion which arose in the arrangement of a modern army's supply requirements.[97]

As Brigadier-General Sir James Edmonds noted in his introduction to the Official History's volume on transportation, "the history of the Transportation Services in France is one of adaptation of the technical resources of the nation to the requirements of an army in the field."[98] By the time the Somme had ground into an attritional slogging match in the deteriorating conditions of late autumn and early winter,[99] the limits of military-led methods of adaptation had been reached. It became clear, to Douglas Haig at least, that in order to apply the "technical resources of the nation" in the most efficient and effective manner possible in future, the BEF had to engage much more substantially with those who knew and employed those technical resources during peacetime. The appointment of Sir Eric Geddes was by no means the panacea to the BEF's transportation challenges, and his frustration at the perceived obstinacy of Britain's hosts and ally on the Western Front demonstrates the powerful position the French Army retained as an influencing factor on the BEF's transport facilities.[100] Furthermore, the army still had to learn vital lessons with regard to the importance of engineering and the provision of suitable transport infrastructure for the prosecution of successful operations on the Western Front in the colossal engagements of 1917.[101] Although it took the "crisis" engendered by the BEF's first attempt at major offensive action to bring about the change, 1916 represented the year in which the

---

97 Grieves, 'The Transportation Mission', p. 65.
98 Edmonds' introduction in Henniker, *Transportation*, p. xxiii.
99 Philpott, *Bloody Victory*, pp. 385–428 provides a comprehensive narrative of this period of the battle.
100 As Haig subsequently observed in March 1917: "E[ric] G[eddes] lunched and we discussed the railway situation afterwards. He gave me a letter giving the history of the whole transaction with the French, and showing clearly how they have failed to keep their agreements. We are now practically being 'rationed' in the matter of trains by the French. Geddes questions the utility of his remaining on, if this state of affairs is to last." See NLS: Haig Papers, Acc3155/111, diary entry, 3 March 1917. Research on the importance of the evolving relationship between the partners in the Franco-British coalition is still in an embryonic state. Despite the work of Elizabeth Greenhalgh and William Philpott, the former of whom dedicates a portion of her work to the administrative aspects of coalition warfare, this is an area which demands further study. See Greenhalgh, *Victory through Coalition*; Philpott, *Anglo-French Relations*.
101 R. Thompson, 'Mud, Blood and Wood: BEF Operational Combat and Logistico-Engineering during the Battle of Third Ypres, 1917', in P. Doyle and M.R. Bennett (eds.) *Fields of Battle: Terrain in Military History* (Dordrecht: Kluwer, 2002), pp. 237–55.

BEF abandoned the short-term, small-scale, reactive policies which were incapable of sustaining the army it had become. Starting with Geddes the BEF began to embrace the "superb leadership in the fields of logistics and administration", based upon experiences learned in the operation of Britain's global production and distribution economy, that were fundamental to the development of innovative, well-supplied, and ultimately successful combat methodologies on the Western Front.[102]

---

102 Brown, *British Logistics*, pp. 1–2.

6

Lessons Unlearned: The Somme Preparatory Bombardment, 24 June-1 July 1916

Bill MacCormick

The subject of the British Army's "learning curve" during 1914-18 and whether or not the word "curve" is an accurate description of the process is one which historians continue to debate. Perhaps "rollercoaster" might be a more appropriate term as British tactical and technical development during the war had more than its share of ups, downs and u-turns. Prior to the BEF's attack on 1 July 1916, however, it might be argued that no upward curve existed at all and that, at best, progress had flat-lined and, at worst – embodied by the disaster at Aubers Ridge in May 1915 and 46th Division's doomed assault against Hohenzollern Redoubt in October 1915 – gone into reverse.

The infantry tactics widely used on 1 July, mainly drawn from Fourth Army commander General Sir Henry Rawlinson's controversial "Tactical Notes" issued in May 1916, have been justifiably criticised.[1] The widespread failures of the largest array of artillery and shells collected for one battle by a British Army to that date have, however, been largely ignored.[2] The romance, if one can call it that, of battle lies in the brave advance of the infantryman against impossible odds rather than with the sweating gunner several thousand yards behind the front, who is trying to kill and maim an enemy he will never see.

---

1 See Sir J.E. Edmonds & A.F. Becke, *Military Operations France and Belgium 1916*, Vol. I (hereafter *Official History 1914, 1915, 1916*), Appendices Vol., Appendix 18.
2 In the preliminary bombardment some 1,500 British guns fired 1.5 million shells of which two thirds were 18-pdr shrapnel intended to cut the German wire. A third of the remaining shells were fired by 4.5 in. field howitzers unsuited to the needs of destroying hardened positions or collapsing deep dugouts. The rest were distributed between the heavier howitzers and the long guns, a proportion of which were expended on counter battery work. See Edmonds, *Official History 1916*, Vol. 1, pp. 302-3.

The First World War was the first in which artillery caused more casualties than bullets, whether from rifle or machine gun, as well as all other weapons combined.[3] Some put a figure of 58 percent on artillery inflicted casualties[4] whilst John Keegan ascribes a proportion as high as 70 percent.[5] The majority of these casualties would have been caused by high explosive shells and their far-flung fragments, as shrapnel was progressively phased out as an effective form of ammunition. In both respects, therefore, the impact of First World War artillery was unlike anything that had occurred before.

Technically the use of British artillery had started to improve by the spring of 1916. By this point gunnery was becoming distinctly scientific. Previously ignored or unknown factors such as air temperature at various heights, humidity and air pressure, were now being factored into the range and accuracy of a gun. The effects of wear on gun barrels, springs and recoil systems were now better understood, although not better dealt with as numerous guns failed during the seven day bombardment because of technical issues and the lack of spare parts. RFC aerial observers were now being more formally schooled to improve liaison with the guns. Set against these improvements, however, was the enormous variability in the quality of both the shells and the fuses at the BEF's disposal. Whilst the impact of the 1915 "shell crisis" was lessening as the new Ministry of Munitions vastly expanded British shells production, quality control, not only in these new factories but, and even more so, in those in the United States where enormous and expensive contracts for both guns and shells had been placed, was inconsistent and often extremely poor. Advancing troops would later report on the startlingly large number of "blinds" – unexploded shells – found in and around newly captured German positions. Of these, some had simply failed to detonate and in others, the fuses had fallen out in flight. With other guns, such as the obsolete 4.7-inch gun often employed on counter battery work, the issues were of more immediate danger to the gunners and the infantry to their front. Many of the shells for these guns were manufactured in the United States and their inadequate copper driving bands were often stripped off as they travelled down the barrel. The result was that these shells sometimes tumbled end over end and landed behind the

---

3   In the Russo-Japanese War of 1904-05 estimates of Russian casualties from Japanese artillery ranged from 14 to 22 percent, the final figure being given in an article in the German publication the *Archiv für Klinische Chirurgie* (1906) written by a Dr Shafer and two Russian doctors. Evidence from the First Balkan War (1912-13) suggested that casualties caused by artillery were likely to be more severe and, therefore, men so wounded were less likely to return to the front. Another article in the previously quoted *Archiv für Klinische Chirurgie* stated that "Statistics confirm the fact that artillery wounds with few exceptions caused a man's absence from his regiment a longer time" whilst an article in the publication of the German Großer Generalstab, *Vierteljahreshefte für Truppenführung und Heereskunde* (1908), p. 169 claimed a higher death rate from artillery instead of rifle fire.
4   Robert Weldon Whalen, *Bitter Wounds: German Victims of the Great War* (Ithaca, 1984), pp. 39-40 & J.B.A. Bailey, *Field artillery and Firepower* (Naval Institute Press, 2004).
5   John Keegan, *The Face of Battle* (Penguin Books, 1978), p. 269.

The Somme Preparatory Bombardment, 24 June-1 July 1916   141

British 6-inch gun.

British 8-inch howitzers of 135th Siege Battery at La Houssoye on the Somme, 1916.

British front lines causing alarm and even casualties amongst friendly infantry.[6] Other shells tended to explode prematurely and the men of the 4.5 in. field howitzer batteries became known as the "suicide club" when asked to fire newly manufactured high explosive shells which suffered from a premature rate of more than one in 5,000 for a time. By comparison, "prematures" for French shells were, at the same time, estimated at one in 100,000 and with the British 18-pdr at one in 27,650.[7]

Technical improvements were, in some respects, off-set by equipment and shell failures. To compound the problems, tactical changes were thin on the ground. The command structure of the artillery gave control of siege weapons (6-inch howitzers and above) and long guns (4.7-inch and larger) to the corps. Divisions retained control of most its field guns and howitzers, and its trench mortar batteries. Consequently, when the infantry left their trenches requests for any alterations to the complex bombardment programmes devised for Z Day had, in the main, to be referred first to Corps before any permitted alterations could be sent on to the various Heavy Artillery Groups (HAGs) and their component batteries. The delays caused by this process often meant that circumstances on the ground had already changed and that the requested alterations were out of date. Reactive fire was all but impossible: delayed and often contradictory information from the ground could not be acted upon and the aerial observation was not yet comprehensive.

The Corps also had control of counter battery work. This was an area of long-standing British weakness. Writing after the war, Brigadier-General Christopher Reginald Buckle, who had been the BGRA of VII Corps Heavy Artillery in 1916, noted: "We did not know enough about counter battery work in those days; but, given the knowledge, we had neither the guns nor the ammunition to carry it out effectively."[8]

This was not a situation which applied to the French troops about to go into battle alongside their Allies. The French, and most especially Ferdinand Foch, the commander of the *Groupe des Armées du Nord* (GAN), had made a close study of the fighting of 1915. He, along with others such as Pétain and Fayolle, the commander of *6e Armée* on the Somme, had come to accept they were fighting an artillery war and, from this, came the famous maxim: "Artillery conquers, infantry occupies." Foch took this notion a step further:

> Against what should fire be opened? Against the obstacles which may delay the march of infantry.
> The first obstacle is the enemy gun. It will be the first objective assigned to artillery masses.[9]

6   Edmonds, *Official History 1915*, Vol. 2, fn. p. 33.
7   Ministry of Munitions, *History of the Ministry of Munitions: The Supply of Munitions*, Vol. X (HMSO, 1922) p. 58.
8   TNA CAB 45/132: Historical Section, Comments, Letters, Personal Accounts, comments with regard to the *Official History 1916*, Vol. I by Maj. Gen. C R Buckle.
9   Ferdinand Foch, *Precepts and Judgements* (H. Holt & Co., 1920), p. 108.

Foch insisted upon, and Fayolle reinforced right up to the day before the offensive, the essential importance of the destruction of the enemy's artillery or, at least, its neutralisation at the time of the infantry's attack. Consequently, there were no hard and fast rules about which guns and of what type could be used for counter battery work. Any gun within range of an active German battery and not already involved in a specific mission was to open fire. Even the light 75mm field gun might be used, though only a shell through the embrasure of an enemy position was likely to do permanent damage. The 75mm, however, had an extremely high rate of fire for limited periods and with its excellent hydro-pneumatic recoil system was very stable and accurate. Thus it could be used to neutralise an enemy battery by pouring shells into an area and, when the weather was suitable, one of the two French lethal gas shells: Shell (Obus) No. 4 contained "Vincennite", a mixture of mainly hydrogen cyanide and arsenic, and Shell No. 5 contained phosgene – could be employed to smother a German battery with a gas cloud.[10] Stopping an enemy battery from firing whilst the French infantry was above ground was nearly as good as destroying the guns. Foch and Fayolle relentlessly pressed these ideas on corps and divisional commanders.

Divisional commanders were relevant because, unlike the British, control of some of the heavier French guns (particularly the 155mm or 6 inch) were devolved to each division so that they could quickly respond to requests for assistance from the infantry. Furthermore, to speed up the process of communication, divisional HQs were brought up close to the front line so that the time lag between request, decision and order were kept to a minimum.

All of which suggests that, since trench warfare had begun, some French commanders had learnt lessons that had yet to be absorbed by the BEF. These lessons extended beyond the importance of counter battery fire and into a formula which limited any front to be attacked to the availability of a particular type of howitzer. The *Canon de 155 Court Mle 1881* was the equivalent of the British 6 inch howitzer and, although the tube was part of the obsolete *Barrière de Bange*[11] designed and constructed in response to the defeat suffered in the Franco-Prussian War of 1870-71, it was now the foundation of the system to destroy the enemy's fixed defences. The

---

10   There were no British lethal gas shells at this time. Groups of French 75mm batteries were attached to each corps on Fourth Army front. With them came gas shells, but they were primarily used for counter-battery work. In addition, there was a small supply of 4.5 in. tear gas shells designated 'SK' as they were designed at Imperial College in South Kensington.

11   Colonel Charles Timothée Maximilien Valérand Ragon De Bange was responsible for the design of a new range of guns and mortars during the period 1877-85. They ranged in size from 80mm to 270mm. None of them had a recoil system and most were emplaced in the border forts constructed by General Raymond Adolphe Séré de Rivières in response to defeat in the Franco-Prussian War. They were removed, mounted on extemporised carriages with either no or a rudimentary recoil system and hurriedly rushed into use in autumn 1914. These guns remained the mainstay of the French artillery until new guns began to appear in 1917.

numbers available dictated the width of front, a formula which the BEF did not then apply. When added to Foch's insistence that the depth of any attack now depended on the ability of terrestrial observers to accurately assess the effectiveness of the French bombardment, this meant that the area to be prepared by the available French artillery for any offensive was tightly proscribed. In the case of French *6e Armée* on 1 July, this essentially meant bombarding and taking only the German first position comprising its fire, support and reserve trenches. This compares to Haig's demand that the VIII, X and III Corps capture three far more robustly constructed German positions and for XV and XIII Corps to seize two.

No French attempt was made with regard to further penetration regardless of how weak the German position appeared. This decision was based on Foch's interpretation of the initial French successes at the Second Battle of Artois and Second Battle of Champagne in the summer and autumn of 1915 respectively. It was during both offensives that French troops broke through in places only to find themselves disorganised and fatigued without infantry or artillery support. Pressing on in such circumstances resulted in chaos, heavy casualties and not just a loss of attacking impetus, but a loss of much of the ground so expensively if temporarily gained.

Setting such limitations, of course, had both positive and negative results. The German held village of Hardecourt aux Bois between Montauban and the Somme could undoubtedly have been taken on 1 July if this restriction not been in place but, on the other hand, the unauthorised entry and rapid ejection of some over-zealous *Sénégalais* troops into the village of Assevillers south of the Somme showed the sense of not attacking locations unless properly prepared in advance by the heavy guns.

For the first phase of the attacks on the southern flank of the Somme the French had, therefore, set themselves limited objectives on fronts restricted to that which the artillery formula demanded. They also planned to fire, proportionately, far more shells per yard of front than did British Fourth Army. South of the Somme, between Frise and Foucaucourt, they were also up against German defences weaker than on the northern wing of Fourth Army and with fewer men and guns deployed against them than elsewhere. The troops involved, the *1er Corps d'armée Colonial*[12] (1er CAC) and *XXXV Corps*, gained all their objectives to timetable, suffering minimal losses and capturing several thousand Germans prisoners. By the end of the week they had achieved the deepest penetration of any allied force since trench warfare began. North of the Somme, where German defences were stronger but still not as formidable as north of the Albert to Bapaume Road, every objective was taken except for the northern tip of the bois Favière in front of Maltz Horn Farm which held out for several days. Strong-points such as the *Bois Y* were overrun in short order. French casualties were around 1,200 men.

---

12 Predominantly made up of white soldiers who had served in the French colonies as well as several battalions of *Sénégalais* (native troops hailing from Imperial possessions in west and central Africa) commanded by white officers.

Fourth Army's tragic 1 July ordeal is well known: for XIII Corps costly success at Montauban on the immediate left of French *XX Corps*; partial success for XV Corps about Mametz and Fricourt, but with some localised disasters; III Corps made minimal gains at ruinous cost about La Boisselle and suffered utter defeat in front of Ovillers; X Corps clung on to a sliver of trench at the Leipzig Redoubt whilst its troops were massacred opposite Thiepval and, after initial gains, the Ulstermen of 36th Division found themselves in the exposed and disorganised condition Foch had described in Artois and Champagne in 1915. For its part, VIII Corps was soundly defeated everywhere with no stretch of German trench gained at any point. The figure of 57,000 casualties killed, wounded and missing on a single day stands testament to the failure of tactics and ideas imposed by the British high command on the officers and men of Fourth Army.

The widespread failure of the British Fourth Army on 1 July 1916 can, and indeed should, be laid at the door of one man: Sir Douglas Haig, the commander in chief of the BEF. It was Haig who over-ruled Henry Rawlinson, the Army commander, in terms of the purpose of the offensive and, most particularly, in terms of the parameters of the attack.[13] It was Haig who determined the width of the offensive and it was Haig who set the depth of the first day's objectives. Finally, it was Haig who further undermined the effectiveness of the already inadequate British artillery by strong-arming Rawlinson into reducing the power of the bombardment only a few days before it was due to start.

These factors flew in the face of the large body of French experience on the Western Front as interpreted by generals such as Ferdinand Foch and Philippe Pétain. Furthermore, previous experience in the small scale British offensives of 1915 should have dictated that even Rawlinson's original plan submitted on 4 April 1916 was over-ambitious. The French sensed this and Pétain, embroiled in the defence of Verdun, explicitly warned against the grandiose breakthrough plan prepared at Haig's behest:

> I hear that they (the BEF) are preparing an assault on the model of those that we conducted in Artois and Champagne in 1915. Currently, that would be the worst of solutions.[14]

There has long been an argument as to what Haig expected from the attack which eventually took place on 1 July. Writing after the battle in his second despatch dated 23 December 1916, Haig described the purpose of the attack thus:

13　For a further discussion of Haig's decision making and an alternative viewpoint, see Andrew Wiest's chapter elsewhere in this volume.
14　Pétain to Joffre, 7th May 1916, *Les Armées Française dans La Grande Guerre* (hereafter *AFdGG*) (Imprimerie Nationale, 1926), Tome IV, Vol. 2, Annexes, Vol. 1, Annexe 129.

> The object of that offensive was threefold: To relieve the pressure on Verdun; To assist our Allies in the other theatres of war by stopping any further transfer of German troops from the Western front; To wear down the strength of the forces opposed to us.

Nowhere in the despatch does the word "breakthrough" appear. Nor is there any reference to the prospect of a "decisive" outcome to the battle. Other than belatedly "rescuing" the French, who had already been fighting at Verdun for four and a half months (and where the key moment of the battle had already passed on 24 June with the failure of the German Green Cross gas attack of 22 June), and trying to pin German troops to the Western Front, the only other objective of the battle was "To wear down the strength of the forces opposed to us". Not rupture their lines, not to unleash cavalry into the open spaces between Bapaume and Arras, but to "wear down" the German forces opposite. On this interpretation, therefore, the Somme was part of a "long game" during which the industrial strength and numerical Allied superiority would erode the Central Powers ability to wage war. Such was Haig's *post hoc* justification for the conduct of the battle and, thereby, for the opening gambit of the Fourth Army's attack between Serre and Montauban on 1 July.

It is an unconvincing justification given Haig's repeated references to breakthrough, starting with his statement made on 10 February at a meeting with Joffre at his Chantilly HQ. When Joffre commented that the main offensive would require the British and French Armies to fight next to one another Haig's response was to declare: "Yes, next, on the Somme and we shall break through."[15] From then on, the plans laid for the Somme offensive were predicated on the basis of being in position as quickly as possible to break into open countryside at Bapaume and to the north. Furthermore, the strains imposed on the manpower and, most particularly, the artillery power of Fourth Army because of Haig's ambitions suggests that little, if anything, had been learnt since the first British offensive conducted by Haig's First Army at Neuve Chapelle in March 1915. Throughout 1915 the French armies had been experimenting with its artillery bombardments gradually, and finally dramatically, increasing their power and concentration as more shells became available to them. Their extraordinary casualty rates in 1914 and in the early fighting of 1915 led some, like Foch and Pétain, to conclude that it was not sustainable to continue to throw infantry against German trenches. More infantry led only to higher casualty rates. More artillery was the solution and many more howitzers were required.

The French armies had gone to war almost entirely equipped with the 75mm field gun, a weapon described in a pre-war official document as sufficient "for all the

---

15 "Oui, à côté, sur la Somme, et nous percerons" according to Buat's *Procès-verbal, AFdGG*, Tome IV, Vol. 1, Annexes Vol. 1, Annexe 221, p. 420.

French *Canon de 75 Mle 1897* battery.

French *Canon de 155 Long mle 1877* battery.

missions which can be entrusted to artillery in field warfare."[16] The result had been the accumulation of a formidable arsenal comprised of the following guns:

3,680 *Canons de 75 Mle 1897*
128 *Canons de Montagne de 65 Mle 1906*
120 *Canons de 120 L Mle 1878 de Bange*
84 *Canons de 120 C Mle 1890 Baquet*
104 *Canons de 155 C Mle 1904 TR Rimailho*[17]

Only these last two weapons were high firing howitzers suited to the destruction of fortified positions and entrenchments. The British too had gone to war mainly equipped with field and long guns. Each division had attached nine 18-pdr batteries (54 guns) and three 4.5 in. field howitzer batteries (18 guns) as well as one battery of 60-pdr guns (four guns). Coming with these guns were their shell supplies which, in the case of the 18-pdrs, were made up entirely of shrapnel, a purely anti-personnel shell. It was not until the first twenty four 6 inch BL howitzers landed in France[18] in September 1914 – by which time the Battle of Mons, Le Cateau, the Marne and the Aisne had all been fought – that the BEF had a weapon capable of causing significant damage to the German trench system which, very soon, was to stretch from the Channel to the Swiss border.

Germany, however, had a rather different artillery arsenal. Its army anticipated that, in a European war, it would have to destroy Belgian, French and Russian fortifications. The most recent example of siege warfare was the Russo-Japanese War; the successful Japanese application of heavy howitzers in both the siege of Port Arthur and at the Battle of Mukden had impressed German observers. As such, it had incorporated field, medium and heavy howitzers into its divisional and corps artillery. These were the 10.5cm *Feldhaubitze 98/09*, the 15cm *Schwere Feldhaubitze 13* and the 21cm *Mörser 10* of which there were 1,260, 416 and 216 respectively available to the

16   Herr, Gen Frédéric-Georges, *L'Artillerie, ce qu'elle a été, ce qu'elle est, ce qu'elle doit être* (Berger Levrault, 1924) translated and published in *The Field Artillery Journal* (United States Field Artillery Association), Vol XVII, No. 3, May-June 1927, p. 224.
17   These figures from Touzin & Vauvillier, *Les Canons de la Victoire 1914-1919* (Histoires et Collections, 2006). Herr provides slightly different figures: 3,840 75mm, 120 mountain guns, 308 'heavy guns for mobile units' (i.e. the *120 L*, *120 C* and *155 C* listed above) and 380 *de Bange* guns of various sorts. Confirmation of the figures of 120mm and above can be found in Gen. Baquet's memoirs. See L.H. Baquet, *Souvenirs d'un directeur d'artillerie* (Charles-Lavauzelle, 1921), p. 118. Herr estimated that there were 7,000 heavy guns of the *de Bange* era and earlier in the fortresses of eastern France and in use for coastal protection. Baquet mentions large numbers of un-adapted *90 Modèle 1877*, *95 Modèle 1878*, *120 L. Modèle 1878* and *155 L. Modèle 1877* guns located in fixed positions, as well as approximately 350 155 *C Modèle 1881* and 230 *Mortiers de 220 Modèle 1880*.
18   Nos. 1, 2, 3 and four siege batteries disembarked at St Nazaire on 19th September 1914, and Nos. 5 and 6, on 27th September 1914. See Edmonds, *Official History 1914*, Vol. I, p. 482.

The Somme Preparatory Bombardment, 24 June-1 July 1916   149

British 18-pdr field gun. (Private collection)

British 4.5-inch howitzer.

German Army in August 1914. France and Great Britain, however, went to war with a combined total of 253 field howitzers (4.5 in. and 120mm) and 190 medium howitzers (6-in and 155mm) and it would take a long time before each Army began to be equipped with anything like the numbers of medium and heavy howitzers required to reduce the defences the Germans were busily erecting on the Western Front.

It took time for the Allies to bridge this gap. For siege artillery the French were dependent on obsolete tubes manufactured as part of the *Barrière de Bange* in the 1870s and 80s and soon found themselves amid an acute shell shortage that was far more immediate and serious than that which faced the British in May 1915. Lacking proper fire support, the infantry suffered shocking casualties for limited gains. Writing in the *Revue Militaire Française* after the war a Colonel Menu made the not wholly reliable comparison between the Champagne fighting in the autumn of 1915 when there was a shortage of 155mm high explosive shells and that of the Somme in 1916 when the deficiency had been made up: Champagne, 21 days fighting – 81,500 dead and missing or 3,880 per day; Somme, 153 days fighting – 65,000 dead and missing or 425 per day.

Previous French experience began to underline the importance of the availability of adequate supplies of high explosive shells of 155mm size and larger as well as the need to concentrate guns to a degree not yet thought necessary within the BEF. During every action in 1915 on the French front the numbers of field and heavy guns per metre of front increased. On the 25 March 1915 in fighting around Perthes – Lès-Hurlus on the Champagne front only 109 heavy guns and howitzers were deployed on a 16 km front, a concentration of one 'heavy' for every 146 metres. This attack was a costly failure. An improved concentration at Les Éparges the following month saw better results, albeit at a high cost in men. Then, on 9 May 1915, the French *10e Armée* launched a major offensive towards Vimy Ridge on the same day as First Army attacked at Aubers Ridge. Their results would be markedly different and, for some at least, instructive.

Aubers Ridge had been an objective of the British First Army's attack at Neuve Chapelle on 10 March 1915. The expectation was that the British would rupture the German lines on either side of Neuve Chapelle and advance quickly to occupy the topographically unimpressive, but tactically important line of low hills which ran south-west to north-east behind the tiny but still significant *Rivière des Layes* (or Layes Brook). To achieve this First Army had concentrated ninety 18-pdrs for wire-cutting and a combination of thirty six field howitzers, eight 4.7 in. guns and twenty four 6 in. 30 cwt howitzers on a front of 1,635 metres (1,790 yards).[19] The field and medium howitzers and the 4.7 in. guns were meant to demolish the somewhat

---

19 There was a gap of 690 metres between the right wing of IV Corps and the left wing of the Indian Corps with the attack intended initially as a pincer movement which would 'pinch out' Neuve Chapelle village before moving on towards Aubers Ridge.

flimsy German front line breastworks.[20] This concentration of guns therefore gave one howitzer/medium gun for every 24 metres of front line trench and one 6 in. howitzer per 68 metres of front. This array of guns proved more than adequate to the task of destroying the weak German front line and the unoccupied support line, with the field howitzers doing the lion's share of the work, firing over 80 percent of the 3,000 howitzers shells utilised.[21] The problems of the battle would come later as the attack became over-extended, communications broke down and the guns began to run short of ammunition; it would be closed down four days later at a cost of some 11,200 casualties and with Aubers Ridge remaining in German hands.

The effect of the initial break-in, however, was tantalising to both Sir John French and Haig and they concluded that only minor tweaking was needed to their plan before the next attack at Aubers Ridge on 9 May. Unfortunately, as seemed too often the case during the first half of the war, the Germans learned lessons faster than their opponents. Their dramatic improvements to their defences proved greater than any changes in manpower deployment, tactics and artillery attempted by First Army.

The assault on Aubers Ridge was conducted by elements of I Corps and the Indian Corps attacking south of Neuve Chapelle and IV Corps assaulting opposite Fromelles. Again, the German front line defences were based on a breastwork. Again the British attacked from two positions over an extended front of 9,000 metres with the idea of joining hands about the isolated *Ferme de la Cliqueterie*. This lay 1,500 metres south of Aubers village and some 4,150 metres from the IV Corps right-hand jumping off trench. The IV Corps attacked on a front of 1,420 yards and I and Indian Corps on a front of 2,200 metres (2,400 yards). To demolish the breastworks the various corps had available:

IV Corps: (12)6 in. and (18) 4.5 in. howitzers
Indian Corps: (8) 6 in. and (18) 4.5 in. howitzers
I Corps: (16) 6 in., (16)5 in. and (14) 4.5 in. howitzers

Other guns were available for counter battery work, the demolition of key strongpoints and the cutting of the wire.

This meant that the northern attack (IV Corps) had one howitzer for every 43 metres of front and the southern attacks (Indian and I Corps) one for every 31 metres of front. Of the heavier 6 in. howitzers there were 36, or one for every 97 metres or 106 yards of front. These two sets of figures compare to 24 and 68 metres of front respectively at Neuve Chapelle. In other words, there was a significant dilution of the concentration of available artillery for trench destruction. To add to British woes

20   The breastworks were four feet high (1.2 m.) and five to six feet wide. Behind this was a 3 feet deep (0.91 m.) trench. Protecting these breastworks was a belt of barbed wire 6-15 yards (1.8-4.6 m.) deep arranged in two to three rows of knife rests.
21   Edmonds, *Official History 1915*, Vol. 1, p. 91.

the Germans had undertaken a major re-building of their breastwork which had expanded from four feet high and six feet wide to seven feet high and up to twenty feet deep. New and concealed wire defences had also been constructed as well as shelters for the men. Wood and iron rail reinforced machine gun posts had been dug into the base of the breastworks. These were thought to be safe from anything except a direct hit from a medium howitzer. When it came to the day, the Royal Artillery's 40 minute bombardment failed to demolish the German positions in the way achieved at Neuve Chapelle. The attackers were shot down in their thousands. After a single day and over 11,000 casualties killed, wounded and missing the attack was called off. The attack posed so little threat to the Germans that they were able to move two divisions away from Aubers to confront the French at Vimy Ridge.

But what of the same day attack on Vimy Ridge? General Ferdinand Foch, commander of the *Groupe Provisoire de Nord* (later known as *Groupe d'Armées du Nord* or GAN) had accumulated numerous guns and a large quantity of ammunition for the attacks on Notre Dame de Lorette, Ablain St Nazaire, Carency, Vimy, Neuville St Vaast, Thélus and Bailleul sir Berthoult. The frontage was some 13 kms long, the German defences robust and its defenders on the alert given the huge tactical significance of control of the summit of Vimy Ridge. Here the bombardment would take six days, not forty minutes. The intention was to erase the German defences before the infantry attacked. But, for all that, the intention was, like at Aubers Ridge, to break through the German line into the wide expanse of the Douai plain beyond the ridge thereby threatening Lens to the north. Foch had 293 heavy guns and howitzers arranged on the front but with concentrations of artillery on the key points in the centre of the attack. This represented one heavy gun or howitzer for every 44 metres of front. There was one field gun for every 17 metres of front of which 90 percent were 75mm QF guns and the rest more elderly 90 and 80mm *de Bange* guns. There was also one trench mortar for every 67 metres of front. Clearly the 293 heavy guns and howitzers had more than the single purpose of demolishing the German trenches as counter battery fire had also been identified as a key priority, but two factors need to be considered:

1. Foch and the commander of *10e Armée*, General Victor Louis Lucien, baron d'Urbal, had not uniformly spread their artillery strength along the entire 13 km front.
2. It quickly became apparent that it was the 155mm Canon Court (155 C) which was the weapon capable of doing the necessary damage both to the German trenches and to hardened machine gun and observation posts as well as being the most numerous howitzer within the French arsenal.[22]

22 As of 1May 1915 the French Army had available 5,940 guns and howitzers (out of a pre-war total of 15,440) of size 65 mm to 270 mm. Of these 43 were 120 C, 258 155 C and 67 were '*M*' (*Mortiers*) *220/270*. A year later these numbers stood at 123, 515 and

The effectiveness, as well as the shortcomings, of the 125 new *Mortiers de tranchée de 58 No. 1, No. 1 bis* and *No. 2* employed to destroy the German frontal position had previously been noted and a vast expansion in their production was already underway.[23]

The primary objective of the attack was the summit of Vimy Ridge between Givenchy en Gohelle and Petit Vimy known as Côte 140. The task was given to the élite *Division Marocaine* which had been thoroughly schooled in the new tactics set out by GQG in a document entitled *But et conditions d'une action offensive d'ensemble* issued on 16 April 1915.[24] These tactics included such innovations as by-passing areas of enemy strength and attacking the weakest point, using 'shock troops' unencumbered by heavy weights to advance swiftly in the first attack and using a rudimentary version of what would come to be described as a "creeping barrage" in front of the advancing men. The *Division Marocaine* rolled over the devastated German front lines and moved forward at rapid pace, arriving at Côte 140, some 4,500 metres from their starting point, in approximately 90 minutes. Some men, indeed, advanced still further penetrating the edges of both Givenchy and Petit Vimy before falling victim to 'friendly fire' and German counter-attacks. This was the deepest penetration of the German lines since trench warfare had begun.

It was, however, unsustainable: the guns ran short of ammunition; the reserves were too far in the rear (as, later, would be British reserves at Loos) and were heavily fired upon when they eventually arrived; the casualties amongst officers at the leading edge of the attack caused confusion; and such a narrow salient was a perfect target for German flanking fire. The position could not be held but the seeds of a method for a successful attack were sown especially in the fertile minds of Foch, Pétain (who commanded the *XXXIII Corps* of which the *Division Marocaine* were a part) and Fayolle of the neighbouring *77e Division* (and who would command *6e Armée* on the Somme in summer 1916). All of them concluded that artillery was the key to the battle, that the infantry needed to be protected from unnecessary risks caused by inadequate artillery preparation, that the accurate observation of fire was essential and, controversially, that the means to break *into* the German lines existed but the means to *breakthrough* were, as yet, absent. Decisive, as in conflict ending, results could not be expected, but a steady gain of occupied territory and successful application of attritional warfare was possible with proper planning and, crucially, enough guns and shells of the right type.

Meanwhile, First Army, following the disaster at Aubers Ridge, attempted to resume the offensive with an attack near Festubert on 15 May. This was after Sir John French informed Joffre that the BEF preferred to attack again rather than take over

---

240 respectively. See Touzin & Vauvillier, *Les Canons de la Victoire, Tome 1, L'artillerie de campagne* (Paris: Histoire et Collections, 2006) p. 22].
23 The *Mortier de 58 T No. 1* was designed by *Chef de bataillon* Duchêne, the commander of the *Gènie* (Engineers) of Fayolle's *77e Division*, in late 1914. There were three variants: *No. 1, No. 1 bis* and *No. 2*. Approximately 5,200 were manufactured during the war.
24 *AFdGG*, Tome III, Annexes Vol. 1, Annexe 52, p. 94.

additional sectors of the line as a means of freeing-up French troops for the continuing assault against Vimy. This battle lasted ten days and cost First Army another 16,000 casualties. The preliminary bombardment involved just the 6 in. howitzers in an attempt to beat down the strengthened German breastworks. Whilst in the attack on the 9 May there had been one of these guns for every 97 metres, at Festubert the distribution was one for every 230 metres of front.

Table 1 clearly demonstrates how, throughout 1915, the concentration of British howitzer firepower on the German lines became increasingly dilute such that, by the time of the opening day of the Battle of Loos on 25 September 1915, the ratio of medium and heavy howitzers per yard of front had more than halved. During this same time frame, however, Foch and others had determined that the Neuve Chapelle ratio of one medium or heavy howitzer per 75 yards was, approximately, that which should be written into French battle orders from now on or until the tactical situation on the Western Front materially altered.

Table 1 British Guns/howitzers as employed in trench bombardments 1915[25]

	Width of front (yards)	No. of Guns (medium/heavy howitzers)	No. of yards per gun (All guns/ howitzers)	No of yards per medium/heavy howitzer*
Neuve Chapelle	1,790	60 (24)	30	75
Aubers Ridge	3,800	102 (36)	37	106
Festubert	5,000	121 (36)	41	139
Loos	11,200	145 (65)	77	172

* 6 in. howitzer and above.

The BEF, on the other hand, went into 1916 with no clear principles on which to base either the width or depth of any new offensive. Rawlinson, for example, when determining the width of the Somme front in early April 1916 wrote that "eight or nine men a yard is none too much" when contemplating an attack of two weeks' duration.[26] When it came to the availability of medium and heavy howitzers (6 in. to 9.2 in.), of which there were to be some 200, his conclusion was that: "This number will not suffice to deal effectively with a larger front than 20,000 yards or a depth greater than 4,000 to 5,000 yards."[27] What should be noted about this sentence is that the depth of 4-5,000 yards mentioned was not the distance to be achieved in one day. Rawlinson initially proposed phased attacks along the guide lines adopted by Foch and these

---

25   Edmonds, *Official History 1915*, Vol. 1, pp. 81-5 and *Official History 1915*, Vol. II, pp. 18-9, 52-5, 163-7.
26   TNA WO 95/431: The Somme – Plan for Offensive by the Fourth Army, G.X.3/1.
27   Ibid.

distances were the ones to be achieved in several attacks not, as was later the case, in one morning's great advance.

Rawlinson entered the planning phase of the offensive sensibly concerned about again incurring heavy losses with little to show:

> [W]e should be foolish to incur them [i.e. losses] without a certainty of success which I cannot guarantee. I shall have to have it out with DH [Haig] perhaps tomorrow after the Army commanders' conference. All my divisions except two are new divisions. Their limit of effort is small compared to those we had last year but we have increased our artillery and munitions greatly.[28]

He was, however, warned by Lieutenant-General Lancelot Kiggell, GHQ Chief of the General Staff, that Haig was in favour of "breaking the [German] line and [was] gambling on rushing the third line on the top of a panic".[29] Despite this, the underlying principle of Rawlinson's initial plan was in line with Foch's way of thinking. It was "to kill Germans at the least cost to ourselves". In other words, the very definition of the battle of attrition which, *post hoc*, became Haig's justification for the extended Somme fighting. But Haig disagreed, commented in his diary on 5 April (the day after receiving Rawlinson's first attack plan draft) that:

> His intention is merely to take the enemy's first and second system of trenches and "kill Germans". He looks upon the gaining of three or four kilometres more or less of ground as immaterial. I think we can do better than this by aiming at getting as large a combined force of French and British as possible across the Somme and fighting the enemy in the open![30]

Thus Haig forced upon a reluctant Rawlinson a vastly more ambitious plan which not only extended the front to take in Serre and Montauban as part of the first phase but also extended it to take in three German positions up to 5,000 yards deep north of the Albert – Bapaume Road and two positions to the south.

Having decided the geographic parameters of the attack the debate between Fourth Army's commander and his superior turned to the length of the preliminary bombardment. The debate was distorted by the fact that GHQ had both underestimated and misunderstood the nature and effect of the initial German bombardment at Verdun on 21 February 1916.

At 4 a.m. on the morning of 21 February 1916, a 750kg shell was fired from a German 38cm *SK L/45* naval gun lurking east of the *Forêt de Spincourt*. Its target lay some 32,000 metres (20 miles) away to the south-west. Clipping the *Cathédrale*

---

28 Churchill Archives Centre, Churchill College, Cambridge, Rawlinson Diary, 31 March 1916.
29 Ibid., 1 April 1916.
30 TNA WO/256/9: Haig Diary, 5 April 1916.

Notre-Dame in the Place Monseigneur – Ginisty, the shell exploded in the courtyard of the 18th Century *Palais épiscopal* which lay on the left bank of the River Meuse just east of the *Citadelle de Verdun*. It was the opening shot of the longest battle of the First World War. It was not followed by an immediate deluge of German shells on the city of Verdun and the snow-covered hills away to the north. There was a pause, pregnant with fear and foreboding for the citizens of the city and the men tasked with defending it. Then, at 7.15 a.m., another great gun opened fire. This was one of the thirteen *42-cm M-Gerät 14 Kurze Marinekanone L/12* super howitzers which ringed the northern and north-eastern edge of the French salient to the north of Verdun. With that, all hell broke loose as 1,225 German guns and howitzers, 542 of them of heavy and super heavy weight, opened fire on the French positions along the length and breadth of the Verdun salient.

Rather more importantly, over 800 guns and howitzers, of which over 360 were howitzers of size 15cm (6 in.) or larger, supported the advance of the three German *Armeekorps* (*III, XVIII* and *VII Reserve*) set to attack along a front of no more than 12 kilometres. This concentration of artillery power represented a ratio of one 15cm or heavier howitzer for every 34 metres of front and one gun/howitzer of all calibres for every 15½ metres of front. There had not been a bombardment of this intensity and concentration in the whole of human history.

It is beyond the scope of this chapter to discuss the nature and impact of the German bombardment. Suffice to say that, despite the intensity, sufficient French troops survived to exact a heavy price upon the attackers at several points.[31] It was during the days *after* the initial attack that French casualties rose dramatically and the defences crumbled in certain places. But Haig drew a faulty conclusion:

> The result of the combination of surprise and an overwhelming artillery preparation was that the infantry appear to have had little more to do in their first advance than to take possession of ground already practically won by the artillery; as a consequence, it appears that in the Verdun area four Corps were enabled to advance on the first day with comparatively little loss, to a depth of nearly 4 miles, on a front of some 9 miles.[32]

The three *Armeekorps* which attacked on 21 February did not achieve a penetration of four miles until 25 February, the day on which the disarmed but psychologically significant Fort Douaumont fell to *Feldwebel* Kunze of the *Infanterie-Regiment Großherzog Friedrich Franz II von Mecklenburg-Schwerin (4. Brandenburgisches) Nr. 24*. Thus on day one of the offensive, the maximum penetration was approximately 2,000 yards.

---

31 Elements of the *56e* and *59e bataillons de Chasseurs à Pied*, commanded by Lt. Col. Emile Driant, held out for nearly 48 hours in the Bois de Caures even though both regiments lost over 50 percent and 60 percent respectively during subsequent fighting.
32 TNA WO 95/3: Document dated 4 March 1916.

But, even if Haig had been correct in his assessment, what seemed unknown was the full scale of the German bombardment. The table below depicts (column A) the number of German guns and howitzers employed along the entire German front line on 21 February 1916.[33] Column B shows the numbers of guns of different calibres employed by Fourth Army in the preliminary bombardment on the Somme. Column C depicts the number of guns the Germans would have employed on a front of the same width as the Somme had they wished to achieve the same concentration of firepower as at Verdun. There were two key differences:

1. The availability of long guns for counter-battery work and to interdict French supply routes and prevent reserves reaching the front. The German concentration of such guns was 2.5 times greater than Fourth Army's on the Somme
2. The number of medium and heavy howitzers available to crush the defences which was more than three times greater that the equivalent concentration achieved by Fourth Army.

Table 2: Comparison between the Verdun and Somme bombardments

Gun type Modern QF Field Guns & Howitzers	A. German guns (Verdun Actual)	B. British guns (Somme Actual)	C. German guns if front same length as British
Field guns	442	868*	789
Field howitzers	108	202	193
100-155 (4.7 in. to 60-pdr) Guns	255	180	455
Heavy & Super Heavy Long Guns	4	2	7
Medium Howitzers	276	104	493
Heavy Howitzers	140	140†	250
Super Heavy Howitzers	26	17	46

*   Includes 60 × 75 mm QF field guns attached from French Army
†   Includes 16 × 220 mm *mortiers* attached from French Army

But even these figures do not provide the entire story. Three German *Armeekorps* attacked in the later afternoon of 21 February. These three units attacked on an initial front of just 7,100 metres and to support them were enough howitzers of size 155mm or greater to provide one for every twenty metres of front and one gun of any type sufficient to one over nine metres of front.[34] These figures need to be borne in mind when one considers the availability of medium and heavy howitzers to Fourth Army:

33   Reichskrieg Ministerium, *Der Weltkrieg 1914-1918*, Vol. X (E S Mittler & Sohn, 1936).
34   Figures calculated from Reichsarchiv, *Die Tragödie von Verdun 1916* (Druck und Verlag von Berhard Stalling, 1925).

XIII Corps: (1) 15 cm/6 in. or heavier howitzer for every 59 metres of front
XV Corps: (1) 15 cm/6 in. or heavier howitzer for every 121 metres of front
III Corps: (1) 15 cm/6 in. or heavier howitzer for every 83 metres of front
X Corps: (1) 15 cm/6 in. or heavier howitzer for every 90 metres of front
VIII Corps: (1) 15 cm/6 in. or heavier howitzer for every 96 metres of front

It should be noted that the most successful British Corps, the XIII Corps at Montauban, was the one with the largest supply of medium and heavy howitzers (backed up by French *Mortiers* and French-assisted counter-battery work).

But it was not only the Germans at Verdun who vastly exceeded the concentration of artillery available to Rawlinson and Fourth Army. So too did Fayolle's *6e Armée* on the Somme. As Table 3 below shows, had the French been about to attack on a front as wide as that of Fourth Army they would have employed nearly 2 1/2 times as many guns of all types as did the BEF. Indeed on a front covered by just five divisions, Fayolle concentrated nearly as many guns as Rawlinson, but on a much shorter front. And, to make matters worse, the German defences opposite Fourth Army were significantly more robust and of greater depth and strength than anything faced by the French and the area to be prepared by the artillery was between two and three times as large.

Table 3: Comparison of French and British artillery employed on the Somme

Gun type (French / British)	A French (Actual)	B British (Actual)	C French if front same length as British
Field Guns & Howitzers			
Field guns all types	787	868*	2,028
Field howitzers	8	202	21
Long Guns			
100-155 (4.7 in. to 60-pdr Guns	277	180	740
Heavy and super heavy guns	58	2	149
Medium & Heavy Howitzers			
Medium Howitzers	128	104	330
Heavy and super heavy How.	144	157†	372
Total	1,412	1,513	3,640

*   60 × 75 mm guns attached from the French Army inclusive.
†   16 × 220 mm *mortiers* attached from the French Army inclusive.

Given the known strength of these German defences how did Haig imagine they might be overwhelmed? Part of the answer lies in Haig's enthusiasm for technical innovations. Unfortunately, he had a tendency to expect too much from such developments. For the Somme bombardment and campaign, he had demanded the recently developed tank[35] and new, lethal gas shells.[36] The availability of these would have been advantageous on 1 July but, when it was quickly established that neither would be ready, the tactics of the attack were not adapted to take account of their absence. This was particularly the case when it came to the use of gas shells which, it had been hoped, might allow lethal gas to be dropped into German trenches where, the gas being heavier than air, it would seep down into the deep dugouts. In Rawlinson's response to Haig's criticisms of his original plan for the attack of the Fourth Army,[37] Rawlinson had referred to the "numerous dugouts and cellars" which sheltered the German defenders. Haig's pencil written response to this was "We must have gas shells for these". Between 29 January and 26 April 1916, Haig wrote seven times to the Ministry of Munitions demanding supplies of both tear and lethal gas shells, initially for the 4.7 in. and 60-pdr guns, and the 4.5 in. howitzers. This request was later extended to the 6 in. Mk VII guns and heavy howitzers. He wrote again on the 16 May with a request for smoke, gas and incendiary shells. The problem was that the War Office had not yet decided which of three possible lethal gasses to use and was reluctant to deploy those which contained cyanide, arsenic or phosgene until convincing evidence of their employment by the Germans had been received. In addition, little was known about the effect on the gas contained in a shell when the shell detonated. What was clear from the exchange was that no lethal gas shells would be available to the BEF before the offensive and, to make matters worse, whilst 10 percent of shell casings were set aside in the hope they might be filled with lethal or tear gas, these then became unavailable for filling with high explosive for use in the offensive.

An alternative method for destroying these dugouts was also suggested, but not taken up. During a conference at Boulogne in June 1915, the French had recommended that all heavy guns should now fire high explosive shells exclusively. Furthermore, they suggested that a portion of these shells should be armed with delayed-action fuses which might allow the heavier shells to penetrate the ground before bursting inside German dugouts.[38] A British artillery officer had suggested something similar two months earlier. Major-General John Philip du Cane had been appointed Sir John French's artillery adviser in 1915 and he, noting the protection given to German machine guns and their teams by dugouts, had suggested the use of delayed-action fuses as a means of collapsing these dugouts. However, when Lloyd George took over the Ministry of Munitions, Du Cane returned to London to advise the new minister and with him, it seems, went this idea. No delayed action fuses were available prior to 1 July. Nevertheless, having acknowledged the existence of

---

35 TNA WO 256/9: Haig Diary, 5 April 1916.
36 TNA WO 95/3: Rawlinson to Haig, 19 April 1916.
37 Ibid.
38 Ministry of Munitions, *History of the Ministry of Munitions*, Vol. I, Part 1, p. 29.

the numerous German dugouts, one might have thought that Haig and Rawlinson would have considered it essential to come up with some solution. Yet, beyond the call for gas shells, no solutions were proposed, let alone developed. Whilst Foch was addressing the numbers and types of shells needed to destroy the various elements of the German defensive system in his pre-battle document, *La Bataille Offensive*,[39] Rawlinson paid scant attention to the employment in his far briefer and considerably less useful "Tactical Notes".

Tactical Notes was written under twenty headings, none of which had very much to say about the use of artillery. Its first section was Selection of Objectives. This ignored Foch's concept of by-passing areas of enemy strength and attacking areas of enemy weakness. Instead, these objectives were to be set with these notions in mind:

1. The ground which could be covered by the artillery
2. The limit of the attacking troops endurance

The former was deemed to be the effective range of the artillery which, given the positioning of the guns, meant that the artillery could cover the German first and Intermediate positions (to be attacked by all five corps) but not the 2nd Position (to be attacked by the VIII, X and III Corps). The anticipated 'limit of endurance' of the attacking troops was rather self-fulfilling: it was the furthest point to be reached as previously decided by the C-in-C. Foch would have been aghast at such reasoning for it flew in the face of French experience so expensively gained in the summer and autumn of 1915. It was, indeed, the recipe for the disasters of 1 July.

The remainder of Tactical Notes focused on issues such as formations (successive waves were recommended but not mandatory), use of reserves (of which there were precious few as nearly every unit had a specific task[40] and, as commented on after the war, a unit with a function could not be a reserve),[41] flank protection, maintaining direction and consolidation. On this latter point great emphasis was laid. Indeed some 20 percent of Tactical Notes focused on this issue. It was not until paragraph 66,

---

39 *AFdGG*, Tome IV, Vol. 2, Annexes Vol. I, Annexe 2, p. 3.
40 For example, two of three of VIII Corps' attacking divisions (i.e. 4th Division and 29th Division) had no immediate reserves, as every battalion had been allocated an objective. The 31st Division had one brigade available to intervene if necessary (it was nearly sent into action opposite Serre in the middle of the night in order to make contact with troops falsely believed to be in the village). The 48th Division had one brigade in the line in the gap between VIII Corps and VII Corps at Gommecourt and its two other brigades were in no position to be actively involved on the first day. See Alan MacDonald, *Z Day. 1st July 1916: The VIII Corps at Beaumont Hamel and Serre* (Iona Books, 2014).
41 See Major General John Kennedy's contribution to the *Report of the Committee on the Lessons of the Great War* (War Office, 1932), p. 50. In it he states: "It should be laid down clearly (in *Field Service Regulations*) that troops committed to a definite role at any state of the battle have ceased to be a reserve; a reserve should be free of any commitment."

approximately two-thirds through the document, that Rawlinson addressed artillery deployment:

> 66. The ideal is for the artillery to keep their fire immediately in front of the infantry as the latter advances, battering down all opposition with a hurricane of projectiles. The difficulties of observation, especially in view of dust and smoke, the varying rates of the advance of the infantry, the varieties of obstacles and resistance to overcome, the probable interruption of telephone communication between infantry and artillery and between the artillery observers and their guns, renders this ideal very difficult to obtain.
>
> 67. Experience has shown that the only safe method of artillery support during an advance is a fixed time-table of lifts to which both the infantry and artillery must rigidly conform.

Rawlinson's tactical prescription for artillery – a system of strictly timed 'lifts' – was to prove a recipe for disaster. Where the infantry were only too often held up the artillery marched impotently away into the distance unable to assist their advance. All the problems hinted at in the second part of paragraph 66 came to pass across the majority of Fourth Army's front. There was no further comment on artillery in Tactical Notes; the phrase 'counter battery fire' does not appear.

With Rawlinson having little to say about artillery usage, it was down to his Corps commanders to fill the gap. Unfortunately, not one senior commander at GHQ, Army and Corps involved in the 1 July attack came from the Royal Garrison Artillery. Haig was a cavalryman; Rawlinson, Congreve, Pulteney and Morland infantrymen, Hunter-Weston a Royal Engineer. Horne, having been Haig's BGRA I Corps, alone had risen through the ranks of the Royal Field Artillery. It was Horne who attempted the rudimentary creeping barrage on XV Corps' front on the opening day of the Somme. This then placed the weight of artillery planning on the shoulders of Rawlinson's artillery adviser – Major-General Noel 'Curly' Birch – and the senior artillery officers at each Corps HQ.

Unfortunately, Haig disrupted this planning process by deciding, in early May, to replace GHQ's current senior artilleryman, Major-General John

Major-General J.F.N. Birch. (John Bourne)

Headlam, with Birch. The latter would be replaced by Major-General Charles Edward Dutton Budworth who, as Brigadier-General Royal Artillery X Corps, had previously devoted his energies to planning the artillery programme for the crucial assault on Thiepval and the Schwaben Redoubt. Despite Rawlinson's request that this change be delayed until after the start of the offensive, Haig refused to wait and both Birch and Budworth took over their new posts in early June and at a time when certain aspects of the preliminary barrage were still very much undecided.

It is beyond the scope of this chapter to go into the detail of the disagreement between Rawlinson and Haig over the duration and extent of the preliminary bombardment. Suffice to say Haig was attracted to the brief but intense barrage which had gained temporary success at Neuve Chapelle and which (at far greater length and infinitely greater intensity) had been employed by the Germans on the opening day of the Battle of Verdun. Rawlinson favoured the lengthy and deliberate bombardment which – out of necessity given the slow rates of fire of their mainly obsolete heavy artillery – was also the French choice, but with the additional reason that "with many new gun detachments we cannot expect very accurate shooting in a hurricane bombardment".[42] Rawlinson eventually got his way and the change of weather extended the bombardment by another two days. But Haig intervened once again just four days before the bombardment was due to start by insisting on the reduction or elimination of certain concentrated bombardments upon areas of tactical significance so as to preserve ammunition for the fighting to come.[43] An already weakened British barrage on the Somme was further diluted in the hope that the shells saved might be employed to hurry along a German withdrawal towards Bapaume and beyond.

In the light of these changes, it is interesting to note related comments made by Birch with regard to prevailing attitudes towards the application of the heavy artillery throughout the war. Writing in response to the first draft of the British *Official History* account of the Somme, his subsequent comments were damning:

> I am not quite sure whether you have sufficiently emphasised the backward state of our artillery and the difficulties of the time. There were miles and miles of wire to cut and no instantaneous fuses, and poor Haig – as he was always inclined to do – spread his guns. The idea of a surprise attack at that time in France was out of the question. After Neuve Chapelle the Germans took every precaution to strengthen their wire both in depth and quantity, and to cut it even with instantaneous fuses would have given away the whole show unless we had cut equally in say three different parts of the long English line. For this there were neither guns nor ammunition. I think I am right in saying it was the first battle for not a few of the gunners and they were put to tasks that had never been contemplated … In truth the problem of semi-siege warfare and the large

---

42 TNA WO 95/3: Amended Fourth Army Plan submitted to GHQ, 19 April 1916.
43 TNA WO 95/4: Kiggell to Rawlinson, GHQ letter OAD 15, 20 June 1916.

concentrations of guns necessary for the work had never been studied by the General Staff in peace, nor by any of the leading gunners, or gunnery schools, so we had to learn our lesson in the pitiless school of war. With the Sappers it was different. I attended a Senior Officers' course at Chatham on fortification and I remember a perfectly excellent lecture by a Sapper officer on the Russo-Japanese war, with most convincing lantern slides of dug-outs, real trenches and tunnels. If only the teaching of Chatham had been absorbed by the General Staff, and they had at the same time understood the gunnery problem that the Sapper demonstrated had been absolutely necessary, thousands of lives would have been saved and the war shortened by some years. Perhaps you will think I am over-stating the case, but I am perfectly certain that I am not. If the lesson of Chatham had been properly understood we should have gone to war with at any rate some munitions reserve, and the problem of demolishing wire would have really been thought out. The Sappers did everything in their power to show us the necessity for this but we had no real school of science of war in those days. We copied French tactics, which were childish, and swallowed the German idea that if you pushed and pushed men at defences you would eventually get there and win.[44]

Birch's negative post-war opinion of the French was not uncommon amongst British officers at the time. What he appears to have missed, or glossed over, is the dramatic improvement in both artillery and infantry tactics enacted by Foch and his juniors during the early fighting on the Somme. As was ever the case, new defensive tactics employed by the Germans stymied the best efforts of both Allied armies to bring about outright victory in 1916. Nonetheless, given the progress made by the French on the Somme and the eventual defeat of the Germans at Verdun, it could be argued that 1916 was France's year; Foch, Pétain and others having paved the way in achieving this result through the creative employment of an artillery arsenal almost all of which had been built before the turn of the century and much of which was technically obsolete. For Great Britain, the failure to learn – either from her ally or previous military experience – would cost the BEF dearly.

44 TNA CAB 45/132: Solicited *Official History* commentary by Maj. General J.F.N. Birch, 8 July 1930, Western Front: Battles: Comments, Letters, Personal Accounts file.

7

"The Battle in Miniature": The BEF and the Art of Trench Raiding 1916

John Pratt

The popular image of warfare on the Western Front in general, and of 1916 in particular, is one of constant high-intensity fighting. In fact, for much of 1916 the BEF was involved in routine line holding where combat was defined not by large scale offensives, but instead by local trench raids. Over the course of the year, countless raids were carried out and trench raiding methods developed dramatically as a result of hard won experience. Whilst the chapter does not focus on the Battle of the Somme *per se*, it is impossible to ignore the great clash as it was the main effort for the British in 1916 and shaped wider operations, of which trench raiding was a part. This chapter will study how the BEF's strategy influenced trench raiding and how it was used as a tool to foster an "aggressive spirit", especially within inexperienced New Army battalions before subjecting them to full scale battle. It will examine how raiding, by virtue of its violent and short lived nature, often enraged the opposing forces and resulted in battlefield repercussions. Finally, the detailed planning and ingenuity that went into the various raids will be considered as will the gallantry displayed by many of the raiders.

Trench raiding was not a new concept to the BEF in 1916. The first raid had been carried out by 1st Coldstream Guards who set out to seize and demolish the German held Fish Hook Trench on the night of 4/5 October 1914, a raid which was considered by the brigade commander as entirely successful.[1] Sir John French, seeing the benefit of raiding and wishing to wrest the initiative away from the enemy at a local level, gave what the *Official History* terms his "Official Authority" in a memorandum dated 5 February 1915 for raids to be carried out "to gain ground, take advantage of

---

1 Spencer Jones "'The Demon": Brigadier-General Charles FitzClarence VC' in Spencer Jones (ed.), *Stemming the Tide: Officers and Leadership in the British Expeditionary Force 1914* (Solihull: Helion & Company Ltd, 2013), p. 247.

any tactical or numerical inferiority on the part of the enemy and capture prisoners for 'identification' purposes i.e. to determine what units were on a particular front."[2]

Raiding, often known by contemporaries by the rather less warlike name "Minor Enterprises", was later summed up in the *Official History*:

> The essence of a raid is that the raiders should enter the enemy's trenches by surprise, kill as many of his men as possible, and return before counter-measures can be taken. Special tasks may be added, such as obtaining prisoners for 'identification', damaging mine shafts, destroying a length of trench or post which is giving particular trouble but cannot be permanently held if captured. The number of men employed was usually 10 to 200.[3]

The BEF believed that trench raiding had other benefits. In *Notes for Infantry Officers on Trench Warfare*, published in March 1916, raiding was seen as a means of "maintaining the efficiency of the troops" during the period of "comparative inactivity, which is the normal condition for life in the trenches."[4] The 9th (Scottish) Division believed that raids raised "the morale of our troops and have a correspondingly depressing effect on that of the enemy."[5] Indeed, a 5th Australian Brigade operation order went so far as to state that one of its raid intents was "destroying the enemy's morale, whilst maintaining the offensive spirit in our troops."[6] In other commands raiding success was perceived as a matter of honour. For example, compliments by 30th Division commander Major-General John Shea and XIII Corps commander Lieutenant-General Walter Congreve VC following a successful raid by 2nd Bedfordshire on 29 April were considered "all the more satisfactory because another Division tried to raid and did not get anybody."[7]

When trying to understand the benefits of raiding, the lack of combat opportunities available to the BEF prior to the Battle of the Somme must be remembered. Considering "the BEF was heavily engaged in major battle for little more than thirty days between the Christmas fraternisation of 1914, and 30 June 1916", leaving most

---

2   James. E. Edmonds, *Military Operations France and Belgium 1915*, Vol. 1(Uckfield: Naval & Military Press reprint of 1932 edition), p. 31, 32.
3   Edmonds, *Military Operations 1916*, Vol. 1, p. 156.
4   General Staff, *Notes for Infantry Officers on Trench Warfare* (London: Harrison & Sons, 1916), p. 8.
5   The National Archives (hereafter TNA) WO95/1734: 'Notes On Conference Held On 3rd January 1916', 9th Division War Diary.
6   Australian War Memorial (hereafter AWM), 3DRL/2316 Papers of General Sir John Monash, 'Fifth Australian Operation Order No 15 Dated 24 June' 1916 <https://www.awm.gov.au/collection/RCDIG0000572/> (Accessed January 2016).
7   F. C. Stanley, *The History of the 89th Brigade 1914-1918* (Liverpool: Daily Post Printers, 1919), p. 125.

of the serious fighting during this period to the French,[8] raiding proved to the Allies that the BEF was not sitting idle. Captain J. C. Dunn, the 2nd Royal Welsh Fusiliers Medical Officer, summed up raiding as the "battle in miniature with all the preliminaries and accompaniments magnified, often manyfold."[9] Raiding therefore also provided commands and units with occasions to plan and execute small operations whilst at the lowest tactical level "furnishing both officers and men with many opportunities in which to display their initiative."[10] As reported by Haig in the first of his despatches there was a "peculiar scope to the gallantry, dash and quickness of decision of the troops engaged" in these raids.[11]

For many junior officers of 1916, the only opportunity to come to terms with their fear, prove themselves as leaders in front of their men and gain actual combat experience before entering the inferno on the Somme was through trench raiding. The theory of "blooding" the young, inexperienced officers in this manner was based upon the assumption they would survive; in fact, the attrition rate of both officers and men in trench raids was high and "many units had to deplore the loss of the cream of their officers, N.C.O.s and men in raids."[12] Despite this high attrition rate, there were clear military benefits to be had, which as Paddy Griffith points out, "have nevertheless been buried in the literature under a mountain of ill feeling since the troops disliked them as being expensive in casualties yet unproductive in ground gained."[13] Yet raiding provided vital experience and was a "dress rehearsal" for what was to come.[14]

Changing Characteristics of Raiding

Despite British efforts at the battles of Aubers Ridge, Festubert and Loos, "the situation with which the Allies were faced at the close of 1915 was not an encouraging one."[15] Whilst Joseph Joffre realised as early as June 1915 that the co-ordination of Allied operations was paramount to success, it was not until 6 December 1915 at Chantilly that a plan of action was finally proposed. As discussed elsewhere in this volume, this plan committed the Allies to a co-ordinated, multi-front "General Offensive" in 1916 during which Great Britain, France, Italy and Russia would deliver

---

8   Paddy Griffith, *Battle Tactics of the Western Front: The British Army's Art of Attack 1916-18* (London: Yale University Press, 1994), p. 11.
9   J.C. Dunn, *The War the Infantry Knew 1914-1919* (London: Sphere Books Ltd, 1989), p. 192.
10 Everard. Wyrall, *The Die Hards in the Great War* (London: Harrison and Sons, 1921), p. 297.
11 J.H. Boraston, *Sir Douglas Haig's Despatches (December 1915-April 1919)* (London: J.M. Dent & Sons Ltd, 1919), p. 4.
12 Cyril Falls, *The History of the 36th (Ulster) Division* (Belfast: Linenhall Press, 1922), p. 71.
13 Griffith, *Battle Tactics*, pp. 61, 62.
14 Ibid., pp. 62, 193.
15 Edmonds, *Military Operations 1916*, Vol. 1, pp. 1, 3.

simultaneous attacks. But until then, the enemy was to be "worn down by vigorous action, to be carried out principally by those powers which still have reserves of man power" namely Great Britain, Italy and Russia.[16] General Sir Douglas Haig, the newly appointed Commander in Chief of the BEF, acknowledged the grave situation that faced the French in terms of available man-power. In his diary on 14 January, he observed:

> There is no doubt to my mind but that the war must be won by the Forces of the British Empire. At the present time I think our action should take the form of
>
> 1. "Winter Sports" or raids continued into spring, i.e. capturing lengths of enemy's trenches at favourable points.
> 2. Wearing-Out fight similar to 1, but on a larger scale at many points along the whole Front. Will last about three weeks to draw in the enemy's reserves.
> 3. Decisive attacks on several points, object to break through. The amount of ammunition for two and three will be very large indeed.[17]

The BEF was now committed to pursuing a policy of wearing down the enemy before the main offensive. In pursuit of the "wearing out" phase, Joffre had directed the British to conduct offensives in April and May, but the BEF lacked the necessary resources. It was short of heavy artillery and its divisions were too inexperienced to conduct vigorous "wearing out" battles.[18] Haig remarked:

> Such attacks, not being carried out to conclusion, would be regarded by the enemy, by the public at home and by neutral countries as Allied defeats, and they would not prevent the enemy from replacing losses from his depots, as well as organising new reserves in time to meet the main effort.[19]

Haig believed such "wearing out" attacks "will wear us out" before the main Somme offensive.[20] In the absence of such operations, he adopted a policy of trench raiding. Numerous raids, carried out across the entire British front, would wear down the

---

16 Ibid., Appendices, p. 5.
17 TNA WO 256/7: 'Field Marshal Sir Douglas Haig, Commander in Chief of British Forces, Western Front: diaries. 19 December 1915 to 31 January 1916'.
18 Lieutenant General Sir W.R. Robertson was to comment that 'The Somme was the first occasion on which our resources in men, guns, and ammunition enabled us to start an offensive with a reasonable chance of success. They were not as good as could have been desired, but they were infinitely superior to anything we had enjoyed before." See W. Robertson, *From Private to Field Marshal* (London: Constable & Company, 1921), p. 281.
19 Edmonds, *Military Operations 1916*, Vol. 1, p. 28.
20 Gary Sheffield and John Bourne (eds.), *Douglas Haig War Diaries and Letters 1914-1918* (London: Phoenix, 2006), p. 179.

enemy, erode their "will to fight" and draw in reserves without the risk of a large scale Allied defeat.[21] On Saturday 29 January, after Haig's army commanders reported on the nature of raiding for the month, Haig was clear on the benefits:

> A few had failed, but a great many had been successful and had raised the spirit and morale not only of the units carrying out the operations, but of the divisions and even of the corps concerned. By getting into and out again of the German trenches with little or no loss, all gained confidence, and also learnt much regarding how to deal with hostile defences.[22]

As the year progressed, Haig's emphasis on raiding shifted from his "Winter Sports" to a wider, more frequent and increasingly aggressive strategy for the BEF. Whilst fulfilling the operational objective of continuing to wear down the enemy on the Western Front, raiding also began to play a tactical part in the main offensive by providing vital intelligence and by misleading the enemy as to the exact time and place of the attack.[23] Raids were now more commonly ordered and coordinated at General Headquarters (GHQ) and army level with complex supporting artillery plans and often incorporating task organised multi-disciplined teams, including Royal Engineer (RE) demolition and mining experts.

Evidence suggests that successful raiding was seen by Haig as an indicator of the combat effectiveness of his armies. On the eve of the Battle of the Somme, he recorded his doubts about VIII Corps, "which has had no experience in fighting in France and has not carried out one successful raid."[24] As history now tells us, VIII Corps' performance on 1 July was unimpressive. Once the Battle of the Somme had begun, Haig continued to evaluate the results of raiding. He demanded raiding reports from the armies along other sectors of the front, which now served a secondary role of holding the line and keeping the enemy alert. Haig felt the "thoroughness with which their duties were performed can be gathered from the fact that in the period of four and a half months from the 1st July some 360 raids were carried out, in the course of which the enemy suffered many casualties and some hundreds of prisoners were taken by us."[25]

Although the operational and tactical focus of raiding in 1916 took on a different character to that of the previous year, the *nature* of a trench raid remained much the same. Consequently, there existed a rich source of "After Action Reports" and

---

21   Edmonds, *Military Operations 1916*, Vol. 1, p. 28.
22   TNA WO 256/7: 'Field Marshal Sir Douglas Haig diaries.'
23   "The Third, First and Second Armies had, during the preparations of the Fourth Army for the battle, kept up the pretence of making ready for an offensive." See Edmonds, *Military Operations 1916*, Vol. 1, pp. 309 -311.
24   Robert Blake (ed.), *The Private Papers of Douglas Haig 1914-1919* (London: Eyre & Spottiswoode, 1952), p. 151.
25   Boraston (ed.), *Sir Douglas Haig's Despatches*, p. 51.

lessons learnt for analysis by the higher echelons who constantly sought to improve the BEF's trench raiding tactics, techniques and procedures. Born from such analysis and seminal in trench raiding doctrine was the dissemination, in March 1916, of SS107 *Notes on Minor Enterprises*, published as a guide only as "no definite rules for the conduct of such operations can be laid down."[26] The various chapters are testament to the evolving character of raiding and give an interesting overview of a raid from the planning through to the execution. It included innovative solutions for solving tactical problems. For example, for conducting raiding operations at night it noted "electric torches fixed to the rifle with black insulating tape have been found useful for men detailed to clear dug-outs."[27] Whether 1st Bedfordshire Regiment was influenced by this direction is difficult to determine, but during a night raid in October the men found "the electronic torches fixed to the rifles near the hand grip proved exceedingly useful."[28] The final section of SS107 covering miscellaneous points identifies a ruse to mislead the Germans by suggesting that "the employment of dummies to deceive the enemy and draw fire to a flank has been found useful."[29] A good example of the use of dummies can be seen in a "small enterprise" carried out on 28 February by a party from the 9th Scottish Rifles who exploded two Bangalore torpedoes in the enemy wire.[30] As the torpedoes detonated, approximately a dozen dummies which had been pre-placed in No-Man's Land were manipulated by lines from the raiders' trenches in order to give the impression of troops moving about. As the enemy manned their parapets to engage the dummies, they were targeted with artillery, mortar, machine gun and rifle grenade fire. The Scottish Rifles suffered just two casualties and according to 28th Brigade war diary "the Scheme was carried out successfully."[31] However, dummies were not just limited to British use. The Germans also employed this ruse as was the case during the *110th Reserve Infantry Regiment*'s successful raid against the 1st Royal Irish Rifles near La Boisselle on 11 April, "to present the appearance of assaulting parties leaving the trenches to charge."[32]

26 SS107 *Notes on Minor Enterprises, Issued by General Staff G.H.Q March 1916* (Stationary Services Press, A-3/16-S56-1,000). It is also worthy of note that Second Army produced the very in-depth *Lessons Drawn from The Various Minor Operations* issued in February 1916. See TNA WO 95/1674: 'Lessons Drawn From The Various Minor Operations', 8 Division Headquarters Branches and Services General Staff War Diary.
27 SS107, *Notes on Minor Enterprises*.
28 TNA WO 95/1570: 'Report on Operations Carried Out On The Night of 31 October/1 November 1916', 5th Division, 15th Infantry Brigade, 1st Battalion Bedfordshire Regiment war diaries.
29 SS107, *Notes on Minor Enterprises*.
30 TNA WO 95/1775: 9th Scottish Rifles War Diary.
31 TNA WO 95/1774: 28thBrigade War Diary.
32 Anon., 'German Raid on the British Trenches Near La Boisselle, April 11th, 1916', *RUSI: Royal United Services Institute for Defence Studies Journal*, Vol. 63, Number 450 (May 1918), pp. 200-225. See also Michael LoCicero's chapter in this volume.

Armed with rifles, revolvers and Mills bombs, a British raiding party poses during training, summer 1916.

SS107 identified surprise as the key to a successful raid with "originality and imagination in planning and carrying out an enterprise" being encouraged.[33] This shows a clear understanding by GHQ of the need to give direction but maintain the freedom for subordinate commands and units to apply their own initiative. Whilst surprise in combat gives the attacker a short-lived period of superiority as confusion reigns in the enemy's ranks, it was always difficult for the raiders to achieve. The German front line trenches were, in most cases, well protected by strong wire obstacles which had to be breached. Overcoming this obstacle was the first challenge faced by a raiding party. The wire could be cut by a local preliminary bombardment but this could alert the defenders and lose the element of surprise. If time allowed, a wire cutting bombardment covering a range of locations and delivered the day before the raid could be used in the hope the enemy did not become suspicious nor repair the wire before the attack. Bangalore torpedoes were also available and could be inserted into the wire by the raiders, with their detonations clearing a small lane.[34] However, as relatively new technology they were unreliable. So much so that Second Army tasked Headquarters

---

33   SS107 *Notes on Minor Enterprises.*
34   The Bangalore Torpedo resembled a drain pipe filled with explosives inserted into the enemy wire at surface level prior to fuse detonation. The resultant explosion cleared an

RE in September to inquire into a number of failures.[35] The last, and least appealing option was to cut the wire by hand. Not only was this very time consuming, it was also a noisy process and was usually only used as a last resort or to finish a job. The 2nd Australian Division discovered this only too well on the night of 5/6 June when a raid had to be aborted when the attackers, cutting wire by hand, realised they were close to an enemy listening post. A clear lesson was learnt:

> Wire can be cut with absolute silence by the large Government Wire Nippers provided that they are set so as not to cut completely through a strand, but only two-thirds or three-quarters of the way through, then being removed and the wire being broken by hand. The man cutting works on his back, one man holds and the other men are available to lay the wire carefully back.[36]

Another problem facing the raider was determining suitable weaponry to fight in the close confines of the trenches, often under cover of darkness. Throughout warfare man has adapted and modified weapons to suit the changing character of combat, and trench raiders certainly learnt to adapt and overcome. Clubs proved popular, being easy to carry and wield in close combat. The British Army referred to most of its clubs as "knobkerrie", an Afrikaans word used to describe the war clubs used by the Zulu and Xhosa peoples. The Australians preferred a specialist club nicknamed the "life preserver", a weapon which was a "cog wheel of iron or steel fixed to an entrenching tool helve" with "a thong of leather for the wrist fixed to the handle."[37] These clubs, of local manufacture prior to production by RE workshops, could easily be brought to bear in the trenches and provided a silent method of disabling the enemy. The service pattern revolver was also found to be a useful weapon. However, there were insufficient numbers to issue to the men and NCOs because the weapon was normally for the exclusive use of officers. Additional service revolvers had to be issued, as did the ammunition for the men to practice with. The nature of trench warfare had already seen the increased utility of the grenade which continued to prove effective, especially for bombing dug-outs. Identifying the enemy was also a problem at night and amidst the confusion of combat when split second decisions had to be made. This was partly overcome by the faces of the raiders being blackened just before the raid. The purpose

---

    open lane in the wire. Sections could be joined together to extend the torpedo for the wider wire defences.
35 TNA WO 95/274: 'Proceedings of Conference on 23 September 1916', Second Army, Headquarters Branches and Services General Staff War Diary.
36 AWM 3DRL/2316 Papers of General Sir John Monash, 'Report on Minor Enterprise Carried out by the 7th Brigade of the Second Australian Division on the night of 6/7 June 1916'<https://www.awm.gov.au/collection/RCDIG0000572/> (Accessed January 2016).
37 AWM 3DRL/2316 Papers of General Sir John Monash, '4th Australian Infantry Brigade Headquarters D.A.D.O.S. dated 23 June 1916'<https://www.awm.gov.au/collection/RCDIG0000572/> (Accessed January 2016).

of this was two-fold; first, to prevent them being seen by the enemy and secondly it enabled the raiders "to easily distinguish between friend and foe",[38] a darkened face indicating friendly forces. Finally, to prevent raiders from being identified, they were stripped of all identifying badges and documentation before the raid preventing the enemy from gaining regimental identification from a casualty or prisoner.

Fostering the Aggressive Spirit

As the BEF began to take over more of the front line it became very apparent that in many sectors the French had a *laissez-faire* attitude to trench warfare and had settled into an "unofficial suspension of arms or truce prevailing,"[39] at any rate above ground."[40] Whilst this style of warfare may have suited the French, it was untenable for the BEF. As celebrated German veteran Ernst Junger observed: "battle brings men together, whereas inactivity separates them."[41] Whilst this is the opinion of a German, it does help demonstrate the risks associated with inactivity during the stalemate of the trenches. As a consequence, GHQ directed "with a view to cultivating an "aggressive spirit", as it was called ... Sniping, fire surprises and raids."[42] The repercussions of such activity were well understood by the General Staff:

> Constant activity in harassing the enemy may lead to reprisals at first, and for this reason is sometimes neglected, but if persevered in, it always results in an ultimate mastery, it gives the troops a healthy interest and wholesome topics of conversation and it achieves the double purpose of raising the morale of our own troops whilst lowering that of the enemy's.[43]

The "aggressive spirit" brought about a sudden end to local truces that the French had enjoyed. 89th Brigade of 30th Division reported, when it first moved into the Carnoy – Maricourt sector of the Somme in early January, "we were having a rotten time in this so-called quiet spot."[44] Even before 30th Division had the opportunity to become familiar with the sector, on 29 January, the 18th King's Liverpool Regiment of 21st Brigade was struck by a German raiding party estimated to be about 100 strong of the Prussian *62nd* and *63rd infanterie regiments*. The Germans succeeded in entering the British trenches but "owing to the preparations made by Captain Adam and the

---

38   TNA WO 95/1674: 'Account of raid carried out by the 17th HLI on 22/23 April', 8th Division War Diary.
39   Often referred to as the "Live and let Live" policy.
40   Edmonds, *Military Operations 1916*, Vol. 1, p. 156.
41   Ernst Junger, *Storm of Steel* (London: Penguin Books, 2004), p. 195.
42   Edmonds, *Military Operations 1916*, Vol. 1, p, 156.
43   *Notes for Infantry Officers on Trench Warfare*, p. 8.
44   Stanley, *The History of The 89th Brigade 1914-1918*, p. 100.

Shot and Shell.

British General Headquarters,
Sunday, 10 p.m.

Last night we carried out a successful raid on the enemy trenches south west of Thiepval. Thirteen prisoners were taken and many casualties were caused by our men bombing enemy dug-outs. Our casualties were very slight.—Official Report, "Glasgow Herald," Monday, 24th April, 1916.

WE take this opportunity of extending to all the raiders our heartiest congratulations on their success. As our Colonel has said, they have enhanced the reputation of the Battalion, and earned the unstinted praise and admiration of all who were unfortunate enough to be outsiders in a scheme that must have been a soldier's highest realization of "fun." We were especially proud to know that not a single man was left in the doubtful care of the enemy in the opposite trench, that all returned safely to our own lines, and that the wounded 'heroes' are all progressing favourably and enjoying their spell in "Blighty." As a result of the raid six awards have been made to the Battalion—an achievement as rare as it is splendid. To each of the recipients we, as a Battalion, offer our warmest congratulations. We wish them the best of luck and may they long be spared to wear and enjoy the honours they have won.

* * * *

Military Cross. A. J. BEGG, Lieut.

Lieut. Begg received his early education at Glasgow Academy and proceeded to Fettes College, where he distinguished himself in athletics as the winner of the School Mile and Half-Mile, and played in the 1st XV. In the Officers' Training Corps he had attained the rank of Colour-Sergeant. He was School Prefect and head of his House. He was about to embark on a business career at the outbreak of the war.

* * * *

Military Cross. J. N. CARPENTER, Second Lieut.

Lieut. Carpenter was educated at Glasgow Academy, where he gained his cap, playing for the 1st XV., season 1912-13. During the same year he was the winner of the School Golf Championship. Previous to the outbreak of war he was serving his apprenticeship with Messrs. Yarrow & Co., Clydebank. He enlisted in the Battalion on its formation as a private, and was one of the 'originals' of No. 8 Platoon. On 26th May, 1915, he was gazetted Second Lieutenant in the Battalion and posted to C Company, where he is in command of No. 12 Platoon. He was the first Officer in the Battalion to take command of a Patrol.

17th Highland Light Infantry trench raid on the night of 22/23 April 1916 as reported by the battalion's newspaper. This article demonstrates how raiding could bolster a battalion's morale. (Royal Highland Fusiliers Museum)

steadfastness of the men the attack was dispersed", at the cost of two Liverpool men killed and eight wounded.[45] For the Germans, two dead and four wounded were left behind, one of which was an officer with the ribbon of the Iron Cross, who later died of his injuries. For gallant conduct and forethought, Captain Arthur de Bels Adam was awarded the Military Cross (MC); he was killed in action on 1 July.[46] While life in the sector was violent and dangerous for 30th Division, its perception was that "the French were on the other side of the river and were having a very quiet time."[47]

When 29th Division entered the line opposite Beaumont-Hamel at the beginning of April, it was described by the divisional historian as being a quiet sector. But "it was not the way of the 29th to leave well alone" and the division soon set about improving the trenches, sniping and patrolling.[48] A few days after taking over the line (night of 6 April) a heavy German bombardment of the front-line trenches held by 87th Brigade completely destroyed the wire east of the area known as Mary Redan. This was then followed up by a German raiding party estimated to be 60 to 100 strong which entered the British trenches, capturing some 14 prisoners.[49] By the end of the raid, 29th Division had suffered "6 officer casualties by wounds and about 100 men dead, wounded, or missing."[50]

This was a rude awakening for the division, so much so that the importance of taking measures to counter raids was insisted on at the divisional conference held on 16 April. At the same time, and a sure sign that 29th Division was not going to take this without retaliation, the conference directed every battalion to "work out a scheme for a raid."[51] The division was quick to respond with two raids planned for the night of 29 April. The north-west face of Hawthorn Redoubt was raided by the 2nd South Wales Borderers of 87th Brigade and the German trenches due east of Mary Redan by the 2nd Hampshire Regiment of 88th Brigade. The Borderers took casualties before even reaching the enemy wire; when they finally made it there, they were lashed by German artillery fire which killed the raid commander, Captain Byrne, and several of his men. At this point the remaining officer realised that all was lost and ordered the raiders to retire. Three of the dead were blown into the enemy wire and were not discovered until daylight. Captain Byrne was amongst them.[52] The price paid by the Borderers was 24 casualties, of which seven were fatal.[53] The Hampshire's

45 TNA WO 95/2330:18th King's Liverpool Regiment War Diary.
46 Ibid.
47 Stanley, *The History of The 89th Brigade*, p. 102.
48 S Gillon, *The Story of the 29th Division: A Record of Gallant Deeds* (London: Thomas Nelson & Son, 1925), p. 77.
49 TNA WO 95/2303: 29th Division, 87th Brigade Headquarters War Diary.
50 Gillon, *The Story of the 29th Division*, p. 78.
51 TNA WO 95/2280: '29th Division Conference No 7 held on 16 April 1916', 29 Division Headquarters, Branches and Services General Staff War Diary.
52 Captain Edmund James Widdrington Byrne has no known grave and is commemorated on the Thiepval Memorial to the Missing.
53 TNA WO95/2280: 'Headquarters VIII Corps', 30 April 1916, 29th Division War Diary.

raid, led by Lieutenants Saunders and Rigg, succeeded in cutting the wire with a 24-foot-long Bangalore Torpedo "but were then met by a determined defence from a party with bombs and machine gun fire from both flanks."[54] One man was killed and two wounded. These two small actions demonstrate just some of the difficulties and dangers of raiding.

In light of the setbacks suffered by the 29th Division it can be difficult to understand how raiding developed the "aggressive spirit." To provide a different reference point, it is worth looking in depth at a single inexperienced division before the battle of the Somme. The 34th Division was a typical Kitchener New Army Division, lacking both training and experience, when it deployed to the Western Front in early January 1916. Once in France, the division was put through some intensive training and courses before moving into the trenches. By early May 1916, the division had taken over the area of the Somme facing the village of La Boisselle, held by the *110th RIR*, an aggressive unit that had successfully raided the 1st Royal Irish Rifles the previous month. Despite its inexperience, 34th Division was relatively quick in establishing itself in the La Boisselle sector, fostering the "aggressive spirit" with active sniping and patrolling. Raids were planned towards the end of May.

For its first raid, the division planned to simultaneously raid two separate positions at La Boisselle; the 24th Northumberland Fusiliers forming the right raiding party and the 26th Northumberland Fusiliers the left.[55] Between the 20 and 22 May the regiments were out of the line in support where,

> The personnel of the party were struck off all other duty, and billeted together and treated just like a team in training for an important sporting event. Every effort was made to get them as fit as possible, and much trouble was taken to ensure that every man knew exactly what he was expected to do. The raid was practised repeatedly over a flagged course, representing the trenches to be attacked.[56]

To support the raid, an artillery plan was drawn up based on the assumption that the bombardment would commence at the designated zero hour and cease at zero plus 1 hour. "Meanwhile Officers and Non-Commissioned Officers of both parties visited the line several times to reconnoitre."[57] Although for an unexplained reason the raid was postponed, training and planning continued as did conferences to ensure cooperation between the artillery and infantry and "great pains were taken to preserve secrecy."[58] The meticulous detail invested in planning and coordinating the raid is reflected in the form of the orders produced for each battalion. The 24th Northumberland Fusiliers

---

54 Ibid.
55 Both 24th and 26th Northumberland Fusiliers were component units of 103rd Brigade.
56 J, Shakespeare, *The Thirty Fourth Division 1915-1919* (London: H. F. & G. Witherby, 1921), p. 81.
57 TNA WO95/2464: 'Narrative regarding previous preparations', 103rd Brigade War Diary.
58 Ibid.

raid orders detailed the composition of the raiding party, command structure, order of advance, method of occupying enemy trenches, retirement and signals. Appendices to the orders provide an interesting insight into the conduct of capturing prisoners:

> [T]hese can be persuaded by the bayonet men to return to our trenches ... In the event of the prisoner attempting to offer resistance, the persuasion should be carried further until if necessary he will be killed. On an enemy being killed the man killing him should if possible endeavour to snatch from the body any identification marks and also feel the pockets for books or papers and bring the same with him. Care must be taken to examine the pocket in the skirt of the tunic. Gas Masks are most urgently required and every effort must be made to secure one or more.[59]

The up close and personal nature of raiding is reflected in the additional kit also listed in the appendices, which detailed every bomber to carry a small hand axe; bomb carriers a "bomb waistcoat" filled with grenades and a small hand axe; and the leading bayonet men to carry electric torches on their rifles. As expected all forms of identification were to be left behind.

However, on 4 June the Germans seized the initiative when a party of between 200 to 300 men from the *110th RIR* entered the trenches held by 21st Northumberland Fusiliers of 102nd Brigade at 01:30 hrs. The raiders were "speedily ejected leaving 1 dead and 1 prisoner – both belonging to the 110th R.I.R."[60] The 21st Northumberland Fusiliers were left with five men killed and one officer and 26 men wounded.[61]

At 20.55 hrs that evening, the enemy commenced a heavy artillery bombardment and continuous machine gun fire on the line held by 21st Northumberland Fusiliers. This lasted for approximately 50 minutes and was followed by a simultaneous attack from two enemy raiding parties; one force of approximately 300 men in two waves and a separate bombing party of 50 men. The larger force was beaten back, but the bombing party entered the British trenches and were only driven out after a close-range fight that left 17 British soldiers missing. According to the brigade war diary, some of the men were believed to have been buried under debris created during the bombardment. The war diary for the 21st Northumberland Fusiliers states that the missing men were taken prisoner.[62] The next morning five German dead were seen lying in the British wire.[63] Despite this blow to the Fusiliers, the General Officer

---

59   TNA WO 95/2432: 'Appendix A to Raid Orders by Major J M Prior', 34th Division War Diary.
60   TNA WO 95/2459: 34th Division, 102nd Brigade Headquarters War Diary.
61   Ibid
62   Ibid.
63   TNA WO 95/2459: 102nd Brigade War Diary.

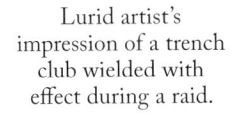

Lurid artist's impression of a trench club wielded with effect during a raid.

Commanding 34th Division was reported as being "of opinion that this Battalion behaved well on this occasion."⁶⁴

It is interesting to note the tactics adopted by the German raiding party. The decision to raid twice within 24 hours was highly unorthodox and likely designed to catch the Fusiliers by surprise. The fact seventeen Fusiliers were apparently taken prisoner would suggest that this approach had merit. Such tactics were not limited to German raids. On 19 August, two consecutive raids were carried out by units of 61st Division at Fauquissart in the sector opposite Red Lamp Salient. The first raid, launched by a single company of the 2/4th Oxfordshire and Buckinghamshire Light Infantry with artillery support, commenced at 22:40 hrs. The plan for the second raid, to be executed by one company of the 2/5th Gloucestershire Regiment, was to hold back until "the excitement following the first fight had died down and then advance against

64   TNA WO 94/2432: 34th Division War Diary.

178   At All Costs

the same objective without any artillery preparation, the guns resuming a box barrage as soon as the enemy's trenches had been entered."[65] The first raiding party reached the enemy parapet but was unable to enter his trenches and suffered ten casualties. In contrast, the Gloucesters found the enemy trenches quiet and managed to enter them, inflicting casualties with bayonet and bomb for the loss of one officer killed and eleven men wounded.[66] The double attack had worked, although not entirely as intended. According to the after action report "the advantage lay more with the second than with the first party."[67] Not only was the experience gained by the raiders seen as being beneficial to them for future operations, it was also seen as having improved the raiders' morale.

Returning to 34th Division, the preparations of the Northumberland Fusiliers finally came to fruition on the night of 5/6 June at 23:40hrs. The 24th Northumberland Fusilier's raiding party was led by Major J. Payne Gallwey whilst Captain H. Price commanded the party of the 26th Northumberland Fusiliers. The 26th Northumberland Fusiliers on the left, "did well entering the enemy's trenches and getting away without loss" but not before bombing some "13 dug-outs apparently full of Germans."[68] Captain Price was awarded the MC for conspicuous gallantry for his part in the action. However, the 24th Northumberland Fusiliers on the right, found that their thorough preparations were for nought as they "were unfortunate in not being able to enter the enemy's trenches, being prevented by artillery fire" from their own guns.[69] All they had to show for their efforts was one man killed, plus Major Payne Gallwey and four men wounded.

Later in the month, on the night of 25/26 June, the two fusilier battalions were ordered to mount another raid. This time the 24th Northumberland Fusiliers found the enemy manning their trenches in strength. After an exchange of bombs the Fusiliers withdrew. The 26th Northumberland Fusiliers actually entered the enemy trenches, but were immediately counter attacked by German bombers to the front and riflemen on both flanks. A fierce fire fight broke out before the Fusiliers were forced to withdraw. Amongst the casualties was Captain Price MC, killed in action.[70]

Just a few days later, on the night of the 29 June at approximately 23:00hrs, the 22nd Northumberland Fusiliers of 102nd Brigade attempted a raid on enemy trenches just

65 TNA WO 95/3063: 'Report on Enterprise carried out against the German lines on the night 19/20 August 1916', 184th Brigade War Diary.
66 Lieutenant John Jackson, 3rd Dorset Regiment, attached to 2/5th Bn. Gloucestershire Regiment, is buried in Laventie Military Cemetery.
67 TNA WO95/3063: 'Report on Enterprise carried out against the German lines on the night 19/20 August 1916', 184th Brigade War Diary.
68 TNA WO 95/2432: 'Summary of Information Appendix B (V)', 34th Division War Diary.
69 TNA WO 95/2432: 34th Division War Diary.
70 TNA WO 95/2464: 103rd Brigade War Diary. Captain Harold Price MC, 26th Battalion, Northumberland Fusiliers is buried in Albert Communal Cemetery.

south of La Boisselle. Unfortunately, the raiding party was prevented from forming up on time, having been held up by its own artillery falling short. The party eventually moved out 30 minutes later but were spotted at 23:35 hrs and targeted by artillery, trench mortars and rifles. For half an hour the raiders were pinned down in No Man's Land, seeking refuge in shell holes, before "the men returned in very good order under fire, and there were no casualties" despite the enemy being "particularly alert."[71] A simultaneous raid carried out by the 23rd Northumberland Fusiliers of 102nd Brigade was also unsuccessful, leaving Second Lieutenant Campbell and two men reported as missing, believed killed, in action.[72]

"Following the unsatisfactory results of the first raid, and in response to the keenness of officers and men concerned therein, a patrol consisting of 1 Officer and 5 Other Ranks" of the 22nd Northumberland Fusiliers was detailed to report on the German wire and the manning of the front line, and if possible capture a prisoner.[73] At 01:55 hrs the following morning, the patrol moved out from the safety of their trenches just 300 yards south of the point of departure for the earlier raiding party. Using the cover offered by shell craters, the patrol made its way across No Man's Land to the enemy's wire, but the party was spotted before it could enter the trenches. Heavy rifle fire was opened immediately and bombs were thrown from the German parapet into the middle of the patrol. The group suffered one man killed, three missing and two wounded. The only intelligence gathered was that the enemy's wire was in a poor condition and easily passable, but the enemy's front line positions were strongly held.[74]

After 1 July it appears the division ceased raiding for two months whilst it recovered from its battlefield casualties. The nature of raids carried out by the 34th Division demonstrate how one of the New Army Divisions' had not only pursued the "aggressive spirit" but persevered despite several failed raids. The actual benefits gained in terms of experience, leadership and the impact the continued pressure had on the morale of the *110th RIR* is difficult to gauge. At the time it was reasoned that even failed raids denied the enemy the advantage of a quiet sector and assisted in wearing them down as "the constant apprehension of attack robs the enemy of rest."[75]

Whatever the benefits, raids must be placed into context. Raiding was a single part of trench routine and the only real combat experience many would get before any large scale battle. The "aggressive spirit" of 34th Division on 1 July at La Boisselle was without question. On 5 July General Sir H. Rawlinson sent his congratulations to the Division, "Please convey to the 34th Division my heartiest congratulations on their

---

71 TNA WO 95/2432: 'Report by Officer Commanding, Right Raiding Party', 34th Division War Diary.
72 TNA WO 95/2432: 34th Division War Diary. Second Lieutenant Ian Stuart Campbell having no known grave is commemorated on the Thiepval Memorial to the Missing.
73 TNA WO 95/2432: 'Report of Patrol', 34th DivisionWar Diary.
74 Ibid
75 H.R. Sandilands, *The 23rd Division 1914-1919* (London: William Blackwood & Sons, 1925), p. 58.

success. Whilst regretting their heavy casualties, I desire to express my gratitude and admiration of the gallantry with which they carried out their difficult task."[76]

On 8 September the 34th Division received instructions for what it termed the "special period for raids and bombardments on the Corps Front."[77] The commander's intent was made clear on 12 September:

> With the object of assisting our operations elsewhere by inflicting as much damage as possible on the enemys [sic] personnel and defences increased activity is to be undertaken on the Second Army Front. This increased activity is to comprise:
>
> a) A series of artillery shoots in connection with which dummy raids are to be undertaken,
> b) A series of raids.[78]

From September 1916 to early February 1917, the divisional history then accounts for some twenty-two of these raids being carried out "of which thirteen may be classed as successes; that is we got into the Boche line and did more or less damage."[79]

Battle in Miniature

Considering the high number of raids carried out throughout 1916, it is easy to underestimate the complexity of the staff work required to plan the attack and the synchronisation of effects required such as the artillery, trench mortars and machine guns. According to the 33rd Division history, planning for a raid could include:

> the study of the ground; compilation and issue of maps, siting of mortar and machine guns; digging of mine galleries; cutting of wire; placing of barrage; getting up bombs, gas cylinders, medical stores, signalling apparatus; deductions by the intelligence branch of the General Staff from aeroplane photographs; and not least, the rehearsal on similar ground behind the line.[80]

A raid carried out by the 6th Somerset Light Infantry of 14th Division in the frontline trenches south of Agny, demonstrates the level of planning and the logistics effort employed in a single small scale raid. To the front of the Somerset Light Infantry,

---

76 Shakespeare, *The Thirty Fourth Division*, p. 54.
77 TNA WO 95/2433: 34th Division War Diary.
78 TNA WO95/2433:'Operation Order no 52', 34th Division War Diary.
79 Shakespeare, *The Thirty Fourth Division*, p. 80.
80 Graham S. Hutchinson, *The Thirty-Third Division in France and Flanders 1915-1919* (London: Waterlow & Sons,1921), p. 6.

the enemy had pushed forward a series of sap-heads, some of which were joined by a specially dug fire trench and others by the natural feature of a road, sunken in places, named on trench maps as the *Tranchee Jocaste*.[81] From here the enemy harassed the British with machine gun and trench mortar fire. To stop the enemy activity, the 6th Somerset Light Infantry was ordered to raid the saps. Complicating matters was the wire protecting the sap-heads, which was reported to be "of a thickness and density which would defy any attempts at cutting by hand."[82] As the sap-heads were believed to be of concrete construction, reinforced with steel loopholes and considered as "impregnable by ordinary means of approach," it was decided a month prior to the raid to commence tunnelling from the British into the German lines.[83] With the aid of aerial photography, the distance of the tunnel was estimated and "certain miners of the battalion were selected for the work and were struck off trench duty until the work was completed."[84] The tunnel was dug approximately five feet below No Man's Land, three feet wide, four feet high and supported with timber props.

The task set for the 6th Somerset Light Infantry for the night of 3 June was to destroy the sap-heads and machine guns in the enemy lines, to investigate and destroy any mine shafts, and to capture and kill Germans. The raiding party, led by Captain G. Manson, consisted of Lieutenants Denton and Rogers and 42 ORs plus Second Lieutenant Mowbray and three Royal Engineers.[85] The Operation Orders for the raid are concise and practical, identifying how the raiding party was to be organised, their duties, the equipment and precautions to be taken, which included "chewing gum for men with coughs."[86]

On 2 June, the tunnellers broke through to the surface only to discover "iron knife rests above and iron screw pegs 2 yds beyond", leaving them about three yards short of their objective. After another day's work, on the 3 June the tunnellers broke through into the German fire trench. "The trench was 4 ft. deep and 3 ft. wide with a small fire step. It had been dug many months ago and had slightly perished in the winter frosts."[87] A quick reconnaissance of the area identified further wire defences and "it was realised that the unexpected discovery of a heavy wired trench and bank added immensely to the difficulties of a successful attack."[88] Postponing the attack was considered, but quickly discounted due to the risk of the tunnel exit being discovered,

81   TNA WO95/1865: 'Report on an attempted minor enterprise carried out by the 6th Somerset Light Infantry', 14th Division Headquarters, Branches and Services General Staff War Diary.
82   Ibid.
83   Ibid.
84   Ibid.
85   TNA WO95/1865: 'Operation Orders', 14th Division War Diary.
86   Ibid. It is worthy of note that SS107 suggested that "men with coughs and colds should be eliminated from raiding party." See 'Miscellaneous Points', p. 7.
87   TNA WO95/1865: 'Report on an attempted minor enterprise carried out by the 6th Somerset Light Infantry', 14th Division War Diary.
88   Ibid

the negative effect on other raids being conducted that night, and the understanding "that the morale of the attacking force is always affected by a postponement."[89]

At 21:30 hrs, Lieutenant Rogers and two ORs went forward to cut the wire and by 23:00 hrs, "the raiding party, Artillery, Trench Mortar batteries, Lewis and Machine Guns, telephonists, Medical, were in position and in perfect order. No hitch occurred anywhere."[90] After two hours of wire cutting, movement was suddenly heard in a nearby trench. This was followed by Very lights being thrown close to the raiders and the Germans firing several rifle rounds into the darkness – a clear indication that the enemy was now alert. Rogers ordered the party to return to the tunnel, re-joining the wire as they withdrew. At the tunnel entrance Rogers discussed the situation with Manson: with the element of surprise lost, they decided to abandon the raid. As the raiders withdrew down the tunnel they covered the entrance and sealed it as best as possible with sand bags and barbed wire.

Although the raid did not achieve any of the set objectives, it was not considered a failure as much had been learnt about the enemy positions. The fact that it was possible to reach the enemy's lines by silent tunnelling and the value of aerial photography in estimating tunnel distance was found to be of great use. Whilst providing the raiders with a silent route into the enemy lines, it was a time consuming and labour-intensive task and required complex planning, which probably explains why this method of overcoming the enemy defences was rarely used.

A raid carried out by the 2nd Royal Welsh Fusiliers on the night of 5/6 July in the Givenchy sector, targeting an area known as "the Warren", gives an insight into planning on a much larger scale. According to Captain Robert Graves this "was a retaliatory raid" carried out in revenge for a mine blown at Red Dragon Crater.[91] Although Graves played no part in the raid itself, only arriving at the battalion on the 6 July, he was to comment on the brutally archaic nature of raiding:

> I noted that for the first time since the eighteenth century the regiment had reverted to the pike: instead of rifle and bayonet, some of the raiders had used butchers' knives secured with medical plaster to the ends of broomsticks. This pike, a lighter weapon than rifle and bayonet, was a useful addition to bombs and revolvers.[92]

Some of the weapons employed may have been crude but the raid itself was complex. It included a deception plan of blowing a mine, a diversionary bombing attack by the 1/5th Scottish Rifles and a feint smoke and gas attack south of the La Bassée Canal

---

89   Ibid.
90   Ibid.
91   Robert Graves, *Goodbye to All That* (London: Penguin Books, 2000), p. 170.
92   Ibid., p. 171.

by 20th Royal Fusiliers with the 1st Scottish Rifles in support.[93] The location of the raid, according to Dunn, was inspired by the capture of a map taken from a German corpse "because every dug-out and feature there is marked."[94]

At 22:30 hrs on 5 July, the artillery and trench mortar bombardment commenced, providing cover for two companies of the Royal Welsh led by Captains Higginson and Moody to get into their jumping off positions. One of the companies had to move across the open front, "this, which appeared the most difficult part of the whole enterprise, was easily carried out."[95]

At 23:00 hrs the smoke and gas were released south of the La Bassée Canal and just five minutes later three mines were blown by the 251st Tunnelling Company, RE. The smoke and gas deception worked as planned, drawing enemy fire to the trenches north and south of the canal. A large mine was then blown at 23:20 hrs north of the Red Dragon Crater, swiftly followed by a further artillery barrage. Startled by this new attack, the Germans redirected their artillery once more. Whilst this was going on the 2nd Royal Welsh Fusiliers dashed forward and were quickly into the enemy trenches where they "soon collected prisoners."[96] Men from 251st Tunnelling Company RE accompanied the Royal Welsh to destroy the enemy mines believed to be there, and men from 222nd Company RE dealt with the trenches, dug outs and a mine shaft in the enemy support line. When the shafts were found, "The German miners put up a stout resistance in the mines, using bombs, and would not surrender, with the result that the mine shafts had to be blown with the miners in them."[97] The Royal Welsh Fusiliers were in the enemy lines for over two hours prior to withdrawal.

The battalion war diary states the objective of the raid was more than fulfilled as some "39 prisoners were captured, 4 dead brought in, 14 identity discs taken off others, and many others known to have been killed and wounded."[98] A great deal of equipment was also taken and a large minenwerfer was destroyed. The price for this was one officer and 10 ORs killed, one officer and 47 ORs wounded and one OR missing.[99] According to Dunn, "It was a Mark 1 success, and went absolutely without a hitch. Our fellows fought like demons."[100] Amongst many messages conveying congratulations to the battalion was a signal received from GHQ on the 5 July, "please convey to 2nd Bn RW Fus the Commander in Chief's congratulations on their very successful raid last night. Raids of this sort are of great material assistance to the main

93 TNA WO 95/2405: 'App AJ dated 6 July', 33rd Division War Diary.
94 Dunn, *The War the Infantry Knew*, p. 218.
95 TNA WO 95/2405: 'App AJ dated 6 July', 33rd Division War Diary.
96 Ibid.
97 Ibid.
98 TNA WO 95/2423: 2nd Royal Welsh Fusiliers War Diary.
99 Ibid.
100 Dunn, *The War the Infantry Knew*, p. 220.

operations."[101] The story of this successful enterprise spread throughout the BEF and was even viewed by the Australian Imperial Force (AIF), then relatively new to the Western Front, as an exemplar of a trench raid. On 9 July the Australians produced a set of notes directing future operations to harass the enemy to their front and assist operations to their south. In this document they set out their immediate policy on raiding, "raids must therefore, take place immediately, and must be on a larger scale than has hitherto been attempted."[102] The AIF referenced the raid carried out by 2nd Royal Welsh Fusiliers:

> The very successful raid the other day by the Royal Welsh Fusiliers was done by 500 men, and was covered by a bombardment and by smoke, both of which were well distributed each side of the point raided. The point was a salient, and while fire was directed on a good length of enemy trench each side of the Salient, the men crept up and laid down close to the enemy's wire opposite the immediate flanks of the salient. When the time for the assault came, a barrage was made immediately behind the salient with the result that practically all Germans in the salient were accounted for. Their success was undoubtedly due to the wide front of smoke and fire, and the planning of the barrage.[103]

Naturally immediate awards for gallantry followed the raid in the form of two MCs, two Distinguished Conduct Medals (DCMs) and two Military Medals (MM) subsequently awarded.[104] The 19th Brigade commander put the success down "to the dash of the 2nd Royal Welsh Fusiliers, to the splendid handling of the artillery, the very full detailed arrangements made before hand, and the splendid way in which each party carried out their respective duties."[105]

A Peculiar Scope to the Gallantry

The nature of raiding gave officers and men alike the opportunity to participate in short lived but intense combat. It therefore provided a natural environment for

---

101 TNA WO 95/2423: 33rd Division, 19th Brigade and 2nd Royal Welsh Fusiliers war diaries.
102 AWM 3DRL/2316 Papers of General Sir John Monash, 'Notes As Regards Future And Present Operations dated 9 July 1916'<https://www.awm.gov.au/collection/RCDIG0000572/> (Accessed January 2016).
103 Ibid.
104 MCs were awarded to Second Lieutenant E Coster and Company Sergeant Major W. Fox. DCMs awarded to Sergeant D. Roberts-Morgan and Private W. Buckley. MMs to Sergeant H. Marke and Private E. Moreton.
105 TNA WO 95/2405: 'App AJ dated 6 July', 33rd Division, Headquarters, Branches and Services General Staff War Diary.

gallantry amongst all ranks. Consequently, countless courageous acts were performed during the many raids, "in fact a raid that was well pressed home, and brought back prisoners and identifications, was a triumph of care in organisation and great gallantry in execution."[106] A raid carried out by the 15th Royal Welsh Fusiliers as part of the 38th Division on the night of 7/8 May in the Laventie sector accounted for eight immediate awards: one Distinguished Service Order (DSO), three DCMs and four MMs.[107] This is all the more remarkable when one considers that the raiding party was only four officers and 51 men strong. The war diary describes the opening action:

> The order to attack was given. 2/Lt H. Taggart sprung forward and shot the sentry dead, and 2/Lt N. O. Jones emptied his revolver into the bay. Another sentry was bludgeoned. This was followed by a shower of bombs into three bays at point of entry, putting the 20 men, estimated to be in them, out of action.[108]

The German garrison, believed to be miners, were found to be mostly unarmed. When the raiders came to withdraw, "2/Lt N.O. Jones was seen to fall as he stood on the enemy parapet directing the retirement of his party."[109] At the same time, Temporary Captain Goronwy Owen, the raid commander, attempted to carry the injured Second Lieutenant Taggart back but was hit and slightly wounded himself. For his part, Owen was to be awarded the DSO:

> For conspicuous gallantry and determination in organising and leading a successful raid on the enemy's trenches. Many of the enemy were accounted for, and Captain Owen covered the withdrawal with great skill under heavy fire. Although slightly wounded, he gave assistance to wounded men.[110]

At the end of the raid two men were reported killed, one was missing and eight wounded. Both second lieutenants were reported missing, believed wounded.[111]

Other raids received even greater rewards for gallantry. Britain's highest award for bravery in the face of the enemy, the Victoria Cross (VC), was awarded in 1916 for at least three trench raids; once to a private soldier and twice to officers. Private Hutchinson of 2/5th Lancashire Fusiliers, part of the 55th Division, was awarded his VC for gallantry during a raid on the night of 28 June which was planned and

---

106 Shakespeare, *The Thirty Fourth Division*, p. 83.
107 DSO awarded to Captain Goronwy Owen; DCMs to Cpl D.W. Bloor, Pte P.F. Witten and Pte J. Heesom. MMs to Sgt G.P. Jones, Cpl F.G Rosser, Pte F. Langdon and Pte I. Downes.
108 TNA WO 95/2556: 'Narrative Of The Raid', 15th Royal Welsh Fusiliers War Diary.
109 TNA WO 95/2556: 'Notes On The Raid', 15th Royal Welsh Fusiliers War Diary.
110 *Supplement to the London Gazette*, 31 May 1916, p. 5405.
111 Second Lieutenants Herbert Taggart aged 22 and Noel Osborne Jones aged 21 are commemorated on the Loos Memorial to the Missing.

executed as part of a wider Third Army operation. 55th Division's part in this was to plan and execute six daylight raids in the Achicourt sector, "in unaccustomed and very difficult circumstances, and in the face of a very determined enemy."[112] The Division's artillery was to cut 20-yard-wide safe lanes in the enemy wire and discharge smoke and a dense volume of gas as follows:

> One half of 8 cylinders per bay to be discharged simultaneously. This to be followed by one cylinder per bay every ten minutes for one hour and forty minutes, then the remaining half of the 8 cylinders to be let off simultaneously. This to be followed by discharging the remaining two cylinders at intervals of ten minutes.[113]

Fifteen minutes after the last of the gas was released, the raiding parties began their advance. Their objectives were to determine the effect of the gas, take prisoners, bomb dug-outs and capture machine guns, but to go no further than the enemy support line. The 2/5th Lancashire Fusiliers raiding group was sub-divided into right, centre and left parties who advanced from their trenches in quick time and entered the enemy lines, but not before taking considerable casualties. The right party, upon entering the enemy's trenches, bombed along an enemy fire trench and threw grenades into two dug-outs before progress was halted by a trench barricade. German bombers deployed to counter-attack and the Fusiliers fell back. Five men from the centre party managed to get into the enemy communication trenches, bombing dug-outs as they moved forward. They were also attacked by enemy bombers and were ordered to retire.

The left party experienced some difficulty entering the enemy trenches with their ladders, so instead they jumped into the position. Hutchinson then led the way "and did some good work with the bayonet."[114] Whilst in the enemy trenches the party was also held up by a barricade but managed to climb over it and bomb the dug-outs that lay beyond. Many of the enemy were shot down as they emerged from these dug outs. When the raiders came to withdraw, Hutchinson "held the enemy at bay until the last of his party got out."[115] The raiders were unfortunately unable to bring back any prisoners or material except for a cap obtained by Hutchinson. For his actions that night he was awarded the VC. The *London Gazette* citation read as follows:

> During an attack on the enemy's position this soldier was the leading man, and, entering their trench, shot two sentries and cleared two of the traverses. After our object had been gained and retirement ordered, Private Hutchinson, on his

---

112 TNA WO 95/2923: 'Special Order of the Day', 2/5th Lancashire Fusiliers War Diary.
113 TNA WO 95/2899: 'Proposals for Attack', 55th Division War Diary.
114 TNA WO 95/2920: 'Report on Operations Carried out by Raiding Parties of 1/4th L.N. Lancs Regt and 2/5th Lancs Fusiliers', 164th Brigade War Diary.
115 Ibid.

own initiative, undertook the dangerous task of covering the retirement, and he did this with such gallantry and determination that the wounded were removed into safety. During all this time this gallant soldier was exposed to fierce fire from machine-guns and rifles at close quarters.[116]

The 55th Division raids provided enough evidence to suggest no Germans had expired from gas except for a few towards the top extremity of Blaireville Wood. According to the raid summary, the Germans were well prepared and the slow deployment of the gas gave them ample time to don gas helmets. Despite their limited success, the raids cost 55th Division 18 killed, 87 wounded and 31 missing.[117] Following the raid, the devotion to duty and gallantry shown by all ranks was commented upon by Major General H.S. Jeudwine, commanding 55th Division, who was "proud to be able to congratulate the West Lancashire Division on the discipline and soldierly spirit exhibited."[118] It was also made clear that the divisional commander felt the division would not forget the losses when the opportunity came to avenge them.

The first VC awarded to a raiding officer was that of Second Lieutenant Edward Felix Baxter. Baxter had joined the 1/8th King's Liverpool Regiment on 14 January 1916, with two fellow second lieutenants as reinforcements, whilst the regiment was conducting training at Airaines.[119] Baxter's first and only raid was planned for the night of 17/18 April 1916, with Captain J.H. Mahon, Second Lieutenant P.O. Limrich and 43 ORs allegedly known as the "Forty Thieves."[120] A wire cutting party under Baxter's command went out to breach enemy wire but had to return as dawn broke at 03:30 hours on the 17 April. Although they had cut through some 13 rows, there was still more wire to cut and enemy activity was audible in nearby trenches. That evening a patrol identified the wire had not been repaired by the enemy and so, just after midnight, Baxter took another patrol out to finish the job.[121] It was during the wire cutting that Baxter "held a bomb in his hand with the pin withdrawn ready to throw. On one occasion the bomb slipped and fell to the ground, but he instantly picked it up, unscrewed the base plug, and took out the detonator, which he smothered in the ground, thereby preventing the alarm being given, and undoubtedly saving many casualties."[122]

---

116 *Supplement to the London Gazette*, 9 September 1916, p. 8870.
117 TNA WO 95/2899: '55th Div No C/37/7 (G)', 55th Division War Diary.
118 TNA WO 95/2920: 'Special Order of the Day', 164th War Diary.
119 TNA WO95/2923: 55th Division, 164th Infantry Brigade, 8th King's (Liverpool Regiment) War Diary.
120 Imperial War Museum, Collections <http://www.iwm.org.uk/collections/item/object/30011287> (Accessed September 2016).
121 TNA WO95/2923: 8th King's (Liverpool Regiment) War Diary.
122 *Supplement to the London Gazette*, 26 September 1916, p. 9417.

By 02:30 hours on 18 April, the wire was cut and the way for the raiders lay open. Leading the left party, Baxter was the "first man into the trench, shooting the sentry with his revolver. He then assisted to bomb dugouts, and finally climbed out of the trench and assisted the last man over the parapet."[123] His party accounted for four of the enemy dead and two of the dug outs bombed. The right party killed three enemy and bombed one dug out, "cries and groans were heard from all the dug outs" but no prisoners taken.[124] When the raiding parties returned, Baxter was missing and could not be found despite another patrol being sent out to look for him; Baxter was reported as missing and appears to have been the only casualty of the raid. Baxter's fate was revealed in a 15 May 1916 report from the Imperial German government which stated he had fallen north of Blairville. It was not until February 1920 that Mrs Baxter was informed that her husband had perished on 18 April 1916 and the Germans had buried him in the parish cemetery at Boiry St Rictrude churchyard. Baxter's personal effects of a cigarette case, silver match box, two knives and two francs were returned in August 1920 by the German government;[125] his body was subsequently relocated to Fillievres British Cemetery in 1924. In addition to Baxter's VC, a DCM and eight MMs were awarded.[126] Second Lieutenant P.O. Limrick and Temporary Captain J.H. Mahon, despite being recommended for awards following the raid never actually received any recognition. Limrick was killed and Mahon mortally wounded at Delville Wood on 12 September 1916.[127]

Second Lieutenant E.F. Baxter VC.

Just a few days prior to the raid for which Hutchinson was awarded the VC, Lieutenant Arthur Hugh Batten-Pooll would be recognised for his gallantry while in command of a raiding party of the 2nd Royal Munster Fusiliers. The action took place in the Colonne sector on 25 June. The objectives set for the raid were much the

123 Ibid.
124 TNA WO 95/2920: 'Operation Carried Out By 1/8th (Irish) Bn', 164th Brigade War Diary.
125 TNA WO 374/4830: Lieutenant E.F. Baxter file.
126 DCM awarded to Sgt W. McClelland. MMs awarded to; Sgt A.J. Burke, Cpls, T. Mahon and F. Brophy, Ptes W.F. Crowe, W.H. Davies, P.W Fussell, J. McEvoy and T Munnerly,
127 Captain J.H. Mahon is buried in La Neuville British Cemetery. Second Lieutenant P.O. Limrick is interred at Delville Wood Cemetery.

Well-known photograph of 1/8th King's Liverpool Regiment raiders following the enterprise launched on the night of 17/18 April 1916. Second Lieutenant E.F. Baxter was the sole fatality.

same as any other; seize prisoners, make identifications, capture equipment, inflict casualties and carry out a reconnaissance of two enemy saps. The main contingent, comprised of eight officers and 152 ORs, was divided into two parts, the northern and southern parties; each of which was allocated an enemy sap to enter. Furthermore, each party was then further organised into a left, right and parapet party.

When the southern raiding party advanced, they found the wire that had been previously cut by the artillery had been hastily replaced. Blocked by the obstacle, they were struck by heavy rifle and rifle grenade fire, suffering several casualties as a result. Despite this, the right party managed to enter the sap and whilst bombing their way along the trenches, passing fire bays, they were counter-attacked by Germans from the parados; "the enemy appeared to be quite indifferent as to his own men holding the front."[128] The right party continued fighting in the trenches until the officer in charge, Second Lieutenant Smith was killed.[129] With casualties mounting and bombs running short, the party began to withdraw, bringing back their dead and wounded, closely pressed by the enemy. The raiders were believed to have accounted for some 30 Germans in combat; four Germans surrendered, but one of the prisoners "attempted

---

128 TNA WO 95/1279: 'Appendix 14', 2nd Royal Munster Fusiliers War Diary.
129 Second Lieutenant William Stanley Smith is interred in Loos British Cemetery.

to push his escort down the entrance of a dug-out en route and was immediately clubbed."[130] The left party, despite heavy casualties from rifle and rifle grenade fire, managed to reach their positions bombing dug-outs on their way.

When the northern raiders advanced, they found the German sap filled with wire and came under heavy fire. Nevertheless, they pushed ahead and entered the enemy trenches. The right party, while bombing their way along the enemy trenches, lost their raid commander, Second Lieutenant Clarke and the leading NCO, both believed to have been killed.[131] "This party, although it lost its leader and senior N.C.O. acquitted itself well."[132] Due to the unexpectedly stiff enemy resistance, the supply of bombs soon ran out and the raiders were forced to withdraw. During the raid the party managed to take some prisoners. However, a grisly incident occurred as one of the Germans was being forced over the parapet by a British officer. One of the raiders, "who seeing this officer was, as he thought, in difficulties, badly battered the prisoner's brains out with a bludgeon."[133] Such was the confusion of war. Another prisoner escaped but was chased and bayoneted by Private Rock, who himself was later killed.[134]

In the left party, Lieutenant Arthur Hugh Batten-Pooll entered the German trenches and was almost immediately wounded by an enemy grenade which maimed his right hand. Despite this painful injury and with some of his raiders urging him to retire, he decided to press on. Leading his party forward, he forced back an enemy bombing post and despatched many of the enemy. Second Lieutenant Jordeson, in command of the "Parapet Party", realised casualties in the raiding party were heavy and discussed withdrawing with Batten-Pooll. Ten minutes later when the time came to fall back, Batten-Pooll who had gone to the assistance of a wounded man, received a further two wounds. Continuing to refuse any assistance he made his way unaided to within 100 yards of the Fusiliers lines where he fainted and had to be carried back.

When the raid was over, the estimated number of Germans killed was 50, but this figure did not include those believed to have been killed by bombs thrown into dug-outs. Royal Munster Fusilier losses were high, in the main caused by grenade blasts, "which testifies to the sternness and closeness of the fighting."[135] As for the prisoners, none were brought back due to the raiders taking heavy casualties, "consequently the men were in no temper to take prisoners, moreover, the evacuation of our own wounded practically occupied the attention of all ranks."[136] Interestingly, after the raid the regiment reported on the usefulness of the bludgeons which "were used with effect. The Irish soldier is fond of this form of weapon. They are perhaps too deadly

---

130 Ibid.
131 Second Lieutenant W.S. Clarke is commemorated on the Arras Memorial to the Missing.
132 TNA WO 95/1279: 'Appendix 14', 2nd Royal Munster Fusiliers War Diary.
133 Ibid.
134 Pte P. Rock is buried in Loos British Cemetery.
135 TNA WO 95/1279: 'Appendix 14', 2nd Royal Munster Fusiliers War Diary.
136 Ibid.

if prisoners are desired. Many of the enemy had their heads smashed to pieces."[137] Batten-Pooll was awarded the VC for his gallantry during the raid. No doubt a man of action, he won the MC and was Mentioned in Despatches in 1917, before being captured near Passchendaele on 10 November of the same year. He remained a prisoner until the Armistice.

Gallantry awards were also earned whilst raiders withdrew from the enemy lines, as made clear by the 8th Division, "casualties occur mostly whilst the raiding party is returning or immediately after its return to our trenches."[138] As the withdrawal was a period of intense retaliation from the enemy, it naturally led to further acts of bravery bringing in and tending to the wounded. Probably the most well-known act of this nature was that of Second Lieutenant Siegfried Sassoon who was awarded the MC for bringing in the wounded under fire following a raid by the 1st Royal Welsh Fusiliers on Kiel Trench near Bois Francais on the Somme during May 1916. A VC would also be awarded to Private Arthur Procter, a stretcher bearer of the 1/5th King's Liverpool Regiment of 55th Division for tending the wounded whilst in the trenches in the Wailly sector. Proctor's act of bravery took place following a raid carried out by the 1/5th King's Liverpool Regiment on 4 June when "unfortunately a certain amount of artillery and trench mortar fire fell short and caused many casualties among the raiding party" necessitating the abandonment of the raid before it reached the enemy wire. Ten men were killed, 39 wounded and 8 were reported as missing.[139] Two missing men observed in no man's land the following day, motivated Proctor to risk life and limb when:

Private A.H. Procter VC.

> [A]n act of extra ordinary daring was performed by 3156 Rfn. PROCTOR, A, a stretcher bearer. This man crawled out of our trench in broad daylight, made his way to where the two wounded men were laying and tended them. He also lent his cardigan jacket to one who was cold. He crawled back across the 75 yards of

---

137 Ibid.
138 TNA WO95/1674: 'Lessons Drawn from the Various Minor Operations', 8th Division War Diary.
139 TNA WO 95/2926: 5th King's (Liverpool Regiment) War Diary.

open ground which separated him from our trench, and reached our lines unhurt in spite of hostile rifle fire.[140]

Both men were subsequently brought in and survived. There were, of course, countless acts of bravery carried out during the many raids that went unnoticed or reported, and many like Mahon and Limrick that did receive recommendations were never recognised for their efforts.

Conclusion

The raids of 1916 were shaped by the Battle of the Somme and the need to extend the "wearing out" battle along the British held front. Consequently, for the first time the direction and organisation of raids was coordinated at the higher echelons of command with a coherent operational focus. Raiding was now carried out on a much larger scale with greater cooperation between the artillery, trench mortars, machine guns and Royal Engineers. Vital for battle planning and understanding the bigger picture, raiding was used to gather intelligence, to deny the enemy a quiet sector and generally wear them down.

Haig also faced the dilemma in 1916 of how to keep his relatively inactive army occupied in the trenches. Discipline had to be maintained and lethargy prevented. When the time came the army would be expected to leave the safety of the trenches and engage the enemy, so maintaining the "will to fight" amongst the troops was key. As articulated by the Guards Division historian, raiding provided a means to "keep up the morale of the troops and be a good antidote to the inevitable slackness resulting from life in the trenches."[141] For both junior officer and man alike, at unit level, raiding provided some combat experience and for the various levels of command, the ability to plan and execute small scale operations. This was important combat experience that would not have been gained had the BEF sat idle in the trenches, and it was especially valuable for Haig's inexperienced New Army battalions.

Whether a raid was a success or not, immediate localised repercussions naturally followed in the form of artillery bombardments to suppress the attack, kill the raiders and generally harass the troops holding the trenches from where the raiders came. There were also clear examples of the British raiding in retaliation and the command structure clearly supported this attitude as it helped cultivate the "aggressive spirit." It therefore appears one inherent outcome of raiding is that it forced an end to the "live and let live" system and prevented it reoccurring.

---

140 Ibid.
141 C. Headlam, *History of the Guards Division in the Great War, 1915-1918*, Vol. 1 (London: John Murray, 1924), p. 108

As raiding had an operational focus, raids were ordered and directed at the higher echelons of command. This meant the decision to enter into the "aggressive spirit" was forced upon both experienced and inexperienced units who had no option but to follow orders. Raiding was no longer a specialism practised by the more aggressive formations but part of trench routine for all units holding the line. This prevented any form of non-aggression being able to flourish in units and especially in those of the inexperienced New Armies. Beyond fostering aggression, raiding played a part in gathering vital intelligence, be that unit identification, capturing prisoners for interrogation or taking vital equipment for analysis. This intelligence alongside raid after action reports helped contribute to the wider "learning process."

Raiding also had a role in "wearing out" the enemy. As demonstrated, wearing down the enemy was not simply about inflicting losses, but psychologically weakening them by denying them a quiet and safe sector. It also demonstrated to the French that the BEF was playing its part as a viable partner in coalition warfare. Trench raiding was of course just one of the many activities designed to "dominate" the enemy: sniping, patrolling and local bombardments of the enemy's lines all played a part. However, none of these methods had the same physiological impact upon the enemy as a successful trench raid.

Whilst the relative value of the "aggressive spirit" has prompted much debate, it is difficult to comprehend what benefits a passive policy would have had on the BEF and it would certainly have contributed to an erosion of discipline, a diminution of combat experience, and a decline in morale and the "will to fight." It is even harder to comprehend how such a policy could have benefited the inexperienced divisions Haig had under his command who were expected to take part in major offensive operations.

Nevertheless, the military value of raiding to the BEF remains difficult to quantify. It does appear that Haig saw raiding as a means of measuring the combat effectiveness of his armies, Haig was also to comment that the final victory in 1918 "would not have taken place, but for that period of ceaseless attrition which used up the reserves of the German Armies",[142] and raiding clearly played a part in the war of attrition. The raid debate is likely to continue as historians seek to assess its value. Whatever the conclusion of this debate, the true value of raiding can only be determined by the commander on the ground at the time, and Haig clearly saw raiding as adding value to the larger situation on the Western Front in 1916. It should, therefore, not be seen in isolation, but instead as part of wider British efforts to wear down and ultimately defeat the German army.

142 Boraston, *Sir Douglas Haig's Despatches*, p. 327

8

"I shall hope to try an officer and at least one corporal for cowardice": The German Trench Raid at La Boisselle, 11 April 1916 and the British Response

Michael LoCicero

> *By hook or by crook this peril too shall be something that we remember.*[1]

Four days after the opening of the Somme offensive on 1 July 1916, a rich cache of documents was discovered within the regimental headquarters of *Badisches Reserve Infanterie Regiment Nr. 110* (*RIR 110*). Elements of 19th (Western) Division stumbled upon this intelligence treasure trove whilst engaged in desperate combat to secure the fortress village of La Boisselle.[2] A corps intelligence summary observed: "A very large amount of documents of all kinds were collected. These included a considerable number of plans & sketches of dugouts & of portions of the trench system opposite this front. Three very excellent large scale trench maps giving every detail of the dispositions of hostile machine guns … were also obtained. Several operations orders were captured …"[3] Amongst the latter were the orders and after-action reports for a highly

---

1   Homer, *The Odyssey* (146-150).
2   La Boisselle was finally cleared of the enemy on 4 July 1916.
3   TNA WO 157/319: Intelligence Summary, 5 July 1916, III Corps Intelligence file. Documents concerning the German Arendt – codenamed "Moritz" – listening device were also found in another La Boisselle dugout at this time. No doubt the translated imminent attack message, transmitted *enclair* in the hours before the opening of the great offensive by a 34th Division staff officer, was discovered there. Official historian Brigadier-General Sir James Edmonds later observed: "Various precautions and restrictions in the use of the telephone were instituted, but were difficult to enforce, and, as the enemy could undoubtedly overhear messages sent through a badly insulated line laid on the earth, the menace of his obtaining information in this manner created a most dangerous situation, although codenames and position calls for units had been introduced." Officers dispatched from III Corps headquarters to retrieve the "German Overhearing Apparatus" from one of the captured dugouts failed to obtain a sample machine. See Sir J.E. Edmonds, *Military*

successful trench raid executed by *RIR 110* on the evening of 11 April 1916. Although of little immediate intelligence value, the enemy raid documents were translated and reproduced as an Army Stationery Office pamphlet concerning German raiding organisation and practice at that time.[4] Subsequent publication followed two years afterwards in the *Royal United Services Institution Journal*.[5] The revelations therein offered insight into an embarrassing episode that aroused the ire of a high command who demanded a court of enquiry and, reliant on its determinations, courts martial proceedings against those deemed to have been in dereliction of duty if not outright cowardice. The unfortunate Irish battalion involved, viewed by some as the worst in the division, appears to have been judged lacking in defensive resolve partially, if not entirely, based on prevailing command attitudes towards Irish soldiers serving in the British Army. However, the Germans, having inflicted casualties before making off with prisoners and captured equipment with little loss, were grudgingly complimentary about encountered enemy resistance.

Set against the backdrop of preparations for the Somme and an increase in raiding enterprises, the 11 April trench raid has been chronicled in a number of recent publications that focus on British or German perspectives only.[6] The primary aim of this chapter is to examine the related military policy of both sides, course of events and resultant consequences in an analytical narrative that places this relatively minor event, one of 33 German raids on the British front between 19 December 1915 and 30 May 1916, in the context of the BEF's learning process.[7]

Operations France and Belgium 1916 Vol. I (London: Macmillan, 1932), p. 71. For the effectiveness of the Moritz apparatus, see Ralph J. Whitehead, *The Other Side of the Wire Volume I: With the XIV Reserve Corps on the Somme, September 1914-June 1916* (Solihull: Helion & Company, 2010), pp. 350-51 and Peter Barton, 'Tolerating Mystery and Challenging History', *Stand To! The Journal of the Western Front Association*, No. 109 (2017), pp. 15-16.

4   General Staff, *SS 462: Translation of a German Document: Raid on the British Trenches near La Boisselle (11 April 1916)* (1916).

5   *Royal United Services Institution Journal* (*RUSI*), Vol. 63, Issue 450, 1918. A facsimile reprint of the *RUSI* article in *Gunfire No. 4*, "An occasional journal produced by members of the Western Front Association, and issued from the York Educational Settlement" (n.d.), was consulted whilst researching this chapter.

6   See James W. Taylor, *The First Royal Irish Rifles in the Great War* (Dublin: Four Courts Press, 2002), pp. 65-73, Stephen Bull, *Stosstrupptaktik: German Assault Troops of the First World War* (Stroud: Spellmount, 2007), pp. 90-92, Whitehead, *The Other Side of the Wire Volume I*, pp. 401-07, Anthony Saunders, *Raiding on the Western Front* (Barnsley: Pen & Sword, 2012), pp. 44-55 and Anthony Leask, *Putty: From Tel-el-Kebir to Cambrai. The Life and Letters of Lieutenant General Sir William Pulteney* (Solihull: Helion & Company, 2015), pp. 376-85.

7   Twenty of 33 German raids were successful. The BEF conducted 63 raids during the same period, 47 of which were successful. See Edmonds, *Military Operations France and Belgium 1916 Vol. I*, p. 242.

196   At All Costs

Fourth Army Arrives

As part of the build-up for the forthcoming Anglo-French offensive, Fourth Army (GOC General Sir Henry Rawlinson) established its headquarters six miles northeast of Amiens at Querrieu Chateau on 24 February 1916.[8] One week later, this new formation took over responsibility for the right sector of the BEF line from General Sir Edmund Allenby's Third Army. Consisting, south to north, of XIII Corps, X Corps and VIII Corps, Fourth Army's front extended approximately 15 miles from Curlu on the Somme to Hébuterne.[9] The area north of the river consisted of open, rolling agricultural country interspersed with towns and hamlets, isolated farms, woods, spinneys and orchards; streams were scarce. British presence here dated back to Third Army's relief of French *Second Army* in summer 1915. With three of four corps already in situ, the next of Fourth Army's expected formations, Lieutenant-General Sir W. P. Pulteney's III Corps,[10] arrived on 24 March. Having travelled by rail from First Army front in French Flanders to north of Amiens by 30 March, its attached 8th (Regular) Division[11] (GOC Major-General H. Hudson)[12] was under orders for the frontline in early April.[13] The 19th Division and 34th Division, also assigned to III Corps, were expected to join their parent formation in early May. Situated between the neighbouring XIII Corps and X Corps, 8th Division would, in its interim capacity as III Corps' only division, take responsibility for one of the

8   See Edmonds, *Military Operations France and Belgium 1916 Vol. I*, pp. 16-51, 246-70 and Robin Prior & Trevor Wilson, *Command on the Western Front: The Military Career of Sir Henry Rawlinson 1914-1918* (Oxford: Blackwell, 1992), pp. 137-70.
9   Major A.F. Becke, *Order of Battle: Part 4. The Army Council, GHQs, Armies and Corps 1914-1918* (London: HMSO, 1945), p. 102.
10 Lieutenant-General Sir William Pulteney Pulteney (1861-1941). Commissioned Oxford Militia 1878; transferred Scots Guards 1881; Egypt 1882; Uganda 1895-97; South Africa 1899-1902; GOC 16th Brigade 1908-09; GOC 6th Division 1910-14; GOC III Corps 1914. Note: Officers are described by the rank they held during spring 1916.
11 Raised from overseas Regular infantry garrisons (India, South Africa, Aden, Egypt and Malta), 8th Division assembled near Winchester in autumn 1914, after which it embarked from Southampton for the Western Front. Its subsequent battles/engagements were 1914: Neuve Chapelle (Moated Grange Attack) 18 December; 1915: Neuve Chapelle 10-12 March; Aubers Ridge 9 May; Bois Grenier 25 September. For a recent analysis of the division's combat performance and somewhat uneven application of lessons learned during this time, see Alun Miles Thomas, 'British 8th Infantry Division on the Western Front 1914-1918' (PhD Thesis. Birmingham: University of Birmingham, 2010).
12 Major-General Havelock Hudson (1862-1944). Commissioned Northamptonshire Regiment 1881; transferred Indian Staff Corps and 19th Lancers 1885; Northwest Frontier 1897; China 1900; Miranzai Expedition 1901; CO 19th Lancers February-July1910; GSO I Directorate of Staff Duties and Military Training August 1910; Commandant Sangor Cavalry School July-September 1912; BGGS Northern Army October 1912; BGGS Indian Corps 1914-15; GOC 8th Division August 1915.
13 Lieutenant-Colonel J.H. Boraston & Captain Cyril E.O. Bax, *The Eighth Division 1914-1918* (London: Naval & Military Press reprint of 1926 edition), pp. 55-62.

Lieutenant-General Sir William Pulteney, GOC III Corps (National Portrait Gallery)

Major-General Havelock Hudson, GOC 8th Division 1915-16.

most notorious parts of the line on a two-brigade front until anticipated relief by the incoming divisional formations.[14]

An acknowledged Somme cockpit since autumn 1914, the Ovillers – La Boisselle sector sat astride the Albert–Bapaume Road.[15] Situated between Bécourt and Authuille, the British line ran along the forward slopes of a long low ridge marked by Tara Hill and Usna Hill. The foremost German position, "with its frontline higher than the British", traversed the upper slopes of three spurs extending south-westwards from the main Poziéres Ridge towards Albert. Distances between the opposing lines varied from 800 to 50 yards.[16] Sector drainage conditions varied; the ground opposite enemy-occupied Ovillers, where no man's land was very wide, was assisted by a gentle slope, but "in front of La Boisselle the trenches were situated in a hollow running from Mash Valley down into Avoca Valley, and on towards Bécourt. There as autumn deepened into winter, the water slowly and irreversibly dissolved the chalk into which the trenches had been cut, creating a slimy ooze which adhered to anything and everything

---

14   Ibid., p. 62 and Edmonds, *Military Operations France and Belgium 1916 Vol. I*, p. 249. XV Corps joined Fourth Army in late April 1916. See Becke, *Order of Battle: Part 4*, p. 225.
15   See Jack Sheldon, *The German Army on the Somme 1914-1916* (Barnsley: Pen & Sword, 2007) and Whitehead, *The Other Side of the Wire Volume I* for the German seizure of La Boisselle in September 1914 and subsequent fighting in the Ovillers-La Boisselle sector during 1915.
16   Edmonds, *Military Operations France and Belgium 1916 Vol. I*, p. 371.

with which it came into contact."[17] La Boisselle, the recognised "key" to the German frontline system "owing to its salient position", was thus a place of unceasing trench and underground warfare.[18] Dorset Regiment subaltern Charles Douie recalled:

> At Millencourt I learned something of the reputation of the La Boisselle trenches. They were among the most notorious in the British lines. For a considerable distance the opposing lines were divided only by the breadth of the mine craters: the British posts lay on the lips of the craters protected by thin layers of sandbags and within bombing distance of the German posts; the approaches to the posts were shallow and waterlogged trenches far below the level of the German lines, and therefore under continuous observation and accurate fire by snipers. Minenwerfer bombs of the heaviest type exploded day and night on these approaches with an all-shattering roar. The communication trenches were in fact worse than the posts in the mine craters to most people; there were, however, some who always felt a certain dislike of sitting for long hours of idleness on top of mines which might at any moment explode. In the craters movement of any kind in daytime was not encouraged.[19]

With the frontline trench just 50 yards from the enemy, Douie's subsequent experience in this central or "Glory Hole" subsector demonstrated that tales of its myriad privations and terrors were no exaggeration. Extending farther south to III Corps' boundary with XIII Corps, the British front extended to Sausage Valley where no man's land increased in depth beyond the La Boisselle mining zone. It was in this sector that a large offensive mine was in the process of being driven towards the German line from a shaft situated near the junction of "Kingsgate Street" trench with "Lochnagar Street" communication trench.[20]

---

17 Michael Stedman, *Somme: La Boisselle: Ovillers/Contalmaison* (London: Leo Cooper, 1997), p. 27.
18 Edmonds, *Military Operations France and Belgium 1916 Vol. I*, p. 375. For offensive/defensive mining operations at La Boisselle, see Captain W. Grant Grieve & Bernard Newman, *Tunnellers: The Story of the Tunnelling Companies, Royal Engineers, during the World War* (London: Herbert Jenkins, 1936), Alexander Barrie, *War Underground: The Tunnellers of the Great War* (Stroud: Spellmount, 1988), Simon Jones, *Underground Warfare 1914-1918* (Barnsley: Pen & Sword, 2010), 'La Boisselle Study Group Archaeological Report 2012'<http://www.laboisselleproject.com/wp-content/uploads/2013/07/La-Boisselle-Study-Group-Archaeological-Report-2012-English-version-low-res.pdf> *The Somme: Secret Tunnel Wars* (2013) <https://www.youtube.com/watch?v=Vc9s3ZMYIec>
19 Charles Douie, *The Weary Road: Recollections of a Subaltern of Infantry* (Stevenage: Strong Oak Press, 1988 reprint of 1929 edition), pp. 87-88.
20 The Lochnagar Mine, a work in progress since 11 November 1915, was begun by 185th Tunnelling Company, 179th Tunnelling Company taking over responsibility in March 1916. Trenches, communication trenches, redoubts, etc. derived their Caledonian sobriquets from 51st (Highland) Division's lengthy occupation of the La Boisselle sector during August – December 1915. See Major F.W. Bewsher, *The History of the 51st*

III Corps, with its headquarters at Montigny Chateau, took full responsibility for the Ovillers – La Boisselle sector from X Corps on the grey, misty morning of 4 April 1916. The exchange occurred simultaneously with 8th Division's relief, commencing 1 April, of 32nd Division[21] on a front (La Boisselle to Aveluy Wood) of 3.36 miles. The 70th Brigade took over the left subsector: 23rd Brigade the right subsector, 25th Brigade remaining in reserve. Division headquarters was established at Hénencourt Chateau.[22] Comparing the discomforts of low-lying French Flanders, where 8th Division had spent so many months, with the Picardy trenches, the post-war divisional history observed:

> The new front was a great change in every respect from the one the division had just left. The trenches were for the most part dry, and provided with fine deep dugouts. From many points a good view could be obtained of the German defences opposite; but this carried with it the corresponding disadvantage that the enemy could overlook equally well some of our own positions. Ovillers Post, for example, was in view of the German lines from two points, and the division had not been in the line two days before "The Glory Hole" was being well "strafed" by "oil cans" and other delights, although no sign of life could be seen in the German trenches.[23]

Major James Jack, second in command of 2nd Scottish Rifles, observed that with the exception of the La Boisselle trenches, the "rest of the line is not so bad, but sniping is active throughout the sector. Almost everywhere, however, the trenches, cut out of the chalk subsoil, have been blasted by shells, in some case blotted out."[24]

(Highland) Division 1914-1918 (Uckfield: Naval & Military Press reprint of 1921 edition), pp. 30-50 and panorama photograph dated 24 August 1915 gatefold in Peter Barton, *The Somme* (London: Constable, 2011), pp. 130-31.

21 Formed in December 1914, the 32nd (New Army) Division embarked for France in November 1915. Concentrated about Ailly le Haut Clocher on the 26th of that month, it was deployed north of the Somme shortly afterwards. See Major A.F. Becke, *Order of Battle: Part 3B. New Army Divisions (30-41); & 63rd (R.N.) Division* (London: HMSO, 1945), pp. 27-28.

22 TNA WO 95/431, Fourth Army War Diary, WO 95/1674, '8th Division Operation Order No. 96', 30 March 1916, 8th Division War Diary and Leask, *Putty*, pp. 376-77. 8th Division's infantry component in spring 1916 was as follows: 23rd Brigade (GOC Brigadier-General H.D. Tuson): 2nd Devonshire, 2nd West Yorkshire, 2nd Scottish Rifles, 2nd Middlesex; 25th Brigade (GOC Brigadier-General J.H.W. Pollard): 2nd Lincolns, 2nd Royal Berkshire, 1st Royal Irish Rifles, 2nd Rifle Brigade; 70th Brigade (Brigadier-General H. Gordon): 11th Sherwood Foresters, 8th KOYLI, 8th York & Lancaster, 9th York & Lancaster. Note: 70th Brigade was transferred from 23rd Division to 8th Division on 18 October 1915, returning to the former on 16 July 1916.

23 Boraston & Bax, *The Eighth Division 1914-1918*, p. 62.

24 John Terraine (ed.), *General Jack's Diary 1914-1918: The Trench Diary of Brigadier-General J.L. Jack, D.S.O.* (London: Eyre & Spottiswoode, 1964), p. 132.

The increased activity heralded by shifting of divisions and newly-arrived units settling into unfamiliar trenches did not, regardless of concerted efforts to keep this hidden from the enemy, go unnoticed.

Festung La Boisselle

The ruined hamlet of La Boisselle and environs was, following a grim two-month occupation, familiar territory to the *Badische* troops of *RIR 110* who had held this position since 4 February 1916. Assigned to *General* Fritz von Below's *Second Army*, 20 months had passed since *28th Reserve Division* (commanded by *Generalleutnant* Ferdinand von Hahn), to which *RIR 110* belonged, detrained on the Somme front as part of *General* Hermann von Stein's *XIV Reserve Corps*.[25] Ensconced in the jutting salient encompassing La Boisselle, the regimental sector extended north and south towards Ovillers and Fricourt (exclusive) respectively. La Boisselle had been transformed into a complex fortress of barbed wire obstacles, trenches, trench mortar positions, observation posts, machine-gun nests and deep dugouts by *RIR 109*, the sector garrison until relief by *RIR 110* in early February: "When we mention La Boisselle, we should not only describe the dangers. We should also praise the efforts the regiment made to develop the position. Over time, at the cost of strenuous labour, we produced a first-class system … which in our sector, not including the long communication trench to Contalmaison, eventually reached twenty-seven kilometres."[26] For their part, throughout *RIR 109's* occupation and thereafter, sappers carried on the subterranean struggle against resolute British tunnellers, dangerous opponents indeed:

> The one occupation which the infantry admitted to be more hazardous and less enviable than their own was that of the men whose daily lot was to descend the mine shafts in and around the cemetery of La Boisselle. I descended a shaft on one occasion, and though assured by the officer on duty that there was no safer place on the Western Front, I ascended again with remarkable speed, preferring the hazards of open-air life in the mine craters to the narrow galleries,

---

25 The *28th Reserve Division* was formed in the Grand Duchy of Baden following mobilisation. Having previously fought in Alsace, it entrained for the Somme in September 1914. One of five divisions (*2nd Guard Reserve Division*, *52nd Division*, *26th Reserve Division*, *28th Reserve Division*, *12th Division*) assigned to *XIV Reserve Corps*, its infantry component in spring 1916 was as follows: *55th Reserve Brigade*: *RIR 109*, *RIR 110 and RIR 111*. See Intelligence Section of the General Staff, American Expeditionary Forces, *Histories of Two Hundred and Fifty-One Divisions of the German Army Which Participated in the War 1914-1918* (London: London Stamp Exchange, 1989 reprint of 1920 edition), pp. 378-82.

26 *RIR 109* regimental history quoted in Sheldon, *The German Army on the Somme 1914-1916*, p. 67. See Whitehead, *The Other Side of the Wire Volume I*, pp. 345-47 for extent and organisation of the improved La Boisselle defences.

driven above and below the German galleries, where men lay listening to the tap of enemy picks, and waiting for the silence which was ever the prelude to the blowing of mine or counter-mine.[27]

Above ground, German trench mortars, machine-guns, rifle grenades and snipers engaged the enemy who, more often than not, responded in kind. Dorset Regiment CSM Ernest Shephard recorded his experience at the receiving end in a pocket journal:

> A tornado of bombs, rifle grenades and more mortars followed, dropping all around, but I dodged and got in alright. This continued at intervals all night, the enemy fired 150 trench mortars [rounds] altogether. These mortars are equal to a Jack Johnson shell, that is the "oil can" or "canister" mortar, but there are smaller kinds.[28] They are the invention of the devil, shell fire by ordinary artillery can very rarely drop plumb into a trench as, having come some distance, they must travel on a curved line and strike parapet first, so that if well down one has a dog's chance of getting no injury. These mortars can, and will, drop anywhere, so they simply lob over from the trenches or point they fire from like an "oil drum". No doubt they are very effective weapons in trench warfare. We have a certain number, but the enemy are miles ahead of us. They have a range of about 700 yards. I can stick rifle and machine-gun fire, ordinary light and heavy artillery guns, bombs, etc., but this mining and trench mortar business is the limit.[29]

Major Jack, having witnessed this almost unrelenting aggression whilst acquainting himself with 8th Division's new line, remarked in his diary: "I have gained the impression that the troops formerly here have allowed the Germans to get the upper hand too easily. One must always hit back as hard and as often as one can; to do less is to invite the bullying to continue …"[30]

With the coming of spring, observers along *XIV Reserve Corps*' 28-mile front began to notice the tell-tale signs of reliefs in progress. *RIR 110's* post-war history observed:

---

27 Douie, *The Weary Road*, pp. 111-12. French and German mining activity commenced at La Boisselle in December 1914. The British followed suit after arrival in summer 1915, detonating 29 mines between August 1915 and June 1916. The Germans detonated 19 mines during the same period. See 'British First World War soldiers identified through DNA testing', *La Boisselle Study Group* <http://www.laboiselleproject.com/2016/09/08/british-first-world-war-soldiers-identified-through-dna-testing/>
28 Packed with high-explosive, these *Minenwerfer* projectiles were the size of a two-gallon oil drum.
29 Ernest Shephard, *A Sergeant-Major's War: From Hill 60 to the Somme* (Ramsbury: Crowood Press, 1988), p. 89.
30 Terraine (ed.), *General Jack's Diary 1914-1918*, p. 132.

According to messages received from Army Supreme Command, a huge attack by the now reasonably well-trained "English" army in conjunction with the French was deemed imminent. Our own regiment's positions could be affected by such an attack. The normal, and largely successful operations planned in the corps sector, which have been ongoing since the previous winter, are intended to create as clear a picture as possible of enemy dispositions and intentions. A [28th] divisional order at that time stated that the Division should strengthen its positions to the point where it could stand firm against repeated enemy attacks for a week.[31]

To what extent this intelligence and recently observed enemy activity were harbingers of major change in the British orders of battle remained unknown.

Raiding, relief deceptions, and the Imperial Strategic Reserve

As discussed by John Pratt elsewhere in this volume, the British Army placed great emphasis on trench raiding prior to the Battle of the Somme. Trench raids were also a fundamental part of German strategy in early 1916. Thus the *Westfront* armies (*Fourth Army, Sixth Army, Second Army, Seventh Army* and *Third Army*), under orders to "demonstrate" from 8 February onwards, were also expected to carry out small-scale local attacks and raiding enterprises in order to draw Allied attention away from *Fifth Army's* impending assault (21 February) on Verdun.[32] For its part, *XIV Reserve Corps* conducted a "great deal of low-level patrol activity, but increasingly night time operations in no man's land took the form of complex and ambitious trench raids" against Fourth Army.[33] Of "debatable" tactical lineage,[34] the latter operations followed a

---

31 Leutnants D.R. Greiner & Vulpius, *Reserve-Infanterie-Regiment Nr. 110 im Weltkrieg 1914-1918* (Karlsruhe: Macklot, 1934), p. 107. Special thanks to Dr Jack Sheldon, Dr Derek Clayton and Hendrik Reuper for the relevant regimental history excerpts, translation and spelling clarification assistance respectively.
32 Edmonds, *Military Operations France and Belgium 1916 Vol. I*, pp. 162-63, Whitehead, *The Other Side of the Wire Volume I*, p. 352 and Hermann Cron, *Imperial German Army 1914-18: Organisation, Structure, Orders of Battle* (Solihull: Helion, 2007), p. 49. The small-scale local operations against the British and French from the River Somme northwards were as follows: Frise 24 January (Somme), Boesinghe 12 February, The Bluff 14-15 February (Ypres) and Vimy Ridge 21 February (Artois).
33 Sheldon, *The German Army on the Somme 1914-1916*, p. 99.
34 Debatable given the extent to which the shock tactics associated with raiding at this time were, as opposed to development and application of this approach by specially raised elite units during 1915-16, "beginning to catch on" in ordinary infantry units. With necessity as the guiding principle, "the strongest single motivating force behind the evolution of Stormtroop tactics was the need to find methods for breaking into, and through trench lines." Contemporaneous with these German developments was the emergence from "precisely the same type of trench-raiding in 1915 that the BEF was conducting with a

similar pattern: A destructive bombardment by artillery and trench mortars firing high explosive, shrapnel and gas shells succeeded by a lift to flanks and rear; entry into the enemy line by volunteer groups of infantry; pre-determined withdrawal with prisoners and booty occurring after a short period of time. Deceptive measures, including bombardments of sectors away from the targeted area and mine detonation, added to the enemy's consternation and confusion. CSM Shephard, remarking on these bellicose forays from across no man's land, observed:

> We call these raids "cutting out". The enemy carry them out by heavily shelling frontline trenches for some 10 minutes or so. Of course the troops keep very low and must get into dugouts. After 10 minutes on trench the enemy raise their range about 10 or 15 yards. This the troops do not notice and meanwhile over comes the raiding party, either bombs causing heavy casualties, or slip into a communication trench and collar 20 or so as prisoners and slip back again before anyone realises what occurred.[35]

The first trench raid on *XIV Reserve Corps* front for 1916, meticulously planned and skilfully executed by *RIR 109*, was launched south-west of La Boisselle against the so-called *Besenhecke* (Broom hedge) salient south-west of La Boisselle on 30 January.[36] The next raid, north-west of La Boisselle, took place on 9 February. Launched against the *Kronenwerk* (Crownwork) – known as the "Nab" to the British – by *RIR 111*, the raiders managed, under cover of a devastating bombardment, to enter the enemy trenches and make off with 15 prisoners of 2nd KOYLI. The contents of British war diaries and subsequent intelligence summaries convey ignorance of the fact that the line had been penetrated and captives, duly recorded as missing, obtained.[37]

---

rather higher frequency and intensity. There was nothing magical about this technique: it was simply an all-arms battle in miniature, and as such it made excellent training for operations later." See Bull, *Stosstrupptaktik*, pp. 79-86 and Paddy Griffith, *British Battle Tactics on the Western Front: The British Army's Art of Attack 1916-18* (New Haven, Connecticut: Yale, 1994), pp. 62-63, 193.

35 Shephard, *A Sergeant-Major's War*, pp. 89-90.
36 The 10th Essex (53rd Brigade, 18th (Eastern) Division) sustained six casualties including the battalion commander killed by direct hit on the telephone dugout. Twelve prisoners, 14 rifles, 10 bayonets, seven anti-gas hoods, equipment belts, steel helmets, shovels, picks, pocket knives and identity discs were brought back without loss by *RIR 109*. See Whitehead, *The Other Side of the Wire Volume I*, pp. 352-58, TNA WO 95/2038: 10th Essex War Diary and Thomas Macdonald Banks & Randolph Arthur Chell, *With the 10th Essex in France* (London: Gay & Hancock, 1924), pp. 84-90.
37 See Whitehead, *The Other Side of the Wire Volume I*, pp. 358-60, TNA WO 95/2367: '32ND DIVISION DAILY INTELLIGENCE SUMMARY from 3 p.m. February 9th to 3 p. m. February 10th 1916', 32nd Division War Diary, WO 95/2402: 2nd KOYLI War Diary and Bill Thompson (ed.), *Morland Great War Corps Commander: General Sir Thomas Morland KCB KCMG DSO: War Diaries and Letters 1914-1918* (Kibworth Beauchamp: Matador, 2015), p. 123.

204   At All Costs

Trench raid spoils: German officers and men pose with captured British booty spring 1916. Regiment unknown, but more than likely a unit of *26th Reserve Division*. (Private collection)

Two more raids, launched by *26th Reserve Division*[38] near Serre and north of La Boisselle on 19 and 22 February,[39] appeared to substantiate *XIV Corps* as "pace

---

38   The *26th Reserve Division's* infantry component in spring 1916 was as follows: *51st Reserve Infantry Brigade*: *Infanterie Regiment* (*IR*) *180*, *RIR 121*; *52nd Reserve Brigade*: *RIR 99*, *RIR 119*. See Intelligence Section of the General Staff, American Expeditionary Forces, *Histories of Two Hundred and Fifty-One Divisions of the German Army Which Participated in the War 1914-1918*, pp. 161-64.

39   Executed by *IR180*, the 19 February raid managed to obtain one wounded officer and 11 other rank prisoners from 2nd Lancashire Fusiliers (12th Brigade, 4th Division). Launched by *RIR 99*, the 22 February raid on the Kniewerk due north of La Boisselle was a somewhat murky affair, the raiders encountering uncut barbed wire obstacles before forcing their way into the British (96th Brigade, 32nd Division) position with some loss and making off with nine prisoners. Curiously, the related British war diaries make no mention of this incursion. See Whitehead, *The Other Side of the Wire Volume I*, pp. 363-66, TNA WO 95/1502, 12th Brigade War Diary, WO 95/2367: 32nd Division War Diary, WO 95/2395: 96th Brigade War Diary, WO 95/2397: 2nd Manchester Regiment, 2nd Royal Inniskilling Fusilier, 15th Lancashire Fusilier war diaries and WO 95/2398: 16th Northumberland Fusilier War Diary.

setter on the Somme front, as far as patrolling and trench raiding was concerned." With experience and reputation in mind, and based on a 29 February tasking by *Second Army*, *XIV Corps* headquarters compiled and issued a detailed report entitled *Patrouillen Erfahrungen* (Patrolling Experiences).[40] Bearing *General* von Stein's signature and distributed to all major headquarters within *Second Army*, it is, Jack Sheldon has observed, "a fascinating document, because it indicates the extent to which the German Army had had to keep its techniques under constant review, in order to retain the initiative in this type of warfare, once the relief of the French Army by the British was completed in the summer of 1915." Itemized into 16 subsections,[41] *Patrouillen Erfahrungen* summarised recent raid developments and best practice as experienced over a period (July 1915 – February 1916) of eight months. It also attests to "how very sophisticated this type of operation had become by this stage of the war and how much attention to detail was required if success was to be assured."[42]

Well aware the enemy was alert and watching, III Corps issued a memorandum concerning sector security and the need for deceptive measures prior to the relief of X Corps:

> [I]t is of great importance to prevent the enemy learning of the arrival of new troops in the 4th Army area ... The country is very different from that which the divisions of the 3rd Corps have passed the winter. It is far more open and the enemy can see from such points as THIEPVAL, POZIERES, CONTALMAISON, etc., considerable portions of the ground behind our lines ... units should be very careful about moving in daylight ... stretches of road which are visible to the enemy must be avoided until it is possible to screen them ... troops must be warned about movement in front and communications trenches. Owing to the irregular tracing of our line and the hilly ground over which it runs the Germans can often look into our trenches ...

Having clearly articulated these pertinent and prudent observations, incoming formations/units were instructed to assume a subtle relief and occupation approach: "It will be advisable for 8th and 34th Divisions to adopt at first the same methods in regard to

---

40 *Patrouille, Patrouillenangriff, Patrouillengang* and *Patrouillenunternehmung* were contemporary German terms for raid. Stephen Bull has observed that "In many instances there was little to distinguish early 'raids' from rather more innocuous-sounding 'patrols', and both had begun before the end of 1914." See General Staff, *Vocabulary of German Military Terms and Abbreviations (Second Edition)* (Nashville, Tennessee: Battery Press 1995 reprint of 1918 edition), p. 113 and Bull, *Stosstrupptaktik*, p. 88.
41 These were as follows: Operational aims; Selection of the break-in point; Infantry: There must be exact knowledge of both positions and No Man's Land based on previous patrolling; Participation; Weapons and equipment; Further preparations; Conduct; Engineers; Mortars; Artillery; Defensive fire; Gas shells; Enemy artillery; Telephones; Machine guns and Praise and Iron Crosses.
42 Sheldon, *The German Army on the Somme 1914-1916*, pp. 100-06.

sniping, patrolling, etc., as have been employed by the troops whom they are relieving. Any alterations in these methods which Divisional Commanders consider necessary should be made gradually ..."[43]

Committed to a major assault at Verdun, the *Oberste Heeresleitung* (*OHL* or Supreme Army Command) remained vigilant for signs of an Anglo-French offensive both prior to and throughout the first four months of the titanic struggle. Speculation as to when and where it would occur remained unclear until mid-June. Incidental to this intelligence enigma was the desire for knowledge of what the British planned to do with the Imperial Strategic Reserve. Composed of 12 divisions evacuated to Egypt from the Gallipoli peninsula during winter 1915-16, information concerning their re-deployment to either the Turkish, Balkan or Western fronts, coupled with the ongoing disembarkation of New Army divisions in France over the same period, would provide further insight into Great Britain's strategic intentions.[44] Thus the coming of spring brought with it indicatory movement and adjustments in and beyond the enemy line opposite; the result being a series of raids prepared and carried out at the behest of higher headquarters by formations of *Second Army* amongst others.

Patrol orders for RIR 110

Patrol and raid activity by both sides intensified during March. The discernible upsurge in the enemy's offensive undertakings alarmed the men of *XIV Reserve Corps* and "there was a greater need to obtain intelligence concerning the British positions, identity of the opposing units and the need to maintain the upper hand in controlling No Man's Land. The size and frequency of the raids went hand in hand with the increase in activity behind the British lines." Tit-for-tat raids occurred throughout the month, with the more experienced Germans having the best of the fighting.[45]

In early April the defenders of La Boisselle were ordered to "carry out a strong patrol[46] intended to capture prisoners and enemy materiel, the timing and exact incursion point to be decided by the regiment." After careful consideration, the headquarters staff of *RIR 110* (commanded by *Oberst Freiherr* von Vietinghoff) selected one of two prospective raid objectives – "the 'Galgen' [Gallows; known as 'Keats Redoubt' to the British] north-west of Boisselle [sic] and the 'Spion' [Lookout Post] opposite Sap

---

43 TNA WO 95/672: 'G.216', 30 March 1916, III Corps War Diary and Thomas, 'British 8th Infantry Division on the Western Front 1914-1918', pp. 140-41.
44 Edmonds, *Military Operations France and Belgium 1916 Vol. I*, pp. 22-25, 316 and Thomas, 'British 8th Infantry Division on the Western Front 1914-1918', pp. 141-42.
45 See TNA WO 95/2367: 32nd Division War Diary, WO 95/2395, 96th Brigade War Diary, Whitehead, *The Other Side of the Wire Volume I*, pp. 369-70 and Thompson (ed.), *Morland Great War Corps Commander*, pp. 128-29 for a costly raid on Y-Sap/*Blinddarm* (27 March 1916) by 1st Dorsetshire Regiment.
46 See fn. 40.

number 3 were possibilities – it was decided to attack the latter and the date for the raid was set for 11 April."[47] Situated south-east of La Boisselle, the *Spion* was a small sap extending from the British frontline into no man's land. One of 11 listening posts established along the frontline from just south of the crater zone to east of Bécourt Wood, "Kirriemuir Street" communication trench led directly to it from the British second line.[48] The *Galgen*, situated at the head of Mash Valley, was no doubt considered too distant. Conversely, the *Spion* and immediate environs' close proximity to the formidable *Schwaben-Höhe* (Swabian Height) position prompted its selection as the more viable raid target.

The raid scheme, amounting to 10 typescript pages including three pages of accompanying fire support tables, emphasised artillery, trench mortar and machine-gun fire suppression roles. In all, 73 guns and trench mortars ranging from 77 mm field guns, 150 mm howitzers and 210 mm mortars would be deployed to engage 27 targets. Battery registration "spread over several days" (5-9 April) was to be carried out without attracting attention except on the right where a feint was to occur. Ordinary ammunition would be expended during the registration period. "Whenever possible, batteries involved in registration did so in conjunction with distant batteries unconnected with the raid as well as in conjunction with retaliatory strikes on British trench mortars." Enemy observation posts on Hill 106 (west of Bécourt Wood) and fronting La Boisselle were to be shelled by "unallotted" batteries.[49]

Finalised two days after 8th Division took responsibility for the La Boisselle – Ovillers sector (6 April 1916), 37 cyclostyle copies were "prepared, including five spares, and sent out to everyone involved in the enterprise from division down to the infantry companies and machine-gun sections."[50] The stated *raison d'être* was identification and intelligence: "As many of the enemy as possible must be made prisoners; in addition, rifles, machine-guns, rifle grenade stands, trench mortars, etc., as well as filled packs, are to be brought back."[51]

---

47 Greiner & Vulpius, *Reserve-Infanterie-Regiment Nr. 110 im Weltkrieg 1914-1918*, p. 107.
48 The Spion sobriquet appears to have been used interchangeably with reference to the British frontline trench/sap.
49 See 'GERMAN RAID ON THE BRITISH TRENCHES NEAR LA BOISSELLE, APRIL 11th, 1916', ORDERS FOR THE RAID, APPENDIX 2: Table of Distribution of Artillery file, APPENDIX A: Corrections to the Tables of Distribution of Artillery Fire, APPENDIX 3: SPECIAL ORDERS FOR THE FEINT ATTACK IN FRONT OF THE SOUTHWEST CORNER OF LA BOISSELLE, REMARKS, *Gunfire No. 4* and Saunders, *Raiding on the Western Front*, p. 46.
50 'GERMAN RAID ON THE BRITISH TRENCHES NEAR LA BOISSELLE, APRIL 11th, 1916', ORDERS FOR THE RAID, *Gunfire No. 4* and Saunders, *Raiding on the Western Front*, p. 45.
51 'GERMAN RAID ON THE BRITISH TRENCHES NEAR LA BOISSELLE, APRIL 11th, 1916', APPENDIX 1: SPECIAL ORDERS FOR A RAID ON THE SPION and REMARKS, *Gunfire No. 4*.

Complex in the organisation and planning, the prospective operation mirrored similar sized British raid schemes at this period of the war.[52] Tentatively scheduled to "take place at dusk" on 11 April, raiding party strength would consist of eight officers and 68 men organised as follows:

> Commander: *Hauptmann* Wagener (*RIR 110's* machine-gun officer)[53] assisted by *Leutnant* Boening, *Assistenzarzt* (Assistant-Surgeon) Wisser, one bugler and six stretcher-bearers
> Stradtmann Patrol: *Leutnant* Stradtmann and 10 men
> Dumas Patrol: *Leutnant* Dumas and 10 men
> Böhlefeld Patrol: *Leutnant* Böhlefeld and 10 men
> Supports: *Leutnant* Freund, 20 men and four pioneers at Wagener's disposal.[54]

On the fixed day, the raiders were to assemble in dugouts "Nos. 1-10, on the right wing of the left-hand battalion", advanced regimental headquarters to be established in Dugout No. 9. The actual raiding party (Stradtmann, Dumas and Böhlefeld patrols) was not "to exceed three officers and thirty men", the remainder to be at "Captain Wagener's disposal for use as supports."[55] Dress and equipment would consist of M1915 *Gummimaske* gas respirators slung and tucked into open tunics and leather waist belts sans ammunition pouches; field caps and greatcoats to be left behind.[56] "To aid identification, every man was to wear a triangle of white canvas on his chest and back." The three patrols would be armed half with the standard *Gewehr 98*, half with *Mauser C96* or *Pistole Parabellum 08* automatics and two grenades per man; designated

---

52 See Appendix 6: Organisation and Execution of a Raid (5th and 7th Canadian Battalions, 16th/17th November 1915) in *Military Operations France and Belgium 1916 Vol. I Appendices* (London: Macmillan, 1932), pp. 42-48.
53 *Hauptmann* Otto Wagener (1888-1971), a wealthy industrialist's son from Durlach.
54 'GERMAN RAID ON THE BRITISH TRENCHES NEAR LA BOISSELLE, APRIL 11th, 1916', ORDERS FOR THE RAID, *Gunfire No. 4*.
55 The translator of the aforementioned captured raid documents converted German ranks into British equivalents i.e., *Hauptmann* to Captain, etc., etc. The latter have been retained in all direct quotations.
56 The M16 *Stalhelm* was not in general distribution throughout the *Westheer* at this time, the troops of *Second Army* relying on the traditional *Pickelhaube* and cloth *Feldmütze*. Nevertheless, small stocks of the new steel helmet were in use, a III Corps intelligence summary noting: "An officer wearing a green cap with black polished peak, and a sentry wearing a shrapnel-proof helmet were seen opposite the right section." Further details of this enemy issue headgear came to light when a photograph of the "NEW PATTERN STEEL HELMET" was subsequently obtained. A rough sketch thereof was accompanied by the statement that "No information is as yet available as to the degree of protection which it affords." See TNA WO 157/315: III Corps Intelligence and WO 157/169: Fourth Army Intelligence files, April 1916.

German M1915 *Gummimaske*.

supports were, except for five men issued with pistols and grenades, to carry rifles and two grenades per man.[57]

On the evening of the raid, "the wire in front of the point of entry" would be cut "on a width of 50 metres" by heavy and medium *Minenwerfer*.[58] Twenty-five minutes prior to Zero, the artillery, having accumulated an authorised stock of 5,250 field gun, field howitzer, heavy field howitzer and gun (9 cm., 10 cm., 12 cm.) shells and 575 'T' and 'K' gas shells,[59] would fire a preparatory bombardment on the British trenches between the "Besenhecke and the Windmühle [Windmill], and also the Weisse Steimauer" [White Stone Wall], before lifting to the British rear defences to cut-off reinforcements. Set aside specifically to bombard the enemy defences, the assembled gas projectile stockpile was to be expended in a fire plan "commencing from the rear

57 'GERMAN RAID ON THE BRITISH TRENCHES NEAR LA BOISSELLE, APRIL 11th, 1916', ORDERS FOR THE RAID, APPENDIX 1: SPECIAL ORDERS FOR A RAID ON THE SPION, *Gunfire No. 4*, Greiner & Vulpius, *Reserve-Infanterie-Regiment Nr. 110 im Weltkrieg 1914-1918*, p. 108 and colour section uniform plates (I 1-3) and accompanying text (pp. 61-62) in Stephen Bull, *World War I Trench Warfare (1) 1914-16* (Oxford: Osprey, 2002).
58 The heavy *Minenwerfer* projectile was so large that anything within 30 feet of impact was considered a direct hit.
59 *K-Stoss* and *T-Stoss* projectiles, first introduced in 1915, contained non-lethal lachrymatory compounds.

210   At All Costs

and working up to the frontline." Machine-guns were to "open fire on positions in rear and on the communication trenches which lead to the objective from both sides."[60]

On the right of the projected incursion, a 30-minute feint bombardment of the British wire and trenches opposite La Boisselle and vicinity was scheduled for the morning of 10 April. This would distract the enemy's attention away from point of entry, "registration being carried out by the heavy field howitzer batteries which have just taken up their positions, the (21-cm.) mortar section, and the heavy and medium Minenwerfer." Participating batteries, *228th Minenwerfer Company* and "close-range weapons"[61] of *1st Reserve Kompagnie, 13th Pionier Battalion* would reprise their assigned roles on the evening of 11 April. Authorised stocks of 390 shells per bombardment were set aside for both diversions. The British were to be further distracted by a pre-bombardment detonation of a "shallow mine" to the left of the crater zone.[62] Thus the anticipated British artillery response to the sudden bombardment would be drawn away from where the raid was actually occurring by a second feint "against the enemy's position just north of La Boisselle Cemetery." Scheduled to begin 15 minutes following commencement of the main 11 April bombardment; the artillery, trench mortars and close-range weaponry were to re-engage enemy positions and barbed wire obstacles opposite the front and south-west corner of the village. Machine-guns, inactive during the 10 April feint, were to engage rear positions, communication trenches and the *Galgen*. Fifteen minutes later, a second mine would be detonated to the right of the crater zone, after which straw-filled dummy figures, situated in the *Blinddarm* and just south of that trench complex, were to be manipulated in order to emulate an imminent riposte during a brief lull before the bombardment reopened again.[63]

60 'GERMAN RAID ON THE BRITISH TRENCHES NEAR LA BOISSELLE, APRIL 11th, 1916', APPENDIX 2: Table of Distribution of Artillery file, APPENDIX A: Corrections to the Tables of Distribution of Artillery Fire, APPENDIX 1: SPECIAL ORDERS FOR THE RAID ON THE SPION, REMARKS, *Gunfire No. 4* and Whitehead, *The Other Side of the Wire Volume I*, p. 401.
61 Possibly light trench mortars, rifle grenades and fixed rifle batteries.
62 The subsequent decision (9 April) to detonate this mine was based on the close proximity of an encroaching British gallery. "As, however, the enemy always showed most activity in his gallery between six and eight a.m., the mine was to be fired during these two hours under all circumstances, with a view of causing him the greatest number of casualties." See 'GERMAN RAID ON THE BRITISH TRENCHES NEAR LA BOISSELLE, APRIL 11th, 1916', APPENDIX 4: SPECIAL ORDER FOR THE FEINT BOMBARDMENT TO BE CARRIED OUT ON THE MORNING OF THE DAY BEFORE THE RAID, REPORT ON THE EXECUTION OF THE RAID ON THE SPION, *Gunfire No. 4* and Greiner & Vulpius, *Reserve-Infanterie-Regiment Nr. 110 im Weltkrieg 1914-1918*, p. 108.
63 'GERMAN RAID ON THE BRITISH TRENCHES NEAR LA BOISSELLE, APRIL 11th, 1916', APPENDIX 3: SPECIAL ORDERS FOR THE FEINT ATTACK IN FRONT OF THE SOUTHWEST CORNER OF LA BOISSELLE, *Gunfire No. 4*.

On the immediate right at the yet to be designated hour, the raiding party was to vacate the "Blaue Stellung [Blue Position] by Sap No. 3 with the object of breaking into the enemy's position in the vicinity of the Süd Spion [Southern lookout post] from which point the enemy's trench will be cleared northwards." Supports were to be held in readiness, "so as to be able to push on after the other patrols" on receipt of orders from Wagener. With a "timetable for all elements of the raid set out to the second", the raiders were limited to 25 minutes in the British line before retiring, on a "signal given by Lieutenant Stradtmann, or on the charge being blown by my [Wagener] bugler", to the *Blaue Stellung* by the shortest avenue of approach.[64]

Subsequent changes to plan by "order of the division" occurred during the days leading up to Zero. These included cancellation of the *Weisse Steinmauer* bombardment, "in order that the enemy's attention might not be drawn unnecessarily to that locality"; attachment of an additional *Minenwerfer* for wire-cutting purposes; adjustment of Stradtmann Patrol's jumping-off time as a ploy to avoid friendly fire losses, and minor modification to available stocks of trench mortar and lachrymatory gas ammunition.[65]

Nothing of importance

No strangers to active trench warfare, the officers and men of 8th Division accustomed themselves to the La Boisselle sector. Deployed and ready, component artillery brigades shelled enemy machine-gun posts, working parties and other tempting targets, whilst battalions carried on with the normal routine of rotating duty in front-line, support and reserve during a period of little offensive activity as recounted in "old corps summaries of 'peacetime warfare.'" This was the ironic "nothing of importance" as chronicled by Royal Welsh Fusilier subaltern Bernard Adams (wounded June 1916) in his classic wartime memoir.[66] Making their way over chalky downland, working parties – the nocturnal role of units in support and reserve – passed through winding communication arteries to haul supplies forward, excavate trenches and construct dugouts. It was during these early days of sector acclimatisation that

---

64 'GERMAN RAID ON THE BRITISH TRENCHES NEAR LA BOISSELLE, APRIL 11th, 1916', ORDERS FOR THE RAID, APPENDIX 1: SPECIAL ORDERS FOR A RAID ON THE SPION, *Gunfire No. 4* and Saunders, *Raiding on the Western Front*, p. 46.
65 'GERMAN RAID ON THE BRITISH TRENCHES NEAR LA BOISSELLE, APRIL 11th, 1916', REPORT ON THE EXECUTION OF THE RAID ON THE SPION, *Gunfire No. 4*.
66 See Lieutenant Adrian Stephen *op. cit.* in Richard van Emden, *The Somme: The Epic Battle in the Soldiers' own Words and Photographs* (Barnsley: Pen & Sword, 2016), p. 275 and Bernard Adams, *Nothing of Importance: A Record of Eight Months at the Front with a Welsh Battalion October 1915 to June 1916* (Stevenage: Strong Oak Press, 1988 reprint of 1917 edition), pp. xxxviii-xxix.

Major Jack remarked on the general distribution of what was soon to be a ubiquitous piece of kit: "Steel helmets have been issued to all ranks; formerly only the company snipers wore them. It is said that while they save some heads they cause more serious wounds to others …"[67]

The 23rd Brigade, of which Jack's battalion was part, took over complete responsibility for the La Boisselle sector by midnight on 5 April. Taking up excavated quarters between Sausage Valley and Avoca Valley, he wrote:

> My bed-chamber is a solitary dug-out hewed eight foot deep in the chalk near the point of the Chapes Spur, an eerie residence, like a sepulchre, dark as a grave save for a flicker from a candle whose beams dimly light up the ghostly white walls. A rough bedframe, a small table and chair from Bécourt Chateau make up the furniture …[68]

The next five days (5-9 April) were described in the brigade war diary as "normal". Broken ground and dense German wire were encountered by patrols after dark. Assigned work consisted of existing trench maintenance, clearing out rubbish from old trenches and firestep and dugout construction. Enemy activity appeared to be confined to the usual *Minenwerfer* and rifle grenade bombardments. In one particularly deadly incident, one officer, two sergeants and two other ranks were killed by a single mortar round. Supporting 18-pdr and 4.5 in. howitzer batteries retaliated with a counter-bombardment "on position from where trench mortar could be seen firing."[69] Effectively masked by this frequent hostile mortar and rifle grenade fire, the subtle pre-raid artillery registration of Sectors 77, 78 – the German designations for the area extending south from opposite the La Boisselle salient to Sausage Valley – was complete by 9 April. Efforts to avoid "attracting attention" appear to have had the desired result, 8th Division's intelligence summaries noting little else except for time and target of the various bombardments.[70]

Having simultaneously taken responsibility for the northern portion of 8th Division's line opposite Ovillers, 70th Brigade appears to have suffered less from hostile bombardments over the same period due to the extreme width of no man's land. Thus little notice was taken, despite deliberate efforts to "attract attention" in this locality, of the pre-feint battery registration of Sectors 75 and 76 – German designation for the "retired lines of trench" separated by the expanse of Mash Valley,

---

67 Terraine (ed.), *General Jack's Diary 1914-1918*, p. 133. One million Brodie pattern steel helmets were received and issued during the first six months of 1916. See Edmonds, *Military Operations France and Belgium 1916 Vol. I*, p. 115.
68 Terraine, p. 133.
69 TNA WO 95/1708: 23rd Brigade War Diary.
70 TNA WO 95/1674: Intelligence summaries, 6-9 April 1916, 8th Division War Diary and 'GERMAN RAID ON THE BRITISH TRENCHES NEAR LA BOISSELLE, APRIL 11th, 1916', REMARKS, *Gunfire No. 4*.

La Boisselle and vicinity – beyond scrupulous narration of sundry shellfire incidents in the aforementioned daily summaries. In total, there were 28 recorded German artillery bombardments of the Ovillers – La Boisselle sector and vicinity during 6-9 April.[71]

Meanwhile, farther north in *26th Reserve Division's* sector, *RIR 119* executed a raid on the night of 6/7 April. The mission was to "ascertain that the British 29th Division had left Egypt", a question which had vexed German intelligence thus far. Penetrating the enemy frontline in the wake of a crushing bombardment, the raiders obtained 19 prisoners of 2nd South Wales Borderers (SWB) (87th Brigade, 29th Division) before the signal to retire.[72]

25th Brigade takes over

The 25th Brigade (GOC Brigadier-General J.H.W. Pollard)[73] relieved 23rd Brigade in the La Boisselle sector on 9 April, 1st Royal Irish Rifles [R. Irish Rif.] and 2nd Royal Berkshire Regiment taking over the frontline on the right and left respectively; 2nd Rifle Brigade, two companies situated at Bécourt Redoubt in Bécourt

---

71 From 5 April onwards, "the artillery repeatedly shelled the trenches and wire at 76y [map reference]. In particular on the evening of April 8th, the wire was shelled continuously for forty-five minutes by the heavy and light artillery. In the same way, the close-range weapons … kept up daily a deliberate bombardment … on the whole extent of the wire from between La Boisselle cemetery and the Galgen. A machine-gun posted every night in the Blinddarm prevented the enemy from repairing the wire." See TNA WO 95/2185: 70th Brigade War Diary, WO 95/1674: Intelligence summaries, 6-9 April 1916, 8th Division War Diary, 'GERMAN RAID ON THE BRITISH TRENCHES NEAR LA BOISSELLE, APRIL 11th, 1916', REMARKS, APPENDIX 3: SPECIAL ORDERS FOR THE FEINT ATTACK IN FRONT OF THE SOUTHWEST CORNER OF LA BOISSELLE and REPORT ON THE FEINT ON THE EVENING OF APRIL 11th 1916, *Gunfire No. 4*.
72 Whitehead, *The Other Side of the Wire Volume I*, pp. 397-400. The 29th Division, sailing from Egypt in early March, disembarked at Marseilles between the 15-29 of that month. Concentrated east of Pont Remy, it had only been attached to VIII Corps for a brief period before confirmation of its presence on the Western Front. See Edmonds, *Military Operations France and Belgium 1916 Vol. I*, p. 254, fn. 1 and Major A.F. Becke, *Order of Battle of Divisions: Part I – The Regular British Divisions* (London: HMSO, 1935), p. 123.
73 Brigadier-General James Hawkins Whitshed Pollard (1866-1942). Commissioned Manchester Regiment August 1886; transferred Royal Scots Fusiliers September 1886; Burma 1887-89; Chin-Lushai 1890; Isazai 1892; Chitral 1895; passed Staff College 1899; South Africa 1899-1902; GSO 1 1914; CO 2nd Royal Scots Fusiliers and GOC 2nd Brigade, 1st Division 1915; wounded October 1915; GOC 25th Brigade 1 April 1916. Pollard's assumption of command followed the recent promotion of his predecessor (Brigadier-General R.B. Stephens) to GOC 5th Division.

Wood, billeted at Dernacourt, and 2nd Lincolnshire Regiment billeted in Albert.[74] Lieutenant W.H.P. Whitfield ('A' Company, 1st R. Irish Rif.) remarked prior to the inevitable change-over:

> While we were in billets during these days, the CO [Major E.C. Mayne],[75] adjutant, and company commanders went up to look at the line which we would take over on the 9th. I remained at HQ and "answered" for Browne [adjutant]. I gathered from Browne on his return that the place was not healthy. ffrench-Mullen [CO 'A' Company] confirmed Browne's view when I went back to my billet for dinner ... The position which the battalion would take over was on the ridge beyond Albert and its left was at the village of La Boisselle which, it turned out later, was a veritable fortress. The enemy, as was usual, was in possession of the highest ground and obtained a fairly good observation into our trenches ... the regiment we would relieve were not, I gathered, very impressed with this position. It was certainly rowdy.[76]

With 2nd Royal Berkshire Regiment taking responsibility for the line facing La Boisselle and immediate vicinity, 1st R. Irish Rif. relieved 2nd West Yorkshire Regiment in the trenches opposite *Schwaben-Höhe*, 'B' Company on the right; 'A' Company in the centre; 'D' on the left, 'C' in the second line providing immediate support. Battalion headquarters was situated at shell-scarred Bécourt Chateau, a two-storey 18th century brick and stone edifice. Whitfield, having had his first taste of the La Boisselle trenches, remarked: "What a difference to the north. No breastwork, shoulder high, just a low battered-in trench. The wire, what we could see of it, seemed good. I did not like the place." Fellow subaltern 2nd Lieutenant W.V.C. Lake observed: "The trench system was largely in chalk and good red soil. This presented a new set of problems. Whereas before we had dugouts down underground with only sacking for doors, now we had to get used to the Nissen type of dugout[77] surrounded on all sides by chalk with only a minimum of chalk on the roof, just sufficient to

---

74 See TNA WO 95/1674: '8th Division Order No. 97', 7 April 1916 and WO 95/1708: '25th BRIGADE OPERATION ORDER NO. 86', 8 April 1916, 23rd Brigade War Diary.
75 T/Major Edward Colburn Mayne, Royal Irish Fusiliers (RIF). Commissioned 3rd RIF 1886; Captain 1893; Sierra Leone 1897-98; South Africa 1899-1901; joined reserve of officers 1903; re-joined 3rd RIF August 1914; embarked for France May 1915, CO 1st R. Irish Rif. since assuming command from his shell-shocked predecessor on 26 February 1916.
76 Whitfield *op. cit.* in Taylor, *The First Royal Irish Rifles in the Great War*, p. 70.
77 Nissen Dugout: Prefabricated structure assembled from half-cylindrical corrugated steel components, a below ground derivative of the celebrated Nissen Hut invented by Major Peter Norman Nissen (1871-1930). See contemporary images in van Emden, *The Somme*, p. 61.

preserve the level of ground."[78] It would take some time before the officers and men of 1st R. Irish Rif. accumulated intimate knowledge of the saps, sniping posts, bombing posts, bomb stores, sandbag dumps, gas alarms, etc. that comprised the perplexing trench maze west and south of La Boisselle.

Morning feint bombardment and Sergeant D'Arcy's amazing discovery

Monday 10 April was fine and hazy with a strong southerly wind. It was on this day that 8th Division headquarters issued a defensive scheme – the general principles of which were "the same as those obtaining in the First Army" – outlining action to be taken by supporting battalions and reserve brigade "in case of an enemy attack." These anticipated movements, in addition to accompanying rocket signalling instructions, were the main elements of a temporary arrangement that would remain in place until a "complete defence scheme can be issued ..."[79]

Following the dawn "Stand To" observance,[80] routine inspections and morning meal, the labouring infantry of 25th Brigade and 70th Brigade continued with maintenance of the frontline system bolstered by 1,185 Royal Engineers [RE]. There was much to do for the general state of wire and trenches were adjudged "insufficient" and "inadequate".[81] Approximately 78 minutes

Brigadier-General James Pollard, GOC 25th Brigade 1916-17. (John Bourne)

---

78 TNA WO 95/1725: 25th Brigade War Diary, WO 95/1729: 2nd Royal Berkshire Regiment War Diary, WO 95/1730: 1st R. Irish Rif. War Diary, Whitfield and Lake *op. cit.*, Taylor, *The First Royal Irish Rifles in the Great War*, p. 71.
79 Sunrise 10 April occurred at 5:22 a.m. British/6:22 a.m. continental time. TNA WO 95/1674: 'G.577/25', 10 April 1916, 8th Division War Diary.
80 Stand To: Shortened definition for "Stand-to-Arms". As enemy attacks were routinely mounted either before dawn or shortly after dusk, both sides took precautions to ensure the firestep was manned an hour before daybreak and nightfall.
81 TNA WO 95/672: '25th Brigade, 207/G., 8th Division', 14 April 1916, III Corps War Diary.

after sunrise,[82] the first of two German mines was detonated, causing "some casualties and wrecked the workings near INCH STREET", to the right of the crater zone at 6:43 a.m. "The mine was fired ... after the presence of the enemy's miners was definitely ascertained by means of the microphone. The effect of the mine was extraordinarily powerful below ground, a new crater, however, was not formed, for the mine chamber was 105 feet below the surface." Immediately after the explosion, German field artillery and close-range weapons "bombarded the enemy's trenches in that neighbourhood" whilst, farther south in the 1st R. Irish Rif. subsector "the heavy and the three medium Minenwerfer registered the point of entry and considerably damaged the wire, firing in all eight heavy and twenty-eight medium Minenwerfer shell." One descending medium projectile was observed penetrating a dugout "from which cries were heard."

Following this violent start, a lull in hostile activity descended until 9:30 a.m. when German artillery dispersed a working party in Waltney Street, "firing 9 rounds of shrapnel over them." This act was part of the pre-registration programme by five light mortars on the "enemy's trenches behind the craters"; 261 rounds were fired. Forty-five minutes passed before the intended feint bombardment opened at 10:15 a.m. "The heavy Minenwerfer and the close-range weapons ... took part ... to the extent of a few rounds." British batteries responded by shelling "trenches in La Boiselle and towards Poziéres, while section of heavy-calibre howitzers (8-in.) shelled the neighbourhood of the [*RIR 110*] command post ..." Relative calm prevailed until 3:00 p.m. when four medium *Minenwerfer* "registered at intervals, with twenty-two rounds" on the wire and trenches opposite Y-Sap/*Blinddarm* until 5:25 p.m.[83]

Fire mission accomplished, the raid after-action report surmised that the 10 April feint "caused the enemy an appreciable number of casualties according to the statements of prisoners" subsequently taken. For the British infantry, new to the sector and some of its hostile weaponry, the fearsome oil can projectiles discharged during the operation engendered "great alarm, as their likes had never been seen before." British losses in these feint operations were relatively light, totalling eight killed and eleven wounded. The wider intention – to distract enemy attention from

---

82   Events will be recounted in British time hereafter, direct quotes exclusive.
83   'GERMAN RAID ON THE BRITISH TRENCHES NEAR LA BOISSELLE, APRIL 11th, 1916', APPENDIX 4: SPECIAL ORDER FOR THE FEINT BOMBARDMENT TO BE CARRIED OUT ON THE MORNING OF THE DAY BEFORE THE RAID, REPORT ON THE EXECUTION OF THE RAID ON THE SPION, *Gunfire No. 4*, TNA WO 95/672: III Corps War Diary, WO 95/1674: 'Intelligence Summary for period of 24 hours ending 6 a.m., 11th April, 1916', 8th Division War Diary, WO 95/1729: 2nd Royal Berkshire Regiment War Diary and WO 95/1730: 1st R. Irish Rif. War Diary,

the projected raid's point of entry – does not seem to have been achieved. The British, so far as can be determined, remained ignorant of the danger.[84]

In the 1st R. Irish Rif. subsector, Captain Ernest ffrench-Mullen's 'A' Company – No. 1 platoon and No. 3 platoon occupying the fire trench – held the centre of the battalion line. Hailing from Templeogue, Co. Dublin and educated at the Jesuit-run Clongowes Wood College in Co. Kildare, the 32-year-old ffrench-Mullen was a pre-war Regular who's R. Irish Rif. commission dated back to 1905.[85] Service with the 4th and 3rd battalions followed until 1913, when, attached to the latter unit, he entered the reserve. Pursuing a post-regimental career as a Malayan rubber planter, ffrench-Mullen contracted malaria during his brief time there.[86] The outbreak of war and a return to the colours was succeeded by promotion to captain and transfer to 1st R. Irish Rif. Posted to France in December 1915, he had been on continuous active service for almost four months.[87]

It was sometime after sunset that a diligent NCO, bearing traces of omnipresent chalk dust from head to foot, entered 'A' Company's headquarters dugout situated in the second line. Lieutenant Whitfield, partaking in a commonplace frontline meal illuminated by paraffin lamp and candlelight, recalled:

> In the evening, when we were having dinner and things had got quieter, Sgt D'Arcy came in and reported to ffrench-Mullen that he thought the Germans were cutting the wire opposite his platoon front which was on the left of mine. We were rather amazed at the idea but went up with Sgt D'Arcy to have a look. We could see nothing so returned.

This warning sign that something was in the offing went unheeded, although the incident appears to have been reported to brigade, which in turn passed it on to

---

84 'GERMAN RAID ON THE BRITISH TRENCHES NEAR LA BOISSELLE, APRIL 11th, 1916', ORDERS FOR THE RAID, APPENDIX 4: SPECIAL ORDER FOR THE FEINT BOMBARDMENT TO BE CARRIED OUT ON THE MORNING OF THE DAY BEFORE THE RAID, REPORT ON THE EXECUTION OF THE RAID ON THE SPION, *Gunfire No. 4*, TNA WO 95/1674: 'Intelligence Summary for period of 24 hours ending 6 a.m., 11th April, 1916', 8th Division War Diary, WO 95/2185: 70th Brigade War Diary, WO 95/1729: 2nd Royal Berkshire Regiment War Diary, WO 95/1730: 1st R. Irish Rif. War Diary, Taylor, *The First Royal Irish Rifles in the Great War*, p. 71 and *Soldiers Died in the Great War 1914-19* [CD Rhom] (Uckfield: Naval & Military Press, 2011).
85 *Riversdale*, ffrench-Mullen's erstwhile suburban Dublin residence, was the home of poet William Butler Yeats (1865-1939) during the final six years of his life.
86 See Margaret Shennan, *Out in the Midday Sun: The British in Malaya 1880-1960* (London: John Murray, 2002) Chapter 9 for the financial lure and rubber planting experience from Imperial apogee to the post-colonial period.
87 TNA WO 339/9059: Captain Ernest FFRENCH-MULLEN. The Royal Irish Rifles file and Taylor, *The First Royal Irish Rifles in the Great War*, p. 243.

division.[88] Whitfield regretfully added, "Sgt D'Arcy was right as we afterwards found out to our cost."[89]

Before the storm

Tuesday 11 April was wet and raw, steady rainfall transforming the chalky subsoil into a clinging black mud that stuck to everything and everyone. Fourth Army GOC Sir Henry Rawlinson, paying his first visit to 8th Division headquarters, noted that he did not get his anticipated horseback ride "on account of the rain." III Corps GOC Lieutenant-General Pulteney, having just returned from home leave the previous day, remarked: "Today it has been horrid nothing but rain besides turning much colder …"[90] Morning Stand To concluded, British sentries, on taking up day positions in the fire trench, peered across no man's land through the fogged lenses of rain-slicked trench periscopes whilst their mates, rifles having been inspected by company officers, tucked into a hot breakfast conveyed to the forward area by battalion ration parties. From mid-morning, infantry and RE working parties, shrouded in rubberized ground-sheet capes, toiled with pick and shovel on trenches and posts. Below ground, the tunnel war of deep and shallow galleries continued unabated. Beyond no man's land and the rusting tangled mass of German barbed wire, here and there interspersed with silver-gray strands denoting recent repairs, *Freiherr* von Vietinghoff issued orders from the regimental command post to "commence the operation at eight o'clock [7:00 p.m. British time] that evening." Watches would be "compared afresh at seven p.m." Owing to the inclimate weather, "the error of the day, for the artillery, was considerable; it had to be worked out by individual batteries and allowed for."[91]

---

88   "During the night the enemy were at work on their wire which had been damaged opposite X.20/4 by our artillery fire." No mention of pre-raid wire-cutting by the German trench garrison before the night of 11/12 April is made in the *RIR 110's* operation orders. It must be assumed, therefore, that the observed parties were, as surmised in the previously quoted intelligence summary, repairing barbed wire obstacles damaged by British counter-bombardments. See 'GERMAN RAID ON THE BRITISH TRENCHES NEAR LA BOISSELLE, APRIL 11th, 1916', ORDERS FOR THE RAID and TNA WO 95/1674: 'Intelligence Summary for period of 24 hours ending 6 a.m., 11th April, 1916', 8th Division War Diary.

89   Taylor, *The First Royal Irish Rifles in the Great War*, p. 71.

90   TNA WO 95/672: III Corps War Diary, WO 95/1674: 'Intelligence Summary for period of 24 hours ending 6 a.m., 12th April, 1916', 8th Division War Diary, Churchill Archive Centre (CAC) RWLN 5/5: Rawlinson Diary, 11 April 1916 and letter from Pulteney to Lady Edith Londonderry (1878-1959), 11 April 1916 quoted in Leask, *Putty*, p. 380.

91   'GERMAN RAID ON THE BRITISH TRENCHES NEAR LA BOISSELLE, APRIL 11th, 1916', REPORT OF THE EXECUTION OF THE RAID ON THE SPION, *Gunfire No. 4*. Prevailing barometric conditions, air temperature and wind direction had to be taken into account by the German gunners.

With Germans guns and mortars deployed and registered since 9 April, subsequent hostile daytime activity, as recorded in the relevant 8th Division intelligence summary, consisted of sporadic shellfire accompanied by the usual trench mortar bombardments. At 10:00 a.m., twenty-five 77 mm shells fell within the Ovillers subsector; an additional 10 projectiles of the same calibre were aimed at the Albert Basilica later that morning. At 3:30 p.m., "a 77 mm battery fired 7 rounds" at map reference X.20/4 in the 1st R. Irish Rif. subsector. This small ammunition expenditure was in keeping with orders that if possible, "Sectors 79 and 80 [extending from the Spion southwards] will not be fired on on the day of the raid." British activity for the same day amounted to artillery retaliation against trench mortars situated in and about La Boisselle and the shelling of observed working parties.[92]

At 3:00 p.m., the raiders, having rehearsed the operation for five days since receipt of orders, "marched from Martinpuich through Poziéres, then by the Latthorf Graben [Latthorf Trench] – Regimentstrichter [Regiment's Crater] – Krebs Graben [Crab Trench] to the appointed dugouts on the left of Sap No. 3, where the evening meal was found ready prepared." *Assistenzarzt* Wisser, installed with his six stretcher bearers in No. 1 dugout, set up an advanced aid post. Established inside advanced regimental headquarters from 5:00 p.m., Vietinghoff, "in the event of the enemy opening a barrage on our trenches", ordered the number of sentries reduced to a minimum. Gas masks and other gas equipment were to be "held ready for use." With the artillery and machine guns registered and ready, the mine gallery tamped and primed, and the raiders fed and eager to attack, all was in place by dusk on 11 April.[93]

Bombardment

Bayonets affixed to rifle nose caps and magazines fully charged, the men of 1st R. Irish Rif. and 2nd Royal Berkshire had been on Stand To vigilance for fifteen minutes when the German main and simultaneous second feint bombardments abruptly opened at 7:00 p.m. Lieutenant Whitfield was preparing for the line with other 'A' Company officers inside the headquarters dugout:

---

[92] TNA WO 95/1674: 'Intelligence Summary for period of 24 hours ending 6 a.m., 12th April, 1916', 8th Division War Diary and 'GERMAN RAID ON THE BRITISH TRENCHES NEAR LA BOISSELLE, APRIL 11th, 1916', REMARKS and REPORT OF THE EXECUTION OF THE RAID ON THE SPION, *Gunfire No. 4*.
[93] 'GERMAN RAID ON THE BRITISH TRENCHES NEAR LA BOISSELLE, APRIL 11th, 1916', ORDERS FOR THE RAID, REMARKS, REPORT OF THE EXECUTION OF THE RAID ON THE SPION and CAPTAIN WAGENER'S REPORT ON THE RAID ON THE EVENING OF 11 APRIL 1916, *Gunfire No. 4* and Saunders, *Raiding on the Western Front*, p. 47.

220   At All Costs

Four of us were just putting on our equipment when it all started, and immediately our exit was plugged with heaps of chalk in the dugout doorway, jamming the door. Shells came in thick and fast and the sacking on the window blew in at every explosion. All we could do was lie low and wait for the end. Our orders had been that in the event of an attack we were to rush up to the front line with all speed. But how was this to be done? It does sometimes happen that orders cannot be obeyed.[94]

Shells saturated "front, reserve and communication trenches in the right section, trench mortars and machine-guns cooperating" with a tremendous din, whilst a fetid vapour of gas, cordite and drifting sandbag scud permeated the twilight time atmosphere. *Hauptmann* Wagener noted: "Shortly after fire was opened, the whole of the enemy's position from Windmühle to Besenhecke was wrapped in a greyish-white smoke, which the wind drove back into our lines." *Freiherr* von Vietinghoff subsequently observed: "[F]rom the start the gas clouds from the 'T' and 'K' gas shell, of which the grouping was perfect, were blown back over our lines by the strong west wind, so that all sentries and machine-gun look-outs were obliged to wear masks."[95]

Their subsector already deluged by trench mortar rounds, 2nd Royal Berkshire headquarters requested retaliatory fire as early as 6:55 p.m. after which La Boisselle was shelled by 4.5 in. howitzers; "Right Group [Artillery] HQ" was "called up and asked by the Right Battalion [1st R. Irish Rif.], as their trenches ... were being bombarded" at 7:05 p.m. 18-pdr and 4.5 in. howitzer batteries replied with "steady rate of fire" on the enemy trenches opposite.[96]

By 7:10 p.m. it was impossible for the raiders to remain in Sap No. 3 without donning gas masks. Major Mayne (CO 1st R. Irish Rif.) recalled: "The lachrymatory shells fired by the enemy caused great inconvenience and trouble to all ranks. Reeking of mustard and cress, the gas "from these shells hung about the trench for many hours and caused great irritation to the eyes. The goggles[97] were found not to be of much use, and most of the men preferred to use the [PH] Gas Helmet[98] which proved very

94 Whitfield *op. cit.* in Taylor, *The First Royal Irish Rifles in the Great War*, p. 72.
95 TNA WO 95/1674: 'Intelligence Summary for period of 24 hours ending 6 a.m., 12th April, 1916', 8th Division War Diary and 'GERMAN RAID ON THE BRITISH TRENCHES NEAR LA BOISSELLE, APRIL 11th, 1916', REPORT ON THE EXECUTION OF THE RAID ON THE SPION and CAPTAIN WAGENER'S REPORT ON THE RAID ON THE EVENING OF 11 APRIL 1916, *Gunfire No. 4*.
96 TNA WO 95/762: '8th Div. G.664/7: Report on the enemy's bombardment on the 11th of April 1916', 8th Division CRA after-action report, III Corps War Diary.
97 Probably Spicer pattern anti-lachrymatory goggles. Approximately three million were manufactured by Messrs Jas. Spicer & Sons for general issue with gas helmets well into 1917. Special thanks to Taff Gillingham for providing details about this particular piece of British issue equipment.
98 The PH (phenate-hexamine) gas helmet adopted in January 1916. See Edmonds, *Military Operations France and Belgium 1916 Vol. I*, pp. 79-80.

effectual." On the immediate left, 2nd Royal Berkshire Regiment, all men except sentries, Lewis Gun posts and "bombing parties near to craters" withdrawn into available dugouts at the start of the bombardment, were unaffected by the gas, although reports were received that the enemy "fired 'tear' shells in the vicinity of SCONE STREET and TUMMEL STREET."[99]

British batteries, on receipt of anxious telephone messages from beleaguered battalions, retaliated; "Whereas at 8:06 a.m. [7:06 a.m.] the enemy's artillery was already shelling the English front-line trenches in Sector 77 and then the trenches in the south-west corner of La Boisselle, immediately after the [mine] explosion it concentrated on the positions adjoining the mine and on the Blinddarm." Telephonic communication, severed by shellfire in the 1st R. Irish Rif. subsector within 10 minutes of the opening of the enemy barrage, remained intact in the 2nd Royal Berkshire subsector.[100]

British PH (phenate-hexamine) gas helmet.

99 Gas projectiles were not included in the feint bombardment ammunition stockpile. See 'GERMAN RAID ON THE BRITISH TRENCHES NEAR LA BOISSELLE, APRIL 11th, 1916', APPENDIX 1: SPECIAL ORDERS FOR THE RAID ON THE SPION, APPENDIX 4: SPECIAL ORDER FOR THE FEINT BOMBARDMENT TO BE CARRIED OUT ON THE MORNING OF THE DAY BEFORE THE RAID and CAPTAIN WAGENER'S REPORT ON THE RAID ON THE EVENING OF 11 APRIL 1916, *Gunfire No. 4* and TNA WO 95/672: 'HQ 25th Inf. Brigade 'B", 1st R. Irish Rif. after-action report, 12 April 1916; 'Report on the enemy's bombardment on the evening April 11th/16', 2nd Royal Berkshire Regiment after-action report, 12 April 1916, III Corps War Diary.
100 See GERMAN RAID ON THE BRITISH TRENCHES NEAR LA BOISSELLE, APRIL 11th, 1916', REPORT ON THE FEINT ON THE EVENING OF APRIL 11th 1916, *Gunfire No. 4*, TNA WO 95/762: '8th Div. G.664/7: Report on the enemy's bombardment on the 11th of April 1916', 8th Division CRA after-action report, III Corps War Diary, WO 95/672: '25th Brigade, 207/G., 8th Division', 14 April 1916, TNA WO 95/672: 'HQ 25th Inf. Brigade 'B", 1st R. Irish Rif. after-action report, 12 April 1916; 'Report on the enemy's bombardment on the evening April 11th/16', 2nd Royal Berkshire Regiment after-action report, 12 April 1916, III Corps War Diary.

At 7:14 a.m., the mine was "fired at the right extremity of the minefield. Forming a crater 50 feet in diameter, "a column of flame shot up to an extraordinary height and stones of appreciable size were scattered to a distance of 330 yards." As prearranged, the German bombardment temporarily ceased at 7:15 p.m. It was at this moment that British field and heavy guns "concentrated on positions adjoining the mine ... opened on the Blinddarm, the majority of the shells being blind." Inside the *Blinddarm*, the previously installed dummies, "arranged in three groups, which were fastened on to lathes, operated by strings leading to dugouts", were "hoisted a few minutes later, because they were partly covered with stones from the mine explosion." This mechanically contrived artifice seemed to have the desired effect, "Immediately the dummies appeared, a brisk fire was opened by two of the enemy's machine-guns, one in the neighbourhood of the Scheere [known as "Dressler Post" to the British] and the other near the Galgen." Having been exposed, lowered and exposed again, the dummies "were greeted afresh with intense fire." Five were hit by machine-gun and rifle fire, "nearly all were more or less knocked about by shellfire or fragments of stone; one was torn off the lathe by a shell." German batteries and trench mortars, recommencing the feint bombardment with "terrific fire" at 7:25 p.m., appeared to silence the hostile machine-guns.[101]

Patrouillen Vorwärts!

Hammered by "large calibre shells", gas shells and "many trench mortars and oil cans", the men of the 1st R. Irish Rif. centre company "had to take cover, the parapet being completely flattened out in many places, and 2 Lewis Guns put out of action." The right and left companies, enduring a comparatively light barrage, were also strafed with machine-gun fire.[102]

The raiders, having quit dugouts 1-10 at 7:20 p.m., were deployed and ready in the *Hohlweg* (Ditch) opposite *Schwaben-Höhe* at 7:25 p.m. Stradtmann's spearhead patrol, "instructed not to leave the Hohlweg at the 23rd minute, but to wait for the conclusion of the intense bombardment in order to avoid at all costs, unnecessary losses from the splinters of our own shells." Blinding "clouds of gas and smoke" enveloping the British trenches opposite made it "impossible to distinguish whether or not our own shells were falling on the point of entry or whether our artillery had already lengthened their range." Finally, at 7:27 p.m., Wagener ordered the Stradtmann patrol

---

101 'GERMAN RAID ON THE BRITISH TRENCHES NEAR LA BOISELLE, APRIL 11th, 1916', REPORT ON THE FEINT ON THE EVENING OF APRIL 11th 1916, *Gunfire No. 4*.
102 TNA WO 95/672: TNA WO 95/672: 'HQ 25th Inf. Brigade 'B", 1st R. Irish Rif. after-action report, 12 April 1916, III Corps War Diary. The trench line objective curving away southwards, only a small portion of the expended gas shell projectiles fell on target. See Saunders, *Raiding on the Western Front*, p. 47.

to advance. Stradtmann, crawling forward with his men, became "violently sick and another man fell down overcome by sudden gas poisoning. However, the latter was on his legs again in a couple of minutes and could not be prevented from hurrying after his patrol." *Leutnant* Boening, accompanied by the six assigned stretcher-bearers, left the jumping-off position simultaneously. Trailing directly behind Stradtmann, he "posted connecting files, whose positions were marked by red signal lamps shaded to the front and to the sides." This human chain to "direct the remaining raiding parties as they advanced across no man's land" now situated; the Dumas and Böhlefield patrols advanced on Wagener's orders one minute later at 7:28 p.m.[103]

Minenwerfer fire had "destroyed the enemy's wire so completely on a width of forty-four yards that on breaking into the enemy's trench, the raiding party did not notice when they crossed the wire entanglement." Stradtmann's patrol entered the shattered British line at "Süd Spion, and at Point 1" before encountering three hapless Tommies in stifling gas helmets exiting a dugout. "They carried hand grenades and rifles with bayonets fixed, but were immediately disarmed by Lieutenants Boening and Stradtmann." The Dumas and Böhlefield's patrols, "following the line of connecting files", arrived moments afterward.[104]

Dumas, brandishing an automatic pistol, led his men left before coming upon a "half-destroyed" machine-gun emplacement in which "Reservist Nadoly, of Stradtmann's patrol was already occupied in digging-out the buried [Lewis] machine-gun." Pressing on, three men under orders to advance overland just beyond the parados, the 11-man party approached the "communication trench [Lochnagar Street] which runs, roughly, along the dividing line between Target Sector 79 and 80, towards the Weisse Steinmauer." It was at this intersection of frontline and communication trench, a large dugout "wrecked, apparently, by a direct hit" nearby, that a "few Englishmen", hastening forward along Lochnagar Street, were surprised and bayoneted by the three above ground men. "Meanwhile, Lieutenant Dumas, with the rest of his men, forced his way further along the trench" before arriving at Tarvis Street communication trench, a "prolongation of the Weisse Steinmauer" just north of the *Besenhecke*. Passing another demolished dugout "in which dead bodies were seen", the patrol reached the entrance of a large and intact dugout adjoining Tarvis Street that they intended to clear. "As, however, a number of Englishmen advanced upon Dumas' patrol from the communication trench and alongside of it,

---

103 'GERMAN RAID ON THE BRITISH TRENCHES NEAR LA BOISSELLE, APRIL 11th, 1916', APPENDIX 1: SPECIAL ORDERS FOR A RAID ON THE SPION, REPORT ON THE EXECUTION OF THE RAID ON THE SPION and CAPTAIN WAGENER'S REPORT ON THE RAID ON THE EVENING OF 11 APRIL 1916, *Gunfire No. 4* and Whitehead, *The Other Side of the Wire Volume I*, p. 402.
104 'GERMAN RAID ON THE BRITISH TRENCHES NEAR LA BOISSELLE, APRIL 11th, 1916', REPORT ON THE EXECUTION OF THE RAID ON THE SPION and CAPTAIN WAGENER'S REPORT ON THE RAID ON THE EVENING OF 11 APRIL 1916, *Gunfire No. 4*.

a mêlée ensued with grenades, rifles and pistols, in the course of which the enemy, after suffering evident loss, either retreated or surrendered" with no injury or loss to the raiders.[105]

Following behind their patrol leader, the 10 men of Böhlefield's party made their way along the trench to the right of the entry point. Encountering three dugouts, "of which one was wrecked and full of dead and wounded", *Leutnant* Böhlefield summoned the occupants to surrender which they did "without more ado." Pausing for a moment to compose a message requesting reinforcements to clear two other dugouts, he ordered the disarmed captives back to the German line under escort before taking up position with the two remaining men "to hold the enemy's trench."[106]

Leutnant Stradtmann, remaining near the entry point with the 10 men under his command, confronted what appeared to be a British counter-attack:

> Whilst our party was breaking into the enemy's trenches, or perhaps before, a party of the enemy, approximately twenty-five to thirty strong, succeeded in getting away from the frontline trench and making their way back to the Weisse Stienmauer, but were again driven back by our artillery fire, and now came running towards Stradtmann's patrol. The latter, apprehending a counter-attack, opened fire.

Ersatz Reservist Walzer, followed by *Unteroffizier* Staiger amongst others, "raised a cheer and charged the Englishmen, bayoneting two of them. Those who did not put up their hands and surrender were killed."[107]

British artillery observers reported "a pair of red rockets" rising from the 1st R. Irish Rif. subsector eight minutes after (7:35 p.m.) the raiders entered the battalion's trenches. Batteries, in response to this recognised SOS signal, fired on prearranged night lines and "swept" forward; "batteries on flanks of zones attacked turning a section on to front attacked, forming a barrage of 50 yards short of hostile trench where distance of 'No Man's Land' permitted."[108]

---

105 'GERMAN RAID ON THE BRITISH TRENCHES NEAR LA BOISSELLE, APRIL 11th, 1916', CAPTAIN WAGENER'S REPORT ON THE RAID ON THE EVENING OF 11 APRIL 1916, *Gunfire No. 4*, Greiner & Vulpius, *Reserve-Infanterie-Regiment Nr. 110 im Weltkrieg 1914-1918*, pp. 108-09 and Abt. Generallandesarchiv, Karlsruhe 456, F54, Nr. 120, Foto 30, Bild 1: Gelünd von Höhe 110 bis La Boisselle, aufgenomen am 21.4.1916 (aerial photograph series), Landesarchiv, Baden-Württemberg. Special thanks to Simon Jones for bringing the latter source to my attention.
106 'GERMAN RAID ON THE BRITISH TRENCHES NEAR LA BOISSELLE, APRIL 11th, 1916', CAPTAIN WAGENER'S REPORT ON THE RAID ON THE EVENING OF 11 APRIL 1916, *Gunfire No. 4*.
107 Ibid.
108 TNA WO 95/762: '8th Div. G.664/7: Report on the enemy's bombardment on the 11th of April 1916', 8th Division CRA after-action report, III Corps War Diary.

No discernible noise emanating from the point of entry, "or from the right of the same, while from a point of some sixty-five yards to the left shots and reports of grenades could be heard", *Hauptmann* Wagener ordered *Vizefeldwebel* Elb to advance and reinforce Dumas' patrol. Stationed close by, Regimental Adjutant *Leutnant* Erb – bedecked in Dräger *Selbstretter* Model 1914 oxygen breathing apparatus – attached himself to Elb's small party on his own initiative as they prepared to cross no man's land. "Shortly after, the sounds of fighting ceased on the left, and the first batch of prisoners were brought back …" Taking stock of the situation, Wagener concluded that "we had the upper hand everywhere, especially on the right, and with a view to exploiting fully our success, I ordered Lieutenant Freund to cross the enemy's trench at the point of entry with fifteen men of the supports, and to attack the Spion from the rear." At the same time, he ordered *Vizefeldwebel* Wölfle to reinforce Böhlefield's patrol with four additional men. His immediate reserve now depleted, Wagener also "ordered up the commanders of the two groups on the flank of the 12th Company, which was stationed immediately to the right of Sap No. 3." These groups had been "warned in the afternoon and given the necessary instructions."[109]

Making their way across no man's land through lingering gas and smoke, the dispatched reinforcements entered the British line at the entry point. Scrambling over tumbledown sandbags and other debris, Elb and Wölfle, "with their men, went in search of Dumas' and Böhlefield's patrols." Trailing close behind, *Leutnant* Freund's patrol "dashed" over the enemy trench and, accompanied by Böhlefield's reinforced patrol, "followed it along to the right as far as the communication trench [vicinity of Inch Street] which leads into the frontline trench near the Spion." Leaping into the frontline on both sides of the communication trench, they surprised and overwhelmed "ten men almost without a struggle, and secured several rifles and articles of equipment." Anyone offering resistance or attempting to escape was mercilessly dispatched with bayonet or bullet. Prisoners and booty thus secured, an "extemporised trench mortar" was discovered close by. Although it was "securely built in", *Vizefeldwebel* Wölfle destroyed it "as best he could with hand grenades and pistol shots." Böhlefield, pushing further ahead with his reinforced command, "came across three or four more wrecked dugouts, which were filled with dead." All "individuals standing about in the trench were killed by the patrol or made prisoner."[110]

Hastening to the left, Elb's party joined Dumas' hard-pressed patrol still heavily engaged near Tarvis Street, "for almost every one of the enemy offered resistance." The desperate close-quarter fighting continued as the Stradtmann, Böhlefield, Freund and Wölfle patrols – on communication of one of two previously arranged return signals – retired from *Süd Spion* to the *Hohlweg*. It was whilst under cover in the latter position

109 'GERMAN RAID ON THE BRITISH TRENCHES NEAR LA BOISSELLE, APRIL 11th, 1916', CAPTAIN WAGENER'S REPORT ON THE RAID ON THE EVENING OF 11 APRIL 1916, *Gunfire No. 4*.
110 Ibid.

that the Dumas-Elb patrols, remaining behind "considerably longer than intended", were determined to be missing. "Hereupon, Lieutenants Boening and Stradtmann, with several non-commissioned officers and men, went back to the enemy's lines and searched the trench" before encountering the overdue party retracing their steps back to the point of entry.[111]

By 7:50 p.m., the "last men of the entire party had returned to the Hohlweg" before seeking cover inside the previously occupied dugouts. One minute passed before the first hostile shell fell on the trenches east of Sap No. 3. The raiders now safely under cover, the German artillery commander, who subsequently switched his guns on to enemy batteries deemed most important to engage, was informed that the feint and main bombardments could be "gradually broken off"; at 8:05 p.m. "the conclusion of the operation" was officially confirmed. At 8:08 p.m. the artillery forward observation officer attached to 1st R. Irish Rif. reported "all quiet – Fire was stopped." The prevailing silence did not last long, 2nd Royal Berkshire Regiment requesting retaliatory fire on La Boisselle at 8:10 p.m. The rounds duly expended "by the battery covering that zone", a reciprocal calm descended across the Ovillers – La Boisselle sector.[112]

"Carried out entirely as pre-arranged"

The enemy having furtively retired from the affected area, cautious elements of 1st R. Irish Rif. re-occupied the shell-shattered frontline as the hovering gas, which left parapets "covered in a black substance", and smoke slowly dissipated. Sentry posts re-established, work commenced on repairs and removal of the dead under the half-light of a waxing gibbous moon intermittently obscured by passing clouds. Inside the German lines, English-speaking *Leutnant* Boening "examined the English prisoners at prearranged points." *Assistenzarzt* Wisser, awaiting the wounded in No. 1 dugout, attended to injured captives in addition to bandaging what appeared to be the raiders' sole casualty; "one man slightly wounded in the forehead by a splinter from a hand grenade."[113] Within 24-hours, the daily *Heeresbericht* (Army communique) reported:

111 Ibid.
112 'GERMAN RAID ON THE BRITISH TRENCHES NEAR LA BOISSELLE, APRIL 11th, 1916', REPORT ON THE EXECUTION OF THE RAID ON THE SPION, CAPTAIN WAGENER'S REPORT ON THE RAID ON THE EVENING OF 11 APRIL 1916, *Gunfire No. 4* and TNA WO 95/762: '8th Div. G.664/7: Report on the enemy's bombardment on the 11th of April 1916', 8th Division CRA after-action report, III Corps War Diary.
113 TNA WO 95/762: "G.353, REPORT OF THE GERMAN RAID ON OUR TRENCHES ON THE NIGHT 11th APRIL 1916', 13 April 1916, III Corps War Diary, 'GERMAN RAID ON THE BRITISH TRENCHES NEAR LA BOISSELLE, APRIL 11th, 1916', REPORT ON THE EXECUTION OF THE RAID ON THE SPION, CAPTAIN WAGENER'S REPORT ON THE RAID ON THE EVENING

"Near La Boisselle (northeast of Albert) a small German detachment brought back 29 captives and one machine-gun from a night-time attack against a British position without any casualties."[114]

Intelligence gathered from the raids on the night of 6/7 April and 11 April refuted *OHL* predictions of a "thrust limited to north of the Ancre, where the British divisions were packed closely together. In fact", a German reserve officer later remarked, "in the middle of April, 52nd Infantry Division was facing odds of six or eight to one. On the right of the brigade, daring patrol work brought Reserve Infantry Regiment 119 the good fortune to discover the presence of 87th Brigade, 29th Division, which only days earlier had arrived from Suez. Left of the brigade, 56th Reserve Infantry Brigade identified the 8th Division."[115]

The remainder of the week (12-15 April) was rainy and windy before the weather finally cleared on Friday the 14th. Bellicose activity in the Ovillers – La Boisselle sector reverted back to artillery, trench mortar and rifle grenade bombardments.[116] Ad interim, both German and British military bureaucracies initiated the process of investigation and analysis in order to determine offensive/defensive lessons of the 11 April trench raid.

Three ex post facto reports were composed by *Freiherr* Vietinghoff, *Hauptmann* Wagener and feint commander *Leutnant* Bachmann, the latter two documents, notwithstanding Bachmann's opinion that "the enemy was completely deceived by the feint attacks", consisting of narrative content only. The recent raid, an effusive Vietinghoff observed, "as far as the infantry, and also the artillery and pioneers, was carried out entirely as planned." All through the period of active operations, "the enemy's artillery was in complete uncertainty as to our point of entry. At about 8:06 p.m. [7:06 p.m.] the enemy's artillery opened a feeble and aimless fire, and or a while shelled the English front line trenches in Sector 77", the feint having drawn the fire to the *Blinddarm* and vicinity "until shortly before 8:50 p.m. [7:50 p.m.] not a single shell fell in the neighbourhood of Sap No. 3." It was also discerned that British batteries did not commence a retaliatory sweep of the general break-in area until 7:47 p.m. when the Bécourt Valley towards *Besenhecke* was engaged with shrapnel. Thus, in Vietinghoff's estimation, "the feint met with entire success, and throughout the entire raid drew

OF 11 APRIL 1916, *Gunfire No. 4* and Moon Phases April 1916 <http://www.calendar-12.com/moon_calendar/1916/april>
114 *Der Deutsche Heeresbericht*, 12 April 1916 < http://www.stahlgewitter.com/16_04_12.htm>
115 *Landwehr Leutnant* M. Gerster *op. cit.* in Sheldon, *The German Army on the Somme 1914-1916*, p. 114. Apprehensive about the obvious Allied build-up, *Second Army* forwarded three pre-emptive attack proposals for *OHL* sanction during the period March to May 1916. *Chef des Generalstabes* Erich von Falkenhayn, maintaining his primary focus on Verdun, refused to entertain the idea beyond discussion stage. See Jack Sheldon, *Fighting the Somme: German Challenges, Dilemmas and Solutions* (Barnsley: Pen & Sword, 2016), Chapter 2.
116 TNA WO 157/315: 'III Corps Intelligence Summary', 12-15 April 1916, III Corps Intelligence file.

almost the whole of the enemy's artillery fire and the fire of several machine-guns." Total ammunition expenditure, feint bombardment inclusive, was as laid down in compiled "Tables of Distribution of Artillery Fire."[117]

The overwhelming "fire for effect" by the 14 heavy and 70 medium *Minenwerfer*, Vietinghoff continued, completely eradicated the enemy's barbed wire defences opposite the point of entry. The cumulative effect of the supporting artillery "on the enemy's personnel and trenches was quite remarkable", the 'T' and 'K' gas projectiles sowing paralysis and confusion, as was apparent from the "condition of prisoners immediately after their capture, and from the fighting in the enemy's position." Nevertheless, that the section of line held by 'A' Company, No. 1 Platoon, 1st R. Irish Rif. demonstrated, "in the opinion of the regiment", a more determined resistance than that of neighbouring No. 3 Platoon. The former's superior performance based "not only on the fact that the commander of No. 1 Platoon showed conspicuous smartness and bravery in encouraging his men to hold out", but was also due to the curvature in the frontline, so that only a small proportion of gas shells fell within the British trench. "Consequently", Vietinghoff continued, "the regiment attaches the greatest importance to a bombardment with gas shell, but considers it necessary that the enemy should, at the same time, be shelled with H[igh] E[xplosives] in the event of strong bodies of troops not being available for the subsequent assault."[118]

Officially recorded German losses, in addition to one man injured by a grenade splinter, amounted to nothing more than "quite negligible" wounds sustained by Dumas' patrol. Unaccountably, another man, *Infanterist* Josef Winkler of *3rd Kompagnie*, appears to have died of wounds in British captivity. Why this went unmentioned in subsequent reports remains unknown. Prisoners and booty, the *RIR 110* commander noted, consisted of "Twenty-four unwounded and five wounded Englishmen. In addition, one Lewis machine-gun, one rifle with telescopic sights, and twenty ordinary rifles, as well as a large number of steel helmets, belts with ammunition pouches, packs, haversacks and gas helmets." Vietinghoff also expressed reserved praise for the "Regiment of Royal Irish Rifles", remarking that the battalion "created a most favourable impression, both as regards the physique of the men and their mode of repelling the assault. But for the effect of the gas shell", he added, it would have been impossible to "clear the section of trench held by one entire company and the flank of the company on its left, so thoroughly that not an Englishman remained alive in

---

117 'GERMAN RAID ON THE BRITISH TRENCHES NEAR LA BOISSELLE, APRIL 11th, 1916', REPORT ON THE EXECUTION OF THE RAID ON THE SPION and REPORT ON THE FEINT ON THE EVENING OF APRIL 11th 1916. Total ammunition expenditure for the raid was as follows: 3,543 field gun; 829 light field howitzer; 540 9-cm. (gun); 30 10-cm. (gun); 110 12-cm. (gun); 984 heavy field howitzer (200 'K' and 178 'T' gas projectiles inclusive); 25 21-cm. (mortar) or 6,061 total. Feint bombardment: 204 *Lanz Minenwerfer*, 26 *Erdmörser*, 57 *Albrecht Mörser*, 48 medium *Minenwerfer*, 474 light *Minenwerfer* or 809 total.
118 Ibid.

Photograph purported to be 1st Royal Irish Rifles prisoners, 11 April 1916. Attired in the first pattern Australian tunic, this image appears to have been taken during the following summer when I Anzac Corps was engaged at Pozières and Mouquet Farm. (Greiner & Vulpius, *Reserve-Infanterie-Regiment Nr. 110 im Weltkrieg 1914-1918*)

the trench", although the number of assumed enemy fatalities was, as we shall see, almost certainly exaggerated in Wagener's report. On-the-spot prisoner interrogations disclosed "many details of especial importance" to *RIR 110*: "For this reason the Regiment considers it desirable that, in all cases, prisoners should be examined by officers with personal knowledge of what is of importance for the regiment to know, and that the majority of prisoners should only be taken away after this examination." According to the post-war regimental history, these captives also related that the fighting had been "'horrible'. Already by the morning of 10th April, during the mortar and heavy artillery bombardment, 'A' Company had suffered 20 killed or wounded." An assault was expected on the night of the 10/11 April. "When nothing occurred, the mood lifted on the 11th and the fear of attack dissipated." The outset of the German "'drumfire' at 8 in the evening therefore came as a surprise and caught 'D' Company in the front line trenches as units were being relieved. Particularly shocking was the detonation of the mines – something the English were particularly anxious about."[119]

---

119 Ibid., Whitehead, *The Other Side of the Wire Vol. I*, pp. 404, 537, Saunders, *Raiding on the Western Front*, p. 51, Greiner & Vulpius, *Reserve-Infanterie-Regiment Nr. 110 im*

Vietinghoff's primary deductions/conclusions were concerned with artillery support and its relation to the number of men deployed for an operation of this size; the effect of flanking bombardments; gas and wind direction; the consequences of wearing gas masks during the attack, and possibilities for deeper penetration into the enemy's defences.

If operations similar to that of 11 April were to be "carried out with the lowest effectives possible, it was essential that the enemy should have already suffered appreciable losses from our artillery, so that patrols were not confronted by strong detachments but only isolated groups whose morale had suffered by the sight of their own dead and severely wounded comrades around them."[120]

The artillery was "most successful" in mastering the British flank defences, "but the regiment considers that the more gas shells are employed the easier this too will be." Present experience also determined that lingering gas was of little risk "to one's own position and one's own raiding party, for the wind could not be more unfavourable than it was in this case." That said, the wearing of gas masks as far as the entry point was recommended, for "[h]owever well the masks are fitted, and however thoroughly the men are practiced, the mask hinders a general survey, and makes it impossible to pick up one's bearings", something deemed crucial for any patrol leader. In addition, the mask overstrained the lungs, "which were already severely tried" by physical exertions and psychological effects inherent to combat.[121]

Depth of advance appeared to be dependent on whether or not the British line could, "as in the present case", be cleared to an estimated width of 150-200 yards and "if the enemy had not, up to that moment, opened a barrage on the point of exit." Then, "in the opinion of the regiment", a further advance into the enemy defences offered "no great difficulty." All that was required were new artillery arrangements and the dispatch of fresh patrols. Furthermore, "in the opinion of patrol commanders", no insurmountable obstacle would have been encountered had fresh patrols "advanced in and parallel to the communication trenches, and cleared out the Weisse Steinmauer position". Patrol leaders were also certain that inroads "into the enemy's third trench and into his last positions in the Labyrinth" would have been possible without risk of serious losses.[122]

In summary, Vietinghoff considered high explosive and gas shell bombardments to be a vital operational component to any successful trench raid. These projectiles, fired in deadly combination, would incapacitate an enemy garrison long enough to allow patrols to complete their mission with a minimum of interference. The enemy

---

Weltkrieg 1914-1918, p. 110. An accompanying appendix entitled 'EXAMINATION OF ENGLISHMEN' was not amongst the raid documents captured on 4 July 1916.
120 'GERMAN RAID ON THE BRITISH TRENCHES NEAR LA BOISSELLE, APRIL 11th, 1916', REPORT ON THE EXECUTION OF THE RAID ON THE SPION, *Gunfire No. 4*.
121 Ibid.
122 Ibid.

thus disoriented and reduced to isolated groups, future opportunities to penetrate as far as the second or third lines might be exploited by fresh patrols following close on the heels of their predecessors. This reliance on a crushing barrage to kill and maim, Anthony Saunders notes, was part of the "destruction strategy at the heart of the major offensives in 1916 such as the one being fought by the Germans against the French at Verdun ... As the British were to discover in a few months' time ... this was a dangerous approach to take as the ideal could never be realised no matter how long or intense the preliminary bombardment might be." Moreover, Vietinghoff's observed operational corollary of incapacitating artillery bombardments and successive patrol advances was the "kind of leapfrogging infiltration ... already practiced in an embryonic form by the new stormtroop battalions" which was further developed during 1917. However, his perspective on the application of firepower to subdue and disorient did not dismiss the "notion of destruction as a means to provide easy access to the enemy lines", something both sides failed to grasp until summer 1916. The use of gas in such operations, the *RIR 110* commander also observed, could be problematic given unpredictable vagaries of the wind that forced raiders to don movement-inhibiting masks during brief but intense periods of combat. In addition to these carefully considered tactical insights, the 11 April raid inflicted notable loss on the enemy and, whilst not providing anything concrete with regard to the expected British offensive, furnished some useful local intelligence.[123] One tantalising "might have been" concerns the close proximity of the Lochnagar mine entrance to the junction of Kingsgate Street and Lochnagar Street. The discovery of this elaborate underground shaft, still in the process of being driven towards *Schwaben-Höhe*, may have occurred had the Dumas patrol pressed down the latter instead of remaining in the enemy frontline as per orders. In any case, it was not in their remit to do so.[124]

"The blighters raided us ..."

III Corps' intelligence summary for 12 April related all that was known in the immediate aftermath of the German trench raid. The enemy bombardment had done a "considerable damage to the trenches" and caused a "good many casualties ..." Actual

---

123 Ibid. and Saunders, *Raiding on the Western Front*, pp. 52-53.
124 Underground warfare historian Simon Jones observed in an October 2016 correspondence with the author: "Although the Lochnagar entrance was in dead ground, the spoil heap had long been visible to the Germans and they had frequently subjected it to mortar fire. They only commenced mined listening galleries from the *Schwaben-höhe* perhaps a week before 22 April 1916 after overhearing mining activity (but they did not locate the gallery before 1 July). Their previous apparent lack of interest in British mining activity in this sector is odd, and I can only speculate that the Germans believed the distances too great to make it worthwhile, both in respect of the width of no man's land and the distance behind the British front line of the apparent spoil heap."

details remained sketchy, but an infantry observer reported "that a party of the enemy left their trenches towards the end of the bombardment." Traces of the brief enemy occupation were determined by the discovery of 27 German hand grenades "picked up in the frontline and dugouts immediately in rear of our trench X.20.4 this morning, so that a raiding party must have got into our trenches." At this stage it was "impossible to say if any prisoners were captured by the Germans until the trenches have been cleared."[125]

Rawlinson, visiting 8th Division headquarters during the 12th, was initially sympathetic with regard to the reverse:

> It appears that during the bombardment yesterday evening the Germans did raid our trenches and took away about 20 men of the RIR [R. Irish Rif.] out of dugouts – the bombardment consisted of about 6 to 7000 shells and our reply was late and very moderate in intensity – the 8th Division do not come out of it well but there is then to be said namely that they have only very recently taken over the line …[126]

Infantry fatalities when finally reckoned were, considering the circumstances, relatively light – one officer and eight men of 1st R. Irish Rif.; one officer and one man of 2nd Royal Berkshire Regiment.[127] The number of wounded sustained by both battalions were 39 and four respectively. This left 28 men of 1st R. Irish Rif. missing and unaccounted for.[128] They were, it had to be assumed, now in enemy hands.

---

125 TNA WO 157/315: 'III Corps Intelligence Summary: Covering a period of 24 hours ending 6 a.m., 12/4/16, III Corps Intelligence file.
126 CAC RWLN 5/5: Rawlinson Diary, 12 April 1916.
127 1st R. Irish Rif.: 2nd Lieutenant Percival Maxwell Harte-Maxwell, 5796 Rifleman William Dodd, 6488 Rifleman Henry Holmes, 5745 Rifleman William Marjury, 6694 Rifleman Patrick Mullen, 7892 Rifleman Francis Parkes, 5454 Rifleman John Rankin, 1365 Rifleman Harry Shaw and 11357 Rifleman Thomas Todd; 2nd Royal Berkshire Regiment: Lieutenant Edward Morley Medlicott and 8084 Private Frederick King. Killed by shellfire, Harte-Maxwell (b. Kingstown, Co. Dublin 1884) was a former Bank of Ireland employee and popular Enniscorthy tennis player who joined 1st R. Irish Rif. from 4th Connaught Rangers on 25 May 1915. The informal active service wills of Riflemen Dodd and Rankin are available at the National Archives of Ireland (NAI). See *Soldiers Died in the Great War 1914-19* (CD Rhom), TNA WO 339/30271: Lieutenant Percival Maxwell HARTE-MAXWELL. The Connaught Rangers file, Thomas F. Hennessey (ed.), *The Great War 1914-1918: Bank of Ireland Staff Service Record* (Dublin: Alex Thom & Co., 1920), p. 8, Taylor, *The First Royal Irish Rifles in the Great War*, p. 257, Paul Rouse, *Sport in Ireland: A History* (Oxford: Oxford University Press, 2015), p. 225, NAI 2002/119: Soldiers' Wills and F. Loraine Petre, *The Royal Berkshire Regiment (Princess Charlotte of Wales's) 1914-1918 Vol. II* (Reading: The Barracks Reading, 1925), p. 80.
128 TNA WO 95/1730: 1st Royal Irish Rifles and WO 95/1729: 2nd Royal Berkshire Regiment war diaries.

A Lieutenant Carson was dispatched from III Corps headquarters to investigate what had happened. An initial report based on his findings was distributed on 13 April. In addition to providing the earliest chronology of events, he determined that "a party of the enemy from 30 to 40 strong came over our parapet & entered our trenches. The part of the line they had chosen was particularly suitable for a raid. Our wire was so weak that it formed practically no obstacle and many of our frontline trenches had no firesteps." This unfortunate state of affairs ensured that "Only about 60% of the frontline garrison could man the trenches in the sector attacked." As for signs of brief German occupation and the missing men, "The enemy left a number of rifle grenades behind them & presumably took prisoners – the 24 [sic] men hitherto unaccounted for." Moreover, "No German corpses have been seen in our trenches or in 'No Man's Land' since the raid. The raiders may have belonged to a travelling raiding party which is reported to be moving up and down the line."[129] Carson concluded: "Their object was to obtain identifications and probably to capture a Lewis Gun. They were successful in both cases. The damage done to the trenches is considerable, the frontline having been severely damaged and the support line to a less extent."[130] III Corps' GOC Pulteney remarked:

> The blighters raided us on my return after a terrific bombardment [;] of course they chose the worst battalion in the corps to take on and they chucked it (between ourselves) so 29 of them are marching to Berlin, they are all Irishmen, I very much doubt they knew which brigade they belong to and am sure they don't know what division [,] so much doubt if they get much information out of them.[131]

Pulteney was indeed correct in his final assertion, *RIR 110's* history noting: "The prisoners know nothing about the expected offensive."[132]

Rawlinson's attitude began to harden following a subsequent successful German raid on Fourth Army front. On 13 April he observed:

---

129 The celebrated *Sturmabteilung* commanded by *Hauptmann* Wilhelm Rohr was, following a three-week tour at Verdun, re-organising and re-fitting at this time, and did not commence the *OHL*-inspired training programme for "small cadres of officers and NCOs" tasked with inculcating the latest *Stoss* tactics throughout the army until May 1916. It must be surmised, therefore, that the erroneously perceived "travelling raiding party" was indicative of the simultaneous adoption of stormtroop tactical methodology at formation and unit level. See Bull, *Stosstrupptaktik*, pp. 83-84.
130 TNA WO 95/672: 'G.353, REPORT OF THE GERMAN RAID ON OUR TRENCHES ON THE NIGHT 11th APRIL 1916', III Corps War Diary.
131 Letter from Pulteney to Lady Edith Londonderry, 13 April 1916 quoted in Leask, *Putty*, pp. 380-81.
132 Greiner & Vulpius, *Reserve-Infanterie-Regiment Nr. 110 im Weltkrieg 1914-1918*, p. 110.

Last night the Bosches made another raid on the XIII Corps[133] and captured some 18 men of the 18th Division who were out as a working party – It was not a good show – The guns did not get on to the place quick enough and from what I can gather the men did not behave any too well – I am much annoyed that two successful raids should have been undertaken by the enemy on this front within the same week, and I have sent out a pretty stormy memorandum on the subject – The answer to the raid should be a counter-raid I think and listening posts should be made to run well out in front of our wire to give warning and to bring flank fire to bear on the enemy as they come across – I do not gather that on either of these occasions there were active measures taken by the inf[antr]y to resist the enemy – Both occasions were preceded by very heavy bombardment – that against the 8th Division was commenced by some 6 to 7000 shells most of which however were from field guns – Our guns were slow and the SOS signal did not work well – Lines were cut and there was no alternative signal.[134]

Rawlinson was anxious "to find some means of preventing these raids in the future" for the recent German incursions "during the last few weeks have not only inflicted considerable losses on our troops in the frontline, but have supplied the enemy with very important information." Corps commanders were, therefore, to carefully consider enemy tactics. It appeared probable that German raiding parties got "into position close to our wire before the hostile barrage opens" and the enemy trenches "where our barrage was likely to come are cleared of troops, so as to avoid loss from our retaliation. We must, therefore", Rawlinson concluded, "consider how best to meet these manoeuvres." Elaborating on his diary passage, he called for listening posts to be pushed out "well beyond our wire all along our line at 100 to 200 yards intervals." As stated during a subsequent conference, these posts were to be occupied by "small bodies of infantry, and, in some cases, Lewis Guns." Strongly wired and "fire-stepped at the end and along the sides", they would serve the dual function of hostile raid deterrent and useful annex for retaliatory operations. Sentries, the 13 April memorandum continued, were to remain in place following commencement of German bombardment in order to "keep a sharp lookout on either flank for any bodies of hostile troops that may be lying out in front of our wire." Cover of darkness offered

---

133 "On the night of the 12th – 13th April the enemy raided our trenches NE of Carnoy. One prisoner was captured and the bodies of several dead Germans show the raiding party to have belonged to the 62nd Regiment, 12th Division …" A German report subsequently recorded 13 prisoners of 12th Middlesex Regiment. Peter Barton, erroneously stating that this particular raid occurred on 15 April, notes that a pocketbook seized from one of the captives provided the Germans with "useful verbal data" relating to a recent training course. See TNA WO 157/169: 'Fourth Army Summary of Intelligence, 1st to 15th April 1916', Fourth Army Intelligence File and Barton, 'Tolerating Mystery and Challenging History', *Stand To! The Journal of the Western Front Association*, No. 109 (2017), p. 10.
134 CAC RWLN 5/5: Rawlinson Diary, 13 April 1916.

maximum opportunities for concealment within outposts thus affording "a difficult target for the enemy to hit." Sufficient occupation of these positions also afforded the opportunity to thin out the frontline garrison, the majority to take up position in support trenches until the bombardment was over. The listening posts constructed, the artillery was to be "very careful that their barrage is not formed close enough to our lines to hit the men in their posts." A series of specific precautions to be immediately implemented[135] were followed by the pronouncement that the "fact that the enemy has succeeded in gaining a footing in our trenches is no reason for the garrison of these trenches to surrender, even if temporarily cut-off from support", therefore, it was the "duty of every man to continue fighting and inflict casualties" as a "deterrent against future enterprises." Major-General Hudson (GOC 8th Division) conveyed the memorandum directives to his brigade commanders at a conference held the same day as the document's general distribution throughout Fourth Army. Discussion with regard to further implementation continued at the next conference on 19 April.[136]

Formations/units affected by the raid were required to submit their after-action reports. Major Mayne, acting CO 1st R. Irish Rif., submitted his report to 25th Brigade on 12 April. Written within a day of the raid, Mayne admitted that he was "unable to ascertain definitely" at what time the enemy entered the British line and that only three men could be found "who actually saw the Germans in our frontline, and these men seem very uncertain as to numbers." 'A' Company officers were equally uncertain as to enemy strength and duration of the hostile incursion:

135 These were as follows: "(a) The order must be strictly enforced as regards men not taking cover in dugouts in the frontline. (b) Steps should be taken to improve the wire along our front. Where there are still dugouts in the frontline another line must be dug in front, the old frontline becoming the support line. (c) The siting of the machine and Lewis guns should be carefully gone into to ensure that there is good flanking and covering fire all along our front, not only from guns in the frontline, but also from guns in emplacements in the neighbourhood of the support line. (d) Instructions should be given to our artillery to continue their barrage for at least half an hour after the infantry have reported 'all quiet". During this half-hour fire must be delivered well on the flanks as well as on the front of the area raided. (e) Our shrapnel must be burst as close in front of our own trenches and listening posts as safety admits, so as to enclose the area threatened. (f) To enable the artillery to be concentrated at the right time and place, every effort must be made to keep the gunners, both field and heavy, constantly informed as to the intensity of the targets of the enemy's fire. This is a factor of great importance, and, in order that information may be passed direct to the guns concerned, each divisional battery charged with the defence of the portion of the front must have direct telephone communication with the HQ of the company or companies whose front it covers. (g) In order to ensure that artillery are able to bring their fire to bear at once, constant tests of the SOS signal should be carried out. (h) In the case of a raid the artillery fire must be as rapid as possible, and there must be no question of husbanding ammunition …"
136 TNA WO 95/672: 'General Staff 4th Army No. III/1(g) v', 13 April 1916, III Corps War Diary and 'NOTES ON A CONFERENCE HELD AT FOURTH ARMY HEADQUARTERS, 16th APRIL 1916', III Corps War Diary, WO 95/1674: 'G. 131 K', 13 and 19 April 1916, 8th Division War Diary.

None of the platoon commanders of the centre company saw any Germans in the trench. They appear to have entered the frontline on the left of the centre (A Coy.). 27 hand grenades (enemy) were found in the frontline and in dugouts immediately in rear after the bombardment had finished. I am unable to say how long the enemy remained in our frontline, but owing to the fact that none of the centre company saw any Germans, and that only three men can be found who did, I am of the opinion that they can have been in our trench only a very short time. The men who say they saw Germans in our frontline can give no indication which would furnish any clue as to what unit they belong.

Casualties – "one officer and eight men killed. 35 men wounded, 26 men [sic] missing" – confirmed, and one Lewis Gun unaccounted for, Mayne concluded, given the obvious success achieved by the enemy, with a case for mitigating circumstances: "I should like to add that the wire along the front occupied by my Battalion is very bad – there is very little of it, and at the point where it seems the enemy entered, there is none at all that can be really considered an obstacle." The frontline, he continued, "is generally not in a good state of defence – there are many long stretches without any firesteps, and in consequence the men cannot man the parapet. During the few days the Battalion has been in the line every effort has been made to remedy these defects."[137]

Major G.H. Sawyer, CO 2nd Royal Berkshire Regiment, had little to add in his report. His battalion suffered light casualties – one officer and one man killed, four men wounded – during the German feint bombardment. A counter-attack company had been held in readiness "for any action" and no SOS or gas signal was sent up by his unit, but at "about 7:55 p.m. I received an SOS message [.] This was passed to Coys and they stood to arms. As the bombardment was at this time ceasing and there was no sign of the enemy making any advance, it appeared the SOS must have been delayed in reaching me." Artillery support was "called for" and duly "rendered." Telephone communication "worked well, only one wire being cut, but in spite of this it was very difficult to know what was happening in the frontline." Sawyer concluded with the observation that "more splinter-proof dugouts are required in the frontline owing to the time it takes to get the men out of the very deep dugouts."[138]

Mayne and Sawyer's reports were passed on to brigade headquarters for consideration. Careful evaluation following receipt thereof, in addition to what appears to have been the sanctioning of a brigade-level investigation, assisted Brigadier-General Pollard, GOC 25th Brigade, with the compilation of his own report. Forwarded to 8th Division headquarters on 14 April, the document was a combination of serious battalion-level criticism tempered by extenuating factors relative to his command's

---

137 TNA WO 95/672: 'HQ 25th Inf. Brigade 'B", 12 April 1916, III Corps War Diary.
138 TNA WO 95/672: 'Report on the enemy's bombardment on the evening April 11th/16', 2nd Royal Berkshire Regiment after-action report, 12 April 1916, III Corps War Diary.

short time in the Ovillers – La Boisselle sector and the poor state of its inherited defences. Pollard began by stating that he had encountered "great difficulty in getting a report of what had occurred, hence the delay in rendering this report, but after enquiries the following appears to be as correct an account of what occurred as is available." Specific details summarising the main features of the enemy bombardment and the fact that it appeared to be specifically directed against the centre company of 1st R. Irish Rif. were succeeded by the surmise that the raiders breached the line "on the front occupied by the left centre platoon of the centre company (about X.20.4 [map reference] thereabouts)." Of the aforementioned platoon, of which 21 of the missing men originated from, "one man escaped from the raiders, and the ration party and a guard at Battn. HQ were absent, the remainder of the platoon were killed, wounded or missing." With regard to communications, "all wires from companies appear to have been cut in the first ten minutes" – the telephone wire to the centre company headquarters dugout almost immediately. "Telephonic communication with the right company was restored and maintained, but that with the remaining frontline companies was not restored until the following day." Patrols were dispatched from battalion headquarters at once but did not reach the centre company until "all was quiet." The "considerable delay", Pollard continued, in "obtaining any accurate account of casualties was the result of "confusion existing in the centre company, although it was withdrawn into support" on relief by the support company."[139] These additional details recounted, the dismayed brigadier remarked:

> As regards the statement by the OC R. Irish Rifles that no officer of the centre company saw any German, I regret to say that investigation has shown that no officers of that company were in the frontline until all was over. I have verbally informed GOC [Hudson] of this, and the step which I have taken in the matter. The fact that no Very Lights were put up by these officers is accounted for in the same manner.

The step taken was, as per the current *Manual of Military Law*, an order for the immediate arrest of 'A' Company CO Captain ffrench-Mullen who would remain in custody pending further instructions from divisional headquarters.[140] Battalion-level failings identified, Pollard concurred with Mayne's contention that the defences were in poor state with little time to put them in order prior to the German raid. Warming to this theme, he concluded with the general observation that "I am bound to say, in my

---

139 Pollard's report recorded 1st R. Irish Rif. casualties as follows: Right company: one killed and two missing; centre company: six killed, 27 wounded and 26 missing; left company: one officer and one man killed, six wounded and one missing; support company: one killed and four wounded (76 total).
140 See TNA WO 339/9059: Captain Ernest FFRENCH-MULLEN. The Royal Irish Rifles file, Taylor, *The First Royal Irish Rifles in the Great War*, p. 72 and War Office, *Manual of Military Law* (London: HMSO, 1914), Chapter IV, sections 1-10.

opinion, a well-planned raid against such trenches, situated as they are in a position where hostile observation is very easy, had every chance of success. But my opinion of the part played by the battalion concerned has been shown in the action which I have taken, with which [the] GOC is acquainted."[141]

Major-General Hudson, the GOC concerned, was, based on the penetrating comments by Brigadier-General Pollard, decidedly unimpressed with the performance of 1st R. Irish Rif. and dismissed Major Mayne's document: "A bad report – not candid. Where was the company commander and his officer?" In reference to Pollard's assertion that flares should have been discharged whilst the raid was in progress, he observed, "I would also like to add that the officer of the centre company should not use many Very lights. In consequence, the sections in the left and right companies were not able to observe the approach of any of the enemy."[142] Reports from battalions and brigade in hand, he composed a highly critical cover document before forwarding all to III Corps headquarters on 15 April. In no uncertain language, Hudson opined that he was "not satisfied with several matters in connection with the behaviour of the unit concerned [,] especially with those referred to in paras. 2 and 3 of the report by Brigadier-General J.H.W. POLLARD, commanding 25th Brigade." In response, he ordered a court of enquiry "to make a full investigation of the whole case, after which I shall be able to give a definite opinion of the matter." Until then, "the officer commanding the centre company of the Royal Irish Rifles has been placed under arrest, and Major SAWYER, 2nd Royal Berks Regt., appointed to take over command of the battalion from Temp[orar]y. Major MAYNE R.I. Rifles."[143] Hudson concluded with the exonerating determination that artillery support throughout the raid "lacked intensity, but this was due to a breakdown in communications since the supporting group artillery had but little information regarding the actual point of attack."[144] To what was deemed an avoidable "breakdown" could also be, by inference,

---

141 TNA WO 95/672: '25th Brigade, 207/G, 8th Division', 14 April 1916, III Corps War Diary.
142 TNA WO 95/672: 'HQ 25th Inf. Brigade 'B'', 12 April 1916, III Corps War Diary.
143 TNA WO 95/672: 'General Staff G.664/7/2', 15 April 1916, III Corps War Diary.
144 Ibid. Hudson's exculpation of the gunners aside, there was "little clear policy governing the defensive use of artillery." Indeed, the instructional pamphlet *Artillery in Holding the Line* (1916) "was published in sufficiently small numbers that none have survived. The title alone suggests a passive or at least rigid defensive mentality. Its contents can be surmised as … approving and elaborating the *ad hoc* system that had grown up in 1915. 'Sectors' were official policy, and SOS lines were normal practice. There was no modification of defensive measures to reflect the evolving and improving command system, nor any consideration in changes in the infantry. This suggests that doctrine was still compartmentalized." For its part, Fourth Army headquarters stated in a March 1916 document: "Corps must have definite schemes made out for the employment of their heavy artillery subject to the requirements of effective counter-battery work in the event of a serious bombardment by the enemy on any part of their front. For the purpose of framing these schemes [,] the enemy's frontline should be divided into sections and mutual assistance by adjoining corps considered." See Sanders Marble, *British Artillery on*

attributed to the perceived failure of infantry officers to signal supporting gunners with rockets as laid down in paragraph IV of the 10 April defence scheme.[145]

At III Corps headquarters, Lieutenant-General Pulteney read through Hudson's collection of forwarded documents prior to forwarding to Fourth Army on 15 April. In the accompanying covering letter he declared, "I concur with the remarks made by General Hudson. As far as I am able to ascertain at present, there is no redeeming feature in the conduct of the Irish Rifles during this action; with the exception of one officer who was killed there does not seem to have been any officer in the front and this matter will be dealt with by the court of enquiry."[146]

With a court of enquiry now set in motion, Major Mayne relieved of command in what was a typical "inefficiency replacement", and an ostensibly incompetent company commander placed under arrest, Rawlinson addressed "Recent Hostile Raids" and remedies to thereof at a Fourth Army conference on 16 April. He remained unconvinced with

2nd Lieutenant Percival Maxwell Harte-Maxwell, the only 1st Royal Irish Rifles officer fatality sustained during the 11 April 1916 trench raid. (Hennessey (ed.), *The Great War 1914-1918: Bank of Ireland Staff Service Record*)

regard to Hudson's exoneration of the gunners, remarking "that the artillery had not been quick enough or strong enough and there was not sufficient volume of fire."[147] Furthermore, he observed during the 16 April conference, "the infantry and machine-guns must do their share in the defence of the line, and not rely on the artillery to do

---

the Western Front in the First World War: "The Infantry cannot do with a gun less" (Farnham: Ashgate, 2013), p. 114 and 'Fourth Army No. 4/A.A./5', 3 March 1916 as quoted in TNA WO 95/672: 'General Staff 4th Army No. III/1(g) v', 13 April 1916, III Corps War Diary.
145 TNA WO 95/1674: 'G.577/25', 10 April 1916, 8th Division War Diary.
146 TNA WO 95/672: 'G.378', 15 April 1916, III Corps War Diary.
147 This perspective had its origins in the "stormy memorandum" of 13 April, in which Rawlinson noted that the "enemy was unlikely to expose his men" to retaliatory fire in the trenches opposite and "howitzer fire on such a target" would more than likely be ineffective.

240   At All Costs

everything."[148] Briefly recapitulating the defensive methodology outlined in the 13 April memorandum, Rawlinson next sought to inculcate the offensive spirit whilst responding to German aggression in kind:

> Each division in the frontline is to have a raid organised and ready to be launched as a counter to any enemy raid. These raids will probably [be] more successful if launched immediately a hostile raid has taken place, and in the same vicinity, as the preparatory bombardment and wire-cutting might then be mistaken for retaliation. At the same time, the Army Commander does not necessarily wish commanders to wait for the enemy, but to undertake raids at their own selected time.[149]

To this end and based on recent "indications that changes in the enemy's dispositions opposite the front held by the Fourth Army have lately taken place", two raids were ordered for the night of 22/23 April. One of these operations would provide 1st R. Irish R. with the opportunity to redeem themselves.[150]

"They are a very bad battalion"

Relieved by 2nd Rifle Brigade on the evening of 13 April, 1st R. Irish Rif. withdrew to brigade reserve billets at Dernacourt. Casualties for the five-day period commencing on 9 April, amounted to two officers and 87 men. Lieutenant Whitfield remarked in the aftermath of this very trying tour, "We are glad to be out. We had a really bad time of it and my nerve, like most of the other officers, was considerably shaken." Major Sawyer assumed command the next day. Returning to the La Boisselle trenches four days later on the 17th, 1st R. Irish Rif. relieved 2nd Rifle Brigade, battalion headquarters being established in a dugout at Chapes Spur.[151]

---

148   Peter E. Hodgkinson, *British Infantry Battalion Commanders in the First World War* (Farnham: Ashgate, 2015), pp. 118-19 and TNA WO 95/672: 'General Staff 4th Army No. III/1(g) v', 13 April 1916, III Corps War Diary and 'NOTES ON A CONFERENCE HELD AT FOURTH ARMY HEADQUARTERS, 16th APRIL 1916', III Corps War Diary.
149   TNA WO 95/672: 'General Staff 4th Army No. III/1(g) v', 13 April 1916 and 'NOTES ON A CONFERENCE HELD AT FOURTH ARMY HEADQUARTERS, 16th APRIL 1916', III Corps War Diary.
150   TNA WO 95/672: 'GENERAL STAFF 4th ARMY 14 6G', 17 April 1916, III Corps War Diary.
151   TNA WO 95/1730: 1st R. Irish Rif. War Diary and Whitfield *op. cit.* in Taylor, *The First Royal Irish Rifles in the Great War*, p. 73.

General Key for All Maps

Formation/Unit National Designators

Red	German
Blue	Allied
ANZAC	Australian and New Zealand Army Corps
AUS	Australian
BR	British
CAN	Canadian
FR	French
Bav	Bavarian
Col	Colonial (French)
Erz	Ersatz
Gd	Guards (British or German)
Ldw	Landwehr
Mar	Marine
Res	Reserve

British and Dominion Regiments

Border	Border Regiment
Buffs	Royal East Kent Regiment
Dor	Dorset Regiment
Essex	Essex Regiment
ES	East Surrey Regiment
HLI	Highland Light Infantry
Kings	King's Liverpool Regiment
KOYLI	King's Own Yorkshire Light Infantry
LF	Lancashire Fusiliers
Manch	Manchester Regiment
Norf	Norfolk Regiment
NF	Northumberland Fusiliers
Queens	Royal West Surrey Regiment
RBks	Royal Berkshire Regiment
Northants	Northamptonshire Regiment
RCR	Royal Canadian Regiment
R Irish Rif	Royal Irish Rifles
RWK	Royal West Kent Regiment
Suff	Suffolk Regiment

XXXXX	Army Group
XXXX	Army
XXX	Corps
XX	Division
X	Brigade
III	Regiment (FR/GE)
II	Battalion or Regiment (BR only)
I	Company
•••	Platoon
⊠	Infantry

——XXXXX——	Army Group to Brigade boundaries (number of crosses denotes which. All armies)
●●●●●●●●●●●●●	Railway
●●●●●●●●●●●●●	Canal
- - - - - - - - - -	Light railway/tramway
≈ ≈ ≈	Marsh/inundation

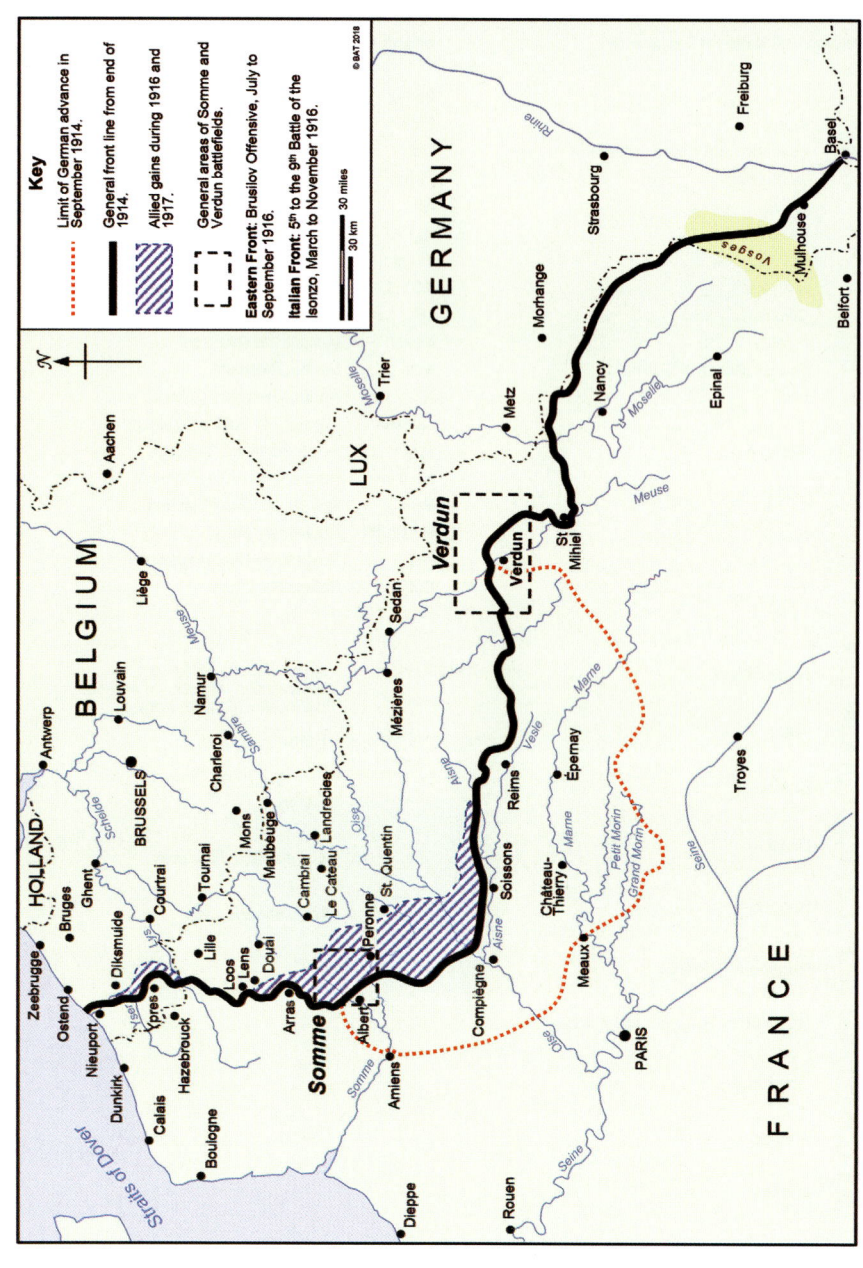

Map 1 Western Front 1916: The year was dominated by Verdun and the Somme. As part of the planned Allied general offensive, the Russians and Italians launched offensives of their own in support of Anglo-French efforts on the Somme.

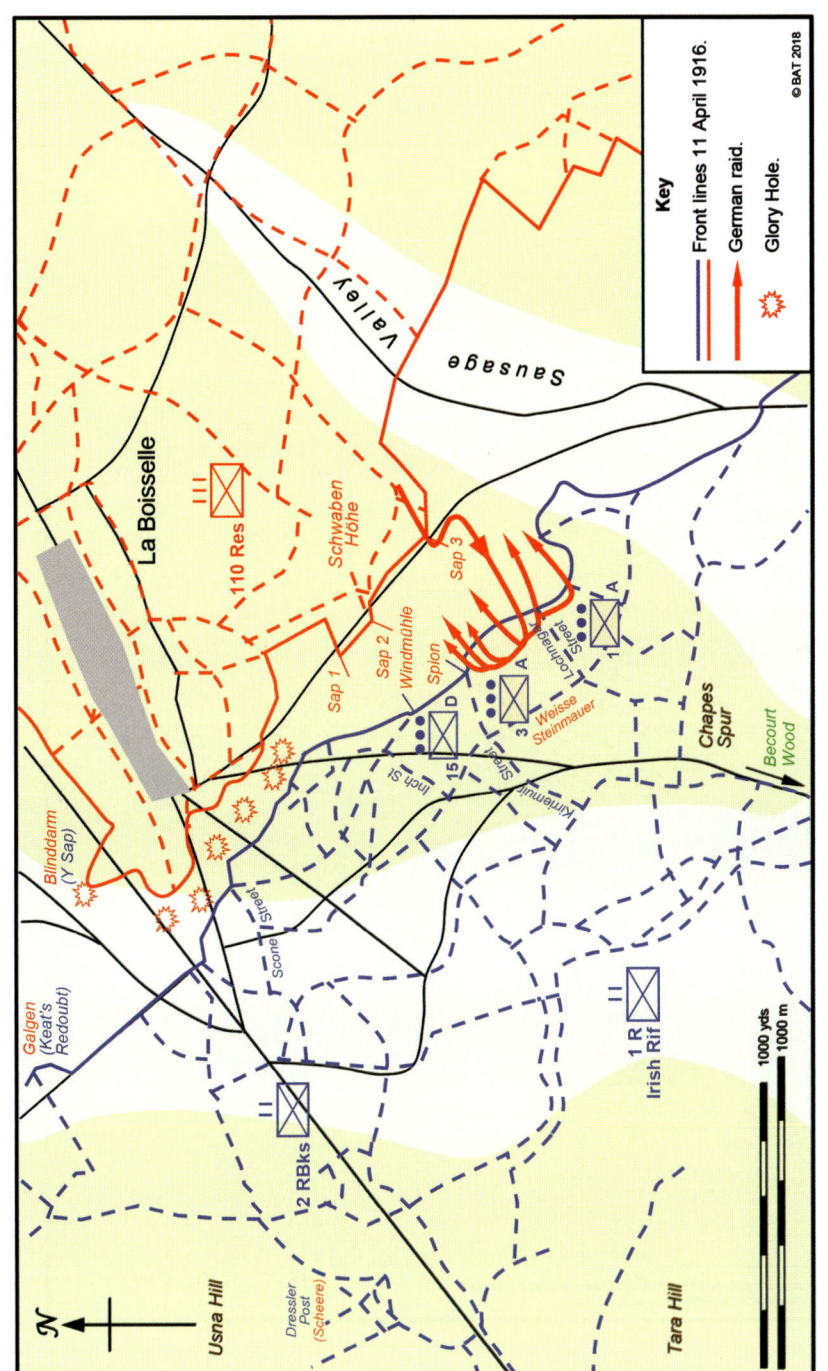

Map 2 German trench raid at La Boisselle, 11 April 1916: Successfully executed by a 76-man detachment of *Badisches Reserve Infanterie Regiment Nr. 110*, valuable offensive/defensive tactical deductions with regard to such small-scale enterprises were obtained by both German and British commanders.

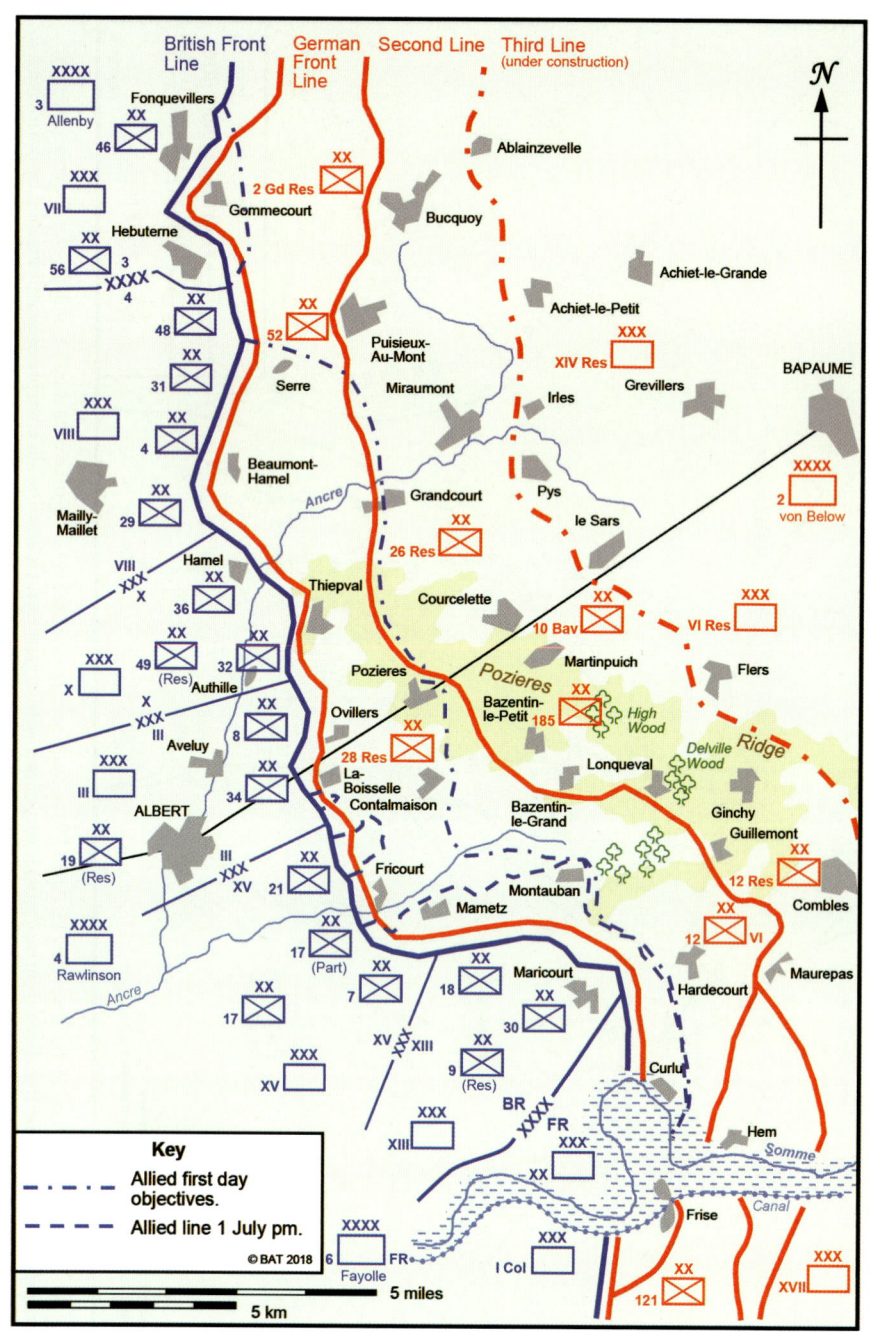

Map 3 Plan and reality, 1 July 1916: The only British success occurred on the southern part of the battlefield. No significant gains were made in the centre and north.

iv

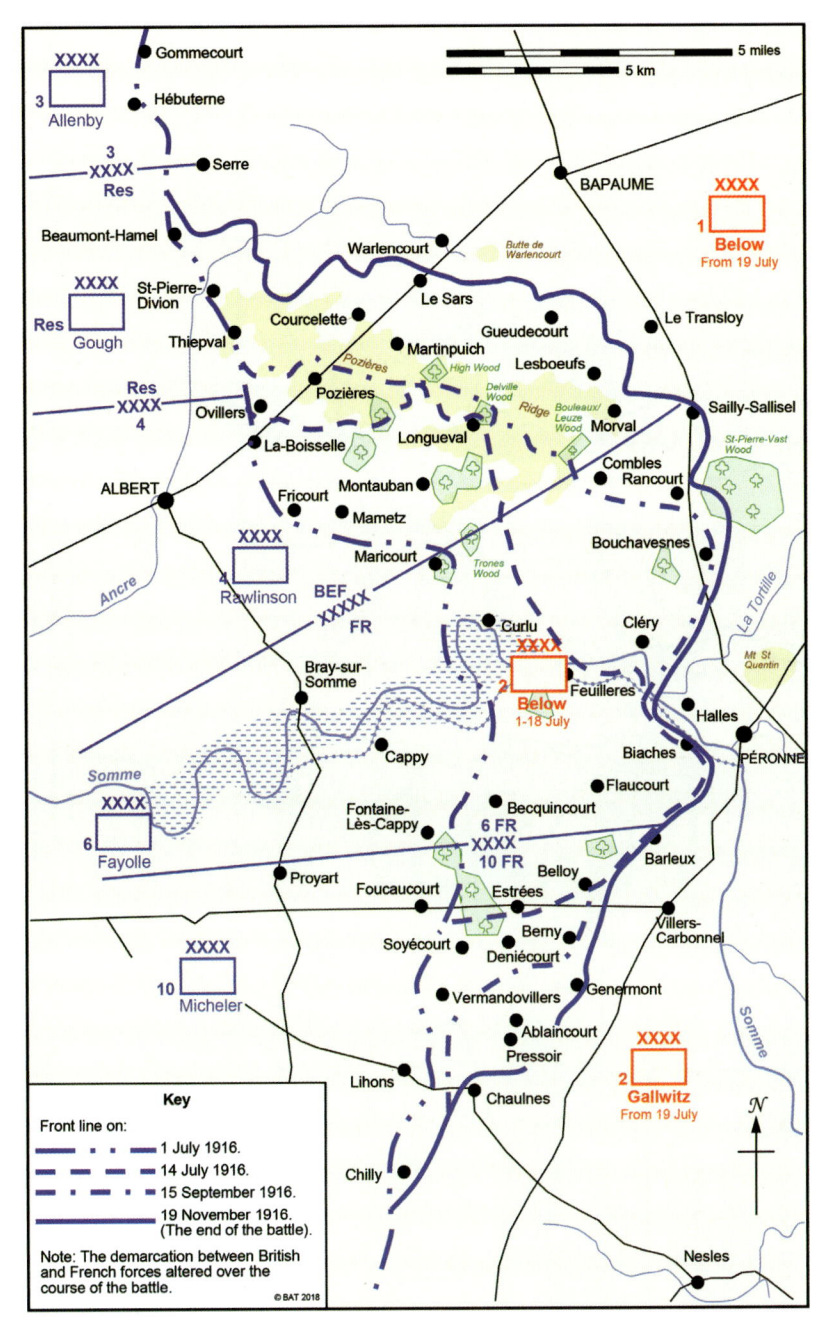

Map 4 Battle of the Somme, July to November 1916: In the aftermath of a horrific opening day, the Anglo-French offensive continued with notable attacks occurring at Bazentin Ridge (14-17 July) and Flers-Courcelette (15-22 September).

v

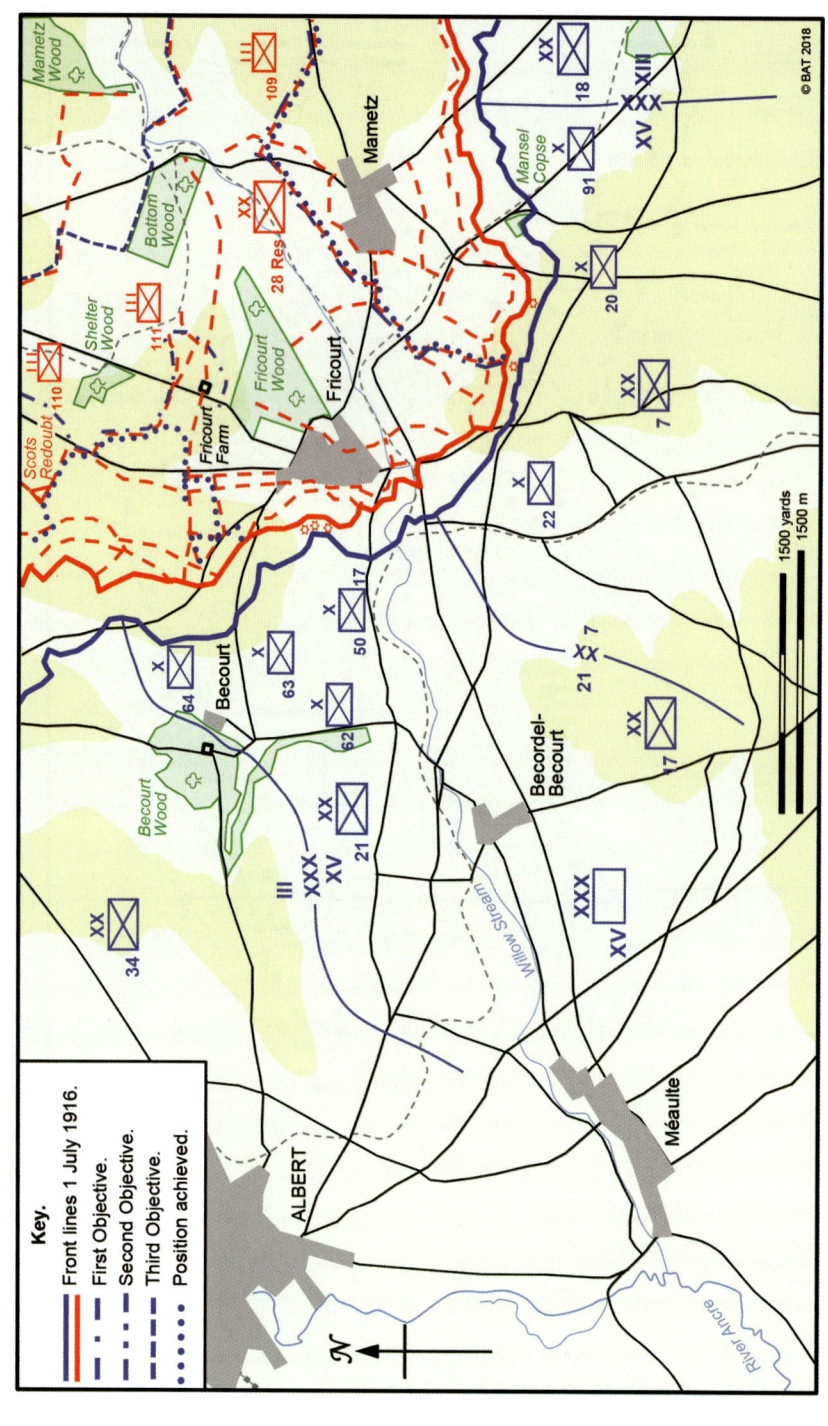

Map 5 XV Corps, 1 July 1916: This operation was intended to envelop Fricourt. After some hard fighting, the fortified village was secured on 2 July.

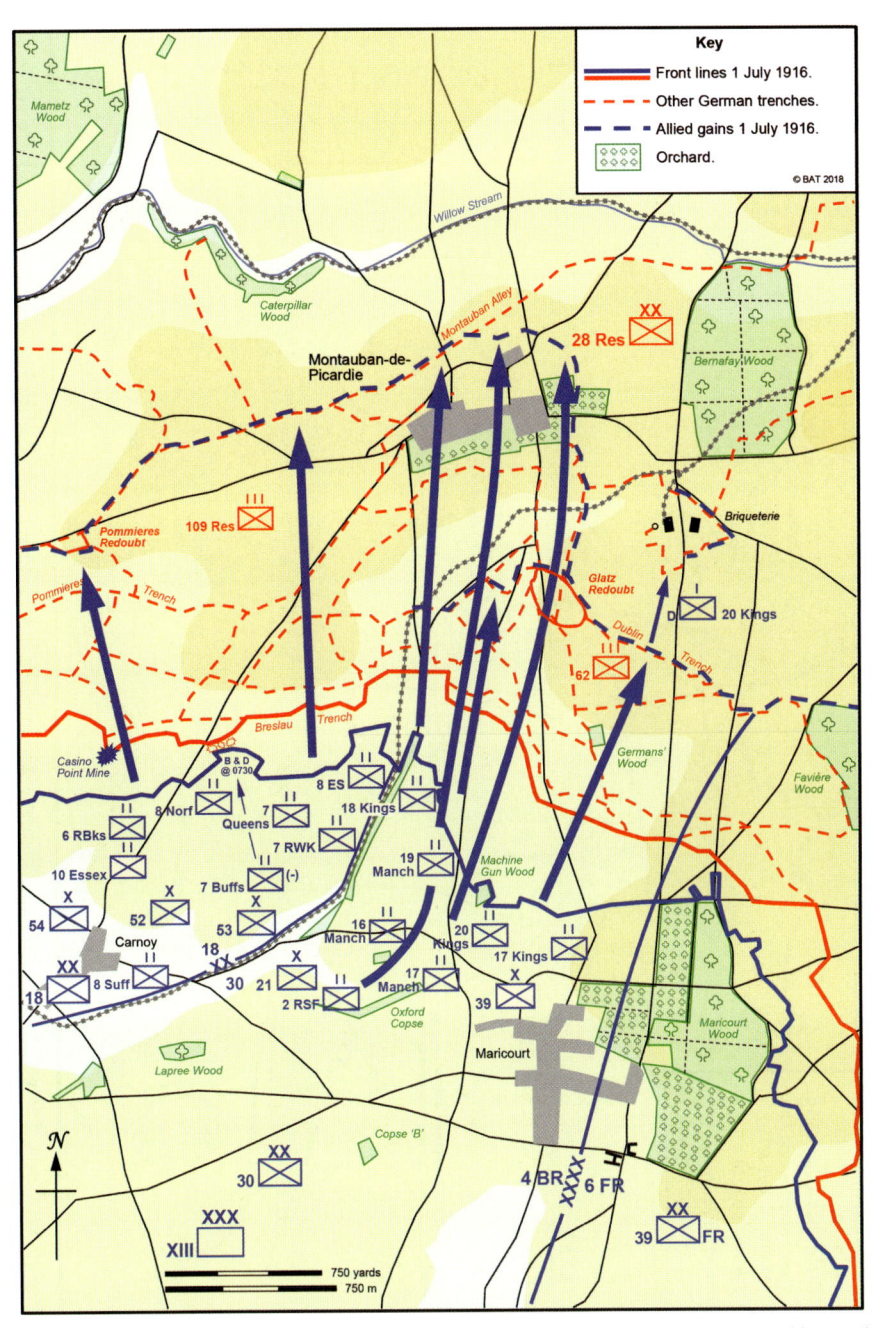

Map 6 XIII Corps, 1 July 1916: Aided by advantages of terrain and the operational/tactical oversight of skilled commanders, the attackers seized all of their objectives and were on the edge of open country by day's end.

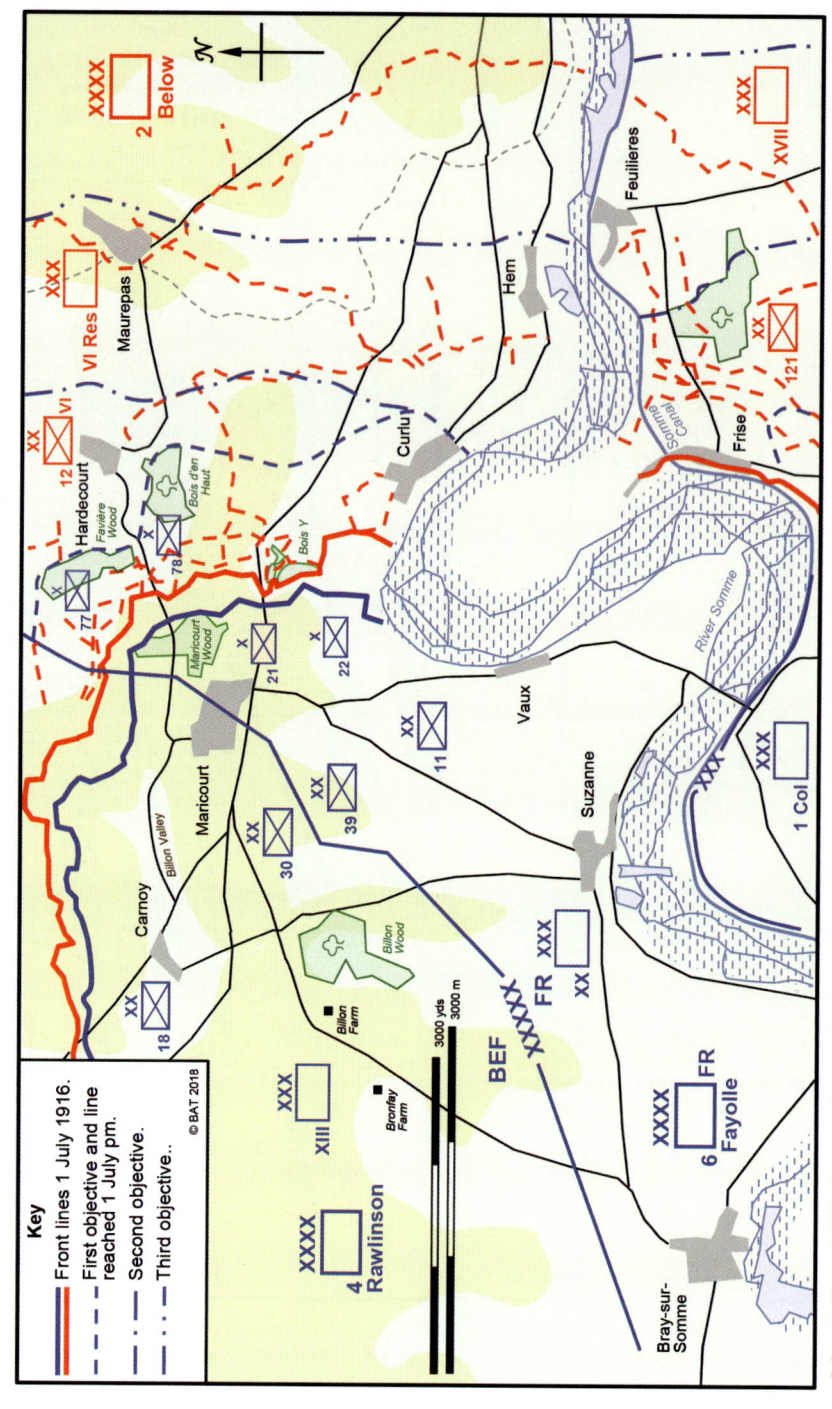

Map 7 French XX Corps, 1 July 1916: In this sector, the battle-hardened French planned a limited offensive backed by concentrated artillery fire. The attackers achieved notable success with comparatively few casualties by day's end.

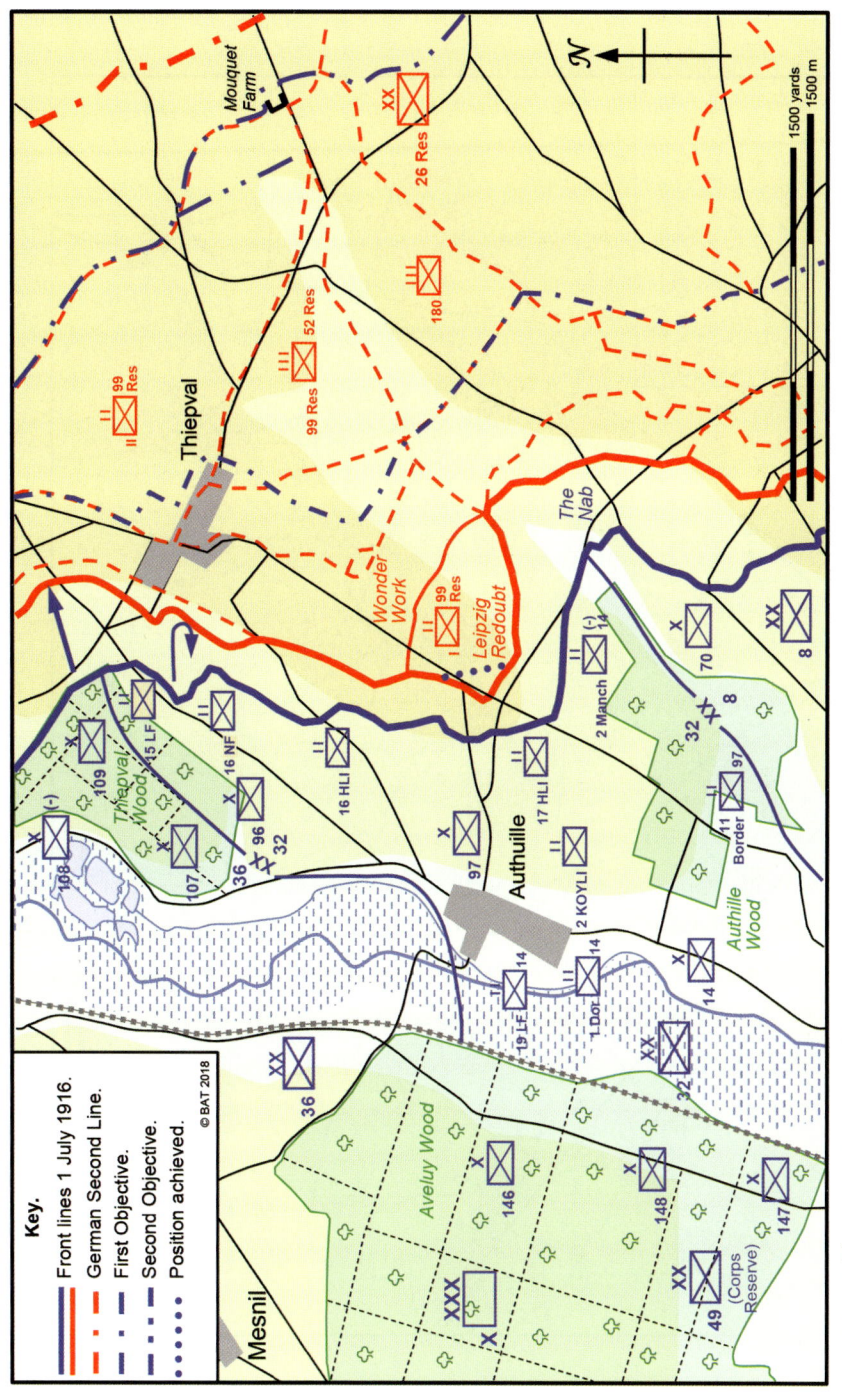

Map 8 Thiepval, 1 July 1916: Although pressed with great courage, the 32nd Division assault made, with the sole exception of a small lodgement in Leipzig Redoubt, almost no progress against powerful German defences.

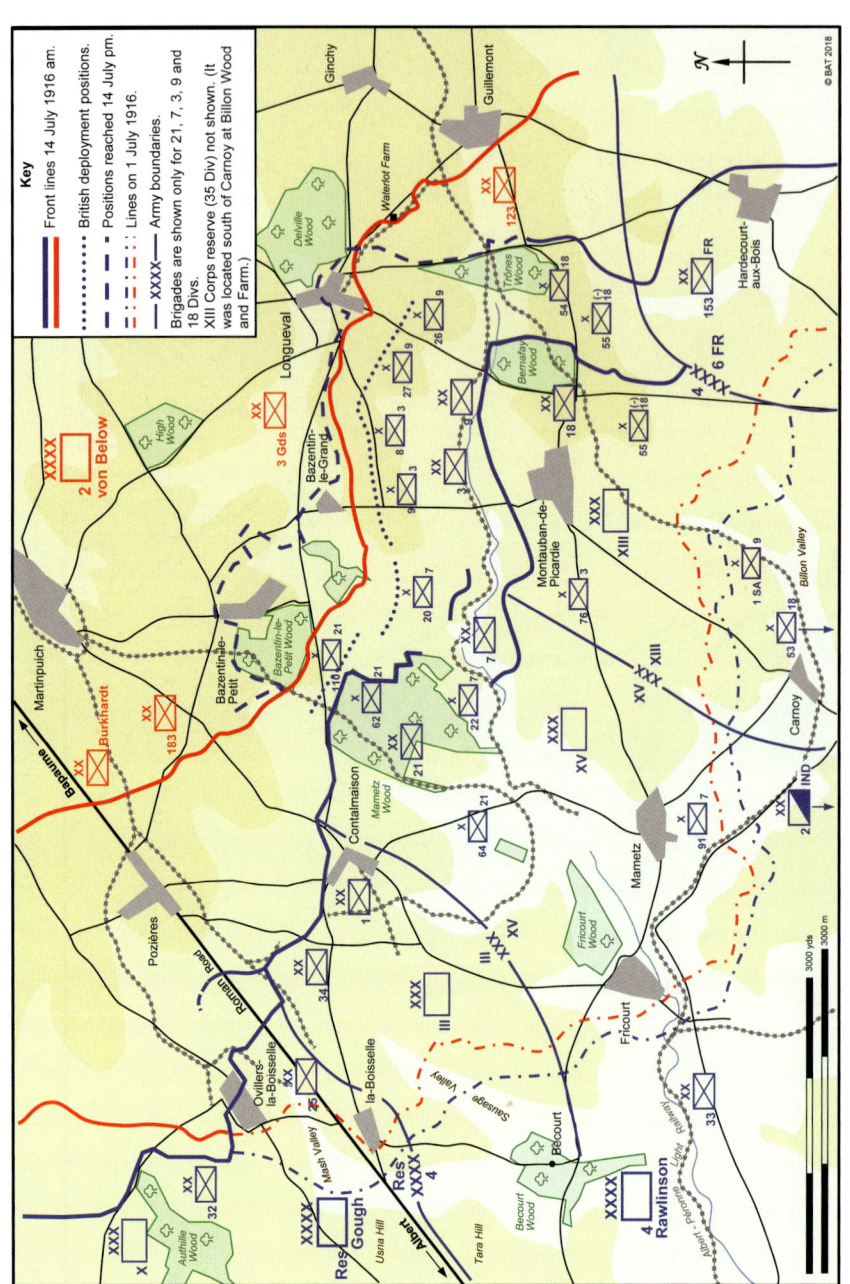

Map 9 Bazentin Ridge, 14 July 1916: This innovative large-scale night attack was supported by a devastating artillery concentration. British success here stood in stark contrast to 1 July.

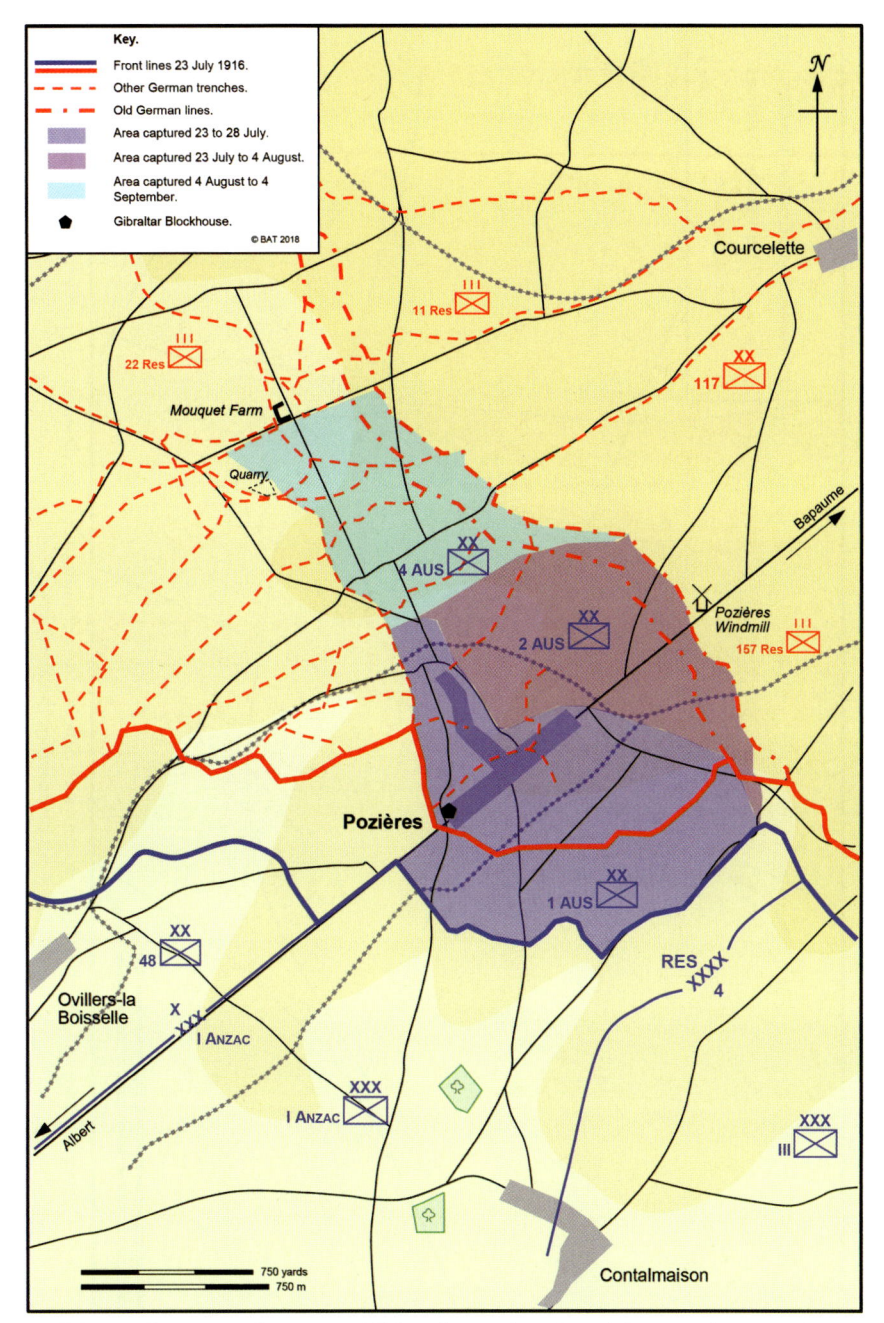

Map 10 Pozières and vicinity, 23 July-4 September 1916: After initial success, the I Anzac Corps offensive towards Mouquet Farm degenerated into a series of piecemeal attacks that secured small portions of ground at the cost of severe casualties.

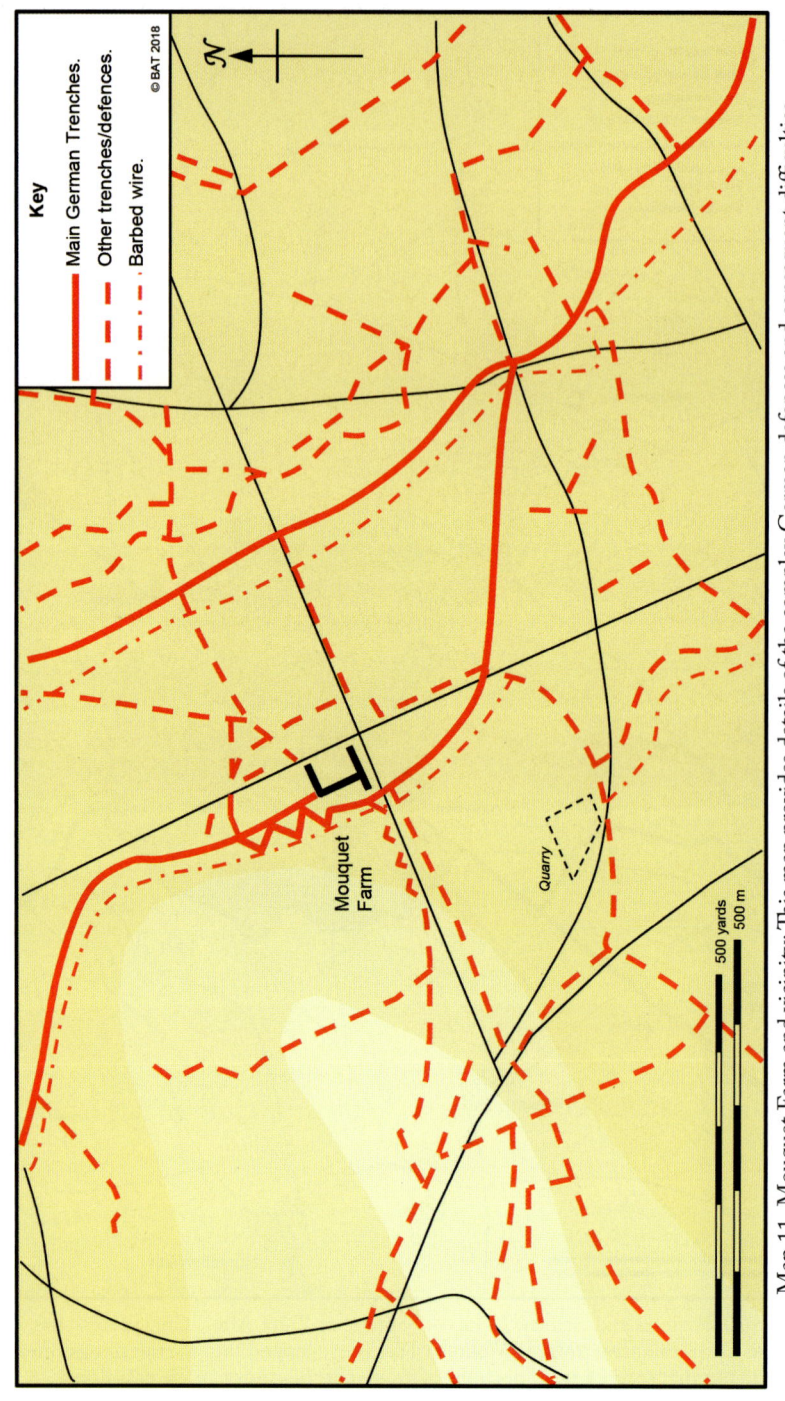

Map 11 Mouquet Farm and vicinity: This map provides details of the complex German defences and consequent difficulties confronting the attackers.

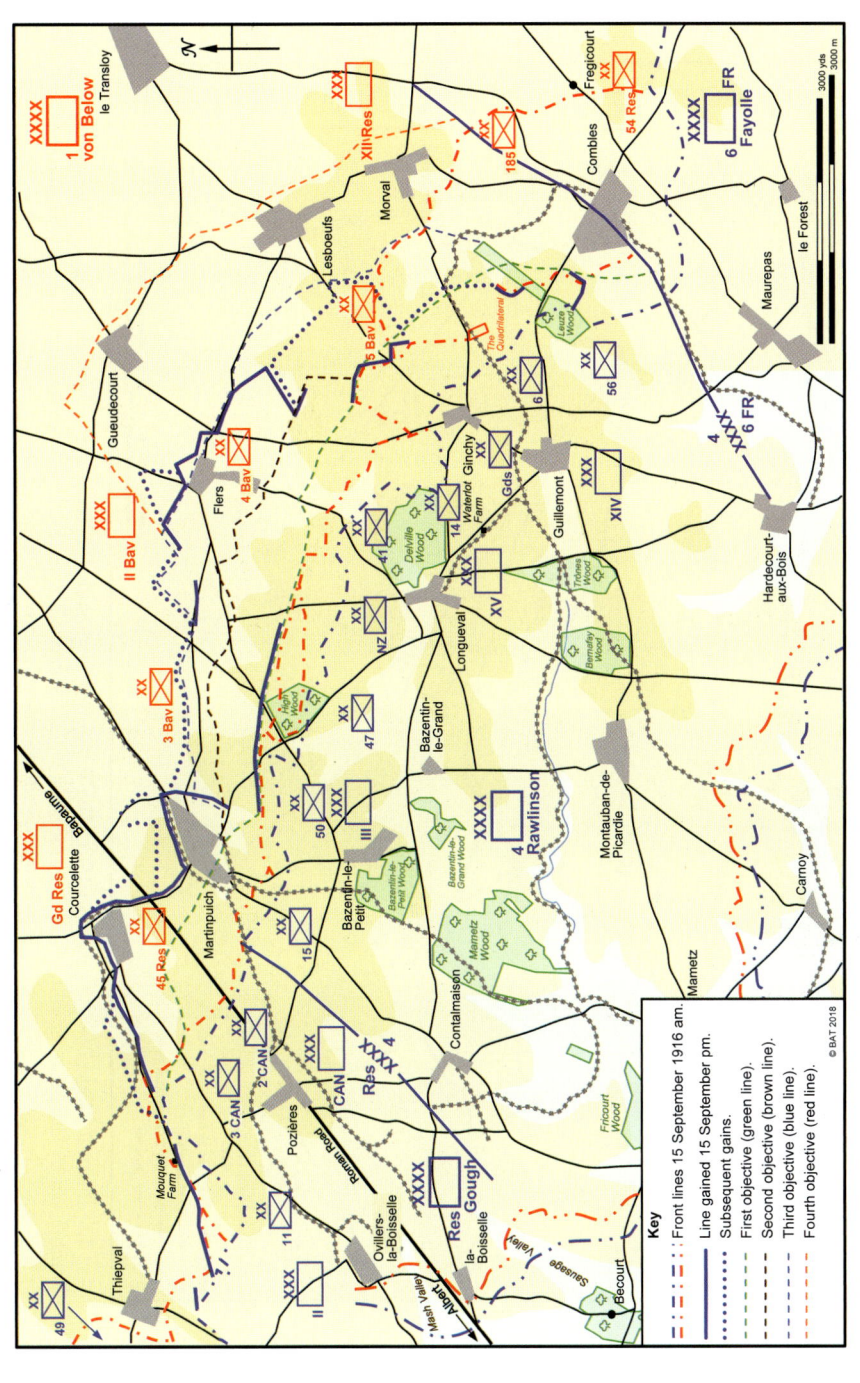

Map 12 The Battle of Flers-Courcelette, 15-22 September 1916: Famed for the introduction of the tank, this ambitious offensive failed to achieve all the planners had hoped for, but still inflicted a severe blow to the German defence.

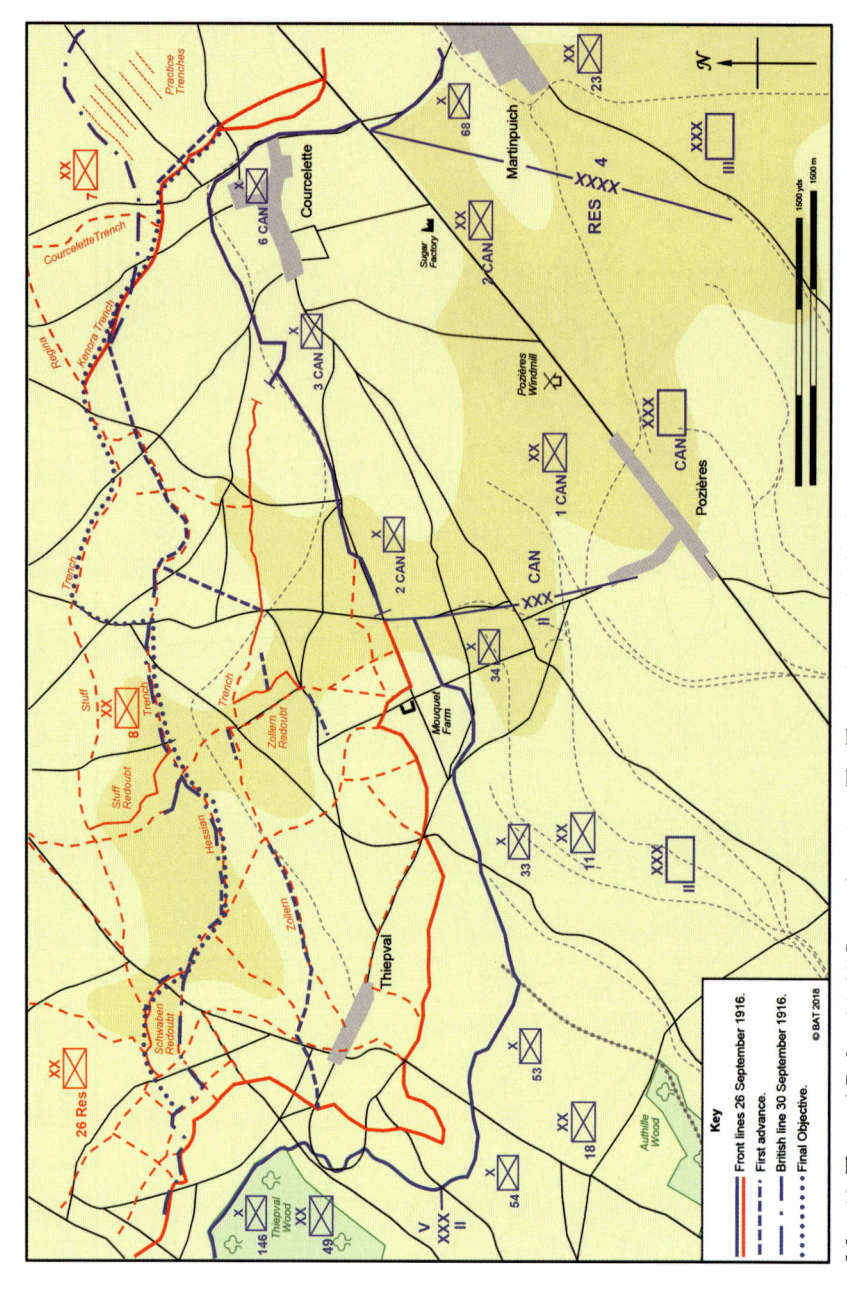

Map 13 Thiepval Ridge, 26-30 September 1916: The Thiepval stronghold had become emblematic of German resistance on the Somme, but by late September it was in the process of being outflanked by operations along Thiepval Ridge. After much bitter fighting, the village was secured on 28 September.

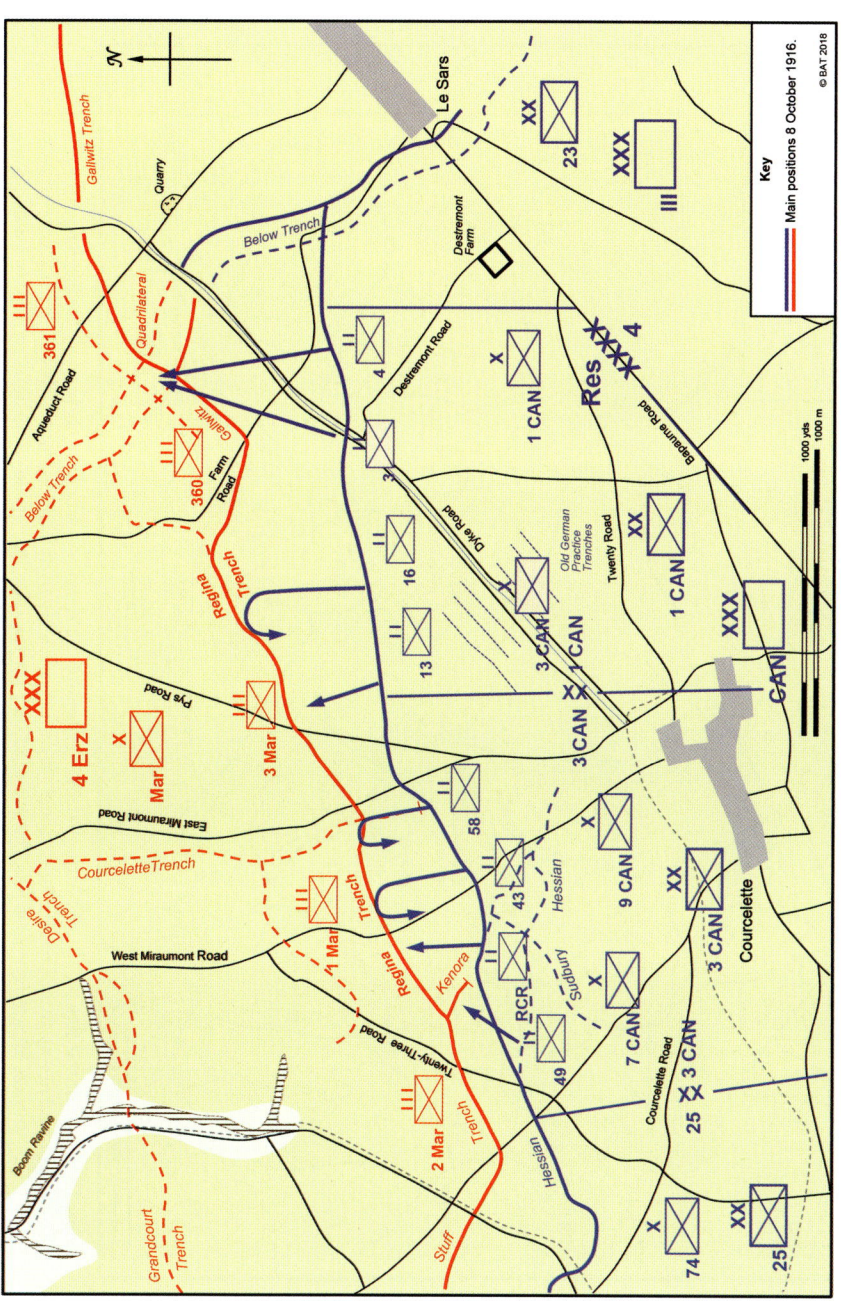

Map 14 Regina Trench, 8 October 1916: Costly errors made prior to and during the assault resulted in a subsequent court of inquiry followed by a great deal of introspection. Lessons learned would inform operations during 1917.

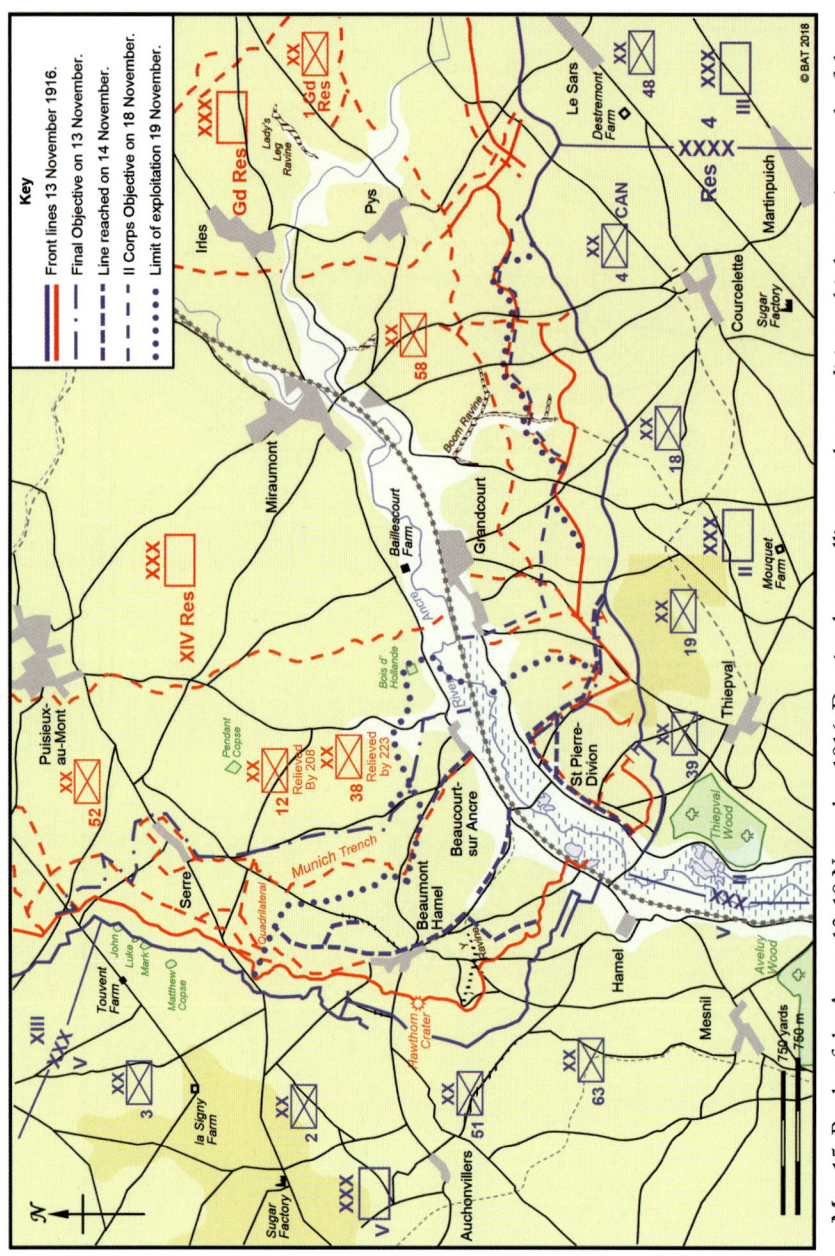

Map 15 Battle of the Ancre, 13–19 November 1916: Despite the appalling weather conditions, this last major assault of the Somme offensive was an impressive local victory for the newly-designated (30 October) British Fifth Army. The apparent success allowed Sir Douglas Haig to fend off political criticism of the campaign's previous conduct.

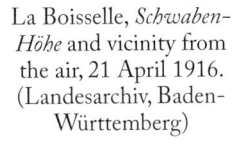

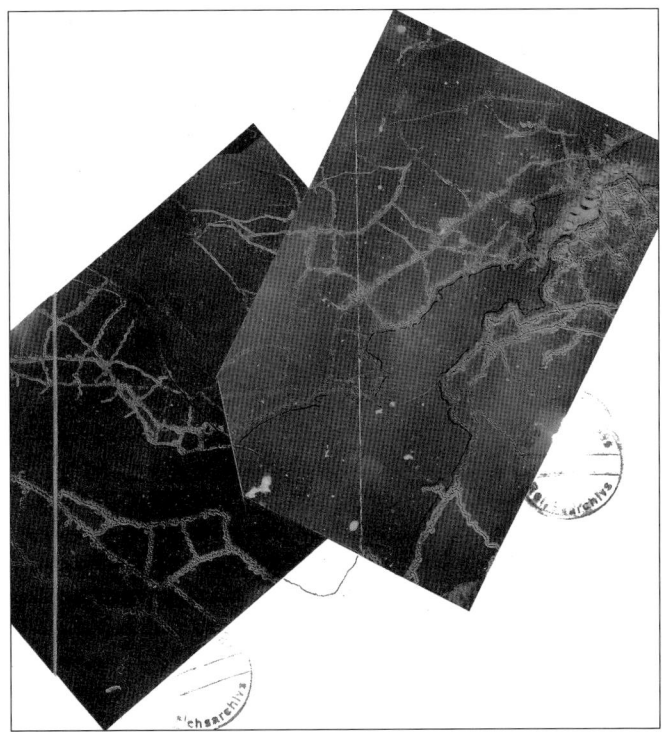

La Boisselle, *Schwaben-Höhe* and vicinity from the air, 21 April 1916. (Landesarchiv, Baden-Württemberg)

The R. Irish R. raid, carried out by 2nd Lieutenant James Lennox Muir[152] and 20 select men, one of whom went sick just prior to the operation, was a modest affair when compared with the recent German incursion. The objective was a small salient due south of enemy-occupied Sausage Redoubt. The raiders, having entered no man's land at 9:45 p.m. on 22 April, crept forward under an artillery bombardment. Hostile machine-gun fire from somewhere in the rear "was high and caused no loss. At 10 p.m., as arranged, 2nd Lieut. MUIR gave the order to rush the enemy trench. At this moment, an enemy machine-gun was brought out of a sally-port,[153] just by the point selected for attack by about 5 men." Muir, immediately comprehending this unforeseen threat, dashed forward and shot down the leading man with his revolver. "The gun however was brought into action and opened a rapid fire." Isolated just to the north of it, the frustrated subaltern later observed that "if he had had a few men with him he could have captured the gun, but apparently his party, except two or possibly three, had thrown themselves on to the ground." Concealed below the enemy's parapet,

---

152 See Taylor, *The First Royal Irish Rifles in the Great War*, p. 302 for Muir's biographical details.
153 Sally-port: A small exit point in a fortification for the passage of troops when making a sally.

Muir tossed a Mills Bomb into the shadowy depths of the trench before seeking cover from bombs thrown back in reply. The advance thus thwarted, he withdrew only to be "severely shaken by a shell explosion" from a retaliatory bombardment. The remainder of the party returned with four wounded; one man later recorded as missing. All was quiet by 10:45 p.m. Whitfield subsequently observed: "Not enough time was given to prepare the men (only two days). The men did not combine and did not back the officer up although all old soldiers. Our artillery fired short. The Hun replied very heavily and it was hard getting back to our own lines again."[154]

To the north in neighbouring X Corps' sector, the second of two projected raids commenced at 9:50 p.m. on the 22nd when two officers and 45 men of 17th Highland Light Infantry (HLI) raided the apex of a German salient south-west of Thiepval. Thirteen prisoners and some very useful intelligence were brought back without serious loss. Lieutenant-General Morland remarked with some satisfaction, "Raid by 17th HLI at 9:30 p.m. [sic] successful, 13 prisoners taken, many Germans killed; our losses 1 seriously, 11 slightly wounded in raiding party …"[155] Fourth Army's intelligence summary for 23 April stated:

> The enemy trenches were raided twice last night. One raid was carried out S. of LA BOISSELLE which failed. The other raid took place S. of THIEPVAL; we secured 13 prisoners; our casualties were slight and none of the raiding party are reported to be missing.[156]

Having read through forwarded reports, Major-General Hudson was unimpressed with the latest 1st R. Irish Rif. reverse. A subsequent interview with 2nd Lieutenant

---

154 TNA WO/95/672: 'B.M.C. /298' Brigadier-General Pollard's after-action report, 'Intelligence Summary for the period of 24 hours ending 8 a.m.', 23 April 1916, 'Intelligence Summary' III Corps War Diary and Taylor, *The First Royal Irish Rifles in the Great War*, p. 73. The La Boiselle Moritz station appears to have predicted the 22 April raid based on intercepted telephone conversations. The following day it reported "the fury and helplessness of the British commander" over the failure of what was erroneously deemed to be two "patrols" instead of one followed by a disparaging reference to the 'Damned Germans." See Greiner & Vulpius, *Reserve-Infanterie-Regiment Nr. 110 im Weltkrieg 1914-1918*, p. 111 and Whitehead, *The Other Side of the Wire Volume I*, p. 406.

155 See TNA WO 95/672: 'Fourth Army No. G.S. 139/2: Account of a raid carried out by the 17th H.L.I. of the 32nd Division on the night of the 22nd/23rd April 1916', III Corps War Diary, WO 157/169: 'Fourth Army Intelligence Summary', 24 April 1916; 'ANNEX TO FOURTH ARMY SUMMARY NO. 59: Report on German Trenches at R.31.a.35/15 raided on the night of 22nd April 1916', Fourth Army Intelligence file, John W. Arthur & Ion Munro, *The Seventeenth Highland Light Infantry (Glasgow Chamber of Commerce Battalion) During the First World War 1914-1918* (Driffield: Leonaur, 2010 reprint of 1920 edition) pp. 44-49 and Thompson (ed.), *Morland Great War Corps Commander*, p. 137.

156 TNA WO 157/169: 'Fourth Army Intelligence Summary, 24 April 1916, Fourth Army Intelligence file.

Muir, still "at present very much shaken from the explosion of a shell which … burst very close to his head", no doubt confirmed a determination that the rot had set in.[157] Battalion morale and discipline, thought to be substantially improved from September 1915, now appeared unsatisfactory in light of the old soldiers' failure to assist a raid commander in dire circumstances.[158] For his part, Rawlinson's previous sympathetic attitude vanished:

> I am displeased with the part taken by the RIR [R. Irish Rif.] in the raid on Sat[urda[y] night – They would not follow their officer who behaved very well and shot two Germans himself. The report of their behaviour when the Bosches raided them is poor reading and I shall hope to try an officer and at least one corporal for cowardice – They are a very bad batt[alion]. Raids are in the course of preparation in the XIII and VIII corps which will I hope come off this week – I rode over to Putty [Pulteney] today and gave him my views as to the RIR …[159]

This desire to take punitive action against the 1st R. Irish Rif. rank and file had already manifested itself during courts-martial proceedings at Dernacourt on 20 April when Acting Sergeant S.J. McIlwaine, Rifleman J. Gribbon and Rifleman J. Kane were tried for cowardice. The accused NCO was found not guilty whilst both riflemen were sentenced to death commuted to 15 years penal servitude, "suspended sentence."[160]

A court of enquiry was convened at 25th Brigade[161] headquarters on 21 April.[162] The final report is absent from available archives, but it may be surmised that, in addition to the personal conclusions reached by brigade, division, corps and army commanders, its findings provided ample justification to bring further general court-martial proceedings against Captain ffrench-Mullen for "neglect to the prejudice of good order and military discipline."[163]

---

157 Muir was awarded the MC for his actions.
158 TNA WO 95/672: '8th Division G. 664/8', III Corps War Diary and Timothy Bowman, *Irish Regiments in the Great War: Discipline and Morale* (Manchester: Manchester University Press, 2003), p. 43.
159 CAC RWLN 5/5: Rawlinson Diary, 24 April 1916.
160 Taylor, *The First Royal Irish Rifles in the Great War*, pp. 73, 192. A general courts-martial could, in addition to trying a commissioned officer, alone award punishments of penal servitude and death. See War Office, *Manual of Military Law*, p. 35.
161 The 25th Brigade was relieved by 70th Brigade on 23 April. See TNA WO 95/1674: '8th Division Operation Order No. 99', 23 April 1916, 8th Division War Diary.
162 2nd Lieutenant Lake later observed: "I had been appointed Lewis Gun officer by this time [11 April 1916] and the Germans had captured one of my guns, together with the crew. I had to face a Court of Enquiry because of this, but the court accepted my account of the raid and I was not punished." See Taylor, *The First Royal Irish Rifles in the Great War*, pp. 72, 243.
163 ffrench-Mullen was prosecuted under Section 40 of the Army Act which covered conduct, disorder or neglect by the individual charged. See TNA WO 339/9059: Captain Ernest FFRENCH-MULLEN. The Royal Irish Rifles file, Taylor, *The First Royal Irish Rifles in*

244   At All Costs

Forty-one days transpired before ffrench-Mullen appeared in front of a court-martial on 2 June 1916. Though completely exonerated, the extended period of uncertainty took a toll on his mental and physical health.[164] Captain C.L.G. Powell RAMC (1st R. Irish Rif. medical officer) stated in a confidential report to the battalion adjutant one day after the trial:

> I beg to report that on several occasions lately I have visited Capt. ffrench-Mullen and that I have been much impressed by the change in his appearance during the last two months. I consider that the strain of awaiting a Court Martial for so long has told most severely upon him and that he is now on the verge of a complete nervous collapse. On these grounds I strongly recommend that he be brought before a medical board as soon as possible with a view of granting him sick leave. I think that this should be done without delay.[165]

The latter duly forwarded the request to 25th Brigade headquarters and No. 5 Casualty Clearing Station in nearby Corbie. Further to this, a related note was sent to 8th Division headquarters by the divisional ADMS on 7 June:

> Captain E. ffrench-Mullen, 1st RIR [R. Irish Rif.], has been sent to hospital by me today. This officer has been in France since 17th December 1915 and has had no leave. He has recently been through a GCM and, although honourably acquitted, the trial and the length of time he had to wait (7 weeks) has told on him. Previous to being put under arrest he had suffered on and off from malaria and although not on the sick list was not in a good state of health. Immediately after arrest he was in hospital for over a fortnight with symptoms of neurasthenia and insomnia. At present, although much better, he is in my opinion unfit for duties at the front and I recommend his being set to base with a view of appearing before a Medical Board.[166]

His constitution broken by the raid and consequent statutory anxieties, ffrench-Mullen embarked for Great Britain on 11 June where he was admitted to No. 4 London Hospital – diagnosis: "neurasthenia".[167]

---

the Great War, p. 73 and Thomas, "British 8th Infantry Division on the Western Front 1914-1918", pp. 143-44.
164   Taylor, *The First Royal Irish Rifles in the Great War*, pp. 72, 243.
165   TNA WO 339/9059: Captain Ernest FFRENCH-MULLEN. The Royal Irish Rifles file.
166   Ibid.
167   Ibid.

Postscript

Rawlinson's unequivocal "counter-raid" policy made certain that trench raiding incidents increased along Fourth Army's front during the final period of preparations for the Somme offensive. Approximately 29 (17 British and 12 German) punitive/intelligence gathering intent operations were launched from 12 April until the opening of the British preliminary bombardment on 24 June.[168] As one German officer observed:

> The enemy seemed to have got the measure of our trench raid tactics and suddenly turned them against us. Generally he just suffered reverses, but occasionally, however, he succeeded in forcing a way into our lines and capturing prisoners. Initially this caused fury and a tendency to blame subordinate commanders and forward troops, but it was soon realised that sufficient expenditure in ammunition in support of a courageous assaulting force meant that such break-ins would almost always succeed.[169]

Whether or not implementation of the defensive measures articulated in the GOC Fourth Army's memorandum of 13 April reduced the threat of enemy incursions can only be speculated, but at least four subsequent German raids appear to have been frustrated between 29 April and 11 June.[170]

Commenting on the three hostile raids[171] during the first half of April, a Fourth Army intelligence summary stated:

> Prior to each raid the registration of the trenches was spread over two or three days so as not to attract attention … It is highly probable that on each occasion the raiding party left their own trenches before the bombardment commenced

---

168 TNA WO 95/431: Fourth Army War Diary. From 1 January to 23 June 1916, *XIV Reserve Corps* captured no less than 207 British prisoners during raids and scouting expeditions. Seventy-six were seized during the period January-March, and 131 for the remaining months. "That the number of prisoners increased alongside the likelihood of a British attack was unsurprising given the demand for up-to-date intelligence" from Corps Commander von Stein. See Andrew Macdonald, *First Day of the Somme* (London: Harper Collins, 2016), p. 100.
169 *Landwehr Leutnant* M. Gerster *op. cit.* in Sheldon, *The German Army on the Somme 1914-1916*, p. 114. See Lieutenant-Colonel J.H. Boraston (ed.), *Sir Douglas Haig's Despatches (December 1915 – April 1919)* (London: J.M. Dent & Sons, 1919), p. 4 for British GHQ's general overview of trench raiding activity from December 1915 to May 1916. The final paragraph states: "The initiative in these minor operations was taken, and on the whole has been held, by us; but the Germans have recently attempted some bold and well-conceived raids against our lines, many of which have been driven back, although some have succeeded in penetrating, as has been reported by me [Haig] from time to time."
170 TNA WO 95/431: Enemy raiders were repelled without gaining entry into the British trenches near Fricourt on 29 April; La Boisselle and Hamel on the night of 1/2 May, and north of Thiepval Wood on the night of 10/11 June.
171 The German raids were as follows: Beaumont Hamel, night of 6/7 April; La Boisselle, 11 April, and northeast of Carnoy, night of 12/13 April.

in order to avoid our barrage on their frontline. Hence the places chosen by them for the raids were where the opposing trenches were 250 to 400 yards apart.[172]

This basic comprehension of the enemy's tactical methodology contributed to the applied defensive response. Yet, given German occupation of the dominating Poziéres Ridge, there was only so much that could be done to secure the frontline. As Brigadier-General Pollard observed in his report on the 11 April setback, "a well-planned raid against such trenches, situated as they are in a position where hostile observation is very easy, had every chance of success."[173]

Comprehension of enemy tactics was further augmented by an act of Teutonic bureaucratic thoroughness. Pleased with the results of the 11 April raid, *RIR 110* produced "no less than three reports at various levels." *Hauptmann* Wagener "appears to have distributed forty copies of one of his reports." It was one of these widely-distributed documents – in addition to a copy of *Oberst Freiherr* von Vietinghoff's report, etc. – that fell into enemy hands on 4 July 1916. Within months "the British had not only Wagener's words translated but a copy of the fire plan and 'deductions' drawn – virtually everything was being studied on the other side of the line by August 1916." Thus the instructive value of this "model raid" proved short-lived, "the German perpetrators" gaining, "at best, four months' headway in digesting the lessons." It is also true, Stephen Bull concludes "that the Canadians were already using similar methods, and information regarding these had already been circulated to British and other Empire formations prior to this date. As in so many fields, the tactical advance was incremental, and learning from the opposition was crucial."[174]

---

172 TNA WO 157/169: 'FOURTH ARMY SUMMARY OF INTELLIGENCE', April 1916, Fourth Army Intelligence file. See also letter from Lieutenant-General Pulteney to Clive Wigram (1873-1960), 2 May 1916 quoted in Leask, *Putty*, pp. 384-85.
173 TNA WO 95/672: '25th Brigade, 207/G, 8th Division', 14 April 1916, III Corps War Diary. Fourth Army losses for April 1916 amounted to 2,318. This figure was broken down by causation as follows: shellfire: 1,243; rifle 415; grenade 557; mines 15, missing 88. See CAC RWLN 5/5: 'CASUALTIES – APRIL 1916', Rawlinson Diary. The determination that "it was well nigh impossible for a unit to protect itself against ... well organised and executed incursions" was also reached by Third Army in the period following the 31 January 1916 raid on 10th Essex. See Banks & Chell, *With the 10th Essex in France*, p. 90
174 See Bull, *Stosstrupptaktik*, p. 92. Such determinations with regard to German complacency and consequent intelligence failures are at odds with some of the contentions put forward by Peter Barton in the television documentary *The Somme 1916 – From Both Sides of the Wire* (BBC2 2016). In a subsequent journal article, Barton concedes that German troops could be just as talkative or careless with sensitive documents, but intelligence gathered by their opponents was of less practical value because the "British (and French) were perpetually on the offensive. This meant that they had no choice but to draw up and distribute detailed tactical arrangements" that often fell into enemy hands. See Barton, 'Tolerating Mystery and Challenging History', *Stand To! The Journal of the Western Front Association*, No. 109 (2017), p. 18. See also Sheldon, *Fighting the Somme* for German

The question remains as to why 1st R. Irish Rif. was subject to such severe censure by the military authorities?[175] This is especially true when considering the reverse experienced by 2nd SWB on the night of 6/7 April 1916. No evidence of an investigation or court of enquiry following this raid has come to light.[176] Clearly, the 1st R. Irish Rif. affair was considered serious enough to warrant further investigation and punishment. In addition to the absence of company officers in the frontline, apparent failure of other ranks to defend the position adequately and the number of men taken prisoner, the battalion was tarred by a poor morale and discipline record and, according to Timothy Bowman, the mind-set that "British Army officers did see the Irish soldier as being distinct from his English counterpart." He also notes that Irish servicemen were tried by courts martial far more often than their English, Scottish or Welsh contemporaries.[177] Pulteney summed up the official point of view in a letter to the King's Assistant Private Secretary and Equerry Clive Wigram: "The Irish Rifles did not do very well when they were raided on 11 April, but the blame is due to the officers and not the men. I have made changes which I trust will have good effect, they have always been the worst battalion in the division."[178] Lieutenant Whitfield, commenting about the then widely accepted stain on 1st R. Irish Rif. reputation, observed:

> The battalion received very severe criticism for their night's work, but some allowance must be made for what appeared to be such a poor fight put up by them. First of all, it was the first occasion that they had ever been subjected to such a bombardment, either in intensity or length. Secondly, it was the first occasion on which gas shells had been used against them in any quantity. Thirdly, those that survived the bombardment were forced to fight in gas helmets (sack type) and being night-time had no idea where they were themselves or where the enemy was coming from. The full German account of this raid was afterwards found during the Battle of the Somme. In this pamphlet [sic][179] the Germans

     strategic and operational missteps/deficiencies perpetrated prior to and during the gruelling *Materialschlacht* that heralded inevitable defeat in two years' time.
175 Commenting on the 31 January 1916 raid, the post-war 10th Essex regimental history observed that successful enemy incursions of this type resulted in the "temporary grave of a good many [unit] reputations." See Banks & Chell, *With the 10th Essex in France*, p. 90.
176 Their relative inexperience of combat on the Western Front and an overly demonstrative paternalism displayed by Lieutenant-General Sir Aylmer Hunter-Weston (GOC VIII Corps) towards formations/units previously under his command at Gallipoli may have been taken into account during review of 2nd SWB's performance. See TNA WO 95/2280: 29th Division War Diary, WO 95/2298: 87th Brigade War Diary, WO 95/2304: 2nd SWB War Diary and British Library 48365: HUNTER-WESTON PAPERS. Private War Diary. Vol. XI. 8th Army Corps [VIII Corps]. Somme and Ypres. 1 Jan.-31 Dec. 1916.
177 Bowman, *Irish Regiments in the Great War*, p. 202.
178 Letter from Pulteney to Wigram, 2 May 1916 quoted in Leask, *Putty*, pp. 384-85.
179 Whitfield was confusing captured documents with the aforementioned *SS 462: Translation of a German Document: Raid on the British Trenches near La Boisselle (11 April 1916)*

paid tribute to the regiment in the following terms: "The Regiment of Royal Irish Rifles created a most favourable impression both by their physique and their mode of repelling assault. Had it not been …" and then goes on to explain that things would probably had not happened as they did if they had not used so much gas. It was a glowing tribute and one in which the regiment may well be proud.[180]

Interestingly, he made no mention of company officer deficiencies, their absence from the frontline considered to be the most egregious of the court of enquiry revelations. Whitfield's assertion that he and his fellow officers "were getting ready for 'Stand To'" when the German barrage opened at 7:00 p.m., confirms intent to proceed there foiled by a matter of minutes.[181]

Overall, the 11 April 1916 trench raid is indicative of a period of the war when the British Army had to "learn many a hard lesson" whilst engaging with a tenacious and skilful enemy. Crippling losses amongst pre-war Regulars and Territorial Force (TF) during 1914-15, and consequent de-skilling throughout the BEF "applied to formations such as 8th Division that were becoming 'Regular' in name only." Decimated during the previous 19 months of conflict, these trained military professionals – army reservists inclusive – were replaced by special reservists, volunteers and, with the passing of the Military Service Acts of March and May 1916, conscripts. Contemporaneous with this, morale and discipline within Regular Irish infantry units from summer 1915 to autumn 1916 "was under pressure" from a "partial collapse" of the army drafting system and the inability of affiliated Special Reserve (SR) battalions to supply competent drafts in satisfactory numbers.[182] This was a consequence of an evident downturn in Irish recruitment[183] well before the Easter Rising and the often

---

pamphlet.
180 Whitfield *op. cit.* in Taylor, *The First Royal Irish Rifles in the Great War*, p. 72.
181 Ibid.
182 Special Reserve: A form of part-time soldiering similar to the TF whereby a man could join the SR for six years with the possibility of call up in the event of general mobilisation, and otherwise undertake all of the same conditions as Army reservists who had completed full terms of service with the colours. Six months full-time training after enlistment was succeeded by three to four weeks training per year thereafter. A man bereft of past service with the Regular forces could extend his SR service for four years up to, but not beyond 40 years of age. Conversely, former Regulars, on completion of their Army Reserve term, could also re-enlist in the SR and serve until age 42. As an institution, the SR was "a fairly botched compromise, especially in Ireland, resulting from the Haldane Reforms" of 1906-08. "The decision not to establish Territorial Force units in Ireland meant that Irish regiments had a larger number of Special Reserve battalions than their counterparts in Great Britain." See *The Long, Long Trail* <http://www.1914-1918.net/reserve.htm> and Bowman, *The Irish Regiments in the Great War*, p. 189.
183 Wartime conscription was never enacted in Ireland. See Thomas Hennessey, *Dividing Ireland: World War I and Partition* (London: Routledge, 1998), pp. 80-123, 202-33.

poor standard of training in SR units.[184] Nonetheless, criticisms levelled against 1st R. Irish Rif. by the high command did not take into account the intensity of the German bombardment or the difficulties of bringing up reserves under heavy shellfire. To this must be added an unwillingness to recognise the need for units to acclimate to unfamiliar trenches or for "any weaknesses caused by tiredness or ill-health." Ensuing harsh penalties were, however, tempered by suspended sentences and medical leave.[185]

Relieved by 34th Division in early May 8th Division shifted its front northwards to opposite Ovillers.[186] Both formations went on to suffer 6,380 and 5,121 casualties killed, wounded, missing and prisoner respectively on 1 July, 1st R. Irish Rif. share in these losses amounting to 17 officers and 429 men.[187] In the months prior to this *Hauptmann* Wagener, raid commander and *RIR 110's* specialist machine-gun officer, arranged the lethal Mash and Sausage valley killing zones swept by at least 12 *Maschinengewehr 08* that contributed more than anything else to the shocking III Corps debacle. Thus, it could be said that Wagener was, at the local tactical level, one of the architects of Great Britain's bloodiest day.[188] The *Blinddarm* and foremost section of *Schwaben-Höhe* obliterated by the Y-Sap[189] and Lochnagar mines just prior to Zero, *RIR 110* defended La Boisselle and vicinity against relentless British assaults until, forced back from trench to trench, the battle-worn regiment was relieved. Amongst

---

184 Bowman, *The Irish Regiments in the Great War*, pp. 104, 189-201. Of the 46 recorded deaths sustained by 1st R. Irish Rif. between 1 January and 11 May 1916, there are some obvious pre-war enlistments, but also, based on assigned regimental numbers, a large number of postings from R. Irish Rif. reserve battalions (3rd (Special Reserve), 4th and 5th (Extra Reserve). These would normally have been special reservists that may have served for some years prior to 1914; others might have been Regular reservists "parked" there following mobilisation. Special thanks to Dr Alison Hine for this illuminating analysis.
185 Thomas, "British 8th Infantry Division on the Western Front 1914-1918", pp. 144-45.
186 TNA WO 95/1674: '8th Division Operation Order No. 101', 5 May 1916, 8th Division War Diary.
187 See Edmonds, *Military Operations France and Belgium 1916 Vol. I*, pp. 370-93, Taylor, *The First Royal Irish Rifles in the Great War*, pp. 74-86 and Martin Grace & John Grehan, *Slaughter on the Somme 1st July 1916: The Complete War Diaries of the British Army's Worst Day* (Barnsley: Pen & Sword, 2016), pp. 326-27.
188 Greiner & Vulpius, *Reserve-Infanterie-Regiment Nr. 110 im Weltkrieg 1914-1918*, pp. 116-17. Wagener transferred to the *Generalstab* later in 1916. He went on to become a member of the right-wing *Freikorps*, prominent Nazi and close economic advisor, travelling companion and confidant to Third Reich *Führer* Adolf Hitler. Rising to the rank of *Generalmajor* during the Second World War, Wagener surrendered the Dodecanese Islands to the British in May 1945. See Henry Ashby Turner Jr. (ed.), *Hitler: Memoirs of a Confidant* (New Haven, Connecticut: Yale University Press, 1987).
189 The Y-Sap Mine extended from the British front line near to where it crossed the Albert – Bapaume Road, but because of existing German underground defences it could not be driven forward in a straight line. About 500 yards were dug beneath no man's land, before diverging right for approximately 500 yards. See Edmonds, *Military Operations France and Belgium 1916 Vol. I*, p. 375.

Approximate 11 April 1916 trench raid jumping-off site, Bécourt Wood in the left distance. (Author)

its 1,089 killed, wounded and missing sustained from 23 June to 3 July were *Leutnant* Dumas and *Leutnant* Stradtmann shot dead; *Leutnant* Böhlefeld was taken captive.[190]

Relieved of battalion command, Major Mayne relinquished his temporary rank to resume company leadership before employment as town major of Millencourt and Vermelles. Discharged duty for health reasons the following September, subsequent postings included instructor and area commandant until demobilized as an honorary major in 1919. Captain ffrench-Mullen made a full recovery and was passed fit for duty by a medical board in August 1916. Home service succeeded by active service in the Middle East earned him an MC, a mention in despatches and the Egyptian Order of the Nile, 4th Class.[191] He died in 1929. Lieutenants Lake and Whitfield survived

---

190 Ralph J. Whitehead, *The Other Side of the Wire Volume 2: The Battle of the Somme. With the XIV Reserve Corps, 1 July 1916* (Solihull: Helion & Company, 2013), pp. 283-327.
191 The Order of the Nile (*Kiladat El Nil*) is Egypt's highest state honour. The award was instituted in 1915 by Sultan Hussein Kamel (1853-1917) for exceptional services to the nation. It was reconstituted under the Republic of Egypt on 18 June 1953.

the war, the former becoming a minister, the latter retiring from the army with the rank of brigadier in 1950.[192]

Today, visitors to the preserved Lochnagar Crater have only to proceed just beyond the western face of the 220 feet (67 metre) diameter depression in order to reach the approximate jumping-off position of *Hauptmann* Wagener's raiding party. Gazing across the gently rolling vista constituting Chapes Spur, Avoca Valley and Tara Hill – Sausage Valley to the left; La Boisselle to the right – it is not difficult to imagine the white ribbon-like trenches that once criss-crossed the open fields ahead.[193] Nearby, within Bécourt Military Cemetery's 713 graves situated in a lovely sylvan enclosure at Bécourt Wood, lie the mortal remains of one officer and eight men of 1st R. Irish Rif. They are only tangible trace of the 11 April 1916 trench raid on the now popular destination battlefield site – *Pulvis et umbra sumus*.[194]

---

192 TNA WO 339/9059: Captain Ernest FFRENCH-MULLEN. The Royal Irish Rifles file and Taylor, *The First Royal Irish Rifles in the Great War*, pp. 243, 275, 295, 332.
193 Bécourt Military Cemetery was begun by 51st (Highland) Division in August 1915, and carried on by 18th (Eastern) Division and other formations until the Battles of the Somme. Its regular usage, chiefly by field ambulances, continued until April 1917. Special thanks to Stephen Barker and Jim Smithson for their assistance in identifying the raid site.
194 Horace, *Odes*, Book IV, ode vii, line 16 (23 BC).

9

Henry Horne as Corps Commander on the Somme

Simon Innes-Robbins

This chapter studies the experiences of a single British corps commander, Henry Sinclair (later General Lord) Horne at the Battle of the Somme, highlighting many of the command problems experienced in action and demonstrating what the better generals learnt from this lengthy and hard fought campaign. Commanding XV Corps during all stages of the Battle of the Somme until promoted to command First Army on 30 September 1916, Horne's performance confirmed his membership of a cadre of competent leaders which was slowly built up during the war and which formed the backbone of the army which had advanced to victory by November 1918.

Given command of XV Corps in the Suez Canal Zone, Horne transferred to France in April 1916 along with his Corps Headquarters, following successful lobbying by the War Office and GHQ.[1] Horne's return to France and his subsequent elevation to an Army command owed a great deal to Douglas Haig's influence.[2] William Robertson also had a high regard for Horne, who attributed the "very great honour" of his subsequent rise to army command to the support of Haig and Robertson, who had "backed me up",[3] and noted that Robertson and Robert Whigham, CIGS and Deputy CIGS at the War Office respectively, were "both good friends to me".[4]

In particular, both Haig and Robertson looked to Horne, as the only gunner to command an Army, to provide artillery expertise during 1914-15, even though he

---

1 The Imperial War Museum (hereafter IWM): General Lord Horne Papers, Horne to wife, 27 February 1916, and Lady Horne to Horne, 4 April 1916.
2 The National Archives (hereafter TNA), WO 256/12, Field-Marshal Earl Haig Papers: Diary, 11, 13 and 20 August 1916; IWM: Horne Papers: Horne to wife, 26 March, 11 April, 28, 29 and 30 August, and 26, 29 and 30 September 1916.
3 IWM: Horne Papers: Horne to wife, 20 August 1916.
4 IWM: Horne Papers: Horne to wife, 23 July 1916.

was no longer Haig's MGRA.[5] At his suggestion the system of artillery command was changed after Festubert,[6] and his ADC noted that "as a gunner one feels that his knowledge of what the artillery can do is a great asset to him in his present position, & his opinion on these matters carries more weight with those above than that of the average Divisional General".[7] A measure of Horne's influence on artillery matters may be gathered by an incident which occurred in May 1916. At the time, Robertson was opposed to the appointment of Noel Birch as the replacement for John Headlam as MGRA at GHQ, but changed his mind after being informed by Horne that Birch was "the best selection".[8] As late as June 1918 Birch, still holding the post of MGRA visited Horne "to stay the night and discuss artillery matters".[9]

Horne also received support from Henry Rawlinson of Fourth Army. Rawlinson was "delighted" when Haig informed him he would have Horne, Indeed, he asked Robertson to send Horne "out as soon as you can". On the grounds that Walter Congreve VC was his "weakest" corps commander and that the five divisions currently under his aegis were "too much for one man to handle in a general action",[10] Rawlinson removed two divisions from Congreve, whose plans were not considered to be "dashing enough", to create a role for Horne's XV Corps.[11] Having arrived in France on 20 April 1916, Horne lost most of his staff,[12] as only three out of fifteen staff officers joined him in France from Egypt.[13] As a result, taking over the section of line on the Somme opposite Fricourt and Mametz, Horne and his new staff had only two months in which to plan and implement his role in the largest British offensive of the war to this point.

Like other senior officers who had not attended Staff College, Horne was heavily reliant on his trained staff officers. On arrival at the recently formed Fourth Army, Horne discovered that Brigadier-General L.R. (later Lieutenant-General Sir Louis) Vaughan was to be his BGGS.[14] Horne's success at XV Corps rested upon a strong

---

5 TNA: WO 256/1, 3-4, Haig Papers: Diary, 23 August and 18 September 1914, 1 March and 11 May 1915.
6 Major-General Sir Frederick Maurice, 'Horne, Henry Sinclair, Baron Horne (1861–1929)', Dictionary of National Biography, p. 430.
7 IWM: Horne Papers: John A Don to Lady Horne, 5 May [1915].
8 TNA: WO 256/10, Haig Papers: Haig, Diary, 10 and 15 May 1916, and Field-Marshal Sir William Robertson to Haig, 15 May 1916.
9 IWM: Horne Papers: Horne to wife, 17 June 1918.
10 The Liddell Hart Centre for Military Archives (hereafter LHCMA), Robertson Papers 1/21/11: General Lord Rawlinson to Field Marshal Sir William Robertson, 8 April 1916. For more on Walter Congreve VC and his command of XIII Corps, see Spencer Jones's chapter elsewhere in this volume.
11 Ian F.W. Beckett, 'Henry Rawlinson' in Beckett and Steven J Corvi, *Haig's Generals* (Barnsley: Pen & Sword, 2009), p. 170.
12 IWM: Horne Papers: Horne to wife, 21April 1916.
13 Major A.F. Becke, *History of the Great War, Order of Battle*, Part 4 (London: HMSO, 1934-45), p. 225.
14 IWM: Horne Papers: Horne to wife, 23 April 1916.

partnership with 'Father' Vaughan, who was a "charming man, with his professional manner, sweetness of speech, gentleness of voice and gesture, like an Oxford Don analysing the war correspondence of Xenophon".[15] Horne noted that Vaughan "was a splendid staff officer", who bore "the burden & heat of the operations like a hero",[16] and, when he was struck down by appendicitis, missed him "very much as he has been my right hand man".[17]

One of "the advantages of Lord Horne's ignorance of staff work" was that "detailed execution was left to his staff, and that staff, once proved in his estimation, were given the fullest trust and confidence".[18] "One of the outstanding features" of XV Corps "was the 'very happy family' of the Corps Staff" and the "intensive training for the issue of operation orders" as Vaughan realized that "it was all important in major operations that orders to units - smallest units - must reach them in plenty of time and that there must not be a second's delay to passing orders from Corps to Division & Division to Brigade etc".[19] One staff officer with XV Corps noted that "as soon as it was known that a Division was ordered to join the Corps, one of the Corps Staff went at once to the Div.'s HQ – even before arrival in the corps area – to give maps, photographs, areas, traffic routes and in fact every scrap of useful information which could be circulated and digested during the move up".[20] As a result "the staff work went like clockwork" and Horne "could get his orders carried out".[21]

Lieutenant-General Sir Henry Horne.

15 Sir Philip Gibbs, *The Realities of War* (London: Heinemann, 1920), p,397.
16 IWM: Horne Papers: Horne to wife, 18 September 1916.
17 IWM: Horne Papers: Horne to wife, 23 September 1916.
18 IWM: Horne Papers: Lieutenant-General Sir Hastings Anderson, 'Lord Horne as an Army Commander', p. 417.
19 TNA: CAB 45/132: Major P.J.R. Currie to Brigadier-General Sir James Edmonds, 23 April 1930.
20 TNA: CAB 45/132: Major P.J.R. Currie to Brigadier-General Sir James Edmonds, 23 April 1930.
21 TNA: CAB 45/136: C.M. Page to Brigadier-General Sir James Edmonds, 25 August 1934.

Horne's experiences on the Western Front during 1915 had taught him to be sceptical about the possibility of achieving a quick victory. Like Rawlinson, Horne favoured the "bite and hold" approach that sought limited objectives. These lessons were outlined in an undated, but presumably pre-Somme, paper dissecting the problems presented by trench warfare. He noted that once the attack was successful, it was essential that the troops should "consolidate at once" whatever ground had been gained and to "take all possible steps to avoid being turned out of it again". Horne was "in favour of having the first objective of the attack clearly laid down" and that "it should be understood that troops do not advance beyond this, until reorganized". In the meantime scouts would "of course be pushed out at once towards the second objective" and Horne warned that consolidation "ought not to prevent the seizing of any important tactical point near at hand which ought to be troublesome to get later", but believed that such decisions would "depend on the sagacity & initiative of the man on the spot".[22] The New Armies lacked these very qualities. Both the Germans and the French noted that, although very brave, the 'green' British junior leaders often reacted slowly, paralysed by their inexperience and indecision.[23] The dilemma of whether to consolidate or exploit haunted the British Army throughout 1916-17.

Horne's plans for 1 July reflected his belief in the "bite and hold" method. Assessing XV's Corps objectives, Horne chose to bypass Fricourt, which was of "exceptional strength" and "the corner stone" of the German line between the Ancre and the Somme,[24] because of the "insuperable" difficulties of a frontal attack. Elsewhere, Horne relied on a long preliminary bombardment to destroy the enemy's main defences, notably the machine guns and artillery. The infantry would follow the barrage which would lift according to a strict time table to ensure that the infantry was never left unsupported. Machine guns were to be used before and during the assault to harass the enemy and to cover the advance of the infantry.[25] Horne was "in favour of a somewhat prolonged bombardment" having concluded that "the bombardment must be hot en[ough] & prolonged eno[ugh] to demoralize" the enemy and that "the short intense bombardment is now played out".[26]

Visiting Horne and Vaughan on 30 June, Haig recorded that the wire was "very well cut" as a result of XV Corps expending "twice as much" ammunition "as was allowed".[27] Indeed, on the fronts of the XIII and XV Corps the wire "had been better

---

22 IWM: Horne Papers 38/3: Horne, 'Attack of Trenches from Trenches', undated, pp. 4-5.
23 Christopher Duffy, *Through German Eyes* (London: Phoenix, 2006), p. 166, and Elizabeth Greenhalgh, '"Parade Ground Soldiers": French Army Assessments of the British on the Somme in 1916', *The Journal of Military History*, Vol.63, No.2 (April 1999), p. 300.
24 Brigadier General J E Edmonds, *Military Operations France and Belgium 1916*, Vol. I (London: Macmillan, 1932), pp. 346-347.
25 TNA: WO 95/921: XV Corps, Scheme of Operations, undated.
26 IWM: Horne Papers 38/3: Horne, 'Attack of Trenches from Trenches', undated, pp. 1-2.
27 TNA: WO 256/10, Haig Papers: Diary, 30 June 1916.

cut" than elsewhere.[28] Horne recorded that the bombardment before the assault had "obliterated" the German trenches.[29] The artillery had "thoroughly completed" its work as the wire "was everywhere well cut" and the hostile trench system had been "severely damaged, and in many parts obliterated" while the villages of Fricourt and Mametz "had practically ceased to exist". Nevertheless, many dugouts had proved "impervious to shell fire" and the infantry would suffer "heavy casualties from hostile MG fire".[30]

Major-General Sir John Headlam of the Ministry of Munitions later compiled a report on the artillery operations on the Somme between 24 June and 3 July 1916, with particular reference to the operations of XV Corps heavy artillery which afforded "the greatest variety in the nature of guns employed and in the nature of the enemy's defences". Headlam commented on the accuracy of the artillery fire, even "on reverse slopes where direct observation was impossible", and the effect of the artillery fire which "was generally fully equal to expectations", causing the trenches to be "knocked out of all shape" and "in nearly all cases" shelters which were above ground to be "completely destroyed". He also remarked that the "formidable" German wire when under "direct observation" had been destroyed by the artillery, and that "many infantry officers & men told me that they had never been in any way retarded by the wire or ever had to use the cutters on their rifles". He hoped that the introduction of the new instantaneous fuze, No.106, in early 1917 would "very materially" increase "the power of the artillery to deal with wire". Headlam noted, however, that "no effect at all had been produced" on the deep dug-outs which had been "quite beyond the reach of artillery fire". He also highlighted the difficulty for the artillery of locating and destroying machine guns which were kept hidden in dug-outs during the bombardment and only brought up at the last moment. Once in action these machine guns could only be destroyed by a direct hit but were "very small and inconspicuous" and therefore difficult to target.[31]

The XV Corps attack on 1 July (Z Day) was generally "very successful" taking most of their objectives and capturing 29 officers and 1,596 men "after hard fighting".[32] Horne noted that the artillery had done "splendid work" ensuring that Mametz, Fricourt and the trenches had been "utterly demolished", while the infantry had "fought splendidly". The 7th Division had "distinguished themselves", taking Mametz, and the 21st Division "also did well north of Fricourt". Moreover, the casualties were not "as heavy" as Horne had expected because "the artillery [had] covered the infantry advance so

28 Brigadier General J.E. Edmonds, *Military Operations France and Belgium 1916*, Vol. I, p. 307.
29 IWM: Horne Papers: Horne to wife, 9 July 1916.
30 TNA: WO 95/925: XV Corps CRA War Diary, 1 July 1916.
31 IWM: Horne Papers 43/2: Major General Sir John Headlam, 'Notes on Artillery Materiel in the Battle of the Somme', 5 July 1916.
32 IWM: Horne Papers: Horne to wife, 1 July 1916.

well".[33] On 1 July 1916 the 20th Brigade (7th Division, XV Corps) followed "what eventually became known as the creeping barrage".[34] Along with XIII Corps, XV Corps achieved the deepest penetration of the German front by Rawlinson's Fourth Army, capturing the important Montauban - Mametz Ridge which protected the flank of the main attack and which was considered to be of "considerable tactical value",[35] and "the pivot of the whole of the second phase" of operations.[36]

The enemy's resistance on the front of the 30th, 18th (XIII Corps) and 7th Divisions (XV Corps) had been "completely broken" but no effort was made to occupy positions beyond the first day's objectives, such as Mametz Wood, which could probably have been captured with small loss and which subsequently proved very costly both in time and casualties to occupy. Instead, the gains were consolidated,[37] as Horne was expecting that "we shall have to stick on hard tonight & tomorrow against counter-attacks". Horne had also received the first indications that, whereas the XIII Corps (Congreve) to the south on Horne's right had also done "very well", the corps "to the north of us have not got on too well",[38] where the gamble by the High Command on achieving a quick and deep advance on the Somme had failed.[39] The subsequent failure to take the German second line and capture Mametz Wood, which was finally secured on 12 July after bitter fighting, meant, however, that momentum was lost. The problem of how to exploit a successful attack and convert it into a breakthrough continued to thwart British ambitions.

Nevertheless, on 2 July Horne received the congratulations of Robertson and Haig,[40] who complemented him "on the success of his operations' which had posed "a most difficult problem".[41] Robertson later telephoned Lady Horne to inform her that her husband had "done splendid work",[42] while his ADC wrote to inform her that Horne and his Corps "have done most exceptionally".[43] The main problem now was how to continue the advance. Between 11 and 13 July the German Second Line was bombarded and the wire cut,[44] in preparation for another set-piece attack by XV

33 IWM: Horne Papers: Horne to wife, 2 and 6 July 1916.
34 TNA: CAB 45/132: Brigadier-General G.H. Boileau to Brigadier-General Sir James Edmonds, 16 February 1934.
35 IWM: Fourth Army Papers, Vol. 5: Lieutenant General Sir Launcelot Kiggell to General Sir Henry Rawlinson, OAD 710, 12 April 1916.
36 IWM: Fourth Army Papers, Vol. 6: Major General A A Montgomery, Conference held at Fourth Army Headquarters, 12th June 1916, Fourth Army No GX3/1C, 15 June 1916.
37 Brigadier General J E, *Military Operations France and Belgium 1916*, Vol. I, p. 366.
38 IWM: Horne Papers: Horne, Diary and letter to wife, 1 July 1916.
39 Royal Artillery Institute (hereafter RAI), Brigadier E C Anstey Papers: Anstey, The History of the Royal Artillery, p. 112.
40 IWM: Horne Papers: Horne to wife, 2 July 1916.
41 TNA: WO 256/11, Haig Papers: Diary, 2 July 1916.
42 IWM: Horne Papers: Lady Horne, Diary, 4 July 1916.
43 IWM: Horne Papers: Major C C Lucas to Lady Horne, 6 July [1916].
44 IWM: Horne Papers: Horne, Diary, 11-13 July 1916.

and XIII Corps. The artillery had "quite got the supremacy", thanks to "the splendid assistance" of the RFC's aeroplanes which had done "splendid work".[45] Horne was instrumental in obtaining Haig's approval of Rawlinson's plan to employ a night attack to capture the German second line. Haig was reluctant to undertake such a night operation as the troops were "not highly trained and disciplined, nor the staffs experienced in such work" but one of the main factors that changed his mind was the knowledge that Horne "was much averse" to attacking "on the lines suggested by the C-in-C" and thought that his plan was "unlikely to succeed".[46]

At 3.25 am on 14 July 1916 XV Corps attacked Bazentin le Petit Wood and Village, and Bazentin le Grand Wood after a intense, 5-minute bombardment. The 7th and 21st Divisions undertook the assault which "went right thro[ugh] to objective without a hitch" capturing about 600 prisoners, including the commander of the Lehr Fusilier Brigade and at least 2 heavy howitzers and 3 field guns. Even though the cloudy weather had handicapped air observation,[47] the wire "had been well cut by the artillery".[48] The losses were slight and no great difficulties were experienced in taking their objectives.[49] The 20th Brigade (7th Division, XV Corps) followed the barrage "very close" as its commander Brigadier-General C.J. (later Field-Marshal Sir Cyril) Deverell influenced by his experiences on 1 July "regarded the immediate entry of the objective as the barrage lifted off as absolutely essential to success in the 14 July night attack".[50] For the attack on 14 July 1916 "the infantry (20th and 22nd Brigades) had evolved a system of creeping forward, and attacking at 3.30 am quickly reached their objective (the enemy's 2nd line) taking 1 gun and 300 prisoners".[51] Deverell, who "had taken a lot of trouble" in planning this "very successful attack" and "was the originator of the creeping forward idea",[52] would soon be promoted to command 3rd Division. The XV and XIII Corps had captured the German second line between Bazentin le Petit and Longueval and "a good many prisoners" who were "in a much demoralized condition",[53] in "a great success" in which "the troops fought brilliantly".[54] Rawlinson

---

45 IWM: Horne Papers: Horne to wife, 13 July 1916.
46 IWM: Fourth Army Papers, Vol. 5: Note of discussion as to attack on Longueval plateau and the C-in-C's decision thereon, OAD 60, 11 July 1916.
47 IWM: Horne Papers: Horne, Diary, 14 July 1916.
48 IWM: Fourth Army Papers, Vol. 2: Fourth Army, War Diary, 14 July 1916.
49 TNA: WO 158/328: 'Operations of the 7th Division', 14 July 1916, and 'Operations of the 21st Division', 14 July 1916.
50 TNA: CAB 45/138: Field-Marshal Sir Cyril Deverell to Brigadier-General Sir James Edmonds, 9 April 1930.
51 TNA: CAB 45/132: Brigadier-General G.H. Boileau to Brigadier-General Sir James Edmonds, 16 February 1934.
52 TNA: CAB 45/132: Brigadier-General G.H. Boileau (C.R.E., 7th Division) to Brigadier-General Sir James Edmonds, 26 January 1930.
53 IWM: Horne Papers: Horne to wife, 14 July 1916.
54 IWM: Horne Papers: Horne to wife, 15 July 1916.

Henry Horne as Corps Commander on the Somme   259

reported that "our corps commanders – Horne and Congreve – have done and are doing splendid work".[55]

Unfortunately, once again, the caution of Rawlinson and Horne prevented exploitation. The failure to delegate to the experienced divisional commanders, Haldane (3rd Division) and Watts (7th Division), meant that reserves, including the cavalry, were not employed to maintain the impetus of the advance and the fleeting opportunity to take High Wood and possibly Delville Wood was missed. High Wood would only be captured after another two months of bitter and bloody fighting.[56] It is debateable whether the cavalry could have done much even if it had arrived. With the benefit of hindsight, Basil Liddell Hart complained that Horne "had stopped the infantry in the morning from exploiting a gap and securing High Wood when it was clearly undefended".[57] Unfortunately, the situation at the time was not quite so clear cut.

Horne reported that the Germans had been reinforced and that it was not possible to advance "without a regular artillery preparation" and so had drawn his men back from High Wood "where they were being too much exposed" so that he could shell it.[58] Horne has been criticized for making this decision to withdraw from High Wood, notably by Liddell Hart on the grounds that it would be two more months before the wood was regained,[59] but Horne did so because he considered that "it was evident that it could only be taken after very heavy bombardment" as part of a larger operation, rather than undertaking "an isolated operation", which would be costly and make success "more difficult".[60] In any case, the real opportunity had already been missed. Once more, the Germans recovered and their opposition around High and Delville Woods prevented further, quick progress. Throughout August XV Corps launched a succession of piecemeal attacks in an attempt to clear the defenders, but the uncoordinated efforts suffered heavy losses and and made little progress. Similarly, in the first half of September Horne's soldiers struggled to secure Ginchy as a precursor to the capture of Guillemont.

Throughout the Somme, new tactics were developed formulating "the artillery doctrine which was to be followed for the rest of the war and which was to form the basis of post-war training".[61] Artillery support was the backbone of any attack and would eventually become the battle winner of the First World War. From mid-1916 onwards the artillery barrage was "a deciding factor in the success or failure of an operation" and "by the end of the Somme techniques had been improved to the state that

55 LHCMA, Robertson Papers 1/21/28: General Lord Rawlinson to Field Marshal Sir William Robertson, 14 July 1916.
56 Brigadier-General J.E., *Military Operations France and Belgium* 1916, Vol. II, pp. 83-84.
57 Sir Basil Liddell Hart, *Memoirs*, Vol. I (London: Cassell, 1965), p. 25.
58 IWM: Horne Papers: Horne to wife, 16 July 1916.
59 B H Liddell Hart, *The Real War* (London: Faber & Faber, 1930), p. 261.
60 TNA: WO 95/921: Brigadier-General L.R. Vaughan, Note on the reason for the withdrawal from High Wood 15/16th July, 1916, 21 July 1916.
61 RAI: Anstey Papers: Anstey, The History of the Royal Artillery, p. 229.

when it was usually possible to put infantry into a succession of trenches with small loss".[62] Horne's greatest contribution was as an innovator in developing the employment of artillery on a large scale to break down the formidable German defences. During the campaign on the Somme artillery techniques developed and improved and there was considerable innovation whose impact would not be fully felt until 1917.

Horne, calling on his background as a gunner, drove artillery innovation in XV Corps. For example, the barrage maps produced by XV Corps for the attack on 1 July were the earliest issued in the BEF.[63] The first occasion on which a barrage map was issued to the infantry for an attack was on 14 July by XV Corps.[64] Horne "gained some notable successes by the skilful handling of his artillery, in particular the development of the creeping barrage".[65] This creeping barrage "was used by the 15th Divn. at the Battle of Loos" and "was always done by the XVth Corps Artillery (including the Heavy Artillery) during the Somme Battle from 1st July on".[66] 1 July 1916 was "the first time" that an advance of such depth was successfully carried out, under a creeping barrage".[67] It took some time for the new creeping barrage to become universal. For example, as late as 23 August 1916 the bombardment of the heavy artillery was ineffective and the barrage by the field artillery was short and lifted early leaving the attacking infantry a considerable distance to go in the face of unsuppressed machine-gun fire.[68]

During August 1916 the British developed an artillery system based on a preparation by an "accurate bombardment with heavy shells throughout 48 hours, or more" and "an intensive barrage with 18-pdr. shrapnel" under which the infantry assaulted.[69] Given sanction by GHQ as early as 16 July as "one of the outstanding lessons of the recent fighting", by early September the creeping barrage was "an established practice" and the troops were accustomed to keeping as close to it as possible.[70] This progress was regularised on 15 September when an Army Order confirmed formally for the

---

62 TNA: CAB 45/132: Lieutenant-General Sir Charles Broad to Brigadier-General Sir James Edmonds, 6 March 1937.
63 Major A F Becke, 'The Coming of the Creeping Barrage', *The Journal of the Royal Artillery*, Vol. LVIII (1931-32), p. 28.
64 TNA: CAB 45/137: Major-General E.W. Alexander to Brigadier-General Sir James Edmonds, 21 February 1930.
65 Gregory Blaxland, *Amiens: 1918* (London: Frederick Muller, 1968), p. 14.
66 TNA: CAB 45/137: Major-General E.W. Alexander to Brigadier-General Sir James Edmonds, 21 February 1930.
67 TNA: CAB 45/136: Major-General S.F. Metcalfe to Brigadier-General Sir James Edmonds, 17 March 1930.
68 TNA: CAB 45/137: Lieutenant-Colonel L.L.C. Reynolds to Brigadier-General Sir James Edmonds, 19 August 1934.
69 TNA: WO 256/12, Haig Papers: Diary, 5 August 1916.
70 Brigadier General J E Edmonds, *Military Operations France and Belgium 1916*, Vol. II, p. 251.

first time the use of a creeping barrage.[71] XV Corps first used the rolling or creeping barrage in its fully developed form during the attack on Flers on 15 September,[72] where it employed 25 percent of its field artillery in the creeping barrage and 75 percent in the stationary barrage.[73]

The development of the creeping barrage on the Somme "was the most important development in artillery tactics that had as yet appeared",[74] and one brigadier-general noted that "the introduction into the battle of the creeping artillery barrage" had "revolutionised all infantry tactics" which "developed into a race between the enemy rushing machine guns out of their dugouts and into position and the attackers rushing forward with the bayonet and bomb to prevent them".[75] An infantry officer reckoned that the invention of the creeping barrage "saved the lives of tens of thousands of the PBI".[76] Although also employed by VIII and XIII Corps,[77] there is enough evidence to support "the belief that the formalised creeping barrage originated in XV Corps".[78] Horne shares credit for the development of the creeping barrage with Major-General E.W. Alexander VC, who was his BGRA at XV Corps on the Somme in 1916 and later became his MGRA with First Army in April 1918. Although refreshingly modest about his own participation, Horne could lay "some claims to the invention and development of the creeping barrage",[79] having with the assistance of Alexander, his "particularly able Artillery Commander",[80] "devised a new method of employing his artillery to assist forward the Infantry attack" which "was quickly improved upon & turned into the 'Creeping Barrage' & taken up by all the armies for supporting Infantry attacks with artillery fire".[81]

71 RAI: Anstey Papers: Major-General E W Alexander to Brigadier-General Sir James Edmonds, 21 February 1930.
72 RAI: Rawlins Papers Box 3: Major General E W Alexander to Colonel S W H Rawlins, 6 January 1919; RAI: Anstey Papers: Note by Brigadier-General Sir James Edmonds and Lieutenant-Colonel A F Becke, 26 July 1926; Major A F Becke, 'The Coming of the Creeping Barrage', *The Journal of the Royal Artillery*, Vol. LVIII (1931-32), p. 30.
73 Brigadier General J E Edmonds, *Military Operations France and Belgium 1916*, Vol. II, p. 295, fn.2.
74 RAI: Anstey Papers: Anstey, The History of the Royal Artillery, p. 126.
75 TNA: CAB 45/208: Bernard Freyberg, *A Linesman in Picardy*, Chapter II, p. 12.
76 TNA: CAB 45/136: Major C.W. Wingrove to Brigadier-General Sir James Edmonds, 12 November 1934.
77 Brigadier-General Sir James Edmonds, *Military Operations: France and Belgium, 1916*, Vol. I, p. 293.
78 Major A F Becke, 'The Coming of the Creeping Barrage', *The Journal of the Royal Artillery*, Vol. LVIII (1931-32), p. 30.
79 IWM: Horne Papers: Anderson, 'Lord Horne as an Army Commander', p. 407.
80 IWM: Horne Papers: 'Our Gunner General, Lord Horne: The Leader of the Stalwart First Army', *The Gunner*, No.2 (February 1920), p. 7
81 TNA: CAB 45/134: Lieutenant-Colonel R.S. Hardman to Brigadier-General Sir James Edmonds, 30 March 1930.

During this period, on-going artillery innovation was matched by the gradual emergence of a combat-hardened cadre of officers which would lead the British Armies at all levels during 1917-18. From the Battle of the Somme onwards several effective commanders emerged within the BEF who had gained experience and were active in pursuing new ideas. At the same time, the weak and ineffective were steadily weeded out. Although the clear-out of senior officers was at times arbitrary and unfair, one must remember that the stakes were high and that incompetence cost lives. There is no doubt that poor leadership and staff work contributed to many of the failures in the period 1915-17. Haig maintained that "if a Divisional General reports any one of his Brigadiers as unfit, I had only one of two alternatives: Either the Brigadier must go or the Div. GOC".[82] Gradually, as the war progressed, the weaker commanders unfit for the strenuous life of trench warfare were ruthlessly replaced at brigade and divisional level by battle-hardened veterans who developed effective operational methods.

On the Somme, Horne was much involved in the process of weeding out the older or less competent senior officers and replacing them with more experienced and professional soldiers. For example, Horne was reported by Haig to be "dissatisfied" and "very disappointed with the work" of Brigadier-General R.S. Oxley (24th Brigade), Major-General T.D. Pilcher (17th Division), and Major-General Sir Ivor Phillips (38th Division) in July 1916 and Haig, trusting in Horne's judgement, approved of their removal.[83] Having been adversely reported on by Lieutenant-General Sir James Babington (23rd Division) as being only "fairly satisfactory as a Brigadier" and "certainly not fit for promotion to command a division",[84] Oxley was replaced on 11 July. Following the capture of Fricourt on 2 July, subsequent attempts by the relatively green 17th and 38th Divisions to take the German second line and seize Mametz Wood had bogged down in poor weather which interfered with the registration of the artillery. A sense of frustration built up within the British high command at the slow progress. GHQ reminded Rawlinson that Mametz Wood on the left flank of the Fourth Army was of "great tactical importance".[85] When in turn informed by Rawlinson that he "had hoped that by this time we might have established ourselves in this Wood", Horne explained that "this is the first time New Army troops have had to undertake a job of this sort, and it is difficult to get the push on that is necessary in open war".[86]

Aware that there had been "too many delays already",[87] Horne was under considerable pressure from Haig, who visited him almost every day and urged him to capture

---

82 TNA: WO 256/14, Haig Papers: Diary, 21 November 1916.
83 TNA: WO 256/11, Haig Papers: Diary, 4, 8, 9 and 10 July 1916.
84 TNA: WO 256/6 and 9, Haig Papers: Diary, 16 November 1915 and 18 March 1916.
85 IWM: Fourth Army Papers, Vol. 5: Lieutenant-General Sir Launcelot Kiggell to General Sir Henry Rawlinson, OAD 52, 8 July 1916.
86 IWM: Fourth Army Papers, Vol. 6: Notes of Conference held at Fourth Army headquarters, 8th July 1916, undated.
87 IWM: Horne Papers: Horne to wife, 9 July 1916.

Mametz Wood.[88] Horne took drastic action on 9 July, removing Philipps (38th Division) and sending Major-General H.E. (later Lieutenant-General Sir Herbert) Watts (7th Division) to supervise the efforts of the inexperienced 38th Division to capture Mametz Wood.[89] He reported to Fourth Army that the 113th and 115th Brigades had failed to deliver attacks and that "this Division is not yet sufficiently trained to take part in an attack", although noting that the GSO1 (Lieutenant-Colonel H E ap Rhys Pryce) "did excellent work" and "rendered great assistance", taking "an active part in re-organizing the men".[90] Some six weeks later, Brigadier-General Horatio J. Evans commanding 115th Brigade, was also sent home, probably because, aged 57 years, he was considered too old.[91]

Major-General Herbert Watts.

On 11 July Horne "spoke to General Pilcher",[92] whose 17th Division was struggling to take the Quadrangle and had "got into trouble with General Horne for allowing the enemy to get the upper hand so much & for not knowing where the enemy front line ran".[93] Pilcher was sacked on 12 July. Haig, trusting in Horne's judgement, approved their removal.[94] The removal of Philipps and Pilcher is a good illustration of the way in which the shortage of experienced commanders and staff officers hindered the operations of the British Army in 1915-16. These shortages were the result of the rapid expansion which the BEF had undergone during the early years of the war. This problem was exacerbated by the poor management of the battle by the high command, which lacked experience of major, sustained operations, and failed to construct an

---

88   IWM: Horne Papers: Horne, Diary, 9, 10, and 13 July 1916.
89   IWM: Horne Papers: Horne, Diary, 9 July 1916.
90   TNA: WO 95/921: Lieutenant General H S Horne to Fourth Army, B65/10, 13 July 1916.
91   Trevor Gordon Harvey, '"An Army of Brigadiers": British Brigade Commanders at the Battle of Arras 1917', PhD Thesis, University of Birmingham (August 2015), fn. 73, p. 32.
92   IWM: Horne Papers: Horne, Diary, 11 July 1916.
93   TNA: CAB 45/135: Major G.H. King to Brigadier-General Sir James Edmonds, 27 March 1930.
94   TNA: WO 256/11, Haig Papers: Haig, Diary, 4, 8, 9 and 10 July 1916.

alternative strategy once the initial plan to breakthrough had failed.

Haking (GOC XI Corps) had already told Haig that he had "no confidence" in Philipps "as a commander", which according to the Commander-in-Chief was "not to be wondered at as the poor fellow has had no training as a commander in the field!"[95] Philipps, originally a Regular soldier who had retired from the Indian Army before the war and was serving with the Pembrokeshire Yeomanry at its outbreak, had been promoted, likely due to his connections as an MP and a friend of Lloyd George, to command the 38th Division in early 1915 "over the heads of many more senior and meritorious officers". It was therefore "hardly surprising that he was ignorant, lacked experience and failed to inspire confidence" while it was Lieutenant-Colonel ap Rhys Pryce (the GSO1), "a thoroughly capable officer in every way", who "in reality commanded the Division".[96] Philipps, aged 54, who was "ignorant" and lacked the skills required,[97] was replaced by Major-General C.G. Blackader, aged 46, commander of a battalion between 1912 and 1915, and a brigade in 1915. Blackader in turn made way for Major-General T.A. (later General Sir Thomas) Cubitt, a younger man, who had commanded a battalion and then a brigade between 1916 and 1918. One staff officer believed that Philipps had "quite rightly" been sent home and "had no claim to a division whatever having done some 20 years in the Indian Cavalry & then left as a Major to become an MP".[98] Under the stewardship of Blackader and Cubitt the division "did extremely well".[99]

Pilcher was an opinionated officer whose provocative writing on military topics before the war had attracted the hostile notice of his superiors. He had received an adverse report from the Commander-in-Chief, India in June 1914,[100] and in November

Major-General Ivor Philipps.

---

95 TNA: WO 256/7, Haig Papers: Haig, Diary, 17 January 1916.
96 TNA: CAB 45/132: Major G.P.L. Drake-Brockman to Brigadier-General Sir James Edmonds, 7 February 1930.
97 Churchill College, Cambridge (hereafter CCC), General Sir Charles Bonham-Carter Papers 9/2: Bonham-Carter, Autobiography, Chapter VIII, pp. 13-14.
98 IWM: Game Papers PWG12: Air Vice Marshal Sir Philip Game to wife, 2 August 1916.
99 TNA: CAB 45/132: Major G.P.L. Drake-Brockman to Brigadier-General Sir James Edmonds, 7 February 1930.
100 See TNA: WO 138/36: Pilcher Papers.

1914 Sir John French had refused the offer of Pilcher for employment with the BEF because he had never been impressed by him.[101] Nevertheless, Pilcher had been given command of the 17th Division, a New Army division, in the UK in January 1915, coming out to France in July 1915. After the loss of the Bluff in early 1916, Haig had wanted to sack both Lieutenant-General Sir Hew Fanshawe (V Corps) and Pilcher, who according to Major General J.A.L. (later General Sir Aylmer) Haldane (3rd Division) rarely visited the trenches, but Plumer (Second Army) had taken "the blame on himself", and Pilcher had survived.[102] Horne's assessment that Pilcher lacked the "initiative, drive and readiness of resource" essential for a divisional commander [103] was supported by Rawlinson (Fourth Army) who agreed that he did not have "the special characteristics" to command a division,[104] and by Haig, who noted that he had "shown himself unequal to the task of commanding a Division in the field", as he "does not possess those qualifications essential for a higher commander in the field".[105]

Pilcher, who was both somewhat inexperienced and at the age of 58, rather old to be commanding a division, was replaced by the younger and more battle-hardened Major-General P.R. Robertson (aged 50), who since August 1914 had commanded the 1st Cameronians (1914-15) and the 19th Brigade (1915-16), which had been part of Horne's 2nd Division in 1915. Robertson remained in command of the division for the remainder of the war. This process of removing incompetent commanders was a continuous one in 1916-17 as the high command sought to ensure that senior officers like Philipps and Pilcher, who were perceived to lack the ability to adapt and learn quickly, were removed and replaced by commanders who were seen to be more competent or perhaps willing to demand the necessary sacrifices. Horne did not however hold a grudge against the 17th Division, meeting all the commanding officers on 28 July and informing them that "the Division had earned a high reputation for holding onto the ground gained".[106]

It must also be recalled that Horne himself felt the pressure from above to gain quick and decisive results. In addition to their perceived slowness, his disillusionment with Philipps and Pilcher may have been influenced by their willingness to argue and challenge his orders. Certainly, Horne favoured the more thrusting and perhaps more pliant Watts (7th Division), who got on with fighting the Germans

---

101 TNA: Kitchener Papers 30/57/49, WA/50: Field Marshal Sir John French to Field Marshal Lord Kitchener, 29 November 1914.
102 The National Library of Scotland (hereafter NLS), General Sir Aylmer Haldane Papers: Haldane, Diary, 24 February and 8 March 1916.
103 TNA: Major-General T.D. Pilcher Papers, WO 138/36: Pilcher to the Military Secretary, War Office, 11 August 1916.
104 TNA: Pilcher Papers, WO 138/36: General Sir Henry Rawlinson to the Military Secretary, GHQ, 11 July 1916.
105 TNA: Pilcher Papers, WO 138/36: General Sir Douglas Haig to the Military Secretary, War Office, 12 July 1916.
106 IWM: Lieutenant-Colonel R. Fife Papers: Fife, Diary, 28 July 1916.

without questioning his orders. Watts was "a splendid fellow", who was "very fit & well, always cheery and confident, and a very nice man indeed" for whom Horne had "a very great regard & affection" as "the best general I have, and the most successful", having done "excellent work" at Mametz.[107] Watts, who was to be promoted to command XIX Corps in early 1917, was according to Haig "a plucky hard little man" and "a hard fighter, a leader of men", who, although "distinctly stupid" with "no great brains" and lacking imagination, inspired "confidence in all both above and below".[108] Like Horne, Watts had never attended Staff College and was heavily reliant on his staff officers but also proved to be "a fine leader and a delightful chief to serve".[109]

Major-General Thomas Pilcher.

By contrast, both Phipps and Pilcher suffered from the perception that they were "dugouts" and thus ill-equipped to command divisions. Moreover, it was believed by at least one officer that General Pilcher "was 'stellenbosched' [sacked]" for "very rightly refusing" to attack a resilient German trench for the fifth time.[110] Pilcher wrote a defence of his actions, accusing Horne of "not consenting to be cross-questioned",[111] and he understandably retained a dislike of Horne.[112] There is the distinct impression that the system tended to reward commanders who did not question orders. As a personality, Horne was much more than a mere martinet, visiting Divisional HQs every day and cheering his subordinates up by creating an atmosphere of confidence.[113] He combined an "inflexible insistence on efficiency with the greatest kindness and

---

107 IWM: Horne Papers: Horne to wife, 12 July 1916.
108 TNA: WO 256/3 and 10, Haig Papers: Diary, 26 February 1915 and 9 May 1916.
109 CCC, Bonham-Carter Papers 9/1 and 9/2: Bonham-Carter, Memoir, Chapter VII, p. 24, and Chapter VIII, pp. 2-3.
110 TNA: CAB 45/132: Lieutenant-Colonel R.W. Caster to Brigadier-General Sir James Edmonds, 6 April 1930.
111 TNA: Pilcher Papers, WO 138/36: Pilcher, 'Narrative ... of incidents on the front of 17th Division...'.
112 IWM: Horne Papers: Horne to wife, 22 October 1917.
113 TNA: CAB 45/123: General Lord Jeffreys to Brigadier-General Sir James Edmonds, 31 July 1931.

courtesy to all ranks" and ran "essentially a 'happy' unit".[114] But he "was impatient of indiscipline, of slackness, of eyewash, and especially of a lack of care in Commanders for the lives and the comfort of their men".[115] In July 1916 Evans, Oxley, Philipps and Pilcher were at the receiving end of this impatience. Thus, the trend was for younger and more competent senior officers to command formations, although the process by which this was achieved could often seem harsh.

At 6.20 am on 15 September the XV Corps was able to launch a more coherent, large-scale operation, employing the 14th, 41st, and New Zealand Divisions and 17 tanks to attack the Switch, Flers and Gueudecourt lines while the XIV Corps attacked Les Boeufs & Morval. The second objective was taken, while the New Zealanders took the third objective.[116] For this attack a heavy concentration of artillery was utilized,[117] while tanks were employed for the first time to "great effect".[118] Having taken the Switch Line, the Flers Line, and Flers village,[119] Horne reported that the attack was "a great success" and that his troops "did splendidly". In particular, the gunners did "splendid work",[120] inflicting "heavy losses" on the Germans.[121] The Battle of Flers on 15 September saw the first employment of organised counter-battery fire,[122] and on the Somme British counter-battery fire was noticeably ahead of the Germans. VIII and XV Corps laid the foundations for the growing ascendancy which the British artillery was to achieve in 1917-18.[123]

The tanks had done "very well on the whole".[124] Fourth Army recorded that the employment of tanks had allowed "portions of the enemy's lines" to be taken "without difficulty". Furthermore, "the value of the tanks was clearly shown by the fact that positions against which the tanks advanced were taken, those against which the tanks did not advance (owing to mechanical difficulties) held out and remained uncaptured at the end of the day".[125] But, above all, the operations had given the British "the high ground" for which they had fought for so long and carried them "forward

---

114 IWM: Horne Papers: General Sir Herbert Uniacke, 'General The Lord Horne of Stirkoke', p. 4.
115 IWM: Horne Papers: Anderson, 'Lord Horne as an Army Commander', p. 418.
116 TNA: WO 158/330: Fourth Army, 'Summary of Operations, September 15th, 1916', 15 September 1916.
117 Brigadier-General J.E. Edmonds, *Military Operations France and Belgium 1916*, Vol. II, p. 293, fn.1 and 2, 298, 306.
118 TNA: WO 158/236: Major-General A A Montgomery, 'Instructions for the Employment of "Tanks"', 11 September 1916.
119 IWM: Horne Papers: Horne, Diary, 15 September 1916.
120 IWM: Horne Papers: Horne to wife, 16 September 1916.
121 IWM: Horne Papers: Horne to wife, 17 September 1916.
122 Albert P. Palazzo, The British Army's Counter-Battery Staff Office and Control of the Enemy in World War I, *Journal of Military History*, Vol. 63, No 1 (January 1999), p. 57.
123 General Sir Martin Farndale, *History of the Royal Regiment of Artillery: Western Front, 1914-18* (Woolwich: The Royal Artillery Institution, 1986), p. 149.
124 IWM: Horne Papers: Horne to wife, 24 September 1916.
125 TNA: WO 158/330: Fourth Army, 'Summary of Operations', 15 September 1916.

a fine step".[126] This was Horne's last major triumph as on 29 September he handed over command of XV Corps and left to take over First Army. Rawlinson, his Army Commander, was pleased for Horne but "desperately sorry to lose him" as he had been "a tower of strength, and full of originality".[127] Rated by one observer as one of the "two best Corps Commanders in France",[128] Horne had earned his promotion.

The story of how, in September 1916, Horne left to assume command of the First Army is interesting.[129] When Monro was appointed as Commander-in-Chief in India, Haking, despite his poor performance as a corps commander at Loos in September 1915 and again at Fromelles in July 1916,[130] was appointed to command the First Army in August 1916 by Haig who claimed that he had been appointed "to 'act temporarily' in Monro's absence" because no other Corps Commander, such as Byng, Birdwood, or Cavan, was available.[131] The War Council, which had to ratify Army Commands, indicated that Haking was unacceptable and the CIGS (Robertson), who "was very angry with Haig for appointing Haking",[132] when it was unlikely to be approved by either the Secretary of State or the Prime Minister, insisted that Haig choose between Birdwood, Cavan, Horne and Henry Wilson instead, declaring a preference for Cavan, of whom he had "the highest opinion", or Horne.[133]

It was rumoured that Haig chose Horne, who was "the least brilliant" instead of Cavan, who had "a great reputation", because "some people talk of him as the most likely successor to Haig".[134] As a result, Haking was merely a caretaker until Horne could be spared from the Somme. With his appointment to First Army, Horne had climbed from the rank of Colonel with the temporary rank of Brigadier-General to that of full General in less than two years. This was a meteoric rise which was equalled only by General Sir Hubert Gough (Fifth Army) amongst the Army Commanders in France. Horne had grasped the career opportunity provided by the outbreak of the war.

Although the Somme campaign was a major disappointment, characterised by heavy casualties and limited success, often as a result of poor and inexperienced generalship, it did nevertheless provide many valuable lessons, notably in the use of new weapons such as aircraft, machine guns and tanks which would help overcome the German defences and ultimately win the war. 1916 also saw the first employment by

---

126 IWM: Horne Papers: Horne to wife, 19 September 1916.
127 Major General Sir Frederick Maurice, *The Life of General Lord Rawlinson of Trent GCB* (London: Cassell, 1928), p. 175.
128 LHCMA, Brigadier Sir Edward Beddington Papers: Beddington, Memoir, p. 92.
129 IWM: Horne Papers: Anderson, 'Lord Horne as an Army Commander', p. 408.
130 IWM: Field-Marshal Sir Henry Wilson Papers: Wilson, Diary, 19 July 1916.
131 TNA: WO 256/12, Haig Papers: Diary, 11 August 1916.
132 IWM: Wilson Papers: Wilson, Diary, 21 August 1916.
133 TNA: WO 256/12, Haig Papers: Field-Marshal Sir William Robertson to Haig, 10 August 1916.
134 Brian Bond & Simon Robbins (ed.), *Staff Officer: The Diaries of Walter Guinness (First Lord Moyne), 1914-1918* (London: Leo Cooper, 1987), pp. 129-130.

Horne and others of the set-piece attack utilising an effective all-arms doctrine under the umbrella of the artillery's fire-power. This operational method would be further developed by the British Armies in France during 1917 to overcome the German defensive system and finally achieve victory in 1918. The 1 July 1916 was the nadir of the British Army, but the lessons learnt by commanders such as Horne during the five-month long Battle of the Somme promised better days ahead and paved the way for the victories of 1918. Horne, who represented the best of what the old army had to offer – a lack of personal ambition; an austere sense of duty; a thoroughgoing professionalism and attention to detail[135] - was one of a group of fine commanders who formed the higher echelons of the high command and made this all possible. His career provides many clues as to how this turn around in the fortunes of the British Army was achieved.

---

135 IWM: Horne Papers: Anderson, 'Lord Horne as an Army Commander', p. 409.

10

XIII Corps and the Attack at Montauban, 1 July 1916

Spencer Jones

A century on, the "tyrannical hold" of 1 July 1916 shows no signs of weakening its grip on the public perception of the First World War.[1] The opening of the Battle of the Somme, notorious as the single bloodiest day in the history of the British Army, remains indelibly associated with the entire conflict. There is no denying the scale of the disaster which engulfed British forces north of the Albert – Bapaume Road, yet events south of this boundary, where British and French troops breached the German defences and captured almost all of their first day objectives, have remained neglected until comparatively recently. In some cases, the events in the southern sector of the battlefield are obfuscated or ignored. In *The First World War* John Keegan described the carnage in the north in detail before making a passing reference to disproportionate German alarm that "astride the River Somme ground had been lost"[2] whilst the foreword to the 2016 edition of *The Missing of the Somme* stated, incorrectly, that "By the end of the [first] day… Not a village had been taken, nor a single major objective achieved."[3]

Recent studies have noted the success in the south.[4] Yet even here, the emphasis on the impressive achievements of the French have sometimes resulted in British efforts being marginalised or portrayed as being dependent on French assistance. Powerful French artillery support was certainly advantageous for British XIII Corps, but victory cannot be ascribed to this alone. In fact, as this chapter will demonstrate, the British

---

1 Peter Simkins, *From the Somme to Victory: The British Army's Experience on the Western Front 1916-1918* (Barnsley: Praetorian Press, 2014), p. 31.
2 John Keegan, *The First World War* (London: Pimlico, 2002), p. 318.
3 Geoff Dyer, *The Missing of the Somme* (Edinburgh: Canongate Books, 2016), p. xiv.
4 A concise account of the action can be found in Robin Prior & Trevor Wilson, *The Somme* (London: Yale University Press, 2016), pp. 105-111. For a comprehensive study, see Jonathan Porter, *Zero Hour Z Day: XIII Corps Operations between Maricourt and Mametz* (Antrim: W & G Baird, 2017).

victory in the south was reliant on several factors, not least the impressive performance of commanders and soldiers in planning and preparation. This chapter focuses upon the efforts of XIII Corps[5] and will show how this formation, through a combination of circumstances and organisation, represented some of the best attributes of the BEF of 1916. In doing so it will cast light on one of the few success stories of 1 July 1916 and add a new perspective to the voluminous literature on how the British Army learned and adapted to modern warfare prior to and during the Battle of the Somme.[6]

In March 1916 Sir Douglas Haig noted in his diary that "I have not got an Army in France really but a collection of divisions untrained for the Field." The post-war typescript diary added "The actual fighting Army will be evolved from them."[7] These statements contained much truth. There is no doubt that prior to the Somme the British Army lacked experience in sustained, large-scale operations. British efforts on the Western Front in 1915 had been minor in comparison to those of the far larger French army.[8] Nevertheless, the proportionate cost in lives had been high, with the bulk of the casualties coming from the BEF's dwindling numbers of pre-war trained Regulars and Territorials. This created a vicious circle, for high casualties in one battle ensured inexperience in the next, in turn leading to heavy losses.[9] The battles of 1915 dashed any hope of retaining a cadre of experienced veterans and using them as a nucleus for the expanded BEF.

Yet it is wrong to assume that the British Army was entirely novice by 1916. Although the previous year had been devoid of victories, it had not been bereft of useful battlefield lessons. The BEF had learned much about mass warfare and the problems of attacking an entrenched position. Important, if occasionally hesitant, steps had been made towards improving co-operation between infantry, artillery and aircraft. Various attempts were made to codify this hard-won knowledge. Divisional schools began to emerge towards the end of 1915 and the Army produced a variety of pamphlets and memoranda outlining best practice, including translations of French tactical advice, throughout the year.[10] It is difficult to say what effect this mass of

---

5 French and German formations/units are indicated in *italics*.
6 The best summary of this process may be found in Simkins, *Somme to Victory*, pp. 12-59.
7 Quoted in Gary Sheffield, *The Chief: Douglas Haig and the British Army* (London: Aurum Press, 2012), p. 147.
8 For discussion of British and French efforts in 1915, see Spencer Jones (ed.) *Courage without Glory: The British Army on the Western Front 1915* (Solihull: Helion, 2015) and Jonathan Krause, *Early Trench Tactics in the French Army: The Second Battle of Artois, May-June 1915* (London: Routledge, 2013).
9 Spencer Jones, "'To Make War as we must and not as we should like": The British Army and the Problem of the Western Front 1915' in Jones (ed.), *Courage without Glory*, p. 54.
10 For example, see The National Archives Kew (Hereafter TNA), WO33/717, 'Object and Conditions of Combined Offensive Action, translated from the French', June 1915; TNA WO33/725, 'Tactical Notes compiled by the General Staff from both British and French Fronts', 1915; WO 95/2015, 18th Division War Diary, "Notes from a young [French] officer who himself led a company in the battles and assaults in Lorraine last

paperwork had upon overworked infantry and artillery officers, and it certainly did not represent any form of centrally approved doctrine, but it did reveal a growing understanding of trench warfare. In late 1915 and early 1916 the production of the famous series of "SS" instructional publications marked an improvement in the way the Army shared its knowledge, although it was still far from the battle-forged doctrine which was possessed by the French army on the eve of the Somme: Fourth Army's chief of staff Archibald Montgomery described the French as being "months ahead of us in practicing these principles."[11] The British approach remained in something of a half-way house between the needs of the small but elite pre-war Regulars, who could rely upon thorough training and a culture of adaptability to solve most battlefield problems, and the demands of the hastily raised mass citizen army which required a great deal more guidance in the nuances of modern warfare.[12] Prior to the Battle of the Somme there was little central guidance for the coming assault, aside from the broad advice contained in Fourth Army's "Tactical Notes" and GHQ's "Training of Divisions for Offensive Action." There is a sense that senior officers of the BEF hoped that the New Army would eventually evolve into a force comparable to the Regulars, but the process by which this was to be achieved was unclear and it was acknowledged that it would only come at the cost of severe casualties.[13]

It was against this background of slow, uncertain and often costly learning that XIII Corps was formed. It was a typical New Army corps, created in late 1915 but only receiving its component divisions in March 1916. By the time of the Battle of the Somme it consisted entirely of New Army divisions: 9th (Scottish) Division, 18th (Eastern) Division and 30th Division. 9th Division had undergone its baptism of fire at the Battle of Loos in September 1915 but the remaining two divisions had not seen any significant action.

---

    autumn, around Ypres last winter, and around Arras this spring." The most famous tactical pamphlet was Captain Laffargue, 'Impressions and Reflections of a French Company Commander Regarding the Attack', translated by HMSO and issued as 'CDS 333' in late 1915. It was subsequently published in booklet format. A good study of the latter may be found at <https://simonjoneshistorian.com/2014/03/05/infiltration-by-close-order-andre-laffargue-and-the-attack-of-9-may-1915/>

11 Quoted in Simon Robbins, *British Generalship on the Western Front 1914-1918: Defeat into Victory* (London: Routledge, 2004) p. 94.

12 Imperial War Museum (Hereafter IWM): Ivor Maxse Papers, 17/2, Maxse to Montrgomey, 31 July 1916. Maxse noted that "The Old Army" could be "hustled on and told to attack at an impossible hour" with an expectation of success but that the New Army needed careful management.

13 Ibid, Maxse to Montgomery, 31 July 1916. Maxse thought that New Army officers required "nursing" as they were "brave to a fault" and should not be asked to attempt "the impossible" as they would sacrifice themselves for no useful gain. On the expectation of heavy losses as the price for inexperience, see Tim Travers, *The Killing Ground: The British Army, the Western Front and the Emergence of Modern Warfare 1900-1918* (Barnsley: Pen & Sword, 2003) p. 145.

Much has been written on the novice status of the BEF's soldiers on the eve of the Battle of the Somme, but it is often forgotten that many of the senior officers were equally inexperienced. This command inexperience had two aspects. Firstly, planning corps scale operations required the co-operation of command and planning staff. This was still a relatively new concept in a British Army which drew most of its experience from small scale colonial warfare where individual decision making was paramount. In 1914, the BEF marched to war under the rather naïve assumption that the commander-in-chief would impose unity through force of personality.[14] The chaotic fighting of 1914 swiftly dispelled this idea and the importance of battle planning became clear during the offensives of 1915.[15] But there was little pre-war experience of this process and limited mechanisms with which to train new staff officers, and thus the rapidly expanding BEF was forced to learn in the field.[16] Secondly, the combat experience gained in 1915 was unevenly spread across the BEF. Britain's battles of 1915 were comparatively small scale and were primarily fought by Douglas Haig's First Army. Experience had tended to develop in clusters, with some formations and their officers being involved in multiple major engagements and others seeing no significant action. As discussed above, the efforts of GHQ to disseminate information were well-intentioned but haphazard, meaning that the practical knowledge gained in battle sometimes remained a trade secret possessed only by participants. When knowledge was shared it was often through informal channels.[17] This meant that comparatively few corps and divisional commanders had the opportunity to gain relevant combat experience prior to the Battle of the Somme.

XIII Corps was emblematic of this latter problem. The commander of XIII Corps, Lieutenant-General Walter Congreve VC, had seen fierce fighting as a brigadier-general in 1914 and had commanded 6th Division during the recapture of Hooge in August 1915, but he had not fought at any of the major set piece offensives of that year. The commander of 18th Division, Major-General Frederick Ivor Maxse, had been sent home in ignominy after the Battle of the Aisne in September 1914 and had not seen action since. Major-General John Shea, commanding 30th Division, had spent most of his career as a staff officer and had the least battle experience of the trio. His introduction to field command had come via a ten-month apprenticeship

---

14 Spencer Jones, *From Boer War to World War: Tactical Reform of the British Army 1902-1914* (Norman, Oklahoma: University of Oklahoma press, 2012), p. 54.
15 Patrick Watt, 'Douglas Haig and the Planning of the Battle of Neuve Chapelle' in Jones (ed.) *Courage without Glory*, pp. 183-204.
16 For more on this process, see Paul Harris, *The Men Who Planned the War: A Study of the Staff of the British Army on the Western Front, 1914-18* (London: Routledge, 2015).
17 Aimee Fox, *Learning to Fight: Military Innovation and Change in the British Army, 1914-1918* (Cambridge, University of Cambridge Press, 2017), pp. 1-18. For an example of informal learning in practice, see Michael Woods, 'Gas, Grenades and Grievances: The Attack on the Hohenzollern Redoubt by 46th (North Midland) Division, 13 October 1915' in Jones (ed.) *Courage without Glory*, p. 415.

commanding 151st Brigade in a quiet sector, and he had only taken command of his division at the end of May 1916.

The inexperienced commanders were given a heavy burden by the planning process prior to the Somme. Although Fourth Army oversaw corps planning, corps and divisional officers were given a great deal of latitude to devise their own assault schemes. In these circumstances, the importance of individual commanders should not be underestimated. Command ability was not the sole determinant of success on the Western Front – factors such as the effectiveness of the artillery preparation, the strength of German defences, and the nature of the terrain were all crucial considerations – but it was a vital ingredient necessary for victory.[18] The combination of inexperienced commanders directing novice divisions against formidable German opposition held the potential for military disaster that would, in many cases, be fully realised on the 1 July 1916. Yet, although in terms of composition and relative experience XIII Corps was typical of its New Army comrades, it achieved striking success. This accomplishment was driven by the skill of its commanders. Despite the lack of relevant operational experience, Congreve, Maxse and Shea were all men of notable military ability. Given the importance of individuals in the BEF of 1916, it is worth considering the three men in greater detail.

Congreve was 54 years old in the summer of 1916 and boasted a career which spanned 31 years. A member of a famous military family – his grandfather had been the inventor of the "Congreve rockets" of the Napoleonic Wars – Walter Congreve stood out as a true iron man in an army that prided itself on physical and mental toughness. His fit, wiry frame concealed the fact that he suffered from chronic asthma and he was prone to severe bouts of bronchitis. But he regarded the handicap as a challenge that could be overcome by sheer force of will. His capacity for pushing himself through pain was matched by his physical courage. He had won the Victoria Cross at the Battle of Colenso 1899 for his part in a doomed effort to rescue abandoned British guns, but he attached no importance to the award and despised the "celebrityship" that came with it.[19] Despite his family's wealth and status, Congreve had the mindset of a warrior ascetic. His wife remembered Walter's "great dislike of luxury of any sort. Dislike is too mild a word – he had a horror of it. A meal in a smart restaurant was a misery to him."[20]

Although famous for his physical exploits, Congreve's pre-war career revealed him to be tactically astute and a "keen student of military science", talents which resulted

---

18   Debate continues on this topic. Prior & Wilson, *Somme*, p. 304, regard artillery as the deciding factor in battle for without adequate fire support commanders "could make no difference whatever." This has been challenged by Simkins, *Somme to Victory*, p. 51, who regards the ascribing of success or failure purely to artillery as "formulaic."
19   L.H. Thornton, *The Congreves: Father and Son* (London: John Murray, 1930), p. xxii.
20   Ibid., p. xxii.

in his appointment as Commandant of the School of Musketry at Hythe in 1909.[21] An officer recalled that during this period Congreve's "dominating idea was the effective use of machine guns and the development of the power of the rifle. He was even then a strong advocate of a machine-gun unit as an integral part of the Infantry Battalion."[22] At the outbreak of war he had commanded 18th Brigade before being promoted to command 6th Division in February 1915. It was in the latter role that he directed the operation to recapture Hooge on 9 August 1915, a bitterly fought but well executed action that was described by the *Official History* as "a model of its kind."[23] Within three months of the victory at Hooge Congreve was promoted to command XIII Corps.

The first eighteen months of the war had served as a tough apprenticeship for Congreve. He confessed in his diary in December 1914 that, despite his Boer War experience, he felt "uninitiated" in trench warfare.[24] Nevertheless, principles he had developed early in his career remained true, notably his overriding belief in the value of thorough training and strict discipline. He summed up his approach in a 1917 lecture to the officer school of VII Corps:

Lieutenant-General Walter Congreve. (Author)

> Be just, yet severe; never overlook a fault, yet be human. Keep up your dignity, but at the same time enter into your men's joys and sorrows and be their friend.

---

21 Congreve's tenure here coincided with the important work of Major N.R. McMahon. On the latter, see Nicholas A. Harlow, 'The Creators of the "Mad Minute": The Careers of Brigadier-General N.R. McMahon and Major J.A. Wallingford', *Journal of the Society for Army Historical Research*, 94 (377), pp. 37-53.
22 Quoted in Thornton, *Congreves*, p. 97.
23 Edmonds, *Military Operations: France & Belgium 1915*, Vol.1, p. 106. (Hereafter *Official History*). A concise account of the retaking of Hooge can be found in Nigel Cave, *Sanctuary Wood and Hooge* (Barnsley: Leo Cooper, 2002), pp. 59-76.
24 Hampshire County Records Office, Congreve Papers, Diary, 20 December 1914.

276   At All Costs

> See to their comforts before your own, which entails knowing what they should receive in rations, clothing, etc.[25]

Congreve was a 'soldier's soldier' who had the ability to share easy conversation with his troops. An officer who served with Congreve recalled his "patience with the men" but also the fact that he "could be very hard on cowardice, slackness or lack of perseverance."[26] Another officer remembered that Congreve "retained far more of the characteristics of the first-class Regimental Officer than any other man in his rank and position I have known, and this gave him great influence over the officers and other ranks."[27] Congreve's innate toughness earned him the affectionate nickname "Old Concrete" from soldiers under his command.[28] Although he maintained a stern countenance in public, it is clear from Congreve's diary that he had genuine affection for his troops. Upon departing 6th Division he recorded: "I left my old Division very sadly ... I had a dreadful day of partings, and then when I thought all done I found the road lined by several Battalions who waved their hats and cheered as I passed. Dear dirty fellows, how I do hate leaving them ... If only I could have brought them with me."[29]

However, the magnetic draw the front line exerted over Congreve could be a negative influence. It sometimes put him in unnecessary danger. Brigadier-General F.C. Stanley took Congreve on a tour of the trenches in March 1916 and noted that "he infinitely preferred walking out in full view and quite close to the enemy than anything else. He simply asked for trouble."[30] Prior to the Battle of the Somme Congreve had taken an aeroplane tour over the front, noting in his diary "an explosion came v. close and Robeson [pilot] jinked the machine at once on a new track. He told me it was of our own how[itzers] firing directly below us and that the shell came v. close to us."[31] Congreve's disregard of danger reached its inevitable conclusion in the summer of 1917 when he was severely injured by German artillery and lost his left hand.[32] Congreve's reckless courage sat uneasily with his duties as corps commander, a position which demanded careful management rather than heroic leadership. Lord Stanhope felt that staff work at XIII Corps was undermined by Congreve's command style, noting that personal animosity between the officers of G and Q staffs resulted in the two departments existing in a state of "armed neutrality", an unwelcome situation

25   Quoted in Thornton, *Congreves*, p. 136.
26   Quoted in Ibid., p. xv.
27   Quoted in ibid., p. 97.
28   Terry Norman (ed.) *Armageddon Road: A VC's Diary 1914-1916* (London: William Kimber & Co., 1982), p. 175.
29   Quoted in Thornton, *Congreves*, p. 153.
30   F.C. Stanley, *The History of the 89th Brigade 1914-1918* (London: Daily Post, 1919) pp. 112-113.
31   Hampshire County Records Office, Congreve Papers, Diary, April 25 1916.
32   For an account of this incident, see Thornton, *Congreves*, pp. 162-164.

that went unnoticed and unaddressed due to Congreve's overriding interest in the fighting line.[33]

General Sir Henry Rawlinson also harboured some doubts about Congreve's ability as a corps commander. After a meeting on 6 April 1916, he criticised Congreve's plans for the initial assault, feeling that it was "too apt to see difficulties" especially given the "overwhelming artillery and paucity of Bosch on our front."[34] Furthermore, XIII Corps was initially composed of five divisions, a number judged too great for one man to command, prompting Rawlinson to reduce the formation by removing two divisions from Congreve's authority.[35] Congreve bristled at this slight, recording in his diary: "Sent for to see A. Commdr who told [me] that he did not consider me fit to take comd. of 5 Divs in coming operations… I had expected something of the sort from the character of Rawly and Haig both of whom consider nothing and no one of use unless from 1st Army. A severe slap in the face all the same."[36] The matter prompted Congreve to seek an audience with Sir Douglas Haig to "put my side of the story."[37] The meeting never occurred, but on 9 May a representative from GHQ reassured Congreve that he had Haig's full confidence and that there was no belief that he was "lacking in push."[38]

Nevertheless, friction between Rawlinson and Congreve lingered throughout the build up to the offensive. Rawlinson visited Congreve's headquarters on ten separate occasions between March and June 1916, considerably more than any other corps commander, and commented in his diary on 8 May "All going well VII, X and III Corps. XIII Corps and Montauban not so satisfactory."[39] It is tempting to see this as an example of the argumentative and clique-ridden

General Sir Henry Rawlinson.

---

33   Richard Holmes, *Tommy: The British Soldier on the Western Front 1914-1918* (London: Harper Perennial, 2005), pp. 232-233.
34   IWM: Henry Wilson Papers, 2/82/104, Congreve to Wilson, 20 April 1916. I am grateful to Dr. Rodney Atwood for bringing this correspondence to my attention.
35   These divisions became part of Henry Horne's XV Corps. For more on this process, see Simon Innes-Robbins's chapter elsewhere in this volume.
36   Hampshire County Records Office, Congreve Papers, Diary, 7 April 1916.
37   IWM: Wilson Papers, 2/82/104, Congreve to Wilson, 20 April 1916.
38   Hampshire County Records Office, Congreve Papers, Diary, 9 May 1916.
39   Quoted in Porter, *Z Day*, p. 480.

"hidden army" proposed by Tim Travers.[40] But a close reading of the evidence reveals a rather different picture. There is no indication in either Congreve's or Rawlinson's private papers of personal ill-feeling after the stormy meeting of 6 April 1916. Indeed, on 20 April 1916 Congreve told Henry Wilson that although the removal of the divisions had angered him, "Rawly and I are excellent friends in every way & I think he has been going out of his way to be extra so."[41] Once the battle began Rawlinson acknowledged Congreve's "splendid work."[42] Seen in this light, the friction between Rawlinson and Congreve appears to be a straightforward disagreement between two strong willed professionals. Rawlinson's decision to reduce the size of Congreve's corps was sensible, but Congreve's indignant reaction to the loss of his "best divisions" was understandable.[43] The resulting tension did not contain any real animosity and the planning of XIII Corp's operation does not appear to have been greatly hindered. Congreve offered a simple summary of the matter when he wrote "I presume Rawly wants to beat the Bosch and thinks this [reorganising XIII Corps] the best way to do it."[44]

Furthermore, the reorganisation of XIII Corps eventually proved to be a blessing in disguise, as it brought to the fore two promising divisions. The more senior of the formations was 18th (Eastern) Division, commanded by Major-General Frederick Ivor Maxse. Maxse had much to prove in 1916. Prior to the war he had built a reputation as an innovative trainer and tactician. He had commanded 1st Guards Brigade at Aldershot and was the principal author of *Infantry Training 1914*.[45] But his peacetime expertise availed him little in the chaotic fighting that marked the opening weeks of the war. Maxse was held responsible for the disaster that engulfed the British rear-guard at Etreux on 27 August 1914 when the 2nd Royal Munster Fusiliers were cut off and destroyed. This incident shook Maxse's confidence; Haig remarked on 6 September that he "seemed to have lost his fighting spirit which used to be so noticeable at Aldershot in peace time!"[46] After a poor showing at the Battle of the Aisne in September, Maxse was 'kicked upstairs' to command the newly formed 18th Division. Although this was a stinging rebuke, it gave Maxse a chance to recover from the stress of campaign, learn from his mistakes, and put his undoubted skills as a trainer of soldiers to good use. By overseeing 18th Division from its inception to its deployment

---

40　Tim Travers, 'The Hidden Army: Structural Problems in the British Officer Corps 1900-1918', *Journal of Contemporary History*, Vol.17, No.3, July 1982.
41　IWM: Wilson Papers, 2/82/104, Congreve to Wilson, 20 April 1916.
42　Liddell Hart Centre for Military Archives, (Hereafter LHCMA), Robertson Papers, 1/21/28, Rawlinson to William Robertson, 14 July 1916.
43　IWM: Wilson Papers, 2/82/104, Congreve to Wilson, 20 April 1916.
44　Ibid.
45　John Baynes, *Far from a Donkey: The Life of General Sir Ivor Maxse* (London: Brassey's 1995), pp. 40-49.
46　Quoted in Simon Batten, *Futile Exercise? The British Army's Preparations for War 1902-1914* (Solihull: Helion, 2018), p. 241.

in action, Maxse was able to put into practice two of his abiding pre-war training principles: firstly, that officers and NCOs down to the rank of lance-corporal should be fully briefed on their objectives and encouraged to show tactical initiative, and secondly that the same officers and NCOs who trained the men should also lead them into battle.[47] 18th Division arrived in France in July 1915 and joined XIII Corps in March 1916. The Battle of the Somme was to be its first major action.

The second spearhead formation was the 30th Division, commanded by Major-General John Shea of the Indian Army. Although he had seen action in the Boer War, Shea had spent most of his pre-war career as a staff officer and had served as an instructor at the Staff College at Quetta. A keen student of military history, his pre-war writing

Major-General Ivor Maxse.

marked him out as an intellectual and he was described by contemporaries as "a very smart fellow" with "plenty of brains and energy."[48] In contrast to Maxse, Shea's star was in the ascendant on the eve of the Battle of the Somme. He had begun the First World War as a staff officer at GHQ with the rank of lieutenant-colonel before experiencing a meteoric rise, ascending to major-general and command of a division by May 1916. Shea had the useful advantage of having previously worked alongside Congreve, having served as Congreve's GSO 1 at 6th Division between May and July 1915. Shea arrived at XIII Corps with a "a great reputation" and replaced the "good natured" but unimaginative Major-General William Fry.[49] 30th Division had spent less time on the Western Front than 18th Division, and Shea was new to the post, but these disadvantages were compensated by the fact that 30th Division had occupied the Maricourt sector since December 1915 and had developed valuable knowledge of the ground. It had also been blooded during a series of violent raids and counter-raids in the winter and spring of 1916.[50]

47 Quoted in M.A. Ramsay, *Command and Cohesion: The Citizen Soldier and Minor Tactics in the British Army 1870-1918* (Westport, Connecticut: Praeger, 2002), p. 102.
48 See for example LHCMA, Shea Papers, 2/5, 'The Doctrine of a Doctrine', n.d.
49 Stanley, *89th Brigade*, p. 118.
50 Ibid., pp. 103-109.

Although the divisional commanders had met with varying fortunes up to this point in the war, they shared the common advantage of possessing a good relationship with Congreve. Prior to the war, Congreve and Maxse had been part of an informal group of reformist officers who promoted the "fire and movement" tactics used by the BEF in 1914. Both men argued in favour of procuring additional machine guns for the army, and the need to reform the old fashioned eight company system employed by infantry battalions.[51] The shared outlook continued once the war began. Maxse had taken a particular interest in the recapture of Hooge and had a short report on the action circulated to his division.[52] The relationship between Congreve and Shea was especially strong and it has been suggested Congreve formally requested Shea be appointed to command 30th Division.[53] Congreve was a firm believer in the value of homogeneity within the corps and having two commanders whom he knew and could trust was a valuable advantage.[54] Congreve would revisit the importance of corps identity throughout the war. In August 1916 he argued that it was "desirable that the Corps should be more generally recognised as the real 'unit of attack'" and that corps should retain the same divisions to ensure "continuity and to avoid the repetition of methods which have been found to be erroneous."[55] The proposals were not adopted and the British Army would retain the policy of rotating divisions for the remainder of the conflict.[56]

Major-General John Shea. (Author)

Beyond their strong professional links, the three officers were all firm believers in the importance of training. This was a valuable advantage for the unevenness of

---

51 For example: Congreve's comments on Captain R.V.K. Applin, 'Machine Gun Tactics in our Own and Other Armies', *Journal of the Royal United Services Institute*, Vol. 54, No. 1, 1910, pp. 62-64; Brigadier-General F.I. Maxse, 'Battalion Organisation', *Journal of the Royal United Services Institute*, Vol.56, No.1, 1912, pp. 53-85.
52 IWM: Maxse Papers, 15/1, 'Notes on the Recent fighting at Hooge'.
53 Porter, *Z Day*, p. 482.
54 Robbins, *British Generalship*, p. 20.
55 Ibid., p. 20.
56 The Australian and Canadian Corps, as proto-national armies, were exempt from this policy and developed a notable *esprit de corps* as a result.

training was one of the greatest barriers to BEF effectiveness prior to 1917. Lack of facilities and a shortage of experienced NCOs and junior officers undermined training in the United Kingdom; once divisions had arrived in France opportunities for exercises behind the lines were limited by the need to carry out endless fatigue duties. One veteran wrote after the war that until 1917 it was "customary to regard trench warfare and training as incompatible."[57] A soldier of 18th Division recalled that in June 1916 "each night during this tour we had every available man at work. There was so much to do that Battalion H.Q. had to send nearly every man out to carry up food and ammunition for the Brigade dumps."[58] The demand for labour was insatiable and seriously diminished training time. A frustrated Maxse complained to Montgomery: "If next year the infantry could be spared such manual labour and taught instead its job of fighting we should do better and have fewer casualties."[59]

Given these limitations, it is notable that XIII Corps was still able to find time to carry out several sophisticated exercises. Congreve briefed his divisional commanders in May and made it clear that "Success now depends almost entirely on training in the back areas."[60] It has been calculated that 18th and 30th Division spent more time in training – 17 full days - than any other division involved in the assault on 1 July.[61] In comparison, other British divisions spent between five and nine days in training.[62] Furthermore, the training of XIII Corps was particularly intensive. The corps was allocated a training area at Picquigny, six miles to the west of Amiens, an area chosen for its strong resemblance to the terrain over which the attack would take place on 1 July.[63] Upon this ground "a complete system of trenches, reproduced exactly from air photographs, was constructed representing the whole of the objectives to be attacked by each brigade."[64] Brigadier-General F.C. Stanley recalled that 30th Division dug "from six to seven thousand yards of trenches, of course not to full depth but enough to show what it looked like."[65] The 18th Division created its own replica trenches; an officer recalled that all trenches "were named by notice boards and we were all bidden to learn these names without delay."[66] To add to the realism, Congreve visited the "camouflage school" and later acquired a number of models that could be added to the trenches to provide realism, including "dead men and dead horses."[67] To supplement

---

57 John Ewing, *History of the 9th (Scottish) Division* (London: John Murray, 1921), pp. 175-176.
58 T.M. Banks & R.A. Chell, *With the 10th Essex in France* (London: Gay & Hancock, 1924), p. 110.
59 IWM: Maxse Papers, 17/2, Maxse to Montgomery, 31 July 1916.
60 IWM: Maxse Papers, 17/2, Divisional Commander's Conference, 26 May 1916.
61 Porter, *Z-Day*, p. 178.
62 Ibid., p. 483.
63 TNA WO 95/895/7, 'XIII Corps Operations on the Somme', Section (Λ), 'Training'.
64 Ibid.
65 Stanley, *89th Brigade*, p. 119.
66 Banks & Chell, *10th Essex*, p. 175.
67 Hampshire County Records Office, Congreve Papers, Diary, 22 April 1916.

the life size trenches, a series of "miniatures" were constructed and kept up-to-date using aerial reconnaissance. These were used to brief officers and NCOs and test their knowledge with tactical problems. Ultimately it was intended that NCOs would reach such a level of expertise that each would "be ready at any moment to take command of his platoon."[68]

The relative lack of experience in 18th and 30th Divisions in large scale action was apparent as they began training. Congreve watched his men carry out a practice attack in April and recorded in his diary "a very poor thing it was."[69] Yet from this inauspicious start the formations improved rapidly. XIII Corps's training began with slow, carefully orchestrated timetabled attacks that "resembled a parade" but gradually increased in complexity. Maxse identified that 18th Division exercises would "Start as a set piece, but Bosch will certainly upset things. Therefore, make officers handy and capable of tackling the unexpected."[70] Stanley recalled that the "training was infinitely harder work than being in the line. There was no rest all day and far into the night for a good many of us…We practiced all day and every day. First battalions singly, and then two or more battalions together."[71] An officer of the 10th Essex remembered "Our training was never once monotonous. Some mornings aeroplanes worked with us and the elements of contact work in battle were demonstrated to us."[72] Maxse placed great value upon these exercises, warning his officers that "assaults require constant practice." He added:

> Now is the time to make every platoon handy and dashing. What do the men feel like in a good platoon which is carefully trained for short, sharp, definite local assault [?] – they must feel certain that all their comrades in the platoon will come on with them and not leave them in the lurch. How are they to be got to feel that? – by the example and confidence inspired by the character and training of their platoon commander. How can that be attained? By constant practice …[73]

Maxse also warned that poor training would produce battalions "useless for fighting" and "likely to be carried off as prisoners to Germany and there to wait, half-starved and thoroughly bullied, until the war is over. What will they then say to their womenfolk at home?"[74]

The effort put into XIII Corps's training was impressive. Maxse later told Montgomery that "No Corps Commander or Corps Staff could possibly have done more for my Division to give it TIME to train, during the four months preceding

68   IWM: Maxse Papers, 17/2, Divisional Commander's Conference, 26 May 1916.
69   Hampshire County Records Office, Congreve Papers, Diary, 24 April 1916.
70   Ibid.
71   Stanley, *89th Brigade*, p. 119.
72   Banks & Chell, *10th Essex*, p. 176.
73   IWM: Maxse Papers, 17/2, 'Notes on Attacks from Trenches with Limited Objectives'.
74   Ibid.

1st July."[75] Full scale brigade exercises were conducted over the replica trenches: the brigades of 18th Division "got an average of ten days on the models" and those of 30th Division received an average of six days.[76] The remaining training time was spent in battalion, company and platoon exercises. The time and effort devoted to training would prove its worth on 1 July. An after-action report from the 7th Bedfordshire Regiment noted: "The chief reasons of the success of the operation are in my opinion as follows…The training of the Battalion at Picquigny. The time and attention to every detail that was carried out there was repaid a thousand-fold."[77]

Time spent in training allowed Maxse and Shea to experiment with an unorthodox attack formation. Traditionally, an attacking British division would put two brigades into the attack and keep its third as reserve which could reinforce or consolidate as required. Both 18th and 30th Division rejected this method as unsuitable for the position which they faced. There were two elements to the decision. Firstly, advancing on a two-brigade frontage would require that each battalion extend its line to such an extent that the attack risked being weak at all points. Secondly, battlefield experience in 1915 had shown that feeding reserve brigades into the battle was fraught with difficulty and often ended in disaster. To solve these problems, Maxse and Shea proposed attacking with *all three* brigades abreast. The assault waves themselves would be subdivided, with reserves following close behind the attackers for, as Maxse observed, "Unless a reserve is actually on the spot it cannot intervene in time to be of use."[78] Rather than relying upon sheer weight in the assault, the attackers were to seek weak points. Brigade orders stated "if a company is held up unexpectedly by uncut wire and hostile machine guns, it should consolidate what it has gained and pass its reserve platoons round to the flanks. Other adjoining companies to press forward without a pause until they reach their objective."[79] This approach to battle bears similarities to the tactics of the much vaunted *stosstruppen* employed by the Central Powers in the latter half of the war. Behind the attackers came specialist teams which included "clearers" who would deal with defenders who had survived the initial assault, and "mopper uppers" who would eliminate dugouts and strongpoints.[80]

The infantry plan was innovative but risky. Lack of dedicated reserves meant that it would be difficult to reinforce success or to consolidate in the event of repulse. However, given the circumstances of the assault, the policy made sense. The 18th and 30th divisions were not expected to go beyond their initial objectives, which made the

---

75   IWM: Maxse Papers, 17/2, Maxse to Montgomery, 31 July 1916.
76   TNA WO 95/895/7, XIII Corps War Diary, 'XIII Corps Operations on the Somme'.
77   TNA WO 96/2043, 7th Bedfordshire Regiment War Diary, [Report on attack on] Carnoy Trenches 1st July 1916.
78   IWM: Maxse Papers, 17/2, 'Additional Notes', 5 August 1916.
79   TNA WO 95/2934, 53rd Infantry Brigade, War Diary, June 1916, Operation Order 38.
80   IWM: Maxse Papers, 17/3, 'Notes on Consolidation of Captured Positions', 3 September 1916.

decision to put maximum emphasis on the opening push logical. Once the ground was taken, there would be a pause in operations before the next attack commenced.

This was a sharp contrast to the last major engagement of the BEF, the Battle of Loos, where attacking forces had been given open-ended "into the blue" targets.[81] It was, however, in keeping with Congreve's own views on trench warfare. During the fighting for Hooge he had observed the difficulty of consolidating a newly won position: his infantry had suffered severe casualties from German artillery fire and Congreve recorded in his diary that had the enemy followed up with a determined infantry attack "we sh[oul]d have had a very hard day."[82] The experience informed his thinking prior to the Battle of the Somme. As already noted, Rawlinson regarded Congreve's initial assault plan as overly cautious and urged him to take greater risks. The original plan does not appear to have survived and thus it is difficult to gauge how far the final scheme differed from that proposed in April 1916. What is clear is that XIII Corps's plan remained wedded to the concept of limited objectives. Issued on 23 June 1916, it stated:

> The Corps Commander wishes to impress on all commanders that the success of the operations as a whole largely depends on the consolidation of the definite objectives which have been allotted to each division. Beyond these objectives no serious advance is to made until preparations have been completed for entering on the next phase of operations.[83]

An enduring legend from the Battle of the Somme claims that, after XIII Corps captured its first day objectives, Congreve telephoned Rawlinson to request that cavalry be sent forward to exploit the crumbling German defences. This claim appears to have originated in Martin Middlebrook's seminal *The First Day of the Somme* and has proved sufficiently intriguing to resurface in several other works.[84] However, the story is almost certainly a myth. There is no contemporary evidence that such a telephone call ever took place and, as discussed above, available archival material shows that Congreve had planned a careful, controlled advance. XIII Corps held 9th Division in reserve on 1 July with the expectation that it would reinforce and relieve the assault units during the night. There were no plans to use it to exploit a breakthrough or to continue the advance. Given the thoroughness of the pre-battle planning, it seems improbable that Congreve would suddenly cast aside his caution and ask for cavalry reinforcements in the midst of battle.

---

81 Nick Lloyd, *Loos 1915* (Stroud: Tempus, 2005), p. 78.
82 Hampshire County Records Office, Congreve Papers, Diary Aug 8, 1915.
83 TNA WO 95/895, XIII Corps War Diary, Operational Order No.14, 23 June 1916.
84 Martin Middlebrook, *The First Day of the Somme* (London: Classic Penguin, 2001), pp. 212-213. Middlebrook gives no source for the claim. Most recently the story has appeared, without any reference to its source, in Robert Kershaw, *24 Hrs at the Somme: 1 July 1916* (London: W.H. Allen, 2017), pp. 281-282.

There were good reasons for Congreve's step-by-step approach. Fourth Army's plan emphasised the importance of the attack around Thiepval in the north and it was here that the main British effort was to be made. There was no expectation that a breakthrough would occur in the south and resources were distributed accordingly. XIII Corps also had to cooperate with French forces on its right, a challenging task that required a clear understanding of respective objectives. A British advance that rushed beyond agreed targets and got too far ahead of the French risked being struck in the flank by a German counter-attack. If the British were repulsed, then this would expose French forces to defeat in detail.

General Maurice Balfourier (centre).

The development of good working relations with the French proved challenging; differences of language, culture and training resulted in a certain degree of mutual mistrust and meant that coordination between British and French forces was haphazard in the first half of the war.[85] Cooperation between XIII Corps and the neighbouring *XX Corps* could not be taken for granted, yet good relations were essential for success. As Brigadier-General Robert Lecky noted "It was decided that from our point of view the operations contemplated were feasible with a great deal of give and take and the utmost good will between us and the French but that GHQ staff must settle the matter."[86] To this end a variety of official channels were created to foster communication between the two corps. A direct line was laid linking Congreve to *XX Corps* headquarters and day-to-day duties were left in the hands of the liaison officers: a British liaison officer, Captain J.V. Williams of the 18th Manchesters, was posted to *XX Corps* and a French liaison officer, Lieutenant Tassart, stationed at XIII Corps.[87] Congreve was essential to the success of liaison. Although not fluent in the language, he could speak a little French and had the experience of working alongside French forces during the fighting at Hooge. He visited his French opposite, General Maurice Balfourier, on six separate occasions between April and June 1916. Relations

---

85 Elizabeth Greenhalgh, *The French Army and the First World War* (Cambridge: Cambridge University Press, 2014) p. 55.
86 Quoted in Porter, *Z Day*, p. 104.
87 TNA WO 95/895, XIII Corps War Diary, June 1916, 'Liaison with French XX Corps'.

between the two men were cordial and Congreve told Henry Wilson "The French XX Corps on our right are fine fellows & old Balfourier & I are great friends."[88] Efforts to secure friendly relations could result in awkward moments. On one occasion, Congreve was a guest of honour at a French army sports day but found himself in an "embarrassing" position "at [the] head of a line of French soldiers standing to the national anthem" and was forced to endure two full verses before he was able to move aside![89] At a lower level, 30th Division was given the responsibility of liaising with French *39th Division*, and in turn the rightmost British unit, 89th Brigade, was to liaise with its neighbouring French brigade. Fraternisation was encouraged leading to "much unofficial friendly liaison" between officers and "many guest nights."[90] British officers discovered that the mess of *I Colonial Corps* provided "an excellent dinner and a capital host."[91]

Practical military problems remained. Disputes over road allocation – a common complaint since the very beginning of the war – continued.[92] There were also difficulties in accommodating the British and French artillery parks which soon filled the countryside. Major Fraser Tyler recalled on 19 June "there are no less than 424 French guns and howitzers packed into the little salient and as we have increased our guns in nearly the same proportion, you can imagine the congestion of batteries in the valley."[93] Two French artillery groups, each named after their commanding officer, were attached to XIII Corps. *Group de Comte* consisted of twelve 75mm field guns and added its weight to the divisional British artillery. Of greater significance was *Group de Menthon* which was armed with sixteen venerable 220mm mortars. These cumbersome siege guns were decades old at the outbreak of the war yet could deliver truly devastating plunging fire. Congreve had seen what a handful of such guns could do during the action at Hooge. On the Somme they were deployed in far greater numbers and provided a valuable addition to the weight of the bombardment.

In addition to *Group de Menthon*, XIII Corps was able to deploy three Heavy Artillery Groups (HAGs) armed with guns and howitzers of no less than seven different calibres ranging from giant 12-inch howitzers to obsolete 4.7-inch guns of Boer War vintage.[94] The combined heavy artillery was tasked with the material destruction of the German position. Their fire was intended to shatter trenches, machine gun nests and fortified villages. British plans placed less emphasis on counter-battery fire than

88   IWM: Wilson Papers, 2/83/55, Congreve to Wilson, 1 July 1916. I am grateful to Dr. Rodney Atwood for bringing this letter to my attention.
89   Hampshire County Records Office, Congreve Papers, 6 May 1916
90   George Herbert Nichols, *The 18th Division in the Great War* (London: Blackwood & Sons, 1922), p. 33.
91   Hampshire County Records Office, Congreve Papers, Diary, 4 May 1916.
92   Ibid., 7 May 1916.
93   Quoted in Porter, *Z Day*, p. 110.
94   TNA WO 95/895, XIII Corps War Diary, June 1916, XIII Corps Plan of Operations: Artillery.

A "monstrous heap of rubble": Montauban after capture.

the French, listing it as the fifth of five priority targets,[95] but the 60-pounders of 29th HAG and the 12-inch howitzers of 31st HAG proved effective in the role. As early as May it was reported that the heavy guns had "carried out several successful shoots against hostile batteries" and the counter-battery duel would grow in intensity as the 1 July approached.[96] The *Official History* later quoted German sources which remarked that on the day of the attack "A great number of [German] guns were smashed up … When the British attacked there were only ten field and thirteen heavy batteries in readiness, and these had numerous unserviceable guns."[97]

The artillery preparation benefitted from the nature of the German position at Montauban. In contrast to the north, where the subsurface chalk allowed the construction of sturdy dugouts and trenches, the ground in the south was predominantly soil and clay. It was difficult to construct defences in the soft earth and there was a constant demand for fresh timber to shore up trenches and dug outs. The reliance on timber made the dugouts far more vulnerable than those built into the chalk of the north. Reverberation from heavy shells could knock timber supports loose, causing

---

95   Heavy artillery was given five key targets, of which counter-battery fire was listed last. See Porter, *Z-Day*, pp. 114-115. Prior & Wilson, *Somme*, p. 107, state that XIII Corps had given "counter-battery operations the highest priority of any British corps during the preliminary bombardment" but do not provide a source for this information.
96   TNA WO 95/895, XIII Corps War Diary, May 1916, Weekly Report W/E 18 May 1916. See also Weekly Report W/E, 8 June 1916.
97   Edmonds, *Official History 1916*, Vol.1, p. 344.

the dug out to collapse and entomb the defenders.[98] As a result the defences here were noticeably weaker than elsewhere on the front: when German *109th Reserve Infantry Regiment* arrived to garrison the line on 18 June they were alarmed by the weakness of the position relative to the one they had previously constructed at La Boisselle.[99] Adding to German woes was the fact that, unusually for the Somme position, British occupation of the high ground at Maricourt Ridge provided Allied artillery observers with a good view of the enemy defences.

The combination of weight of Allied artillery, the vulnerability of the front line and the superior observation available to the attackers meant that the German position was pulverized prior to the 1 July. The front-line trenches were reduced to "sand dunes, enormous mounds and holes of earth, absolutely untenable" and "with very few exceptions the wire was beautifully cut."[100] Behind the line, the fortified village of Montauban "was all wreck and ruin, a monstrous heap of rubble stinking of death, brick-dust and high-explosive" and many of its defenders were buried alive in their own dugouts.[101] Those who survived the preparatory barrage endured further punishment on the day of the offensive as both 18th and 30th Division advanced under the cover of an early type of creeping barrage fired by their divisional artillery.[102] The destruction wrought by the artillery was in evidence the following day. When Congreve went forward to inspect the position on 2 July he recorded "I was surprised how completely the line was demolished and how little remained of trenches. A good many dead Germans were lying about & the usual debris of a battle… Their trenches were not so good as I expected nor were the dug outs particularly in evidence, in the back lines anyway. The front ones too much destroyed to tell."[103]

Yet even with this devastating preparatory bombardment the surviving defenders fought hard on 1 July. It is testament to the professionalism and tenacity of the German army that it was capable of such stout resistance. Surviving machine guns were able to inflict severe losses on the attackers. Congreve noted "After zero hour the Bosch still held out in pockets of trenches & did a great deal of damage there from rifle and machine gun fire. The way these pockets held out was very fine [.] One in the craters in the front line tho' surrounded from 1st held out for several hours."[104] Some attacking battalions were caught in the open by machine gun crossfire and

98 I owe this information to a discussion with the late Colin Hardy.
99 Porter, *Z-Day*, p. 55.
100 Stanley, *89th Brigade*, p. 130; TNA WO 96/2043, 7th Bedfordshire Regiment War Diary, [Report on attack on] Carnoy Trenches, 1 July 1916.
101 Quoted in William Philpott, *Bloody Victory: The Sacrifice on the Somme* (London: Abacus, 2014), p. 181. See also Prior & Wilson, *Somme*, p. 111.
102 TNA WO 95/895, XIII Corps War Diary, June 1916, XIII Corps Plan of Operations: Artillery. Interestingly, Brigadier-General E.C. Anstey claimed that only 18th Division used a true creeping barrage and that 30th Division used a system of timed lifts. See Royal Artillery Archive, Anstey Papers, 'History of the Royal Artillery 1914-18', p. 117.
103 Hampshire County Records Office, Congreve Papers, Diary, 2 July 1916.
104 Hampshire County Records Office, Congreve Papers, Diary, 1 July 1916.

Eyewitness artist's depiction of the attack on Montauban. (*Illustrated London News*, 22 July 1916)

became pinned down.[105] Others that made progress could only do so at a high cost: the 18th King's Liverpool Regiment, fighting towards Montauban, had suffered more than 50 percent casualties by the end of the day.[106] It was in the chaos of battle that the value of training was revealed. Officer casualties and the resulting confusion had lain at the heart of many battlefield disasters in 1915, but XIII Corps continued to press forward regardless of loss. For example, an officer of the 7th Bedfordshire recorded: "I may quote that only three officers in the entire Battalion got beyond Emden Trench, most of the platoon and very many section leaders had gone, yet so thorough was the training beforehand that the men carried on entirely by themselves, knew where to go and to do when they got there."[107] Pre-battle training that emphasised turning the flanks of strong points and leaving their destruction to the "mopper uppers" proved its worth. Maxse noted with satisfaction "The 18th Division's mopping-up parties effectually put an end to any obstinate Bosches who had been passed over during the advance. I was pleased to discover that none of the forward men, to my knowledge, had been shot in the back" whilst a report from the 7th Bedfordshire Regiment praised "The good work done by the clearing up parties. The work done by the Northampton Regt was splendid and we had no shooting

---

105 Philpott, *Bloody Victory*, p. 180.
106 Graham Maddocks, *Liverpool Pals: A History of the 17th, 18th, 19th and 20th (Service) Battalions* (Barnsley: Pen & Sword, 2015), pp. 90-91.
107 TNA WO 96/2043, 7th Bedfordshire Regiment War Diary, [Report on attack on] Carnoy Trenches 1 July 1916.

from behind."¹⁰⁸ Instead, it was German defenders who found themselves under fire from unexpected directions. *Oberst* Leibrock, commanding *6th Bavarian Reserve Infantry Regiment* from a reinforced dugout, recalled that by mid-morning:

> [It was] reported that the British were indeed behind the dugout. I went out myself to take a look. Hardly had I put my head up when I received a burst of small arms fire from the rear. I could not be absolutely certain about the situation, but it was at least clear that it was not our men standing around firing from the Second Trench, but rather the British digging in.¹⁰⁹

Leibrock and his command post were surrounded and, with no possibility of a counter-attack to relieve them, were forced to surrender.¹¹⁰ By the early afternoon XIII Corps had taken the majority of its objectives and were consolidating their position. To the north, Germans were observed "fleeing backwards in hopeless confusion."¹¹¹ Fierce fighting continued on 18th Division's front, especially around the Pommiers Redoubt, until around 6pm. By 7pm XIII Corps "had secured the whole of its objective."¹¹² With no intention of any further advance all efforts were turned towards consolidation of the hard-won ground. The position was in a strong state of defence by the early hours of the morning. The Germans discovered this to their cost: a series of poorly coordinated counter-attacks launched by *12th Reserve Division* ended in "complete fiasco" as the attackers advanced over open ground into remorseless British fire.¹¹³ A veteran of the Manchester Regiment described how "long lines of grey figures in greatcoats and helmets" were spotted in the pre-dawn light:

> There was no need to issue fire orders. As the Germans topped the ridge our men opened rapid fire with deadly precision, many climbing out on to the parapet to get a better field of fire. The Lewis guns served splendidly. It had been said 'You can take the village, but can you hold it?' 'We can do it', said the men and they did.¹¹⁴

---

108 Quoted in Porter, *Z Day*, p. 483; TNA WO 96/2043, 7th Bedfordshire Regiment War Diary, [Report on attack on] Carnoy Trenches 1 July 1916.
109 Quoted in Philpott, *Bloody Victory*, p. 182.
110 Ibid., p. 182.
111 Quoted in Ibid., p. 183.
112 TNA WO 95/895, XIII Corps War Diary, July 1916, 'The Attack and Capture of the Enemy's First Line System of 1st July'.
113 Jack Sheldon, *Fighting the Somme: German Challenges, Dilemmas & Solutions* (Barnsley: Pen & Sword, 2017), p. 70.
114 Anon., *Sixteenth, Seventeenth, Eighteenth, Nineteenth Battalions: The Manchester Regiment – A Record 1914-18* (Manchester: Sherratt & Hughes, 1923), p. 26.

The repulse of the German counter-attacks capped an impressive victory on an otherwise black day. 18th Division's history aptly described the first day of the battle as "a triumph first of preparation and construction and then of grit and determination."[115] Maxse later reflected on the battle and attributed success to a variety of factors including "practice over exact models of the hostile trenches" which not only contributed to an effective attack but also allowed rapid consolidation.[116] The comparative weakness of the German defences, the French artillery support and superior observation available to attackers were key advantages, but even with these assets victory was by no means assured. The use of three infantry brigades abreast was also cited as a key factor with Maxse noting that it "greatly facilitated the close and intimate co-operation" of infantry and artillery.[117] The latter point was especially important. The assault on XIII Corps' front was an all-arms attack which contained many elements that would be recognised as war-winning by 1918. Thorough training, careful preparation, close co-operation between infantry and artillery and individual initiative from sections, platoons and companies were all vital ingredients to success. In many ways this was a refinement of the informal 'art of attack' which had been devised by the BEF by the end of 1915. It has been suggested that 30th Division "seemed to adopt no particularly innovative tactics" and that success was almost entirely due to artillery.[118] Whilst it is true that, other than the unorthodox assault formations, there was no startling innovation in the attack, this explanation neglects the extent to which existing methods had been refined and solidified via thorough training and effective commanders.

XIII Corps' assault demonstrated what the New Army could achieve when the objectives demanded matched the means available. In the victory one can perceive the beginnings of the British Army that would come of age in the summer of 1918. It would take another two years of bitter fighting before this process was complete.

115 Nichols, *18th Division*, p. 35.
116 IWM: Maxse Papers, 17/2, Maxse to Montgomery, 31 July 1916.
117 Ibid., 'Additional Notes', 5 August 1916.
118 Prior & Wilson, *Somme*, p. 115.

11

French XX Corps and Preparations for the Somme Offensive

Tim Gale

The first two years of the First World War were brutally hard for the French army. It had begun the conflict in a state of doctrinal chaos and still largely armed with nineteenth century equipment, particularly in respect of its heavy-artillery.[1] Although it halted the tide of German invasion in 1914, this came at a terrible cost and left the invaders occupying a large swathe of French soil. Attempts to evict the enemy from the occupied territories during 1915 proved fruitless. Despite some encouraging tactical successes throughout that year – for example at Artois[2] on 9 May – the French offensives failed at the cost of nearly 350,000 dead, with over a million men wounded or missing.[3] The French commander-in-chief, General Joseph Joffre, his senior officers, and the French nation itself could not afford another year of costly setbacks and were determined to improve the army's offensive performance in 1916.

As discussed elsewhere in this volume, the Allies planned a great Anglo-French attack on the Somme, originally envisaged as involving up to 40 French divisions, but the German assault on Verdun in February 1916 considerably reduced French commitment to the Somme campaign. Despite the reduction in the size of its contributory component, the thorough planning for the offensive by the French army was impressive. This chapter examines the doctrinal and organisational framework that a French corps worked within and how this influenced its planning and execution of offensive action in the initial stages of the Battle of the Somme. The focus of this chapter is *XX Corps*, commanded by General Maurice Balfourier, part of General

---

1 For the state of the French army up to 1914, see Douglas Porch, *The March to the Marne: The French Army 1871-1914* (Cambridge: CUP, 1981) & on doctrine see Dimitry Queloz, *De la Manoeuvre Napoléonienne à l'Offensive à Outrance* (Paris: Economica, 2009).
2 Jonathan Krause, *Early Trench Tactics in the French Army: The Second Battle of Artois, May-June 1915* (Farnham: Ashgate, 2013), pp. 88-90.
3 See Jonathan Krause, 'The Evolution of French Tactics 1914-16' in Matthias Strohn (ed.), *The Battle of the Somme* (Oxford: Osprey, 2016), p. 201.

Émile Fayolle's *6e Armée*. *XX Corps* was chosen for study specifically because it was on the right flank of British XIII Corps and thus makes an interesting comparison with British best practice. It should be noted that *XX Corps* was somewhat atypical; it had been in the thick of the fighting since the war began and had established a reputation as an elite formation known as the *Iron Corps*. However, this could equally be said about the other corps from *6e Armée* involved on 1 July such as *I Colonial Corps*, another hard-fighting unit made up of professional soldiers that were originally tasked with defending the French colonies. Nevertheless, *XX Corps* was operating under the same body of doctrine and standard procedures that other French corps were and thus its preparation and planning can be considered as indicative of French army practice in this period. This chapter therefore offers a point of comparison for British and Empire corps performance during the intense fighting of 1916.

Doctrinal Framework

The Battle of the Somme would be *XX Corps'* first engagement under the new French doctrine. The new doctrine was informed by the experiences in Artois and Champagne during 1915 and was issued in two instructions: *Instruction sur le combat offensif des petites unités* 8 January 1916 and *Instruction sur le combat offensive des grandes unités* 26 January 1916, the former being for units from section (four sections being in each company) to brigade level (essentially the infantry) and the latter being for divisions and above.[4] In addition, there were detailed instructions issued by General Ferdinand Foch, commander of the Northern Army Group (*Groupe d'Armées du Nord* - GAN) of which *6e Armée* was part. Foch's instructions primarily used established doctrine but drew attention to specific issues that he wanted to emphasise and this document would shape how *XX Corps* would undertake its preparation for its battle on the north side of the Somme river.[5]

The approach of *XX Corps* to planning was dictated by the *Instruction sur le combat offensif des grande unités*. The main aim of the *Instruction* was to clarify and determine the roles of the army commander and his subordinates, the corps and divisional commanders, in the preparation and development of an offensive action against fortified positions.[6]

The *Instruction* makes clear that the corps was the centrepiece unit of an offensive, largely because at this point in the war it was still the smallest all-arms formation; "the corps is the unit of attack, within which the divisions undertake combat, following

---

4 GQG, 3 Bureau, *Instruction sur le combat offensif des petites unites* (Paris: Imprimerie Nationale, 8 January 1916). GQG, 3 Bureau, *Instruction sur le combat offensive des grandesunités* (Paris: Imprimerie Nationale, 26 January 1916).
5 GAN, *L'Instruction du Général Commandant du GAN sur le bataille offensive*, 20 April 1916, 18N148.
6 *Instruction sur le combat offensif des grande unités*, p. 3.

the overall plan of the Corps Commander, combining the actions of the different arms."[7] As with the *Instruction* for the smaller units, this *Instruction* made clear that the infantry in an offensive was reliant on the artillery for success; "*it* [infantry] *cannot act offensively except with the help of the artillery* ..."[8]

The *Instruction* also emphasised preparation of the offensive, this being of "fundamental importance" and in two stages.[9] The first stage was the work required prior to the assault troops arriving in the sector, and comprised general reconnaissance, the establishment of an engagement plan, the general organisation of the ground and of the rear area, as well as the emplacement of the heavy artillery batteries.[10] Once the troops undertaking the offensive had entered the sector, plans and work could be finalised, although at this point it had to be expected that the enemy was now alert to the possibility of an offensive.

While the army-commander oversaw devising the plan for the offensive, the corps commander was tasked with executing this plan in his sector. The corps commander was expected to arrive with his staff well before the bulk of his troops in order to have as much time as possible to study the situation and devise his plan. This plan would identify the objectives to be taken by the front-line divisions, how to deploy the divisions in the second line, the distribution of the non-divisional elements within the corps and, perhaps most importantly, the artillery plan, the last being made in close conjunction with the corps artillery commander.[11] The divisional commanders would then create a divisional engagement plan that followed the instructions of the corps commander. At some point during the final stages of the preparation for the offensive, a definitive Attack Order (*Ordre d'attaque*) would be issued by the corps and divisional commanders to their subordinates.[12]

The role of the corps commander was further delineated in a detailed list of what was expected of his engagement plan. It was to consist of an overall attack plan, with details of the missions of both the first and second line divisions, the fixing of immediate and potential objectives, the positioning of the corps artillery, the distribution of corps assets to the divisions, along with special instructions for the use of gas and mines. The corps commander was also expected to make carefully considered plans for both the resupply of his corps and for efficient casualty evacuation.[13]

In addition to the published *GQG* doctrine, *XX Corps* had also received detailed instructions from Foch in *L'instruction du général commandant du GAN sur le bataille*

---

7 *Instruction sur le combat offensif des grande unités,* p. 1. The division would, as a matter of course, be transformed into the smallest all-arms formation, but this would not transpire until mid-1916.
8 Ibid, pp. 1-2. Emphasis in the original.
9 Ibid., p. 2.
10 Ibid.
11 Ibid, p. 3.
12 Ibid. See the translation of 20 Corp' attack plan in Appendix 3.
13 Ibid, pp. 22-23.

offensive.[14] This document built on the ideas contained in the January GQG doctrine but added information that GAN had collected from its meticulous analysis of the 1915 offensives and extensive artillery testing, as well as initiating a new air to ground (and vice versa) signalling system. It illustrates Foch's developing ideas about "the scientific battle"; Foch emphasised that an offensive needed to be seen (and planned) as a series of actions, each being over an area of ground where the enemy defences, generally only one of the enemy's lines (i.e. first position or second position), had been destroyed by the artillery.[15] As with the primary doctrine, Foch declared that the artillery was the key to offensive success and determined what could be done by the infantry; "the depth of the ground battered by the artillery is the definitive fix of the space that can be assigned to capture by the infantry."[16]

Foch emphasised that the artillery preparation required a methodical approach; "a regulated fire with very great precision, observation throughout its execution and the quantity of shells known to be required to guarantee success."[17] The required number of shells for specific targets is given in one of the appendices.[18] This appendix gives the number of shells required to destroy a lengthy list of various trench defences. For example, a field-artillery (75mm) battery would need to fire 600 shells at a range of 2500 metres to make a 20-25 metre breach in a barbed wire network.[19] In respect of the trench artillery, similar calculations had been made at GAN; at a range of 400 metres, the 58mm trench-mortar would need to fire 200 16kg shells to make a breach of roughly 40 metres in a barbed-wire network.[20]

Fayolle issued a note to his commanders on 8 June that largely reiterated the existing doctrine and the instructions of Foch.[21] He emphasised that operations now required "an organised combat that is conducted from objective to objective, always with an artillery preparation" and thus the primary role for the commander was to determine these objectives.[22] While conceding that some officers were concerned that this approach emphasising the artillery's role would dampen the infantry's *elan*, Fayolle

---

14 For the development of Foch's military thought and its effect on planning for the Somme, see William Philpott, *Bloody Victory: The Sacrifice on the Somme and the Making of the Twentieth Century* (London: Little, Brown, 2009), pp. 129-30 and Elizabeth Greenhalgh, *Foch in Command: The Forging of a First World War General* (Cambridge: CUP, 2011), pp. 140-65.
15 *L'Instruction du Général Commandant du GAN sur le bataille offensive*, p. 1.
16 Ibid.
17 Ibid., p. 23.
18 *Annexe 2 Renseignements sur les tirsd'artillerie (Résultats obténus dans les cours de tir du GAN)*, pp. 1-8.
19 Ibid., p. 2.
20 Ibid., p. 3. In addition to barrage and counter-battery fire guidance, there are also instructions for the engagement of *chevaux de frise*, trench works and gun emplacements. See pp. 4-8.
21 6e Armée, 3 Bureau, 6494/3, *Note Relative à la préparation et l'éxecution des attaques*, 8 June 1916, 19N1089
22 Ibid., p. 1

pointed out that the infantry's morale was more likely to be seriously damaged if they were struck by flanking machine-gun fire or if they ran into undamaged barbed-wire networks.[23] The fact that he had to state this suggests that many officers retained belief in pre-war notions of morale and the 1913 regulations. Fayolle summarised the new approach thus; "it is better to act surely rather than quickly. Speed will be obtained by not losing any moment in the organisation and the preparation of each partial attack."[24]

Infantry

The infantry of *XX Corps* followed the doctrine contained within *Instruction sur le combat offensif des petites unités*, issued by GQG in January. The *Instruction* is quite clear that the artillery defined what could be achieved on the battlefield; "The infantry does not have, in itself, sufficient offensive power against positions defended by fire and garnished with defensive accessories [i.e. barbed-wire, bunkers, etc...]."[25] Therefore "one should never launch an [infantry] attack without an artillery action both preceding and accompanying the action. One must not fight with men against material."[26] Thus, whilst acknowledging that only the infantry were able to occupy and retain captured ground, the *Instruction*'s primary message to the infantry commanders (to whom it was mainly directed) was; "the artillery destroys, the infantry occupies."[27]

Parts of the *Instruction* retained ideas that were becoming rapidly outmoded such as "the combat formation is a line of riflemen. The normal interval between the riflemen is two paces. Exceptionally, and for advancing over battered spaces, the interval can be augmented."[28] However, doctrine was beginning to change to reflect ideas that the infantry had already began to implement themselves. So although the infantry was still expected to advance in lines of riflemen, the *Instruction* also now talks of movement by infiltration, the advance taking place "step by step", from cover to cover.[29] The spacing of the infantry as they advanced was increased by the *Instruction* but this had to be increased again in a *Note Annexe provisoire du 27 Septembre 1916* (the two first waves now having 30 metre gaps, with subsequent waves being less dense).[30]

It also recognised that in combat the organisation of smaller units was liable to be disrupted and that officers should realise that they may find themselves in charge of

---

23 Ibid.
24 Ibid., p. 2.
25 *Instruction sur le combat offensif des petites unités*, p. 3.
26 Ibid.
27 Ibid., p. 4.
28 Ibid., p. 12.
29 Ibid., p. 13.
30 6e Corps d'armée, 3 Bureau, 8.570/3, *Rapport sur les enseignements à tirer des Opérations de la Bataille de la Somme*, 12 December 1916, p. 1, 19N1089.

extemporised formations; "the incidents of the struggle and the exigencies of the terrain [often] create temporary *groupements* of combat …."[31] In other words, infantry commanders were expected to be flexible in combat, something that had not been encouraged in earlier doctrine. Battalions would normally deploy in square-formation (two companies forward with two supporting directly behind them), although if circumstances required it there might be three companies in the front line with only one in support. There was no manoeuvre expected of the infantry company, it would advance directly to its front in most circumstances. Each company would advance in two waves, with the battalion normally advancing in four successive waves. The overall density of infantry on the front had been considered carefully and was half that of the Battle of Artois; 1600 men per kilometre of front as opposed to 3500, which significantly lowered the casualty rate on the Somme compared with previous years.[32]

General Émile Fayolle.

In terms of organisation, the standard French division in 1914 was overwhelmingly manned by riflemen, with two infantry brigades, each comprising two regiments of three battalions (12 battalions of infantry), a *groupe* of field-artillery with thirty six 75mm guns, some engineers and a squadron of cavalry, in all around 16,000 men, of whom 85 percent were infantry with 10 percent being in the artillery arm. As one post-war writer characterised it; "Lots of men, little material."[33] Although in 1916 the brigade was being phased out as a unit of command, to be replaced by one senior officer commanding the division's infantry, the *infanterie divisionnaire*, this was in the early stages of implementation and *XX Corps*' divisions still had their infantry regiments organised into brigades.[34] The brigade commander was expected to formulate plans with his infantry commanders and the divisional artillery in the period

---

31 Ibid., p. 11.
32 Michel Goya, *La Chair et l'Acier: L'invention de la guerre moderne (1914-1918)* (Paris: Tallandier, 2004), p. 265.
33 Lieutenant-Colonel Laure and Commandant Jacottet, *Les Étaples de Guerre d'une Division d'Infanterie* (Paris: Berger-Levrault, 1928), p. 140.
34 Indeed, many divisions would not move to the *infanterie divisionnaire* system until mid-1918. For example, *XX Corps' 153rd Division*.

leading up to combat. In combat, the brigade commander was expected to handle the brigade's infantry without recourse to the divisional commander, other than in exceptional conditions, although he was expected to keep the latter informed in detail at all times about the condition and the positions of the brigade infantry.[35]

The battles of 1914-15 had revealed that French infantry lacked firepower. To remedy this, it received three new weapons in early 1916 that would significantly increase its combat power. The Viven-Besières rifle-grenade came into operation, along with the light-machine gun, officially the *Fusil Mitrailleur Modèle 1915* (FM-15) and a 37mm infantry gun. The V-B rifle-grenade had an effective range of 180 metres and two were issued to each rifle-squad. The FM-15 was a light machine gun with a crew of three and an effective range of only 600-700 metres, after which it became very inaccurate. It was not an easy gun to use, particularly in trench conditions, and its major faults were still being ironed out in July 1916. But, fabricated from stamped-steel parts, it was simple to manufacture and thus the army could introduce it in large numbers relatively quickly. The 37mm gun was designed primarily to give the infantry a means of engaging enemy machine guns nests and had an effective range of 1500 metres.[36] However, the January doctrine from GQG was issued prior to the introduction of these new infantry weapons and had no provisions for their usage. The use of these weapons on the Somme was thus largely doctrinally un-codified and training was difficult to arrange for units in constant movement and action.

The *11th Division's* experience is an illustration of the difficulties encountered with bringing these weapons onto line. The entire division only had two operational FM-15s when it left Verdun on 10 April rather than the regulation eight *per company*.[37] By 22 May, only *37th RI (regiment d'infanterie)* had its full complement of FM-15s and the last regiment to be supplied, *79th RI*, was only at full strength by 19 June, after it had arrived in the attack sector.[38] A 37mm gun peloton, of one gun and its crew, was organised in each infantry regiment but the guns only arrived on 20 June, minus much of their essential kit including binoculars. This left no time for training and the 37mm guns of *11th Division* did not get into combat until mid-July.[39] Whilst grenade training had been "satisfactory", the rifle-grenades only arrived on 25 June and the troops had, for the most part, to learn how to use them during combat.[40]

Only the rifle-grenade was an instant success, despite the lack of training. The other weapons proved problematic; the FM-15 was very fragile and badly affected by rain and mud, while the 37mm gun was a little too heavy for easy manoeuvring.

---

35 *Instruction sur le combat offensif des petites unités*, p. 24.
36 See Anon., 'Évolution de l'armement de l'infanterie pendant la Guerre', *La Revue d'infanterie,* August and October 1920, pp. 348-361 & 567-577.
37 Ibid., p. 358.
38 11th Division d'Infanterie, Etat-Major, *Historique des opérations de la 11o Division d'Infanterie du 1erJuillet au 21 Août 1916*, 29 August 1916, p. 1.
39 Ibid.
40 11th Division, *Historique des opérations*, p. 2.

In addition, indirect fire from the 37mm gun was difficult due to a lack of observers, whilst the smoke issued by it when firing made direct-fire hazardous.[41] These problems would be addressed as the Battle of the Somme continued, but on 1 July they were a major impediment.

Artillery

At the start of the war the French army found itself seriously deficient in modern artillery and this deficiency had not been made up by 1916. The French artillery in 1914 was comprised largely of the *Mle1897* 75mm field-gun, the "glorious 75." This was an excellent field-gun on its introduction in 1897 but was prone to manufacturing faults that were exacerbated by the stress of wartime production, and were exposed as the guns were fired more intensively than they had been designed for. In relation to heavy-artillery equipment, nearly all of France's heavy and medium artillery was obsolete by 1914, not having been replaced because discussions within the army and government over various large-calibre guns had become so politicised that it had been impossible to resolve either the technical or bureaucratic arguments.[42] Although various heavy-artillery projects were underway by the time of the Battle of the Somme, in the first half of 1916 the French army was still largely reliant on outmoded equipment such as the *155mm de Bange* model from the 1880s. Most of the heavy artillery used up to 1 July was from the nineteenth century, although many models had been updated to some extent prior to or during the war.[43] New modern guns were coming into service, such as the rapid-fire *155L Schneider*, but these would not play a part until later stages of the battle.[44]

The trench-artillery units (*Artillerie de Tranchée* – AT) were the only part of the artillery entirely equipped with modern weapons, which consisted of the *58mm Mortier de 58 No 2* and the *240T* (*Mortier de 240 Mle 1915*) trench-mortars, both introduced in 1915. The 58mm could fire a 16 kilogram shell with a range of 600 metres while the *240T* fired an 87 kilogram shell nearly one kilometre.[45] While the 58mm was, after some modifications, successful, the *240T* had to be replaced by an updated model towards the end of 1916 due to a lack of precision and range. Like the *240T*, most of the heavy artillery was serviceable but in the process of being replaced by newer models. Another problem was that there were a bewildering number of different guns

---

41 XX Corps, 3 Bureau, SC no. 3254, *Compte-rendu des opérations du XX Corps d'Armée sur la Somme- Appendix Infanterie*, 6 September 1916, 19N1089.
42 See Porch, *The March to the Marne*, Chapter 12.
43 See Colonel Aublet, 'L'Artillerie Francaise de 1914 à 1918,' *Revue Militaire Francaise*, July 1929, pp. 234-252, 238-40.
44 Étude sur l'Artillerie dans la preparation de l'attaque du 1 Juillet, p. 29.
45 Ed., Colonel de la Porte du Theil, *Organisation des Matériels d'Artillerie – Volume VII – Artillerie de Tranchée* (École d'Application d'Artillerie, 1935), p. 19, 27.

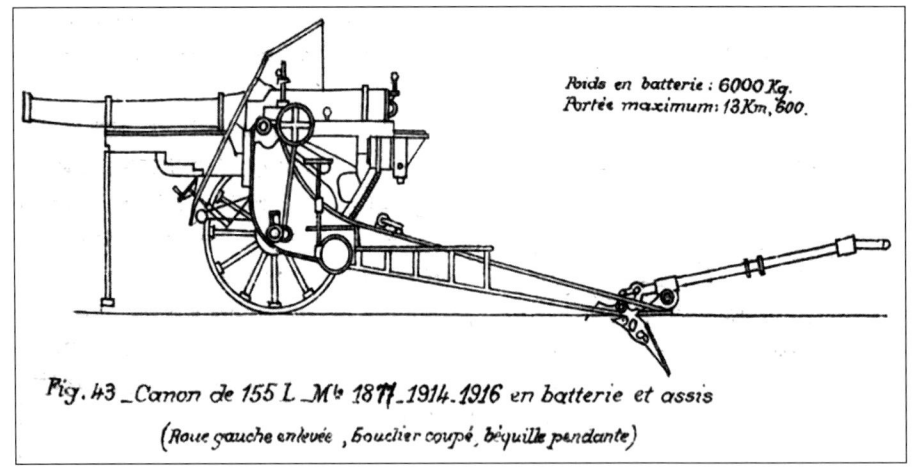

Mle 1877-1916 155L Gun unlimbered. Captain Leroy, *Cours de l'artillerie – Historique et Organisation de l'Artillerie* (École Militaire de l'Artillerie, 1922)

in use. There were no less than ten different 155mm gun models in service in the first half of 1916.[46]

In addition, the French were still investigating the optimal organisation of artillery within the corps and divisions. Although field artillery practice was well thought out, there was a necessity to issue new doctrine for the heavy artillery after the experiences of 1915; the *Instruction sur l'emploi de l'artillerie lourde*, which contained the lessons believed to be derived from the 1915 offensives.[47] One of the main changes introduced by this *Instruction* was to give the corps greater control over the heavy artillery than hitherto and an Army commander was expected to devolve his heavy artillery as much as was prudent.[48]

Air Component

Foch was insistent on the importance of air power in the modern battle and devoted an appendix to this subject in his instructions; "the essential role of aviation in the battle is to act as an observer for the Commander and for the artillery and to prevent

---

46 Lt. Colonel Rimailho, *Artillerie de Campagne* (Paris: Gauthier-Villars, 1924), p. 119.
47 GQG, 1 & 3 Bureaux, 11239, *Instruction sur l'emploi de l'artillerie lourde* (Paris: Imprimerie Nationale, 20 November 1915 plus errata issued on 13 February 1916). The trench artillery primary doctrine was; Ministère de la Guerre, Artillerie, *Réglement de manoeuvre de l'artillerie de tranchée*, 18 March 1916.
48 *Instruction sur l'emploi de l'artillerie lourde*, p. 19

at the same time the enemy's observation."[49] It also stated that mastery of the air was a "necessity."[50] As elsewhere, the air appendix emphasised that there must be only one commander of air assets in the "zone of attack."[51]

The air component of a corps had different tasks as the preparation for the offensive unfolded. Initially, the main role of the aircraft of *XX Corps* was identifying as many of the enemy positions as possible, as well as keeping the French commanders informed about the preparatory work going on in the German lines.[52] A new section had been formed within the army & corps artillery staffs, the *Service des renseignements concernant les objectifs de l'artillerie – SRA*, to centralise intelligence interpretation for the artillery, which was used during this period to monitor the enemy positions.[53] On the front of *XX Corps*, to avoid alerting the enemy unduly, only a single balloon was ever in the air at one time during the reconnaissance phase of the offensive's preparation, which gave the aircraft an essential role.[54] Three observations balloons were employed, as a commencement of the preparatory bombardment approached, two spotting for the divisional artillery and one for the heavy artillery.

During the artillery preparation, the intelligence missions for the artillery continued and aircraft were used to direct heavy artillery and counter-battery fire. Four wireless-equipped (TSF) aircraft were used across *XX Corps'* front to direct the artillery, the maximum that could operate simultaneously within that area.[55]

Once the attack commenced, *XX Corps* had two aircraft, one attached to each division, which were tasked with liaising between the infantry and both the corps staff and the artillery. Two other aircraft kept watch on the areas beyond the French front line in order to direct counter-battery fire and fire on any counter-attacks that appeared. Two of the balloons were attached to the divisions, with the third reserved for the artillery.[56]

Planning the offensive – XX Corps

Fayolle sent his first instructions to Balfourier on 15 May, along with a large dossier of maps and passes for the French officers to enter the British zone.[57] Fayolle gave

---

49 GAN, *Le bataille offensive – Annexe 3 – L'Aeronautique dans la Bataille*, p. 1.
50 Ibid., p. 2.
51 Ibid.
52 20 Corps, 2 Bureau, CCN 165, *Plan d'emploi des unités Aeronautique du CA,* 19 June 1918. 22N1364.
53 GQG, 1 & 3 Bureaux, 11239, *Instruction sur l'emploi de l'artillerie lourde* (Paris: Imprimerie Nationale), 20 November 1915 and errata issued 13 February 1916, p. 27.
54 *Plan d'emploi des unites Aeronautique du CA.*
55 Ibid.
56 Ibid.
57 6e Armée, 3 Bureau, no 6205/3-GO, *Le Général Fayolle, commandant la 6 Armée, à Monsieur le Général Commandant le XX Corps d'Armée,* 15 May 1916, 22N1365.

302   At All Costs

Balfourier the information needed for the corps' commander to be able to orient himself to the commander's intent and the work that needed to be done within the corps. Fayolle's *Instruction* contained material on: the manoeuvre plans of the army commander, the overall planning to be undertaken by each corps, the additional artillery being made available to the corps, the projected emplacements for the heavy artillery, the organisation of the corps' zones (placement of the rear divisions, camps, roads, railways, water supply, all depots, hospitals), as well as details on such matters as air support and the required telephone network.[58]

XX Corps was codenamed 'Corps A' in the planning. It would be the army's most northern corps with one division and one brigade in the first line, the final brigade being stationed on the right bank of the Somme as the corps reserve. A further two divisions stood on the left bank of the Somme, acting as army reserve. The mission of *XX Corps* was two-fold; to cover against the intervention of enemy artillery situated north of the Somme on the attacks executed south of the river in the region of Herbécourt and Flaucourt and to advance in close liaison with the British army as per Joffre's instruction of 2 May 1916 (included within the dossier).[59] Balfourier was instructed to send his staff immediately to the front to make the necessary reconnaissance and other preparations.

Fayolle sent further instructions to Balfourier on 3 June, detailing how the operation should unfold and how *XX Corps'* advance would run parallel with that of British Fourth Army.[60] Fayolle also notified Balfourier of the artillery that would be available to him and added an important additional note that the artillery of *XX Corps* would be free to fire south of the Somme in support of 1 CAC, whose artillery would in turn be available to support *XX Corps*.[61] Fayolle kept a close eye on his subordinate units; from 28 June, a liaison officer (a captain) from *6e Armée's* 3rd Bureau was permanently stationed in each of the army's corps, tasked with ensuring the army command received timely information from its subordinate units.[62]

Balfourier constructed his engagement plan according to the instructions of Fayolle and the January doctrine.[63] His initial engagement plan of 8 June covered the following required issues:

a)   The overall plan of attack (divisions of the first line and second line), the mission of each division and their attack sectors.

---

58   6e Armée, 3 Bureau, no. 6187/3-GO, *Instruction Personnelle et secrete no. 1120 pour le Général Commtle 20 CA,* 14 May 1916, 22N1365.
59   6e Armée, 3 Bureau, no. 6187/3-GO.
60   6e Armée, 3 Bureau, no. 6848/3 GO, *Projet d'action d'ensemble,* 3 June 1916 [Fayolle], 22N2420.
61   6e Armée, 3 Bureau, no. 6848/3 GO, p. 4.
62   6e Armée, 3 Bureau, 6743/S, *Instruction No. 1194, relative au fonctionnement du service de l'Etat-Major,* 26 June 1916. 22N1364.
63   See list in *Instruction sur le combat offensive des grandes unités,* pp. 22-23.

b) Fixing of objectives (both immediate and those that might unfold during the battle).
c) Determining positions of corps artillery.
d) Distribution of resources (mainly artillery) between divisions.
e) Employment of the corps' elements not attached to component divisions.
f) Possible employment of special means; gas clouds, special shells of all categories, mine warfare.
g) Supply and casualty evacuation plans.[64]

Supply was carefully organised. As well as three CVAD sections,[65] carrying 120,000 bread rations and 30,000 rations of oats, there were sector depots on the first line with two days of water rations and one day of food rations, as well as a depot at Cerisy-Gailly, which could supply two infantry divisions for a day and hold larger items such as oats, hay and coal. This meant that there were enough supplies in *XX Corps*' sector to supply 50,000 men and 15,000 horses for 3 days, even if resupply from the rear was somehow interrupted.[66]

Organisation of XX Corps' sector

The preparation of the ground in the corps sector prior to the attack troops' arrival was extensive. When the infantrymen of the *26th RI*, part of *21st Brigade, 11th Division*, arrived in their sector in early June they were very impressed at the amount of preparation of the rear positions that had already been made.[67] The work on preparing the rear-area for the offensive had in fact started long before they arrived; for example, planning for the road network had started in March 1916 and work on it a month later.[68] Twelve new large railway stations had been built to carry the men and munitions to the front.[69] At the end of April, six officers and 700 men began work which would ensure the water supply for *6e Armée* was guaranteed for the offensive.[70] Although *XX Corps* had to be supplied by one main road-route, Froissy – Bray – Suzanne (transferred from the British army), the *DSA* managed to move large number of vehicles along this road; moving, for example, over 8572 vehicles on the Bray – Cappy road in

---

64 XX Corps d'armée, 3 Bureau, SC 1768, *Projet d'Engagement du XX Corps d'Armée*, 8 June 1916, 22N1354.
65 CVAD – Supply Convoy.
66 XX Corps d'armée, 3 Bureau, SC 1768, *Projet d'Engagement*.
67 Anon., *Historique du 26e Régiment d'Infanterie – campagne 1914-1918* (Paris: Berger-Levrault, undated, circa 1920), p. 72.
68 *Les Armées françaises dans la Grande Guerre* (Paris: 1933) [AFGG], Tome XI, p. 375.
69 Ibid, 345.
70 Ibid., p. 427.

one day.[71] Despite assistance from neighbouring divisions and corps, not to mention assistance from the army, most of the work had to be undertaken by troops from the corps. The corps' infantry had to construct the heavy battery emplacements, as well as building temporary depots, strengthening the front line trenches and rebuilding the communication trenches. To the east of Suzanne, the communication trenches were built by the divisional infantry, to the west, the corps' troops were used for this task (the corps' *génie* and 142 RIT).[72]

Before the infantry arrived in the attack sector it had to be prepared for the artillery. This involved creating new rail access as well as the improvement of existing roads and paths in *XX Corps*' sector. As this was a significant amount of work with large numbers of workmen involved, this had to occur before the divisions arrived to avoid paralysing the transport network. In addition, the heavy-artillery required a narrow-gauge railway for supplies which had to extend all the way to the batteries.[73]

In respect of *XX Corps*' divisions, these were alerted in May to their coming role in the offensive. For example, on 18 May, General Eugene Vuillemot, commander of *11th Division*, received secret instructions from Balfourier regarding future operations and was notified that his division was going to replace British 30th Division on the Somme – Maricourt sector.[74] Three days later, Vuillemot and his subordinate commanders (brigade, regimental and artillery) began reconnaissance of their new sector but this was restricted by their distance from it, the number of days available and that fact that the commander of British 30th Division limited the number of French officers who were allowed in his sector due to fears over security. Unlike the well organised French rear-area, the officers of *XX Corps* did not think much of the state of the British positions they were taking over, grudgingly describing them as "good enough" for defence but quite inadequate to launch an offensive from.[75] The main communication trench to the rear area was only covered in part and did not extend all the way to the front line, there were no depots set up for the storage of material and the main transport road left by British 30th Division for the French *11th Division* and *39th Division* was in a "very bad state."[76]

The French were left with a great deal of work to prepare their new sector as they not only had to install new infrastructure for the offensive, such as telephone

---

71   Ibid, pp. 376, 378.
72   XX Corps, 3 Bureau, SC no. 3254, *Compte-rendu des opérations du XX Corps d'Armée sur la Somme*, 6 September 1916. 19N1089. The communication trenches to the rear of the front line past Suzanne were in the event hardly used due to the weak German artillery response, with only a few shells a day falling in this area and thus exposing troops to little danger when they were moving to the front.
73   XX Corps, artillerie, No. 7, *Rapport concernant les operations auxquelles a pris part l'Artillerie du XX Corps d'Armée entre le 1 Juillet et le 21 Août 1916*, 27 August 1916, p. 2.
74   11th Division d'Infanterie, Etat-Major, *Historique des opérations de la 11o Division d'Infanterie du 1er Juillet au 21 Août 1916*, 29 August 1916, p. 2. 22N1364.
75   Ibid.
76   Ibid.

networks, but also build new shelters as the British had left "insufficient" numbers of them.[77] By 5 June, *11th Division* had taken over the entire sector and work commenced preparing the ground. However, this work was to prove difficult due to lack of materials and men.[78] When Vuillemot was originally informed of the operation on the Somme, he had assumed he would have several months to prepare his sector but in the event he only had 15 days.[79] After drafting in troops from *72nd Division*, the work was completed on time and *11th Division's* front was ready for the offensive.[80] By 1 July, each of the brigades had built a large and fully equipped communications trench from the front line back to Suzanne.[81] During June, *XX Corps* received an enormous amount of equipment for the offensive, including 650 acetylene lamps, 1200 axes, 13,000 spades, 18,000 logs and nearly 500,000 sandbags.[82]

Great efforts were made to ensure that communication within the corps was as efficient as possible during the attack, within the limited and rather crude means available at the time. Pigeons were still a major means of communication, each corps having a unit with between 100 and 200 messenger-pigeons, these units being commanded by officers from the staff of 2 Bureau.[83] There would also be phone-lines, wireless-telegraphy (TSF), optical signalling and runners available, all of which were the subject of detailed liaison plans drawn up by the corps and its divisions.[84]

Artillery Preparation

Balfourier received instructions in May from the commander of *6e Armée's* artillery, Général de Brigade Lucien Lizé, that the corps artillery plan would conform to a uniform model determined by *6e Armée*, the instructions including an example of such a plan.[85] This was passed to Colonel Alexandre, commander of *XX Corps* artillery, who agreed his artillery plan with Balfourier in early June and issued his fire-plan on 17 June 1916.[86] The corps artillery was divided into three *groupements*; Groupement

---

77 Ibid., p. 3.
78 Ibid., p. 4.
79 Ibid. This point is underlined in Vuillemot's report.
80 Ibid., p. 5.
81 Ibid.
82 XX Corps, Commandant du Génie, 1592/A5, *Materiel Recu en Juin et Juillet 1916*, 13 December 1916, 22N1365.
83 6e Armée, 2 Bureau, no 3511/2, *Instruction pratique sur la liaison par pigeons-voyageurs à l'intérieur des corps d'armée*, 25 May 1916. 22N1364.
84 XX Corps, 39th Division d'Infanterie, 978/PC, *Note sur les Liaisons*, 11 June 1916, 22N1364.
85 6e Armée, Artillerie, Etat-Major, *Le Général Lizé Commandant l'Artillerie de la Sixth Armée à M. le Général Commandant le XX Corps d'Armée*, 14 May 1916, 22N1365. Lizé (b. 25 February 1864) was killed in 1918. *Leonore*.
86 XX Corps, Artillery, *Concentrations – Note*, 17 June 1916, 22N1364.

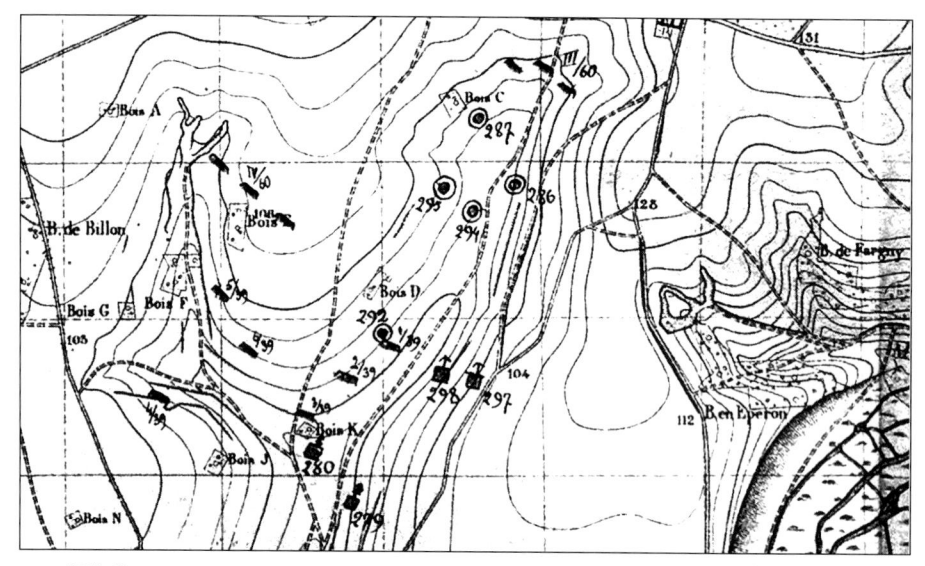

XX Corps: *Groupement Anglade* heavy artillery emplacements, June 1916. (22N1364)

Anglade (named after the colonel commanding *XX Corps* heavy artillery), *Groupement Walch* (named after *11th Division's* artillery commander) and *Groupement Vouillemin* (named after *39th Division's* artillery commander).

Groupement Anglade was tasked with counter-battery and long-range fire and was armed with a variety of heavy pieces. It was divided into four *sous-groupements*, each being equipped in accordance with its mission; for example *Sous-Groupement 2*, with one *groupe* of *120L* and one of *155L* based in the Maricourt ravine, was tasked with counter-battery fire.[87] The two other *groupements*, also sub-divided for specific missions, would conduct what the French army termed "destruction-fire" on their respective divisional fronts.[88] These divisional *groupements* had a wide variety of guns to control; for example *Groupement Walch* (*11th Division*) had eighteen batteries of field guns, twelve batteries of heavy artillery and six batteries of trench-mortars to control. The artillery *groupement* commanders were expected to closely liaise with their divisional commanders and to keep them current with both the fire-plan and its implementation.[89] As required by the regulations, Colonel Alexandre kept Balfourier

---

87 They were used for counter-battery fire because both guns had a range of five kilometres, unlike the other heavy artillery pieces with ranges of three kilometres, *Instruction sur l'emploi de l'artillerie lourde*, p. 6.
88 Destruction fire comprised artillery attacks on trenches, defensive positions, barbed-wire etc. For a complete list of the artillery in divisional *groupements*, see Appendix II.
89 11th DI, Artillerie, 28, *Le Colonel Walch Cdt le 8eRégimentd'artillerie à M. le GénéralCdt la 11 DI*, 20 June 1916, 22N1364.

appraised on a daily basis as to the development of the artillery plan and its implementation.[90] The corps artillery plan was carefully coordinated with British XIII Corps and *I Colonial Corps*.[91]

6e Armée received 26 batteries of 58mm trench mortars and seven batteries of *240T* trench mortars on 7 June adding to its organic complement of six batteries of 58mm and four batteries of *240Ts*. These were all devolved to the army's divisional batteries, meaning that on the army's front of 12 kilometres there was one 58mm battery per 300 metres and one *240T* battery per 1090 metres.[92] Although most of the batteries were below full strength, these formations represented an impressive 320 58mm and forty *240T* trench mortars, double the number per metre that had been deployed in the Champagne offensive of September 1915.[93] In relation to *XX Corps*, *39th Division* received four 58mm batteries and one *240T* battery, with *11th Division* receiving six 58mm batteries and two *240T* batteries.[94]

Resupplying the trench artillery, being so close to the front line, was a lengthy and hazardous undertaking; General Nourisson of *39th Division* reported that the overnight resupply of a trench battery required between 150 and 200 men operating in "perilous conditions."[95] This difficulty meant that *6e Armée* had been stockpiling trench-mortar shells for the offensive since 1 May.[96] In the event, fewer trench artillery shells were fired than had been expected, which illustrates how carefully the fire had been regulated during the preparation.[97] Nonetheless, the trench artillery of *6e Armée* hurled a prodigious amount of shells at the German positions on the Somme, firing nearly 3000 tonnes of shells during the preparation, which represents 200 kilograms of shells per metre of enemy trench attacked.[98] The 58mm batteries fired an average of 410 shells per day, with the highest daily consumption per battery being on 27 June (751 shells) and lowest on 24 June (128 shells), with the 240T batteries firing an average of 90 shells per day.[99]

---

90 See, for example, XX Corps, Artillerie, 807, *Le Colonel Alexandre Commandant p. i. l'Artillerie du XX Corps à M. le Général Commandant le XX Corps d'Armée - Compte-Rendu*, 24 June 1916, 22N1364.
91 Ibid.
92 6e Armée, 3 Bureau, Étude sur l'artilleriedans la préparation de l'attaque du 1 Juillet 1916 à la *Sixth Armée et pendant la bataille de la Somme*, 29 March 1917, p. 2, 19N1089.
93 Ibid, pp. 2-3.
94 Ibid., p. 4. This was rather fewer than received by *I Colonial Corps*, which had thirty 58mm batteries and eight *240T* batteries. Note that the number of 58mm batteries given to *39th Division* had been increased from the number envisaged in XX Corps' engagement plan of 8 June.
95 General Pierre Nourisson, 39 DI, *Observations faites sur les opérations dans la période du 1 Juillet au 20 Août sur la Somme*, 28 August 1916, 19N1089.
96 6e Armée, *Ètude sur l'Artillerie*, p. 8.
97 Ibid., p. 6.
98 Ibid., p. 7.
99 Ibid, pp. 7-8.

The large-scale concentration of trench artillery was matched by the heavy artillery; *6e Armée* received 228 howitzers & mortars (largely the *M.220*), 300 heavy guns (with calibres from 95mm to 155mm) and 56 large-mortars (with calibres from 270mm to 370mm).[100] This gave *6e Armée* one piece of heavy artillery per 28 metres of front, which was nearly double the density of heavy artillery on the Champagne front in September 1915 (one piece per 50 metres of front), and consisted of a greater proportion of howitzers than deployed in 1915 (43 percent as opposed to 39 percent in Champagne).[101]

There had been questions asked prior to the Somme operation as to whether the *M.220s* would be as effective as the *155Cs*, the bulk of which were left on the Verdun front due to the difficulty of moving them, but experience on the Somme demonstrated that the former were just as efficient as the latter in destruction fire.[102] In fact, in terms of attacks against solidly-built fortified positions, the *M.220s* "played a superior role to that of the *155C*."[103] However, the *M.220* was extremely cumbersome to move, a process taking days, which made its use after the initial artillery preparation significantly more difficult than the *155Cs* and thus limited its use over the course of operations after 1 July.

There was a prodigious amount of field artillery deployed by *XX Corps*, largely comprising the 75mm guns of the infantry divisions, of which *XX Corps* had 39 batteries (156 guns), giving a density on the corps' front of one battery per 144 metres.[104] The 75mm guns fired on average 392 shells per day during the six days of the preparation.[105] There were, however, still problems with the manufacture of the guns and this rate of fire tested the quality of the barrels. Five times as many guns self-destructed as were destroyed by the Germans over the first four months of the Somme campaign.[106] However, despite the problems a considerable amount of shells were fired from the 75s; during the preparation they fired a total of 1,151,372 shells, which weighed-in at an impressive 6,119,542 kilograms.[107]

Once the attack began, the field artillery had planned a detailed programme of support for the infantry. The *11th Division's* field artillery was divided into three *groupements* of six batteries, each covering the zone of an infantry regiment and given specific targets and times to fire, although the field-guns were told to ignore time limits if they could actually see the infantry's progress.[108]

---

100 Ibid., p. 18.
101 Ibid., p. 7.
102 Ibid, pp. 19-20.
103 Ibid., p. 20.
104 6e Armée, *Ètude sur l'Artillerie*, p. 56. The field-artillery also comprised of a number of 105mm pieces.
105 6e Armée, *Ètude sur l'Artillerie*, p. 59.
106 Ibid., p. 60.
107 Ibid.
108 11th DI, Etat-major, *Complement au plan d'action de la 11 DI - Action de l'artillerie de 75 en liaison avec d'Infanterie pendant d'attaque*, 26 June 1916, p. 4, 22N1364.

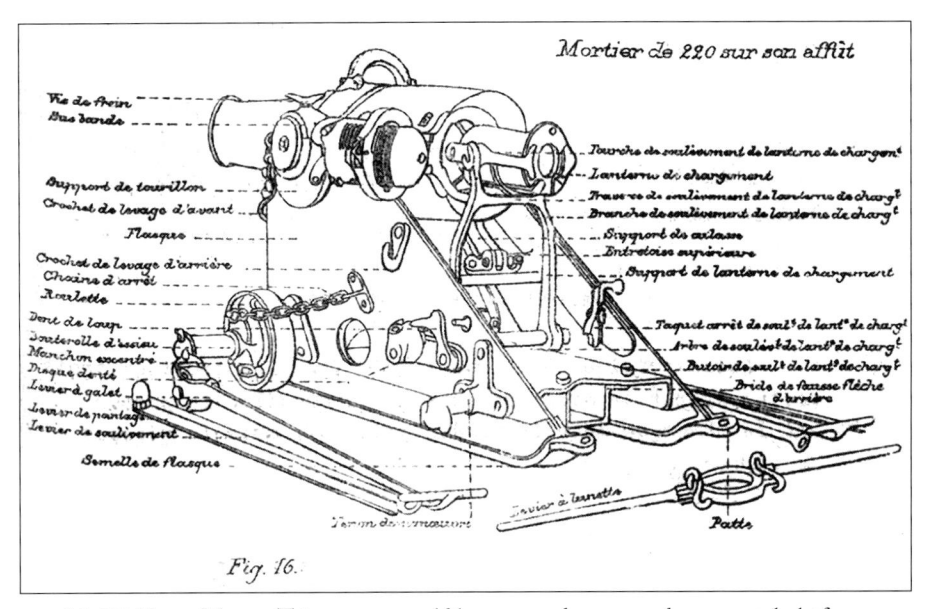

M. 220 Heavy Mortar. This weapon could be mounted on a wooden or metal platform. (Captain Leroy, *Cours de l'artillerie – Historique et Organisation de l'Artillerie* (École Militaire de l'Artillerie, 1922)

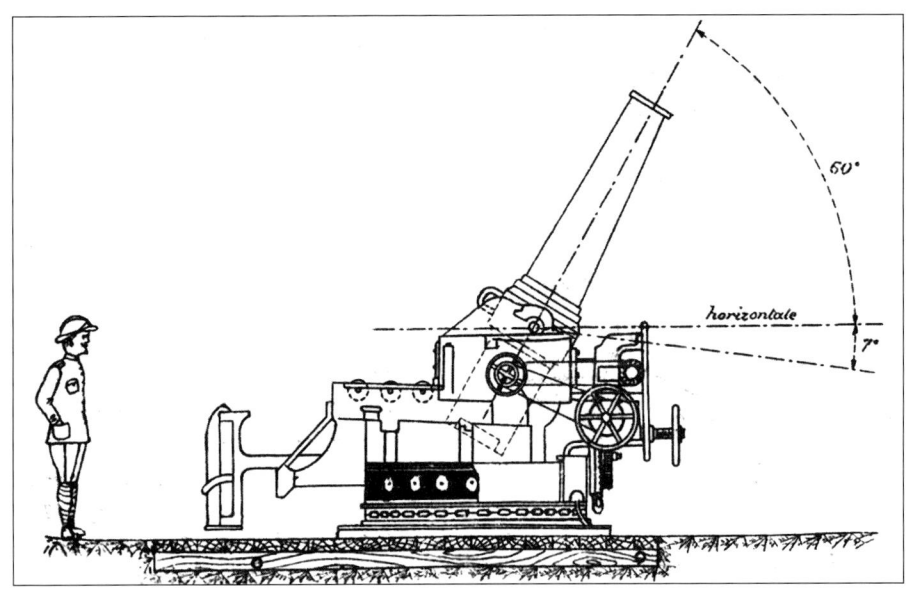

C–270 de Côte coastal heavy mortar. (Captain Leroy, *Cours de l'artillerie – Historique et Organisation de l'Artillerie* (École Militaire de l'Artillerie, 1922)

Although not under the control of *XX Corps*, mention must be made of the super-heavy artillery, the *Artillerie Lourde à Grande Puissance* (High Power Heavy Artillery – ALGP) and the *Artillerie Lourde sur Voie Ferrée* (Railway Heavy Artillery – ALVF), as their use was almost completely unprecedented. There had been some super-heavy guns (190mm, 240mm and some colossal 305mm rail guns originally designed for use on battleships) on GAN's front since the spring of 1916 but, to maintain surprise, none had been fired during this period.[109] The ALGP guns were therefore something of an unknown quality at this stage of the war, although a battery of 305mm rail guns had been utilised during the Battle of Artois in 1915.[110] There was little specific experience to draw on and there was much debate within GAN as to whether the ALGP would be able to fulfil a useful part in the Somme operation.[111]

The use of super-heavy guns was complicated by the fact that the French, unlike the British, were not prepared to fire on French villages and towns far behind the German lines. Thus the potential targets upon which the ALGP guns could engage were necessarily limited.[112] In addition, directing the long-range artillery fire from aircraft required putting up a spotter aircraft with fighter escort, requiring a "true air expedition" and thus the fire of the super heavy guns was limited to the day of the attack and was not to be repeated during the rest of the battle.[113]

While it was generally held that the ALGP had been a useful addition to *6e Armée*'s firepower, the commander of *XX Corps* artillery believed that the good service from the super-heavy guns had not been worth the considerable effort that had to be made to get them emplaced in his sector in the first place.[114]

A large part of the heavy (as distinct from super heavy) artillery was devoted to counter-battery programme. The lessons of 1915 had revealed the need to suppress German artillery fire and the French put considerable effort and thought into the counter-battery struggle with the Germans prior to the Battle of the Somme. Indeed, a 1917 report stated that the counter-battery fire programme of *6e Armée* was more carefully considered than in any previous operation.[115] The number of *155Ls* (the main counter-battery gun at this stage of the war) on the front, one *groupe* per kilometre, was as per the 20 November *Instruction*[116] and a total of 300 guns were assigned to the counter-battery preparation, the *155Ls* representing 140 of these. Although the *155Ls*

---

109 6e Armée, *Ètude sur l'Artillerie*, p. 68.
110 Ibid.
111 Ibid,, p. 69.
112 Ibid., p. 76.
113 Ibid.
114 XX Corps, Artillerie, No. 7, *Rapport concernant les operations auxquelles a pris part l'Artillerie du XX Corps d'Armée entre le 1 Juillet et le 21 Août 1916*, 27 August 1916, p. 10, 19N1089.
115 6e Armée, *Ètude sur l'Artillerie*, p. 30.
116 *Instruction sur l'emploi de l'artillerielourde*[116], p. 19.

were rather inefficient, there were enough of them and they were well handled by their crews, which resulted in considerable success as detailed later in this chapter.

The French artillery was flexible and prepared to change methods in the light of experience. For example, prior to the Somme operation, it was not thought within the ALGP that it could be an effective counter-battery tool but ideas changed as the Somme artillery preparation developed and some ALGP guns were brought into the counter-battery struggle, with good effect.[117] An example of a specific lesson learned from 1915 was that the artillery observers were pushed much further forward than hitherto, in some cases beyond the front line trenches, a practice that a *XX Corps* report suggested was taking a good idea to the "extreme."[118]

Infantry Organisation

For the attack on *39th Division*'s front, the infantry were organised as follows. 78th Brigade on the right of the division had two battalions from *156th RI* in the first line, as well as two sections of *genie* (engineers) and a territorial infantry company and was advancing on the Bois d'En Haut, Bois Sans-Nom and the quarry north of this wood. *77th Brigade* on the left of the division and in contact with the British army had two battalions from *146th RI* in the first line, with one battalion from *146th RI* and one from *153rd RI*) in the second, as well as two sections of *genie* and a territorial infantry company. It was advancing on strong-point 155-163, the Bois Favière, in liaison with the British attack. Two battalions of *153th RI*, and its commander, with four sections of *genie* were in the divisional reserve in the Bois de Maricourt and south of Maricourt.[119]

On *11th Division*'s front, the infantry were organised as follows; *21st Brigade* on the left of the division had two battalions from *26th RI* in the first line, with a reserve of one battalion from *26th RI* and three sections of *genie* (the latter also being tasked with liaising with the British) and was advancing north of the Peronne Road. *22nd Brigade* on the right flank had *79th RI* (minus two companies), one battalion from *69th RI* and two and half battalions from *37th* in the first line, with a reserve of two companies from both *79th* and *37th RI* and a *genie* company. The brigade was advancing south of the Peronne Road. The divisional reserve consisted of two battalions of *69th RI*.[120]

---

117 6e Armée, *Ètude sur l'Artillerie*, pp. 88-89.
118 XX Corps, Etat-Major, 3 Bureau, SC No 4151, *Rapport du Général Commandant le XX Corps d'Armée sur les enseignements tires des opérations de la Bataille de la Somme*, 15 December 1916.
119 XX Corps, 39 DI, *Rapport concernant les opérations auxquelles à pris part la 39 Division pendant la période du 1 Juillet au 10 Août 1916*, 22N1364.
120 11th DI, *Projet d'Engagement de la 11 DI - Infanterie - (Etablicon formément aux indications données dans la "Bataille offensive" du Général Foch, Commandant le GAN)*, 17 June 1917, p. 10, 22N1364.

312   At All Costs

Artillery preparation results

There was little reaction from the German artillery when the French began the artillery preparation, due to both the superiority of numbers that the latter had over the former but also because *6e Armée*'s air component quickly acquired complete air-superiority in its sector, eliminating German artillery observation from the air.[121]

The trench-artillery preparation began on 24 June and then intensified from 26 June onwards: "The effect of this rain of shells falling in an uninterrupted fashion for five days on the German first line was without precedent; having a great material and moral effect."[122] The first German line was seriously damaged and while the deep shelters had largely withstood the attack, many entrances had been blocked and their occupants buried alive.[123] The effect on German morale had been equally strong; many accounts from prisoners testified to the fear engendered by the heavy and seemingly endless shelling of the trench mortars.[124]

As mentioned above, *6e Armée* conducted a highly efficient counter-battery programme and, in particular, was very successful in locating the enemy batteries during the artillery preparation; for example, *3rd Colonial Division* (*I Colonial Corps*' front) reported that it found in its sector only one battery that had not been previously identified and then destroyed.[125] Indeed, the German artillery reaction to the French advance was described as "absolutely passive."[126] Putting so much of the control of *6e Armée*'s heavy artillery in the hands of the corps and divisions had been considered "audacious" before the Somme preparation but it was widely held to be a great success after the operation.[127]

The French artillery fired a *faux* preparation on the nights of 27 and 29 June in order to get the German batteries to fire barrages in response and thus establish their barrage zones. The German gunners, their nerves strained by the knowledge an assault was inevitable, fell for this ruse and duly opened fire, giving the French accurate information about what might be expected on the day of the attack.[128]

By the night of 29/30 June, so many German positions had been destroyed that it was considered safe enough to move a French infantry company into the Bois de

---

121   XX Corps, 3 Bureau, SC no. 3254, *Compte-rendu des opérations du XX Corps d'Armée sur la Somme,* 6 September 1916, p. 3, 19N1089.
122   6e Armée, Étude sur l'Artillerie dans la preparation de l'attaque du 1 Juillet, op. cit., p. 9.
123   Ibid.
124   Ibid., p. 10.
125   Ibid., p. 31.
126   Ibid., p. 32.
127   Ibid.
128   20 Corps, Artillerie, No. 7, *Rapport concernant les opérations auxquelles a pris part l'Artillerie du XX Corps d'Armée entre le 1 Juillet et le 21 Août 1916,* 27 August 1916, p. 3, 19N1089.

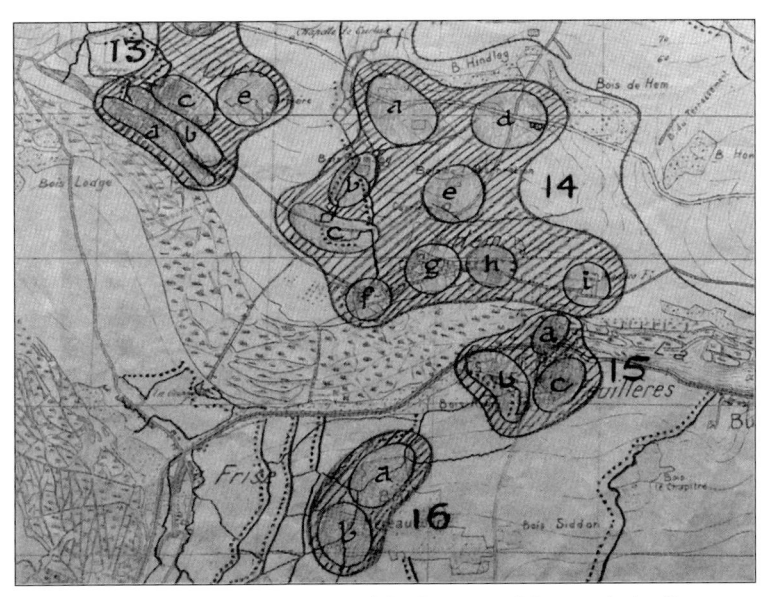

French XX Corps and Preparations for the Somme Offensive 313

XX Corps bombardment zones 4-12 (Hardecourt to Maurepas). Artillery map abstract, 17 June 1916. (22N1364)

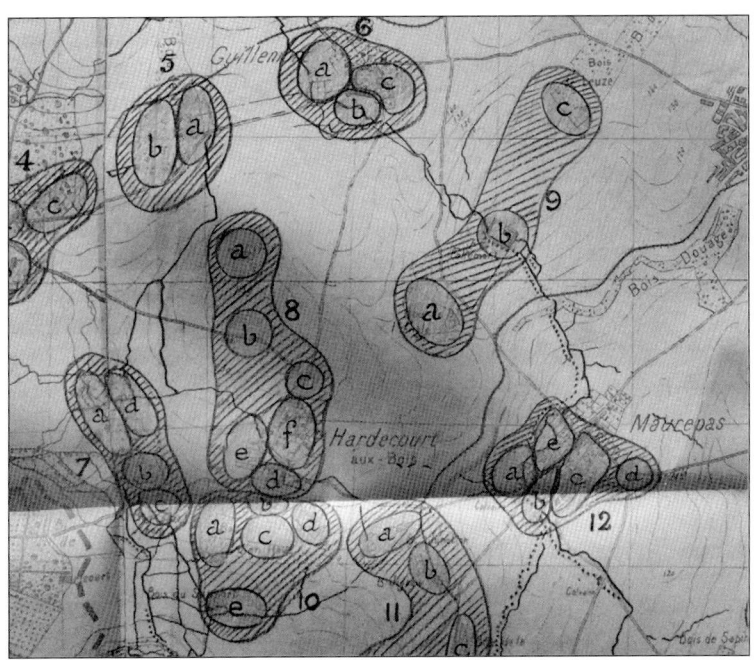

XX Corps bombardment zones 13-15 (Curlu to Frise). Artillery map abstract, 17 June 1916. (22N1364)

314   At All Costs

Loges and establish six observation posts on the eastern edges of the woods, giving clear views over the loop of the Somme and across to the outskirts of Curlu.[129]

XX Corps' artillery commander reported that the distribution of the corps' artillery had given "excellent results" but that the organisation could be improved, as, for example; the divisional artillery commanders had inadequate staffs (the size of an infantry regiment's) to command and control an entire artillery sector.[130]

Infantry Attack, 1 July 1916

The effort devoted to planning and preparation paid off on *XX Corps*' front on 1 July. General Vuillemont, commander of *11th Division*, reported that the surprise of the attack "seemed complete."[131] The *faux* artillery fire on 29 June had established that the Germans would take at least 30 minutes to respond to an attack; the German artillery did not react until 08.00, firing mainly on the line Moulin de Fargny and the Bois de l'Endurance.[132] The artillery preparation had been very successful; most of the German strong-points in the division's sector were destroyed and the area from the French lines to their objectives in the German positions was reduced to "a series of conjoined craters."[133] The assaulting infantry overran the German positions on most of the front and only ran into difficulties at the fortified village of Curlu. The *3rd Battalion/37th Infantry Regiment (RI)*, part of *22nd Brigade* situated on the right flank of *XX Corps*, entered the village, but met determined resistance from hard-pressed elements of *6th Bavarian Reserve Infanterie Regiment* and *63rd Infanterie Regiment*. In the sharp action that followed, the French quickly lost seven officers and 200 men.[134] Although the village had been subject to heavy artillery fire, machine-guns carefully emplaced in cellars, as well as the church and cemetery, had survived and were able to unleash punishing fire on the French attackers.[135] Vuillemont wanted to mount a rapid infantry assault on Curlu, as the advance of *2nd Battalion/37th RI* was halted by enfilading fire from the village. Balfourier ordered Vuillemont not to assault the village with his infantry and ordered instead an artillery bombardment; 500 heavy-artillery and 6000 field-artillery shells were fired on Curlu between 18.00 and 18.30.[136] As night fell, the third battalion of *3rd Battalion/37th RI* was able to

129   Ibid.
130   Ibid., p. 2.
131   11th DI, *Historique des opérations*, p. 6.
132   Ibid.
133   Ibid.
134   Anon., *Historique du 37eRégiment d'Infanterie pendant la Guerre 1914-1918* (Paris: Berger-Levrault, c. 1920), pp. 45-46.
135   Jack Sheldon, *The German Army on the Somme* (Barnsley: Pen & Sword, 2005), p. 168.
136   XX Corps d'Armée, 3 Bureau, SC No 3254, *Compte-rendu des opérations du XX Corps d'Armée sur le Somme*, 6 September 1916, p. 4, 19N1089. However, *11th Division*

capture the village; patrols crept into the village ahead of a series of small infiltration columns, who cleared the rubble and captured 150 German prisoners,[137] including a number of buried Germans that were disinterred from the few shelters that had not been destroyed in the village.[138] This action freed *2nd Battalion/37th RI* to advance right up to the Eulenbourg Quarry and thus fulfil its objectives by 19.00.[139]

There was equal success on *39th Division*'s front. The first infantry waves left their trenches at 07.30 and five minutes later they were at the first German line. 10 minutes later a battalion of *153rd RI* had taken its objective (Strong-point 155-163) without losses. *146th RI* had successfully penetrated the Bois Favière and *156th RI* was at the eastern edge of the Bois Sans-Nom and into Varlope Trench.[140] There was little enemy reaction until 08.15 when a German counter-attack was launched from Hardecourt. This was struck by heavy French fire and the Germans retired in disorder. By 08.50, the division's sector was under control except for in the Bois Favière where *146th RI* was involved in heavy fighting and had to request artillery support. By 09.00, most of the attack troops were now entrenched in their new positions, although in the north-east edges of the Bois Favière there were small groups of Germans still holding their ground. However, the attack had been an overall success. Casualties had been light in most places and the division's command post had received 259 prisoners including four officers. A further 300 prisoners caught by the division were sent straight to the command post of *XX Corps*.[141]

It was only during the afternoon that the German artillery began to fire against *39th Division*. German shelling proved particularly effective against strong-point 155-163 at 15.45 and the north edges of the Bois Favière. The division's rear area was also bombarded, as was the Bois de Maricourt.[142]

During the night there were five German counter-attacks; each was repelled by *39th Division*. Indeed, *156th RI* was attacked four times starting at 20.00, with the last assault occurring at 05.00 on 2 July; *146th RI* was attacked once at 04.00. French artillery and machine-gun fire forced the Germans back to their lines in disorder, leaving some 450 prisoners behind.[143]

    headquarters subsequently reported its commander had sanctioned this. See 11th DI, *Historique des opérations*, pp. 6-7.
137 11th DI, *Historique des opérations*, p. 7.
138 Ibid, pp. 7-8.
139 *Historique du 37e Régiment d'Infanterie pendant la Guerre 1914-1918*, p. 46.
140 Ibid.
141 Ibid.
142 Ibid.
143 Ibid.

Conclusion

The results on the 1 July 1916 were a triumph for the French army's meticulous planning. The unqualified success demonstrated its general effectiveness at this stage of the war. After 1 July, the French Army operations on the Somme continued with some success, but were hampered by both the comparative failure of their British neighbours and the inherent difficulties of continuing a high tempo of operations once an offensive had commenced on the Western Front.

Indeed, French operations on the Somme were not limited in success by inadequacies in planning or execution but by the limitations of the equipment available. By the end of 1916, the French army would begin to be armed with formidable modern artillery pieces, many of which would continue in service well into the 1950s, but until then there were difficulties with the artillery equipment that would only be overcome when the new guns came into the line.[144] For example, the main counter-battery gun of the Somme preparation, the *155L Mle 1877*, was simply not well-suited for counter-battery work due to its slow rate of fire, which made aircraft direction of fire difficult and landing sufficient shells on an enemy battery very difficult.[145]

A close examination of French military planning for the Battle of the Somme demonstrates that it was an important step forward in its institutional adaptation to modern warfare and was carefully thought out given the circumstances.[146] As Fayolle conceded in his diary, the theory was easy; it was putting it all into practice that was difficult: "If one is too quick, one risks failure, if one is too slow, the enemy has the time to remake successive positions. Here is the difficulty, and it is extreme."[147]

---

144 Aublet, 'L'Artillerie Francaise de 1914 à 1918,' p. 242.
145 6e Armée, *Ètude sur l'Artillerie*, p. 29.
146 For a full discussion of this process see Goya, *Le Chair*, pp. 231-270.
147 Emile Fayolle, *Cahiers secrets de la Grande Guerre* (Paris: Plon, 1964), p. 142.

Appendix I: XX Corps Orders of Battle

XX Corps – General M. Balfourier[148]

11th Infantry Division (General E. Vuillemot)[149] – 21st Brigade (26th & 69th Infantry Regiments), 22nd Brigade (37th & 79th Infantry Regiments).

39th Infantry Division (General P. Nourisson)[150] – 77th Brigade (146th & 153rd Infantry Regiments), 78th Brigade (156th & 160th Infantry Regiments).

153rd Infantry Division (General G. Magnan)[151] – 306th Brigade (418th Infantry Regiment & 2nd and 4th Chasseurs Battalions), 3rd Moroccan Brigade (1st Mixed Zouaves/Tirailleurs Regiment & 9th Algerian Zouaves Regiment).

72nd Infantry Division (General L. Ferradini)[152] – 143rd Brigade (164th & 62nd Infantry Regiments and 56th Chasseurs Battalion), 144th Brigade (324th & 365th Infantry Regiments and 59th Chasseurs Battalion).

XX Corps component units – Staff and four squadrons of 5 Hussars Regiment, 142 Territorial Infantry Regiment, two *groups* from 60th Field Artillery Regiment (75mm field guns), one *groupe* (two batteries) of 120mm guns and one *groupe* of 105mm howitzers from 120th Heavy Artillery Regiment, Air Squadron F.35, four companies of 10th Engineer Regiment.

---

148 General Maurice Balfourier (1852-1933). Assumed command of *11th Division* on mobilisation; assumed command XX Corps from Foch on 28 August 1914. *Leonore*.
149 General Eugene Vuillemot (b.1864). Served with various infantry staffs prior to assuming command of *11th Division* in April 1916. *Leonore* & AFGG X/2, p. 85.
150 General Pierre Nourisson (b. 1862). Staff colonel prior to assuming command of *39th Division* in March 1916. *Leonore* & AFGG X/2, p. 313.
151 General Georges Magnan (b.1860). Brigade commander 1914; assumed command of *153rd Division* on March 1916. *Leonore* & AFGG X/2, p. 839.
152 General Louis Ferradini (b. 1868). *Infanterie de Marine*; 17 CA staff lieutenant-colonel 1914, assumed command *72nd Division* in March 1916. *Leonore* & AFGG X/2, p. 549.

Appendix II: XX Corps *Artillerie Divisionnaire*[153]

	AD 39	**AD 11**
AC	*AD/39* 9 batteries *AD/153* 9 batteries *AD/41* 6 batteries **Total 24 batteries**	*AD/11* 9 batteries 3 groups of 75mm 9 batteries **Total 18 batteries**
AL	2 groupes *155C* 4 batteries 2 groupes *M.220* 4 batteries 1 battery *M.220* plat 1 battery 1 groupe *280* 2 batteries **Total 11 batteries**	2 groupes *155C* 4 batteries 2 groupes *M.220* 4 batteries 4 batteries, *270, 280* or *295* 4 batteries **Total 12 batteries**
AT	4 batteries 58 – 4 batteries 1 battery 240 – 1 battery **Total 5 batteries**	3 batteries of *58* 3 batteries 2 batteries of *240* 2 batteries 75mm 1 battery **Total 6 batteries**
Total	40 batteries	36 batteries

AD - *Artillerie Divisionnaire* – Divisional artillery.
AC = *Artillerie de campagne* – Field Artillery
AL = *Artillerie Lourde* – Heavy Artillery
AT = *Artillerie Trenchée* – Trench Artillery

---

153 6e Armée, 3 Bureau, *Ètude sur l'Artillerie dans la preparation de l'attaque du 1 Juillet à la VI Armée et pendant la bataille de la Somme,* 29 March 1917, p. 36. 19N1089.

Appendix III

20 Corps D'Armée[154]   HQ 22 June 1916
3 Bureau
No. SC 2073
Secret
General Order of Operations no 45, for the attack of 20 Corps

I. Mission of the Corps

20 Corps has the mission to cover the right of British 4 Army and to attack in conjunction with it.
   The first operation will take place on D-Day.
   On that day, the right of British 4 Army (13 British Corps) will attack Montauban. The provisions concerning the advance of the first line are as follows:

- the front 155-149 will be achieved by H + 20
- the front 155-145 at H + one hour
- the front 155-support trench Pissenlit, Cornichons trenches at H + 2 hours 25 mins
- the edges north of Montauban at H + 2 hours 40 minutes.

The plan of attack does not envisage the immediate occupation of the Briqueterie but its neutralisation by constant bombardment. This strong-point will be taken during the day or the following night.
   To the right of 20 Corps, 1 Colonial Corps will attack on the left bank of the Somme, its premier objective being marked towards the north by the Boucher Garenne, the Hospice Garenne, the Hélène trench. Subsequently 1 Colonial Corps will attack Frise, the Bois de Méréaucourt and Feuillères.

II. Composition of the Corps

20 Corps is reinforced by 72 Infantry Division and a complement of heavy and trench artillery.

---

154 *Les Armées francaises dans la Grande Guerre* (Paris: 1933), Tome IV, Vol. 2, Annexes 2, pp. 372-376.

III. Objective of the Corps during the course of the operation

The objectives to be taken by the Corps during D-Day are;
The Bois de Favière, the Bois Sans Nom, the Bois d'En Haut, the plateau that runs between the Bois de l'Endurance and the Curlu Chapel [north-east of Curlu] and the village of Curlu.
The liaison of the Corps with 13 British Corps will be:

a) on the Cassis trench, at the point where it crosses the Maricourt-Briqueterie road.
b) from the Framboises trench to point 155.

From the point when 20 Corps attains the objectives listed above, all of the artillery not employed in counter-battery fire against the enemy and able to intervene south of the Somme will be employed to facilitate the progress of 1 Colonial Corps in the direction of the Bois de Méréaucourt. The generals commanding 11 and 39 Infantry Divisions will make known which of the batteries in their groupements they judge available for this mission.

The colonel commanding the Corps artillery will receive from the commander of the army's artillery instructions concerning the assistance to be given to the action of 1 Colonial Corps and other provisions for the action of 20 Corps' artillery.

IV. Missions of the divisions and the attack sectors

The attack will be made by two divisions:
The 39th Infantry Division on the on the left, 11 Infantry Division on the right.
39 Infantry Division has the mission to support the flank of the British attack. In liaison with the right of British 13 Corps, it should take the Bois Favière, the Bois Sans Nom and the Bois d'En Haut and to establish observatories in front of Hardecourt having a good view of the slopes south of plateau 140.

The front to be reached by the end of the attack is marked by; point 155, the northern and eastern edges of the Bois Favière, the point north-east of the Bois Sans Nom, the northern and eastern edges of the Bois d'En Haut, the emplacements of [enemy] battery 4640.

11th Infantry Division has the mission to take the first enemy position north of the Somme, to take Curlu and advance up to the eastern part of the Bois de l'Endurance and the Curlu Chapel. It should avoid advancing beyond the line where the ground ceases to be observable by our artillery observers.

The front to be attained by the end of the attack is marked by the emplacements of [enemy] batteries 4640 and 4434, le Calvaire, the point north-east of the quarry at Eulenbourg and the point south-east of Curlu.

The limit of the divisional sectors is as follows; the crossroads 1000 metres east of the Maricourt bell-tower, the point south of the bois d'En Haut, the emplacements of [enemy] battery 4640. At the end of the attack, the liaison between the two divisions will be at that last point (included in the sector of 39 Infantry Division).

The front indicated here represents the minimum to be attained by each division. The divisions will have all latitude to occupy positions beyond this front if their action will improve their attack or make their defence more assured.

The commander of 11 Infantry Division[155] will have all of his [organic] elements available, as well as the divisional artillery of 72 Infantry Division and a complement of heavy and trench artillery. He will ensure the occupation of the passive loop of the Somme to the south of the Fargny Windmill; a detachment of 2 squadrons from 5 Hussars Regiment and a mixed company of machine guns (from 142 Territorial Infantry Regiment and 5 Hussars Regiment) are placed under his orders for this special mission.

The commander of 39 Infantry Division[156] will have all his [organic] elements, minus 160 Infantry Regiment, and also the divisional artillery of 153 Infantry Division and a complement of heavy and trench artillery.

160 Infantry Regiment will be the Corps' reserve and held at Suzanne.

153 and 72 Infantry Divisions are at the disposal of the commander of 20 Corps and will be stationed south of the Somme; 153 Infantry Division from Cerisy-Gailly (exclusive) to Hamel (inclusive), 72 Infantry Division from Vaire-s-Corbie to Aubigny (inclusive).

V. Employment of non-divisional elements

A *groupement* consisting of the Corps heavy artillery and some other heavy batteries constitutes the counter-battery and long-range artillery for the Corps.[157]

The aviation of the Corps will consist of MF35 & MF32 (two squadrons) as well as the aircraft from the heavy artillery and MF204 & MF208. Their employment is to be regulated by the Corps aviation plan, dated 18 June.

During the period of the [artillery] preparation, the task of the aviation will be to control the artillery fire, check its results and reveal any undiscovered enemy batteries.

During the attack, one aircraft [each] will be made at the disposition of both 11 Infantry Division and 39 Infantry Division to assure permanent liaison with the front line, two other aircraft will be in the air at the same time to maintain surveillance over the battlefield, watching the counter-battery fire and the assembling of enemy reinforcements.

155 General Vuillemot.
156 General Nourrisson.
157 *Groupement Anglade.*

The Corps will have three balloons available.

During the attack, *Balloon 51* will be attached to 11 Infantry Division, *Balloon 68* to 39 Infantry Division and *Balloon 50* to the counter-battery artillery. One of the divisions' balloons will act as the Corps commander's balloon.

The two companies of *génie* will remain in place in the region of Bray during D-Day at the disposition of the Corps' commander. They will be tasked with organising any conquered positions.

142 Territorial Infantry Regiment, three days before D-Day, will make available to the infantry divisions a battalion each, with the third battalion remaining under the orders of the Corps' commander in order to guarantee operation of the stations and depots.

5 Hussars Regiment will detach two squadrons on foot to 11 Infantry Division to guarantee surveillance on the Somme loop, the other squadrons will have diverse missions.

VI. Command Posts

Army HQ – Méricourt-sur-Somme.
   Corps HQ – will be 1500 metres south-west of the bell tower of the last village on the Bray to Suzanne road.
   11 Division HQ – will be on the north-eastern edge of the bois de Vaux.
   39 Division HQ – at the Maricourt Brewery.
   153 & 72 divisions HQ at Méricourt-sur-Somme.

VII. Artillery Preparation

From today, the designation of D-Day can be announced at any moment.

The artillery preparation will be over five days. It will be made under the following conditions.

D minus 5 and D minus 4 - this is the struggle against the enemy artillery and the destruction of his observatories, both aerial and terrestrial.

To force the enemy artillery to unmask itself, the trench-artillery batteries will engage the enemy shelters from D minus 5 and all the heavy batteries and field-artillery batteries that are able to will concentrate on destroying the enemy artillery. Fire will only be made on known enemy artillery emplacements and this is always to be properly regulated and controlled.

From D minus 5, there will be equal attention on the enemy rail network to the rear of the attack front, destruction of which will continue during the entire period of preparation. The commander of the Corps' artillery will give this mission to whichever long-range pieces he chooses.

The ALGP will take part in this destruction by acting against the stations, assembly points etc … according to the established plan. During this period, the aviation will destroy all the enemy balloons under the conditions laid down by the army commander.

In order to unmask any remaining enemy batteries, there will be false preparation fires made on D minus 5 & 4, under the conditions laid down by the Corps' commander, as advised by the Corps' artillery commander. This should be a short preparation in order avoid expending excessive munitions.

D minus 3, 2 and 1 – destruction of enemy defences and trenches along different lines of the first position by the field artillery, the trench artillery and the howitzers. All batteries not engaged in this work will continue action against the enemy artillery.

D-Day - the divisional commanders will have discretion as to how the regulate the artillery preparation immediately before their attack.

In the course of this preparation, artillery fire will return to the first objectives, if practicable, in order to mislead the enemy into exposing themselves to our fire when leaving their shelters. The fire will be progressively elongated from H-Hour, following the instructions of the divisional commanders, and will continue until H+30 on the front; west edge of the Bois d'En Haut, Bois de l'Endurance, west of Crucifix, west edges of Curlu.

At H+30, the fire will be regulated by the divisional orders.

Special Shells[158] – these shells will be fired in the last days of the preparation (D minus 1 & 2) and during the day of the attack. They will be used thus;

For the artillery – against batteries that fire had not been effective against, for example, those in woods or villages and anywhere where effective fire is difficult. These enemy batteries will be neutralised on the day of the attack by gas shells.

For the infantry – against trenches that the [French] infantry signal are full of shelters, against villages and woods, where reserves may be found, against sunken roads where troops are or might be assembling. Gas shells are to be used on the flank of the attack as well.

VIII. Departure of the attack

H-Hour will be notified later.

The first waves of infantry will begin their advance no later than H-Hour precisely and in all cases where it is possible before H-Hour in order to be in the first enemy line as the artillery fire moves on.

Signed General Balfourier

NOTE – This order replaces or annuls that of the engagement plan of 8 June.

158 Gas shells.

12

Learning from Defeat: 32nd Division and 1 July 1916

Stuart Mitchell

This chapter will examine how a single, representative division of the BEF planned, executed and learned from their experiences on the 1 July 1916. It will argue that the pre-war principles of war laid down in *Field Service Regulations Part One: Operations* (1909) remained broadly relevant throughout the conflict, but that these principles were not always appropriately applied. The ethos and intellectual values of the Edwardian era British Army encouraged practical changes in tactics and operational methods when circumstances demanded it. However, this approach, which valued flexibility for commanders facing different tactical problems, discouraged direct intervention by senior commanders. It will be shown that this led to grave errors on the 1 July 1916 which otherwise may have been avoided.

The structure of the British Army, and in turn its system of learning, was shaped by its cultural and social make up. This influenced its intellectual values and created a "unifying philosophy", which Albert Palazzo has described as ethos.[1] This would influence the guiding principles of the institution as outlined in *FSR I*.[2] By looking at the 32nd Division, a formation that went through both Rawlinson's Fourth and Gough's Reserve Army, this chapter will demonstrate how the pre-war principles of war and ethos of delegation to the 'man-on-the-spot' could have both positive and deleterious effects. Furthermore, the division fielded both Regular and New Army battalions and fought over the heavily fortified village of Thiepval, a vital lynchpin in the German first line defences.[3] They had not seen any major action before the

---

1   Albert Palazzo, *Seeking Victory on the Western Front* (Lincoln, Nebraska: University of Nebraska Press, 2000), pp. 8-17.
2   General Staff, *Field Service Regulations Part I: Operations* (London: HMSO, 1909).
3   The 32nd Division was comprised of the following units in June 1916: 14th Brigade: 1st Dorsetshire Reg., 2nd Manchester Reg, 15th Highland Light Infantry, 19th Lancashire Fusiliers, 14th Bde Machine Gun Company, 14th Bde Trench Mortar Battery; 96th Brigade: 16th Northumberland Fusiliers, 15th and 16th Lancashire Fusiliers, 2nd Royal

Somme, nor were they considered an elite division. As such they offer an important insight into how the British Army analysed its successes and failures.

In recent years, the British Army's learning process has received much attention. The orthodox image of brave men slaughtered by the orders of incompetent, callous and detached British generals, perhaps best epitomised in Alan Clark's *The Donkeys*, has been replaced by a much more nuanced and contextualised view of the British Army as one facing the profound difficulties of mastering industrial warfare.[4] The Battle of the Somme has formed a crucial part of this historiographical shift; Gary Sheffield, William Philpott, Christopher Duffy and Paddy Griffith have all identified it as a turning point in the British conduct of operations and indeed the war.[5] This scholarship has demonstrated many of the changes brought about during or after the battle but it has not been as successful in probing the underlying mechanisms for learning.[6] Andy Simpson's *Directing Operations: British Corps Command on the Western Front 1914-1918* is a noteworthy exception to this, highlighting the importance of pre-war ideas in shaping the BEF's conduct and and development of corps command.[7] This chapter will first consider how ethos and doctrine influenced one another, before assessing the planning, the execution and the aftermath of the battle. The learning

Inniskilling Fusiliers, 96th Bde Machine Gun Company, 96th Brigade Trench Mortar Battery; 97th Brigade: 11th Border Reg., 2nd King's Own Yorkshire Light Infantry, 16th and 17th Highland Light Infantry, 97th Brigade Machine Gun Company, 97th Brigade Trench Mortar Battery.

4 See Alan Clark, *The Donkeys* (London: Hutchinson, 1961). For the development of the part the First World War has played in British society since the end of the war see Dan Todman, *The Great War: Myth and Memory* (London: Hambledon, 2005); for a more international approach see Jay Winter & Antoine Prost, *The Great War in History: Debates and Controversies, 1914 to the Present* (Cambridge: Cambridge University Press, 2005).

5 Gary Sheffield, *Forgotten Victory. The First World War: Myths and Realities* (London: Headline, 2001), *The Somme* (London, Cassell, 2003); William Philpott, *Bloody Victory: The Sacrifice on the Somme and Making of the Twentieth Century* (London: Little Brown, 2009), Paddy Griffith, *Battle Tactics on the Western Front* (London: Yale University Press, 1994); Christopher Duffy, *Through German Eyes: The British & The Somme 1916* (London: Orion Books, 2006).

6 The doctrinal development in the form of manuals and pamphlets has regularly been identified but few have traced how these lessons were extracted. Paddy Griffith, *Battle Tactics* (1994), pp. 179-191, 'The Extent of Tactical Reform in the British Army' in Paddy Griffith (ed.), *British Fighting Methods in the Great War* (London: Frank Cass, 1996), pp. 1-22 and Jim Beach, 'The Division in the Attack 1918, SS 135, T/1635, 40/WO/7036', *SCSI Occasional Number 53*, pp. 3-5 are notable exceptions, but the conclusions are often too generalized and much more work remains to be done. In less strictly doctrinal terms Peter Simkins has touched upon the theme of development and performance at divisional level in: 'The War Experience of a Typical Kitchener Division: The 18th Division, 1914-1918' in Hugh Cecil & Peter H Liddle (eds.) *Facing Armageddon* (London: Leo Cooper, 1996), pp. 297-313.

7 Andy Simpson, *Directing Operations: British Corps Command on the Western Front 1914-1918* (Stroud: Spellmount, 2006).

system encouraged self-reflection, distillation and dissemination of lessons both up and down the chain of command. But like any system, it was only as effective as the individuals working within it and as the personnel and operational environment changed so too did the effectiveness of the system. This was not always for the better as the division's experiences under Gough's command will show. Nevertheless, there was an administrative and cultural system of learning in place within the BEF in 1916 and despite flaws in practice, it was generally fit-for-purpose.

Doctrine and Ethos

The pre-war British Army had both an ethos and a doctrine. Albert Palazzo defined ethos as "the characteristic spirit and the prevalent sentiment, taste, or opinion of a people, institution, or system."[8] Developing this idea, Palazzo then applied the changes that were occurring in British society prior to the outbreak of war to the army, demonstrating that it reflected the nation's willingness to accept radical change when it was required. This, in his eyes, "obviated the need for doctrine. Ethos provided the continuity of thought that welded the army into a whole."[9] Palazzo's argument holds much merit. By reintroducing societal values it helps explain how doctrine which was not always universally read could still be carried out in practice. Doctrine, on the other hand, has remained a point of discussion for historians. Shelford Bidwell and Dominick Graham defined doctrine by rooting it in the study of past campaigns, resources and weapons. This would lead to "the correct strategic and tactical principles in which to base both training and the conduct of war."[10] They concluded that the pre-war British Army lacked a formal doctrine, combined arms co-operation was ignored and fire-power was misunderstood. The authors build on these conclusions by drawing upon Jack Snyder and John Gooch's work which leads to a definition of doctrine which emphasised standardisation and uniformity in its application across the army.[11] This view of British doctrine has been challenged by Stephen Badsey, Timothy Bowman and Mark Connelly who have observed that definitions and expectations were contextually different during the Edwardian period. As such any attempt to find doctrine in its modern interpretation is destined to fail.[12] The pre-war British Army never imposed the sort of uniformity of training

---

8 Palazzo, *Seeking Victory on the Western Front*, p. 10.
9 Ibid., p. 9.
10 Shelford Bidwell & Dominick Graham, *Fire-Power: British Army Weapons and Theories of War 1904-1945* (London: Allen & Unwin, 1982), p. 2.
11 Ibid.
12 Stephen Badsey, *Doctrine and Reform in the British Cavalry, 1880-1918* (Farnham: Ashgate, 2008), pp. 2-3; Timothy Bowman & Mark Connelly, *The Edwardian Army: Recruiting, Training and Employing the British Army, 1902-1914* (Oxford: Oxford University Press, 2012), p. 76.

and process that would meet some modern scholars' ideas of 'formal doctrine'. Yet the intellectual heartbeat of the army may be seen by looking at the principles of war published in documents such as *FSR I* and recognising the cultural willingness to embrace change.

One of the more damaging effects of the supposed absence of doctrine has been the proliferation of the idea that the Edwardian Army was a hide-bound, insular and unthinking institution. Palazzo, while generally sympathetic to the ability to adjust in war, contends that the ethos of the army led to a rigidity in principles being applied; citing the *Army Review* he claims: "The British Army did not encourage self-criticism, and it lacked the formal mechanism for its members to perceive and debate flaws, except at the price of their careers."[13] While some dissenting voices may have been drowned out by the chorus of the traditionalists, to extrapolate from this that the culture was closed to self-criticism is a sweeping generalisation; if anything the opposite was true.[14] In the years preceding the outbreak of the First World War forums such as the *Royal United Services Institute* saw a number of important military debates puncture the parochialism of the Victorian and early Edwardian army. Officers such as Reginald Kentish and Ivor Maxse debated the reorganisation of infantry battalions from eight companies to four at the *RUSI* and in the pages of its journal. The cavalry suffered a serious identity crisis during this period. An argument regarding the role and requirements of the cavalry played out on the pages of the 1904 and 1907 *Cavalry Training* manuals and drew in the major military figures of the time. Lord Roberts's 1904 publication advocating dismounted tactics was replaced in 1907 by Douglas Haig's manual emphasising the need for cavalrymen to be proficient in mounted shock action as well as dismounted skills such as marksmanship.[15] Other debates included infantry formations when facing the fire swept battlefield, the integration of modern weaponry and the most effective use of fire-power. The debates were reflective of the major challenges facing all European armies in the early twentieth century. Technology had increased the power of defensive weapons while communications were still lacking. The full implications of this fire-power revolution were still to be seen but the debates began long before the first shots of the Great War were fired. It is therefore difficult to maintain the line of argument that the British Army did not encourage self-criticism and was insular or out-of-touch with the realities of

---

13 Ibid., p. 26.
14 Captain Wetherell (1st Bedfordshire Regiment) can be identified as one such dissenter, but even he was "congratulated for speaking out" see Bidwell & Graham, *Fire-Power* (1982), pp. 30-31.
15 For the infantry debate, see Bidwell & Graham, *Fire-Power* (1982), pp. 35-37; Imperial War Museum (IWM) 98/12/1, Brigadier-General R. J. Kentish Papers; Spencer Jones, *From Boer War to World War: Tactical Reform of the British Army, 1902-1914* (Norman, Oklahoma: University of Oklahoma Press, 2012), for cavalry debates see Gary Sheffield, *The Chief: Douglas Haig and the British Army* (London, Aurum, 2011), pp. 55-56; Stephen Badsey, *Doctrine and Reform in the British Cavalry 1880-1918* (London: Ashgate, 2008).

modern war. By addressing these debates through publication, doctrinal or otherwise, the army supported a process which would persist throughout the war and prove to be a major part of the learning process.

FSR I would set the tone for British learning during the First World War.[16] It was not written as a prescriptive set of rules, but as a guide to the principles of war. It drew upon the lessons of imperial campaigns and the careful study of military theory by the key architects; the most influential of these being Sir Douglas Haig.[17] The demands of Empire had ensured Britain's small professional army adhered to a structure which preserved the maximum flexibility in how operations were conducted, but recognised that to achieve this the army would need to be well versed in sound military principles. Central themes emerge from *FSR I*. Historians have tended to emphasise sections remarking upon the importance of moral factors in overcoming the dangers posed by fire-power, and offensive action at both the strategic and tactical levels.[18] Yet, although these themes are prominent they do not sit in isolation. It is certainly true that the human element of war was present in statements like: "The advance of the firing line must be characterized by **the determination to press forward at all costs**" but placed fully in its context on the page it becomes clear that the importance of fire-power and gaining fire superiority through mutual support is given significant discussion:

> When once the firing line comes under effective fire, its further advance will be greatly assisted by covering fire from the rear, and by the mutual support which neighbouring units in the firing line afford one another. **All leaders, down to those of the smallest units, must endeavour to apply, at all stages of the fight this principle of mutual support**. Aided in this way the infantry will fight its way forward to close range, and, in conjunction with the artillery and machine guns, will endeavour to gain superiority of fire.[19]

The modern weapons of war, chiefly quick-firing artillery and machine guns, were understood to be critical components of the twentieth century battlefield. There are also significant sections in *FSR I* covering the flexibility of command in war, understanding the role and purpose of the different arms of the army and empowering

---

16 Stuart Mitchell, 'An Inter-Disciplinary Study of Learning in the 32nd Division on the Western Front, 1916-1918' (PhD thesis, University of Birmingham, 2015), pp. 33-34. See also Simpson, *Directing Operations* (2006), pp. 6-7.
17 Sheffield, *The Chief* (2011), p. 60.
18 Tim Travers, 'The Offensive and the Problem of Military Innovation in British Military Thought', *Journal of Contemporary History*, Vol. 13, No.3 (July 1978), pp. 531-553; 'Technology, Tactics and Morale: Jean de Bloch, The Boer War, and British Military Theory 1900-1914', *The Journal of Modern History*, Vol. 51, No. 2 (June 1979), pp. 264-276; Tim Travers, *The Killing Ground* (London: Allen & Unwin, 1987), pp. 37-61; this is not confined to Travers. See also Palazzo, *Seeking Victory* (2000), pp. 17-40.
19 General Staff, *FSR I* (1909), p. 116 (original in bold).

the man-on-the-spot to make decisions – or decentralised command. These would become cornerstones of the learning system.[20] The historiography has tended to see the German Army as the principal pioneer of decentralised decision-making at the tactical level; often coupled with an unfavourable comparison to their Entente opponents.[21] Indeed, as David Zabecki has observed:

> The Allies generally tried to centralize both planning and execution at the highest levels, which in the end robbed subordinate commanders of all initiative and made it almost impossible to exploit rapidly tactical opportunities as they arose.[22]

Yet the British, even in 1909, were stressing the importance of subordinate commanders in the conduct of tactical operations. *FSR I*'s explanation of the guiding principles in framing orders for the attack are especially illuminating: "iv. The choice of the manner in which the task assigned to each body of troops is to be performed should be left to its commander."[23] Despite the challenges of rapid expansion and the introduction of civilian volunteers into both the officer corps and ranks, this principle would not fundamentally change; delegation of command to the man-on-the-spot remained an immutable principle of war, moreover it formed part of the ethos. This image of decentralisation of command jars with the conventional view of battalion after battalion blindly charging to their deaths across the machine gun swept No Man's Land of the Somme on 1 July 1916. But, as shall be shown later, the fault lay in the operational difficulties that led to poor and inconsistent execution rather than the principle.[24]

Decentralisation of authority posed certain problems to the British Army. If decisions were made down the chain of command, how could the results be communicated upwards? *FSR I* and its counterpart the *Field Service Pocket Book* (1914) set the expectation and criteria for giving feedback in the form of reports.[25] The advice given was firmly with an eye on the immediate tactical situation rather than any long-term

---

20   *FSR I* (1909) for examples of flexibility, see pp. 129-130, 171; co-operation and understanding of different arms, pp. 11-12 and 14-20, delegation to the man-on-the-spot, pp. 27-28.
21   See Bruce Gudmundsson, *Stormtroop Tactics* (London: Praeger, 1989), pp. 21-24, 171; David Zabecki, *The German 1918 Offensives* (Abingdon: Routledge, 2006), pp. 60-63.
22   Zabecki, *The German 1918 Offensives* (2006), p. 61.
23   *FSR I* (1909), p. 113; see also n.17 above; for a similar challenge regarding the French decentralisation see Jonathan Krause, *Early Trench Tactics in the French Army: The Second Battle of Artois, May-June 1915* (London: Ashgate, 2012), p. 261.
24   It is perhaps coincidental but the British Army's most recent 'capstone' doctrine, *Army Doctrine Publication: Land Operations* (MOD, 2017) 6-4 (paras. 6-09) has adopted elements regarding the limits of mission command that bear a striking similarity to that found in *FSR I* (1909), p. 102.
25   Ibid., pp. 30-31; General Staff, *Field Service Pocket Book* (London: HMSO, 1914), p. 211.

development, but as the scale of warfare expanded they became an integral facet of the learning system. Delegation of responsibility remained pivotal in filtering information to be passed up the chain of command. *FSR I* advised any soldier reporting that: "Common sense and a moderate capacity for sifting evidence should prevent inaccurate or misleading information being sent."[26] In the wake of 1 July 1916 this emphasis helped officers quickly draw valuable lessons from the experiences of the 32nd Division and send them up the chain of command.

In *FSR I* the British army had published a codified set of principles which were relevant to both the challenges of maintaining security within the empire and facing a continental opponent. Nonetheless it was hamstrung in one critical respect. While the manual provided a "sound basis for problem solving" it frequently lacked the sort of specific advice which might facilitate the implementation of the principles on the ground.[27] It remained unclear as to which level of officers the principle of decentralisation was most relevant to, and no advice was forthcoming over when a subordinate might best exercise their initiative as the 'man-on-the-spot'. The army would take time to learn that the general principles needed to be fleshed out with more prescriptive examples.[28] As the army rapidly expanded to meet the immense continental commitment, demand for more prescriptive manuals arose. To meet this, several private authors produced works imparting new officers with their wisdom. Yet, these essentially mirrored the principles of *FSR I*. Major J. L. Sleeman published *First Principles of Tactics and Organisation: War Edition 1915* and prefaced his work with: "Throughout the instruction it must be remembered that this book is written to be read in conjunction with 'Field Service Regulations.' Without frequent reference to this excellent text book much useful instruction will be lost."[29] What emerges throughout Sleeman's and other such works, are reiterations of the core intellectual ideas, supported with practical advice and ways of approaching problems. A new generation of eager professionals was exposed to both the principles and ethos of the army.

While ethos shaped the standards and expectations, it did not preclude sub-cultures arising. While army principles stressed inter-arm co-operation it was common for specialists to develop their own *esprit de corps*. R.E. Grice Hutchinson, a 32nd Division chaplain to the artillery, remarked on this: "the nature of its organisation was entirely different from an Infantry Brigade." He continued by adding: "Each [battery] was

---

26 Ibid., p. 30.
27 Sheffield, *The Chief* (2011), p. 60.
28 This is most clearly observed in the evolution of the instructional pamphlets published by the Army Printing and Stationery Service. See, for example, SS 143, *Instructions for the Training of Platoons for Offensive Action, 1917* (February 1917, April 1917, June 1917, September 1917) and SS 143, *The Training and Employment of Platoons 1918* (February 1918) and finally SS 143, *Platoon Training, 1918-1919* (March 1919).
29 Major James Lewis Sleeman, *First Principles of Tactics and Organisation: War Edition 1915* (London: Gale & Polden, 1915), p. vii.

British 2-inch Medium Trench Mortar. (Private collection)

entirely separate in character and far more independent of one another."[30] Hutchinson was not the only one who saw differences, Lieutenant F. D. Hislop was the Lewis Gun Officer to the 5/6th Royal Scots in October 1916; he wrote a memorandum to the battalion adjutant requesting fewer fatigues for his men on the grounds of their Lewis gun specialisation.[31] It is clear that he and the men he represented took a certain pride in their uniqueness: "Machine gunners have always been specially picked men, as their work makes a greater intellectual demand, and from time to time a greater physical demand than feels to the average private."[32] Paddy Griffith described this as "The problem of Cap Badges".[33] Nevertheless, it is easy to overstate the prevalence and impact of these divided loyalties.

Despite the boasts or complaints of some soldiers, more often than not relations were amicable and co-operation existed. Sergeant J.E. Prince of Heavy Battery (V/32) 32nd Division Trench Mortars referred to our "Infantry friends in the line" and Lieutenant A.B. Scott (Reconnaissance Officer for X and W Trench Mortar Batteries) recounts a request from the Colonel of the 2nd King's Own Yorkshire Light Infantry (KOYLI)

---

30 R. Whinyates (ed.), *Artillery and Trench Mortar Memories: 32nd Division* (Uckfield: Naval & Military Press reprint of 1932 edition), p. 99.
31 All units are component parts of 32nd Division unless stated otherwise. The 5/6th Royal Scots joined 32nd Division in late July 1916.
32 IWM, Capt. F. D. Hislop, 95/16/1, Memo on Employment of Lewis Gunners on Fatigue. pp. 1-2.
33 Griffith, 'Tactical Reform in the British Army', *Fighting Methods* (1996), p. 5.

to fire on a certain troublesome machine gun.[34] This was successfully carried out, to some unpleasant heckles from the nearby infantry, but despite this Scott saw that they "always lined the trench, and we [the gunners] felt somewhat compensated by their cheery remarks when a good hit was made."[35] There is a tendency to see cap badge or specialist loyalties as mutually exclusive to other identities. There is little evidence to suggest that this was the case within the 32nd Division. Captain E.B. Lord of 15th Lancashire Fusiliers would refer with some pride to the division's nickname as the "Mad Division" on account of its enthusiasm for raiding, while R.L. Venables a driver in 164th Brigade RFA, commented that different divisions were used for different roles, promoting the idea of the 32nd Division as assault specialists: "Our Division was usually moved to where a battle was planned to take place, so that if they captured a gun or vehicle of ours and know to which Division it belonged they would be prepared."[36] These were boastful claims yet the very fact that they existed demonstrates that identity and pride extended beyond a soldier's battalion. Identities within the BEF were akin to *matryoshka* dolls: the section, platoon, company or battalion affiliations may well have been the strongest but they did not preclude individuals identifying with the division or as a part of the whole expeditionary force. The strengths of these varied, but the overall ethos was accommodating and complementary to these sub-cultures precisely because it allowed them to flourish within a set of principles and guidelines.[37] These sub-divisions played an important role in the British Army's overall learning system. To understand how this was the case the concept of 'communities of practice' needs to be considered.

John Seely Brown and Paul Duguid's "communities of practice" idea, explains both the interaction between internal "sub-cultures" and indicates how the sum of individual learning contributed towards the development of the whole army. Individual experience is the basis for "communities of practice". Brown and Duguid build on this by recognising that organisations tend to perceive work done by their employees as "canonical" – that is, they see jobs to be completed as being carried out according to a set of instructions which generally ignore the practical complexities that carrying out the task might entail. The subordinates on the other hand tend to work in "non-canonical" ways, developing "communities of practice" that obviate these sorts of problems. Individuals build up methods through experience, but quickly share them within their working community through observation and discussion. Brown and Duguid draw the conclusion from this that if "internal communities have a reasonable degree of autonomy and independence from the dominant world view, large organisations

---

34 Whinyates (ed.), *Artillery and Trench Mortar Memories* (1932), pp. 26-27, 665.
35 Ibid., p. 27.
36 See IWM 79/12/1, Captain E.B. Lord page 41and R.L. Venables, 76/225/1, p. 13.
37 It of interest to note that both Gudmundsson and Zabecki promote this as a strength within the German Army, but deny it to both the British and French armies. The latter's ultimate victory should perhaps have prompted pause for thought.

might actually accelerate innovation."[38] They note however that this is only possible if the organisation avoids regular wholesale shifts in structural practices.[39] This idea might be applied to the BEF; a coherent learning system needed to be able to draw upon the practices within the smaller communities at the lowest level, draw their lessons upwards and then disseminate them.[40] This was especially crucial for an army whose communities could be weakened by casualties as a consequence of their actions. Autonomous "communities of practice" certainly have benefits in a stable environment, but in a war where units and formations could lose significant portions of their manpower there also needed to be a robust centralised system of accumulation of lessons which could be quickly shared within the wider organisation. The system of feedback and dissemination the BEF used to do this will be looked at in more detail later.

It has been suggested that rather than one "learning curve" there were numerous curves, starting at different points for different arms and specialisms.[41] This is an eminently sensible development of the "learning curve" idea, but it still fails to address how these different "competences" managed to interact to create a cohesive system. Furthermore, how individual learning extended to the group remains vague, the idea of a "community of practice", held together by a broadly principle-based system however, fleshes this out. Ethos promoted a manner of thinking which bled through to the officers and men and left them accommodating to change; it encouraged the serious study of war and through the "principles" promoted in *FSR I* provided a loose framework in which "communities of practice", or subordinate commanders could freely apply their diverse experience and knowledge. This was observed, experienced and communicated by subordinates, peers and superiors contributing towards the overall development. It is all very well to set out with the structures in place, but how did it work when faced with the strains of the 1 July and the later actions on the Somme?

Preparing for the Push

On 7 March 1916 after a conference at X Corps HQ at Toutencourt, the 32nd Division began their preparations for the Somme offensive in earnest.[42] They would be attacking

---

38 John Seely Brown & Paul Duguid, 'Organizational Learning and Communities-of-Practice: Toward a Unified View of Working, Learning, and Innovation' in *Organization Science*, Vol. 2, No.1, (February, 1991), pp. 40-57.
39 Ibid., p. 54.
40 Brown & Duguid, Organizational Learning and Communities-of-Practice (February, 1991), p. 54.
41 Mike Senior, 'Learning Curves and Opportunity Curves on the Western Front', *Stand To!*, No. 93 (December 2011/January 2012), pp. 11-14.
42 TNA WO 95/2367: 32nd Division: Headquarters Branches and Services: General Staff, 7 March 1916; Memorandum on the Front held by the 32nd Division (n.d.). For corps conference details see Simpson, *Directing Operations* (2006), p. 32.

what General Horace Smith-Dorrien described as "the hardest nut to crack in the whole line": the village of Thiepval and the adjacent Leipzig Spur.[43] Despite having four months to prepare, one of the biggest criticisms levelled at the 32nd Division, and its General Officer Commanding (GOC), Major-General Rycroft, was the overworking of the infantry. The General Staff Officer Grade II (GSO), Major Austin Girdwood was to comment to James Edmonds, compiler of the *Official History* (1922-48), "The real cause of the failure of the 32nd Division is that the wretched Infantry were literally exhausted long before the day of the attack."[44] He would direct this criticism at Rycroft and his GSO I, F. W. Gosset: "I did protest to General Rycroft that he was not treating the Infantry fairly and I said so often to Gosset."[45] There can be little doubt that the infantry were subjected to significant manual labour in the months leading up to the battle, but this was not wholly down to the commander. The picture that emerges is one of delegation, inexperience, and poorly prioritised planning which, while conducted with the best of intentions, left the infantry making up the shortfall in labour. The 32nd Division was a microcosm of the wider army: overworked infantry, delegation of planning to specialists and a task too large for the available resources. Prior and Wilson have identified these at the Army level in *Command on the Western Front*, and their critical conclusion of Rawlinson's role in allowing inconsistencies, especially in the artillery plan, is understandable.[46] This failure may partly be attributed to the uncertainty of senior commanders in knowing how far to intervene or defer to specialists. In practice how should they apply the army's core principles? Senior commanders during the battle of the Somme faced the same problem of balancing their own experience against the proposals of their subordinates and judging when to intervene to make changes. This would not be easily rectified in 1916.

If the performance of the 32nd Division at the battle of the Somme was judged by feats of engineering then there is little doubt they would be considered a success.[47] In the months leading up to 1 July the division completed 15 major building works including: 19.65 miles of trench for telephone wires dug (of which 11.25 miles was 6 feet deep; 8.4 miles 4 feet deep), these trenches then filled back in; "the completion of a water supply system throughout the front lines"; 28 bridges for artillery tracks were

---

43 Perth and Kinross Council Archive (PKCA), Rycroft Papers, MS35/50: Horace Smith-Dorrien to William Rycroft, 20 August 1916. Similar sentiments existed at X Corps HQ. See TNA CAB 45/191: Colonel H.W. Wynter to Brigadier-General James Edmonds, 6 October 1930.
44 TNA CAB 45/134: Girdwood to Edmonds, 30 June 1930.
45 Ibid. 30 June 1930; interestingly Girdwood fails to mention Major E.G. Wace who replaced Gosset as GSO I in May 1916.
46 Robin Prior & Trevor Wilson, *Command on the Western Front: The Military Career of Sir Henry Rawlinson 1914-1918* (London: Blackwell, 1992), pp. 159-165.
47 The 32nd Division was far from unique in this respect. The Fourth Army as a whole had to cope with these problems. Prior & Wilson, *Command on the Western Front* (1992), pp. 156-157.

erected, as well as "numerous bridges for infantry"; while construction of "additional sidings on the trench tramways to Thiepval and Authuille Woods" was completed.[48] The three companies (206, 218, 219) of the Royal Engineers carried out the specialist aspects of this work, but the infantry were frequently called upon to furnish working parties and conduct labour intensive tasks.[49] The bane of the platoon commanders' existence, the working parties prompted one officer, Charles Clifford Platt – 19th Lancashire Fusiliers to playfully describe the life of the "common or garden infantry subaltern" as the "rottenest job in the world".[50] There was an opportunity cost to excessive labour. Time spent on working parties or fatigues limited time to train. The effect on morale was equally damaging.

Major-General W.H. Rycroft. (John Bourne)

If Girdwood's account is accepted the effects were serious: "[T]he men and officers lost heart and were simply worn out physically and morally."[51] This testimony warrants scrutiny. Girdwood was removed from his position as GSO II on 16 July 1916 to assume command of the 11th Border Regiment. In his post-war letter to Edmonds he suggested that he had predicted the impending "disaster" and was "'given command of a Battalion to get me out of the Staff Office."[52] This has led Peter Simkins to conclude that "all was not well in the command and staff echelons of the division."[53] Girdwood's

---

48　TNA WO 95/2368: 'Report on Operations by the General Staff', 32nd Division, pp. 1-2; all of this was in addition to the construction of frontline, support and communication trenches, "Russian saps" and mortar emplacements, as well as the usual maintenance and repairs necessary while in the line.
49　Labour was also drafted in from the batteries of the Corps Reserve Division. TNA WO 95/2368: Report on Preparation and Action of the 32nd Divisional Artillery During Operations of July 1916, p. 1.
50　IWM, C.L. Platt, 78/72/1, 15/4/1916 writing in a generally jovial tone to his enlisted letter brother Glyn, Platt urged him to become a specialist where he might avoid supervising the outings described.
51　TNA CAB 45/134: Girdwood to Edmonds, 30 June 1930.
52　Ibid.
53　Peter Simkins, 'Somme footnotes: The Battle of the Ancre and the Struggle for Frankfurt Trench, November 1916', *Imperial War Museum Review No.9* (1994), pp. 84-101.

testimony certainly suggests a serious breakdown in the relationship between the GOC and his staff. However, new archival evidence paints a more complicated picture.

Girdwood's letter to Edmonds in 1930 suggests a hardening of opinion which was more much accommodating during the war. Although Rycroft and Girdwood could not be considered friends, they continued to correspond after Rycroft's removal from command of the division in November 1916. In May 1917 Girdwood wrote to Rycroft, ostensibly to seek his support for a promotion, however, he also recalled how:

> All the old hands still talk of you when we meet and recall the happy days we had under your command. I often think of a conversation I had with you about only quick + rapid thinkers and writers being any good for Staff. I did not agree at the time and have watched many of the rapid type come to bitter grief through being rapid. If they have had practical experience they are all right but so many of that type have propelled themselves upward by their peers that they have not had time to see things. As C.O. I have seen the Staff from both ends and I know quite a lot about it now. The quick fellow is always very sketchy and the results of his orders are often totally different to what he thought they would be.[54]

This frank exchange of views may not have been the best way of currying favour with his old commander, but it demonstrates that their relationship was perhaps not as frosty as might have been expected. The fact that Girdwood felt comfortable discussing his different views on staff work just six months after Rycroft had left the division indicates that the divisional headquarters was not quite as closed to views as the post-war correspondence with Edmonds suggests. Even so, the warmer relationship between Girdwood and Rycroft does not necessarily invalidate the criticism made of the GOC. It is worth looking at the claims made against Rycroft to evaluate just how culpable he was.

In March 1916, the 32nd Division faced the gargantuan task of preparing the front and rear areas for a major attack from scratch. No buried cable system existed, gun positions needed to be dug and supply routes developed. Such planning was not subject to one man's oversight but was rather the product of delegation to those logically best placed to oversee the work. Corps and division passed much of the responsibility of planning to the specialist arms. The artillery's communications network, for example, was a product of a consultative process:

> There was no system of buried cables in existence and so a suggested scheme was drawn up by Divisional Artillery and forwarded to Corps Signals for sanction.

---

54 PKCA, Rycroft Papers, Austin Girdwood to William Rycroft, 28 May 1917.

The original scheme was modified and placed under the control of an Officer of the Divisional Signal Co.[55]

This scheme itself proposed centring communications around the two Artillery Group HQs (Right and Left) while an Observation Exchange at these Group HQs allowed forward communication to be maintained with the observation posts. This meant that if they lost contact with the batteries the messages could be brought forward from the Group HQ.[56] This emphasis on backup communications was understandable given the practical difficulties commanders had faced keeping in touch with their units and formations once the attack had begun. The priorities in construction were incorrectly established though. Observation exchanges proved to be complicated and unnecessary, while the Group HQ wires to the front line dugouts, which were not fully finished by the time of the attack, "were of the greatest value and should have been first to be completed."[57] German shell-fire posed a further problem. Centralising the Artillery Group HQ network would, if struck by hostile shellfire, have a disproportionate effect on communications with subordinate batteries. While the Artillery HQs of both Brigades remained safe, some of the left group's batteries, collected under the commander of 155th Brigade's Lt-Col. Ponson J. Sheppard, were to struggle with their telephone exchange. This was sited across the marshy ground of the Ancre where wires could not be buried to the usual depth of 6 feet: instead they were dug to a depth of 2 feet with 4 feet of sandbagged breastworks above. Consequently, "by midday there was no communication – all the lines being cut. Communication was established during the afternoon, but it was very precarious…"[58] Shell-fire was not the only issue, in planning a complex and labour intensive system the division had very little time once functional to familiarise themselves with it:

> As the system was only completed just before operations, R.A. operators did not have an opportunity of thoroughly learning the lines and test boxes. This was a great drawback when repairs became necessary.[59]

Undoubtedly, the inexperience of building a satisfactory communications network in a very limited time frame on a scale hitherto unknown by the divisional artillery

---

55 TNA WO 95/2368: 32nd Div., General Staff, 'Report on Preparation and Action of the 32nd Divisional Artillery During Operations of July 1916', p. 1.
56 To complicate matters, the 'Group' was not an official designation but an administrative one which seemingly denoted the existing RFA Brigades as they were expanded with incoming batteries. Special thanks to Rob Thompson for his assistance with the attempt to unravel this issue.
57 Ibid., p. 1.
58 TNA CAB 45/191: Lt-Col. Ponson J. Sheppard to Edmonds, 26 May 1930. This is also corroborated by Major R. B. Warton in TNA CAB 45/191: Major Warton to Edmonds, 26 May 1930, p. 3.
59 TNA WO 95/2368: Report … 32nd Divisional Artillery, p. 1.

and signals staff led to errors. The scale of the forthcoming offensive, the lack of time to train and familiarise and the prioritisation of work proved to be the major errors in planning. The topography of the ground was out of the division's control but it also added to the difficulties on 1 July. Nevertheless, Brigadier-General J.A. Tyler (Commander of Royal Artillery, 32nd Division) would conclude: "The system on the whole worked very well."[60] Girdwood was right to point out the difficulties facing the infantry in the build-up to the battle, but the blame cannot solely be laid at Rycroft's feet. By delegating in line with the prevailing principles he avoided dictating on matters where he lacked personal expertise. The size of the task and the general inexperience of those within the specialist branches meant there was simply too much to do in the time allotted and with the manpower provided.

Decentralisation was mirrored in other branches of the Division as well as at corps and army level. When deciding upon the tactical approach to the battle the division, corps, and army employed a consultative process completely in keeping with the ethos of the pre-war British Army. In 1916 it did not always function as intended as the experiences of the 97th Infantry Brigade demonstrates. As Andy Simpson has observed, conferences were a crucial forum for the process of consultation.[61] During April 1916, when the bulk of the tactical planning was formulated by division, Rycroft regularly visited and hosted meetings with his brigade commanders.[62] The topics discussed in these conferences and meetings varied, but the general structure was a familiar one for all concerned. Brigadier-General James Jardine, GOC 97th Brigade, described a conference held by General Rawlinson: "As was the custom it took the form of the senior officer asking each brigadier in turn what he noticed worthy of remarks & criticism."[63] Conferences and meetings were a part of broader framework of discussions, inspections and informal "pow-wows" that comprised an integral part of the BEF's decision-making process. In February 1916, a relatively average month, 48 discussions, inspections and conferences involving either senior commanders or DHQ's general staff officers were significant enough to be noted in the War Diary.[64] Conferences were thus a vital part of the planning process and provided a mechanism, albeit an imperfect one, for subordinates to discuss their ideas and opinions.

In theory this custom of consulting subordinate commanders drew upon the experience of the "communities of practice" at the lower levels of the army. Practically though, the utility of this was hampered by individual perceptions, prejudices and scepticism. At the aforementioned conference with Rawlinson, Jardine explained his views that the infantry should follow the protective barrage within 30-40 yards, and expect some

---

60   Ibid., p. 1.
61   Simpson, *Directing Operations* (2006), p. 32.
62   TNA WO 95/2367: 32nd Div., April 1916.
63   TNA CAB 45/135: Brigadier-General James Jardine to Edmonds, 13 June 1930.
64   TNA WO 95/2367: 32nd Div. February 1916. Excluding inspections which may involve much less constructive dialogue there were still 23 occasions for discussion. Ranks considered: GSO III upwards and brigadier upwards.

casualties from their own shells. Jardine recalled how this was met with a polite degree of scepticism.[65] At first glance, this may seem like the logical response; no army ever won a war by shelling their own troops. However, Jardine's advocacy was based upon his experiences as an observer during the Russo-Japanese War. He had seen the battles of Sai-Ma-Chi, Yu-shu-lin-tzu and Mukden and recognised the importance of being first to positions of tactical importance.[66] This was reinforced by the results of raids on German lines conducted by his brigade in the run up to 1 July.[67] He knew that the best way to save the lives of his men would be to win the race to the parapet. This would incur loss but "it was worth it." In spite of the strong basis for ideas Jardine felt that some remained sceptical owing to his background: "I fancied – of course I may have been wrong – that there was a little bit of unconscious prejudice against my ideas, being a cavalryman." Moreover once he explained that this was inspired by "what the Japanese did", he got the "sneering" reply of: "Oh, the Japanese" from Rawlinson.[68] Looking more widely at the tactical plans for the infantry on 1 July it seems unlikely that Rawlinson's view was motivated by prejudice. Major-General Sir Oliver Nugent, GOC 36th (Ulster) Division, employed a similar tactic in the neighbouring sector, as did Major-General Sir Ivor Maxse, commanding 18th (Eastern) Division attacking Montauban Ridge and Pommiers Redoubt.[69] Both were infantrymen. Rawlinson, whatever the rationale behind his scepticism, did not alter Jardine's plans. He allowed his subordinate commander the freedom to use the tactics he saw as most appropriate. Nonetheless, Rawlinson did little to promote or disseminate these ideas. He was permissive of tactical variation but only went so far as recommending small parties of Lewis guns be pushed forward into No Man's Land in his *Fourth Army Tactical Notes*.[70] This criticism should not be taken too far though, Rawlinson presided over a system which was in keeping with the pre-war ethos and gave significant latitude to his subordinate commanders to apply their own experience. Although it would take time to refine so that good ideas were disseminated more rapidly, it was superior to the alternative of an overly centralised and impractical battle plan.

65 TNA CAB 45/135: Jardine to Edmonds, 13 June 1930.
66 General Staff, *The Russo-Japanese War. Reports from British Officers Attached to the Japanese and Russian Forces in the Field Vol.I* (London: HMSO, 1908), pp. 135-141, 210-220, 405-430, 647-668; General Staff, *The Russo-Japanese War. Reports from British Officers Attached to the Japanese and Russian Forces in the Field*, Vol. II (London: HMSO, 1908), pp. 493-500, 526-541.
67 For example, the 17th Battalion Highland Light Infantry trench raid on the night of 21/22 April 1916. See John W. Arthur & Ion S. Munro (eds.), *The Seventeenth Highland Light Infantry (Glasgow Chamber of Commerce Battalion)* (Glasgow: David J. Clark, 1920), p. 35. See also TNA WO 95/2399 97th Brigade, Appendix 8, 25/4/191, April 1916.
68 Ibid., 13 June 1930.
69 Simkins, 'The War Experience of a Typical Kitchener Division: The 18th Division, 1914-1918' in Cecil & Liddle (eds.) *Facing Armageddon* (1996), p. 301.
70 Sir J.E. Edmonds, *Military Operations France and Belgium 1916*, Vol. I (hereafter *OH 1916*, Vol.1) (London: Macmillan, 1932), Appendices.

Execution

At 7.30am the bombardment lifted and the leading brigades of 32nd Division, 96th (GOC Brigadier-General Clement Yatman) and 97th (GOC Brigadier-General James Jardine) assaulted the fortified village of Thiepval and the Leipzig Salient. On the right of the divisional line, the 17th Highland Light Infantry had crawled into No Man's Land where they awaited zero hour close to the bombardment. Once the guns lifted they stormed the Leipzig Redoubt, the German strongpoint on the tip of the salient. This was to be the division's only meaningful gain on the 1 July and the scene of intense fighting throughout the next 24 hours. Yatman's 96th Brigade were less fortunate. Despite also waiting in No Man's Land, albeit 60 yards further away than 97th Brigade, the initial waves of the 15th Lancashire Fusiliers and 16th Northumberland Fusiliers were caught in the open by machine gun fire from Thiepval. Some elements of Lancashire Fusiliers were reported to have made it into the German lines but reports remained tentative and imprecise. The confusion over these reports and the status of the attack would prove costly and highlight the frailties of the decentralised command system in 1916. As the day went on enfilade fire from Thiepval and the "Nordwerk" strong point pinned down the now mixed up troops of 97th Brigade, while the bulk of 96th Brigade remained stranded in front of the German first line positions; all attempts to push on met with bloody failure. 14th Brigade, in reserve, struggled to reach their own front lines under the weight of machine gun fire, but some companies were able to reinforce the gains in the Leipzig Redoubt.[71]

One of the major challenges facing Major-General Rycroft and the staff of the 32nd Division once battle had commenced was communications. As Wyn Griffith, of 15th Royal Welsh Fusiliers (38th Welsh Division) subsequently observed: "A General without a telephone was to all practical purposes impotent – a lay figure dressed in uniform, deprived of eyes, arms and ears."[72] In principle the decentralised system of command should have compensated for this neutering of the generals; in practice uncertainty seeped back from brigade and poor choices spread up the chain of command. The trouble centred around Yatman's 96th Brigade, General Rycroft, and

---

71   Primary source narrative of events drawn from: TNA WO 95/2368: 32nd Division Headquarters, Branches and Services: General Staff, 1 July 1916 and appendices, WO 95/2399: 32nd Division: 97th Brigade Headquarters, 1 July 1916 and appendices; WO 95/2395 32nd Division: 96th Infantry Brigade Headquarters,1 July 1916 and appendices, For a more detailed general narrative of events see Edmonds, *OH 1916*, Vol.1, pp. 394-423, William Philpott, *Bloody Victory: The Sacrifice on the Somme and the Making of the Twentieth Century* (London: Little, Brown, 2009), pp. 172-208; Gary Sheffield, *The Somme* (London: Cassell, 2003), pp. 41-74; Michael Stedman, *Salford Pals: 15th, 16th, 19th & 20th Battalions Lancashire Fusiliers A History of the Salford Brigade* (Barnsley: Pen & Sword, 1993), pp. 87-116.

72   Wyn Griffith, *Up to Mametz* (London: Severn House, 1981 reprint of 1931edition), p. 185. See also Paddy Griffith, 'The Extent of Tactical Reform in the British Army', Paddy Griffith (ed.), *British Fighting Methods in the Great War* (London: Frank Cass, 1996), p. 1.

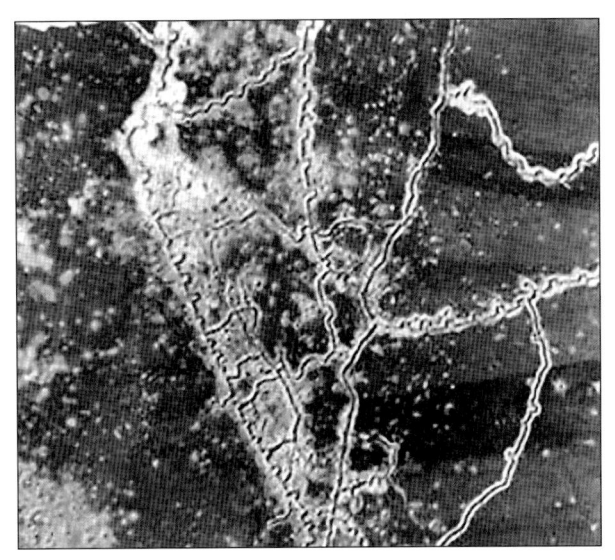

Leipzig Salient from the air, 1 June 1916.

X Corps Commander, Lieutenant-General Sir Thomas Morland. By 8am reports had reached Yatman that the leading companies of his left battalion, 15th Lancashire Fusiliers, were making good progress through the German front lines.[73] This was supported at 9.22am when Lt. McRobert reported from the Coniston Observation Post that British troops had been moving forward east of Thiepval 12 minutes earlier.[74] Further reports trickled in from the artillery observers and possibly aerial reconnaissance. By late morning Rycroft and Yatman believed that a portion – although the exact strength remained maddeningly vague – of the leading two companies of the 15th Lancashire Fusiliers were in or isolated near the eastern edge of the village.[75] This information coloured Yatman's decisions throughout the day. When new plans were formulated to attempt to flank the village from the north he dissuaded both Rycroft and Morland from re-bombarding the forward positions in the village and the fortified Thiepval Château. Instead he recommended concentrating the artillery on the strong-points to the south and east until the outcome of his attack, by two companies of the 2nd Battalion Royal Inniskilling Fusiliers and 16th Lancashire Fusiliers, was known.[76] This effectively deprived the attacking companies of any meaningful

---

73 TNA WO 95/2368: 32nd Div., 1 July 1916, 8.20 a.m.
74 Ibid., 1 July 1916, 9.22 a.m.
75 Ibid., 1 July 1916, aerial reconnaissance, see TNA WO 95/2397 15th Lancashire Fusiliers, 1 July 1916.
76 TNA WO 95/2368: 32nd Div., 1 July, 11.45 a.m.; 11.57 a.m.; 1.50 p.m.; CAB 45/191 R. B. Warton, 155th Brigade RFA to Edmonds 26 May 1930, Edmonds, *OH 1916*, Vol.1, pp. 410-411.

artillery support, and the result was a costly failure. Furthermore Thiepval remained unsuppressed and its defenders were able to wreak a deadly toll upon the flank of the neighbouring 36th (Ulster) Division.[77]

This was not simply bad leadership but a flawed implementation of decentralised command. The acceptance of Yatman's reservations demonstrated that during the conduct of battle there was a meaningful system of opinion and feedback. Yet decentralisation as explained in *FSR I* did not promote the removal of higher command from the decision-making process. A balance needed to be struck between stifling, impractical intervention, and giving subordinates the freedom to decide how best to proceed according to the local conditions. In this instance, with all three commanders operating within an information vacuum, a decisive corps or divisional commander may have overruled Yatman's fears on the hard calculation that the risk of friendly fire against two depleted companies was better than sending many soldiers forward without sufficient artillery support. That this did not occur can only reflect the thorough uncertainty of the position. The learning system relied upon experience, and it would take more days like 1 July before commanders would understand the balance between intervention and delegation. Ultimately, this was Clausewitzian friction at its most destructive.

The artillery on 1 July has been much criticised. The long arm has been portrayed as inflexible, detached over-centralised and insufficient.[78] Yet in this particular case it provides an excellent example of decentralised initiative. Having captured the Leipzig Redoubt, it had become clear that the artillery barrage was moving away from the infantry faster than they could advance. At this point Jardine liaised with Lt-Col. Cotton, commanding 32nd Division's Right Artillery Group, and arranged for two batteries to be pulled from the standard fire-plan in order to protect the gains that had been made. Uncertainty remains over whose idea this was: Edmonds, in the *Official History*, suggests it was an order from Brigadier-General Jardine prompted by Lt-Col. Cotton's consultation, although the wording indicates this is based mainly upon Jardine's letter.[79] Yet the divisional records state:

> Lieut-Colonel Cotton, the officer commanding the Artillery Group with 97th Brigade, hearing from his O.P.s [Observation Posts] that the Infantry were unable to keep up with the Artillery lifts…rightly drew back the fire from some of his batteries from their pre-arrange objectives and thereby enabled the 97th Brigade to hold on to the captured trenches.[80]

77 Cyril Falls, *The History of the 36th (Ulster) Division* (London: Constable, 1922), p. 54.
78 Simpson, *Directing Operations* (2006), p. 32; Bidwell & Graham, *Fire-Power* (1982), p. 84; Travers, *The Killing Ground* (1987), pp. 161-162 and Jonathan Bailey 'British Artillery in the Great War' in Griffith (ed.), *British Fighting Methods* (1996), pp. 23-49.
79 Edmonds, *OH 1916*, Vol.1, p. 401; TNA CAB 45/135: Jardine to Edmonds, 13 June 1930.
80 TNA WO 95/2368: 32nd Div.: 'Report on Operations', p. 6.

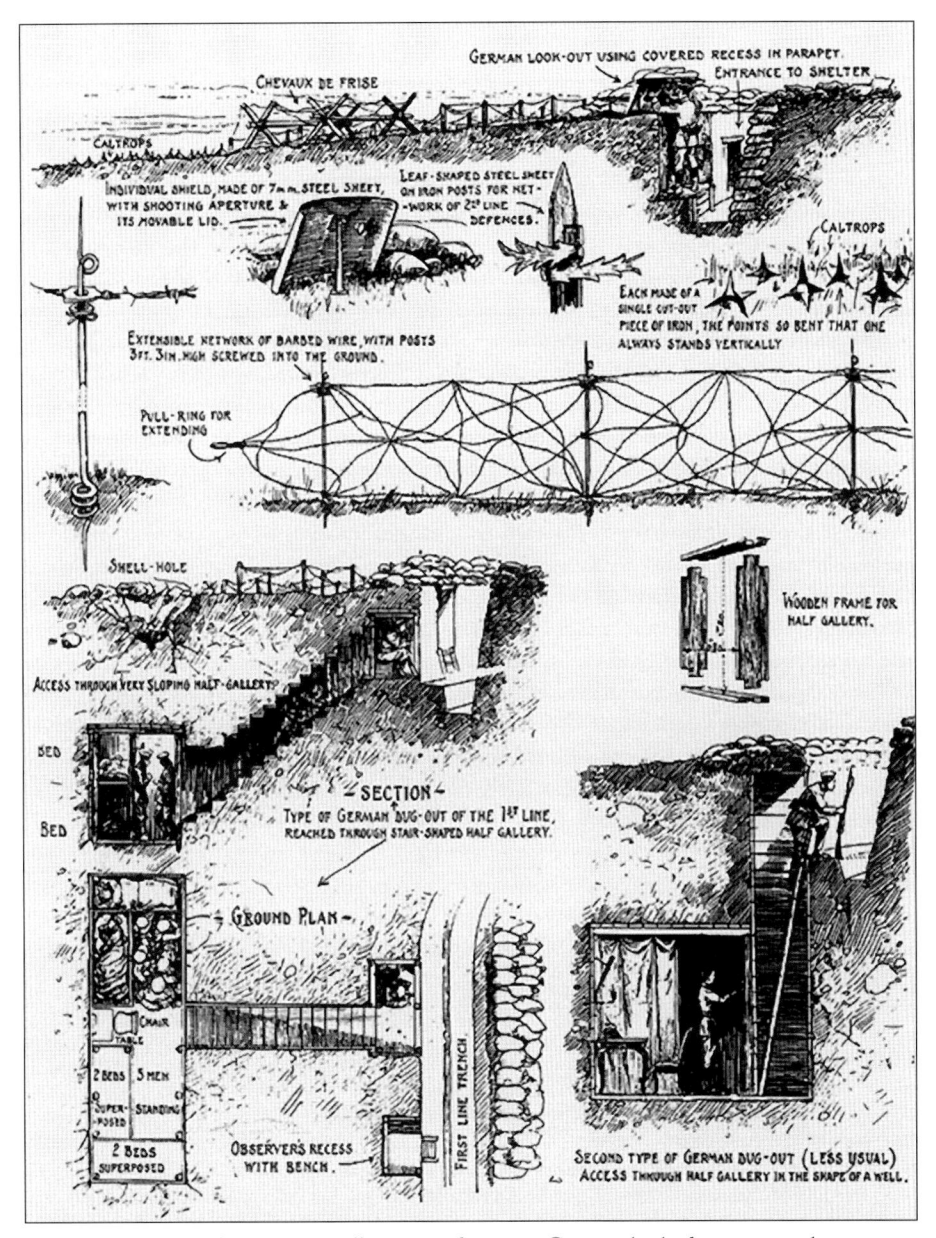

Contemporary diagrammatic illustration depicting German barbed wire entanglement arrangements, observation posts and mined dugouts of the kind constructed by the Thiepval defenders during the period 1914-16.

The testimony of Major E. Pease Watkins suggests that the observation of the front line was conducted by Lt J.W. Buckley (161st Brigade, RFA), rather than by Lt-Col. Cotton himself, as Edmonds suggests.[81] From the available evidence it is likely that upon receiving the reports of the 97th Brigade's advance, Cotton suggested the idea to Jardine and the decision was at least reached mutually. Whoever ordered the withdrawal of batteries from the fire plan is an interesting point, for neither had the authority to do so. Both Jardine and Cotton demonstrate that when acting upon sound intelligence and in co-operation with the other arms, decentralisation could have positive, and tangible effects. This largely relied upon commanders' confidence to break from the plan, and faith that the system would recognise the merits of the actions taken. Jardine knew the implications of the action: "This was of course, strictly contrary to orders but I believe, & some one [sic] later on told it me, that at G.H.Q. my action was quoted as being a case when orders should be disobeyed!"[82] That Rycroft warmly praised the action of his subordinates in his report to corps, should show that the BEF was not a centralised autocracy run through top down control.[83] On the ground it was up to individual commanders and leaders to evaluate the orders against the situation they found themselves in and act accordingly within the spirit, but not always the letter of the plan.

So far the examples have concerned the implementation of the pre-war principle of decentralisation at relatively senior levels of command. What about the lower ranks? At the lowest levels of the army men were willing to bend the rules or side-step impractical orders, but under the stricter conditions of a large structured attack the opportunities to do so were limited. More often than not it fell upon only a few individuals, namely the battalion commanders, to make such decisions.[84] The experiences of the supporting battalions on the right of the 32nd Division's line demonstrate that the same process was taking place on the front line. Between 8 and 8.30am the 11th Border Regiment (Lonsdales), 97th Brigade's reserve debouched from the relative safety of Authuille Wood.[85] Under the erroneous impression that the attack was proceeding well they were immediately hit by a hail of gunfire from the German strong points south of Thiepval. Shortly afterwards, at approximately 8.45am, the 1st Dorsetshire Regiment pushed forward towards the front line but were engaged on an artillery bridge near Dumbarton Track in the same wood.[86] Charles Douie recalled

---

81 TNA Cab 45/138: Major E. Pease Watkins, 15 May 1930.
82 TNA CAB 45/138: Brigadier- General James Jardine to Edmonds, 13 June 1930.
83 TNA WO 95/2368: 32nd Div., 'Report on Operations', p. 6.
84 Stuart Mitchell, '32nd Division on the Western Front' (2015), pp. 144-164.
85 There are some minor discrepancies on the timing: TNA WO 95/2399: 97 Infantry Brigade Headquarters. Appendix A suggests 8am; TNA WO 95/2368: 'Report on Operations', p. 6 places it at 8.30am as does Edmonds, *OH 1916*, Vol.1, p. 401; the latter are more likely correct.
86 TNA WO 95/2368 Report on Operations p. 6 records 8.45 a.m.; War Diary 1 July: 8.40 a.m. entry records 8.35 a.m., Edmonds, *OH 1916*, Vol.1, p. 409 recorded 8.45a.m.

the "unerring accuracy" of the German machine-gunners; "a platoon forty-eight strong on one side emerged with a strength of twelve".[87] Upon seeing the danger at the edge of Authuille Wood the 1st Dorsets attempted to find an alternative route but they were blocked by "barbed wire and other obstructions". Consequently when they left their position to reinforce the Leipzig Redoubt they did so in sectional rushes. Casualties were still heavy. Things got worse: still following the pre-battle plan, the 19th Lancashire Fusiliers, followed the Borders and Dorsets. Further casualties were incurred until Lt-Col. Graham co-ordinated the Trench Mortars who dropped a smoke screen, then used covering fire from the Vickers and Lewis Guns to allow his men to advance in platoon rushes.[88] Despite attempts to mitigate losses all three battalions suffered heavily and only fragments reached the newly captured positions. Many remained in the now chaotic British front line trenches. The 32nd Division's report to corps refrained from any criticism of these units, but the "Extract from Diary of 32nd Division 1st July to 3rd July 1916" found in "Ryecroft's [sic] General Diary" was blunt:

> The 11th Borders, which seeing that the right was held up should have been kept back in AUTHUILLE WOOD […] The 1st Dorsets, the leading battalion of the 14th Brigade was held up, should have remained under cover but also debouched into the open, followed later by the 19th Lanc. Fus.[89]

It is clear that Rycroft felt that the planned orders should have been countermanded on the ground when the results were clearly going to be disastrous. That they were not reflects both the inconsistencies in application, inexperience of the men, and the uncertainty of the situation. The fates of the three battalions contrasts unfavourably with that of the 2nd Manchesters, who were attached to 97th Brigade at 12.10pm and faced the similar challenge of getting forward. Rather than take the artillery bridge, Lt-Col. 'Corky' Luxmoore commanding the Manchester battalion had earlier consulted the nearby Trench Mortar crew to gauge the situation for the Borders, Dorsets and Lancashire Fusiliers. In doing so he was made aware of the dangers and told of another route "round by Rock Street". Luxmoore ordered the route reconnoitred and once found clear it was used. The battalion thus avoided the disaster that befell the others and two companies, under the cover of an intensive barrage, would reach the Leipzig Redoubt, where they played a vital role in consolidating the gains made.[90] Luxmoore's decision to break from the original plan was certainly significant. However it should be recognised that he had the benefit of forewarning and an

87   Charles Douie, *The Weary Road* (London: John Murray, 1929), p. 162.
88   By this point men and units begin to become muddled and the situation confused, the 19th Lancashire Fusiliers appear to have reached the front line by 10.25 a.m.
89   TNA WO 95/2398: 32nd Div., General Ryecroft [sic], General Diary, 1 July 1916.
90   J.E. Prince, 'Reminiscences of "Tock-Emma" Days' in Whinyates (ed.), *Artillery and Trench Mortar Memories, 32nd Division* (1932), p. 669. Luxmoore was known as 'Colonel Corky'

opportunity to liaise with his brigade commander, Brigadier-General C.W. Compton, who by 10.30am was aware of the disaster unfolding in the front lines.[91]

On 1 July 1916 there were command system failures at all levels. Decentralisation led to an abdication of responsibility at division and corps while battalion commanders generally stuck to the plans as they were set down before the battle. Criticism of the lower echelons should be limited. The battalion commanders were operating in the toughest of circumstances with little information and the chaos of battle unfolding around them. There were some notable occasions where initiative was exercised effectively and gains were made, and in time leaders would become more willing to take such actions. Rawlinson was not wholly wrong when he observed that the troops had "become accustomed to deliberate action based on precise and detailed orders."[92] The system was in place to be developed, the army had to relearn how to implement it effectively. This was perhaps best summed up by Charles Carrington who observed: "Enthusiastic amateurs when fighting began, the British were soldiers at the end, with the cynical notions and the prudent habits that professionals exhibit."[93]

Appraisal

An effective learning system requires a reliable method of feedback. By 1916 the BEF had developed an effective administrative system that encouraged analysis and reflection at the lower-levels. This system however, could be seriously hampered by authoritarian command structures. In the days following the 1 July the 32nd Division's feedback process began. Officers and men were consulted, reports were written and questions were asked. Units were required to write up narratives of their actions including any noteworthy observations. The result was a series of narratives at each level of command that highlighted the sequence of events as could best be discerned. Thus, battalions wrote accounts for brigade, who then analysed these and compiled a report of its own to be sent to the divisional staff, sometimes along with copies of the battalion reports. The division then brought these together to form its own report to be sent to corps. This continued until it reached GHQ.

Unit and formation war diaries also played an important role in the appraisal process. War diaries kept a record of day-to-day events, conditions, casualties, reports, orders and often opinions for each discrete unit and formation within the BEF. The quality of these diaries was highly variable with accounts of the first day

---

    on account of his prosthetic cork leg. TNA WO 95/2392: '2nd Battalion the Manchester Regiment July 1916, Reports on Operations', p. 2.
91 TNA WO 95/2392: 2nd Manchester Regiment, July 1916, 'Reports on Operations', p. 2.
92 See 'Fourth Army Tactical Notes' May 1916, Edmonds, *OH 1916*, Vol.1, Appendix 18, p. 131.
93 Charles Carrington, *Soldier from the Wars Returning* (London: Hutchinson & Co, 1965), p. 134.

Ruins of Thiepval Château, July 1916. (Anon., *Die 26. Reserve Division 1914-1918*)

Thiepval Château Park, July 1916. (Anon., *Die 26. Reserve Division 1914-1918*)

of the Somme running from one line in the case of the 11th Border Regiment to three pages in the case of 16th Lancashire Fusiliers. The war diaries were conceived of as a didactic tool from the outset. *Field Service Regulations Part II: Organization and Administration* (henceforth *FSR II*) laid out their purpose as "an accurate record from which the history of the war can subsequently be prepared" and secondly "to collect information for future reference with a view to effecting improvements in the organization, education, training, and administration of the army for war."[94] Copies would be made and compiled monthly before being sent up the chain of command. Eventually they would be sent to GHQ before being forwarded to the War Office at which point they would become the permanent record of a unit's movements, operations and methods. Pre-war doctrine established war diaries as an integral post-war source of information, and there is evidence that they played an important role during the war itself, helping diligent new commanders familiarise themselves with the service history of the formation or unit they were joining. The personal papers of Major-General Thomas Stanton Lambert include a significant collection of the war diaries and official reports for the 32nd Division covering their service in 1917. Lambert only took over command of the division on 29 May 1918 so it is likely these were the GOC's copies of the divisional war diaries and were retained by the divisional staff to be passed on to new commanders. It is difficult to say whether this was general practice or a novel quirk within one division but it would be entirely in keeping with the ethos of the army.

Perhaps the most notable products of the system of narratives were the "lessons learned". These discussed successful practices and advice for front line commanders. Frequently discrete lesson learned reports were produced.[95] More often lessons were captured in post-action reports and fed up the chain of command rapidly. In the fallout of the first day of the Somme, 97th Brigade's report hailed one of the few successes of the day: the opening of the Sanda Sap linking the British lines to the Leipzig Redoubt by the Pioneer battalion, 17th Northumberland Fusiliers. This was described as a "godsend" for both supply and communications.[96] The corresponding Divisional Report also recognised that it "proved of inestimable value" and furnished further specifics such as timings and the unit involved drawn from other reports and communications.[97] Reports were nothing new to the BEF: by 1916 the bureaucratic system extended beyond the assessment of major battles to encompass most actions.

---

94 General Staff, *Field Service Regulations Part II: Organization and Administration* (London: HMSO, 1909), pp. 174-175.
95 TNA WO 95/2368: '32nd Div., Points with regard to operations, 27 October 1916', Appendix 28; 'Lessons derived from experiences of 32nd Division in Recent Operations', November 1916, Appendix 26a.
96 TNA WO 95/2399: '32nd Div., 97th Infantry Brigade, 'Report on the Operations of the 97th Infantry Brigade 1st/2nd July 1916'.
97 TNA WO 95/2368: '32nd Div., Report on Operations', p. 7.

Learning from Defeat: 32nd Division and 1 July 1916   349

Feedback was gathered on patrols, raids and intelligence gathering to name but a few.[98] Furthermore, these were not restricted to narrative but contained practical feedback on new developments, techniques and technologies being employed. After a night raid by the 15th Lancashire Fusiliers, the after-action notes pointed out: "The protection afforded by the steel helmet was exemplified in several instances."[99]

Despite a degree of standardisation of procedure, different information was emphasised depending upon the branch concerned. After the Thiepval attack infantry units included large sections of narrative. The reports by the Commander Royal Artillery, Brigadier-General Tyler, and the Trench Mortar Batteries followed a template which did not include any substantial narrative but focused almost exclusively upon technical, practical and logistical points.[100] This pattern would continue beyond the Somme. The Trench Mortar report noted: "The general design of the Heavy T.M. Emplacement brought out by the 4th Army School of Mortars was adhered to and found quite satisfactory. Several minor changes however were found to be necessary."[101] Specialist feedback at divisional level, after the 1 July, made a concerted effort to bridge the gap between the best-practice being taught and that which was being used on the ground.

The system of post-action appraisal relied upon honest and straight-forward assessments at each level of command. This was not always forthcoming. As has already been documented, Rycroft avoided criticising his brigades and battalions after 1 July despite harbouring personal doubts about their conduct.[102] This was, perhaps, in part due to two commanders becoming casualties in the attack. Lt-Col. P. W. Machell of the 11th Borders was killed and Lt-Col. J. V. Shute of the 1st Dorsets was wounded. Rycroft slightly changed his approach after a failed follow-up attack by the 14th Brigade and attached 75th Brigade on 3 July 1916. He offered a critique on the conduct and employment of the attached brigade without overtly attributing any blame: "I believe that every possible assistance was given by my Staff and that of my Brigades but without doubt mistakes and delays did occur."[103] In truth evidence from the war diary suggests Rycroft was far from happy with his staff. On 15 July 1916 it was noted (and signed by the GSO I Lt-Col Wace) that: "The value of an untrained

---

98   For an example of 97th Brigade patrol reports from June 1916, see IWM, Major J. A. Jellicoe, P455; for raids see TNA WO 95/2397: '32nd Div., Raid Carried out 5/6th May 1916'; for intelligence summaries see TNA WO 95/2368: 32nd Division Daily Intelligence ssummaries, June 1916.
99   TNA WO 95/2397: 32nd Div., Raid Carried out 5/6th May 1916.
100 Information on shell usage, and tasks were included though. For example, 32nd Division 18-pdr batteries were targeting the German second line barbed wire defences. See TNA WO 95/2368: 32nd Div., 'Report on Operations … Divisional Artillery', July 1916.
101 TNA WO 95/2368: 32nd Div., 'Report on work of V. 32 Heavy Trench Mortar Battery During Bombardment and Subsequent Operations: 24/7/16 [sic] to 3/7/16'.
102 TNA WO 95/2368: 32nd Div., General Ryecroft's [sic] General Diary; Report on Operations General Staff.
103 TNA WO 95/2368: 32nd Div., S.G. 142/169.

GSO3 in active operations of this kind is very small."[104] Rycroft was more overt in his attempts at exonerating 75th Brigade's commander Brigadier-General Jenkins who "was confronted with many difficulties".[105] He failed and Jenkins was later removed by Reserve Army commander, General Sir Hubert Gough. Reading between the lines of Rycroft's report on 3 July attack, it is clear that he felt the failure was due to the changes in plans rather than personal errors.[106] That this was not explicitly stated, strongly indicates that reputation, self-preservation, and the preservation of others could 'soften' the honesty of reports, but even in the case of the fearsome Gough it did not fully remove it. Without a doubt, obfuscations, half-truths or outright lies were concocted in certain reports throughout the war, but even when the commanders of the 32nd Division had every reason to fabricate events they still stuck to the truth, albeit one that (wisely) avoided overtly criticising the Army Commander.[107] This was by no means a perfect system, but the infrequent abuses should not obscure the fact that generally reports were accurate representations of the salient problems; furthermore, there were no real alternatives to the system.

Feedback was not just sent up the chain of command. More assertive commanders would seek answers to specific points. General Sir Hubert Gough was one such commander. On 2 July 1916 the X Corps was moved to the newly formed Reserve Army under Gough's command where they were thrown into action the following day. After 14th and 75th Brigades' failure Gough had questions that needed answering. In a memorandum to 75th Brigade, he wanted to know where losses were incurred, by what means were units driven back and how the German machine guns could affect the attacking waves in the enemy lines.[108] He followed this up that same evening by descending upon 32nd Division's HQ and questioning Rycroft over the use of Stokes mortars, and his exact dispositions in the Leipzig Salient.[109] All of this brought a swift response from the 32nd Division, reports were gathered and answers supplied within 24 hours.[110] This process does not appear to have stifled recommendations from the lower ranks either. In response to the almost perpetual bombing battles being fought in the chokepoints of the Leipzig Salient, Captain Kentish, Brigade Major of 14th Infantry Brigade, hand wrote a note observing the German grenade's practical superiority and the ineffectual counter-measures available to the British infantry.[111]

104 TNA WO 95/2368: 32nd Div. General Staff, 15 July 1916.
105 Ibid. p. 5.
106 TNA CAB 45/138 Lt-Col E.G. Wace to Edmonds, 30 October 1936; TNA WO 95/2368 32nd Div. General Staff, July 1916, S.G. 142/169: Statement of Facts, p. 5.
107 Perhaps the most infamous example is Rawlinson's blaming of Major-General J. Davies in the immediate aftermath of the Battle of Neuve Chapelle (10-13 March 1915). See Prior & Wilson, *Command on the Western Front* (1992), pp. 70-73.
108 TNA WO 95/2368: 32nd Div., 3 July 1916: A.G. 142/167.
109 Ibid., 4 July 1916: S.G. 148/170.
110 Ibid., 4 July 1916: S.G. 140/170.
111 TNA WO 95/2368: 32nd Div., 13 July 1916, GI 8.

In recent years Gough's autocratic command style has been the subject of criticism, but, while flawed in application, his methods did draw feedback up from the front quickly.[112] Too often though Gough coupled this investigative style with overbearing control of his subordinates. This resulted in the effective abandonment of the decentralised system and *FSR I*'s principles.[113] Subordinates were deprived of the opportunity to apply earlier lessons leading to a series of poorly conducted attacks imposed upon them by Reserve Army.

3 July was not the only hasty, ill-prepared and ill-co-ordinated attack. After a period of rest and line-holding the 32nd Division was brought back to the Somme to take part in the final actions of the Battle of the Ancre. On 18 November Gough committed the division to an attack on the Munich and Frankfort trenches without their own artillery, any significant input into the proposed plan, nor a tactical reserve at brigade level. After the inevitable failure the division disseminated a memorandum on the lessons learnt from the operation.[114] These could be read as a charge sheet against Gough's decision making. It criticised the lack of available reserves, poor familiarity with the objectives and one of the final sections concluded: "In my opinion time and organisation are the keys to success".[115] The attack had neither. Yet it also demonstrated that despite the errors and strict oversight, internal divisional development still occurred, even if it was not always heeded universally, this was not "an entire system that did not work" but one commander who had failed to adhere to the ethos and principles that already existed.[116] The subordinate formations suffered accordingly.

The contrasting fortunes of 1 July for the British and French armies prompted analysis of the differing operational and tactical methods. The main driver behind this was Captain Edward Spiers (later Spears) who had penned a general report dissecting the reason for the French success in the South within 24 hours.[117] This was first sent to the Chief of the General Staff, Lieutenant-General Sir Launcelot Kiggell and then subsequently distributed down the chain of command to the Brigade level. It arrived at 32nd Division's HQ on 6 July where Rycroft dissected

---

112 Helen McCartney & Gary Sheffield, 'Hubert Gough' in Ian Beckett & Steven Corvi (eds.), *Haig's Generals* (Barnsley: Pen & Sword, 2006), pp. 75-96 and Simpson, *Directing Operations* (2006), pp. 38-39, 42-43.
113 TNA WO 95/2368: Notes G.S. 406/48, 5 July 1916; S.G. 142/175, 5 July 1916; CAB 45/138 E.G. Wace to Edmonds 30 October 1936. See also Simpson, *Directing Operations* (2006), pp. 46-47 and McCartney & Sheffield, 'Hubert Gough', pp. 81-83.
114 Simkins, 'Somme Footnote: The Battle of the Ancre and the Struggle for Frankfort Trench, November 1916', *Imperial War Museum Review No.9* (1994), pp. 84-101; Travers, *The Killing Ground* (1987), pp. 188-189.
115 TNA WO 95/2368: 'Recent Operations, [n.d.] November' 1916, Appendix 26a.
116 Travers, *The Killing Ground* (1987), p. 189.
117 Edward Spiers changed the spelling of his name to Edward Spears in 1918. In order to avoid anachronism, the original spelling has been utilised. Spiers was subsequently knighted for his liaison work during the Second World War.

the report and distributed it to his subordinate commanders the same day.[118] The report itself reflected the greater emphasis the French Sixth Army had placed on methodical, overwhelming artillery preparation and counter-battery fire. The role of liaison between levels of command, successful mopping-up, and well-handled reserves were also regarded as pivotal to the success of the French.[119] Rycroft saw the value in the artillery lessons, he noted at the end: "Our lifts were on experience much too quick."[120] Having also suffered at the hands of Gough's hasty, overzealous plans on the 3 July, it is also notable that Rycroft highlighted: 'The influence of the Army made itself especially felt in preventing a headlong advance …'[121] The Spiers report was not revolutionary but it drew attention to key areas of improvement which the British would take steps to address. Rycroft's comments show how the lessons of the first day of the Somme were interpreted through the lens of the commander's own experience. But perhaps the most important element of the report was how quickly it was disseminated down the chain of command. The administrative system that supported learning within the BEF worked rapidly and was generally successful in identifying the key areas of improvement.

The 32nd Division was an inexperienced formation when it went into battle on 1 July 1916. Yet, behind its failure lay a learning system based upon correct principles and reinforced by a widely accepted ethos that was ready to adapt in response to the baptism of fire on the Somme. Planning even if over-cautious and the implementation even when too ambitious were both rightly delegated to those who were in the best position to judge what was required. Under Rawlinson the tactical views of subordinates were discussed and commanders were given the freedom to adopt their own plans. Good ideas may have been inhibited by certain prejudices and concerns but in deferring to the 'man-on-the-spot' each commander could judge for himself. The feedback system reinforced this by establishing a common framework of reports and conferences, providing a mechanism through which experiences and lessons could be shared. The more technical branches overtly compared their practice on the ground with recommended best-practice; continually refining both in light of what was determined to be effective. While reports were subject to mild manipulation, they generally drew the pertinent lessons out, and quickly disseminated them both within the division and outwards across the army. The extent to which divisional lessons could be applied was limited by micromanagers like Gough, but this did not stop the process of feedback or learning. Inter-allied co-operation existed although it was interpreted through the lens of the commander's own experiences. Perhaps the biggest strength was the speed that

---

118 TNA WO 95/2368: '32nd Div., S.G. 142/177', 6 July 1916. This document was signed-off and dated by all commanders.
119 TNA WO 95/2368: 32nd Div., General Staff, 'L.S. 98', 2 July 1916.
120 Ibid., p. 3. Rycroft's emphasis.
121 Ibid., p. 2.

lessons could be shared. The ethos of decentralised command gave commanders freedom to experiment while the administrative system provided an effective tool to appraise the whirlwind of different approaches. Throughout 1916, the BEF had a solid systemic basis for learning based upon pre-war principles. It certainly had its faults, and was inconsistently applied by high command, but it ultimately proved to be the foundation stone for later success.

13

Cooperation on the Somme: The Application of Firepower on Pozières Ridge

Meleah Hampton

The Battle of Pozières Ridge lasted precisely six weeks from 23 July 1916 when I Anzac Corps captured the shell-shattered village of Pozières, to 3 September. Recently arrived on the Western Front from Egypt, I Anzac Corps was put into the British Reserve Army under General Sir Hubert Gough. The offensive against Pozières Ridge was the first major Western Front operation conducted by the antipodean corps and the beginning of the first extended series of operations conducted by Reserve Army.

Warfare on the Western Front was a complicated business. The British Army had learned painful lessons on the importance of combining infantry, artillery and other auxiliary arms. Arrangements and coordination had to be worked on and developed at each level of command from Army down to battalion and platoon. While it was possible for decisions and actions at each level of command, not to mention the ever present friction of war, to derail an operation, there were certain fundamental factors which dictated whether the attack would succeed or fail. One of the most important was the application of firepower, that is, the way the artillery would support the infantry advance. If this was ineffective, there was little chance of the infantry crossing no man's land, let alone fighting their way into the German position. One of the most striking lessons from 1 July 1916 was the absolute requirement for effective fire support.

Despite their lack of experience in the conditions of the Western Front, the commanding officers of Reserve Army, I Anzac Corps, and their subordinates were expected to plan and execute their attacks with little, if any, guidance from above. While the newly-appointed Army commander, General Sir Hubert Gough, had experience of conditions on the Western Front,[1] the commanding officer of

---

1   Gough had benefited from a meteoritic rise. He began the war as a Brigadier-General commanding 3rd Cavalry Brigade. In 1915 he commanded 7th Division at the Battle

the I Anzac Corps, Lieutenant-General Sir William Birdwood, had spent the previous year on Gallipoli or training in Egypt, and would find the change to the main theatre of the war a difficult one. His application of artillery was consistently poor, and in fact worsened over the six weeks of the Battle of Pozières Ridge. Operational plans that had proved successful in the past were not repeated. Instead, rushed, ad hoc operations with shortened objectives, little preparation and inadequate artillery barrages became the norm. The net result of this costly series of errors was 23,000 casualties in six weeks, with an advance of little over a mile.

The stagnant battlefields of the Western Front were a very different prospect from that anticipated before the war. Preparations for a war of movement and outflanking the enemy soon proved to be useless in the face of a deadlocked trench system hundreds of miles long. These defences would have to be faced head on, but with few established methods to do so. It was immediately obvious to all sides that technology was the answer, but the method of applying modern firepower to the problem varied widely both among and within different national forces. The Australian forces formed a contingent of the British Expeditionary Force, and as such were privy to the latest operational developments used by the British Army in its attempt to break the stalemate. For the first months of the war the artillery did not have the accuracy to do much more than destroy enemy trenches and barbed-wire entanglements.[2] From 1915 various British units had experimented with the use of falling curtains of shellfire that protected the infantry in the field, or even preceded them as they advanced.[3] The use of these barrages was still in its infancy in 1916. Technological advances improved the situation, but the correct use of barrages was not entirely established within British forces on the Western Front on the eve of the Battle of the Somme.

Thus when, on 23 July 1916 1st Anzac Corps' successful capture of Pozières involved a closely integrated artillery barrage, it was operating at the forefront of

General Sir Hubert Gough.

---

of Festubert and I Corps at the Battle of Loos. From 22 May he commanded Reserve Army.

2 John R. Innes, *Flash-Spotters and Sound-Rangers: How They Lived, Worked and Fought in the Great War* (London: Allen & Unwin, 1935), p. 21.

3 Major A.F. Becke, 'Coming of the Creeping Barrage', *Journal of the Royal Artillery*, Vol. 58, p. 20; Spencer Jones 'Toothless Lions: Firepower and Equipment in the British Army on the Western Front 1915', in Peter Liddle (ed.), *Britain and a Widening War, 1915-1916: From Gallipoli to the Somme* (Barnsley: Pen & Sword, 2016).

technical developments in warfare at that time. The division conducting the assault, the 1st Australian Division,[4] was new to the Western Front, and was heavily reliant on guidance from Reserve Army. While I Anzac Corps headquarters was still moving south from Belgium to establish itself on the Somme, Gough and his staff wrote the battle plan for the taking of Pozières, including the artillery barrages and circumventing corps command. The operation produced by Reserve Army headquarters was well-structured and incorporated a lifting artillery barrage. Three objective lines were given, each around 400 yards ahead of the last, leading up to the Albert-Bapaume Road which ran through the village. The first objective, Pozières Trench, would be subjected to three minutes' fire before the barrage lifted onto the second objective and the infantry moved forward to attack. After half an hour of firing on the second objective, the artillery would lift away to the third, a line along the Albert-Bapaume Road, as the infantry attacked and captured the second objective. Finally the artillery lifted to a fourth line and dropped a standing barrage of fire onto German positions just north of the road to provide protection to the third line of infantry as it rushed and captured its objective.[5] Each of these objective lines had to be consolidated once captured; the attacking wave of infantry that took it remaining there to work on defensive measures to ensure it could not be recaptured. This was an attack "in depth" that established and maintained a deep defensive line.

The plan worked. By 9am on 23 July, some 8 1/2 hours after the operation began, most of the objectives were in Australian hands and were being consolidated. The attack on the far right of the line had not been as successful, with infantry being held up by two particularly strong German trenches known as the OG Lines. This would become important for the next advance. But the positions that had been captured enabled the infantry to infiltrate the northern half of Pozières, which had not featured in the initial operational order, and within two days all the village was in British and Australian hands.

The artillery barrage on 23 July had been well-paced, well-spaced and heavy enough to keep the German defenders pinned down. It should be noted, however, that whilst an effective bombardment was a requirement of success, it was not enough *alone* to ensure victory. Myriad other factors, from a failure to properly address the threat posed by the OG Lines by Reserve Army, to clashes of personalities between battalion commanders on the field of battle, could have had enough impact to cause the operation to fail.[6] But without the overarching firepower from the artillery and the protection it afforded the infantry in the field, none of those factors had a chance

---

4   Unless otherwise noted, all references to numbered divisions refer to Australian divisions of I Anzac Corps.
5   Australian War Memorial (hereafter AWM): 4/13/10/22: 'Table of Artillery Tasks attached to First Australian Divisional Artillery Order No. 31', 21 July 1916, 1st Australian Divisional Artillery War Diary.
6   Meleah Hampton, *Attack on the Somme: 1st Anzac Corps and the Battle of Pozières Ridge, 1916* (Solihull: Helion & Co., 2016), pp. 31-59.

to come into play. The first factor to get right in trench warfare was the application of firepower, without which nothing could be done.

The immediate problem facing the Australian garrison in Pozières village was the presence of the German force holding the OG Lines. This pair of strongly defended trench lines were part of the German second line of defence on the Somme and as such were the main defensive position in the area. The attack on Pozières had resulted in the capture of an outpost position, and while Pozières was occupied, it was under constant threat of counter-attack from these lines. As a result the OG Lines were an obvious, and urgent, objective for I Anzac Corps. The 1st Division was exhausted following the capture of the village, and was relieved by the 2nd Australian Division on 27 July 1916. I Anzac Corps headquarters also had time to establish itself following the move to the Somme from Belgium, and would play its proper role in the operation to take the OG Lines.

Accordingly, whilst Gough set the basic parameters for this attack, it was left to Birdwood to give orders for "wire cutting, preliminary bombardment and subsequent artillery lifts."[7] The objectives for this attack were of necessity different from those at Pozières. In the first attack there was enough room for three well-spaced parallel objectives one after the other. But the assault on the OG lines featured just two objectives, the parallel trenches OG1 and OG 2, which were around 50 to 100 yards apart. Neither objective was close to the jumping-off trench, being around 400 to 500 yards distant. If an artillery plan similar to that for 23 July was to work, it would have to be modified considerably to deal with this different battle-field layout. Of necessity, the depth of the infantry attack employed at Pozières would be absent as the priority was capturing the OG Lines themselves, with little beyond.

Lieutenant-General Sir William Birdwood.

---

7   TNA WO 95/518: 'Artillery Arrangements No. 2 Reserve Army,' attached to Reserve Army Operation Order No. 15, 28 July 1916, Headquarters Branches & Services: General Staff.

The artillery plan in the first attack on the OG Lines was markedly different from that at Pozières and was completely inadequate. The preliminary bombardment was aimed at OG1, but it was timed to last just a single minute before moving on. From there, the artillery would fire a barrage upon OG2 for ten minutes. The barrage would then make two more smaller lifts at five minute intervals to a standing position beyond OG2. This programme was very fast – lasting just 16 minutes from preliminary bombardment to final standing barrage – and comparatively light, being fired at a rate of two rounds per gun per minute in comparison to Pozières' two to five rounds per gun per minute.[8] Furthermore, there was a worrying disconnection between the infantry and the artillery plans. Infantry orders called for the men conducting the attack to leave the safety of their jumping-off trench *before* the preliminary bombardment, creeping out into no man's land to be as close as possible to the bombardment once it started. This may have been inspired by the approach used by some British units on 1 July 1916 but differed in a critical respect: British units had crept into no-man's land whilst a heavy bombardment was *in progress*. The Australians planned to exit their trenches without any covering fire whatsoever. This was completely inadequate for the operation proposed, and paid no more than lip service to the concept of employing a lifting barrage to protect advancing infantry. Worse, it appears that the commanding officers of the Australian units, Birdwood at corps level, and Major-General James Gordon Legge, commanding officer of 2nd Australian Division, had made moves to modify – and almost certainly weaken - the barrage. In fact, Douglas Haig's artillery adviser, Major General Noel Birch, believed that Legge wanted to do away with it altogether, reporting that "the Australians had at the last moment said that they would attack without artillery support and that 'they did not believe machine gun fire could do them much harm'."[9] After hearing the reports, Haig put a stop to this, reinstating the original programme, but without any comment on its inadequacy.

On 29 July 1916, the artillery began its bombardment on time, and the infantry - most of which had, perhaps surprisingly, arrived at its jumping off point in no man's land with minimal casualties - launched its attack. But while the artillery successfully completed its programme, the infantry attack failed all along the line. As soon as the attack began it was obvious that the artillery had completely failed to suppress German machine-gun fire. In fact, the movement of troops into no man's land had alerted the Germans and they were fully prepared to meet the attack.[10] German flares were seen all along the line as much as half an hour before the assault began, and once it was launched, the advancing infantry was immediately met with a hail of machine

---

8   AWM: AWM 26/53/2:1st Australian Divisional Artillery War Diary Summary of Events, 28 July 1916.
9   Gary Sheffield & John Bourne (eds.), *Douglas Haig: War Diaries and Letters* (London: Weidenfeld & Nicolson, 2005), p. 210.
10 AWM: AWM 26/57/27: 'Report on Operations 28/29 July 1916,', 29 July 1916, Operations File Somme 1916, 6th Infantry Brigade & Battalions.

gun fire. Men later reported that "it was impossible to move without being seen."[11] The artillery not only failed to protect the men advancing across no man's land, it had also failed in its task of cutting the German barbed wire, either in preliminary bombardment or in the attack itself. Those men who reached the German wire found no way through, and many lost their lives trying to cut it with wire clippers. The operation was an abject failure.

Haig was thoroughly disgusted, writing in his diary that the Australian commanders "cannot be trusted to work out unaided the plans of attack."[12] He had good evidence for this statement. Most of the blame could be placed on the inadequacy of the artillery orders Birdwood put in place, namely those for the preliminary bombardment and wire-cutting, as well as the lifting barrage for the operation itself. At least part of the blame for this lies with Gough, however. He had a well-earned reputation as a "thruster" which manifested in impatience and a tendency towards reckless haste in pushing operations through. Major-General Harold Bridgwood Walker, commander of the 1st Australian Division, had resisted Gough's attempts to rush his formation into battle shortly before 23 July, gaining a few valuable days to prepare before launching the operation to capture Pozières.[13] Legge, on the other hand, had acquiesced to Gough's demands and rushed into the assault on OG Trench without even ascertaining if the wire had been cut during the preliminary bombardment. Gough's attitude throughout the Battle of Pozières Ridge was that it was "imperative to press the enemy constantly and continue to gain ground as rapidly as possible";[14] this attitude limited the amount of time allowed to complete staff work, or indeed preparation at the front, beforehand. Despite some attempts, like Walker's, to slow the pace of operations, I Anzac Corps soon took on a "culture of rapidity" which saw its divisions conducting a greater number of smaller, hurried operations, rather than pausing before taking larger, measured bites out of the German line as it did at Pozières.[15]

This lay in the future. First, the OG Lines had to be captured. Haig continued to observe the situation, and insisted that zero hour for the next attack should be determined by the completion of pre-battle preparations, rather than the amount of preparation possible being determined by an approximate zero hour. He told Birdwood that

11 AWM: AWM 26/56/4: 'Report on Action of 28/29th July Part I,' 14 August 1916, Operations File Somme 1916, 2nd Australian Division General Staff.
12 Robert Blake (ed.). *The Private Papers of Douglas Haig 1914-1919* (London: Eyre & Spottiswoode, 1952), p. 156.
13 For more on this, see G.D. Sheffield, 'Australians at Pozières: Command and Control on the Somme, 1916,' in David French & Brian Holden Reid (eds.), *The British General Staff: Reform and Innovation c.1890-1939* (London: Cass, 2002), pp. 112-26.
14 AWM: AWM 26/42/1: Reserve Army SG.43/0/1, 3 August 1916, Operations File Somme 1916, Reserve Army General Staff.
15 Hampton, *Attack on the Somme*, p. 210.

he was not "fighting Bashi-Bazouks[16] now – this is serious, scientific war, and you're up against the most scientific and most military nation in Europe."[17] Birdwood would have to come to terms with the role technology played in warfare on the Western Front to appease high command. Gough's impatience, too, was a problem. In this instance he was also reined in, not being allowed to rush the operation through until preparations were complete. Instead, he chafed as an appropriate jumping-off trench was constructed, and reports from artillery observers slowly came in to say that the firing plan had been successful in cutting the wire. When the attack finally went ahead on 4 August 1916, the battalions found the barbed wire thoroughly demolished. More importantly, the artillery barrage was both slow and strong enough to ensure that the German defenders were only just coming out of their dugouts to meet the attack as the Australians arrived. As with the success at Pozières, commanding officers responsible for the fighting along Pozières Ridge had another example of what could work – engaging in "serious, scientific" warfare methods through appropriate artillery barrages and useful preparatory measures to ensure as much safety for the attacking infantry as possible. Neither Gough nor Birdwood would heed these lessons.

The 2nd Division was exhausted following the capture of the OG Lines on 4 August 1916. In twelve days in the line it had lost 6,848 officers and men, and was relieved on 7 August by the 4th Australian Division. Under the command of Major General Herbert Vaughan Cox, the division was almost immediately called into action. With both the village and the OG Lines in Australian hands, the time had come to turn attention back to the overall objective for the operations along Pozières Ridge. This had originally been little more than keeping the enemy occupied while Fourth Army, to the right, conducted the majority of the Somme operations. However, success at Pozières had changed that. The day after Pozières was captured, it was revealed that "further operations of the Reserve Army will be conducted with a view to establishing ourselves at Mouquet Farm",[18] a fortified farm building to the north of Pozières. From there, I Anzac Corps would push to the north, dragging the rest of Reserve Army on its left flank with it. Eventually, Gough envisaged that I Anzac Corps would drive beyond Thiepval, cutting off the German stronghold and reaching a position to circle around to the left and attack it from the rear, before Reserve Army advanced the rest of its line to meet it.[19] The more advanced I Anzac Corps became, the less it would be obliged to coordinate with neighbouring Fourth Army.

---

16 Bashi-bazouks were irregular soldiers of the Ottoman Empire, known for their brutality and indiscipline. A Turkish word, bashi-bazouk translates literally as "damaged head", a reference to the wild conduct of these troops.
17 C.E.W. Bean, *Two Men I Knew. William Bridges and Brudenell White: Founders of the AIF* (Sydney: Angus & Robertson, 1957), p. 137.
18 TNA WO 95/518: Malcolm, Reserve Army to II Corps, VIII Corps, X Corps, I Anzac Corps, 15th Wing RFC, 24 July 1916.
19 TNA WO 158/334: 'Outline of Plan of Attack on Thiepval,' II Corps, 28 July 1916, Scheme "F."

Accordingly, Cox turned his division's attention away from the OG Lines and towards Mouquet Farm. The farm stood no more than 1,100 yards from the northernmost point of the village, around the same distance covered in the operation of 23 July. However, there were no plans for an operation similar to that at Pozières to cover the distance, either from Reserve Army or from I Anzac Corps. Instead the first operation undertaken by 4th Division was a diversion to distract German attention from Fourth Army's attack on the village of Guillemont some five miles distant.[20] The objective chosen by Reserve Army was a German trench on the way to Mouquet Farm, known to the British as Park Lane. It was an insignificant position, and accordingly, a small-scale attack on a frontage of around 900 yards was arranged for 8 August, the day after 4th Division took over the front line.

Although a small, diversionary operation, this attack still required an artillery barrage. It was designed to fall on the first (and only) objective for three minutes, before lifting on to a series of deeper targets. The infantry was not expected to advance beyond Park Lane. Conducted in lifts, this barrage plan attempted to produce a type of creeping barrage that became available only later in the war, following further technological developments in ranging and calibration. Each lift was around 50 yards further on from the last, and perhaps could have helped the infantry to follow it across no man's land. Unfortunately, the barrage began on the only objective for the infantry's operation – Park Lane. Each subsequent lift took the artillery away from the objective, with the smaller distances between each lift benefitting nobody. In fact, any lift beyond the first objective that was not a standing barrage – designed to block off the approach of German reinforcements – was pointless. What was to be achieved through such an intricate plan, if anything, is hard to say. Before the attack went ahead, Birdwood boasted that the 4th Division might be able to push on beyond the objective towards Mouquet Farm itself.[21] Although Gough put a swift stop to this loose talk, there is the possibility that Birdwood saw the artillery plan as a means to advance further than ordered. However, it is more likely that neither Birdwood nor Cox was entirely sure of the purpose of a lifting barrage, and they were unable to integrate one appropriately into their plans. It was a great deal of effort for little purpose.

This attack was successful, and the 15th Battalion, a well-trained and well-prepared unit, captured its objective. Although Park Lane was of little, if any, significance in terms of the overall position on Pozières Ridge, the ability of I Anzac Corps to report a success was considered important. In fact, it became of such importance that it overshadowed any previously planned movement towards Thiepval. It gave otherwise pointless, small-scale operations validity, and allowed Birdwood to repeatedly shorten

---

20 AWM: AWM 26/42/3: 'Reserve Army Operation Order No. 17', 7 August 1916, Operations File Somme 1916, Reserve Army General Staff.
21 AWM: AWM 26/50/16: Handwritten note signed RHS, 7 August 1916, Operations File I Anzac Corps General Staff.

the objectives given to him by Reserve Army. This further encouraged the "cult of rapidity", with each small scale success being celebrated despite the limited gains and growing loss of life associated with these 'victories'.

And so the next operation was against a single German strongpoint, Point 78, which lay on the far left of the previous Australian operation. It had withstood an assault by the 7th Suffolk Regiment that had been launched at the same time as the Australian advance of 8 August. The Suffolk attack had been little more than a strong bombing raid, so Birdwood took the initiative and planned to capture it with I Anzac Corps. Birdwood's fascination with Point 78 can only be explained through reference to the "cult of rapidity." The position, like Park Lane, had little material value in and of itself. A far greater prize lay ahead - the fortified compound of Mouquet Farm – which was comfortably within reach of a three-objective set-piece attack from Park Lane. Nevertheless, the minor operation against Point 78 was given precedence over preparations for any major advance, and the attack was ordered for the following day. It was so hastily arranged that there was not enough time to organise a formal artillery barrage. Instead a hasty bombardment was fired in the general area of the strongpoint, and the trench mortars were ordered to attempt an ad-hoc lifting barrage in coordination with the infantry. This was beyond the technical and tactical capabilities of the mortar batteries, which could do little more than fire on the objective for a short time, and then lift their fire away to an unspecified distance.[22] There was no sophistication or finesse to be found here – the objective was bludgeoned quickly with firepower before being stormed by the infantry. In this case it worked, with the 16th Battalion being able to report that the operation was successful, and that the battalion had captured 70 prisoners. This report was used to mask the fact that this "operation" was little more than a raid – less than a battalion's worth of troops capturing a single German stronghold. It was a success, but an extremely limited one.

More operations of this nature followed. They were all extremely small-scale attacks against nearby objectives with only a preliminary artillery bombardment of the enemy position before the attack was launched. Given their extremely limited aims, many were successful, resulting in some triumphant reporting. But these successes came at the cost of hundreds, if not thousands, of casualties. Although I Anzac Corps was inching the line ever closer to Mouquet Farm, none of these small operations coalesced into a larger-scale attempt to do something meaningful, and none addressed any but the least significant German strongholds and trenches in the sector.

On 12 August, Reserve Army ordered an attack which should have advanced I Anzac Corps' line by between 50 and 400 yards. This was far from the 1,200 yards captured on 23 July, but was at least designed to seize the major defensive obstacle in I Anzac Corps' sector: Mouquet Farm. But for reasons that remain unclear, Birdwood passed those orders on to Major General Cox, without listing Mouquet Farm as an explicit objective. Instead he left it up to his divisional commander to decide whether

---

22   AWM: AWM 26/60/6: '4th Australian Infantry Brigade Order No. 31,' 9 August 1916.

Australian 18-pdr field gun in action, July 1916.

or not to capture the farm at all. Cox chose to remove it from the objectives.[23] In this plan, success would be achieved when the front line skirted the southern edge of the old farm buildings, without attempting to enter or capture it. The artillery barrage for this operation made even less sense. On the far right, where the front line was intended to push out a marked salient, the advance was to be around 400 yards, or similar to a single artillery lift on 23 July. On the left, however, the artillery barrage was designed to fall on or only just ahead of the trenches already held by the 50th Battalion. The range was so close and the risk of friendly fire so great that battalion had to leave their current position and fall back 250 yards to facilitate the barrage, and then advance to recapture their own front line positions. At the same time the 145th Brigade, 48th Division of II Corps would conduct a bombing operation towards the 50th to try to establish a stronger link between the two corps. Therefore, on the left of this operation, the largest since 23 July, the advance was almost certain to dribble away into little more than empty attempts at conducting movement for its own sake.

This operation was launched at 10pm on 14 August and soon ran into trouble. On the right, where the 51st Battalion was making the greatest advance, the barrage had been very weak and began too far from the objective. At least four German machine guns were able to continue firing whilst the barrage was supposed to have been falling on them. A handful of small infantry detachments managed to advance and hold

---

23   AWM: AWM 26/59/6: '4th Australian Divisional Order No. 14,' 12 August 1916.

Pozières sector bombardment, August 1916.

on for some hours, but were forced to withdraw at sunrise.[24] On the left the 50th Battalion had been under heavy shellfire for the previous 48 hours, but remained organised enough to evacuate and "recapture" its own trench. However, the inaccurate artillery barrage fell on their old position rather than the German line. As a result, the 50th came under constant machine gun and rifle fire from the minute they evacuated their trench to the minute they recaptured it. The advancing infantry also ran into their own shellfire which failed to lift as scheduled.[25] The attack was a complete disaster. No ground was gained, and in fact the 50th Battalion managed to *lose* ground due to a nonsensical plan. The battalion recorded 45 men killed and 105 wounded before noon that day.[26]

This operation marked the half-way point of I Anzac Corps' period on Pozières Ridge. The corps had conducted more than six operations of varying sizes during this time, and had used a variety of different approaches. It had made significant advances at least twice, once in the capture of Pozières, and again during the successful capture of the OG Lines. These two operations had demonstrated the value of a preparatory barrage in destroying enemy defences and the benefit of a heavy, well-paced artillery barrage accompanying the infantry advance. They had also demonstrated some

---

24 AWM: AWM 26/61/15: '51st Battalion Operation Report August 13th-17th 1916', 15 August 1916, Operations File Somme 1916, 13th Infantry Brigade.
25 AWM: AWM 26/61/15: '50th Battalion Summary of Intelligence Received', 15 August 1916.
26 AWM: AWM 4/23/67/2: 50th Battalion War Diary, August 1916.

approaches to battle that would be detrimental. Rushing into operations without preparing "jumping-off" trenches or communication trenches, and failing to allow sufficient time for the guns to destroy enemy barbed wire, had resulted in failed operations and heavy casualties. During a number of attacks the enemy was able to maintain fire against the Australians, demonstrating that the artillery barrage accompanying the attack was not doing what it was supposed to do. And the most recent attack on 14 August showed the folly of targeting objectives that were too close to the Australian line– so close in fact that battalions were forced out of their existing positions and then obliged to recapture them. The fact that the 50th had not been able to do so should have reinforced the idea that this was a very poor tactic.

Unfortunately, it would appear that no time was taken to assess the results. Although there were many reports on "lessons learned from recent operations", these appear to have had no influence on higher level operational planning. The ability of commanders at every level, but particularly division and higher, to report the word "success" without a sensible assessment of whether that success was a significant contribution to the campaign meant that tactical development stalled and ultimately failed.

I Anzac Corps crept ever closer to Mouquet Farm – an objective it could have reached in a single determined attack similar that to which had taken Pozières – and at the end of five weeks held a line so close to the southern perimeter that the men in the trenches could literally reach out and touch the rubble of the wall. Australian soldiers regularly entered the destroyed farm compound; Lieutenant William Hoggarth of the 50th Battalion being the first credited with doing so on 12 August,[27] but were driven out by the Germans occupying the cellars and dugouts below. No attempt was made to organise the farm's permanent capture, and the small groups that probed inside the perimeter were ordered out on a regular basis. By mid-August all significant attempts to drive along the Pozières Ridge had ceased.

The 4th Australian Division was withdrawn after the operation on 14 August and replaced by the 1st Division which was now on its second stint in the front line. With the refreshed division in place, Gough began planning an attack to be conducted simultaneously by II Corps and I Anzac Corps. It was to take place on 18 August 1916, the same day as an operation conducted by Fourth Army to the south. The plan developed over the coming days and changed shape several times. It could have been used for one of two purposes – to further the plans of Reserve Army to advance beyond Thiepval before encircling it, or to act in close support of Fourth Army's operation. In the event Fourth Army's operation ended near the village of Martinpuich, some four kilometres from Pozières, and was completely disconnected from I Anzac Corps. But neither did the operation – ordered by Gough – serve Reserve Army's desire to advance beyond Thiepval. Instead, this new operation was little more than a

---

27   C.E.W. Bean, *The Official History of Australia in the War of 1914-1918. Volume IV: The AIF in France 1917* (Sydney: Angus & Robertson, 1936), p. 213.

jump from one trench system to another. In fact, 1st Division's attack would be further diminished by being split in half, one small force making the advance in the direction of Mouquet Farm, and the other making a small advance of around 150 yards towards Fourth Army. Its conception was similar to the small operations that were by now commonplace on I Anzac Corps' front and it promised equally limited results.

Walker, the commanding officer of the 1st Division, objected to a number of elements in the attack. He felt it wrong to treat the two operations as part a single, divisional action. The second operation near Fourth Army should, he reasoned, be deliberately coordinated with that Army's efforts. It was not. He also pointed out that the small advance towards Mouquet Farm constituted "a wedge driven along the main ridge, and as it advances is susceptible to enfilade fire from both flanks."[28] This extension of the salient which I Anzac Corps occupied was risky and ignored the overriding operational options: the Australians could either capture Mouquet Farm as a necessary precursor to further attacks or they could cease the advance along the ridge entirely. Yet Birdwood ignored these choices and instead chose to make yet another small step forward that worsened his overall position. Walker's protestations were ignored. Exasperated, Walker wrote to I Anzac Corps the day before the attack to say that "if due preparedness is to be permitted, the main operation should now be postponed till or after the 20th."[29] No inquiries were made as to the state of preparation of the 1st Division, or the viability of the operation; instead Walker was simply ignored and the two operations went ahead the following day. Although Walker had been successful in lobbying Gough for more preparation time before the assault on Pozières, he could not win this battle, probably at least in part because Birdwood failed to present his case to the Reserve Army commander strongly enough.

Both the main attack towards Mouquet Farm and the secondary one towards Fourth Army were launched under cover of a lifting barrage, but both barrages were very light and the fastest-moving yet, with each lift lasting just three minutes or less. Neither suppressed the defenders who directed a hail fire against the Australians. Worse still was the proximity of the barrage to the jumping off trenches. All of the objectives were extremely close to the Australian position. In the case of the attack towards Mouquet Farm, a significant part of the objective line was just 50 yards from the Australian trenches. Nowhere was the objective more than 200 yards distant. In many cases those conducting the attack were forced out of their own jumping off trench, either to deliberately facilitate the barrage, or to avoid it for the sake of their lives. Both of the barrages then raced away, leaving the attackers scrambling to reorganise and keep up.

---

28 AWM: AWM 26/51/30: Walker (GOC 1st Div.) to 1st Anzac Corps HQ, 17 August 1916, Operations File Somme 1916, 1st Australian Division General Staff.
29 AWM: AWM 26/51/30: Walker (GOC 1st Div.) to 1st Anzac Corps HQ, 17 August 1916, Operations File Somme 1916, 1st Australian Division General Staff.

It should come as no surprise that both of these operations failed miserably. Past experience with faulty artillery barrages were ignored and there was no consideration of the limitations of the weapon system itself. Although there had been significant advances in ranging and calibration of artillery in the first two years of the war, field guns could not guarantee consistent accuracy against a single target. Two rounds fired in succession by a single gun would not necessarily land in exactly the same place for a variety of reasons, ranging from barrel wear to meteorological conditions.[30] In July and August 1916 the "safety distance" from a target was 200 yards. That is, a shell fired at a objective could reasonably be expected to fall within 200 yards of that target and still be considered to be accurate. And so, when artillery barrages were drawn up for an objective 50 yards from the existing front line, there should have been a reasonable expectation that a good portion of the shells would fall amongst friendly troops. Every time these close-range barrages were delivered they resulted in heavy "friendly fire" casualties. More than one subsequent attack required the infantry to vacate their current positions to facilitate the barrage before attacking close objectives, and at other times the infantry complained that they should have been asked to do so but had not.[31] Yet despite these manifold problems such bombardments were used on multiple occasions. These artillery plans were invariably the responsibility of Birdwood and I Anzac Corps headquarters, and they were never corrected either by Gough or by his superior, Haig. Even at the end of August, objectives were too close to the front line for effective artillery barrages. They fatally undermined Australian efforts.

Reserve Army operations on the Somme had originally been limited to a supporting role on the left flank of Fourth Army. Gough required initial success in I Anzac Corps' sector in order to justify his actions in his area of operations, and hoped that an Anzac advance would pull the neighbouring corps along with it, and so on.[32] However, as time passed, Gough began conducting operations further to the left of his line without I Anzac Corps making the advance required. Rather than pulling the rest of Reserve Army along, I Anzac Corps stagnated. By late August, even the small successes against insignificant obstacles had dried up, and the high casualty rate was rewarded only with tactical failures. The blame for some of these problems can be laid at Reserve Army's door. Gough's impetuosity led to a constant push to hurry operations through, particularly in the early days of the battle. There were only a few occasions when it possible to thwart him; generally the rush to attack went unmodified and gradually became a feature of operations generated at corps and divisional level. At the same time, Gough removed himself from the planning process, spending

30 Innes, *Flash-Spotters and Sound-Rangers*, p. 21.
31 AWM: AWM 26/60/9: Durant (CO 13th Bn) to 4th Bde, 29 August 1916, 9.05pm, Operations File Somme 1916, 4th Infantry Brigade.
32 TNA WO 158/334: 'Outline of Plan of Attack on Thiepval', II Corps, 28 July 1916, Scheme 'F'.

much more of his time and resources on operations to the left of I Anzac Corps and leaving Birdwood to fill the gap.

The frustration for the historian in this process is that several important factors were clearly demonstrated as being of benefit in the attack. Strong, well-paced artillery barrages had been a noticeable element in the capture of Pozières and the OG Lines. Conversely, light, swift-moving barrages were disastrous, with many reports coming from the field complaining about unsuppressed German fire stopping the advance. But there is no evidence that either positive or negative reports made any difference to any subsequent plans. Birdwood and his staff were primarily responsible for the deterioration of artillery tactics at Pozières Ridge. Birdwood especially failed to demonstrate any development in his understanding or application of artillery barrages in the attack, and his actions went unamended as Gough either refused to recognise problems that might delay his plans, or turned his attention elsewhere along the line. Birdwood seemed to feel that technology lessened the level of achievement in any success. He once wrote to Senator George Pearce that the capture of Pozières did "not compare with the attack on Lone Pine in actual hand to hand and determined fighting."[33] He also displayed a marked reluctance to assign significant targets to operations, preferring always to shorten the objective to limit the difficulty of the operation and to be able to report a success – no matter how insignificant – to his superiors. His near daily small-scale attacks in mid-August were enough to appease Gough's desire for constant activity; without closer scrutiny of his methods, Birdwood had little incentive to reassess his method of command or the tactics of his corps.

I Anzac Corps first captured a fortified village on Pozières Ridge. It then captured a significant portion of the German second line of defence on the Somme. From there it took nothing of importance – in fact, nothing that could even be described without the use of map coordinates. Its dreary advance along the ridge achieved nothing to further Reserve Army's stated intentions and contributed little except attrition to the Somme campaign as a whole. As operations along the ridge wore on, the bar by which success was measured was steadily lowered. Throughout July the advance was measured by hundreds of yards, by late August success was reported when a battalion had evacuated its front line to facilitate an artillery barrage and then recaptured it. This farce may have resulted in reports of success, but it was not an accurate one, and it was not without its cost.

The infantry, slowly detached from their main form of firepower support, were put under further pressure by the hurried, small-scale operations. This was the war the Australian infantry knew on the Somme. Too often the "poor bloody infantry" were required to conduct operations that were so badly planned that on most occasions they were doomed to fail from the start. Lack of artillery support was combined with such problems as illogically reduced objective lines, unprepared jumping-off trenches and narrow-fronted, disjointed attacks, resulting in heavy infantry losses.

33 AWM: 3DRL/2222/3/3, Birdwood to Pearce, 1 August 1916.

Although I Anzac Corps began the campaign on Pozières Ridge with no experience in large-scale operations, it began well, with the capture of the village. But over the following six weeks, operational planning deteriorated until the infantry were attacking with little or no artillery cover – or worse, actually under fire from their own artillery – and attempting to take insignificant objectives that did not correlate with overarching plans on the Somme in any significant way. Too many orders given on Pozières Ridge were illogical and impossible to fulfil. The price for this folly was paid by the Australian infantry who lost large numbers of men dead, wounded, and missing.

There is little if any evidence of learning from previous operations at Pozières. The tragic August follies left I Anzac Corps in a shattered state by early September. The six-week campaign was costly and inconsequential. Whilst the capture of Pozières was an important gain, the failure to capitalise upon its seizure by continuing to advance against important objectives, and the stubborn refusal to learn lessons from previous operations, suggests that the Battle for Pozières Ridge was an abject failure.

14

Lessons and Legacy: Notes on 1st Canadian Division Attack, Regina Trench, 8 October 1916

Kenneth Radley

> Let us admit it fairly, as a business people should,
> We have had had no end of a lesson: it will do us no end of good.
>
> Rudyard Kipling, *The Lesson* (1901)

The attack on Regina Trench was no end of a lesson for the Canadian Corps. It helped to confirm and propel change, as evidenced by a December 1916 instruction by Brigadier-General Percy P. de B. Radcliffe: "Recent experience has proved that the present organisation and training of our infantry have not succeeded in developing the maximum offensive power bestowed by the weapons with which it is now armed." While Canadian experience during 1915 and at Mount Sorrel in June 1916 had resulted in a transition – "bees from flies" – Radcliffe's remarks reflected the earnest desire of Lieutenant-General Julian Byng, the General Officer Commanding (GOC) the Canadian Corps, and his staff and subordinate commanders, for more change, this time "hornets from bees." Arthur Currie, GOC 1st Division, in his dogged pursuit of the lessons of 8 October, during his official visit to Verdun in January 1917 and afterward, confirmed himself, most decidedly, as a "hornet" and a man for all seasons.[1]

---

1 Radcliffe, a British officer on loan to Canadian Corps, was the senior staff officer, the Corps' Brigadier-General General Staff (BGGS). Widely regarded as an "outstanding planner" and the "ablest tactician" in the British Army, Radcliffe joined the Canadian Corps from II Corps where he had also been BGGS. For further biographical information him and the contemporary staff system, see Kenneth Radley, *We Lead Others Follow: First Canadian Division 1914-1918* (St. Catharines: Vanwell Publishing Ltd, 2006); Library and Archives Canada (hereafter LAC) RG9IIIC1, Vol. 3839, Folder 34, File 1, Radcliffe to divisions, 12 March 1917; Martin Luther, *Whether Soldiers Can Also be in a State of Grace* (1526).

This chapter examines Currie's reaction to the failure of his division to secure and hold its assigned objective during the attack on Regina Trench. The primary focus is 1st Brigade, just as it was during the three investigations that followed the attack: first, Reserve Army's demand for a full account; second, the Court of Inquiry convened by Currie; and third, Currie's personal investigation. The records of the attack and the investigations add up to a stack of archival documents, all on foolscap-size pages, two inches high. Currie's diary provides additional information. Collectively these highlight the required remedial action, the impact on command relationships and the influence on Canadian Corps organisation, training and doctrine. Equally noteworthy and beneficial are Currie's notes on his visit to Verdun in January 1917.

Lieutenant-General Sir Julian Byng.

At first sight the reader may think the topic restrictive since Canadians also participated in the September attacks, five in all, but given the complexity of these battles and the confines of a single chapter, the topic had to be limited. An aspect that makes the October attacks stand out is structural, stylistic too, since the month displays, as an early account put it, a neat "unity of its own afforded by its main objective – Regina Trench."[2] While October encompasses the attacks on the first and eighth of that month, the essay mostly concerns the latter. There are several reasons for this: first, failure, which always cries out for explanation, especially when it comes at very high cost; second, the three investigations afterward (one would be inevitable, two unusual, three phenomenal); third, Currie's reaction during which he displayed an uncommon ability to clearly see the woods *and* the trees; and, finally, the stirring of some internal and external command dissent and controversy. While these may seem negative, a saving grace arises in the immediate aftermath and in the longer-term: "We learn wisdom from failure much more than from success. We often discover what will do by finding out what will not do."[3]

On 30 August the three divisions of the Canadian Corps (a fourth had just formed) joined General Sir Hubert Gough's Reserve Army, which had relieved the Fourth Army in the northern part of the Somme front. By this time 18 months' experience had

---

2 Sir Charles Lucas, gen. ed., *The Empire at War*, 5 vols. (Oxford: Oxford University Press, 1921-26), Vol. 2; F.H. Underhill, *Canada* (London: Clarendon Press, 1923), p. 139.
3 Brigadier-General J.J. Collyer, *The Campaign in German South West Africa 1914-1915* (Pretoria: Government Printer, 1937), Preface.

given the Corps a solid reputation. Robert Graves, recollecting a debate about which divisions were "dependable on all occasions" and which were generally recognised as "top notch," listed in that category the 2nd, 7th, 29th, Guards' and 1st Canadian Divisions. A German assessment of 26 August largely agreed when it grouped the divisions that might come against their *First Army* into three groups according to "combat-worthiness":

> Good: 47th, 6th, 20th, 50th, 18th, 1st Canadian, 2nd Canadian
> Medium: 11th, 39th, 41st, 3rd Canadian, New Zealand
> Poor: 61st, 40th, 60th, 63rd, 3rd and 5th Australian, 4th Canadian

These categories "were not intended to indicate absolute worth, but [their] effectiveness ... at a given time, as influenced by ... training, freshness, experience and battle losses." Six of these divisions would participate in the forthcoming attacks.[4]

The Canadian Corps was well led. Lieutenant-General Sir Julian Byng had commanded a cavalry division in 1914, then the Cavalry Corps in France. Thereafter he was GOC IX Corps in the Dardanelles and then GOC XVII Corps from February 1916. He joined the Canadian Corps under protest: "Why am I sent to the Canadians? I don't know a Canadian ... I am ordered to these people and will do my best." His best efforts were rewarded. He became familiar with his troops and they came to respect him. Three days after he joined the Canadian Corps at the end of May, he took it through the hard times at Mount Sorrel where in twelve days it suffered the loss of approximately 8,000 men. In the end, "The first Canadian deliberately planned attack in any strength resulted in an unqualified success."[5]

Byng's divisional commanders were Arthur Currie, Richard Turner and Louis Lipsett. At Second Ypres Currie had been far and away the best of the Canadian brigadiers, this bringing him command of the 1st Division in July 1915. Turner, GOC 2nd Division since August 1915, who had not shown well at Second Ypres or at St Eloi in March 1916, had come at that time close to dismissal. Still, on the Somme 2nd Division would "prove its prowess and re-establish its reputation."[6] The Germans had thought well of it at the Somme. Louis Lipsett, who took command of the 3rd Division after his predecessor's death at Mount Sorrel, had been the outstanding

---

4   Robert Graves, *Goodbye to All That* (Harmondsworth: Penguin, 1960) p. 152; Christopher Duffy, *Through German Eyes: The British and the Somme 1916* (London: Weidenfeld & Nicolson, 2006) p. 65. 4th Canadian Division would debut at Regina Trench in November.
5   Jeffery Williams, *Byng of Vimy: General and Governor General* (Toronto: University of Toronto Press, 1992) p. 115. Byng in both appointments came to like Canadians and Canada. The affection was heartily reciprocated by all Canadians, especially by "Byng's Boys," the veterans of the Canadian Corps. Brigadier-General Sir J.E. Edmonds, *Military Operations France and Belgium, 1916*, Vol. I (London: Macmillan, 1932), p. 241.
6   Colonel G.W.L. Nicholson, *Official History of the Canadian Army in the First World War: Canadian Expeditionary Force, 1914-1919* (Ottawa: Queen's Printer, 1962), p. 145.

Canadian dead near Courcelette, September 1916.

battalion commander at Second Ypres and in displaying equal proficiency as a brigade commander had become the best choice for a division. His 3rd Division, if not equal to the 1st, came a very close second. Of the "October" brigadiers George Tuxford (3rd Brigade) Archie Macdonell[7] (7th Brigade) and Frederic Hill (9th Brigade) would demonstrate their sound battlefield sense. One, Garnett Hughes, GOC 1st Brigade, would be found wanting by Arthur Currie. The eight battalion commanders would prove a solid lot, two later rising to brigade command.

When the Canadian Corps relieved I Anzac Corps near Poziéres, 2nd and 3rd Divisions[8] began preparations for the Battle of Flers Courcelette (15-17 September 1916) which would feature a creeping barrage and, for the first time, crawling machines known as tanks. The offensive enjoyed only minor success at a cost of over 7,000 casualties. A subsequent attack ten days later by Fourth Army gained more ground, but not Thiepval, an objective that had to be left to Gough's Reserve Army. His attack, when it came, aimed at seizing the whole of the Thiepval Ridge since doing so would prevent the Germans observing Reserve Army's rear area while giving British forces observation over the Ancre river valley.

---

7   This Macdonell, later Sir Archibald, would in time command 1st Division. His cousin, A.H. Macdonell, commanded 5th Brigade, 2nd Division.
8   All numbered divisions referred to from this point onwards are Canadian, unless otherwise noted.

374   At All Costs

At this time a boundary change split the front evenly, 3,000 yards each to the Canadian Corps on the right and II Corps on the left. For the subsequent attack 1st Division had successive objectives: Zollern Graben, then Hessian Trench and, ultimately, Regina Trench with its branching Kenora Trench. However, Currie was ordered not to go beyond Hessian Trench "owing to the uncertainty as to the condition of the wire in front of Regina Trench." Another obstacle, Sudbury Trench, which formed a partial intermediate line before Kenora Trench, proved to be "one of the deepest and strongest trenches" ever seen. Turner's 2nd Division had as an objective the extensions of these trenches beyond Courcelette.[9]

On the 26th the two-corps attack began. 1st Division quickly seized Sudbury Trench, but Kenora Trench, while entered briefly, could not be held, nor did the division get any closer to Regina Trench, extremely heavy casualties making further progress impossible. 2nd Brigade on the divisional left had partially cleared Zollern Graben and the left end of Hessian Trench by nightfall of the 27th, but not Regina Trench. Overall, a "not unsatisfactory" situation, as Corps Headquarters (HQ) somewhat nebulously phrased it, since 1st Division had "almost" reached the crest of the ridge. As for II Corps, it had secured most of Thiepval and the western half of Zollern Graben. Closing the gap that had opened between the two corps as they attacked became another task ordered by Gough for the next morning, 1st Division to seize Regina Trench and link up with II Corps. The former proved impossible since the enemy retained Kenora Trench and would do so for several more days. On the 28th, 1st Division was relieved by 2nd Division and 3rd Division's 8th Brigade also came into line.[10] Although attacks by 5th Brigade that day failed to gain Regina Trench, most of Hessian Trench was taken. No advance northward could commence until Regina Trench was secured as the new jumping-off line. This task would fall to 2nd and 3rd Divisions. At this point, Major-General Turner again expressed his concern that Regina Trench had not been hit hard enough – it lay beyond the crest – and the German wire had suffered very little damage.[11]

Hugh Urquhart, commenting specifically on the Canadian attack that was to come on 8 October, later offered this summary: "From their very inception, misfortune dogs the steps of certain enterprises and here we seem to be dealing with an undertaking of that nature." His assessment applies equally well to the attack on 1 October, for as Zero Hour (3:15 pm) approached and the troops waited in drizzling rain, "many were hit by our own shells falling short all along the line." Captain Robert Clements of

9   LAC, War Diary, Canadian Corps General Staff, Operation Order 55, 24 September 1916; Brigadier-General Sir J.E. Edmonds, *Military Operations France and Belgium, 1916*, Vol. II (London: Macmillan, 1938), pp. 396, 449; Kim Beattie, *48th Highlanders of Canada, 1891-1928* (Toronto: 48th Highlanders of Canada, 1932), p. 180.
10 Nicholson, *Official History of the Canadian Army*, p. 177; Edmonds, *Military Operations 1916*, Vol. II, p. 399.
11 LAC, War Diary, Canadian Corps General Staff, 1 October 1916. The diary noted that Regina Trench's garrison consisted of fresh troops of a Marine Infantry Brigade.

25th Battalion ascribed this to "confusion at some gun pits, one battery of 6-inch guns was given incorrect ranges and target information." Eventually the friendly fire stopped. That enemy fire added to the din - and the casualties – suggests that little counter-battery work had been planned or undertaken. Zero hour, when it came, must have seemed a relief, albeit a short-lived one. The rush forward brought worse conditions.[12] The intense machine-gun fire convinced the attackers that artillery had not dealt with the enemy trench to the extent anticipated. Further, uncut wire posed a terrible problem, one made more formidable by great quantities of concertina that had been set out to thicken the belts of wire. The results were tragic. One company was virtually obliterated in no-man's land. Two other companies lost half their men. While the second wave managed to enter a communication trench leading into Regina Trench a vicious bombing contest erupted and a block had to be built in the communication trench to stop enemy penetration. While this held, it also prevented further progress. An element of 5th Canadian Mounted Rifles (CMR) did get into Regina Trench, but repeated counter-attacks had driven the few survivors out by the morning of 2 October.[13]

Major-General Arthur Currie.

5th Brigade, to the right of 8th Brigade, had an equally severe trial. In view of the heavy casualties suffered in earlier assaults, the GOC, A.H. Macdonell, used three battalions for his attack, the 22nd, 24th and 25th. The first, which had to advance about a half-mile to reach Regina Trench, lost heavily under intense artillery and machine-gun fire while enroute to wire entanglements that displayed little evidence

---

12   Hugh M. Urquhart, *The History of the 16th Battalion (The Canadian Scottish Regiment) Canadian Expeditionary Force in the Great War 1914-1919* (Toronto: Macmillan, 1932), p. 179; LAC, 8th Brigade War Diary, October 1916, Appendix A, "Report on Operations 27 September–3 October 1916"; Brian Douglas Tennyson, ed., *Merry Hell: The Story of the 25th Battalion (Nova Scotia Regiment) Canadian Expeditionary Force 1914-1919: Captain Robert N. Clements, MC* (Toronto: University of Toronto Press, 2013), p. 155.

13   Captain S.G. Bennett, *The 4th Canadian Mounted Rifles 1914-1919* (Toronto: Murray Printing Company Limited, 1926), pp. 37-40. The 1st, 2nd, 4th and 5th CMR were raised as cavalry, but served as infantry. The title CMR was an historically based salute to the volunteer cavalry units that had fought in the South African War.

of damage. Fewer than 50 men actually reached Regina Trench from which bayonet and bomb attacks quickly drove them out. 24th Battalion's advance, which struck at the junction of Regina and Kenora Trenches, established blocks 50 yards either side of the junction. The 25th, the centre assault battalion, soon saw that the Germans had managed to repair any damage to their wire: "great rolls of concertina rolled out… to plug gaps" defeated any attempt at penetration. Relentless artillery fire stopped a second try an hour or so later, the men scrambling into shell holes as they were created. When the fire gradually died away an observer described "heads [popping] up from shell holes…There was not anything funny about it, but they did look almost like a field of gophers." A third attempt proved equally fruitless. Casualties were now so severe that the 25th could muster just 89 officers and men by the end of the day. 5th Brigade, after five days' fighting, stood at 770 all ranks. On the right, 4th Canadian Brigade advanced some 400 yards coming into line with Fourth Army. Weather then shut down any further large-scale operations.[14]

During that week of relative quiet, redeployment gave the left brigade sector to II Corps and 1st Division relieved Turner's worn-out 2nd Division. Come Zero day on the 8th, the Canadian sector would have in line from the left A.C. Macdonell's 7th Brigade and F.W. Hill's 9th Brigade, both of 3rd Division, and then 1st Division's 3rd Brigade (Tuxford) and 1st Brigade (Garnett Hughes). Canadian Corps objectives were Regina Trench from 500 yards west of the Regina-Kenora junction east to and including the infamous "Quadrilateral," a feature formed by the "intersection of a double row of trenches…with the dual trench system of the old German Third or La Sara Position" and, ultimately, a German trench on the high ground between Courcelette Trench and the West Miraumont Road. Once secure, Regina Trench would be Reserve Army's jumping-off line for the attack northward.[15]

Prior to the attack all advanced posts were linked to form a new jumping-off line that at some points lay only 300 yards short of Regina Trench. The artillery was kept busy, too, thanks to the Germans who nightly repaired the wire cut daily by the gunners. Both sides of this fearful symmetry were remarked upon by daily reconnaissance patrols; fearful for sure, the tiger in the night, so to speak, being wire that would once again prove its power to deny success. The antonym – failure – usually gives way

---

14 LAC, 5th Brigade War Diary, 'Report of 22nd Battalion, 5 October 1916' and 'Summary of Operations, October 1916,' Canadian Corps General Staff War Diary, 1 October 1916; Tennyson, *Merry Hell*, pp 156-58.
15 Nicholson, *Official History of the Canadian Army*, pp. 180, 184; Edmonds, *Military Operations 1916*, Vol. II, pp. 449-51 and Sketch 43 (facing p. 449). George Tuxford had raised the 5th Battalion in Saskatchewan at the outbreak of war. Despite his rough and outspoken manner he made a solid reputation for himself as a battalion commander and did likewise as a brigadier. Hughes, on the other hand, had a mixed reputation. Some thought he had been pushed on too fast (he had not commanded a battalion) thanks to the interference of his father, Major-General Sir Sam Hughes, Minister of Militia. However, others thought him a really good soldier and a fine brigade commander.

to stronger terms. There being no suspense to ruin, one can say at this point that the attack on 8 October on Regina Trench failed, a failure later described variously as debacle, disaster or fiasco. Debacle it was not, or so the *Concise Oxford Dictionary* informs us; disaster, in the sense of "sudden misfortune" it was, but only partly, the "sudden" not fully applicable; fiasco – failure – it certainly was. It remains to say why.[16]

During the night of the 7 October the assault battalions of 7th Brigade, the 49th and the Royal Canadian Regiment (RCR) moved into the line, the 49th being the most westerly battalion of the brigade and of the Canadian Corps. The next morning at 4:50am the brigade would attack into the mouth of the "Y" formed by the West Miraumont and the "Twenty-Three" Roads. That night, once relief of the 42nd Battalion ended, patrols sent to check enemy wire found it remained a substantial obstacle. The RCR also had a crucial responsibility in that once it seized Kenora Trench it would have to work westward along Kenora to where it joined Regina Trench. Should it fail in this, the attacking 49th would face fire from its front and from the right. The RCR made a good start, gaining Kenora Trench quickly and securing it along a two-company frontage, losses having been fewer than expected. Bombing along the trench toward the junction progressed well, but slowed when the bombers began taking fire from the right rear because the neighbouring battalion of 9th Brigade (43rd) had not kept pace. Soon the RCR found both flanks in the air and counter-attacks coming in from three directions. In the end, the RCR was ejected from Regina Trench, the 130 or so survivors being forced to withdraw to where they had begun the day.[17]

Brigadier-General Garnett Hughes.

---

16 Paddy Griffith, *Battle Tactics of the Western Front: The British Army's Art of Attack, 1916-1918* (London: Yale University Press, 1994), p. 187; R.C. Fetherstonhaugh, *The 13th Battalion Royal Highlanders of Canada 1914-1919* (Montreal: The 13th Battalion Royal Highlanders of Canada, 1925), p. 142; Nicholson, *Official History of the Canadian Army*, p. 186.
17 R.C. Fetherstonhaugh, *The Royal Canadian Regiment 1883-1933* (Montreal: Gazette Printing Company, 1936), p. 254; G.R. Stevens, *A City Goes to War* (Brampton: Charters Publishing Company, 1964), p. 61.

From the start the 49th Battalion endured extremely heavy shelling that caused many casualties. Soon it became apparent that the attack had lost direction, having veered northeast instead of northwest toward Regina Trench. No entry had been made there; indeed, two of Lieutenant-Colonel Griesbach's three companies were "in the blue." By noon, fearing a counter-attack on his attenuated and scattered battalion, which had no appreciable stock of bombs and with no organised defence possible, Griesbach ordered the remnants to join the RCR, some of whom were still clinging to Kenora Trench. When the fighting ended and there was time to take stock the toll was grim: of the 49th every other man was a casualty; 10 officers and 203 other ranks (ORs) were killed, wounded or missing. The RCR, the only Regular regiment in the Canadian Army, lost 289 all ranks.[18]

Griesbach's report is clear as to what had caused failure. The loss of direction by two companies he believed was due to a misaligned guiding tape, it having being put down more nearly parallel to Kenora Trench than to Regina Trench, which accounted for the deflection. Of his missing companies he wrote "They went straight for the objective; they disappeared over the crest...and have not been seen since." But the primary cause of failure came down to this: enemy trenches and strong points not touched by heavy artillery. One of his officers reported Regina Trench "practically untouched: very deep, very strong and filled with men." As for field artillery, Griesbach called it quite useless for wire cutting and for destroying enemy positions. Wire remained an obstacle even though the outer wire was cut to pieces. The officer referred to reported even worse news: "Our own artillery fire which came on about 3:30 pm and was evidently directed at the Trench was all short and fell to the rear...It consisted of 18 pounder shrapnel and H.E. and of heavier guns...None of it reached the enemy trench, nor his wire." Unsuppressed enemy machine-guns swept the front and accounted for many casualties. In the actual fighting in the trenches "enemy bombers out-threw our bombers by ten or twelve feet...a disparity very noticeable." It is clear which arm of the service Griesbach blamed for the failure of the attack.[19]

Little can be said about 9th Brigade's attack, which is not to disparage it. Both attacking units found the enemy wire mostly uncut, the 58th Battalion's War Diary describing the entanglements as not damaged by artillery fire "to any appreciable extent." In his report Lipsett summarized it as "Not satisfactorily cut" along the whole of his division front, this one of two causes for failure, the other in his mind, being the inadequate artillery support that left enemy trenches largely undamaged. Very few

18   Edward Fraser and John Gibbons, *Soldier and Sailor Words and Phrases* (London: George Routledge and Sons Ltd., 1925), p. 28. In the Blue meant "Failure. Something gone wrong. An attack that broke down, or troops who got out of touch, would be said to be in the blue." Fetherstonhaugh, *The Royal Canadian Regiment*, pp. 62, 254; Stevens, *A City Goes to War*, p. 64.
19   LAC, 49th Battalion War Diary, Appendix to October 1916; 3rd Division War Diary, Appendix, Statement of Lieutenant W.S. Hefferman to Canadian Corps, 14 October 1916.

men got into German position. Of the one company that did only 10 men returned. 9th Brigade's casualties totalled 34 officers and 907 Other Ranks, 43rd Battalion being particularly hard hit. Major Charles Gordon, chaplain of the 43rd, recalled after the war how his commanding officer had refused to allow him to accompany the battalion at Regina Trench: "I said goodbye…with an ominous foreboding … An awful sense of desolation swept over me…Except for a poor remnant I never saw them again."[20]

Next in line to the 9th Brigade stood Tuxford's 3rd Brigade, his assault battalions being the 13th, on the left, under Lieutenant-Colonel G.E. McCuaig, who had been CO for only 12 days, his predecessor having been killed in action in the attack on 26 September. On 7 October as the Battalion practised "battalion in the attack" McCuaig issued his first ever operation order as CO. Sharp at Zero (4:50 a.m.) the first wave was over the parapet, about 800 yards to go to Regina Trench, direction for once not a problem since a line of telegraph poles led straight to the objective. Considerable time elapsed, no news being perhaps good news, but then McCuaig and his battalion headquarters were shocked by the arrival of a wounded, mud-coated runner who delivered an immediate and graphic report: "Sir, we're buggered." More reports revealed that the 13th had encountered "a great mass of uncut wire." As dawn broke and efforts to get through it continued, the strong garrison cut the attackers down, leaving long ribbons of dead and dying. One observer counted over 300 bodies "hanging on the wire." Of the 17 officers and 360 men who attacked, only four and 72 remained: "Surely the Battalion bore the mark of…that place of evil which was the Somme."[21]

Of Lieutenant-Colonel J.E. Leckie's 16th Battalion, the right assault unit, perhaps 100 men got into Regina Trench. Checked by uncut wire they had persevered, despite the high cost, and had been played in by Piper James Richardson who then exchanged his pipes for bombs, materially assisting in beating off a series of counter-attacks. Hand-to-hand fighting raged in the trenches, the bombers doing their best to prevent enemy reinforcements getting into the 16th's enclave, using German stick bombs when their own stock ran out. Before the retirement, necessitated by the withdrawal of units of 1st Brigade, Richardson disappeared; probably the victim of the rain of German grenades that had driven in both flanks of the 16th. This young piper would not know that his valiant action had won him the Victoria Cross. At nightfall the battalion's

---

20   LAC, 9th Brigade War Diary, 'Narrative,' October 1916; Military Advisory Board, *Canada in the Great World War; an Authentic Account of the Military History of Canada from the Earliest Days to the Close of the War of the Nations, Vol. IV. The Turn of the Tide* (Toronto: United Publishers of Canada Limited, 1920), p. 76; Charles W. Gordon, *Postscript to Adventure: The Autobiography of Ralph Connor* (New York: Farrar & Rinehart, 1938), pp. 263-64. Gordon, who wrote under the name Ralph Connor, became the most successful Canadian novelist of the early 20th century.
21   Fetherstonhaugh, *13th Battalion*, pp. 6, 138-41; McCuaig was appointed Adjutant of the battalion on mobilization in 1914. Canon Frederick George Scott, *The Great War As I Saw It* (Vancouver: Clarke & Stuart Co., 1934) p. 95.

remnants managed to return to their departure point of that morning.[22] Afterward, as the 16th marched out of its trenches Private H. Hines and his chums in the 72nd Highland Battalion, hearing that the 16th was coming, lined the road to cheer them, but "there was no cheering. There wasn't 110 men in the whole unit." Private Stewart Scott added when seeing the 3rd Brigade pass, "We didnt like what we saw. Battalions commanded by Subalterns and what were units of company strength were battalions. We were sobered." In November, when the new 4th Division moved into the 16th's old trenches, Private C. Swanson remarked as to how the 16th "had got pretty badly shot up. The trench was filled with bodies of the 16th Canadian Scottish. That was our baptism."[23]

Turning now to Garnet Hughes' 1st Brigade, its two assault battalions, the 3rd, temporarily under Major W.M. Yates of 2nd Battalion, and Lieutenant-Colonel William Rae's 4th Battalion, would experience the "serious mauling" inflicted on all the assault battalions by the Marine Infantry Brigade of the 8th German Division. However, 1st Brigade's attack did begin rather well: it advanced "to the Le Sars line without a check and secured it from Dyke Road to a point 400 yards beyond the Quadrilateral." In itself, capture of this feature posed a considerable challenge, it being a "task of special difficulty [and] great strength." Both units had "little" difficulty in reaching Regina Trench, within a mere 10 minutes, according to the history of the 3rd Battalion. This unit also found no particular difficulty entering the Quadrilateral.[24]

Rae's 4th Battalion did not fare as well. Unlike the 3rd, it encountered uncut wire, thick belts of it, and in trying to find gaps Lieutenant W.H. Joliffe, then the most junior Subaltern in the unit, described the sinking feeling of being "sitting ducks" as the men bunched up, becoming easy targets for enemy fire. Eventually the 4th veered left around the wire and in so doing entered the enemy trenches at the same point as the 3rd, resulting in great congestion until the two units commenced bombing to the south and east, in the process taking almost 200 prisoners. However, rapid

---

22 Urquhart, *16th Battalion*, pp. 180-84; Scott, *The Great War As I Saw It*, p. 95; LAC, RG9IIIC3, Vol. 4080, Folder 4, File 2, statements of Lieutenant-Colonel C.W. Peck, Lieutenant E.B. Hart and Sergeant F.M. Watts; Colonel C.W. Peck, VC, DSO, "The Story of Piper Richardson, VC," *Canadian Defence Quarterly* 7 (October 1929): 93-96; News Release, Office of the Premier of British Columbia, 8 November 2006: "War Hero's Pipes Received in Ceremony." Richardson's pipes, considered lost forever, were found decades later at Ardvreck School in Crieff, Scotland. In 2006 they were repatriated and are now on display at the Parliament Buildings at Victoria, BC.
23 LAC, RG 41, Canadian Broadcasting Corporation (hereafter CBC) Interviews of Great War Soldiers, No. 8, 'The Somme.'
24 Jack Sheldon, *The German Army on the Somme 1914-1916* (Barnsley: Pen & Sword, 2005), p. 318; Edmonds, *Military Operations 1916*, Vol. II, p. 451; Military Advisory Board, *The Turn of the Tide*, p. 74; Nicholson, *Official History of the Canadian Army*, p. 184; Major D.J. Goodspeed, *Battle Royal: A History of the Royal Regiment of Canada, 1862-1962* (Toronto: The Royal Regiment of Canada Association, 1962), p. 163.

expenditure of bombs depleted the stock available and with none coming forward, soon none were to be had.[25]

When around 1 pm the first of the inevitable counter-attacks began coming in from both northeast and northwest the situation took a rapid downward turn. Private William Thomas, 4th Battalion, recalled how "We ran out of Mills grenades and… we had just our rifles, and he certainly gave it to us." A series of attacks in strength and characterised by an endless rain of bombs, eventually drove a wedge between the 3rd and the 4th and then drove them down the trenches in opposite directions. With no bombs and no ammunition for the one surviving Lewis gun, some survivors kept to the trenches while others moved to shell craters. At this stage, only two of the 14 officers of the 3rd remained. Lieutenant W.A. Chatterton, the sole surviving Subaltern, in attempting to organise a bayonet counter-attack, had to act very sternly, shooting "some of our men…who could not be induced to counter-attack." His desperate charge, accompanied by a handful of men, failed. Shot through the shoulder, Chatterton crawled into the trench, tied his arm in a sling, rallied more men and launched another bayonet charge. He was killed, as was an officer of the 4th who attempted a similar effort. In the end, as Arthur Currie wrote, "After Chatterton's gallant effort, the men drifted back to our old line. They had seen two bayonet rushes broken up with the officers leading them killed, the bombs were gone and it seemed impossible to hold on any longer." By 6 pm the few survivors of the 4th were forced into the lines of the 23rd British Division. Private Charles Brown was enormously fortunate. Lying in a shell crater he was found by a German medical corps sergeant who tended to his wounds and said in excellent English "There you are, Canada, that'll do until they find you. I've got to hurry up and get out of here. I'll be caught myself." Brown never forget this incredibly honourable act. Later he was picked up by men of the 8th Battalion which relieved the 4th on the night of 9 October. What was left of the 3rd withdrew to the original Canadian line covered by Corporal W. Walsh who collected a few bombs from the dead and acted as rear-guard. He, too, was killed. Of the 14 officers and 481 ORs who had attacked, just one officer and 85 men remained.[26]

On coming out of the line on Monday 9 October, few in 1st Brigade would have thought that an ordeal of a different kind awaited it. For some, officers primarily, there would be the prying interrogations of not one, but three "investigations." Of the four brigades that attacked on 8 October only the 1st would be singled out, which may seem strange since it had done no worse than the others. In fact, its "better" performance,

25 LAC, RG 41, CBC interview, Lieutenant Joliffe, No. 8, 'The Somme.' Joliffe after the attack found himself the Senior Subaltern. War Diary, 3rd Battalion, 8 October 1916.

26 LAC, 1st Division General Staff War Diary, Appendix 16, report of Major-General Currie's investigation with "Finding of Court of Inquiry," 16 October 1916; RG 41, CBC interviews of Privates William Thomas and Charles Brown and Lieutenant Joliffe, No. 8, "The Somme;" Goodspeed, *Battle Royal*, pp. 164-65; Military Advisory Board, *The Turn of the Tide*, p. 75.

and especially how prematurely success was reported, "fingered" the 1st Brigade. The key is in Currie's diary, his entry for the day of the attack reading "Attack … in conjunction with 3 Division. They fail absolutely. Our 13th Battalion fails on account of uncut wire. 16, 3 and 4 Battalions succeed." He made no entry for 9 October, but for the 10th we read "Order Board to investigate action of 3 and 4 Battalions" and for the 14th (the next entry) "Conduct personal investigation of retirement of 3 and 4." On the Somme, a word like "success" going up the chain of command and/or the staff net, formally or informally, would put a smile on many a face, each of which would settle into gloom and a glower of disappointment when a correction such as "retirement" appeared. That word in itself, like withdrawal or retreat, conjures up all sorts of evil and screams out for answers. In the resultant search for how and why success faded into "retirement", Garnet Hughes and his brigade became the centre of attention. Whilst 3rd Brigade, which had been next to the 1st during the attack, would be questioned, the process there would be far less arduous.[27]

The chain of investigation began on Tuesday, 10 October, with the receipt of Reserve Army's demand for a full report on the attack of 8 October. Corps sent this immediately to 1st and 3rd Divisions directing "report by 12 noon on 12th Oct." Currie wasted no time: that same day his order for a "Board" went to Brigadier-General G.S. Tuxford, GOC 3rd Brigade, as President. The other members of this Court of Inquiry, selected by Currie, were Lieutenant-Colonel C.E. Bent, CO 15th Battalion, and Major L.P. Page, 5th Battalion. Their battalions had not been engaged on 8 Oct. Currie, as ordered, submitted his response to Reserve Army's demand on 12 October. Realizing the limitations of a Court of Inquiry on Saturday, he began his personal investigation into 1st Brigade's attack. The results went to Corps on the 16th together with the findings of the Court.[28]

Brigadier-General George Tuxford.

27 LAC, MG30E100 (Currie Papers) Diary, Vol. 52, 2 June 1916-8 Feb. 1917, Nicholson, *Official History of the Canadian Army*, p. 184; Edmonds, *Military Operations 1916*, Vol II, pp. 451-52.
28 LAC, RG9IIIC1, Vol. 3843, Folder 45, File 6, Reserve Army to Canadian Corps and minute Corps to divisions, 10 October; MG30E100 (Currie Papers) Diary, Vol. 52 and Vol. 35, File 176, 1st Division to Corps, 12 and 16 October 1916.

Not surprisingly, while the three investigations are similar they varied when it came to purpose, primarily due to the differing levels of command: as Victor Odlum, GOC 11th Brigade, during 4th Division's attack in November, would say of the Somme as a whole "Those higher up can always see a clean map. The man who works in the mud can never see a clean map. So there was a difference in their viewpoint." General Sir Hubert Gough, GOC Reserve Army, sought a "full report upon the attack [including] the reasons for failure … particular attention" to be given to the following questions:

1. The jumping-off place. Did the Infantry start from trenches or did they line up in the open? Was the jumping-off place satisfactory as to siting, and what was the average distance from the objective?
2. The artillery barrage. What was the rate of advance and was the Infantry able to keep close up to it?
3. Was the wire satisfactorily cut? What reports had been received from the Infantry on this point prior to the attack?
4. Was the liaison between Infantry and Artillery satisfactory? Were the directions given in Reserve Army No. G.A. 15/0/1 followed?
5. What were the reasons for the retirement of the 1st Bde from the Quadrilateral? Had this Brigade made proper preparations for the supply of bombs? When the counter-attack was delivered was the artillery support properly forthcoming?
6. Was the communication between 1st Brigade Headquarters and the Battalion headquarters satisfactory?
7. What lateral communications was there with the left of III Corps? Was that Corps promptly informed of the withdrawals?
8. What orders were issued by the Brigade Commander and why was it that no counter-attack was ordered and organised?

Currie's most recent biographer, quite forgetting that Army level and divisional level lessons differ, described these points as being of a "perfunctory nature [and] consequently he [Currie] conducted a private survey." In fact, the eight points were not that at all. While the first two are fairly straightforward, the third was the latest reiteration of a long series of unresolved questions; for example, it had been the case in 1915 and later that artillery and infantry reports on the efficacy of wire-cutting seldom coincided. After Givenchy the Commander Royal Artillery (CRA) of 1st Division had insisted that in future the infantry had to say, before an assault, whether or not the wire-cutting was satisfactory. Currie's response, discussed below, to Reserve Army's query shows this controversy had not disappeared. Nor had artillery-infantry liaison always been satisfactory, hence that query. Some of Gough's points also suggest concern about 1st Brigade's leadership. Gough sought the reasons for failure since from these he could draw lessons relevant to Reserve and other Armies of the BEF. Moreover, the biographer's comment is fair neither to Gough, nor the relevant corps and division commander. It fails not only to appreciate the needs of the various command levels, but also fails to credit Byng and Currie with the sense that allowed them to realise what Gough's purpose was and that he quite rightly had left tactical and technical matters for them to resolve.[29]

As for the Court of Inquiry, Currie knew one simply could not be avoided. The Court's assigned challenge was to "investigate the circumstances under which the 1st Canadian Infantry Brigade retired from captured positions on the 8th October." The Court translated this into "to investigate and enquire into certain matters relating to the operations of the 1st Canadian Infantry Brigade during ... 8 October." A separate instruction prepared by Currie's General Staff Officer (GSO1) Lieutenant-Colonel R.H. Kearsley, posed 22 questions that the Court had to answer, five of which contained the "retirement" word. Currie, of course, also knew that the court would not prove satisfactory since by its very nature its purpose was to describe events, determine what had gone wrong, assign causes of failure and, if warranted, assign blame. On 14 October Currie commenced his personal investigation with a five hour stay at 3rd Battalion where he conducted interviews and compiled statements.[30]

Currie's determined and diligent investigation pursued "local," tactical lessons, which is not to say he only looked downward; corps lessons, too, were critical for he knew that he had good prospects of being the next GOC of the Canadian Corps. He assembled the most complete picture he possibly could, milked the reports for every conceivable lesson and planned how to implement each in order to prevent future repetition of shortcomings. His investigation, would, of course, reveal personnel, as well as organisational, logistical, planning, preparatory and executive failures. While there would be no courts-martial, for some participants there would be unpleasant consequences.

A curious feature about 1st Brigade and the attack concerns its planning and execution. The GOC, Garnet Hughes, played no part, his responsibilities falling to Lieutenant-Colonel A.G. Swift, Commanding Officer (CO) of 2nd Battalion, who assumed command when on 26 September Hughes "proceeded to England on leave."

---

29 LAC, RG 41, CBC interview, V.W. Odlum, No. 8, 'The Somme;' A.M.J. Hyatt, *General Sir Arthur Currie: A Military Biography* (Toronto: University of Toronto Press, 1987), p. 60; LAC. RG9IIIC1, Vol. 3843, Folder 45, File 6, Reserve Army to Canadian Corps, 10 October 1916.

30 LAC, RG9IIIC3, Vol. 4026, Folder 11, File 3, Lieutenant-Colonel G. Frith, Assistant Adjutant and Quartermaster-General (AA&QMG) 1st Division, to 1st Brigade, 10 October; Lieutenant-Colonel R.H. Kearsley, GSO1, to Brigadier-General G.S. Tuxford, 10 October; *The King's Regulations and Orders for the Army. 1912, Reprinted 1916* (London: HMSO, 1916) pp. 148-51; *Manual of Military Law* (London: HMSO, 1914; reprint ed., 1917), pp. 637-39. Courts of Inquiry investigated specific failures of discipline, general failures and tactical failures. Where a Court determined or suspected that any individual had violated the Army Act courts-martial generally adhered to. A Court examining a particular situation might also have terms of reference ominously stating: "[T]o enable higher authority to fix responsibility for." Such wording focused attention wonderfully.

It seems an odd time for a brigade commander to be absent on leave, but he must have had authority to do so. Currie appears to have had full confidence in Swift. The 2nd Battalion, after its capture, on 9 September, of the last enemy held portion of the Poziéres Ridge, had received the congratulations of Haig and Currie. The latter wrote when the 2nd was holding the line at Courcelette saying how glad he was that the battalion was there and that he was "counting on the 2nd…with all possible confidence." Later, Currie expressed his appreciation of the 2nd's "work on the Somme," especially for the "splendid" attack on the ridge. The battalion history also notes that on 26 September "Captain W.O. White, the Adjutant of 2nd Battalion, accompanied [Swift] temporarily as Brigade Major." This appointment, then as now, is key, for it is one of the most demanding in the Army; Currie believed that if it was not "filled by a trained staff officer loss of efficiency will occur and too great additional responsibility [will be] thrown upon the Brigadier." Hughes returned from leave on 6 October at which time he attended the final conference for the attack.[31]

1st Brigade's attack report is not dated and is signed by Captain Adams over his signature block, not the brigade commander's. This, as per Staff Duties, says Adams wrote it. The body of the report reveals some unfamiliarity with the conventions of staff writing. The covering letter, dated 18 October, ten days after the attack, is signed by Hughes over his block. That the date may be an error is indicated by the fact that 3rd and 4th Battalion Operation Orders are attached. In his report of 16 October Currie made extensive use of these orders. No mention of them is made in his report of 12 October.[32]

Currie's seven-page response to Gough's demand for a full account provides exactly that, including his "opinion as to the reasons for failure" and, as a bonus, what he believed were the "principal lessons to be learned." Also attached were the reports of Brigadier-Generals H. Burstall and H.C. Thacker, respectively General Officer Commanding Royal Artillery (GOCRA) and CRA 1st Division. Currie used the same headings as Gough's demand, the critical ones being the last six. Wire-cutting was never out of mind, in this instance "Not satisfactorily cut, in some cases practically undamaged by our artillery." But Currie also noted infantry shortcomings: inaccurate reports on the state of enemy wire due to inexperience of patrols, reduced infantry

---

31   LAC, 1st Brigade War Diary, 25 September, notes Hughes' departure and Swift's assumption of command. Colonel W.W. Murray, *The History of the 2nd Canadian Battalion (East Ontario Regiment) Canadian Expeditionary Force* (Ottawa: Mortimer Ltd., 1947), pp. 119-20, 135-36, 138; LAC, MG30E75 (Urquhart Papers) Vol. 2, File 3, Currie to GOC Canadian Corps, 11 September 1916. There was no permanent Brigade Major (BM) at 1st Brigade starting in September: 1-10 September, Major P.F. Villiers; 11-20 September, Captain W.D. Adams; 21-25 September, Captain J.K. Bertram; 25 September–2 October, Captain W.O. White (ex-2nd Battalion); and afterward until January 1917, Captain W.D. Adams (all dates from War Diary). Such a turnover would not bode well for any brigade.

32   LAC, MG30E100 (Currie Papers) Vol. 35, File 176, 1st Brigade report. Currie may have received the Operation Orders directly.

familiarity with the front because of the brief time in situ and unsettled weather, which made observation of wire difficult. He them summarized the state and impact of wire: 13th Battalion, "almost all … held up by wire"; 16th Battalion, "one half … got through"; 3rd Battalion, "got through but found uncut wire between front and support trench"; 4th Battalion, "Wire … very strong and undamaged." Infantry-artillery liaison he described as satisfactory, with a gunner officer at each headquarters. He did not think the artillery could have stopped the enemy counter-attacks, which came in great strength down all four trenches that converged on the Quadrilateral. Liaison with Corps Heavy Artillery had been good, although Reserve Army direction that artillery liaison officers should be senior officers could not always be achieved given the limited number of field officers available.

Regarding Reserve Army's fifth point on retirement, bombs and counter-attack, Currie briefly summarised events before the counter-attack. 3rd Battalion took its objective without "great difficulty," not much wire, few losses, captured 150 prisoners, established contact with flanking battalions and set blocks in the trenches to prevent enemy penetration. 4th Battalion also took about 150 prisoners. Its second objective could not be attacked due to uncut wire. Enemy counter-attacks, which began in early afternoon, drove a wedge between the two battalions and when their bombs ran out men of the 3rd gradually "drifted" back to the jumping-off trench while the 4th "under orders of an officer" withdrew into 23rd Division's lines. The two battalions each carried 3,200 bombs into the attack. Additionally, 2nd Battalion provided carrying parties, one party to each of the 3rd and the 4th, with 900 bombs. More carriers and bombs were available at brigade. However, getting the bombs across No Man's Land proved problematic. Here Currie could say little more for he was not in possession of the details that his personal survey would reveal. As for artillery support against the counter-attack, field artillery fire had been prompt and accurate, heavy artillery the same and "as close as possible." In summary, Currie said 1st Brigade "Did not retire from the Quadrilateral." Rather, it was forced back, fighting all the way, it being overcome by sheer numbers and without the means – bombs - to stop the enemy. Points 6 and 7 – communications -he considered good throughout. A liaison officer kept the flanking brigade of III Corps informed at all times and promptly advised that corps when the two battalions "had been driven" from the Quadrilateral. Elements of the 4th Battalion did counter-attack, but were repulsed. At 4pm Currie ordered 1st Brigade to counter-attack with the 1st and 2nd Battalions, at which time the brigade commander went forward and at 6pm issued the attack order. Currie cancelled this at 7:40pm. No counter-attack was made.

Currie saw four reasons for failure. First, uncut wire forced the infantry to try to gain the trenches, not by going overland, but by bombing while in the trenches. In so doing the bombs were quickly used up, leaving the men no recourse but to "get out." If overland had been possible Curie believed the bomb supply would have lasted until dark when more could have been brought forward. Had Zero hour been later, any time after noon, Currie believed "we would be there yet." Second, a "fairly large proportion" of officers and men had never been in a trench and many had never thrown a bomb.

Third, infantry reports on the state of the wire had been inaccurate. Finally, artillery fire over "nearly a fortnight should have had greater destructive results."[33] The report of the GOCRA, Harry Burstall, focussed on wire-cutting, which he assessed as "not satisfactory throughout," but he added that on the extreme right no infantry reports from 3rd and 4th Battalions were received prior to the attack. CRA 1st Division made no mention in his report of wire-cutting.[34] Lastly, Currie listed "the principal lessons to be learned" as follows:

- The necessity of dependable patrolling.
- The getting of the trench does not mean the getting of the objective.
- We must not only clear the enemy out of the trenches but we must also control all his approaches to it.
- Making the bomb supply sufficient, as far as humanly possible.
- Development of qualities of leadership and resolution in officers.
- When drafts [arrive] they should be already trained.

These lessons would be amplified in Currie's report of 16 October. To his mind, things were greatly amiss when it came to training and leadership.[35]

To his personal investigation report Currie attached the findings of Tuxford's Court of Inquiry. Most of its three pages relate the events of the day, these having been described above. Essentially, with all bombs gone the two battalions were unable to repulse German counter-attacks. Enemy fire prevented more bombs getting to them. No orders to retire were issued; rather men "drifted" back to the jumping-off line. The inexperience of the men was noted. From a training point of view new men being "unaccustomed to the use of the Lee Enfield Rifle and the Mills Bomb" would not only worry, but anger officers of any rank who had to command them. There would be repercussions for training staffs in England. Only one finding was made: "there was no general retirement."[36]

Currie's six-page report related that he had interviewed all surviving unwounded officers of both battalions, plus a "great many" ORs, at least three per company. Time probably dictated that he had to focus on one battalion, which he did, the report being largely about 3rd Battalion. Perhaps his choice of unit was based upon the rank of its acting CO, a Major, Currie possibly thinking that more lessons might therefore surface than with Lieutenant-Colonel Rae, DSO, who had commanded the 4th Battalion since June 1916. Rae had a reputation as a meticulous officer. Currie's account of the actual attack, start to finish, is very detailed in every respect, with each circumstance and

---

33   Ibid., Currie's report of 12 October 1916.
34   LAC, RG9IIIC1, Vol. 3843, Folder 45, File 6, Burstall to Canadian Corps, 12 October; Thacker to 1st Division, 11 October.
35   LAC, MG30E100 (Currie Papers) Vol. 35, File 176, report of 12 October 1916.
36   Ibid., 16 October 1916 report.

development being analysed in his search for lessons. He made three general criticisms unrelated to 3rd Battalion's performance. First, he thought the attack should have been a half-hour later when the light was better. This would have meant "less confusion," specifically the supporting companies would not have become mixed, although he identified too wide a distance between attacking waves as a contributory factor. Second, few bombs were brought forward. The carriers provided by 2nd Battalion suffered 60 percent casualties, this proof of their determined effort to sustain the assaulting troops. Finally, the wire not being "sufficiently cut" caused delay and considerable losses, as did enemy artillery, which from 9 am until the enemy counter-attacks began at 3 pm rose from "intense" to "hurricane." Currie also stressed that the 3rd had fought hard, hand-to-hand and with clubbed rifles once all their bombs were gone. Of the 15 officers in the attack four were killed and eight wounded. He took pains to identify those who had showed the "greatest gallantry and determination."

The 3rd Battalion's failure to conduct a pre-attack rehearsal despite "oft repeated orders" to always do so clearly displeased Currie. This "neglect" also contributed to the mix up that occurred in the supporting companies. The "lack of clearness" in the battalion's Operation Order and the failure of unit officers to properly brief their men disturbed him even more. One example of ambiguity in the battalion Operation Order came up repeatedly in interviews of NCOs who reported finding themselves following the wrong company and others who were confused about which units were on which flank. Currie commented at length on the poor briefings given by company officers, a shortcoming that does not reflect well on them. What he discovered was this: company tasks were explained to the men using a map as a reference, but this simply did not suffice: "To tell a Machine Gunner to take up his position at M.14.b.2.6 or a Bomber to establish a block at M.8.d.3.0 is an absurd order unless some other means of fixing this point has been explained." Currie from personal experience knew the folly of this for at Festubert he had been ordered to take "K4," a point that could not be confirmed on the map or on the ground. Currie also spoke to NCOs who could not tell him from the map where they were had to go or where they had been. Had objectives been set out and briefed on the Practice Trenches men would have known their task. To Currie such neglect equated to "grave misdemeanour." His questioning also revealed that NCOs did not know the extent of their objective, how far away it was or who they were to link up with. Notwithstanding these grievous faults, Currie concluded "Yet had none of these things occurred, the wire would still have been uncut and the supply of bombs would have run out just as soon." He clearly intended remedial action:

> All the lessons to be learned … all the points, and they many, which can be improved, all the things left undone, done badly or which may have been done better, I shall take up not only with the 3rd and 4th Battalions, but with all the Battalions of this Division.[37]

37 Ibid. and Findings of Court of Inquiry.

One remarkable aspect of all the reports is the paucity of comment about what damage artillery inflicted upon the enemy trenches. In the 12 October report one comment described the northeast face of the Quadrilateral as "badly smashed in." Another, speaking generally, described enemy trenches as "little damaged." Only one such comment – the Regina support trench was "badly knocked about" – is in the report of 16 October. This leaves one to share Colonel Nicholson's conclusion: "More important (though this was given little prominence in post-operation reports) was the failure of the artillery to destroy or even substantially damage Regina Trench." Nicholson continued:

> In the Somme fighting heavy batteries did not attain the high accuracy of fire on unseen targets that came in later battles, and although there was no serious shortage of howitzer ammunition, the expenditure seems frugal when compared with what was used in subsequent operations.

GOCRA Canadian Corps reports state that at least one round Heavy or two Medium Howitzer were allowed per yard of trench and divisional howitzers (4.5 inch) having completed other tasks were to fire any surplus (of their allotted 1,000 rounds) on Regina Trench. Spread over the divisional frontage such amounts could not create much damage. In comparison, attacks after 8 October on Regina Trench and the Quadrilateral set no limit on what could be fired: "each section of trench must be completely obliterated." On 14 October these targets received 5,700 rounds, compared to the 3,000 expended on the 8th. William Griesbach, CO of 49th Battalion, spelled out what these figures had meant to the men who attacked on the 8th:

> The wire was considered to be passable upon the assumption that the enemy trench had been well battered in and that the garrison had been severely shocked. With the enemy trench in being and the enemy garrison unshocked, the flimsies wire constitutes an impassable obstacle.[38]

In the immediate aftermath, changes occurred in the officer slate. Lieutenant-Colonel Swift, who had planned and executed 1st Brigade's attack, departed for Great Britain on 26 October to take command of a training brigade. He did not return to the Western Front. Major Yates, who had been placed in command of 3rd Battalion temporarily, returned on promotion to command 2nd Battalion. Critically injured in an accident before Christmas, he was invalided to England. Garnet Hughes remained GOC 1st Brigade until February 1917 when he departed for England, there eventually

---

38   LAC, MG30E100 (Currie Papers) Vol. 35, File 176, reports of 12 and 16 October; Nicholson, *Official History of the Canadian Army*, p. 186; LAC, War Diary, GOCRA Canadian Corps, Instructions 38 and 39, Appendix A, October 1916; War Diary 49th Battalion, Appendix, Griesbach's report to 7th Brigade.

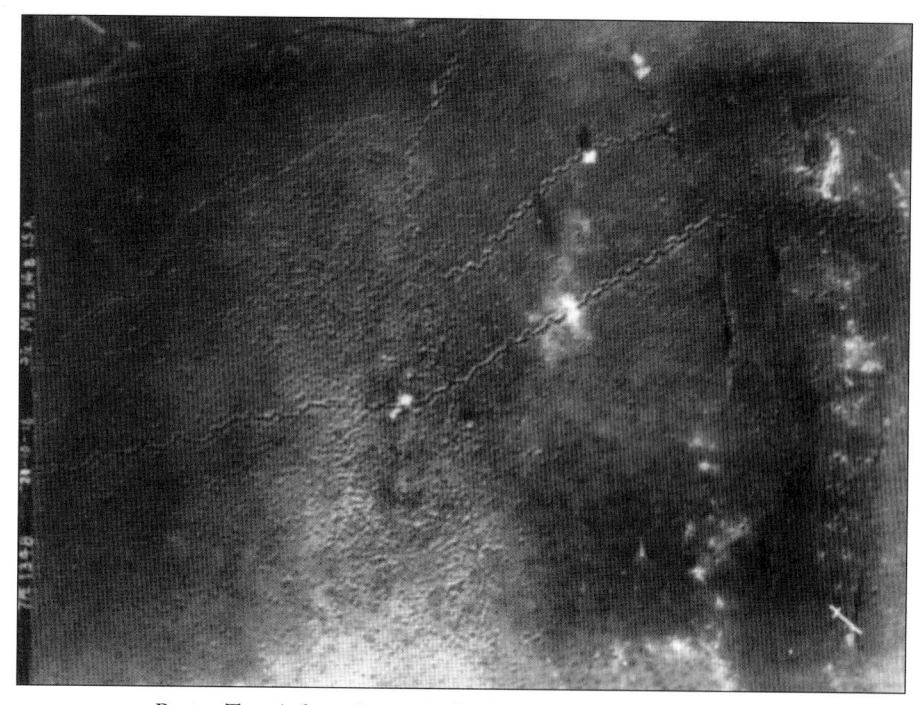

Regina Trench from the air, 21 October 1916. (Private collection)

to be involved in the formation of 5th Division which he hoped to command and take to France. None of this happened partly because of the long-standing antagonism between Hughes and Currie that had begun at Second Ypres where Hughes had been Brigade Major 3rd Brigade. Currie, who had not been impressed then, later thought Hughes "unfit for higher command." His replacement, William Griesbach, would shine as a brigade commander just as he had as a battalion commander.[39]

One relationship that began during the Somme would prove an unhappy one according to several studies. In fact, it proved very difficult indeed. The attack on Regina Trench caused "considerable antipathy" for the GOC Reserve Army (Gough) by his Canadian subordinates who believed that the Corps had been ill-used. Nor was it just Canadians who found Gough impossible. Australians, too, had a very poor opinion of him, a "disenchantment" that spread. Geoffrey Powell describes Gough's primary fault as not realising that the defects of his staff, especially his Major General General Staff (MGGS) Neill Malcolm, had engendered a strong reluctance in many

---

39 Murray, *2nd Battalion*, pp. 148, 150; Desmond Morton, *A Peculiar Kind of Politics: Canada's Overseas Ministry in the First World War* (Toronto: University of Toronto Press, 1982), p. 121.

divisions, British as well as Dominion, to serve under Gough. When told before Passchendaele that Gough would again have Canadian Corps under command Currie refused, whereupon Haig wisely re-allocated Corps to Plumer. While Canadians did not work well with Gough, Haig knew that Currie and Plumer got on well together, the same true of other Dominion commanders. To Canadians and Australians, officers and men alike, Plumer was "Plum" or "Daddy Plumer."[40] Gough was never "Daddy."

Despite his efforts to determine exactly what had gone wrong, and the undoubted excellence of his two reports, neither could have entirely satisfied Currie and probably not Byng, the situation simply one where no more could be usefully said or done beyond making the changes that would prevent repetition. When in December Currie travelled to Verdun with a party of British and Dominion senior officers to study French operations, it was obvious he was delighted with the opportunity to attend the related tours, lectures and conferences. According to one attendee, "He [Currie] was an inveterate questioner. He pumped everyone dry." His deep interest shows in the many pages of notes he made during the visit. How he put these together with his distillation of what 1st Division experienced at the Somme, and his further reflection upon the Verdun visit, and the subsequent use made of Currie's study, is an interesting story, an important one, considering its impact upon organisation, communications, artillery support and training within the corps and within the BEF.[41]

Currie took with him to Verdun a "Proof Copy" of SS 135 *Instructions for the Training of Divisions Withdrawn from the Front Line* (December 1916). Upon the backs of its 46 pages in small and closely set manuscript are his 40 pages of notes on the French attacks at Verdun in October and December. When he returned on 9 December, Currie spent many days working up his notes and reflections, "intending it to be a formal report [but] while writing it I was asked to lecture at the Corps [and at each Canadian Division] and I finished it with that object in view." The typed version (16 pages) dated 23 January and entitled "Notes on French Attacks North-East of Verdun in October and December 1916," would be widely distributed within the BEF. Lieutenant-Colonel G.R. Frith, AA & QMG 1st Division, who attended the lecture, was "greatly struck by the lucidity ... and power of observation ... I do not believe any

---

40   Gary Sheffield & Dan Todman, *Command and Control on the Western Front: The British Army's Experience 1914-18* (Staplehurst: Spellmount, 2004) p. 75; Robin Neillands, *The Great War Generals of the Western Front 1914-1918* (London: Magpie Books, 2004) pp. 290-91; Ian F.W. Beckett, 'Hubert Gough, Neill Malcolm and Command on the Western Front,' in British Commission for Military History, *Look to Your Front* (Staplehurst: Spellmount, 1999), p. 5; Geoffrey Powell, *Plumer: The Soldiers' General* (London: Leo Cooper, 1990), p. 203; Robert Blake, ed., *The Private Papers of Douglas Haig 1914-1919* (London: Eyre & Spottiswoode, 1952), p. 257.

41   Hugh M. Urquhart, *Arthur Currie: The Biography of a Great Canadian* (Toronto: J.M. Dent, 1950), p. 142. During the war Urquhart served with 16th Battalion, thereafter as Staff Captain at 3rd Brigade, then BM and finally as CO 43rd Battalion (3rd Division). His history of the 16th (853 pages) must surely be one of the most thorough battalion histories ever.

among the generals in the [visiting] party deduced with greater acumen the lessons [taught] by the fighting there [Verdun]."[42]

Accompanying Currie's "Notes" was an undated, unsigned five-page document entitled "Notes on a Visit of a Party of British Officers to Verdun, January 5th – 8th, 1917." Comparison must reflect the fact that Currie's 16 pages looks and reads like a lecture while the five-page document is a report. The two differ in their approach and format. Currie organised his chronologically, as his title says, October and then December, then discussion of common elements such as maps, liaison and organisation, followed by eight lessons to be learned. The British document is thematic, which allows specific matter to be highlighted, but does result in some duplication, apparent in phrases like "as already stated." Currie's notes, on the other hand, are a dense read, one that topical headings would have helped. Overall, the two papers are similar in content, one more detailed than the other, but both very useful in any study of BEF doctrinal and tactical developments.[43]

Byng, too, pursued the lessons of the Somme, asking division commanders on 3 November to report lessons. Currie responded on 25 November with a comprehensive report eleven foolscap pages long that represented the consensus of his brigade and battalion commanders, plus his own reflections. A subsequent study focussed on adjustments required to infantry tactical organisation in light of the lessons. Byng later summed up the lessons thus:

> The reasons for lack of success were many. The artillery had failed to gap the German barbed wire or to destroy Regina Trench. German shelling had inflicted heavy casualties on units moving up from reserve. Objectives had been hard to identify. Reinforcements had been inadequately trained. Most important of all, the infantry formation for attack was suspect.[44]

The content of all the documents mentioned or discussed above cannot be assessed here; moreover, they deserve study in their own right. Each listed a number of lessons or factors in French success at Verdun. The British report on the Verdun visit listed

---

42   SS 135 *Instructions for the Training of Divisions Withdrawn From the Front Line* (London: Harrison & Sons, December 1916); LAC, MG30E100 (Currie Papers) Vol. 49, "Notes on French Attacks North-East of Verdun in October and December 1916."
43   Ibid., LAC, RG9IIIC1, Vol. 3871, Folder 115, File 8.
44   Williams, *Byng of Vimy*, p. 141; LAC, RG9IIIC3, Vol. 4011, Folder 17, File 1, Corps to divisions, 3 November, and 1st Division to Corps, 25 November; RG9IIIC1, Vol. 3864, Folder 99, File 3, Corps to divisions, 27 December 1916. In February 1917 GHQ published *The Organisation of an Infantry Battalion* in O.B./1919, followed that same month by SS 144 *The Normal Formation for the Attack*, these to be read in conjunction with SS 135 *Instructions for the Training of Divisions for Offensive Action, 1916* and SS 143 *Instructions for the Training of Platoons for Offensive Action, 1917*, the latter regarded by regimental officers as the "most important publication issued during the war." See Graves, *Goodbye to All That*, p. 215.

these as careful staff work, thorough artillery preparation and support, surprise and a high state of infantry training. Currie offered eight lessons:

1. Greater chance of success if attack is on a wide front.
2. All assault troops must cross the barrage line as quickly as possible.
3. Objectives should be tactical features.
4. No attack unless all enemy trenches destroyed and machine-guns "done in."
5. Methodically destroy enemy guns; blind those not destroyed with smoke.
6. Platoons must be self-reliant and self-sufficient. Develop platoon commander initiative.
7. Surprise
8. Attack with fresh and highly trained troops.[45]

Clearly, much of the above had begun or was contemplated before the visit to Verdun and even before the October attacks on Regina Trench, but much remained to be done and such documents provided impetus for change. Christopher Pugsley summed up Currie's report and his earlier investigations as "an evaluation of what [was] learnt from what [had been] done wrong … It was a thoughtful assessment of how organisation, communications and training in the Canadian Corps had to improve and what the artillery had to do to get the infantry across No Man's Land and at the enemy." The changes themselves go much beyond this essay. Here we can only say, as Charles Carrington did, that "The British Army learned … during … the Somme and, for the rest of the war, was the best army in the field."[46]

In the end, Canadian casualties at the Somme totalled 24,029.[47] On 17 October the Corps departed for First Army which was then between Arras and Lens. Vimy loomed. There the Corps would show that the lessons had been absorbed. What had gone before and what lay ahead testifies to the validity of the Russian proverb which says the roads that lead to war are very wide, but the path that leads to home is very narrow.

---

45 LAC, MG30E1ll (Currie Papers) Vol. 49; RG9IIIC1, Vol. 3871, Folder 115, File 8; Urquhart, *Arthur Currie*, p. 142. On some points Currie felt there was nothing to learn from the French and on others he thought them no news to the BEF.
46 Christopher Pugsley, "Learning from the Canadian Corps on the Western Front," *Canadian Military History* 15 (Winter 2006) p. 13; Charles Carrington, *Soldier From the Wars Returning* (London: Hutchinson, 1965), p. 120.
47 Nicholson, *Official History of the Canadian Army*, p. 198.

15

Early Tank Tactical Doctrine and Training

Philip Ventham

On 15 September 1916, after nearly two years of development and numerous setbacks, 21 British tanks rolled into action on the Somme.[1] Manned by hastily trained crews, "the trickle of tanks only made a slight contribution to the day's success, such as it was."[2] The tactical employment of the tank evolved over the following years largely as the result of experience gained on the battlefield. The crews and commanders needed to be trained how to drive and maintain the new vehicles, how to navigate them over the battlefield and how to fight from them. Initially, their training was rudimentary, hampered by a dearth of vehicles and inadequate facilities.[3] It concentrated on basic driving and gunnery skills, and was given by instructors barely more knowledgeable than their students.

The novel weapon was untested in warfare. The early tactical and operational employment was based on the best guesses and assumptions of a number of self-proclaimed experts. Higher commanders needed to be educated in the most effective use of this weapon. The tactical development of the tank was hampered by a paradox. To get the most from the new weapons, a standard doctrine was required which could serve as a guide for training. Yet the novelty of the vehicle meant that it was impossible to develop a doctrine without gaining combat experience. As a result the first tank

---

1   There are conflicting opinions on how many tanks actually went into action on 15 September. Harris, quoting Liddell Hart and Terraine, endorses 50 tanks sent to France plus 10 in reserve, 48 fit for action of which 36 reached the assembly point. Thirty started and 21 subsequently went into action. See J.P. Harris, *Men, Ideas and Tanks* (Manchester: Manchester University Press, 1995), p. 65.
2   B.H. Liddell Hart, *The Tanks: The History of the Royal Tank Regiment and its Predecessors, Heavy Branch Machine-Gun Corps, Tank Corps And Royal Tank Corps, 1914-1945*, Vol. I (London: Cassell, 1959), p. 71.
3   John Glanville, *The Devil's Chariots* (Stroud: Sutton, 2006 [2001]), pp. 215-238; Frank Mitchell, *Tank Warfare* (London: Nelson, 1934), pp. 68-87.

crews were forced to learn in the field and develop their doctrine in the midst of battle. The dilemma was neatly summarised by Major-General Hugh Elles, the commander of the Tank Corps in France: "There was no guidance as to training – the entire system had to be thought out from the beginning, and continuously modified by the experience of the battlefield – instructors had not only to be found but trained – *esprit de corps* and discipline had to be built up: and all this against time."[4]

This chapter will chart the efforts of a few enlightened individuals to overcome the stalemate on the Western Front by the use of tanks. It will describe the early attempts to produce a body of tank tactical and operational doctrine for the benefit of both crews and commanders. Finally, it will describe the difficulties encountered in training the first tank crews before their initial experience of battle in September 1916.

The evolution of early tactical doctrine

It was Lieutenant-Colonel Ernest Swinton who first articulated the tactical requirement for an armoured fighting vehicle on the Western Front. As the Assistant Secretary to the Committee of Imperial Defence, he was sent to the Western Front in October 1914 to serve as the official war correspondent under the pseudonym 'Eyewitness'. Here, he saw the power of German machine guns first hand and became deeply concerned about the difficulty of breaching barbed wire entanglements. He described this worrying impasse to Maurice Hankey, the Secretary of the Committee of Imperial Defence (CID).[5] Influenced by Swinton's reports, Hankey produced his so called Boxing Day Memorandum in late December 1914.[6] This paper included various proposals for overcoming the stalemate on the Western Front, including Swinton's idea of an armoured "caterpillar" vehicle capable of crushing barbed wire and crossing enemy trenches Hankey's proposals were taken up enthusiastically by Winston Churchill, the First Lord of the Admiralty, who, unbeknownst to the War Office, was already sponsoring independent trials of various armoured vehicles for use by the Royal Naval Air Service (RNAS) and the Royal Naval Division (RND) in Flanders.

The concept of the armoured fighting vehicle had been born. What was lacking was a considered appreciation of the tactical requirement for the proposed machine; in effect, a military doctrine. Swinton, frustrated at the apparent disinterest shown by GHQ towards the concept of armoured vehicles despite his "verbal and personal representations", sent a memorandum entitled *The Necessity for Machine Gun Destroyers*

---

4   Major-General Hugh Elles, Introduction to C.A. Williams-Ellis, *The Tank Corps* (London: Country Life, 1919), p. vi.
5   Major-General Sir Ernest Swinton, *Eyewitness* (London: Hodder & Stoughton, 1932), pp. 81-83.
6   The National Archives (hereafter TNA) MUN 5/210/1940/13. Maurice Hankey, Memorandum, 28 December 1914.

to Major-General Henry Wilson, the British liaison officer at the French HQ, on 1 June 1915.[7] In many ways this document represented the first attempt to outline tank tactics. Swinton identified German machine guns as the "chief factor which has rendered abortive our attempts to penetrate their positions", for which he proposed two solutions: the use of "artillery and high explosive ammunition to blast a way through the German positions", or "other means of destroying these weapons." As sufficient artillery was not yet available, "Armoured Machine Gun Destroyers" might be "the other means". His description of such a vehicle was remarkably close to what was actually produced in January 1916. He emphasised the need to build the machines in secrecy and not to disclose their existence until enough were available.

Lieutenant-Colonel Ernst Swinton.

Swinton suggested that 50 destroyers might be available for an attack, deployed in line at 100 yard intervals, covering a frontage of around 5,000 yards or three miles. A preceding artillery bombardment would cut the wire entanglements and, at dawn, the destroyers would climb from their pits and advance on the German lines at the rate of three miles an hour. They would crush enemy strong-points and enfilade trenches using their 2-pounder guns and machine guns. Artillery would thus be freed to concentrate on counter-battery fire. With the German machine guns destroyed and their artillery silenced, British infantry would advance "practically unscathed." Once through the first line of trenches, the destroyers would turn and attack again from the rear, then proceed forwards supporting the first wave of attackers and "the mass of troops forming the main body of the attack." In defence, Swinton saw tanks as "mobile strong points" to be driven forward against any enemy penetration. Interestingly, this tactic was employed with considerable effect during the German spring offensives in 1918.[8]

Swinton's memorandum was the first attempt at formulating a tactical doctrine for the use of armoured vehicles on the Western Front. In hindsight, it is easy to identify

---

7   Bryn Hammond, 'Practical Considerations in British Tank Operations on the Western Front, 1916-1918', in Alaric Searle (ed.) *Genesis, Employment, Aftermath: First World War Tanks and the New Warfare, 1900-1945* (Solihull: Helion, 2015), p. 34.
8   Tank Museum Library, Bovington (hereafter TM) E.2006.1095.3. The Necessity for Machine Gun Destroyers', 1 June 1915. Swinton's pencilled note on his copy of the memorandum reads "NB. This was written on 1 June 1915 after efforts from October 1914 to get the matter taken up by verbal or personal representations."

its flaws. For example, the use of artillery ignored several associated problems. Firstly, the ammunition and fuses available at the time were ineffective at cutting barbed wire and destroying deep dug-outs; secondly, a preliminary bombardment would surrender the vital principle of surprise and allow the defenders to man their trenches once the bombardment had lifted and finally, intense preliminary bombardments would crater the ground and render it difficult, if not impossible, for machines to cross. However, Swinton must be credited with giving constructive thought to overcoming the impasse on the Western Front and producing an early attempt at tactical doctrine for the entirely new vehicles.

The Commander-in-Chief (C-in-C) of the British Expeditionary Force (BEF), Field Marshal Sir John French, thought: "[T]here appears to be considerable tactical value in the proposal" and forwarded the memorandum to the War Office, suggesting that Swinton's proposal be placed in secret before an experienced engineering firm for further investigation.[9] He stated that he understood that the Admiralty was already conducting experiments indicating the lack of co-operation between the Navy and the War Office, a peculiar state of affairs considering that the weapon was of greater use to the Army than the Royal Navy.

Swinton returned to Great Britain in July 1915 as the Acting Secretary of the CID and was in a position to push forward the development of a suitable machine. He was determined to co-ordinate the separate efforts of the Admiralty and the Army: "I am doing my best to help to get the different designs of machines under consideration co-ordinated."[10] Swinton subsequently convened an Inter-departmental conference on 28 August 1915 with representatives from the War Office, the Admiralty, and the Ministry of Munitions. The conference was held specifically to "Consider future procedure as to the design and construction of 'land cruisers' or armoured motor cars propelled by the 'caterpillar' principle, for the use of the Army. "It was agreed that Churchill's Land Ship Committee would continue to supervise the experimental work in design and construction of the land cruiser but taking instructions about the design requirements from the War Office. The whole was to be co-ordinated by the Inventions Department of the Ministry of Munitions.

As the possibility of a suitable machine was fast becoming a reality, thoughts turned to the manning and training of the future crews. The C-in-C had already indicated in his letter of 22 June 1915 that he wanted the training to be carried out in the UK. The conference reported that:

> For the manning of these machines, also, special technical men will be required. The crews must include drivers experienced in handling caterpillar vehicles who will have to be trained almost as trick drivers in order to get the best out of the

9 TM E.2014.695: French to Secretary of State for War, 22 June 1915.
10 TNA WO 158/818: Swinton to Major Guest, Secretary of the BEF Experimental Committee at GHQ, 23 August 1915.

cruisers; mechanics in order to maintain and repair the machines; and skilled machine gunners able to shoot from moving platforms. These duties will have to be, to a large extent, interchangeable; and to enable them to be carried out will necessitate the collection of a body of men of a far higher class than that usually found in the ranks or amongst military motor transport drivers.[11]

The next significant move in the development of a tactical doctrine came from Winston Churchill. Despite being demoted from First Lord of the Admiralty in May 1915 he remained closely involved in the development of a "land cruiser" by the Admiralty. Whilst serving as a battalion commander in France and witnessing the stalemate first-hand, he considered the problem of breaking the trench deadlock on the Western Front. In early December 1915 he forwarded a paper entitled *Variants of the Offensive* to Sir John French and others.[12]

Under the heading "Attack by Armour", Churchill envisaged the use of small armoured shields to protect advancing infantry. These could be propelled by hand "during the short walk across from trench to trench." In addition, he had a vision of larger "caterpillar engines" which would pass "through or across our trenches at prepared points." Armed with two or three Maxim machine guns and "flame apparatus" they would turn parallel to the enemy trenches sweeping them with fire. The engine would be capable of crossing any known obstacles and be invulnerable to anything other than a direct hit from a field gun. In his enthusiasm, Churchill stated that that 70 such machines were nearing completion and should be inspected. What he clearly did not know was that a tentative order for 70 machines had been abandoned and that experimental work was concentrated on a single machine that showed some promise. Although much of his paper was fanciful and did not reflect the practicalities of the new technology, his tactical proposals were remarkably similar to those propounded by Swinton earlier. There is no evidence that the two men had colluded in their proposals.[13] Churchill's paper prompted action within the Government departments involved. In late December, the existing Land Ship Committee was replaced by an inter-departmental Tank Supply Committee under the presidency of Lieutenant Albert Stern, RNVR, who had been responsible for much of the Admiralty's earlier experimentation.

A further meeting of the Tank Supply Committee sat on Christmas Eve 1915, and recommended an approximate establishment based on the suggested number of

---

11 TNA ADM116/1339: 'Report and Recommendations of an Interdepartmental Conference held on the 28 August 1915'.
12 TNA WO 158/ 831: W.S. Churchill, Variants of the Offensive, 3 December 1915. See also Wilfrid Miles, *Military Operations France and Belgium 1916*, Vol. II (London: Macmillan, 1938) (hereafter Miles, *OH 1916*, Vol. II), Maps & Appendices, Appendix 17.
13 See Gary Sheffield, *Forgotten Victory* (London: Headline Review, 2001) pp. 176-178 for a general discussion on Churchill's antebellum views on deployment of tanks during the Battle of the Somme. Sheffield describes this document as "pure fantasy".

50 tanks, of one officer and 10 ORs for every tank plus a 50 percent reserve. They therefore needed to recruit 75 officers and 750 other ranks. It was "thought both officers and men should have some mechanical knowledge and aptitude, and that they should be drawn from those now serving in any branch of the forces or from civil life." It considered "that each member of this body of men should be trained to perform every duty which he might be likely to be called upon to carry out." Personnel from 20th Squadron RNAS, who had provided the original drivers for the experimental machines, were to be given the opportunity of transferring into the new formation which would form a "Tank Detachment" of the Machine Gun Corps.[14]

Albert Stern.

In early January 1916, the first experimental tank, nicknamed "Mother", was demonstrated in Lincoln in front of several members of the Tank Supply Committee. General Sir Douglas Haig, the new C-in-C of the BEF, had read Churchill's paper and, after enquiring "is anything known about the Caterpillar referred to in para. 4, page 3?" sent the then staff officer and future Tank Corps commander Major Hugh Elles to observe the new weapon and report back. Demonstrations of the tank were held in late January at a secret location in Hatfield Park. The vehicle tested its capabilities over an obstacle course representative of British and German trenches and wire entanglements. The Secretary of State for War, Lord Kitchener, attended and was apparently unimpressed.[15] The King attended a trial a few days later, indicating the importance attached to the new weapon.[16] However, Elles forwarded a positive report to Haig, who informed the War Office:

> The reports of the officers who represented me at the trials ... lead me to the conclusion that these 'Tanks' can be usefully employed in offensive operations by the forces under my command.[17]

Haig requested that between 30 and 40 tanks be ready by mid-May and asked whether further tanks might be ready by mid-July. In common with his predecessor, Sir John

---

14 TNA ADM 116/1339: Report and Recommendations of an Interdepartmental Conference held on December 24, 1915.
15 Swinton, *Eyewitness*, p. 169.
16 Liddell Hart, *Tanks*, Vol. I, pp. 48-50.
17 TNA WO 32/5754: Haig to War Office, 8 February 1916.

"Mother" prototype tank undergoing trials.

French, he recommended that personnel should be "supplied and trained at home." He emphasised that "Secrecy is of the highest importance in order to get full advantage from the use of these machines." Buoyed by the moderate success of the trials and by Haig's evident enthusiasm, 100 machines were ordered by the War Office, later increased to 150.[18]

Until now, any consideration of the training of tank crews and commanders had been directed towards the mechanical aspects of their role; gunnery, driving and maintenance. There had been no mention of tactical training and, beyond Swinton and Churchill's formative ideas, little in the way of doctrine on which to base it. However, once the acceptance of the tank was assured, Swinton expanded his earlier thoughts into a more substantial paper, *Notes on the Employment of "Tanks"*, published in late February 1916.[19] This seminal document formed the basis for tank tactical doctrine for the remainder of the war, although it was much altered in the light of combat experience. A note inserted at the beginning of Swinton's document read:

> These notes as to measures of preparation and suitable tactics for tanks are not intended to imply that the whole of our offensive operations are to be subordinated to their action. They are put forward as a basis for early discussion of the possibilities and requirements of an entirely new weapon, so that by the time that

18 TNA WO32/5754: Kiggell (CGS BEF) to War Office Secretary, 5 April 1916.
19 Liddell Hart Centre, King's College (hereafter, KCL): Fuller Papers I /1/3, Swinton, Lieutenant-Colonel, 'Notes on the employment of 'Tanks', February 1916.

it is ready for employment everything possible may have been done to ensure its success.

The first sentence is significant in that it foreshadows the debate that ensued over the operational role of the tank.[20]

Tanks had evolved since Swinton first penned his doctrine for "Machine Gun Destroyers." The trench crossing ability had been increased to 10 feet as a result of the analysis of captured German trenches. However, the crossing of rivers and canals would be difficult as existing bridges in the battle zone could not carry the weight of the latest tanks. For the male tank, the current armament was four Hotchkiss machine guns and two naval Hotchkiss 6-pounder quick-firing [QF] guns mounted either side of the machine in detachable sponsons. The female tank carried six machine guns: two Vickers in each sponson and one Hotchkiss at front and rear of the vehicle. Enemy machine guns would be destroyed either by direct fire from the 6-pounders or by being crushed beneath the tracks of the tank. The tank was protected by 12mm hardened steel plate which made it practically invulnerable to rifle, machine gun fire and shell splinters. However, the enclosed nature of the vehicle made communication with the outside world difficult. Swinton proposed various methods of communicating with the accompanying infantry; small "wireless telegraphy" sets, a trailing telephone cable, miniature kite balloons and smoke rockets. In practice, effective communication with the infantry remained a problem throughout the rest of the war.[21]

In tactical terms, the chief weakness of the tanks was their vulnerability to direct fire from artillery or even to high velocity, small calibre rifle fire which the Germans were thought to be developing for use against sniper shields. They would also be vulnerable to land mines. However, it was thought that preparatory artillery countermeasures could be devised to deal with these problems.[22]

Swinton re-emphasised the important point that successful use of the tank depended on "its novelty and in the element of surprise." Therefore, they should "not be used in driblets"and "the fact of their existence should be kept as secret as possible until the whole are ready to be launched."[23] The operational sector needed to be carefully chosen in view of their limitations and in good time to allow for their deployment. Deployment routes needed to be reconnoitred, bridges strengthened and river crossings prepared. The tanks would assemble about two miles to the rear of their start line, before proceeding along previously reconnoitred routes marked by lanterns. Alternatively, tanks would move by night into previously dug pits close to the frontline from which they would emerge when the attack began. In action the line of tanks should not be extended more than 150 yards between vehicles. With the 100 tanks

20 Swinton, Notes, Introduction.
21 Swinton, Notes, para.7.
22 Swinton, Notes, paras. 9,10.
23 Swinton, Notes, para.11. Emphasis in original.

ordered, allowing for reserves and flanking operations, a total frontage of some 9000 yards or three miles was envisaged. In a footnote, Swinton observed:

> This calculation as to the extent of frontage will hold good whether the tanks are forward in one continuous line or in groups with intervals between the groups so that certain areas may be 'bitten off' by a lateral movement as soon as sufficient forward progress has been made. The selection of either method is a matter of general tactics, and not one specially connected with the employment of tanks.

This comment indicated an early, less prescriptive tactical doctrine resulting from the general uncertainty about how the vehicles would perform in battle.

The timing of the advance of the tanks in conjunction with the infantry was to become the subject of much debate over the following years. Swinton believed that the ideal time was at first light when there was sufficient daylight for the tank commanders to make progress. The tanks would advance first, sweeping the enemy trenches with machine gun fire. When they had advanced about three-quarters of the way through No-Man's-Land, attracting enemy fire onto themselves, the infantry would advance – the movement timed so that the attackers would arrive just as the tanks crossed and enfiladed the enemy trenches. Swinton rejected the alternative view that the infantry should advance first and the tanks would then only advance if the infantry was stopped by uncut wire or machine gun fire. He reasoned that the tanks would be needed from the outset to maintain the momentum of the attack.[24] In Swinton's vision, once the infantry had closed up, the tanks would then proceed at "full speed" – four miles per hour! – towards the enemy second-line trenches before advancing along the line of communications trenches and crushing them to prevent the arrival of reserves and reinforcements.

If this phase of the battle proceeded well, it would produce an opportunity for exploitation. Swinton was not prescriptive about "the Extent to which the Attack is pressed." He debated the merits of the step-by-step operation with a strictly limited advance after artillery preparations, followed by a pause for consolidation and further artillery fire before another advance took place. The alternative operation was of an all-out, violent effort to burst through the enemy defensive lines. Swinton rightly left this decision to the field commander but noted that the advent of the tank made the breakthrough of the German defensive zone a feasible proposition. His enthusiasm was apparent in a section that envisaged an advance of 12 miles in a day into the heart of the enemy artillery positions, providing plans were made for the replenishment of the tanks and their crews.[25]

On the question of co-operation with other arms, Swinton emphasised that "tanks cannot win battles by themselves. They were purely auxiliary to the infantry." The

---

24   Swinton, Notes, para. 21.
25   Swinton, Notes, paras. 22-30.

vulnerability of tanks to German shellfire meant that they in turn were reliant on the close support of the Royal Artillery. Pre-battle bombardments were needed to silence German artillery positions, leaving the first-line defences to the tanks themselves. Swinton concluded by saying that experiments were being conducted on methods of clearing wire entanglements.[26]

Swinton's groundbreaking paper represented his vision of the employment of tanks rather than a prescriptive tactical doctrine. He acknowledged that there were several questions which needed to be considered and which could not be resolved until the tanks had deployed in action, such as, how effective the tanks would be in destroying strongpoints and in crossing and clearing trenches.

On 26 June 1916, a conference at GHQ, attended by Swinton, agreed on the tactics that would form the basis of training:

> [T]he tanks should move forward so as to reach the German first-line trench before dawn followed up by our infantry which is to start forward from our line as soon as the tanks reach the first line of the enemy; that in the further operations that will ensue by day-light, tanks should proceed the infantry from place to place as quickly as possible; that the ultimate objectives of the tanks during this period of attack should be:
>
> 1. The German artillery positions
> 2. The German 2nd or 3rd lines
>
> That the German artillery positions might be assumed at an approximation to be at a distance of 2000 to 3000 yards from the German front line; that the training of the Tanks should proceed on these lines and that the maximum interval at which they should be spaced for the attack should be 150 yards; that the crews should be trained to drive in the dark; that the movement from the position of assembly to the starting point tapes may be laid forward up to a distance of about 1,000 yards from our firing line or the tanks may be led forward by guides up to that distance; further progress will be guided by disks painted with luminous paint.[27]

Finally, Swinton had some firm guidance on which to base the training of the tank companies. In a letter of 8 July enclosing a copy of a provisional memorandum on tactical training addressed to the BGGS, he showed that he was anxious to proceed and could not wait to receive further views based on the experiences of the fighting on

---

26 Swinton, Notes, para. 45.
27 TNA WO 32/5754/14: Digest of Decisions reached at Conference on the 26 June 1916.

1 July 1916.[28] He was no doubt aware that the likelihood of a major offensive, using tanks for the first time, was not far away.

The next significant progress in the production of tactical doctrine came with Swinton's memorandum produced in July 1916, entitled *The Handling of the Heavy Section, Machine Gun Corps*. The memorandum emphasised, in capital:

> THE PRIMARY OBJECT OF THIS UNIT [Heavy Section, Machine Gun Corps] IS TO ASSIST THE INFANTRY BY DISPOSING OF THE PRINCIPAL DIFFICULTIES IN THE WAY OF THEIR ADVANCE IE, BARBED WIRE AND MACHINE GUNS.
>
> BATTLES CANNOT BE WON BY TANKS ALONE AND IT IS BY INFANTRY AND INFANTRY ALONE THAT A DECISION CAN BE REACHED.

The section on training emphasised the following: "all officers should be able to read a map – particularly a trench map – and understand the compass fitted in the Tank … should be practiced … in synchronising their watches … they should be trained in the issue of precise and concise verbal orders to subordinates … must also be taught to exercise their imagination and to inspire that of their subordinates." Section commanders were to be encouraged to find rapid solutions to problems set by the company commander and to decide exactly how they would overcome various obstacles. Tank crews should be taken on foot around the training area in all weather conditions to identify likely enemy machine gun posts. Practice in laying out the routes of deployment needed to be carried out by day and night. Training with infantry should be carried out to ensure that they *followed* the tanks rather than precede them.[29]

Swinton produced some further "hints on the use of tanks" on 27 July 1916 for "circulation amongst those who will have control of them in action." For the first time, these included observations by Captain Gifford Martel, a staff officer at Tank HQ, who had seen action on 1 July 1916. Martel thought it "absolutely imperative" that the "hush-hushes" should be used without the usual preliminary bombardment. He did not think they would be in any danger from artillery once they reached the enemy front line as the Germans would not risk "friendly fire", and therefore they could and should precede the infantry. He also recommended that the tank should not advance beyond the first enemy line until all Germans had been "mopped up" and

---

28 TNA WO 32/5754/54: Swinton to Major General Burnett-Stuart (BGGS, GHQ), 8 July 1916.
29 KCL: Fuller papers I/3/1: A pencilled annotation on this memorandum states that it was written by Swinton and staff, HS MGC.

their deep dug-outs cleared. Swinton's letter included a single page of "Tank Tips", clearly written for the benefit of tank commanders, although it is not known if the advice ever made it to the battlefield.[30]

All these various views were coalesced into a succinct paper issued by Major-General Launcelot Kiggell, CGS at GHQ, on 16 August 1916. It was sent personally to the commander of the Fourth Army, General Sir Henry Rawlinson, and of the Reserve Army, General Sir Hubert Gough, as they prepared for the forthcoming September offensive. The covering letter gave a brief summary of the C-in-C's intentions, listed the characteristics of the tank and invited Rawlinson and Gough to consider how they could best employ the new weapons. Kiggell listed a number of points for consideration by the commanders and emphasised that "the objectives of the 'tanks' must be clearly stated and as simple as possible, as it is difficult for the 'tanks' to manoeuvre."[31]

The paper reiterated the primary object of the tank; "to help the infantry forward and especially to deal with enemy machine guns." It realistically pointed out that the original concept of an advance in line of large numbers of machines involving "an approach march and deployment under cover, a surprise start, accurate keeping of alignment and direction … renders this a difficult operation." It cautioned that a tank cannot, except at great risk, cross a heavy barrage of H.E. or gas shells and it cannot lie out in the open under shell fire." The employment of the tanks would be limited "unless we are prepared to risk the loss of all the tanks by pushing them as far forward as they can go, if possible right through to the enemy's gun positions."[32]

By the time the guidance was issued it was clear that only a handful of tanks would be available by September. The document suggested a number of ways that this small quantity could be best deployed:

a)   The advance in line in large numbers;
b)   The attack in groups, or pairs, against selected objectives;
c)   Employment singly, or in pairs, for special purposes;
d)   Employment as mobile light artillery

The document concluded on a cautious but realistic note:

> The tank is a novel engine of war, and untried. Its use will require careful study and preparation on each separate occasion…every attack by tanks must be combined with an infantry attack and it will be the special duty of the infantry to co-operate closely with the tanks …

30   TNA WO 32/5754: Swinton to DSD, 27 July 1916.
31   TNA WO 158/235/172: Kiggell (CGS GHQ) to Commanders 4th and Reserve Armies, 16 August 1916. See also Miles, *OH 1916*, Vol. II, Appendix 15.
32   TNA WO 32/5754: Preliminary Notes on Tactical Employment of Tanks (Provisional), 16 August 1916. See also Miles, *OH 1916*, Vol. II, Appendix 15.

It is not known who the author of the document was, possibly Kiggell himself, but it is clear that the paper did not take Swinton's original proposals at face value. It was a more thoughtful and considered appraisal of the limitations of the new weapon as well as of its potential. It was an important document in that it encapsulates GHQ's views on the tactical employment of tanks on the eve of their debut on the Somme in September 1916. It illustrated the fact that elements of GHQ had given considerable thought to the practical use of this new addition to its armoury. The document could be criticised for being unduly cautious but, on balance, the author was pointing out the known limitations of the new, untested weapon.

What is remarkable is that, in the very short period between the first appearance of an entirely new weapon of war in February to its first deployment in September 1916, a body of tactical doctrine had emerged, been refined and disseminated to the commanders involved. All this was done against a background of uncertainty as to how many weapons would be available and how they would actually perform, with the added constraint of maintaining secrecy. Meanwhile Swinton, the man charged with both finding and training the crews, had very limited time and resources in which to do so.

Early Crew Training

First, authority had to be sought for the formation and organisation of the new corps. At a War Office conference held on 14 February 1916 attended by the Director of Operations, and representatives of the Staff Duties, Adjutant General and Finance branches, it was recommended that the new "tank detachment" should form part of the Motor Machine Gun Service [MMGS] of the Machine Gun Corps [MGC], as no further MMGS batteries were being formed. The committee felt it unlikely that many RNAS personnel would transfer from 20th Squadron into the MGC as the rates of pay were inferior. It was more likely that personnel would come from the MMGS.[33] On 17 March 1916, Swinton was approved as the commander of the "special Corps" which was to be located in part of the barracks at Bisley occupied by the MMGC Training Centre. The need for secrecy was again emphasised and all matters regarding training and resources were to be addressed directly and confidentially to the Staff Duties branch at War Office.[34] On 1 May 1916, the War Office confirmed that the "Tank Detachment" of the MGC would be renamed the "Heavy Section, Machine Gun Corps" [HSMGC] in order to preserve the secret nature of the unit.[35]

33 TNA WO 32/5754/6: Recommendations of Conference held at War Office, 14 February 1916.
34 TNA WO 32/5754: Letter Major-General Whigham for CIGS to the C-in-C Home Forces, 17 March 1916.
35 TNA WO 32/5754: Letter Secretary of the War Office to C-in-C Home Forces, 1 May 1916.

HSMGC officer and NCO in 1916 issue leather tank helmet.

Initially, Swinton wanted the unit organised into three battalions of five companies. Each company would contain two sections with six tanks apiece. GHQ rejected this idea and wanted a company to be an independent tactical unit.[36] Therefore, the organisation was set at six companies each with 25 tanks in four sections of six tanks and a spare. This arrangement required an establishment of 184 officers and 1,610 other ranks.[37]

Attention turned to the recruitment of suitable manpower. Swinton had recommended that the officers and men be "trained at home … to steer and operate over an imitation British and German trench zone by the aid of trench maps similar to our aeroplane maps of the German defensive positions."[38] Confidential letters were sent out in January 1916 to the COs of Special Reserve and Training Regiments in the UK for officer volunteers. Officers had to be under 25 and capable of driving cars. No particular requirements appear to have been laid down for the NCOs and soldiers, although a number of ASC Motor Transport drivers who had worked on the experimental Admiralty machines elected to transfer.

The former commander of the MMGC, Lieutenant-Colonel R.W. Bradley, transferred to become Swinton's second-in-command. In April, he and Swinton toured officer cadet units, in particular the 18th, 19th and 20th (Public Schools) battalions of the Royal Fusiliers, to spot potential officers with some mechanical experience.[39] They

36 No reason was given for this decision. It is possible that, at this stage, GHQ regarded a company of tanks as a tactical addition to an infantry unit rather than part of a newly-created, independent organisation.
37 Liddell Hart, *Tanks*, Vol. I, p. 55.
38 Swinton, 'Notes on the Employment of Tanks'.
39 William-Ellis, *The Tank Corps*, p. 16.

even enlisted the help of the popular magazine, *The Motor Cycle*, to attract men from the motor engineering trades.[40] Some personnel from the MMGC transferred into the new unit but, as the War Office had predicted, not a single man of 20th Squadron RNAS volunteered to join. This was hardly surprising as naval pay was almost three times that being offered by the Army.

Training was carried out initially at Siberia Camp, Bisley, the former training centre of the MMGC. Two new companies of the MGC were formed K and L, which together formed the HSMGC. No tanks were yet available to train on, so exercises concentrated on the weapons; the Vickers and Hotchkiss machine guns and the Hotchkiss 6-pounder QF gun. Captain D.G. Browne who joined the Tank Corps around this time, described those early days at Bisley:

> There being as yet no tanks available for training purposes, the programme of work at Bisley was limited virtually to drill and courses on the Hotchkiss guns. It would be absurd to pretend that any of this was taken very seriously…the new formation suffered inevitably from a lack of competent and energetic senior officers … Of the subaltern officers probably about 75 per cent represented as good material as could be found anywhere- a high proportion, in view of the extraordinary and haphazard processes by which the commissioned ranks of the New Army were filled, and one that compared favourably with that of most infantry units.[41]

One of the first officers to volunteer, Lieutenant Raikes of the South Wales Borderers, met his section of recruits for the first time in April 1916. They were mainly men who had enlisted under the Lord Derby recruiting scheme and "no attempt had been made to pick men with mechanical experience or who could even drive a lorry!." They were taught how to handle the Hotchkiss and Vickers Machine Guns and the 6-pounder gun at Bisley and with the Royal Navy at Portsmouth. But their first encounter with an actual tank was not until June when part of the Heavy Section had moved to Thetford to conduct its training in greater secrecy. They then had less than two-and-a-half months to learn how to drive and maintain the machines before going into action for the first time in September 1916. Raikes remarked:

> It is amusing to think that the first tanks were actually taken into action by men who had not been in the Army for more than four months although a lot of the Officers had seen service in France before.[42]

---

40   Liddell Hart, *Tanks,* Vol. I, p. 54.
41   Captain D.G., Browne, *The Tanks in Action* (London: Blackwood, 1920), p. 24.
42   TM E2007:2411: Colonel Raikes correspondence to *Tank Journal*, 8 January 1951.

The training facilities at Bisley proved unsuitable. The training area was not sufficiently remote to provide necessary security. Attempts to fire practice rounds from the borrowed 6-pounders proved dangerous when the shots strayed outside the range boundary. Thus, 6-pounder practice had to be carried out on the Naval ranges at Portsmouth and Chatham and on the artillery ranges at Larkhill, although firing at sea with the Royal Navy provided useful training for engaging moving targets from the tanks.[43]

A more remote and suitable area was sought and found on Lord Iveagh's estate at Elveden, near Thetford, Norfolk to which the Heavy Section began to move in June.[44] A secure training area was created with a branch railway line to receive and despatch tanks. A practice area was constructed:

> The area was turned into an imitation of the trench front in France … this practice battlefield was designed by Captain G.LeQ. Martel RE, who was sent over by GHQ for the purpose and constructed by three Pioneer battalions. The 'section' was one and a half miles in width and in depth embraced the British support and front line, No Man's Land and the German first, second and third lines. It included all forms of obstacle and entrenchments likely to be met in the enemy's defensive zone.[45]

Delays in the production of tanks meant that driver training could not start until the arrival of the first batch in mid June. "The men were both clever and keen, and the most serious trouble was the insufficient supply of tanks on which to train them. Many drivers had spent no more than an hour or two in a tank before they left for France."[46] The GHQ imperative was to employ whatever tanks were available for an offensive in mid-September. Even when a few arrived in late June, there remained the problem of what form the instruction should take, other than the mechanical and gunnery skills.

> It would be difficult to over-estimate the difficulties which confronted those officers responsible for the preliminary training of the Heavy Section of the Machine Gun Section; no-one had actually fought inside a Tank … There was no manual to guide them.[47]

Training concentrated on mechanical knowledge of the tank and peculiarities of particular vehicles; thorough knowledge of the 6-pounder gun and machine guns;

---

43 Liddell Hart, *Tanks*, Vol. I, p. 55.
44 For more information, see David Fletcher 'The First Tanks at Elveden', *Stand To!: The Journal of the Western Front Association* (February 2016).
45 Liddell Hart, *Tanks*, Vol. I, p. 56.
46 Browne, *Tanks in Action*, p. 27.
47 Williams-Ellis, *Tank Corps*, p. 19.

crew duties; physical fitness and revolver shooting. Some aspects were not covered either through lack of time, lack of resources or lack of knowledge of what was needed:

> We had no reconnaissance or map reading ... no practices or lectures on the compass ... we had no signalling ... and no practice in considering orders ... We had no knowledge of where to look for information that would be necessary for us as Tank Commanders, nor did we know what information we should be likely to require. We had no signalling and only one day revolver drill and one day revolver shooting on the range. In England we were issued with goggles and the old type of the gas helmets but the men never had a gas drill and did not know how to put on their helmets and goggle when we got to France. Nearly all these things would have been rectified had we had longer time in which to do the training which was on the syllabus. Perhaps the most important point of all is that we had only once fired from a moving tank ... I cannot emphasise too strongly how much I feel that it is essential that the crew and Tank Commander should fire from a moving tank at unknown targets.[48]

Swinton was under constant pressure from GHQ to provide more tanks and trained personnel. In April, GHQ had increased their order to 150 tanks and, following a meeting in London with Haig on 14 April 1916, Swinton was invited to produce these tanks by June for the planned Somme offensive. This was an entirely unrealistic request and on 26 April 1916 Swinton wrote to GHQ to explain the supply position stating: "it is best to be categorical as to what we expect can or cannot be done, and so as to avoid disappointment and the reversal of plans." He explained that no tanks would be ready by 1 June, that some tanks would be available by July but these were un-armed tanks used for training only and not suitable for combat. He thought that all tanks would be ready by 1 August, "strikes and Acts of God excepted", and that 75 trained crews would be ready by then, provided sufficient tanks were received to train on.[49]

On 15 May 1916, Swinton wrote again to Butler, stating that the supply position was unchanged and that he had got nearly all the officers he wanted and most of the men; machine guns were arriving but there was a "hitch" with 6-pounder ammunition. Driving was progressing slowly as he only had one tank, Big Willie, to train on.[50] On 14 June 1916 he sent a detailed progress report to Butler. Having sent Stern to the manufacturing works at Lincoln to check on progress, he provided a breakdown of when he anticipated tanks would be ready for despatch to France. He was optimistic that all 150 would be ready, in batches, by the beginning of September, but there were delays in the supply of machine guns, 6-pounders and sponsons.[51]

---

48 Ibid., p. 20.
49 TNA WO 32/5754: Swinton to Butler (DCGS GHQ), 26 April 1916.
50 TNA WO 32/5754: Swinton to Butler, 15 May 1916.
51 TNA WO 32/5754: Swinton to Butler, 14 June 1916.

Training on the 6-pounders was limited by the fact that he had had to borrow five guns – four from the Navy and one from the Royal Military Academy, Woolwich – and even these had different mountings. He had difficulty finding suitable ranges but hoped that problem would be solved when the entire unit moved to Elveden. Driver training was progressing but with only one tank, progress was slow. He anticipated getting another 25 tanks by the end of July which would coincide with the completion of the practice battlefield. At that point three companies would be located at Elveden and tactical training could begin in earnest. In reality, as Swinton later observed:

> There was no time for practicing the Tanks in accordance with any elaborate tactical scheme. All that could be taught was the art of manoeuvring together with the straightforward object of searching out and destroying machine guns emplaced in every kind of artfully concealed position. Had there been time the next step would have been combined operations with the infantry.[52]

By 21 July, training had advanced to the extent that a tactical demonstration using 25 tanks could be held at Elveden for the benefit of the CIGS, representatives from GHQ and David Lloyd George, the new Secretary-of-State for War. On 8 August 1916, Swinton reported to DSD that because of problems with the delivery of "accessories and spares" which would not be available until 1 September, tanks that had already been sent to France could not be used in battle although they would be suitable for training with the infantry. "Accessories" referred to tank guns and sponsons.[53]

Three companies of tanks were allocated to the September offensive. The first company of tanks was sent to France on 13 August 1916 in two batches. The tanks were in such a poor state of maintenance, having been used continuously for training, that they were only made battle-ready with the help of a large volunteer party of fitters sent from the manufacturers. The companies went first to an improvised training facility at Yvrench then onto a concentration area at The Loop close to the front. A second company followed in late August arriving just two days before the planned attack. The third company arrived in France too late to take part in the attack.

The precious little time available for further training, critically with their supporting battalions, was curtailed by essential battle preparations and constant demonstrations of the new weapon to "embarrassing numbers" of staff officers and curious on-lookers.[54]

> Meanwhile, the Tank crews and commanders had been enjoying three or four days of almost comically complete nightmare. In the first place they had all manner of mechanical preoccupations- newly arrived spare engine parts to test, new guns to adjust, box respirators to struggle with, and an astonishing amount

---

52 Ernest Swinton, *Eyewitness*, p. 272.
53 TNA WO 32/5754: Swinton to DSD, 8 August 1916.
54 Miles, *OH 1916*, Vol. II, p. 296.

Mark I 'Female' tank, September 1916. This photograph provides a clear impression of its camouflage paint scheme.

of "battle luggage" to stow away. But worst of all they found themselves regarded as the star variety-turn of the Western Front. At Yvrench they had performed in front of General Joffre, Sir Douglas Haig and the greater part of the GHQ staff.[55]

Swinton remarked:

> Some of the machines were asked to force their way through a wood and knock down trees – tricks which they had not been designed to play and which were likely to damage them seriously. I protested against these 'stunts' and the frequent exhibitions, which were wearing out both machines and personnel. In addition to the almost continuous work of repairing, learning and tuning up their Tanks, the men barely had time to eat sleep and tend themselves. I speculated as to how many machines would be one hundred per cent to go into action when the day arrived.[56]

At a demonstration with 7th Middlesex on 26 August,[57] Haig made his prescient remark: "Altogether the demonstration was quite encouraging, but we require to clear our ideas as to the tactical handling of these machines."[58]

---

55 Williams-Ellis, *Tank Corps*, p. 26.
56 Swinton, *Eyewitness*, p. 279.
57 TNA WO 95/2950: 7th Middlesex War Diary, 26 August 1916.
58 TNA WO 256/12: Haig diary entry, 26 August 1916.

On 13 September 1916, the tanks moved out of the concentration area at the Loop to their assembly areas and the following night to their starting locations just behind the frontline. It was a salutary experience for the debut of the tank. Exhausted crews, many now gaining their first experience of a battlefield, faced the reality of two short night moves across muddy, shell-cratered ground. At this stage, reconnaissance and planning of routes for the tanks was the responsibility of the supporting divisional staff. "It is to be feared that in many cases young and inexperienced tank commanders found themselves overburdened with directions and instructions, which, in many cases, had to be memorised, as there were not enough copies to go around."[59] Only 36 of the 49 tanks reached their starting points for the attack the following morning. The time for training was over; the day of battle had arrived.[60]

Conclusion

Had a credible body of doctrine evolved in the eight months between the first appearance of a practical fighting vehicle in February 1916 and its deployment for the first time on 15 September 1916? Did the commanders involved have sufficient knowledge and guidance in the tactical use of the new weapon? Were the first crews adequately trained for their initiation into combat? Credit must be given to Swinton for his tireless efforts to produce a workable body of doctrine for the employment of the tanks. In addition to his early unofficial and verbal lobbying, Swinton produced no less than three substantive memoranda on the subject, the last in July 1916. He sought the views of other experienced commentators and sent a staff officer to GHQ to elicit their views. His recommendations were eventually amended and condensed into the "Notes" sent to the two Army commanders in mid-August, giving them just over a month to prepare their plans for the offensive and the part that the tanks were to play in it.

Swinton had the unenviable task of not only setting up the new unit, recruiting officers and men for it, writing the tactical doctrine, acting as a liaison between the demands of GHQ for more tanks and the realities of supply from the manufacturers, agreeing modifications and improvements to the vehicles, finding a suitable training area and moving his organisation to it and in addition supervising the training of the crews and commanders with insufficient resources. All this was achieved in the short space of eight months. The fact that any tanks went into action on 15 September to achieve a modest degree of success reflects greatly on Swinton's often ignored efforts. In a final irony, he was ultimately denied the opportunity of commanding tanks in action, that honour being given to former subordinate Hugh Elles.

59 Miles, *OH 1916*, Vol. II, p. 297, fn. 2.
60 For accounts of the tank actions on the Somme in September 1916, see Liddell Hart, *Tanks*, Vol. I; Williams-Ellis, *Tank Corps* and Trevor Pidgeon, *The Tanks at Flers* (Cobham: Fairmile Books, 1995).

16

"A Ragged Business": Officer Training Corps, Public Schools and the Recruitment of the Junior Officers Corps of 1916

Timothy Halstead

> *Mobilisation for war is for every Power a ragged business. We have our peace establishment of Regular officers. There is practically no deficiency there. But when we pass to mobilisation we want a great many more officers.*[1]

When Britain went to war on 4 August 1914 it is generally acknowledged that the mobilisation of the British Expeditionary Force was a well-planned and executed exercise, the details of which had been set out in the 'War Book' which had been prepared by the Government in the years leading up to 1914. This highly-detailed volume laid down the administrative arrangements for the actions to be taken by each government department in the event of war.[2] The clearest demonstration of the success of the 'War Book' was the speed with which the railways were mobilised so that the regular army could be transported to the south coast prior to deployment to France. The plan specified that the troops were to be sent to Southampton to be embarked and the detailed timetable allowed for troop trains to arrive at the port every twelve minutes for sixteen hours each day. By 31 August 1914, 670 trains had carried nearly 120,000 soldiers to the port.[3]

However, while the plan successfully addressed the immediate problems of mobilising for war it did not address the long-term strategy required to sustain or develop the British Army beyond deployment. The pre-war government's view was that Britain's main contribution would be at sea, which would include a naval blockade

---

1 Lord Haldane, *Parliamentary Debates 1912*, Vol. II, 13 May 1912, House of Lords, columns 984-6.
2 David French, *British Economic and Strategic Planning 1905-1915* (London: George, Allen & Unwin, 1982), p. 82.
3 Christian Wolmar, *Engines of War: How Wars Were Won & Lost on the Railways* (London: Atlantic Books, 2010), p. 155.

of Germany, but a comparatively low level of involvement on the continent. Britain would support the war through its economic strength and by providing financial and logistical support to its allies. The appointment of Lord Kitchener as Secretary of State for War on 5 August 1914 led to a radical change in the Government's policy. He quickly disabused the cabinet of the notion that the war would be a short one and informed them that a large army to fight on the continent would be needed if the war was to be won. To lead this new army it was necessary to identify and recruit suitable men as junior officers. At the outbreak of the war the British army had 24,896 officers but by November 1916 this had grown into an officer corps of 122,352.[4] The vast majority of this expanded corps were new junior officers. As Peter Simkins points out, during Kitchener's term of office it was necessary to find *at least* 30,000 officers to lead the infantry battalions which he had created. This figure took no account of replacing the casualties suffered or the officers needed for other parts of the army such as the Royal Engineers, Royal Artillery and the Army Service Corps.[5] With no plans or mechanisms in place to initiate such an expansion it was inevitable that the process of recruiting junior officers would be, as Lord Haldane predicted a "ragged business."

To understand the composition of the Junior Officer Corps in 1916 it is necessary to examine how the men who formed it were recruited in 1914 and 1915. Inevitably, carrying out a rapid expansion from such a low base of preparedness would require a great deal of improvisation. To understand the capabilities of the junior officer corps in 1916 it is necessary to study the system which had produced them. Although by the beginning of 1916 a more coherent and formal system for recruiting junior officers had evolved, the officers who served in the opening of the Battle of the Somme were primarily products of the early, ad-hoc approach to recruitment. This improvised approach means that the expansion of the junior officer corps cannot be solely explained by factors such as drawing on young men with experience of serving in the Officers Training Corps (OTC) of the leading public schools. The expansion of the junior officer corps was complex and nuanced. It is the purpose of this chapter to explore the process with reference to the Officer Training Corps (OTC) system. The chapter will consider how recruitment and training evolved between 1914 and 1916 and will show how a nascent informal approach became more structured during this period. Although far from perfect, it proved to be successful in building, from scratch, the junior officer corps of a citizen army.

---

4   War Office, *Statistics of the Military Effort of the British Empire During the Great War 1914-1920* (London: HMSO, 1922), pp. 30-31.
5   Peter Simkins, *Kitchener's Army: the Raising of the New Armies 1914-1916* (Barnsley: Pen & Sword, 1988), p. 212.

A Low Base

In the years before the war there were several factors which had constrained the preparation of the British army for war. Both long and short term political factors led to the army being, until 1914, a relatively small body. Up until the start of the twentieth century it was not necessary for Britain to have a large army. A standing force of continental proportions was not required by the British government, which could rely on its command of the sea for defence. In the event of war, the island geography of Britain and its naval mastery provided an insurance policy; if faced by a sudden attack by powerful enemies, Britain would have time to build up the necessary land forces to achieve victory.[6] Further, the Royal Navy could simultaneously protect the maritime trade routes upon which the prosperity of the Empire depended whilst denying them to any enemy. Therefore, it is unsurprising that Britain devoted its resources to supporting its navy, assigning relatively little to the army. In addition, especially amongst Liberals, the legacy of Cromwell in the seventeenth century continued to cast a shadow. After 1689 the annual passing of the Mutiny Act formed the basis on which the army existed, funded and governed itself. The events which followed the English Civil War had left British parliamentarians with a fear of military dictatorship. Even after the end of the Napoleonic threat in 1815 both the main political parties endeavoured to keep army expenditure as low as possible.[7] Such constitutional and political luxuries were the privilege of an island nation with a strong navy; the countries of mainland Europe with substantial land borders were not in the same position and conscription was a necessity.

The landslide victory won by the Liberal party in 1906 gave them the opportunity to implement a peace dividend after the Boer War.[8] To fund the planned programme of radical social reforms the well-off needed to be taxed more heavily, and savings had to be found elsewhere. The army, with its ambivalent relationship with politicians, was a natural target. Its annual budget was reduced and restricted to £28million per annum. It was within the constraints of expenditure and political suspicion of the army that the new Secretary of State for War, Richard Haldane, had to act. Haldane, a Liberal Imperialist in a party split between imperialists and radicals, was concerned about the German threat to the British Empire and used his considerable skills to address it while working under these political constraints. Despite the stringent financial limitations, his pragmatic approach and a notable ability to manage the resources available efficiently allowed him to make considerable progress. He concentrated on building a small professional army and developing the Territorial Force (TF) and

---

6   Michael Howard, Introduction in Michael Howard (ed.), *Soldiers and Governments Nine Studies in Civil-Military Relations* (London: Eyre & Spottiswoode, 1957), pp. 13-14.
7   Robert Blake, 'Great Britain The Crimean War to the First World War', in Howard (ed.) *Soldiers and Governments*, pp. 27-28.
8   Niall Ferguson, *Empire: How Britain Made the Modern World* (London: Penguin, 2004), p. 287.

Special Reserves (SR) to provide ready access to additional trained men in the event of war.[9] His reforms also created other organisations including the OTC to feed recruits into the TF and SR. The OTC, which came into effect in 1908, made the system of university and school rifle corps which had existed since the late nineteenth century considerably more efficient. Instead of being attached to their local regiments, the OTC contingents came under the direct control of the War Office for the first time. This allowed the development of an OTC training programme which was integrated into that of the army as a whole. As a result, cadets in the OTC received training which equipped them to gain commissions as junior officers relatively quickly. This was a notable improvement from the situation which Britain had found itself in during the Boer War when it recruited "suitable gentlemen" as officers but sent them into action without any training.[10]

Haldane's reforms were limited by the political circumstances of the day. He preferred to achieve consensus rather than push for radical changes. Although the reform of the OTC was a positive development it only provided a small number of officer candidates for the Army. As Lord Kitchener recognised at the start of the war, Haldane's reforms did not place the British Army in a position where it could make a significant military contribution to victory. In August 1914 Britain not only needed to expand its army rapidly, but on a scale far greater than it had ever done in the past.[11]

Starting from Scratch

When Kitchener assumed the post of Secretary of State for War in 1914 he in effect tore up Haldane's approach to growing the army to fight the war. The TF was sidelined and no longer a key part of feeding men into the army. Instead it was decided to create a new army through a massive expansion of existing regular battalions; the men would be provided by a nationwide call for volunteers. This sudden change of approach meant that there was no mechanism in place to recruit and train the junior officers in sufficient numbers to lead this new army and, in effect, it was necessary to start from scratch. Until 1910 the army had drawn its officers from a relatively small social group consisting mainly of "families with military connections, the gentry and peerage and to some degree the professions and clergy."[12] The need to develop a more professional officer corps led to a widening of the social groups the army drew on in

---

9   E.M. Spiers, *Haldane: An Army Reformer* (Edinburgh: Edinburgh University Press, 1980), p. 191.
10 John Mason Sneddon, 'The Company Commander' in Spencer Jones (ed.) *Stemming the Tide: Officers and Leadership in the British Expeditionary Force 1914* (Solihull: Helion, 2013), p. 317.
11 Simkins, *Kitchener's Army*, p. 40.
12 Gary Sheffield, 'Officer-man Relations: Morale and Discipline in the British Army 1902–22' (PhD thesis, King's College London, 1994, p. 3.

Dulwich College OTC camp inspection 1913.

Cranleigh School OTC summer camp postcard 1914.

the following years but even this expanded base was insufficient to provide all the officers that new army would need.

Considering this lack of preparation, it is unsurprising that the approach to recruiting officers was haphazard. On 10 August the first appeal was made for 2,000 officers; *The Times* contained an announcement from the War Office that it required 2,000 unmarried men for commissions in the regular army. It asked for men who were, or had been, cadets in university OTCs or had a good general education.[13] The War Office also took a more pro-active approach and wrote to potential candidates; Philip Howe, who ended the war as a captain in the West Yorkshire Regiment had graduated from Sheffield University and served in its OTC contingent, received a letter inviting him to apply for a commission. The policy of the War Office to recruit gentlemen as officers was clear but somewhat simplistic.[14] It was fortunate that applications for commissions far exceeded the 2,000 initially required.[15] As recruitment continued apace it became clear that the War Office could not identify and recruit all possible candidates, and by September 1914, Kitchener had devolved the recommendations for commissions to battalion commanding officers. With no equivalent of the detailed modern day 'person specification' to fill the positions it is dangerous to overemphasise the importance of qualifications such as membership of the OTC. Battalion COs were left to judge for themselves what constituted a suitable candidate (and gentleman). In these circumstances there was inevitably a combination of factors which led to a successful application for a commission. These included membership of the OTC, the sort of school attended, having the right connections and sometimes even bribery.

The idea of getting the "right sort" of man was such an esoteric concept that it is difficult to identify even an informal methodology. Analysing the recruitment of cadets from the Junior OTC demonstrates how any attempt to apply a model to junior officer recruitment is flawed. By March 1915, at least 16,000 former cadets from Junior OTC contingents had been awarded commissions. However, the proportion of candidates who enlisted and were granted commissions varied a great deal. At Harrow, the 370 former cadets had all been granted commissions whereas in the case of Wellington College in Somerset only forty-three of the 105 who had enlisted had won commissions. Indeed, the ten leading schools who contributed the most officers to the army before the war (Charterhouse, Cheltenham, Clifton, Eton, Haileybury, Harrow, Marlborough, Rugby, Wellington College and Winchester) provided thirty-eight percent of OTC cadets who held a commission by March 1915. In total, they provided just under twenty-one percent of all OTC cadets recruited during the period demonstrating that the cadets of the ten leading schools were far more likely to be

---

13   *The Times*, 10 August 1914, p. 5.
14   Christopher Moore-Bick, *Playing the Game: The British Junior Infantry Officer on the Western Front 1914-18* (Solihull: Helion, 2011), p. 19.
15   Simkins, *Kitchener's Army*, p. 213.

awarded commissions. On average, ninety-four percent of the cadets from the ten leading schools were awarded commissions. The cadets from these schools were a known quantity to the army and therefore it is no surprise it significantly drew on these schools for cadets.

Further analysis reveals that fifty-nine schools had had over seventy-five percent of their former OTC cadets accepted for commissions by March 1915. These fifty-nine schools made up thirty-six percent of the 166 schools with OTC contingents in March 1915, but provided sixty-seven percent of the cadets from the Junior OTC who gained commissions by March 1915. In other words, just over one third of the OTC contingents had provided over two thirds of OTC officers. The table below shows a sample of nine schools from the fifty-nine which had had over seventy-five percent of their former OTC cadets accepted for commissions by March 1915. From this sample can be seen the dangers of taking a one size fits all approach to understanding the contribution of the OTC and public schools to providing officers for the new army.

Table 1   Enlistment Analysis – Selection of Junior OTC Contingents with over 75-percent of Cadets obtaining commissions[16]

	Former Cadet Officers at 14 Aug	Commissions 14 Aug to 15 March	Serving in the ranks 15 March	Total enlisted to 15 March	Commissions to 15 March	Officers as percent of total
Charterhouse	198	411	79	688	609	88.5
Clifton College	192	206	34	432	398	92.1
Eton	145	850	13	1,008	995	98.7
Grimsby Municipal College	0	25	0	25	25	100.0
Harrow School	117	253	0	370	370	100.0
Lancing College	59	143	41	243	202	83.1
Oakham School	46	65	17	128	111	86.7
Oundle School	29	197	75	301	226	75.1
Uppingham School	61	215	74	350	276	78.9
Westminster School	39	88	41	168	127	75.6

The data shows that of the 166 schools with OTC contingents in March 1915 ninety were members of the Headmaster's Conference (HMC). Discussion amongst educationalists about what constitutes a public school can descend into some very fine semantics but a broad definition of a public school in 1915 was one that was a member of the HMC. Of the fifty-nine schools mentioned above, only forty four

---

16   The table and accompanying text is based on analysis of Captain Alan R. Haig-Brown, *The O.T.C. and the Great War* (London: Country Life, 1915), pp. 97-106.

were members of the HMC. Less than half of the public schools had converted the vast majority of their OTC cadets into officers by 1915. Indeed, of the fifty nine OTC contingents which had had done so, twenty-five percent were not members of the HMC at all. In other words, there was a not a straight forward prejudice within the army towards those contingents with a public school background. Within this list are four schools which had traditionally been public schools long before the great Victorian expansion in the movement: Charterhouse, Eton, Harrow and Westminster. Four schools in the table were members of the group of the ten leading 'army' schools: Charterhouse, Clifton, Eton and Harrow. One, Uppingham, thanks to the efforts of the great Victorian educationalist, Edward Thring, had become one of the leading public schools in the second half of the nineteenth century. Three schools listed (Lancing, Oakham and Oundle) were considered to be less significant public schools and one, Grimsby Municipal College, was a technical college.

Examining these last four schools demonstrates how the army could draw on sources outside its traditional base. Grimsby Municipal College OTC demonstrates that the selection of officers went beyond relying on the top 'army' schools. Its cadets provided many officers to the local Pals battalion, the Grimsby Chums. The elevation of these cadets to commissions was in response to the unique character of the Pals battalions and the unusual circumstances of Grimsby. The fishing town had only expanded in the 1850s with the arrival of the railway and was to all intents and purposes a new town. As a result, there was no tradition of wealthy local men sending their sons away to public school. These young men were educated locally, continued to live in Grimsby and therefore did not have a background which the army would normally have expected of a gentleman (and junior officer). Pals battalions were based on a shared background such as a regional identity or common place of work; it was natural, therefore, for the Pals officers to come from the same background. The existence of an OTC in Grimsby provided an obvious source of officers for the Chums. All twenty five cadets from the college's OTC had gained commissions by March 1915, almost certainly because they were judged to have an adequate mix of skills and local background to make them suitable officers. Officers for the Chums were also drawn from Worksop College (a Woodard boarding school in north Nottinghamshire which, while not an HMC member, also had an OTC contingent).[17] Ernest Stream, principal of the college and the CO of its OTC, was a dynamic figure who had played a leading part in the formation of the Chums.[18] Although the national OTC had been designed to provide common and integrated training for potential officers it is clear from the example of Stream and others that dynamic leadership was important in providing effective training. The CO of Lancing College OTC, Alan Haig Brown was a leading figure within the OTC movement and in 1915 published *The O.T.C. and*

---

17 Peter Chapman, Grimsby Chums correspondence, 3 July 2015.
18 Major General C.R. Simpson (ed.), *The History of the Lincolnshire Regiment 1914-1918* (London: Medici Society, 1931), pp. 51-52.

OTC cadets, Hare Hall Camp, Romford, Essex 1915.

Dulwich College OTC 1915.

the Great War which celebrated the movement's contribution to the war. He was CO of the college's OTC from its formation in 1908 to 1915 when he left to serve with the army. At Lancing, it is claimed that the contingent was the first one where every boy was a member on a voluntary basis.[19] This was quite an achievement due to the competition between sporting clubs and the OTC for members. Although there was pressure within the school to enlist this would have been countered by the demands of games for leading sportsmen. Many of the latter in schools where membership was voluntary chose not to join their OTC contingent.[20]

The recruitment of officers from a restricted range of OTC contingents points to their reputation and efficiency being an important factor. The War Office carried out annual inspections of all OTC contingents; this was not just a cursory examination but a thorough exercise to confirm their efficiency. The reports on the inspections were not bland and uncritical and the War Office developed a strong impression as to which were the best contingents. The reputation and background of the school was not the only factor in judging its efficiency. Oakham, just under eighty-seven percent of whose cadets had become officers by March 1915, had no military tradition and was far from a typical public school. Although a founder member of the HMC in 1869 it had then left the organisation, as its fortunes waned at the same time as nearby Uppingham expanded under Thring. It had only been readmitted into the HMC in 1911 after the school's decline was halted by the awarding of direct grant status so that it became Rutland's grammar school as well as a boarding school. The OTC at Oakham was only established in 1911; unlike many other schools it had not established a rifle corps, such as Oundle which had established one in 1903 after the Boer War, which had then become part of the OTC in 1908. The Headmaster of Oakham had decided in 1911 that the interesting training provided by the OTC made it a useful addition to the school's curriculum; the same year he had also increased the amount of Army class work at the school.[21] That 111 of its 128 cadets who had enlisted had gained commissions by March 1915 when many other schools with a longer military tradition lagged behind, indicates that Oakham's OTC contingent and its Army class was highly regarded.

Nevertheless, the reputation of a school still played an important part in its success at providing men to take up commissions. Oundle under Sanderson had gained a reputation for its emphasis on the sciences and bringing the best out of every boy.[22] In early 1915, when Cecil Lewis was interviewed by Captain Lord Hugh Cecil for a

---

19 Lancing College War Memorial, Lieutenant Colonel Alan Roderick Haig-Brown DSO <http://www.hambo.org/lancing/view_man.php?id=132> (Accessed 31 December 2016).
20 Timothy Halstead, 'The First World and Public School Ethos: The Case of Uppingham School', *War and Society*, 34: 3 (August 2015), pp. 209-229.
21 *Grantham Journal*, 5 August 1911, p. 2.
22 Richard John Palmer, *The Life of F.W. Sanderson (1857-1922) with Special Reference to His Work and Influence at Oundle School (1892-1922)* (Hull: University of Hull Department of Education, 1981), pp. 365-366.

commission, Cecil clearly held Sanderson in high esteem and the connection was of great assistance in gaining Lewis a commission, despite being underage.[23] This reputation rubbed off on other old boys from Oundle; boys who had not served in the OTC, although they may have served in the Rifle Corps, were clearly attractive to recruiters because of the school's reputation. By March 1915, Oundle had provided 301 former OTC cadets to the army; 226 had gained commissions. The Oundle figures demonstrate that many who had not served in the OTC had enlisted and become officers. By November 1914, 440 men had enlisted. A year later, in November 1915, the figure had risen to 657; 45 of whom had been killed in action.[24]

It was often the school itself, rather than the OTC exclusively, which provided officers. At Uppingham, only thirty-seven percent of those who served in the Great War had been OTC cadets, yet over seventy-seven percent of Old Uppinhamians who joined the Army became junior officers. It is clear that junior officers were drawn from a wider catchment than merely the OTC. Indeed, by February 1916 and the introduction of conscription, an impressive seventy-percent of all the Old Uppinhamians who served in the war had already enlisted.[25]

The development of the junior officer corps by 1916 suggests that there was some sort of unofficial method to the process, if not a formally documented approach. Although the army did use some criteria in the recruitment of many officers this was not set in stone. More nuanced judgements were also made about the suitability of men to be officers. The case of St Georges, Harpenden illustrates how this could work. Founded in 1907, St Georges was the first co-educational boarding school and in 1914 was not yet a member of the HMC. It did not have an OTC contingent, instead having a Cadet Corps unit; the Cadet Corps was designed to prepare men to be soldiers whereas the OTC was designed to prepare men to be officers. Therefore it would appear St Georges was unlikely to be a good source of officers, especially as it was a relatively small school. However, during the war, of the seventy-eight boys who served sixty-two (seventy-nine percent) became officers.[26] To place some context on this, of those old boys from Wellington College, Somerset, which had an OTC contingent before the war, only thirty-nine percent were awarded commissions.[27] By the end of 1915, at least twenty-four Old Georgians had been granted commissions.[28] Examination of officer files for Old Georgians suggests a variety of reasons for this

23 Cecil Lewis, *Sagittarius Rising* (London: Penguin, 1977), pp. 18-19.
24 Palmer, *The Life of F.W. Sanderson*, p. 219.
25 Halstead, 'The First World and Public School Ethos: The Case of Uppingham School', pp. 222, 224.
26 Paddy Storrie, *"Here I am; Send me": The War Dead of St George's School 1914-1918* (Harpenden: St Georges School, 2004), p. 2.
27 Based on analysis of Asher C.J. Pirt MA, *WSS Old Boys and the Great War 1914-1918* (Watchett: Private publication, 2013).
28 Based on analysis of *The Great War 1914-1919: Old Georgians' Roll of Honour and Record of Service*, St Georges School Archive (SGSA).

decision. In some cases, it was because they were members of a University OTC. Some had brief experience of service in another school's OTC contingent. Others still were chosen simply because they had the right background. Old Georgians nearly all had a professional or middle class background.[29] The boys of Wellington, Somerset were drawn from an agricultural background.[30] In addition, to the more professional and commercial background of its pupils, St Georges had a distinctive educational ethos. The front page of its first prospectus in 1907 contained a long extract from Thring of Uppingham's educational ethos.[31] At the heart of Thring's approach to education was an aim to bring out the best in every boy so that they possessed independence, inquisitiveness, and self-confidence.[32] Men who displayed these qualities were attractive material to the army.[33] One of these men was Philips Muirhead, who was awarded a commission in October 1914 after enlisting in September 1914. Paddy Storrie suggests that Muirhead did not care for being in the ranks and that strings were pulled to get him a commission.[34] However, if strings were pulled it appears that it was easy to pull them to great effect. A letter from the Royal Horse Artillery, Woolwich, (the signature is indecipherable) makes enquiries about whether his application is likely to be successful. The writer describes him as being "an intelligent fellow well above the normal gunner." As further support the letter points out that Muirhead had been captain of the St Georges rugby team and had also played for his county. Sporting ability was a further qualification which could only help him to find a way through the heavy load of commission applications the War Office was handling.[35]

Sports qualifications were not the only path to a commission, especially as the war proceeded. Arthur Francis Scroggs had seen a short period of service with the St Pauls OTC; but the use of Form MT393 (which was for men who had not served in the OTC) to apply for a commission demonstrates it was not long enough to count. His file recommends him for a commission on the grounds that he was a mathematician and had a scholarship to Merton. With this background, he was granted a commission in the Royal Garrison Artillery where mathematical ability was a much-needed skill.[36]

29 Storrie, *"Here I am; Send me"*, p. 1.
30 J. de Symons Honey, *Tom Brown's Universe: The Development of the Victorian Public School* (London: Millington, 1977), p. 68.
31 SGSA: 1907 Prospectus.
32 Halstead, 'The First World and Public School Ethos', p. 227.
33 There was an indirect connection to Uppingham. A major figure in St Georges governance was Canon Hardwicke Rawnsley – one of the founders of the National Trust – who was an OU and protégé of Thring. See Malcolm Tozer, *The Ideal of Manliness: The Legacy of Thring's Uppingham* (Truro: Sunnyrest Books, 2015).
34 Storrie, *"Here I am; Send me"*, p. 44.
35 The National Archives (TNA) WO 339/17988: Lieutenant Phillips Quincy Muirhead, Royal Field Artillery.
36 TNA WO 339/72553: Lieutenant Arthur Francis Scroggs, Royal Garrison Artillery.

Other Old Georgians could draw on social connections and enrol with the socially exclusive Artists' Rifles. The Artists' Rifles, which rapidly became an OTC unit, had to use unconventional methods to select men. When war broke out the regiment searched the London telephone book for men with socially acceptable addresses. The men identified were sent handwritten invitations to join the regiment. However, the response was overwhelming and large crowds gathered outside the barracks. Unable to handle the volume of enquirers, some NCOs changed into civilian clothing and mixed with the crowds, giving out written invitations to those who appeared suitable to attend an interview the next day. The rest were left to look elsewhere.[37] Given the elite background of the Artists' the vast majority of the men recruited were quickly awarded commissions.

Connections of various types were often important in speeding up the process of gaining a commission. The father of Arnold and Cyril Christopherson, W.B. Christopherson, a doctor at Barts, used legal connections to help his sons to gain commissions. On 9 December 1914, H.W. Host of 6 Grays Inn Square wrote to him to report that a James Roche had arranged for Colonel Ommaney of the 12th Service Battalion Welsh Regiment to sign the required forms and make the necessary arrangements for the two men to be gazetted to his regiment.[38] This was, no doubt, a mutually acceptable agreement; Christopherson had gained his sons a commission and the status that went with it, and Ommaney had dealt with part of the responsibility devolved to him of finding officers for his battalion.

However, by December 1914 it appears that both the measures to recruit officers and to find commissions were becoming increasingly desperate. The 16th Public School Battalion lost many new recruits as with their educational background they were recognised as potential officer material and poached by other battalions. The CO, for fear his battalion would never to get to the front because of the high turnover, tried to block this by declining to sign the relevant forms and some candidates were forced into desperate measures to gain a commission. Charles Lawson was only successful because he found a replacement by visiting a recruiting office and giving the Recruiting Sergeant ten shillings for his next recruit![39]

A More Formal Process

The process of recruiting officers in 1914 lacked formality and at times involved manipulation of the system, but it nevertheless produced an impressive number of

---

37   Barry Gregory, *A History of the Artists Rifles 1859-1947* (Barnsley: Pen & Sword, 2006), pp. 122-123.
38   TNA WO 339/17833: Lieutenant Arnold Bayley Christopherson, Welsh Regiment.
39   Steve Hurst, *The Public Schools Battalion in the Great War* (Barnsley: Pen & Sword, 2007), pp. 27-28.

suitable candidates. However, recruiting men was only part of the problem; they then needed to be turned into officers. In the early days of the war training was extremely limited and sometimes non-existent. Some new officers started with a brief attachment to an OTC unit (such as the Inns of Court), or with a course at Sandhurst. Many new officers lacked even this benefit and had to learn alongside the men that they were to command. Most new army units took nine months to be prepared for war.[40] This was inevitable as a mass citizen army was built up from scratch.

However, especially from 1915, a more structured system started to develop. Up until then although training had been provided it did not reflect conditions on the Western Front.[41] The outbreak of trench warfare was unanticipated and it took time to assess the lessons learned from the war so far and revise officer training. In March 1915, the *Uppingham School Magazine* reported a reorganisation of the school's OTC meetings to twice a week with an entire afternoon made available for "Field work" to provide a more efficient use of time. Training concentrated on the lessons of trench warfare and providing potential officers with the skills to instruct their men. The information that several members of the school's OTC contingent had spent Christmas 1914 with mobilised units indicates that by late 1914 considerable thought was being given by the Army Council to preparing young men to be officers.[42] Within the army from mid-1915 their preparation became more structured when Young Officer Companies were formed so that those awarded commissions could be grounded in their duties before joining a service battalion.[43]

The system for recruiting officers had also become more formal and by January 1915 commanding officers no longer had the power to recommend men to become officers.[44] This centralisation of the recruiting process is demonstrated by the example of the OTC. From early 1915 announcements of commissions in the *London Gazette* often reported that the candidate was an OTC cadet or ex-cadet. For example, taking two days as examples, on 9 April 1915 the *Gazette* announced that fifty-two cadets or ex-cadets were to be temporary Second Lieutenants and on 25 June 1915 fifty-nine names were announced.[45] The training at Uppingham and other schools with OTC contingents was at the direction of the Army Council and demonstrates how the OTC was being used to train young men so that they became effective officers as soon as possible. However, there was still no formal assessment of men to assess their aptitude to be officers and occasionally men who gained commissions fell short of the mark and had to be removed. Maurice Ellinger of the 9th Service Battalion Sherwood Foresters was allowed to resign his commission after two attempts at suicide by drug overdose

---

40 Simkins, *Kitchener's Army*, p. 297.
41 Simkins, *Kitchener's Army*, p. 306.
42 *Uppingham School Magazine* (USM, March 1915), pp. 55-56.
43 Simkins, *Kitchener's Army*, p. 313-314.
44 London Metropolitan Archives (LMA): F/PEY271: Hugh Peachey correspondence with Father, 14 January 1915.
45 *London Gazette*, 9 April 1915, pp. 3454-3455 and 25 June 1915, p. 6174.

on 6 and 9 November 1914. The original intention had been to remove him from the regiment on the grounds he was unlikely to be an efficient officer, but after lobbying from his father the army agreed to allow him to resign on grounds of ill-health to protect his career.[46] Nevertheless, it is noticeable how few officers were removed or allowed to resign because they were not up to the job.

From February 1916, the introduction of Officer Cadet Battalions (OCB) provided a greater element of quality control for new officers. Men could no longer apply directly for commissions and either had to come from the ranks or the OTC. All the cadets in an OCB underwent a four and a half month training course with a commission only being granted if the course was successfully completed. This was, however, the formalisation of a system to identify gentlemen (temporary or otherwise) to lead the army. It would not be until the Second World War that the British army introduced aptitude tests for candidates to be officers.

Conclusion

In popular culture, the perception of the First World War junior officer is coloured by characters such as *Blackadder's* The Honourable George Colthurst St. Barleigh, who is portrayed as a parody of the public school officer – brave but profoundly stupid. He cannot wait to fight the Germans but is ignorant of danger and lacks the skills to be an effective leader. This chapter argues that this is a gross distortion of many young men who became junior officers. Those who had service in the OTC had received training which was integrated into the army's wider scheme. Within the OTC scheme the army appears to have concentrated on recruiting from the most efficient contingents. Men gained commissions not merely because of their background but also because of the effectiveness of their OTC training and general education.

It was the recruitment and training activities of 1914 and 1915 which had built the junior officer corps which was in place at the start of 1916. The lack of preparation for total war in 1914 meant that there was no adequate system for rapidly recruiting and training Kitchener's new army. To speedily build a citizen army a great deal of improvisation was required. However, despite appearances, the approach to recruiting officers was not entirely unstructured. The evidence suggests that the more efficient OTC contingents were favoured as a source for the recruitment of officers especially up to March 1915. The army wanted gentlemen to be officers and as the case of St Georges demonstrates, was prepared to exercise some flexibility in finding suitable men. There was no specific formula up to that point which led to a totally unquestioning recruitment of public school boys and cadets from the OTC. Guy Chapman compared his development as an officer to the middle of 1916 as being forced to grow

---

46   TNA: WO 339/11428: 2nd Lieutenant Maurice Reginald Ellinger, The Sherwood Foresters (Nottinghamshire & Derbyshire Regiment).

"like a plant in a hot house."[47] Training of officers was unsystematic and often took place on the job. As 1915 progressed and some order was brought to affairs a more formal approach to recruitment and training developed. The development of training in OTC contingents from early 1915 demonstrates that the Army Council was already looking at how to have young men as fully prepared as possible to take on commissions before enlistment. The men who took on commissions in 1914 and 1915 were still relatively raw in 1916. However, in the "hot house" they had developed skills which would form the basis, with the greatly improved training from 1917, of the men who led the British army to victory in November 1918.

47   Guy Chapman, *A Passionate Prodigality* (London: Buchan & Enright, 1985), pp. 138-139.

17

Infantry Battalion Command on the Somme 1 July-18 November 1916

Peter Hodgkinson

This chapter explores the nature, evolution and combat experience of infantry battalion commanders in Fourth and Third Army attached units who were in the order of battle on 1 July 1916 – the opening of the Somme offensive – until the official conclusion of the battle on 18 November 1918. The rapid expansion of the British Army from 1914 created a significant demand for competent battalion commanders. To meet this, the army had to dig deep into its resources. Within the 703 New Army battalions raised,[1] five principles emerge in the initial filling of battalion commands. First, active Regular officers were employed; as, second, were retired Regular officers. Third, the most senior remaining officers, many full colonels who had experience of battalion command, were used. Fourth, Indian Army officers who for various reasons were in Great Britain were pressed into service. Lastly, retired Special Reserve and TF officers were employed. Of the 416 new second-line Territorial Force (TF) battalions,[2] either active or retired Territorial officers were almost universally initially employed as COs. The army was therefore clearly pursuing a "business as usual" approach to battalion command in respect of the New Army units, with an emphasis (not unreasonably) on the all-round military ability implied by Regular status, and in its initial appointments, an emphasis on seniority. The Territorial County Associations, on the other hand, attempted to retain a local and TF character in command of their new units, with a similar emphasis on seniority.

Many of these officers proved unsuitable, particularly as active service approached. Thus within the New Army units, whilst 65 per cent of the first-raised K1 units went on active service with their first CO (a number of whom had already been sent to the Western Front to reinforce depleted units of their regiment), only 42 per cent of the locally raised units did so. Within the second-line TF units, 80 per cent of those units

1   Of these, 404 would see active service.
2   Of these, 104 would see active service.

who went overseas in 1915 did so with their first CO, whilst in 1916; only 28 per cent did so. Excessive age and the linked issues of poor physical fitness and lack of stamina were prominent causes of replacement, as were poor general attitude and outdated military knowledge.

There were three peaks in monthly appointments to battalion command during the war. The first, unsurprisingly, was from September to November 1914, self-evidently corresponding to the creation of the New Armies. The two other peaks were related to operations – from July to October 1916 (Somme offensive), and March to May 1918 (German spring offensives). It is the second of these three peaks that is the subject of analysis here. Looking between the second and third peaks, however, the monthly averages of number of CO appointments in 1917, when the BEF had its fullest year of campaigning, were only a little higher than those of the first half of 1916, when no major campaigns were in progress. Despite a "business as usual" approach, the army appears to have shown a dedication to quality control, reviewing and replacing where necessary those appointed. In the six months prior to the opening of the Somme offensive there was thus a significant turnover of COs, indicating proper preparation.[3]

Two hundred and sixteen infantry battalions were represented in the order of battle on 1 July 1916, including five Dominion units.[4] Of the British units, 23 per cent (48) were TF (all first line), a similar percentage were Regular, and 54 per cent (115) were New Army. It is, perhaps, unsurprising that 47 of the 48 Regular battalions were commanded by Regular officers on 1 July 1916. The sole exception was 1st South Staffordshire, who were commanded by Major R.J. Morris, a Special Reserve officer of the regiment who was deputising for his (Regular) CO. Except for two retired officers, all had all been serving in 1914. Attrition meant that none of these units retained their original COs of 1914, although regimental particularism largely remained.[5] In terms of starting rank, in August 1914 one of those commanding on 1 July had been a brevet lieutenant-colonel, 15 were majors, 29 were captains and three lieutenants. These latter three offer a clear indication of how attrition through death, wounding, transfer to staff posts and promotion had offered opportunity for rapid promotion. Major J.N. Bromilow, a lieutenant of 2nd Royal Lancaster in August 1914, had been commanding since the end of April 1916 due to his CO's wounding. His tenure would be brief as he was killed on 1 July. Lieutenant-Colonel E.T.J. Kerans, 4th Worcestershire, a lieutenant and adjutant of the battalion in August 1914, had achieved particularly rapid promotion having commanded since October 1915. Lastly, Lieutenant-Colonel M.B. Stow, 1st East Yorkshire, had been a lieutenant serving as adjutant to Indian Volunteers in August 1914. Distance meant that he escaped the

---

3   See P. E. Hodgkinson, *British Infantry Commanders in the First World War* (Ashgate: Farnham, 2015) for a full discussion of these issues.
4   The Newfoundland Regiment and the four battalions of the South African Brigade.
5   For example, in 5th (Regular) Division, 83 per cent of CO appointments were within regiment, and 65 per cent were within battalion. Hodgkinson, *op. cit.* p. 70.

attrition of his regiment in the initial months of the war, arriving on the Western Front only in August 1915. He had commanded since March 1916 but would be wounded on 1st July, to die at Heilly the following day. The average age of Regular COs was dropping rapidly. On 1 July it was 41, whereas the age of a Regular battalion commander in 1914 was 48.[6] The youngest was Stow at 32; the oldest was Lieutenant-Colonel H.M. Cliff of 2nd Royal Dublin Fusiliers, who, at 52, would be replaced twelve days after the opening of the battle.

Of the 115 New Army units, 92 were commanded by Regulars, including 15 officers from the Indian Army. Of these, nearly half (45 per cent) were "dugouts", officers retired by August 1914. There were 13 COs with origins in the Special Reserve (only two being retired Regulars), six from the Territorial Force (one a retired Regular), two from empire units, and two civilians. Eighty-three percent of New Army battalions were therefore commanded by professional soldiers. The two COs of 1 July 1916 with apparently no previous military experience were Major Alfred Plackett, a 33 year-old bank manager called upon the day previous to command 12th York & Lancaster, his CO going sick; and Captain K.E. Poyser, a 33 year-old barrister, similarly newly elevated to command 8th King's Own Yorkshire Light Infantry, the CO and two majors being sick. Both would be wounded on 1 July. The average age of New Army COs was 44, which likely reflects the presence of the "dugouts". The youngest was Lieutenant-Colonel R.L. Norrington of 7th Border Regiment, at 29 a comparatively young "dugout", having resigned as a lieutenant from the regiment in 1911. The oldest, at 57, was Lieutenant-Colonel J. Forrest, 7th Lincolnshire, a retired Regular major of that regiment, who would be replaced at the end of July.

Of the 48 TF battalions, 68 per cent (33) were still commanded by Territorials, eleven by their original COs. Twelve had been majors in August 1914 and ten had been captains. Fourteen were now commanded by Regulars, two from the Indian Army, with only one a "dugout". The army's bias against TF officers was thus manifesting itself. One was commanded by a civilian, the CO of 1/6th Warwickshire, Lieutenant-Colonel W.H. Franklin, having previous martial credentials only as a senior officer of the Church Lads Brigade. He had been commissioned into the Newfoundland Regiment in September 1914. He would join the list of those wounded on 1 July. The average age of TF COs was also dropping. In comparison with an average age of nearly 48 for a TF CO in 1914, the average on 1st July 1916 was 42. The youngest, and the youngest across all units on 1 July at the tender age of 27, was Lieutenant-Colonel J. Micklem of 1/6th Gloucestershire, who had been a captain of 1st Rifle Brigade in August 1914. He was indeed an individual with promise – by the end of the war he was commanding 4th Tank Brigade. The oldest was Lieutenant-Colonel E.J. King, 1/7th Middlesex, who had been commanding at the outbreak of war, and who would be invalided in September 1916 aged 56.

---

6   During the Hundred Days campaign, the average age would drop to 35.

The overall picture on 1st July was therefore of the Regular army keeping an exclusive grip on the command of Regular battalions, with younger officers coming to the fore. Regular officers commanded 80 per cent of New Army units, albeit nearly half of these being "dugouts"; and Regulars were also extending their command of TF units. The strain for the army inherent in pursuing this approach was enhanced by the fact that the stock of Regular officers, only 12,738 being active in 1914, was being eroded through death or wounding whilst subject to a multiplicity of demands. Sir Douglas Haig had noted in his diary on 25 June 1915 that progress, "even if ample guns etc. provided", would be achieved only when "young capable commanders are brought to the front. Captains to command Battalions; Majors Brigades etc."[7] Haig's words bear close scrutiny – his early view was that youth and ability were the key to command, and would be the mainspring of success. The drop in the average ages of battalion commanders by 1 July 1916 should not, however, be interpreted as representing policy in favour of youth – it was an inevitable outcome of attrition.

The opening of the offensive is most often viewed through the distorting prism of death. As has been endlessly retold, of the 57,470 casualties, 19,240 were fatal. Commanding Officers were as vulnerable as any that day. Sixteen of the COs of the 67 battalions which attacked at 07.30 were killed or died of wounds and eleven were wounded; whilst of the 69 supporting battalions, ten COs died and eight were wounded. Of the 79 reserve battalions, some of whom were pressed into action and others not, three COs were killed and two were wounded. Overall, therefore, 29 COs in the whole order of battle were killed and 21 wounded; a 23 per cent casualty rate. Over the period of the whole war 11 per cent of COs were killed. Their risk was thus doubled on 1st July.

War diaries naturally give some insight into the ways battalion commanders attempted to influence the course of action on 1 July. It is a vagary of these sources that descriptions of the actions of battalion commanders are sometimes only given when they were either killed or wounded. Lieutenant-Colonel W. Burnett (1/5th North Staffordshire) "on hearing that the attack was not developing as arranged, personally went forward to the advance trench and … tried to reorganise and push on."[8] Here he was seriously wounded in the abdomen. Lieutenant-Colonel G.S. Guyon (16th West Yorkshire) had made his way to the frontline with his entire battalion HQ, and after two minutes was shot through the temple by a bullet. Lieutenant-Colonel M.N. Kennard (18th West Yorkshire) did exactly the same thing as Guyon, only to be killed by a shell. Lieutenant-Colonel A.M. Holdworth, 2nd Royal Berkshire, was also mortally wounded in a sap leading from the front line, 15 minutes after zero; his second-in-command Major G.H. Sawyer, who was with him, being wounded. In addition to the risk of injury or death in combat, COs were not immune to psychological trauma. Lieutenant-Colonel A.V.

---

7 National Library of Scotland, Acc. 3155, Field-Marshal Sir Douglas Haig, Manuscript Diary, 25 June 1915.
8 TNA WO 95/2685: 6th North Staffordshire War Diary, 1 July 1916.

Johnson of 2nd Royal Fusiliers was in his front-line trench at Beaumont Hamel when he was subject to friendly fire and invalided "severely shaken."[9] These five COs therefore met their varied fates in the front lines where they were attempting to ascertain what was happening in order to restore command and control. Other COs made the same attempt but died before they could even get there. Men of 1st Somerset Light Infantry had penetrated the Quadrilateral (north of Beaumont Hamel) and Lieutenant-Colonel J.A. Thicknesse and his adjutant Captain C.C. Ford were both killed whilst going forward to clarify the situation, these officers falling before they even reached their original front line. Similarly, Lieutenant-Colonel H.A. Johnson, of the 17th Manchester, a support battalion, was struck by machine-gun fire 100 yards in front of his unit's assembly trenches. Lieutenant-Colonel H.C. Bernard of 10th Royal Irish Rifles, whose battalion was also in support, was killed before zero by a shell.

Others led from the front and perished before the enemy positions. Lieutenant-Colonel L.C.W. Palk, 1st Hampshire, attacking the Hawthorn Ridge, led his battalion HQ and unit into No Man's Land, wearing white gloves and carrying a stick, only to die trapped, wounded, in a shell-hole. Lieutenant-Colonel W. Lyle of 23rd Northumberland Fusiliers was "last seen alive with walking stick in hand, amongst his men about 200 y(ar)ds from the German trenches."[10] Lieutenant-Colonel J.E. Green (1st East Lancashire) was pinned down in "a depression near the German barbed wire" three hours after Zero and was hit in the shoulder.[11] Lieutenant-Colonel B.L. Maddison of 8th York & Lancaster also died in No Man's Land with his adjutant; whilst Lieutenant-Colonel A.J. Ellis, 1st Border Regiment was brought in wounded from No Man's Land at Beaumont Hamel at 09.15. The deeply unpopular Lieutenant-Colonel C.W.D. Lynch of 9th King's Own Yorkshire Light Infantry was killed soon after emerging from a Russian sap near Fricourt. Others would be wounded or die re-establishing command and control in captured enemy positions. Lieutenant-Colonel A.E. Fitzgerald of 15th Durham Light Infantry established his advanced battalion HQ in the Sunken Road near Fricourt, and set about reorganising men from different units. Supervising dispositions to repel an enemy counter-attack, he was hit in the thigh by machine-gun fire. Colonel H. Lewis of 20th Manchester was killed in No Man's Land before reaching the same Sunken Road. Others died whilst providing personal examples, often attempting to rally a stalled attack. Lieutenant-Colonel P.W. Machell of 11th Border Regiment was killed at Authuille Wood, being cut down after climbing onto the parapet to encourage the remains of his battalion on. Similarly, Lieutenant-Colonel H.F. Watson, 11th Sherwood Foresters, was wounded at Ovillers "walking diagonally across the front collecting men as he went" giving "a fresh impetus to the advance by his personal example."[12]

9 TNA WO 95/2301: 2nd Royal Fusiliers War Diary, 1 July 1916.
10 TNA WO 95/2463: 23rd Northumberland Fusiliers War Diary, 1 July 1916.
11 TNA WO 95/1498: 1st East Lancashire War Diary, 1 July 1916.
12 TNA WO 95/2187: 11th Sherwood Foresters War Diary, 1 July 1916.

Leadership from the front, where a number of the fatalities amongst COs of 1 July 1916 occurred, was a respected characteristic of British officers. Lieutenant C.E. Carrington, 1/5th Royal Warwickshire, whose CO, Lieutenant-Colonel G.C. Sladen, was "my hero", was isolated and under counter-attack beyond Ovillers in late July 1916, when suddenly Sladen dropped into his trench. Carrington highlighted the dilemma: "I feel ten times more confident that the Colonel should merely be in the trench with us … where Colonels have no business to be."[13] When the adjutant of 2nd King's Royal Rifle Corps attempted to prevent Lieutenant-Colonel H.W.F. Bircham from being "right up with" the attack, Bircham responded: "You know very well … where a Colonel of the Rifles should be on such occasions."[14] The adjutant was tragically blessed with foresight as Bircham was killed in Munster Alley, Pozières, that day, 23 July 1916. Lieutenant-Colonel J.G. Mignon, 8th Leicestershire, also demonstrated the cost of this attitude, dying eight days prior to Bircham on the Bazentin Ridge, "leading a bombing party like a subaltern."[15]

It is instructive to consider the experiences of two COs of 1 July 1916, one whose unit did not get forward, and another whose did. The experiences of Lieutenant-Colonel G.D. Goodman, 1/6th Sherwood Foresters (139th Brigade, 46th Division), in support at Gommecourt, must have been fairly typical of units that could not make any progress that day. Godfrey Davenport Goodman, a 47 year-old solicitor and Territorial major at the outbreak of war, had commanded the battalion from October 1914, and would have two spells of brigade command (52nd and 21st Brigades), beginning as the Somme battle ended. Given the prejudice against TF officers, he must have been exceptional. He noted: "At 07.45 I and my Adjutant went along GREEN STREET towards REGENT STREET to watch my leading Companies advance and to follow them." He had thus left battalion HQ to set up an advanced HQ, and was planning to follow his companies and set up a further advanced HQ in the German positions. He was doomed to fail – the trenches were too congested and under

Lieutenant-Colonel Godfrey Davenport Goodman.

---

13 C. Edmonds, *A Subaltern's War* (London: Anthony Mott, 1984), p. 75.
14 G.E.M. Eyre, *Somme Harvest* (London: London Stamp Exchange, 1991), p. 225.
15 D.V. Kelly, *39 Months with the "Tigers" 1915-1918* (London: Ernest Benn, 1930), p. 32.

heavy artillery fire, his adjutant being wounded. His men could barely leave their own front line, and the only thing he could do was send "messages to Coy Commanders to organise men in old front trench and retrenchments." Goodman took six principal actions in the exercise of command during the day. The first was, as observed, personal reconnaissance and an attempt to restore command and control. He then returned to his battalion HQ, now two hours after zero, "and reported by telephone to Brigade." His second action was, therefore, the transmission of information to his parent formation. Fifteen minutes later he "received [a] telegraphic message" from brigade that Captain Naylor of 1/5th Sherwood Foresters was in the German front line, and needed support. He sent a message to one of his company commanders to organise this advance, and went back to the frontline to confer again with another two of his captains. His third action as CO was thus to issue new orders and go forward again to assess the situation personally. Here he learnt that Captain Naylor "was back and advance impossible." At 12.30 he received orders to attack at 13.15 under cover of smoke. "There was no smoke however and I did not attack", he later wrote. His fourth action was therefore negative, a decision to ignore an order. Another attack at 14.30 was ordered under smoke, which was not ready. He then received fresh orders that the smoke would be put down at 15.25 and his battalion should advance five minutes later. He conferred with a North Staffordshire officer (i.e. from the battalion to his right), about how the flanks of their units should advance. His fifth action was therefore consultative with another battalion, following which fresh orders were issued. However, "a small film of smoke appeared but in no way interfered with the view of the enemy trenches. I accordingly at 3.35 p.m. ordered the men not to go over the parapet." His sixth and final action for the day was again negative, ignoring an order.[16] It should be noted that this refusal to follow orders that risked useless casualties was entirely in line with the principle established in *Field Service Regulations 1909* of the primacy of the "man on the spot" to make decisions.

At the other end of the British line that day, some success was achieved. The War Diary of 8th East Surrey (55th Brigade, 18th Division) gives a picture of the movements and actions of Major A.P.B. Irwin that day in the attack before Montauban. Alfred Percy Bulteel Irwin had been a lieutenant of 2nd East Surrey in August 1914, but had only commanded the unit since 28 June 1916, and would command with brief absences related to wounds and acting brigade command, until falling wounded once more in September 1918. Five principal actions can be observed in his command of his battalion. After zero hour, Irwin remained in battalion HQ receiving reports from his adjutant, Captain C.C. Clare, who was at the advanced report centre in the front line, and by 07.50 knew that his battalion was in the enemy trenches but had lost a number of officers. In response to this, just after 08.00 he ordered the battalion bombing section, followed by two Stokes mortars, forward. He followed this by requesting reinforcement of two platoons from the adjacent 7th Buffs to deal with an enemy counter-attack. Irwin's first two actions were, therefore, the receipt of information and the transmission

---

16   TNA WO 95/2694: 1/6th Sherwood Foresters War Diary, 1 July 1916.

of same to brigade, and the issuing of orders involving tactical adjustments. Up to this point, he had been receiving a flood of information, some confused and confusing, and at 09.44 "handed over command of the Report Centre to the Adjutant, and went forward to ascertain and if possible bring back news as to the actual position." His third action was therefore to personally reconnoitre to re-establish command and control, which indeed he did. Irwin found himself having to reorganise the battalion for the push on to the next major enemy line (Pommiers Trench). Following his departure, the CO of the support battalion, 7th Royal West Kent, arrived. Clare hastily sent two signallers and a telephone line forward to locate Irwin, unsuccessfully. An hour after his departure, the Battalion Report Centre moved forward to discover that Irwin was now in Pommiers Trench. The view from the new report centre position revealed the whole of the British dispositions and Clare was able to make a report to brigade. Contact was only established with Irwin, after two and a quarter hours of silence, at 12.00. He was now able to give orders over the telephone for advance on both left and right. This advance was achieved and at 12.55 Irwin assumed command of all troops of 55th Brigade west of Montauban. (No order concerning this can be found in 55th Brigade's War Diary, so it is likely that this is a role that Irwin, in his forward position, took upon himself). His fourth and fifth actions were therefore the issuing of orders and the assumption of personal command at the front of the advance to ensure his orders were achieved. Once the brigade objective was reached at 13.30, Irwin shared a bottle of champagne on that spot with his eight surviving officers.[17]

Goodman and Irwin faced very different situations but acted in much the same way. They received information and transmitted it up the chain of command. When the information became unclear, they went forward to make personal reconnaissance and re-establish command and control dependant on the situation they found. They both made tactical dispositions. Only in their last actions did circumstances dictate the shape of what they could do next – Goodman disobeyed an order and did not advance, whilst Irwin assumed control of the whole brigade front and went forward. Both COs used the accepted final judgement of the "man on the spot", in effective yet entirely different ways. Goodman's refusal to execute orders to attack suggests great personal confidence, for although regulations supported independent decision making, lack of "offensive spirit" was often a reason for officers to be dismissed from command. Leaving aside the obvious danger of death and injury, Goodman's decisions were personally riskier than those of Irwin.

As nearly a quarter of the COs of attacking battalions had become casualties on 1 July, there was considerable, and urgent, enforced turnover. Yet, of the 216 infantry battalions, 87 (40 per cent) still retained their official CO of 1 July on 18 November when the campaign formally ended. Whilst divisions spent variable amounts of time on the Somme after 1 July, this still speaks to a greater stability in command than might perhaps have been imagined. This may indicate that the Army was satisfied

---

17   TNA WO 95/20150: 8th East Surrey Regiment War Diary, 1 July 1916.

with its efforts to get suitable COs in place prior to the battle. In terms of turnover, 105 battalions (49 per cent), had two COs at the rank of lieutenant-colonel during the period of the campaign. This means that the replacement for the CO commanding on 1 July was still commanding on 18 November 1918. Twenty-one (ten per cent) had three; and one unit had four.[18]

In addition to those who became casualties on 1 July, a further nine original COs were killed in action and twelve were replaced because they were wounded after that date. Taking into account three COs who were temporarily absent on 18 November, and 15 who were invalided, 46 were replaced for other reasons. This group (36 per cent of the total replacements) therefore represents changes in command made out of choice. Seven of these were COs transferred to another active battalion, and ten were promoted to brigade command. Assuming that the cases of COs being invalided were genuine (the respective war diaries indicating this was the case), and not euphemisms for sacking, 29 (23 per cent) of replacements of COs in post on 1 July during the rest of the campaign were removals from command, the CO either sent back to Great Britain or transferred to a non-active command. It has been determined that up to 38 per cent of turnover in infantry battalion command during the war was a matter of removal.[19] This leads to the conclusion that either replacement due to lack of confidence in ability etc. was lower in the COs of 1 July 1916, or the BEF was putting up with a higher number of inadequate COs because of lack of suitable replacements. Those in post on 1 July who remained in post on 18 November served on average a further nine months in charge of their battalions. This favours the suggestion that they were originally a well selected group. Some, of course, went out of post within days or weeks of the formal end of the battle – fourteen did so, but of these eight were promotions to brigadier-general. Others served long periods. Ten served for a further 20 months or over. Lieutenant-Colonel A.J.N. Bartlett, a Regular captain in August 1914, served until the Armistice in command of 1/4th Oxfordshire & Buckinghamshire; whilst Lieutenant-Colonel L.L.C. Reynolds, a Territorial captain at the outbreak of war, also commanded 1/1st Oxfordshire & Buckinghamshire until the end. Both had had taken command of their units a month before the opening of the Somme campaign.

Of the 40 replacement COs who were *not* in post on 18 November 1916, three had been killed, four wounded and ten invalided. In terms of the end of tenure of command within this group, five were transferred to another active battalion; two were promoted, whilst 16 were removed. Forty per cent of replacements were thus removals. This suggests that the COs transferred in at short notice were less satisfactory than those who were in post on 1 July. This level of replacement further reminds us of the army's commitment to quality control. Those from the replacement group who were still in command on 18 November 1916 served for a fraction under a further 12 months. They were clearly competent COs.

18 These figures ignore majors in temporary command, sometimes only for a matter of days.
19 Hodgkinson, *op. cit.*, p. 117.

Infantry Battalion Command on the Somme 439

Table 1 Military backgrounds of infantry COs, 1 July-18 November 1916

	Regular	Indian Army	Special Reserve	Empire	Territorial Force	Citizen 1914
Regular						
1 July 1916	47		1			
18 Nov 1916	46	1	1			
New Army						
1 July 1916	77	15	13	2	6	2
18 Nov 1916	75	7	12	2	11	8
Territorial Force						
1 July 1916	12	2			33	1
18 Nov 1916	15		1	1	31	

Table 1 contrasts the military backgrounds of those in post on 1 July in comparison with those in post on 18 November. There are three main, if unspectacular, indications of evolution. All concern New Army units. Regular units continued to be commanded almost exclusively by Regular officers. TF units continued to show roughly the same balance between Regular and TF COs. The New Army units, however, showed a decreased reliance on Indian Army officers[20] and an increased reliance on Territorial and citizen COs. The BEF's negative attitude to TF officers was therefore not universal.[21] If 55 of the COs in post on 1 July had been dugouts, the total on 18 November was 50. The BEF's reliance on Regular officers, if diminishing, still required the employment of those who had been retired at the opening of the war.

Another matter that also showed change was the fact that the COs of November 1916 were a younger group. The average age of both Regular and TF battalion commanders was 38 years six months, and that of New Army COs was 40. The average age of Regular COs had therefore dropped by two and a half years; and the age of TF COs had dropped by 3.5 years. The age of New Army COs showed the greatest drop, namely four years. Again, however, this was an inevitable result of attrition of older, more experienced officers, rather than any organised investment in youth.

The experiences of the COs of 18th Division at certain key points during the remainder of the offensive will now be considered to further illustrate how command was exercised. This division was not selected because of its illustrious commander, Major-General Ivor Maxse, but because of its participation in key actions in the later stages of the Battle of the Somme. Maxse had put effort into his recruitment of COs,[22]

20 The return of Indian Army officers to their parent units did not occur until 1917.
21 However, Territorial and citizen officers rarely rose to command formations.
22 Hodgkinson, *op. cit.*, p. 40.

and both their performance and careers from 1 July onwards indicate that he chose well. The division had a preponderance of professional soldiers as COs. Thirteen of the 16 COs commanding during the period (see Table 2) were, or had been, Regulars. Francis Aylmer Maxwell (12th Middlesex), who had been awarded the Victoria Cross for saving guns during the action at Sanna's Post, March 1900, in South Africa, was, however, a major of the 17th Lancers, Indian Army, in August 1914. He had served in both the Sussex Regiment and Bengal Infantry, and also had seen active service in the Chitral (1895) and Tirah (1897-8) campaigns. A third were "dugouts" – four had been retired in August 1914. The splendidly named Henry Gaspard de Lavalette Ferguson (8th Norfolk), had served in the militia of the East Yorkshire Regiment (retiring as a lieutenant in 1895). He had subsequently joined the militia of the Norfolk Regiment where he was seconded to the Sierra Leone police force and saw active service there (1898-9, being awarded the DSO), as well as serving on the staff in South Africa 1900-2. He retired as a captain in 1906. Charles Cattley Carr (11th Royal Fusiliers), had retired as a major from that regiment in 1905, having seen active service in South Africa, being present at the relief of both Ladysmith and Mafeking. George Eustace Ripley (6th Northamptonshire), who would die in October 1916 following the amputation of his right arm, had seen active service as a captain of that regiment in South Africa, but had retired in 1903. He had then been appointed lieutenant-colonel of the regiment's 1st Volunteer Battalion, retiring as CO of the 4th Battalion only months before the war started. Sidney Herbert Charrington, who would succeed Ripley, was another cavalryman. He was commissioned in 1901, and had retired from the 15th Hussars in 1912.

Of those who were serving at the outbreak of war, Gerald Victor Wilmot Hill (8th Suffolk), had been a captain of the Royal Irish Fusiliers in August 1914; Hugh Lawrence Scott (10th Essex), was a captain of that regiment; and his successor on wounding, Charles William Frizzell, was a captain of 1st Royal Berkshire. Bertie Gordon Clay (6th Berkshire), was a cavalryman, a major of 7th Dragoon Guards in August 1914. George Dominic Price (7th Bedfordshire), was also a major at this point in time, of the West Yorkshire Regiment.[23] His successor, George Pilkington Mills, a 49 year-old civil engineer, was a retired Territorial captain. The dominant English racing cyclist of his generation, he had retired from the 3rd Volunteer Battalion of the Bedfordshire Regiment in 1906. He must have shown promise for Maxse to have accepted his appointment. The other outsider to the Regular fold was William Hamilton Hall Johnston, Maxwell's successor at the helm of 12th Middlesex, had been appointed a temporary lieutenant in October 1914. A railway engineer who was working in the Far East, he is one of the signs of evolution in command on the Somme - the rise of the civilian. Amongst the remaining Regulars, Martin Kemp-Welsh (7th West Surrey), was a lieutenant of that regiment in 1914; and Alfred Irwin (8th East Surrey), had held a similar rank with his regiment at the outbreak of war. Algernon

23   Price would fall victim to an aerial bomb dropped on Exmouth in 1943.

Table 2 18th Division COs, 1 July-18 November 1916

	CO 1 July 1916	Reason for departure	CO 18 Nov 1916	Total months as CO
53rd Brigade				
8th Norfolk	H.G. de L. Ferguson		H.G. de L. Ferguson	15
8th Suffolk	G.V.W. Hill		G.V.W. Hill	24
10th Essex	H.L. Scott	Wounded	C.W. Frizzell	25
6th Royal Berkshire	B.G. Clay		B.G. Clay	15
54th Brigade				
11th Royal Fusiliers	C.C. Carr		C.C. Carr	36
7th Bedfordshire	G.D. Price	Promoted	G.P. Mills	16
12th Middlesex	F.A. Maxwell	Promoted	W.H.H. Johnston	11
6th Northamptonshire	G.E. Ripley	KIA	S.H. Charrington	4
55th Brigade				
7th Queens	M. Kemp-Welsh		M. Kemp-Welsh	1
7th Buffs	A.L. Ransome		A.L. Ransome	31
8th East Surrey	A.P.B. Irwin		A.P.B. Irwin	27
7th West Kent	J.T. Twistleton-Wykeham-Fiennes		J.T. Twistleton-Wykeham-Fiennes	1

Lee Ransome (7th Buffs), was a captain of the Dorset Regiment in August 1914; and the triple-barrelled John Temple Twisleton-Wykeham-Fiennes (7th Royal West Kent), was a captain of that regiment as the war began.[24] The oldest was Ripley at 52, the youngest Irwin at 29.

As is well known, 18th Division had more success than most on 1 July 1916, as the exploits of Alfred Irwin demonstrated. Their second major action was the capture of Trônes Wood on 14 July, a necessary precursor to the Battle of the Bazentin Ridge. 18th Division received orders to achieve this as it came back into the line on the morning of 13 July and in turn issued orders for an attack by 55th Brigade at 19.00. Maxse noted that it was "difficult for any Brigadier to collect his C.O.'s and give them attack orders at short notice." Battalion commanders "were unable to make that personal reconnaissance which everyone knew was most desirable."[25] The 55th Brigade, however, did collect their COs – at 11.30 Brigade ordered a conference which took place between

---

24 He was an ancestor of the explorer Sir Ranulph Fiennes and actors Ralph and Joseph Fiennes.
25 G.H.F. Nichols, *The 18th Division in the Great War* (London: Blackwood, 1922), p. 53.

13.00 and 14.00. The attack, during which it is impossible to identify the movements of COs, did not achieve its objective. At 23.30 that night, 18th Division ordered a fresh attack by 54th Brigade, utilising 6th Northamptonshire and 12th Middlesex, to take place at 04.25. The stage was set for the celebrated actions of Frank Maxwell, commanding the Middlesex.

Brigadier-General T. H. Shoubridge met with Maxwell and Lieutenant-Colonel Ripley at 02.00 on the 14th. Owing to communication difficulties caused by the heavy enemy shellfire, Shoubridge "decided that Lieutenant-Colonel Frank Maxwell ... was to command both his own battalion ... and the 6th Northants during the actual assault, subject to the orders issued for the attack." This act of devolved command was swiftly taken advantage of by Maxwell. Unable to collect his unit together in time he "ordered the Northants to carry out the assault and the Middlesex to do the clearing up."[26] Ripley was ordered to remain at Brigade HQ as a liaison officer, and thus Maxwell entered the wood with Major S.H. Charrington of the Northants unit, Major G.M. Clark having just previously led the battalion into the trees, only to be immediately killed for his pains. Charrington, the Northants battalion HQ having been left in the Sunken Road outside the wood, proceeded into the tree-line accompanied by four runners. The communication route was therefore stretched, and information was thin on the ground. Charrington, down to one runner, did as Irwin did two weeks previously, and "collecting as many bombs as they could carry ... went forward to ascertain the situation."[27] Maxwell left Charrington at this point in order to locate his battalion. Receiving no information as to the Northants' progress – the price often to be paid for a CO going forward – he returned, located Charrington, and told him to remain where he was whilst he went to reorganise the scattered companies. Charrington took no part in what subsequently happened.

Lieutenant-Colonel Francis Aylmer Maxwell VC.

The War Diary of 12th Middlesex contains virtually no reference to Maxwell's actions, and reliance must be placed on his own account. Maxwell decided to organise a sweep of the wood south to north, using his own battalion and the Northants companies. "I had meant only to organise and start the line, and then return to my loathsome ditch his [HQ]", he wrote to his wife, going on to emphasise the important role of placing himself

---

26 TNA WO 95/2041: 54th Brigade War Diary, 14 July 1916.
27 TNA WO 95/2044: 6th Northamptonshire Regiment War Diary, 14 July 1916.

in communication with brigade HQ by runner he was thus forsaking. "But ... I immediately found that without my being there the whole thing would collapse in a few minutes. Sounds vain, perhaps, but there is nothing of vanity about it, really." He ordered his men to fix bayonets and advance in line, and "by way of encouraging themselves, to fire ahead of them into the tangle all the way."[28] The approach worked and the wood was cleared.

Maxwell took full advantage of devolved command. He exercised the latitude of the "man on the spot" in two ways. First, in ordering 6th Northants to make the initial attack on the wood rather than his own unit; and, second, in restarting the operation in a different way, determining the infantry tactics used. Like Goodman and Irwin on 1 July, both Charrington and Maxwell were almost completely devoid of information on what the situation was deeper in the wood. Both left their battalion HQs and ended up in the front line. In this position, as Maxwell was keenly aware, he could no longer take responsibility for passing information to his battalion HQ and thence back to brigade. Indeed, he was absent for so long that at 13.30 the Advanced Report Centre of 6th Northants noted that nothing had been heard from him since 09.05 and "it was thought that possibly he had become a casualty."[29] Maxwell, Ivor Maxse's "best platoon commander", was an exceptional soldier, and the divisional history does not employ hyperbole when it describes that: "In temperament and in every other attribute, physical and mental, Colonel Maxwell was fitted for the task assigned him."[30] Yet he only did the same as Alfred Irwin on 1 July – he simply did it with greater audacity. Blind as to the course of the action, both commanders went to find out for themselves, reorganised their troops, and pressed on, even though that course of action disabled them in terms of some of their other functions as CO.

Before 18th Division could depart the Somme for a rest in a quiet part of the line, 53rd Brigade, not employed at Trônes Wood, travelled down its own *via dolorosa* in Delville Wood 19-20 July. Here the division lost its first CO of the Somme campaign. Progress into the wood on the 19th was slow, and after some four hours Lieutenant-Colonel Scott of 10th Essex was conferring with Lieutenant-Colonel Clay of 6th Royal Berkshire, "when a shell burst in the air some 200 yards away." The Adjutant, Captain R.A. Chell went on to describe how: "A second later, a whizz, a small, dull thud, and Colonel Scott had toppled over into my arms." A piece of shrapnel had entered his head just above an eye. Chell continued: "The superb coolness of the man! While reclining in my arms his first act was to test the sight of his injured eye. He placed his hand over the other eye and found he could still see."[31] Clay, "who was established at Essex R(eport) Centre, took over the command of the batt(alion)n at the request of the Adj(utan)t."[32] Clay cannot have served in this capacity for long as both divisional and

---

28 Nichols, *op. cit.*, p. 64.
29 TNA WO 95/2044: 6th Northamptonshire Regiment War Diary, 14 July 1916.
30 Nichols, *op. cit.*, p. 60.
31 T.M Banks & R.A. Chell, *With The 10th Essex in France* (London: Gay & Hancock, 1924), p. 134.
32 TNA WO 95/2038: 10th Essex War Diary, 19 July 1916.

unit histories refer to Captain A.S. Tween, the only surviving company commander, taking over command. In a situation in which the 10th Essex "never again played a part in a battle anything like as unsatisfactory", the only course the battalion commanders could do, given that no progress could be made, was to encourage their battalions to "hang on." Tween epitomised this function: "His work during those two days stamped him as a leader of men." Padre David Randall said of him: "His character rose to wonderfulness."[33] Tween was subsequently awarded the DSO:

> For conspicuous gallantry in action. He took command of four companies after nearly all the officers had become casualties. By his fine example he held the men together, consolidated his position, and repulsed several counter-attacks.[34]

Alfred Stuart Tween would die leading the battalion (his CO being on leave) on 23 March 1918, showing the same spirit he had demonstrated in Delville Wood, leading a counter-attack with battalion HQ personnel against overwhelming enemy numbers.

On 21 July 1916, 18th Division began its move away from the Somme, spending August in the line in front of Armentières. The divisional history notes "there was intensive training."[35] 54th Brigade, for instance, underwent a week of training in the week ending 2nd September. Brigadier-General Shoubridge held a conference with his battalion commanders for more than ninety minutes on 26 August, after which COs met with their company commanders on the training area to arrange an exercise scheme for the following day. The surviving agenda for the conference likely reflects the pooled concerns of the battalions' COs. Items discussed included: "The Attack: Possible future forms of (a) Formations and strength; (b) Forming up; (c) Clearing up." Similarly, "consolidation" was a topic, as was (given recent bitter experience): "Wood fighting – necessity for Brigade to work on some general principles." Bombing was discussed: "Probable greater use. But must not supersede rifle and bayonet."[36] After a further conference with COs, a full brigade training exercise was held on the 31st, in front of Maxse, involving the taking and consolidation of an enemy position.

The 55th Brigade underwent training the following week. Its concerns were much the same as 54th Brigade's. Individual battalions had training weeks organised by COs and Alfred Irwin's scheme for 8th East Surrey survives. After section and platoon training, the whole battalion practiced attack: "Preceded by scouts who must bring in reports … strong points and machine guns to be dealt with. Keeping direction and touch. Consolidation of position." That night the battalion practiced night

---

33 Nichols, *op. cit.*, p. 74.
34 *London Gazette*, 23 October 1916, p. 1881.
35 Nichols, *op. cit.* p. 75.
36 TNA WO 95/2041: 54th Brigade War Diary, 26 August 1916.

operations: "Night advance and attack at dawn."[37] Training was to be put to the test – in early September the division returned to the Somme for its assault on Thiepval.

On the very right of the attack of 26 September on that fortress which had so bloodied the units thrown against it on 1 July, was 8th Suffolk of 53rd Brigade. Between 25 July and 20 September the unit had undergone four days of brigade training, 15 days of battalion training, 15 days of company training and two of platoon training, everything from battalion training downwards having been agreed at a conference between Colonel Hill and his company commanders on 12 August. Hill had reconnoitred the Thiepval trenches himself on 14 September and returned the following day with his company commanders. On the 23rd the whole battalion was taken to a representation of the Thiepval trenches near Varennes, and "each Coy went over the entire ground, followed by a Bttn practice attack."[38] On the 26th, when the details of the way companies would attack was handed down in brigade orders, the assault began at 12.25, and Hill appears to have largely remained in his battalion HQ throughout the successful operation in the direction of Schwaben Redoubt, with one exception, liaising with adjacent battalions and passing information to brigade. Hill's main role in the attack was therefore in training, preparation, and liaison. In the neighbouring battalion, 10th Essex, Lieutenant-Colonel Frizzell, who had only taken over command eight days previously, went round his companies at 10.10, but otherwise did much the same. Frizzell, whom the divisional history describes as "young, likeable, and forceful", was accompanied forward by his 8th Suffolk counterpart at 16.30 "to determine the exact situation."[39] As with Irwin and Maxwell, they felt the need to make personal reconnaissance, but returned to their respective HQs.

On the left, 54th Brigade was assaulting the Thiepval position itself. The leading battalions were the redoubtable Maxwell's 12th Middlesex, paired with 11th Royal Fusiliers under Lieutenant-Colonel Carr. At 13.15, Carr "took headquarters forward",[40] arriving at the Thiepval Chateau ruins at the same time as Maxwell. Uncertain as to what was happening on the battalion's left, Carr took his adjutant forward with him to ascertain the position and was hit by three machine-gun bullets at close range. As demonstrated on 1 July, personal reconnaissance had its costs. Command devolved for the rest of the day on the previously civilian and future CO, Captain W.H.H. Johnston, a 32 year-old cotton importer. The day before the attack, Maxwell had sought to put fire in his troops with a message that ended: "Be out to kill, and get THIEPVAL on our colours",[41] and the battalion orders were detailed in terms of the tactics to be employed. Thus Maxwell instructed, for instance: "No man is to get in enemy's front or second line trench but carry on at a steady pace, those men nearest

---

37 TNA WO 95/2046: 55th Brigade War Diary, 14 August 1916.
38 TNA WO 95/2039: 8th Suffolk Regiment War Diary, 23 September 1916.
39 Nichols, *op. cit.*, p. 82 and TNA WO 95/2038: 10th Essex War Diary, 26 September 1916.
40 Nichols, *op. cit.*, p. 88.
41 TNA WO 95/2044: 12th Middlesex Regiment War Diary, 25 September 1916.

the trenches firing into them." He understood the importance of keeping momentum. Maxwell had been ill for three days, but "happily the tonic of battle seized my rotten carcase."[42] His after-action report, again, does not mention his own actions. Maxwell had, of course, moved his battalion HQ up to the chateau at the same time as Colonel Carr. The supporting battalion, 6th Northamptonshire, also moved up, and the brigade now suffered its second mishap in terms of battalion command. The Northants CO, Colonel Ripley, was mortally wounded en route. Major Charrington thus found himself in charge once more. He sited his battalion HQ where the brigade signal section was located, but as all lines were cut, he moved forward to join Maxwell at 17.15. In order to repulse any counter-attack, as the divisional history notes, "Colonel Maxwell took command of every one of the 54th Brigade on the spot", a necessary but self-assumed role, forming "the scattered units of three battalions into two defensive lines with about fifty yards between the two lines."[43] The chateau, where Maxwell was located, became the pivot of the defensive system.

Lieutenant-Colonel Price, of 7th Bedfordshire, was ordered to relieve the units under Maxwell's command that night, and Ivor Maxse specifically noted his "excellent arrangements"[44] for both this and his plan for clearing the rectangular part of Thiepval still held by the enemy the following day. Maxwell himself noted: "A busy night and not unmixed with anxiety – in fact, very much to the contrary. Perhaps the most trying business is to keep your generals informed of how things are going." After the relief, however, Maxwell would not budge. "Much to the CO's delight", (but not his brigadier's), "I disobeyed the order and stayed on to see him through the attack on the stronghold that had beat us till then. I had no mind to lose what we had so hardly won by going before he had done his job."[45] The operation was successful, but no mention is made of any help that Maxwell offered on the 27th, beyond advice on the enemy's dispositions. Price's supposed "delight" did not find its way into the official record. The 18th Division followed with its successful assault on the Schwaben Redoubt.

On the final "official" day of the campaign, 18 November, 18th Division assaulted Desire Trench as part of a larger operation with the Canadians. 7th Buffs were part of this attack. Lieutenant-Colonel Ransome positioned himself at 05.00 in a dug-out in the front line, Regina Trench, and this advanced HQ was shared with the CO of 7th Royal West Kent. Ransome's adjutant remained in the battalion report centre in Hessian Trench about 500 yards to the rear. He would experience a day in which, no doubt frustratingly, he was unable to fulfil nearly all of a CO's functions for any extended period. At 06.00 he watched A Company assemble, and the attack commenced at 06.10. Minutes later the enemy brought down a heavy barrage on Regina Trench. At 07.20, Ransome sent forward two runners to establish communications, but both were

---

42 Nichols, *op. cit.*, p. 98.
43 Nichols, *op. cit.*, p. 94.
44 Nichols, *op. cit.*, p. 96.
45 Nichols, *op. cit.*, pp. 99-100.

killed by snipers. Over the next hour or so, he sent out five more runners but only one returned – and with no information. Ransome then received a message from brigade that the situation to his front must be "cleared up." At this stage his only information came wounded men crawling back to British lines bearing tales of slaughter and disaster, adding to the confusion. He could not get anyone forward to clarify the situation (some of his unit had actually entered Hessian Trench and were holding out there) due to lethal German sniping. He could "clear up" absolutely nothing at all. Although the two COs tried to organise two platoons from each battalion to attempt to reach Hessian Trench, nothing was possible until gloom settled over the battlefield at 16.15 when two of Ransome's platoons got across to Hessian, found none of their battalion there, and fell back.[46] Ransome had endured a dreadful day. He had been brought into the attack unexpectedly, and there had been no opportunity for detailed planning on his part. The attack had failed, and all his officers bar one were dead – the sole survivor being seriously wounded. He himself had been unable to leave his advanced HQ due to shellfire and sniping. No good information could be obtained, and personal reconnaissance was out of the question. Conditions meant that Ransome had, to all intents and purposes, been unable to exercise command.

Leaving aside those whose battalion command careers in 18th Division were ended by wounds sustained on the Somme, namely Hugh Scott and George Ripley, and ill-health which would force William Johnston out of command and then out of the army in September 1917, the remaining thirteen COs illustrate the difference between "good fighting battalion commanders" and men "suitable for commanding larger formations."[47] That a number had prospects, is indicated by the fact that half (seven) were later promoted to brigade command. "The Brat" Maxwell commanded 27th Brigade from October 1916 until his death at the hands of a sniper in September 1917. Bertie Clay would command 34th Infantry Brigade from August 1917 to the armistice. George Price commanded 55th Infantry Brigade from October 1916 to November 1917. Martin Kemp-Welsh would command 123rd Infantry Brigade from June 1918 to the Armistice; and Algernon Ransome would command 7th Buffs until September 1918 when he would be promoted to the command of 170th Infantry Brigade. Charles Frizzell would command 75th Infantry Brigade from October 1918. Sidney Charrington, who transferred to the Tank Corps, would take command of 5th Tank Brigade nine days before the end of the war. Of those who did not progress with promotion, Henry Ferguson would be rested for six months in Great Britain in October 1917, having commanded for 27 months, and would command a Graduated Battalion before returning to lead 1/9th London August-September 1918. Charles Carr would recover from his wounds to command until September 1917. Gerald Hill would command battalions of the Suffolk Regiment into mid-1918. Alfred Irwin

---

46   TNA WO 95/2049: "Report on Operations 18th and 19th November 1916", 7th East Kent Regiment War Diary.
47   Hodgkinson, *op. cit.*, p. 206.

would lead 8th East Surrey through to September 1918; and George Mills would command 7th Bedfordshire until January 1918. Whilst it cannot be said that they might never have been promoted, their longevity in battalion command without elevation suggests that they fell into the "good fighting CO" category. Only John Fiennes would leave battalion command sick in early October 1916 and not return to active duty, moving into officer training.

The vignettes of infantry battalion COs in action during the Somme offensive allow insight into the principal responsibilities and functions of these individuals, both in preparing for and during combat, and into the possibilities and limitations of the role. As has been seen within 18th Division, a central role of the CO was in preparing his men for battle. That division held conferences, mostly at brigade level, about training schemes, with COs pooling areas of concern or deficit, but it was the CO who was responsible for planning, with his officers, platoon company and battalion training schemes. Most of the actions of COs in battle, unsurprisingly, reflect their attempts to exert command and control, either in the face of adversity or in ensuring success. A CO's actions could only be based on knowledge, and this would be obtained either before (to assist preparation) or during action. Thus Colonel Hill personally reconnoitred the Thiepval trenches prior to taking them over, as was the habit of battalion commanders going into the line. This enabled the CO to issue battalion orders for an attack, fine tuning the brigade scheme. Colonel Price earned accolades from Ivor Maxse for his careful and detailed planning of the relief of 12th Middlesex in Thiepval Chateau on 26 September. Obtaining information during action often became a very personal matter for the CO. The vignettes give a number of examples of them going forward during battle, in the face of confused or confusing accounts, to find out what was happening. On 1st July, this often resulted in mishap, sometimes fatal. Colonel Irwin's experience at Desire Trench demonstrates the fog of war enveloping a CO when no information could be obtained. Another aspect of command and control was liaison. In making decisions, as seen, there was sometimes deliberate consultation between battalion commanders in the heat of the battle as to how to proceed. Some even chose to pool battalion HQs. On other occasions, obtaining information that might save the unit or help it forward resulted in the CO being out of contact with his HQ for long periods of time. This could frustrate another central allied role of the CO, i.e. transmitting that information to brigade, so that the higher formation could form a composite picture of progress across its entire front. Frank Maxwell had this dilemma in Trônes Wood – he knew that on one hand he should be in his HQ, even if it was only a ditch, where he could supervise the relay of information. On the other, he recognised that if he did not personally restore command and control, the operation might fail. Whilst COs often made routine tactical adjustments during action, in these crucial moments, where success might be obtained or disaster averted, they exerted the judgement of the "man on the spot". This lassitude (although sometimes resulting in criticism or even the "degumming" of those who deployed it) was enshrined in *Field Service Regulations 1909*. These emphasised the danger of overly prescriptive operational orders issued at a distance where a subordinate might "be better able to decide on the spot, with a fuller knowledge of local conditions." The negative result of being too prescriptive might "cramp his initiative in dealing with unforeseen developments."[48] The man on the spot was thus specifically encouraged to use initiative, and Colonels Goodman, Irwin and Maxwell all did this in different ways. These decisions were either negative, as in Goodman twice disobeying an order to advance on 1st July; or positive, as in Alfred Irwin's actions at the other end of the line. Above all, in maintaining command and control, the personal element was always important, as in Irwin's leading his men on at Montauban, or Tween's encouragement of his men to "hang on" at Delville Wood. That personal example could be hazardous is well illustrated by the death of Colonel Machell at Authuille Wood.

Lieutenant-Colonel Percy Wilfrid Machell.

Captain D.V. Kelly, in describing the death of Colonel Jepson George Mignon, who as previously recounted, died leading a bombing party, noted: "In the later stages of the War commanders of ... battalions were constantly being enjoined to stay at their headquarters while a battle was in progress." Lieutenant-Colonel F.P. Crozier thought "this whole idea" of remaining in the rear "repulsive. It cut right across the foundations of mutual trust, emphasized in training, between private soldier and officer."[49] Crozier, who commanded 9th Royal Irish Rifles, described how he and Lieutenant-Colonel H.C. Bernard, commanding the 10th battalion, decided to disobey the edict to remain at battalion HQ on 1 July 1916 at Thiepval. Bernard, as noted above, paid with his life. Crozier's point was that one could only command with knowledge, which was only obtained by being "in the fight." Bernard's point, in retrospect, might have been that command is impossible from beyond the grave. The experience of Lieutenant-Colonel G.H. Brush, 11th Royal Irish Fusiliers, who "had been ordered not to lead his men in the attack" on 1 July 1916, highlights the dilemma. "He was to command and control the attack from Bn. H.Q. in the trenches" with "telephone, signal flags, runners and scouts." Unfortunately, "the sheer volume of the German fire made this system of communication almost impossible. The result of having the Commanding Officer at Battalion Headquarters meant the troops on the battlefield lacked specific direction."

48 General Staff, *Field Service Regulations Part 1* (London: HMSO, 1912), p. 27.
49 F.P. Crozier, *The Men I Killed* (London: Michael Joseph, 1937), p. 81.

The balance had to be struck between inspiration and communication.[50] The model of battalion command present in the British army prior to and during the First World War was one of leadership integrated *within* the unit. The CO lead, both in trench warfare but particularly in the mobile warfare of 1914 and 1918, from the front. In a war fought without the benefit of effective voice control, this served the battalion commander and his unit well, whatever the risks, fulfilling the two key functions of getting the "best possible information in the shortest time possible" to make the best possible tactical decisions; and providing an "inspiring personal example."[51]

In terms of evolution, battalion commanders became younger during the Somme offensive, and the period saw the emergence of civilian COs. These individuals emerged in two tranches. The first, representing a trickle, marked by exceptional individuals, occurred during the Somme offensive. The second occurred during 1918, when the trickle became a healthy stream. Evolution was enforced both by circumstances and by the army's clear insistence on quality control. Yet at this point in the war, when the distinctions between Regular, New Army, and TF units were still marked, the army still largely pursued a "business as usual" approach to command, which would only be much more clearly eroded during the final year of the war. But perhaps the most important aspect of this evolution was silent – the officers who commanded battalions, and who would come to command them in due course, became wiser men.

---

50 W.J. Canning, *Ballyshannon, Beloo, Bertincourt* (Enniskillen: Trimble, 1996), p. 66.
51 Doron Almog, "Positioning the Battalion Commander: The Advance and Pursuit from Awali to Beirut, 6-13 June 1982", *Military Operations*, No. 1 (2012), pp. 13-16.

18

Muddy grave? The German army at the end of 1916

Tony Cowan

> *The Somme was the muddy grave of the German field army, and of the faith in the infallibility of the German leading, dug by British industry and its shells…The most precious thing lost at the Somme was the good relationship between the leaders and the led. The German Supreme Command, which entered the war with enormous superiority, was defeated by the superior technique of its opponents. It had fallen behind in the application of destructive forces, and was compelled to throw division after division without protection against them into the cauldron of the battle of annihilation.*[1]

The opening sentence of this quote is well known from its frequent appearance in books about the battle of the Somme.[2] The quote is part of a two-page note in the British official history's first volume on 1916 which is titled "German Views on the Somme Fighting" and cites several German writers on the serious damage suffered by the German army during the battle. It is ascribed to a book by "Captain von Hentig, of the General Staff of the *Guard Reserve Division*." Its authorship by an officer of the famed German general staff lent it weight, adding to its value as part of the British effort to justify the very heavy casualties during the battle.

There are, however, problems with the official history's use of the quote, beginning with the man who wrote it, Hans von Hentig. Although Hentig played an honourable

---

1 Brigadier-General Sir James E. Edmonds (ed.), *Military Operations: France and Belgium 1916*, Vol. I (London: Macmillan, 1932), p. 494 (hereafter *BOH 1916*, I and so on). Ellipsis as per original quote.
2 Examples include John Terraine, *Douglas Haig: the Educated Soldier* (London: Leo Cooper, 1990; first published by Hutchinson & Co. Ltd, 1963), p. 232; Gary Sheffield, *The Somme* (London: Cassell Military Paperbacks, 2004), where the quote appears on the front cover; and William Philpott, *Bloody Victory: The Sacrifice on the Somme and the Making of the Twentieth Century* (London: Little, Brown, 2009), pp. 381-382 quoted in Alain Denizot, *La bataille de la Somme (juillet-novembre 1916)* (Paris: Éditions Perrin, 2002), p. 145.

role in the war, he did not serve in either *Guard Reserve Division* (there were two, not one as implied in the official history); he was not an "active" – i.e. in British terms, regular – officer; and most importantly, he was not a general staff officer. There is therefore no particular reason to take seriously what he has to say about muddy graves, especially as he did not even fight at the Somme. In addition, he had become a leading communist and presumably had an interest in discrediting the wartime German government and military.[3]

There are further problems with the British official history's use of Hentig's text. The ellipsis in the quote implies that a few words or at most sentences have been cut. In fact, the "muddy grave" part of the quote which has attracted so much attention appears twenty pages earlier than the longer, second part. And it is the last sentence in an extended footnote: so to Hentig it was not really important at all.[4] In addition, the focus of the original German sentence is not on the muddy grave but on the British industry which dug it: in other words on the cause rather than the operational outcome.[5]

Summing up, the British official history cobbled together a quote and then mistranslated and misattributed it in order to inflate its importance; this was part of the effort to justify heavy British casualties on the Somme. Hentig's testimony in itself simply does not bear the weight put on it by the official history and subsequent historians.

This chapter examines whether Hentig's text, despite the historiographical problems, nevertheless reveals a deeper truth about the German experience on the Somme. Drawing on examples and statistics, the chapter illustrates the great strain to which the German army was subject in 1916. It then analyses the variable quality of the army as both cause and effect of this strain, together with linked problems of tactical performance. The resulting difficulties and casualties naturally affected morale and trust between leaders and led: Hentig therefore had some justification for his views. But despite its dire situation, the army survived: how it did so is the subject of the second part of the chapter. Contingent factors such as the weather and Allied shortcomings played a major role, but in addition the Germans took important steps to raise

---

3   Autobiographical details of Hentig's wartime career are in Hans von Hentig, *Mein Krieg* (Berlin: August Kuhn Verlag, 1919); full biographical details are in the Bundesunmittelbare Stiftung des öffentlichen Rechts entry for him at <https://www.bundesstiftung-aufarbeitung.de/wer-war-wer-in-der-ddr-%2363%3b-1424.html?ID=4443> (Accessed on 23 July 2017). It is not clear why the British official history misidentified Hentig, but it perhaps confused him with another Hentig who by the end of the war was in a probationary general staff position in the *Guard Reserve Corps*. See Deutscher Offizier-Bund (ed.), *Ehren-Rangliste des ehemaligen Deutschen Heeres auf Grund der Ranglisten von 1914 mit den inzwischen eingetretenen Veränderungen* (Osnabrück: Biblio Verlag 1987 reprint of 1926 edition), p. 566.
4   Hans von Hentig, *Psychologische Strategie des großen Krieges* (Heidelberg: Carl Winter's Universitätsbuchhandlung, 1927), pp. 63, 82.
5   I am grateful to Dr Markus Pöhlmann for his help on the linguistic nuances of the quote; and to Dr Jim Beach and Dr Andy Simpson for their comments on the chapter.

their performance. The chapter focuses on organisational change and the resulting improvement in the handling of reserves. This was key to operational success: the analysis here of the state of German reserves offers fresh insight into the reality of Allied prospects for success during the crisis of the battle in September.

In December 1915, the leaders of the four main Allies – France, Russia, Britain and Italy – had agreed to launch simultaneous offensives on their respective fronts with the maximum force possible.[6] In fact, of course, the Germans pre-empted this with their offensive at Verdun. Famously, the first day of the battle of the Somme on 1 July was the 132nd day of Verdun. By then, the Brusilov offensive on the Eastern Front had scored great initial success against the Austro-Hungarians, and there was heavy fighting in Italy too. As a recent historian of the German and Austro-Hungarian war effort has put it, in the context of these simultaneous battles and the entry of Romania into the war on the Allied side in August, "an Anglo-French victory on the Somme offered a chance to deal a death blow to the now vastly outnumbered and overstrained Central Powers."[7]

In a letter of 21 August, General Erich von Falkenhayn, the head of the *Oberste Heeresleitung* (*OHL*, German Supreme Army Command),[8] described the resulting strain:

> Under the enormous pressure to which we are subjected, we have no spare margin of forces. Any movement of troops in one direction leads inevitably to dangerous weaknesses in another place, which could mean our destruction if we make the slightest error in our assessment of the enemy's intentions.[9]

Falkenhayn's point about there being no room for error is illustrated by the fate of *39th Bavarian Reserve Division*, one of the German formations involved in a powerful French attack at Verdun in December 1916. The division had spent about two years in the quiet Vosges sector and had no experience of major combat. In autumn 1916 it had to give up 1,600-1,800 of its younger men for the Romanian campaign. In return it received inexperienced *Landsturm* men, most of whom had never been under artillery fire, and recovered wounded; this composition was thought perfectly satisfactory for a quiet sector. When asked, the division said it was not fit for deployment to Verdun. It was sent anyway. On arrival, the division briefed the *Fifth Army* commander, General

6   Philpott, *Bloody Victory*, p. 58.
7   Alexander Watson, *Ring of Steel: Germany and Austria-Hungary at War, 1914-1918* (London: Allen Lane, 2014), p. 311.
8   Falkenhayn's formal title was "Chief of the General Staff of the Field Army".
9   Reichsarchiv, *Der Weltkrieg 1914 bis 1918: Die militärischen Operationen zu Lande*, 14 vols. (Berlin: E.S. Mittler, 1925-1956), X: *Die Operationen des Jahres 1916 bis zum Wechsel in der Obersten Heeresleitung* (Berlin: E.S. Mittler, 1936), pp. 675-676 (hereafter *Weltkrieg* X and so on); the quote is slightly mistranslated in *BOH 1916*, II (London: Macmillan and Co., Ltd, 1938), p. 555. In fact, Falkenhayn had misjudged the enemy's intentions. By late August, his failure to foresee Romania's imminent declaration of war was the final straw which led to his sacking and replacement at the head of *OHL* by Hindenburg and Ludendorff.

Ewald von Lochow, on its true combat effectiveness. Lochow arranged for it to receive one month's training before deployment to the front.[10]

When the French attacked on 15 December, *39th Bavarian Reserve Division* was said to have "completely failed."[11] *OHL* described this and an earlier defeat at Verdun in October as "serious tactical failures such as our army has seldom suffered since the start of the war." It demanded the dismissal of the division's commander, Lochow and another senior general. Court martial proceedings were threatened against other commanders; most recommendations for decorations were refused; and a sharp order was issued reminding officers and men of their duty.[12]

This engagement, in which the German army may have suffered some 25,000 casualties, was just the coda to a year of attrition.[13] German losses in 1916 totalled about 1.2 million, of which some three-quarters of a million were suffered in the battles of Verdun and the Somme.[14] Scholarly attention has focused on such raw casualty figures; particularly relating to the Somme, there has been much controversy over whether the British or the German army suffered worse.[15] But in fact another set of statistics is more helpful in understanding attrition. This is what the German army called "total wastage" [*Gesamtausfall*], meaning men who were permanently or long-term unavailable for field service and therefore needed replacement. The term covered killed and missing, together with those wounded and sick who had to be sent back to Germany for treatment.

Figure 1 demonstrates just why the German army was under such strain in summer 1916 when it was fighting major battles at Verdun, on the Somme and in the east simultaneously: nearly 250,000 men were lost to the army in July, either permanently or long-term.[16] Note that the chart covers only the German army, not the Austro-Hungarians who suffered disastrous losses during this period, especially during the Brusilov offensive.

---

10 Reichsarchiv, *Weltkrieg* XI: *Die Kriegführung im Herbst 1916 und im Winter 1916/17. Vom Wechsel in der Obersten Heeresleitung bis zum Entschluß zum Rückzug in die Siegfried-Stellung* (Berlin: E.S. Mittler, 1938), pp. 151-152. *Landsturm* men were either those who had not previously been required to do military service, or those who had served and were aged 39-45.
11 Bundesarchiv-Militärarchiv (hereafter BA/MA): RH61/970: Hermann von Kuhl, unpublished manuscript, 'Persönliches Kriegstagebuch des Generals der Inf. a.D. von Kuhl (Nov 15-Nov 18)', 19 December 1916.
12 *Weltkrieg* XI, p. 165.
13 Ministère de la Guerre, *Les armées françaises dans la grande guerre*, Tome IV vol. 3: *Bataille de la Somme (fin). Offensives françaises à Verdun (3 septembre-fin décembre 1916)* (Paris: Imprimerie Nationale, 1936) (hereafter AFGG, IV/3), p. 487.
14 Watson, *Ring of Steel*, pp. 300 and 324; James H. McRandle & James Quirk, 'The Blood Test Revisited: A New Look at German Casualty Counts in World War I', *Journal of Military History*, 70/3 (2006), Tables 8 and 11.
15 McRandle & Quirk, 'The Blood Test Revisited' is the best modern source on this controversy.
16 Reichskriegsministerium, *Sanitätsbericht über das Deutsche Heer (Deutsches Feld-und Besatzungsheer) im Weltkriege 1914/1918*, 5 vols. (Berlin: E.S. Mittler, 1934-1938), Part III: *die Krankenbewegung bei dem Deutschen Feld-und Besatzungsheer*, Tables 148 and 149.

Memorial card commemorating one of 1.2 million German casualties sustained during 1916.
(Private collection)

The case of German *IX Reserve Corps* illustrates the effect on the ground of this wastage and the fighting that caused it. The corps was deployed in the Pozières-Flers sector of the Somme from 24 July to 10 August. At this stage of the war, a German corps still commanded the two infantry divisions which were organically part of its order of battle and also other divisions posted in and out as the situation required. In this 17-day stint in the battle, the corps' two divisions suffered casualties of 4,800 and 6,800 respectively. After relief and so-called rest, the corps returned to the front in the French sector from 29 September to 16 October; in this 18-day period, the two divisions lost 3,500 and 3,600 men. So their grand total of casualties was over 8,000 and over 10,000 respectively, against a divisional infantry establishment of about 10,000.[17] This compares with an average, conservatively estimated, of 6,100 casualties suffered by the 118 divisions which fought at either Verdun or the Somme or both.[18]

17   These figures do not include other divisions under corps command.
18   "Conservatively estimated" because casualty figures are incomplete and in some cases entirely lacking, individual divisions involved after 15 December 1916 inclusive. All statistics for divisions, their performance and problems have been compiled from the author's databases: see Anthony Cowan, 'Genius for War? German Operational

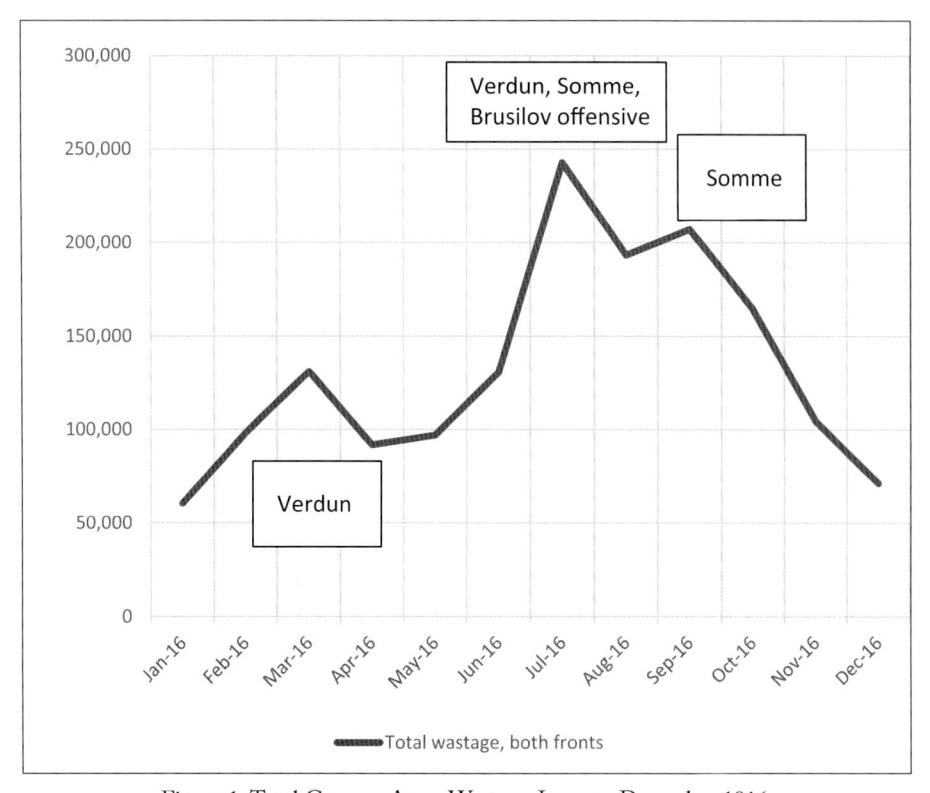

Figure 1 Total German Army Wastage, January-December 1916.

These very high casualties naturally had a severe effect at both the human and tactical levels. The corps chief of staff, Lieutenant-Colonel Albrecht von Thaer, wrote on 7 August towards the end of the first deployment:

> These are *terrible* days … Our good old *IX Reserve Corps* is now so to speak exhausted after 14 days of battle *without* a break. The infantry has lost about half its strength if not more. Those who are left are for the moment no longer men but more or less insane, shattered beings, capable of no impulse of energy, let alone attack. Officers whom I know to be otherwise *particularly* vigorous are reduced to tears.[19]

Command on the Western Front in Early 1917', unpublished Ph.D. thesis, King's College London, 2016, pp. 37-39 and Appendix 2.
19 Albrecht von Thaer, *Generalstabsdienst an der Front und in der O.H.L. Aus Briefen und Tagebuchaufzeichnungen 1915-1919*, p. 81 (7 August 1916).

After the corps' second stint in the line in October, Thaer's superior, *IX Reserve Corps* commander General Max von Boehn, wrote an important and widely-copied memorandum on his experiences.[20] Boehn asked why most German attacks and counterattacks during the battle failed:

> I seek the actual reason in the current quality of the troops, which is no longer adequate. Because of the heavy casualties, we have had to deploy replacements who are partly of lower value ... and without exception poorly trained. Discipline, which in trench warfare can only be maintained with the greatest effort, has been badly affected ... We could cope with all that if we had available trained and energetic junior leaders. But that is precisely what we lack. Battalion commanders are at best young captains, often reserve officers at that; company commanders are almost exclusively young reserve officers commissioned in 1914-15, and some even from 1916. It is obvious that we can no longer expect from units which are so loosely composed the performance we used to be accustomed to from our infantry.

Boehn added:

> [I]n two separate phases of the Somme battle, apart from my own corps I had six different divisions under my command. I noticed these phenomena to a greater or lesser extent in all of them: none was in a position to carry out a successful attack. I am convinced that this observation would apply to most corps on the Western Front.[21]

Is this last observation by Boehn right? He may have been thinking especially of *15th Infantry Division*, which had been through his corps in October. The division was reported to have completely failed: Boehn commented that he had never come across "such an appalling unit."[22] In one incident, out of 40 men who should have gone into the front line to relieve the garrison there, only one had followed his lieutenant; the rest had all slipped away and even shot at their officers.[23] The divisional commander was removed and there was a series of court martials of the men held responsible.[24]

---

20 BA/MA: PH1/9: Boehn memorandum to the Chief of the Military Cabinet, 24 October 1916, folios 284-289. There are further extracts from this document in Jack Sheldon's seminal *Fighting the Somme: German Challenges, Dilemmas and Solutions* (Barnsley: Pen & Sword Military, 2017), pp. 173-176; his translation slightly differs.
21 Boehn memorandum, fn. 282. *Second Army*'s chief of staff had made some of these points at the important Cambrai meeting between Hindenburg, Ludendorff, and Western Front commanders and staff officers on 8 September 1916. See *Weltkrieg* XI, p. 16.
22 Kuhl, 'Kriegstagebuch', p. 30 (13 October 1916).
23 Bayerisches Hauptstaatsarchiv, Abteilung III Geheimes Hausarchiv, München: Rupprecht Nachlass Nr. 705: Crown Prince Rupprecht of Bavaria, unpublished diary, 12 October 1916.
24 Crown Prince Rupprecht of Bavaria, *Mein Kriegstagebuch* (Eugen von Frauenholz ed.), 3 Vols. (München: Deutscher National Verlag, 1929), II, p. 116 (15 March 1917).

Similar problems and sackings continued throughout 1917. Even in September that year the division was being described as having failed everywhere.[25]

Crown Prince Rupprecht of Bavaria, the army group commander, believed that such serious cases were rare.[26] Nevertheless other divisions were of concern too. In early September, Rupprecht himself recorded that "Unfortunately our units on the Somme front are for the most part not exactly the best…"[27] Elsewhere he noted problems in seven other divisions in the last quarter of 1916.[28] In all, in late 1916-early 1917 there is evidence of disciplinary or performance problems in 23 divisions which fought at Verdun and/or the Somme, some 19 per cent.

Underlying these problems and greatly adding to the strain on the whole army were issues relating to the intrinsic quality of formations. Despite efforts to make all

Crown Prince Rupprecht of Bavaria.

divisions as homogeneous as possible, nowhere near all were suitable for major battle: as the German official history states, the highest demands were made of the best divisions.[29] How and where *OHL* actually deployed divisions helps clarify its assessment of their quality. In 1915 the Eastern Front had been Germany's main theatre.[30] But from the start of the Verdun offensive in February 1916, the Western Front took priority. It became increasingly obvious that divisions fighting there needed to be of higher quality: one of the most experienced divisions from the Eastern Front suffered serious problems after arriving at Verdun.[31] *OHL* clearly placed most trust in active divisions – the ones which existed in peacetime – and the reserve and *Ersatz* divisions raised on mobilisation in August 1915 following detailed peacetime planning:

25 BA/MA: RH61/986: Gerhard Tappen, unpublished manuscript, 'Meine Kriegserinnerungen', p. 376.
26 Rupprecht, *Kriegstagebuch*, II, p. 116 (15 March 1917).
27 Ibid., p. 10 (4 September 1916).
28 Rupprecht, unpublished diary 17, 18, 29 October, 3, 13 November and 9 December.
29 *Weltkrieg* XI, p. 481.
30 Giving rise to the jingle: "the brave army is fighting in the East, while in the West the fire brigade is spraying around": Tappen, 'Kriegserinnerungen', fn. 93.
31 Ibid. Tappen does not identify the division. In the opposite direction, Boehn mentioned (but equally did not identify) a division which was seen as inadequate on the Somme but did well enough in the East: Boehn memorandum, fn. 283.

although these formations comprised only 43 per cent of all divisions existing by the end of that year, 80 per cent of them spent 11 or 12 months on the Western Front in 1916.[32] Only two additional active divisions were sent to the Eastern Front in summer 1916 to face the Brusilov offensive.[33] Only one active division fought in Romania in 1916, and it was already on the Eastern Front. No reserve or *Ersatz* divisions formed on mobilisation were sent east for either campaign.

An analysis of divisions' participation in the battles of Verdun and the Somme confirms these patterns. Of the 197 infantry divisions available to the Germans by the end of the Somme, 118 fought there or at Verdun (60 per cent); the other 79 fought at neither. 24 of the 118 divisions fought and suffered appreciable casualties in both battles (Table 1).[34]

Table 1 Divisions deployed at Verdun, the Somme or both

Battle	No. of divisions	% of the 118 divisions	% of total divisions
Fought at Verdun	51	N/A	26
Fought at the Somme	94	N/A	48
Seriously engaged at both Verdun and the Somme (i.e. from the previous 2 categories)	24	20	12

OHL appears to have seen these 24 divisions as the mainstay of the army during 1916. This illustrates the German official history's comment above that the highest demands were made of the best divisions. 75 per cent of the 24 were active divisions or reserve and *Ersatz* divisions raised on mobilisation. Separately, five of them were among the divisions mentioned above as causing concern, suggesting that their multiple deployments in major battle had caused them lasting damage.[35]

The performance problems of divisions which were a cause of concern of course had an effect on the battlefield. The case of *39th Bavarian Reserve Division* at Verdun was

---

32 *Ersatz* (reinforcement) and *Ersatz* reserve units were comprised of supernumerary men including those with no peacetime training as well as wartime casualty replacement recruits.

33 In addition, *1st Infantry Division* was sent back to the Eastern Front where it had been from August 1914 till March 1916; it had suffered nearly 11,000 casualties at Verdun.

34 The sources for these calculations are *Weltkrieg* X, Anlagen 2 and 3 and XI, Anlage 4. Cavalry are excluded. The figure of 197 divisions is calculated from the total available at the end of September 1916, the month when the newest divisions which took part in either campaign were raised. Appreciable casualties are defined as over 1,000 men; three other divisions fought during both campaigns, but suffered under 1,000 casualties in one. *Weltkrieg* X, Anlage 2 (Verdun) covers from 12 February to 28 August only for the East Bank, and to 20 June only for the West Bank.

35 *5th, 38th, 103rd, 113th divisions* and *44th Reserve Division*.

not an isolated example. On 12 September, a French chasseur brigade won a tactical victory at Bouchavesnes on the Somme. The lesson normally drawn from this – as for instance taught on the British army "Somme 100" staff ride in September 2016 – is that the victory was due to rapid exploitation of a fleeting opportunity, which in turn depended on successful application of mission command. But what is overlooked in such accounts is that some of the German defenders were poor quality as well as being heavily outnumbered. French prisoners interrogated after the action reported a string of tactical deficiencies in the defence. These included that German defensive barrage fire had started too late, was wrongly placed and had not hit the first assault waves at all; the German infantry had in many cases been overrun in their shelters (some accounts suggest they were drunk); and finally the second German line had been too weakly garrisoned and therefore easily captured.[36] One of the defending formations, the Saxon *53rd Reserve Division*, had been having problems since spring 1916; was regarded as having "completely failed" during the French attack; was then found no longer suitable for deployment on the Somme; and shortly after moved to the Eastern Front, increasingly a backwater where all less capable troops were being sent.

Certain specific factors contributed to the heavy casualties and resulting problems of quality, in particular the tactical system initially employed by the German army on the Somme. In 1914-15 the army had gradually moved away from the pre-war defensive concept that there should be "one line and a strong one."[37] Doctrine issued at the end of 1915 called for the construction of at least two positions, far enough apart to force the enemy to mount a separate operation to attack each. Experience at Verdun had indicated that manning the defensive front thinly reduced casualties.

However, tactical instructions in the early period of the Somme partly reverted to the older thinking. General Fritz von Below, commanding the Army fighting the battle, ordered:

> I forbid the voluntary evacuation of positions. Every commander is responsible for ensuring that this firm determination to fight is known to every man in the Army. The enemy must only make his way forward over corpses.

Below repeated this order in October. Corps were to make all incoming divisional commanders aware of it, and then to confirm this to him. To ram the message home, Below added that "In every case the planned, voluntary evacuation of positions is to be decided by my headquarters." He also insisted on counter-attacking to regain any ground lost.[38] These tactics did indeed prevent an Allied breakthrough, but at great

---

36 *Weltkrieg* XI, p. 65; British Army, *The Battle of the Somme, 1916: Study Guide* (London: Ministry of Defence, 2016), pp. 62-66.
37 *BOH 1917*, II: (London: HMSO, 1948), p. 295.
38 Hauptstaatsarchiv Stuttgart: M660/038 Bü 16: *Second Army* Order, Ia Nr. 575 geh., 3 July 1916 and *First Army* order, Ia Nr. 1438 geh., 22 October 1916.

cost. Some divisions complained that the casualties incurred bore no relationship to the successful defence or recapture of the ground concerned.[39]

There were also problems in implementing all-arms co-operation, by 1916 meaning co-operation between infantry, artillery and aviation in particular. The Germans themselves believed that the British and French were now superior in this area, an idea which runs counter to the received view of the Western Front and is worth closer examination.[40] German doctrine had long seen all-arms co-operation as essential to solving the problem of modern defensive firepower.[41] Implementing the doctrine was another matter. Hindenburg considered that before the war only the infantry's tactics were common property throughout the army; knowledge of the technical arms was seen as unimportant and to be handled by a few specialists.[42] Statistics show that the infantry occupied a disproportionate number of higher posts: in 1914, 84 percent of divisional commanders were from the infantry and this changed little during the war. The 1914-15 campaigns saw a mixed German tactical performance. At Verdun, the effect of the artillery was less than expected; co-ordination between the arms frequently failed, and the infantry then faced an impossible task no matter how brave they were.[43] An important *OHL* circular of late 1916 commented that when trench warfare began, better training, discipline and drill had given the Germans the upper hand; however, the British and French had in some ways learned more quickly and by mid-1916 had begun to overtake the Germans.[44]

The initial phases of the battle of the Somme demonstrated just how far behind the Germans had fallen in all-arms co-operation. Superior British and French artillery-air co-operation enabled accurate artillery fire, causing heavy casualties to the German infantry and serious damage to the artillery; also, the fixed defences then in vogue became an

General Fritz von Below.

---

39 Report by the Bavarian Military Plenipotentiary at *OHL*, 12 September 1916, quoted in Jakob Jung, *Max von Gallwitz (1852-1937): General und Politiker* (Osnabrück: Biblio Verlag, 1995), p. 74.
40 *Weltkrieg* XI, pp. 109-110.
41 Antulio J. Echevarria II, *After Clausewitz: German Military Thinkers Before the Great War* (Lawrence, Kansas: University Press of Kansas, 2000), pp. 5, 217.
42 Bayerisches Hauptstaatsarchiv, München, Abteilung IV, Kriegsarchiv (hereafter KAM): HKR neue Nr. 378: *OHL* circular to general staff officers, 'Kriegführung und Generalstab', M.J. Nr. 10000, 22 November 1916.
43 Ludwig Gold and Alexander Schwencke, *Die Tragödie von Verdun 1916* (*Schlachten des Weltkrieges* Bde. 13-15), 3 Vols. (Oldenbourg i. O.: Gerhard Stalling, 1928-1929), Vol. I: *Die deutsche Offensivschlacht*, p. 254.
44 *OHL* circular, 'Kriegführung und Generalstab'.

easy target for Allied guns.[45] The German official history points out that control of the airspace over the battlefield had become a basic precondition of success in the land battle; the British were effective in dominating the air over and far behind the German lines, as well as in reconnaissance for and support of their infantry.[46]

At the time, the situation was described in even starker terms. In late September, a senior officer reported that British offensive successes on the Somme threatened to become a crisis. For the moment, the relatively favourable outcome was largely due to the inadequate tactical training of the British, but not to any inadequate moral characteristics. German troops had been once again psychologically and physically shelled to bits. He continued:

> The main cause of the continual loss of positions lies in the fact that north of the Somme it has been completely impossible to get the artillery to cooperate properly with the infantry, and that all attempts to get the field and heavy artillery to work together… have also so far failed. The defence suffers from an unbelievable lack of artillery organisation.[47]

So the problem for the Germans in the first half of the campaign was that the policy of rigid defence from carefully constructed positions, together with frequent counter-attacks, exposed the infantry to the full weight of Allied material superiority, delivered by superior all-arms co-operation. They had not expected this, certainly not from the British whom they regarded as generally less experienced and skilful than the French. As the historian of the Royal Artillery has pointed out, the Somme was the first time the British army was able to fight "a rich man's war"; it was a turning point in the way the army fought, and in the war itself – it showed the British Empire mobilising its strength. Matériel was replacing man.[48]

The Germans called this *Materialschlacht*, the battle of matériel. A senior officer wrote:

> [The enemy] plough up the battlefields with a hail of metal and level our trenches and fortifications, the fire often burying the defenders of the trenches in them. [The enemy] expend metal, we expend life.[49]

---

45   Robert T. Foley, 'Learning War's Lessons: The German Army and the Battle of the Somme 1916', *Journal of Military History*, 75/2 (April 2011), pp. 492-494.
46   *Weltkrieg* XI, p. 110. For a recent analysis of the German, British and French air forces in the battle of the Somme, see James S. Corum, 'Air War over the Somme' in Matthias Strohn (ed.), *The Battle of the Somme* (Oxford: Osprey Publishing, 2016), pp. 75-91.
47   National Archives and Records Administration (NARA), Washington: M958-1: Oberstleutnant Hermann Ritter Mertz von Quirnheim's seventh report to the Bavarian Minister of War, 30 September 1916.
48   Spencer Jones, 'The Royal Artillery at the Battle of the Somme 1916', British Army "Somme 16" Study Day lecture, 8 September 2016.
49   Robert T. Foley, *German Strategy and the Path to Verdun: Erich von Falkenhayn and the Development of Attrition, 1870-1916* (Cambridge: Cambridge University Press, 2005), p. 149.

That was actually a Russian officer, writing about the fighting on the Eastern Front in 1915. The German army then, and modern proponents of its excellence now, have often argued that the Allies only gained their successes in both world wars from material superiority. But naturally the Germans took full advantage when *they* had the upper hand in matériel, as on the Eastern Front in 1915.

As Allied material superiority increased throughout 1916, the German infantry's feeling of helplessness began to cause serious morale problems. A well-attested hatred of officers by other ranks arose. This was certainly not universal, but was of course very damaging.[50] From autumn 1916 there were signs of abuse of troops in the field army by their superiors.[51] Desertion increased.[52] Towards the end of September, Crown Prince Rupprecht informed *OHL* that shirking was occurring even in good units.[53] A battalion commander reported in October that morale was generally adequate, but various factors were having a negative effect including cold rations, the violence of enemy artillery fire, constant short firing by German artillery, the large number of casualties and the great many unburied corpses.[54]

OHL had been systematically examining the state of morale since at least April 1916.[55] Its judgement by the end of the year was that the army was exhausted but its spirit and morale were good. A post-war research paper by the central German military history organisation, the *Reichsarchiv*, concluded that the army's ability to hold out on the Somme showed this judgement was generally correct. There were, however, danger signals: the *Reichsarchiv* thought that *OHL* was not blind to these, but because of its belief in the fighting abilities of the German soldier seemed not to realise the full seriousness of the morale issue.[56]

The *Reichsarchiv* paper considered ration cuts had a particularly negative effect, especially given complaints that officers received or bought better food. Other causes of concern were low pay, perceived injustice in the allocation of decorations, and frequent problems over allowing men to take leave. Letters from home complaining about conditions there also had a major influence on morale at the front. The *Reichsarchiv* paper highlights "the warning signal from Verdun", meaning the December 1916

---

50 See Alexander Watson, *Enduring the Great War: Combat, Morale and Collapse in the German and British Armies 1914-1918* (Cambridge: Cambridge University Press, 2008), pp. 124-133 for a recent discussion.
51 Up to that point such complaints had been limited to the Home Army (*Besatzungsheer*): see BA/MA: RH61/1655: unpublished Reichsarchiv research paper, 'Die Entwicklung der Stimmung im Heere im Winter 1916/17', Sections 2 and 3.
52 Holger H. Herwig, *The First World War: Germany and Austria-Hungary 1914-1918* (London: Arnold, 1997), p. 198.
53 Rupprecht, *Kriegstagebuch*, III, p. 107, quoted in Christopher Duffy, *Through German Eyes: the British & the Somme 1916* (London: Weidenfeld & Nicolson, 2006), p. 288.
54 Jack Sheldon, *The German Army on the Somme 1914-1916* (Barnsley: Pen & Sword Military, 2005), p. 323.
55 'Die Entwicklung der Stimmung im Heere im Winter 1916/17', Sec. 1.
56 Ibid., Conclusion.

defeat there mentioned above. Particularly worrying was that the troops had not fought to the last: when surrounded, they had failed to break out with fixed bayonets and had instead surrendered. The large number of officers, machine guns and mortars captured by the French showed that not only had enemy fire damaged the vigour of the troops but that the morale of some units was no longer at its old level.[57]

There is no doubt then that by the end of 1916 the German army was in a very bad way. Indeed, echoing the German officer quoted above, William Philpott argues that a succession of British and French attacks in September brought the German defence to a crisis point.[58] Overall battle casualties and the total wastage statistics in Figure 1 both reflect this. Hentig therefore had some right on his side when he referred to the superior technique of Germany's enemies and the resulting relative German disadvantage in "the application of destructive forces."

But nevertheless the German army held out for the rest of 1916 – and of course for much longer – as well as preventing an Allied breakthrough on the Somme. The question how it was able to do so can be answered at various levels. Most fundamentally, to quote Philpott again, "Strategic victory in a battle of attrition was undoubtedly a chimera – hoped for, planned for, even on occasion apparently imminent, but unrealisable."[59] Behind these comments lie some of the basic and well-known characteristics of the First World War, especially on the Western Front. In particular, the contemporary technological balance favoured firepower over mobility; inadequate battlefield communications hindered all-arms co-operation; and the force/space ratio, in other words too many men and guns crammed into too small an area, prevented manoeuvre. These factors affected both sides of course, but generally favoured the defence over the attack.

In addition, some more contingent developments aided the German defence as the battle continued. The travails and heavy casualties of the inexperienced British army are analysed elsewhere in this book. By the end of September, the British and even more the French were running out of fresh divisions to feed into the offensive; supply and movement of ammunition were also increasingly difficult. Part of the reason for this was the weather, which as always played a major role in the course of the battle: prolonged periods of rain from the beginning of October caused serious problems for artillery observation and for logistics, as well as misery for the infantry. Sir Douglas Haig in particular has been criticised for failing to realise the likely impact of the weather and not accelerating the tempo of operations accordingly.[60] This criticism may be justified, but there were good reasons why it took time for a still raw army to mount

---

57   Ibid., Section 7.
58   Philpott, *Bloody Victory*, pp. 382-383.
59   Ibid., p. 383.
60   J.P. Harris, *Douglas Haig and the First World War* (Cambridge: Cambridge University Press, 2008), pp. 259, 266, 273.

Shattered German trench near Combles. (Private collection)

major operations, including the need to deploy fresh divisions and artillery and then give them the opportunity to acquaint themselves with the ground.[61]

Not least of the reasons why the German army held out was the quality of its troops and lower-level units. Despite the genuine problems described above, the frequent complaints from senior commanders such as Max von Boehn and concerns about the early calling up of recruitment year classes, the wartime officers and men were still capable of carrying out a tough, courageous and competent defence which proved more than good enough to defeat Allied offensives.[62] *OHL* belief in the fighting abilities of the German soldier was ultimately justified; and Hentig thought that "The German lance-corporal wins the battle of the Somme which the staff have lost."[63]

Tactical and organisational change also played a major role in the German army's ability to resist the storm. If, as is often claimed, the British army learned much from the Somme, so too did the Germans. Attention has generally focused on tactical developments, in particular the introduction of a more mobile defence and a gradual shift from prepared defences which were too easily located and destroyed to improvised shell-hole positions. As the battle continued, increased emphasis was placed on

---

61 Sheffield & Bourne (eds), *Douglas Haig: War Diaries and Letters, 1914-1918* (London: Weidenfeld & Nicolson, 2005), p. 224 (27 August 1916).
62 Philpott, *Bloody Victory*, p. 625. Watson, *Enduring the Great War* explores in depth how the German army at the lower levels of command resisted the continually increasing strain in 1916-1917 and well into 1918.
63 Hentig, *Mein Krieg*, p. 37.

thinning the front line garrison, defence in depth and retaining sufficient strength for counter-attacks of differing scale.[64] Infantry firepower increased during the battle, and in the slightly longer term, new infantry and artillery weapons arrived. From late September, *OHL* began the process of identifying and codifying best practice from these changes; this was eventually promulgated to the army as new doctrine in December 1916, just after the end of the battle.

Although less glamorous, organisational changes were at least as important to German survival as improved tactical performance, and in fact facilitated it. In recognition of the ever-increasing importance of aviation, especially for all-arms co-operation, the air force was established as a separate arm of service. A new post of "commanding general of air forces" took control of all air-related assets in the field and in Germany. The number of squadrons continued to grow, and in particular the formation of specialist fighter units with superior aircraft contributed to German predominance in the air from the autumn.[65] This in turn led to an improved though still patchy all-arms performance.

Corps headquarters increasingly gave up their role commanding an integrated tactical formation and instead became more or less static controllers of Groups or *Gruppen*, through which divisions rotated. This change was much disliked but was unavoidable because of the need to move divisions in and out of combat at different rates while also ensuring continuity of effort in defensive sectors. The roles of *Gruppen* and divisions could then be more clearly distinguished. Divisions became responsible for the close and short-term battle. *Gruppen* handled the deep battle; they also provided continuity in space and time by running the local framework of supporting arms, fixed defences and supply networks into which the divisions fitted.

Perhaps the most important of these organisational changes, however, was the establishment of a self-standing army group level of command. It was no accident that the first to be set up on the Western Front was *Armee Gruppe Rupprecht*, tasked with co-ordinating the German defence on the Somme and in particular improving management of the crucial flow of reserves. The state of German reserves is key to assessing the progress of the battle of the Somme and the prospects for an Anglo-French victory. Various factors complicate our understanding, including differing nomenclature; the location, quality and composition of formations in reserve; the level of command which had authority over them; and the sources now available to study the question.

Modern scholars sometimes refer to the German "strategic reserve", but the Germans themselves used the term *Heeresreserve* (army reserve, meaning the army as a whole rather than individual field Armies). Formations in *Heeresreserve* were under *OHL*

---

64 The best account of this process is Foley, 'Learning War's Lessons'.
65 *Weltkrieg* XII: *Die Kriegführung im Frühjahr 1917* (Berlin: E.S. Mittler, 1939), pp. 8-10 for an overview; Peter Hart, *Bloody April: Slaughter in the Skies over Arras, 1917* (London: Weidenfeld & Nicolson, 2005), pp. 30-34 on the new German fighter aircraft units.

control, and might therefore also be described as "at *OHL*'s disposal".[66] They did not comprise a fixed group, nor were they geographically co-located. Formations moved in and out of *OHL* reserve and were generally placed in the rear of specific Armies; most of them were on the Western Front, but some were in the east. Their quality and state at any given time also varied; in particular, during periods of heavy fighting, formations in *OHL* reserve would not necessarily be fresh. Apart from infantry divisions and corps, *OHL* also created a reserve of heavy artillery (*Heeresartillerie-Reserve*), though it was not always possible to maintain this; and during the battle of the Somme a field artillery reserve (*Heeres-Feldartillerie-Reserve*) was established.[67]

In addition, the German army – like its allies and enemies – held reserves at all levels of command. Of particular relevance to this study, *Armee Gruppe Rupprecht* (from its establishment in late August 1916) and *First Army* and *Second Army*, actually fighting the battle of the Somme, all controlled reserves; as with *OHL*, these varied in number and quality.

A major means of creating or supplementing reserves was to remove forces from less important sectors to reinforce the Somme front. This could be done either by reducing the establishment of the Armies concerned, or by exchanging their fresh or at least fresher divisions with ones exhausted on the Somme. Either method could be problematic, for two reasons. Armies jealously held on to their subordinate formations and might not give them up without a fight, a problem already known to Clausewitz.[68] In addition, the formations might already have been through Verdun or the Somme, raising the question whether they had recovered their full fighting power. Not surprisingly, from summer 1916 the German army paid increasing attention to the condition of its divisions in terms of strength, period of rest or combat and state of training. From early November this was formalised into weekly reporting on every division, allowing more accurate assessment of which divisions could safely be deployed or redeployed to major battle fronts.[69]

This already complex picture is further complicated by three other factors. First, German sources on reserves are not particularly good and tend to vary in terms of period and sector. Few cover both fronts, and many record details of the Somme sector rather than the whole Western Front. Second and linked to this, on the relatively small Western Front with its good transport facilities it was possible to move formations quickly: so a snapshot of reserves on one day might not reflect the true position the next. Third, German sources covering 1916 tended to amalgamate army group or

---

66 William Philpott, *Attrition: Fighting the First World War* (London: Little, Brown, 2014), p. 240. KAM: Heeresgruppe Rupprecht alte Nr. 150: *Armee Gruppe Rupprecht* telegram to *Second Army*, Ia 997 geh., 12 October 1916.
67 *Weltkrieg* IX: *Die Operationen des Jahres 1915. Die Ereignisse im Westen und auf dem Balkan vom Sommer bis zum Jahresschluß* (Berlin: E.S. Mittler, 1933), p. 388, and *Weltkrieg* XII, p. 7.
68 Carl von Clausewitz, *Vom Kriege* (Bonn: Ferd. Dümmlers Verlag, 1973), p. 521.
69 Cowan, 'Genius for War?', p. 46 and Chapter 8.

468   At All Costs

British prisoners with armed escort, August 1916. (Private collection)

Army reserves in one figure; this changed for 1917, when statistics for *OHL* and army group reserves were amalgamated instead.

An example will illustrate the resulting problem of analysing German reserves, faced both by Allied intelligence at the time and modern scholars now.[70] The German official history says that at the end of August, when Hindenburg and Ludendorff took over at *OHL*, reserves had been used up except for tiny remnants. Crown Prince Rupprecht noted in his diary that on 4 September there were absolutely no reserves behind the Somme front. And Ludendorff told a conference of high-level commanders and staff officers on 8 September that no reserves were available.[71] Yet a map in the German official history shows that on 4 September one division and one brigade were in army or army group reserve behind *First Army*, with four more divisions arriving; and two behind *Second Army*, with two others arriving.[72] So if the official history's "tiny remnants" and Ludendorff's comments mean anything, they must refer to lack of *OHL* reserves rather than lack of all reserves. Similarly, if correct, Rupprecht's diary entry must mean there were no army group reserves behind the Somme front, rather than no reserves at all. The 4 September map can of course tell us nothing about the intrinsic quality or current state of the reserves; nor whether part or all of them had already been sucked into the battle. And since it only covers the *First Army* and *Second*

---

70 For British intelligence on German reserves during the Somme campaign, see Jim Beach, *Haig's Intelligence: GHQ and the German Army, 1916-1918* (Cambridge: Cambridge University Press, 2013), Chapter 9.
71 *Weltkrieg* XI, pp. 4, 14; Rupprecht, *Kriegstagebuch*, II, p. 17 (12 September 1916).
72 *Weltkrieg* XI, Sketch 1.

Men of the *185th Infanterie Regiment, 208th Division*, November 1916. This wartime-raised unit entered the line north of the Ancre on the 18th of that month. (Private collection)

Army sectors, it says nothing about reserves elsewhere on the Western Front, let alone in the east.

Given the complexity of the reserve situation, it is not surprising that historians argue whether the glass of Allied prospects during the September crisis was half-full or half-full. In his chapter in this volume, Stephen Badsey views the battle of Morval of 25-28 September as one of the most critical points of the campaign; and the British official history says that at this period "Rupprecht had been obliged to put into the line all his available troops."[73] The German official history too describes the seriousness of the situation: September saw both the most extensive loss of ground since 1 July and the highest casualties of the whole battle. *Armee Gruppe Rupprecht* had to cut back its ambitions to relieve all divisions after 14 days at most; there were concerns about the failing resistance put up by divisions committed to the battle for the second time, and more broadly about the lack of replacements arriving from Germany.[74]

On the other hand, *OHL* was able to lend *Armee Gruppe Rupprecht* both divisions of its reserve in late September – and note that there were two divisions in *OHL* reserve – as well as sending three further divisions a few days later. Strikingly, none of these five divisions was deployed in the front line till early October: this suggests that

---

73 *BOH 1916*, II, p. 425.
74 *Weltkrieg* XI, pp. 75-79.

though the situation was serious, it was not desperate. On 3 October *OHL* allocated five further divisions to *Armee Gruppe Rupprecht* to relieve those in the front line, and moved forward two divisions from its reserve: once more, note that there were again (at least) two divisions in *OHL* reserve. And two days later it announced the early deployment of five fresh (i.e. up to strength and rested) divisions from *Armee Gruppe Kronprinz* to *Armee Gruppe Rupprecht*.[75]

Analysis of the composition and recent experience of the first five divisions mentioned in the previous paragraph further illustrates the "glass half full" nature of the reserve situation (Table 2).[76]

Table 2   Composition and recent experience of five divisions assigned to *Armee Gruppe Rupprecht* in late September 1916

Division	Date of establishment and composition	Experience during 1916
6th Infantry	Pre-war active	Verdun February-May; 9,500 casualties
211th Infantry	Early September 1916; one pre-war active regiment and two reserve regiments raised on mobilisation	New. Regiments were from divisions which had already fought on the Somme, averaging 5,000 casualties
29th Infantry	Pre-war active	Quiet sector
206th Infantry	Late August 1916; one *Ersatz* regiment, one *Ersatz* reserve and one drawn from men of a reserve division formed on mobilisation	New. *Ersatz* and *Ersatz* reserve regiments deployed to quiet sectors; reserve division deployed to Somme sustaining approximately 5,000 casualties
5th Ersatz	June 1915; one *Ersatz* reserve and two *Landwehr* regiments[1]	Quiet sector

Note
1   *Landwehr* units comprised men of earlier year classification and were primarily intended for static defence in quiet sectors.

75   Ibid., pp. 77, 80-81, 83 and Anlage 4.
76   The *6th* and *211th divisions* were the two from *OHL* reserve.

These divisions clearly differed both in their basic quality and their state at the time they were allocated to *Armee Gruppe Rupprecht*. The best was *29th Infantry Division*, a pre-war formation which had been in a quiet sector for the whole of 1916 and had therefore not been cut up by participation in the heavy fighting of the year. In addition, it was from the Baden contingent, whose troops were always highly regarded.[77] The worst was probably *5th Ersatz Division*, composed of lower quality troops. Its deployment on the Somme was not a success: it was regarded as having failed in action, its commander was sacked and it was sent to the Eastern Front, where as noted above all less capable formations were being transferred.[78]

French intelligence believed that the large-scale use of such "less reliable" (*moins sûrs*) units in the battle was new, and a first sign that the German army's freedom to deploy its forces was weakening.[79] But as suggested earlier, though the quality and number of reserves sometimes fell to alarming levels, matters never actually reached breaking point. One important reason for this emerges from the total wastage figures above, now broken down into different fronts (Figure 2). The spike to about 250,000 permanent and long-term casualties in July 1916, caused by simultaneous action on both fronts, was never equalled in the rest of 1916 or the whole of 1917. The increase in September 1916 reflects the crisis of that month, but by then activity on the Eastern Front was declining so total wastage never reached July levels. After September, wastage on both fronts continued to drop and this trend continued until the Allied spring offensive of 1917. This decrease of pressure let the German army off the attritional hook.

At the same time, the overall strength of the German field army was still sharply increasing.[80] This partly reflects the decline in wastage shown in Figures 1 and 2. But it also demonstrates the extent of Germany's remaining manpower, one reason why the German army was able to create so many new divisions at this period. The 164 divisions available at the beginning of the battle of the Somme rose to 197 at its end and 228 at the opening of the Allied spring offensive in April 1917. The quality of the new divisions varied as Table 2 suggests, but at least these formations gave the German high command increased flexibility to man quiet sectors with lower-quality units and to use the better ones for major battle.

---

77 For an assessment of regional differences within the German army, see Tony Cowan, 'A Picture of German Unity? Federal Contingents in the German Army, 1916-1917' in Jonathan Krause (ed.), *The Greater War: Other Combatants and Other Fronts, 1914-1918* (London: Palgrave Macmillan, 2014), pp. 141-160.
78 Rupprecht unpublished diary, p. 2116 (9 December 1916).
79 GQG paper, 'Exposé comparatif des ordres de bataille sur le front occidental établis le 29 août 1916 et le 1er novembre 1916', 2 November 1916, in AFGG, IV/3, Annexe 1445.
80 Cowan, 'Genius for War?', p. 251.

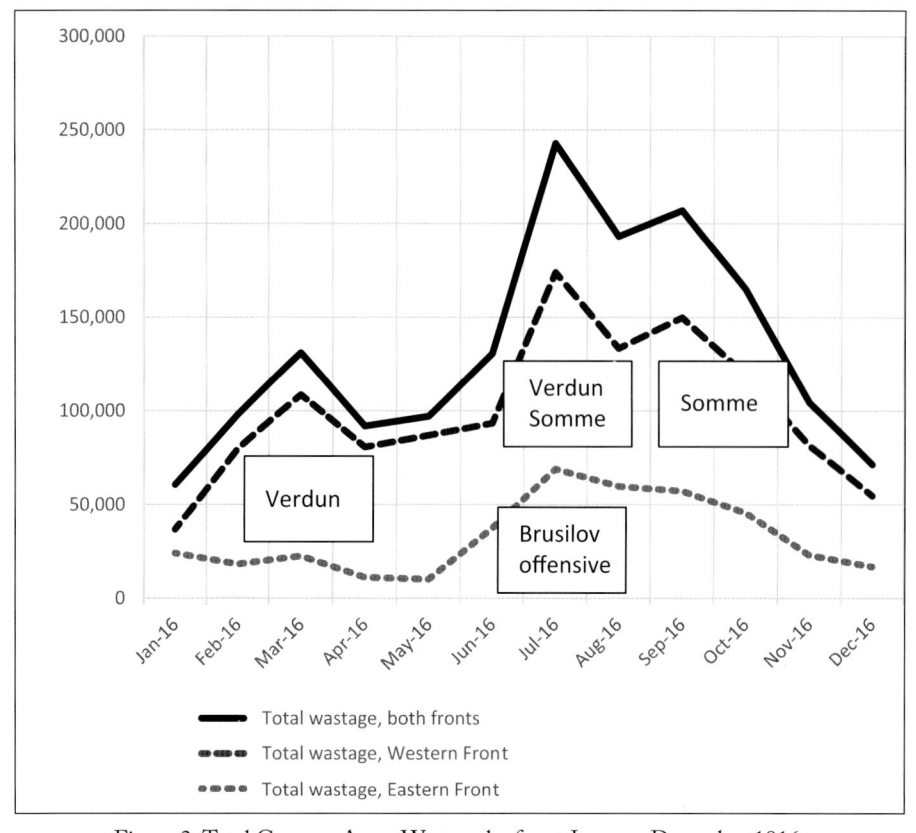

Figure 2 Total German Army Wastage by front, January-December 1916.

In conclusion, the British official history clearly misused the "muddy grave" quote which begins this chapter, as well as inflating the importance of its author, Hans von Hentig: his testimony in itself cannot bear the weight put on it by the official history and subsequent historians. That said, many of Hentig's points were justified. The German army did not find its "muddy grave" on the Somme: but it was very badly damaged there as well as in the other fighting in 1916, especially at Verdun and on the Eastern Front – an important reminder that the Somme was by no means the only major battle in 1916 as British historiography sometimes implies.

Various factors helped the German army survive the crisis of 1916. These included the basic difficulties of the Western Front, and the Allies' own problems there: they too of course were suffering heavy casualties. Despite the forebodings of senior commanders, the quality of German officers and men was still high enough to defeat repeated Allied assaults. In addition, the German army took steps to improve its tactics and organisation. Most importantly, it was able to maintain the flow of reserves which was crucial to operational success. Reserves were often limited in quantity and quality, but they were never as scarce as British intelligence believed at the time or some modern scholars have claimed since. In 1916 conditions, the Allies simply could not inflict enough attrition on the German army to enable a breakthrough.

So the army survived – but for the first time began to doubt whether Germany would win the war.[81] Its difficulties at the turn of the year are reflected in the record of a trip Ludendorff made along the whole Western Front in January 1917. The writer of the record gloomily suggested that though the battle of the Somme had been a German defensive victory, the very heavy casualties, especially in junior commanders and trainers, had caused a watering down of the army and lowered its powers of resistance in the coming year; in addition, there were few reserves of ammunition and a serious threat to the hoped-for increase in production – perhaps even a decrease at the moment.[82]

This is the context of the belief expressed by Ludendorff and other senior officers at the time that the German army would not be able to fight another Somme.[83] The need to relieve pressure on the army was Ludendorff's strongest reason for supporting the unrestricted submarine warfare campaign launched in February 1917. So the poor state of the army following the fighting of 1916 contributed directly to what has been described as "the worst decision of the war" because it led to United States entry into the war and so to Imperial Germany's ultimate defeat.[84]

81 Watson, *Ring of Steel*, p. 326.
82 BA/MA: Hermann Geyer papers, RH61/924: 'Gesamteindrücke der Westreise', *OHL* Memorandum, 21 January 1917, fn. 32.
83 One of these senior officers was General Georg Fuchs commanding *XIV Reserve Corps*: Kuhl, 'Kriegstagebuch', 20 January 1917.
84 Watson, *Ring of Steel*, pp. 422-423, 448-449.

19

Ripples of the Somme: Commemorating and Remembering the Battle, 1919-2016

Mark Connelly

Since 1916 the Somme has gradually come to be invested with an elegiac quality. Viewed almost entirely through the lens of the disastrous first day of the battle, it has come to symbolise the passing of one world and the beginning of another. That day of blazing sunshine, blood and blue skies compresses Paul Fussell's entire thesis about the impact of the conflict on British culture. On 1 July 1916, the era of imperial glory was brought to a shattering end; the Edwardian summer broke that evening and autumn set in. "Never a sunny day in the trenches", as Alan Bennett had it in his bitter-sweet play, *Forty Years On* (1968). The Somme brought storm, rain and misery. "Rain on Armistice Day. Rain on the queues that wait for the Dole", as two of Bennett's characters go on to say. Thus, the Somme destroyed innocence and gave birth to the world of irony and binary visions. From 1 July onwards it was a road towards decay and decline in a process made bitter thanks to incompetence and useless sacrifice. And yet, this interpretation of the Somme does not represent the only narrative of the battle and its meaning. Over the decades, the Somme's significance in British and Commonwealth culture has changed and altered greatly according to specific socio-cultural circumstances. This chapter provides a brief overview of the major shifts in emphases since the end of the conflict and the media through which they were constructed and presented.

Perhaps the biggest surprise in tracing the profile of the Somme in the immediate aftermath of the Great War is its junior position compared with that of Ypres.[1] Given the fact that the Somme marked the debut of the citizen-soldier armies in a significant role this position seems rather odd. After all, it might be expected that such men, coming from the ranks of the educated middle-classes as so many of them did,

---

1   For a study of the dominance of Ypres as a memory site, see Mark Connelly & Stefan Goebel, *Ypres* (Oxford: Oxford University Press, forthcoming 2018).

would have been the formulators of post-war British remembrance culture, and that their families might also have focused on the battle above all others in memory of lost loved ones. Yet it was Ypres that dominated the interwar conception of the conflict in popular culture and discourse. This chapter will argue that it was, in fact, the fiftieth anniversary that catapulted the Somme forward due to a transformation in the position of Britain internally and externally. By the same token, this does not mean that the Somme was anonymous in the twenties and thirties, merely that it was clearly subordinate to the Ypres salient.

Contrary to the position advanced by many studies of the literature generated by the conflict, there was no ten year gap or period of silence.[2] This silence exists only if the now accepted canon of high literature is used as the indicator of significant discourse about the war. Rather, from the moment the conflict ended there was a cacophony of voices debating its meaning and legacy. In terms of the Somme, one of the earliest attempts at a dispassionate historical judgement on the battle was made by John Buchan in his masterly four-volume *Nelson's History of the War* (1921-22), which revised the original 24-volume series which had been released during the conflict. Buchan's opinion was balanced and judicious reflecting the knowledge gleaned from his extensive range of military and political connections. He rejected the idea that ground gained during the battle was a useful measure of achievement, and instead argued that the Somme constituted a strategic victory in terms of its undoubted success in wearing down the enemy's ability to wage war. Nonetheless, he added that though "it was a sound plan", it was also "uninspired and expensive".[3]

It took a further ten years for the first official British statement on the Somme, and that concluded its overview with the situation at nightfall on 1 July. Brigadier-General Sir James Edmonds's *Military Operations France and Belgium 1916,* Vol. I was published in January 1932. Archibald Wavell, reviewing for *The Times Literary Supplement*, believed the author had achieved a fair balance delivering critical and positive judgements based on a close reading of the evidence. Among the points Wavell drew from the text was the over confidence of the British high command and the poor tactical training of the British forces due to 'insufficient skill and experience' among the higher command.[4] Published at a moment when Britain was in highly introspective mode having elected a coalition government to deal with its looming financial difficulties, the *Official History* added to an environment in which British conduct of the conflict was beginning to be questioned with cynical intent.

A wider political drama was also the immediate back-drop to the publication of the second volume, coming as it did in the aftermath of the Munich conference of

---

2 For example, see Dominic Hibberd, *The First World War* (London: Macmillan, 1990), p. 193; Randall Stevenson, *Literature and the Great War* (Oxford: Oxford University Press, 2013), pp. 88-92.
3 John Buchan, *A History of the Great War* (London: Nelson, 1922), p. 218.
4 *The Times Literary Supplement*, 21 January 1932.

September 1938. This time the reviewer for *The Times Literary Supplement* was Basil Liddell Hart and he brought a more acidic approach to the task. Whilst congratulating Captain Wilfred Miles for his admirably succinct approach to such a massive task, and his relevant criticisms of British operational and tactical shortcomings, he found his "unqualified defence of the 'Western School'" a significant weakness of the macro-level issues. He was equally unimpressed with the casualty calculations deeming them "very far from convincing".[5] Perhaps fortunately for the British state, it is very difficult to tell how far these volumes penetrated the popular consciousness. They were hardly easy reads and although they mentioned many units by name, they lacked the intimacy and immediacy of regimental and divisional histories and memoirs.

By contrast, the everyman's edition of Lloyd George's *War Memoirs* – also published in 1938 – was a far more engaging way of understanding the higher level direction of the war due to their journalistic style and no-holds-barred approach. Initially published in 1934, Lloyd George had the advantage of using the *Official History* for his own purposes when discussing the Somme campaign and he relished quoting Edmonds's judgement that the finest men of the nation were lost for minimal gains on 1 July 1916. Adding his own colour, the former prime minister deemed the conduct of the battle "bull-headed" resulting in a "slaughter" from which no strategic advantage was gained. It was only the "inexplicable stupidity of the Germans" in goading the United States into war that prevented the Somme from being adjudged as an undoubted Allied military disaster.[6] However, the continued dominance of the Ypres salient in British visions of the war was revealed in the fact that there was far greater public comment over Lloyd George's treatment of Passchendaele.[7]

Although readers of such works were given the opportunity to combine their personal memories with a greater understanding of the war from these macro-views, it left untouched the emotional need of many, particularly the bereaved, to understand exactly what occurred on the ground and where a lost loved one was buried or commemorated. To answer this need there was a boom in guidebooks to the Western Front which were purchased by those who went on physical pilgrimages and those who travelled there in the imagination only. Within these works, the Somme is often presented as having a distinct 'feeling' through its geography, which was so different to that of the Ypres salient. Consequently its emotional associations for veterans and relatives were unique.

The New Army's close association with the Somme, and as such its geographical position as the conduit to the wider war being waged by the British on the Western Front, was underlined by H.A. Taylor in his 1930 *Good-Bye to the Battlefield*.[8] Part

---

5   *The Times Literary Supplement*, 26 November 1938.
6   David Lloyd George, *War Memoirs*, Vol. I (London: Odhams, 1938), p. 321.
7   David Lloyd George, *War Memoirs*, Vol. II (London: Odhams, 1938), pp. 1247-1333.
8   H.A. Taylor, *Good-bye to the Battlefields* (London: Stanley Paul, 1930).

guidebook, part reflection on his experiences, Taylor stated in the preface that the work grew out of an excursion he took to the Somme front as part of a summer holiday in France, which spurred him to cover the entire British zone with the structure of the book driven by the territory he explored in each subsequent visit. The work therefore opens with four substantial chapters on the Somme during the course of which he highlighted a conclusion that has become an underpinning concept of much contemporary military history about the battle:

> Because they were inadequately trained, and because anyhow, problems novel even to old soldiers were arising every day, these citizen-soldiers bought their experience at a terrible price; but while they suffered, they learned, and made themselves masters of the techniques of warfare.[9]

Former infantry officer and author of the best-selling *Spanish Farm Trilogy* of novels, R.H. Mottram, revisited the battlefields in 1935 and published his reflections a year later in *Journey to the Western Front*.[10] Mottram used his quiet, middle-class insight in the work which was more a set of reflective musings than a true guidebook. He categorised each region as having a particular relationship with a particular British Army; thus, for the Somme, it was Fourth Army.

The visitor attempting to make sense of this particular landscape could therefore draw on a range of guidebooks for assistance, but many also required the input of an expert guide. By the mid-twenties the pre-eminent British guide resident in the region was Captain Stuart Oswald. Based in Amiens, Oswald was an enthusiastic member of the Ypres League and acted as its representative in the Somme region, which also revealed the extent to which the battlefield was regarded as in some way subordinate to the salient in the interwar period. Oswald organised cars employing only British ex-servicemen to act as drivers, and produced a map showing all the main positions of the battles of 1916 and 1918.[11] B.S. Townroe, author of the 1937 work, *A Pilgrim in Picardy*, was very pleased to have come across Oswald who provided a wealth of advice including the tip "that although Albert is more central, all visitors are advised to ascertain the price they will be asked to pay there. 'Otherwise they will find it very expensive,' states Captain Oswald ominously."[12]

The tours organised by the Ypres League included most of the key 1916 sites as well as a nod to the 1918 fighting such as Proyart and Villers-Bretonneux, which lacked the focal point of the main IWGC memorial and cemetery until its completion in 1938. Also included was Chuignolles-Chuignes, which are now not mentioned at all

---

9   Taylor, *Good-bye to the Battlefields*, p. 40.
10 R.H. Mottram, *Journey to the Western Front* (London: G. Bell & Sons, 1936), See Parts IV and V for Somme sections.
11 *Ypres Times*, Vol. 3, No. 3, July 1926, p. 66; Vol. 5, No. 2, April 1930, p. 58.
12 B.S. Townroe, *A Pilgrim in Picardy* (London: Chapman & Hall, 1937), p. 193.

Ruins of La Boisselle, 1919.

in any standard guide to the Western Front. Their significance in the interwar years was due to the extensive remains of a major German gun position, which was tucked away down a track known only to those with great local knowledge. Townroe was taken to it by a French guide hired locally and described it as "a rusting war trophy" on which "tourists have amused themselves by writing their names over every part which they could reach".[13] Such responses reveal that visitors to the Western Front in the interwar years hovered between the reverential mode of pilgrims and that of tourists interested in the spectacular and grotesque.

For those keen to experience a familiar environment, the Somme offered the chance to mingle with the permanent British community. Although not as extensive as that in Ypres, Albert and its immediate hinterland was home to a number of British and Anglo-French families with most employed either by the IWGC or in servicing the needs of British visitors. H.A. Taylor found them a solid bunch on his trips and was especially pleased to hear from an IWGC inspector that the British guides often charged the poorest visitors next to nothing for their services.[14] Characters abounded among this collection of expatriates. At remote Thiepval visitors had the chance of visiting a bar which appears to have been jointly run by two ex-servicemen. They were clearly very engaging personalities who had the ability to "tell many stories of the battles that raged in the area".[15]

For many visitors to the Somme battlefields nowhere struck as melancholy a note as Thiepval, which carried with it the same kinds of resonances as Passchendaele

---

13   Townroe, *A Pilgrim in Picardy*, p. 194.
14   H.A. Taylor, *Good-bye to the Battlefields* (London: Stanley Paul, 1928), pp. 25-26.
15   *Ypres Times*, Vol. 8, No. 6 April 1937, p. 137 gives the owner as a Mr C. Smith, formerly a divisional runner. But Sir John Hammerton listed the owner as a Mr Opie, ex-D.C.L.I, *I Was There*, Vol. II (London: Waverley, 1939), p. 830.

for the Ypres Salient. Largely inaccessible due to the difficulty of building roads through the chaos of the old battlefield up to such a high and remote point, Thiepval lagged behind the reconstruction noticeable in other Somme sectors. A prosperous village dominated by its chateau in 1914, it never recovered its size and was only a small hamlet by the mid-1930s. One of the earliest guides, T.A. Lowe's, *The Western Battlefields* (1920), recommended the "reader to walk from Thiepval to Pozières … [to help] him to understand perhaps a small part of one of the bitterest struggles in the world's history".[16] Taylor observed that "so completely devastated is Thiepval that no permanent rebuilding has been attempted in its ruins. No bright new farmhouses or tilled fields are to be seen here, nothing but uneven earth, rank grass and weeds."[17] In September 1924 Captain Malcolm Cockerell wrote to the Northern Ireland government on behalf of the Ulster Tower caretaker, William MacMaster. He requested that a wireless be purchased for MacMaster to help him endure the winter months during which "visitors are few and far between. The days are short and the evenings exceedingly long" and were a trial for anyone living marooned "on the lifeless heights of Thiepval".[18]

Probably drawing on earlier reflections, Mottram also pointed out the slow recovery of the landscape around Thiepval noting that as late as 1929 it was possible to see collapsed trenches, rusty wire and all sorts of equipment littering the area.[19] Little had changed by 1936. Indeed, just before Mottram's book reached the shops, the IWGC received a letter from a recent visitor to the Thiepval memorial. The correspondent stated that whilst taking a photograph from a nearby field he slipped into an old shell hole "and was surprised to find among the debris therein an old army boot containing human bones in perfect position". An investigation by IWGC officers in France quickly identified it as the remains of a German soldier who had "no doubt, been turned out … by one of the many metal searchers".[20]

Its significance as a location and its difficulty to access and restore partially explain both how it came to be the site for the main IWGC memorial to the 1916 fighting and the length of time it took to complete. Now regarded as an icon of the Somme, and indeed of the work of the IWGC across the globe, Lutyens's masterpiece was located at Thiepval as the result of a series of debates involving much delicate negotiation. Originally destined for a prominent site, possibly straddling the road like the Menin Gate in Ypres, at St Quentin, with additional memorials sited at, or near, the Butte de Warlencourt and Pozières (ensuring that both would dominate the Albert-Bapaume

16 T.A. Lowe, *The Western Battlefields. A Guide to the British Line* (Aldershot: Gale & Polden, 1920), p. 43.
17 Taylor, *Good-bye*, p. 53.
18 Public Records Office of Northern Ireland (hereafter PRONI), PM7/4/9 Provision of radio set for caretaker. Cockerell to Wilson Hungerford correspondence, 17 September 1924.
19 R.H. Mottram, *Journey to the Western Front* (London: Bell, 1936), p. 243.
20 CWGC WG 1294/3 Part 5. Correspondence 20 and 30 April 1936.

Road), the whole programme became entangled in the complex web of memorial politics. As the IWGC's vision matured, it caused the French to become restive about the number of imposing memorials the agency wished to erect within a fairly concentrated geographical region of France. The fear was that the dominant legacy of the conflict French people in these districts would experience was one driven by a British imperial narrative. Anxious to ensure continued French collaboration, the IWGC scaled back its plans and as a consequence a new location for a central Somme memorial was required.[21]

In settling on Thiepval a number of interlocking objectives were met. From a French point of view, although it was in a dominant position, it was well away from the main routes of communication and seemed likely to remain isolated for a considerable period. It was, therefore, very unlike the Menin Gate which was within easy walking distance of the main railway station and on a prominent city landmark. From the British and imperial point of view, Thiepval had the qualities already mentioned: it had been sanctified and reified by the amount of blood spilt to wrest it from the Germans and its height ensured that in that treeless, boundary-less landscape it would be seen from every angle regardless of its remoteness. However, this also meant a very slow building process as the environment proved extremely challenging. To erect such a massive memorial an immense preparatory scheme of clearing the debris of battle had first to be undertaken, and only then could the main project commence.

Lutyens's memorial arch to the 73,000 missing of the Somme covering the period 1915 to spring 1918 is a paean to architectural abstraction and, unlike Reginald Blomfield's Menin Gate, makes very few concessions to the visitor wishing for immediate gratification and easy engagement. Built on sixteen massive, red brick, pillars providing faces to contain the names, it takes the form of an ascending ziggurat pyramid with the flanking arches leading to a vaulted central arch; each arch being exactly two and half times higher than they are wide.[22] Although the memorial was also designed to commemorate Anglo-French solidarity and the feats of arms its combined forces had achieved on the Somme, as symbolised in the addition of staffs to fly the flags of each nation on commemorative days and the inclusion of a joint cemetery of British and French graves, there is nothing obviously triumphalist about the arch. Instead, the visitor is faced with the dominant, and austere, inscription "The Missing of the Somme". In that inscription lays, to paraphrase Churchill's description of the USSR, the genius of Lutyens's enigma wrapped up in a riddle. By stripping it of any obvious and immediate rhetorical flourish, Lutyens actually achieved the greatest of rhetorical statements. In effect, the Thiepval Memorial forces the visitor to either accept or ignore a challenge: consider the 73,000 missing of the Somme;

---

21   For a fuller study of this issue, see Gavin Stamp, *The Memorial to the Missing of the Somme* (London: Profile, 2006), pp. 101-114.
22   For architectural details see Stamp, *Memorial*, pp. 129-144; A.S.G. Butler, *The Architecture of Sir Edwin Lutyens*, Vol. III (London: Country Life, 1950), pp. 41-42.

consider them if you can; consider them without obvious aid from immediately accessible architectural symbol, ornament or flourish; consider what it means to, and for, you here and now. It is magnificent in the extreme, but it is also an architectural examination paper of immense complexity designed to produce an intellectual and emotional response of equal depth.

Perhaps partly for these reasons the Thiepval Memorial never quite captured the imagination of the British Empire in the 1930s, and outside of architectural circles, arguably never has since. But, not only did the memorial pose a challenge to the visitor in the form of its architectural abstraction, it also had to contend with the difficulties already mentioned. Namely, that of being far more inaccessible than other major memorials, particularly the Menin Gate, and due to its protracted gestation, it was not formally unveiled until 1 August 1932 – a full five years after the main Ypres Salient memorials. This precise date is crucial for if ever there was a moment in the interwar period when the people of the British Empire were disillusioned with the war it was in the early thirties. Hit by the recession radiating out from the Wall Street Crash of 1929, Britain, and much of its Empire, seemed to be caught in a trail of misery axiomatically linked to the war. A terrible underlining of the point was seen in the reportage of the unveiling itself when the front page of the *Daily Express* carried the story of the event right next to the headline, "HITLER STORM TROOPS AMOK. EXECUTION SQUADS RAID HOMES. PRUSSIAN TOWN IN GRIP OF PANIC".[23] Striking the right note at the unveiling ceremony and ensuring that this already enigmatical memorial carried the effective core message that the dead had sacrificed their lives in the noblest of causes and were now respectfully honoured and commemorated, was an extremely challenging task.

The correspondent covering the unveiling for *The Times* certainly felt the weight of the past, and the ambiguities of the war memory, describing the memorial as castle-like, "massive and magnificent", built on ground of "glorious and terrible memories".[24] For the *Daily Express* the memorial was one "stupendous gravestone" which "dominates the whole countryside" forcing viewers to crane their necks to comprehend it, and that perhaps also summed up the issue of its challenge to the visitor.[25] Leading the ceremony was the Prince of Wales who declared it the opening of a new chapter in which all were beholden to build a new civilisation in the name of the dead.[26] It was the problem of delivering this lofty ideal at a time when Nazi gangs were running amok that helped marginalise the Thiepval Memorial compared with the Menin Gate, especially as the latter had already stamped its presence into the mind of the Empire.

Of course, many specific locations were embedded in the interwar discourse, but often at a regional level in the UK and Empire due to their associations with particular

23 *Daily Express*, 2 August 1932.
24 *The Times*, 2 August 1932.
25 *Daily Express*, 2 August 1932.
26 *The Times*, 2 August 1932.

Newfoundland Memorial dedication, June 1925.

units. These bonds had been strengthened by the British League of Help, a charity established in 1921 to encourage British (and, occasionally Empire) towns and cities to adopt French communities devastated during the war.[27] Unsurprisingly, the Somme featured strongly in this programme. For example, Birmingham adopted Albert; Sheffield took on Bapaume, Serre and Puisieux; Gloucester formed an association with Ovillers; and Canterbury with Lesboeufs and Morval. Practical assistance was provided in the form of cash and material contributions such as Evesham's donation of apple trees saplings, heifers, seeds, a ton of fertilizer and a goat.[28]

As well as the adoption programme, many communities, civic and military, built their own memorials on the Somme. When set alongside the work of the IWGC the combined effect was the creation of micro-geographies and the sense of ownership of particular districts. The traumatic experiences of 1 July were often the driver and saw the erection of four major memorial schemes, which may be taken as representative of the huge number dotted across the Somme landscape: the Ulster Tower

---

27 For a full history see Bryan Lewis, 'Adoptive Kinship and the British League of Help: commemoration of the Great War through the British League of Help', unpublished PhD, University of Reading, 2006.
28 Lewis, 'Adoptive Kinship', p. 189.

at Thiepval; Newfoundland Memorial Park, Beaumont-Hamel; the 51st Highland Division memorial erected in the Newfoundland scheme; and the South African national memorial at Delville Wood.

Arguably the strongest, and most enduring, emotional links were those between Thiepval and Northern Ireland, and Beaumont-Hamel and Newfoundland.[29] With Ireland reduced to a state of near anarchy at the war's end, the intensity of the symbolism of Thiepval, and therefore its political utility, for the Protestants of Ulster was revealed in the extreme haste with which a major memorial project was conceived and executed. Dedicated on 19 November 1921, long before any other major memorial was completed, the Ulster Tower at Thiepval was a political statement as much as it was one of grief. Modelled on Helen's Tower on the Clandeboye estate, it told the world of Ulster's loyalty to the monarch and its commitment to the Union. The tower served its purpose as no commentator of the twenties or thirties failed to remark upon its significance. Sir John Hammerton's 1938 part-work, *I Was There*, described the assault by the division as "one of the greatest epics of the Somme, and on Thiepval Ridge this stone tower stands in honour of those gallant Ulstermen", which accompanied two photographs of the memorial.[30] A striking photograph was also published in another mid-thirties part-work, Sir Ernest Swinton's, *Twenty Years After*, with the equally forthright caption: "The Spirit of Ireland has been most worthily perpetuated by the erection of this Irish tower".[31] In using such a formulation, Swinton and his collaborators made Protestant Ulster the essential definition of the whole of Ireland. Custodian of the tower, and guide to the battlefields sites in the area, was William MacMaster, former sergeant-major in the 36th (Ulster) Division. His presence added another layer of authenticity and ownership through being a significant mediator. H.A. Taylor described a tour with him as being unlike "the conventional 'patter' of the professional guide. When he speaks of the attack, his eyes light up, and he talks with a fervour that suggests he is living over again those hours of hell in the old redoubt".[32]

The Newfoundland Memorial at Beaumont-Hamel was a tribute not only to the regiment but also to the remarkable persistence and endurance of Thomas Nangle. The Roman Catholic padre of the Newfoundland Regiment, Nangle gained an almost legendary status through his dedication and it was little surprise when in 1919 he was given the rank of lieutenant colonel and made Newfoundland's representative on the Directorate of Graves Registration and Enquiries and subsequently the IWGC. As well as investigating Newfoundland war graves, he envisaged a series of connected memorials to tell the history of the regiment which he labelled "The Trail of the

---

29 For detailed studies of these two memorials see Catherine Switzer, *Ulster, Ireland and the Somme. War Memorials and Battlefield Pilgrimages* (Dublin: The History Press, 2013) and Norm Christie, *For King and Country: The Newfoundlanders in the Great War, 1916-1918* (Ottawa: CEF Books, 2003).
30 Sir John Hammerton (ed.), *I Was There*, Vol. II (London: Waverley, 1939), p. 828.
31 Sir Ernest Swinton (ed.), *Twenty Years After*, Vol. II (London: Newnes, 1936), p. 808.
32 Taylor, *Good-bye*, p. 56.

484   At All Costs

Locally-produced Thiepval Memorial to the Missing postcard c. 1930.

Caribou". Identifying a series of key sites for these memorials, Nangle commissioned the British sculptor, Basil Gotto, to carve a massive caribou known as "The Monarch of the Topsails", replica casts of which were to dominate each of the memorials.

From the start it was obvious that Beaumont-Hamel would be the predominant site and Nangle entered into negotiations to purchase the land after completing an exhaustive round of fund-raising events across Newfoundland. He then engaged Rudolph H.K. Cochius, a Dutch landscape architect who had worked in Newfoundland throughout the war and witnessed the devastation caused by the losses suffered on the Somme and elsewhere. Moving to Albert with his family, Cochius established the Newfoundland War Memorials Office in the town and set to work. With great sensitivity, Cochius reshaped the landscape into a subtle mix of the scars of war, in the form of preserved trenches and shell holes, contrasted with redemption achieved through the planting of native Newfoundland species such as white spruce, birch, dogberry and juniper, plus some 35,000 trees imported from Scotland, Holland and Newfoundland itself. At the same time, this reshaping of the landscape also influenced it as a memory site by privileging a single moment in an extremely long battle. The conception was so impressive that Lord Haig himself presided over the unveiling ceremony on 7 June 1925 and told the crowd that: "This spot will become a place of pilgrimage which, generation after generation, will draw Newfoundlanders to France".[33] Much the same

33   *Daily News* (St John's, Newfoundland), 8 June 1925.

sentiment was expressed by 'Viato', writing in the St. John's Daily News, deemed it "the hallowed soil" of France "which will ever be to us part of Newfoundland".[34]

For the Dominion of South Africa the Somme was also an iconic site and was adopted as the location for the Union's central war memorial.[35] Herbert Baker, a principal architect of the IWGC and the designer of a large number of significant private and public buildings in South Africa, was offered, and accepted, the commission to design the memorial scheme. Convinced that the British Empire was the successor to those of Greece and Rome, Baker believed that his official buildings should reflect what he perceived to be the dignity, majesty and benignity of the British imperial ethos. For Baker, and others of a similar mind, South Africans had proven themselves to be the new hoplites and legionaries on the battlefields of France and Flanders, and they deserved a fitting memorial which reflected the lofty classical values he so passionately believed in.

He deployed one of his favourite motifs in the form of a high flint semi-circular wall, as also seen at Tyne Cot, terminating in two shelter buildings, which Baker "modelled after the summer-house built by an early Dutch Governor on the Groote Shuur estate".[36] This provided the frame for the central feature of a classical domed pavilion (which Baker also replicated at Tyne Cot) topped by statuary. Giving full rein to his classical allusions and sense that the two European races of South Africa were destined to carve out a new civilisation, he used the twin gods often depicted as helmeted horsemen, Castor and Pollux. In Baker's arrangement they hold hands across the back of a war horse completing the sense of two peoples perfectly in tune with the forces of nature. Balancing the pagan symbolism was Reginald Blomfield's Cross of Sacrifice framed through the arch of the pavilion. At the same time, Baker completed the Delville Wood Memorial landscape by designing the large Delville Wood Cemetery which contained 5000 graves.

At Delville Wood, Baker very much sought to stamp pride at martial achievement on to the site. This was reinforced by the retention of the trench names on stone plinths sitting at the junctions of the rides in the wood, which was still a collection of brambles and shattered stumps in the 1920s. A regenerated sylvan landscape was part of the intrinsic vision, but as with so many other memorial sites, the intention was not to restore the wood to its precise former condition through the work of nature, but to alter nature through the inclusion of native South African plants. Special variants were nurtured in Cape Town designed to survive the northern European climate and acorns were gathered from the south-west cape, the district where Huguenot farmers had settled. Thus, a symbolic journey of France to South Africa refracted through an

---

34 *Daily News* (St John's, Newfoundland), 6 June 1925.
35 For a detailed study of the Delville Wood memorial see Bill Nasson, 'Delville Wood and South African Great War Commemoration', *English Historical Review*, Vol. 119, No. 480, 2004, pp. 57-86.
36 Herbert Baker, *Architecture and Personalities* (London: Country Life, 1944), p. 90.

Anglo-Saxon lens was translated back to France. Such was the importance attached to the 'natural' environment that Baker even wanted to introduce fallow deer, similar to the South African springbok, to the site.

The memorial was unveiled in October 1926 in a ceremony overtly presented as a symbol of Anglo-Afrikaner collaboration. The *Natal Witness* was emphatic in its assertion that it was a tribute to "the great white stocks that form the South Africa of today".[37] Unable to ignore the ceremony, the nationalist Prime Minister, J.B.M. Hertzog, attended despite his indifference to the British war effort during the conflict. Avoiding that issue and the fact that South Africa had witnessed open rebellion during the war was well-nigh impossible for Hertzog, and he therefore had to choose his words carefully. Using the totality of recent events, he stated that the bitter conflict they had lived through should teach all South Africans to live without division. Of course, every reference to the races of South Africa, whether in architectural symbolism, speech or print, connected with the Delville Wood memorial meant *white* South Africans: the native and other peoples of the country were ignored almost entirely. The sole exception were wreaths laid towards the end of the ceremony. Leo Weinthal, the Jewish editor of the London-based, *African World*, placed his floral tribute in memory of the native peoples. Rose petals were then scattered by members of the Natal Indian Congress in memory of the Indian Bearer Corps. The gesture was appreciated by the *Abanthu-Batho* which deemed it proof that the efforts of "loyal Bantu subjects of the crown was not being completely forgotten".[38] But a 1923 request by an ex-Labour contingent officer that the men of the S.S. *Mendi*, a ship wrecked in an accident whilst carrying a large number of Native Labour Corps members, be recognised on the memorial was rejected by the Committee. Ostensibly this was done on grounds of military status rather than race: the memorial was about commemorating the fighting men of South Africa. Although it is easy to read this as a fig-leaf covering a racist stance, the significance of the reason should not be dismissed lightly. Many memorial committees across the Empire were debating who had the right to be inscribed and remembered with precise military status often being the point of contention. The men of the *Mendi* eventually came to be commemorated at the site after the end of apartheid rule in South Africa in a move which reinforced the sense of Delville Wood as the pre-eminent site of national commemoration.

Much more modest than any of the memorial schemes discussed above, but equal in terms of significance to a particular group, was that of the 51st Highland Division located within the boundaries of the Newfoundland Memorial Park. Nangle had offered the site after the originally planned location in Beaumont-Hamel proved unstable not due to the remains of German trenches, but ancient tunnels and caves which had, ironically enough, been completely unknown to the German forces despite

---

37 Quoted in Bill Nasson, *Springboks on the Somme: South Africa in the Great War 1914-1918* (Johannesburg: Penguin, 2007), p. 231.
38 Quoted in Nasson, *Springboks*, p. 233.

their huge engineering feats in and around the village. Unlike the overarching narrative of the rest of Newfoundland Memorial Park, which was driven by a sense of pride emerging from devastating loss, the 51st Highland Division Memorial was unequivocally associated with the victorious assault of November 1916.

The memorial scheme, overseen by the architect, A.G. Bryett, was dominated by a figure of a highland soldier sculpted by G.H. Paulin. The Reverend Archibald Fleming, formerly a padre in the division, found a fitting redemptive end in the figure tinged with grief and pride, and was doubtless designed to assuage the pain of the bereaved: "He was modelled from the life, and a more wonderful Highland face surely never spoke, over the wilds, of grit and martyrdom, endurance and eternity; of things beyond that are seen and temporal, which are unseen and eternal."[39] Revealing something of the influence of the divisional war memorial committee and the profile of the unit, Marshal Foch consented to preside over the unveiling. The ceremony took place on 24 September 1924, and unsurprisingly, much was made of the vaunted military prowess of the highlanders as well as paeans to the historic amity of the Scottish and French peoples. Like many other monuments, it was regarded as a piece of home transubstantiated from its original status by the outpouring of blood. The *Scotsman* spoke of "the silent figure ... [who] keeps watch over soil that is forever hallowed by Scottish blood" in a process confirmed by the many floral wreaths and poesies made up of highland plants and heather.[40]

For those unable to attend such ceremonies, trying to understand and visualise the landscape in which their loved ones served and died was a great challenge. Veterans also strove to make sense of the battles in which they fought and place themselves in the narrative. A crucial communicator was the part-work. Lavishly illustrated, and written in the style of extended newspaper articles, each issue provided a wealth of detail and anecdote accessible to a broad range of readers. But perhaps the most important element was the juxtaposition of then and now photographs which allowed the reader to understand in a glance the violence unleashed followed by the scale of the reconstruction. At the same time, it meant the relatives who heard their loved one mention 'Albert', 'Bapaume', 'Courcelette' or 'Ovillers' got the chance to pin their knowledge to a photograph enhancing their understanding of the experience no matter how partially.

Cinema had the ability to enhance visual understandings of the Somme battle, and many people in the twenties and thirties would have had a direct memory of the original release of *The Battle of the Somme* film in 1916 and its Somme-focused successor, *The Battle of the Ancre and the Advance of the Tanks* in January 1917. *The Somme*, a postwar film produced by the New Era Film Company and released in September 1927, reconstructed key moments of the campaign by utilisation of footage from the 1916

---

39 Quoted in *51st (Highland) Division War Memorial: Beaumont-Hamel (Somme)* (Glasgow: Aird & Coghill, 1924), p. 21.
40 *Scotsman*, 25 September 1924.

original. Like the battle reconstructions found in British Instructional Films, the narrative drive was provided by the detailed depictions of Victoria Cross-winning incidents one of which was re-enacted by the winner himself, Corporal T.W.H. Veale. Although the fighting is depicted as bloody and equally awful for soldiers on both sides, it is never presented as a futile waste. Instead, *The Somme* encouraged a sense of awe-struck admiration for the endurance and heroism of the British soldiers who fought it. It was reviewed enthusiastically by most film critics revealing that horror and glory could be intertwined in the public discourse about the war.[41]

The linking element between macro military histories, the guidebooks anchored in the post-war memorial landscape and the visual interpretations was the huge outpouring of veteran memoirs in the twenties and thirties. These provided the insights and details so many required to understand the experience in its entirety. Unsurprisingly, published veteran testimony referred continually to the Somme in the interwar period. For some it was the central focus of their experiences and reflections, particularly if New Army officers and men, while for others it was a component. Four may be taken as representative of the differing shades of opinion and recall; taken in order of publication they are Mark VII (pseud. Max Plowman), *A Subaltern on the Somme* (1927); Llewellyn Wyn Griffiths's *Up To Mametz* (1931); Sidney Rogerson's *Twelve Days: The Somme, November 1916* (1933) and Giles Eyre's grim *Somme Harvest: Memories of a P.B.I. in the Summer of 1916* (1938).

Written in a laconic style, as if little more than a transcribed diary, and thus implying great authenticity and rawness, *A Subaltern on the Somme* is in fact an artfully conceived narrative. It follows what might be deemed the canonical approach to the Great War being the narrative of a young officer who witnesses the misery of life on the Somme front erode the physical and emotional stock of his battalion. Deemed an account of the "all-pervading mud of that dreadful winter [1916-17] … as vivid as anything that has been written about the Somme fighting" by Cyril Falls, *A Subaltern on the Somme*[42] is a rediscovered text insofar as it received relatively little attention at the time, but it spoke to a

Max Plowman.

---

41 For review examples, see *Daily Express* and *Daily Mail*, 1 September 1927.
42 Cyril Falls, *War Books: A Critical Guide* (London: Peter Davies, 1930), p. 217.

later generation, most notably Paul Fussell, who saw it as a classic example of the Great War's influence on the key tropes of modernity and modern culture.[43]

Equally low-key and deliberately understated is Rogerson's *Twelve Days*. Also framed by the winter of 1916, Rogerson, his fellow officers and men, suffer at the hands of nature almost more cruelly than from attention by the enemy. Although there is little in the way of glory as traditionally defined, neither is there anything of disillusion. Instead, there is a quiet pride in the sheer stoicism displayed by all as they endure with little serious complaint or breakdown in discipline. Fussell-esque juxtapositions, but without any of his instance on biting irony, are celebrated as evidence of the essential qualities which saw the soldiers through the battle. The moral is summed up in the observation tinged with a distinct dash of nostalgia: "Did not a mess-tin of stew, a tot of rum or whisky and water in a tin-mug, taste more like divine nectar than the best champagne drunk out of the finest cut-glass to-day?"[44]

By concentrating on short time periods and particular locales, the Somme battle front is broken down into its component parts. This served two functions: first, it emphasizes by omission the sheer amorphous, anonymous scale of the engagement; second, it underlines the association of certain units with particular locales. This was clearly seen in *Up To Mametz* which added another layer to the deep connection between the 38th (Welsh) Division and its role in the capture of the aforementioned village and wood. The utter centrality of Mametz to the narrative and the sense of Welsh identity is clear from the title. Indeed, it dominates the narrative structure with the assault coming at the end of the work: there is no "after Mametz" in this memoir, leaving the reader with the impression that the division had reached the end of its war. Ending the narrative in this way without coda or epilogue implied utter destruction and thus had the potential to be read as a tale of futility and disillusion. It was the foretelling of John Harris's comment in his 1961 novel, *A Covenant With Death*, about the Sheffield Pals: "Two years in the making. Ten minutes in the destroying."[45]

By contrast, Eyre's 1938 account, *Somme Harvest*, tells of the sharp end of the war from the point of view of a sardonic, hard-bitten, but not entirely cynical, private soldier. Like *Twelve Days*, Eyre's memoir emphasizes the ultimately dependable nature of the average British soldier. This is mingled with the pride of the veteran for his former unit. The book is dedicated to his "pals and comrades who 'passed over as the barrage fell' upholding the proud traditions of our regimental motto: *Celer et Audax* ['Swift and Bold']." Introduced with this memorial function, the work reveals how hard it is to categorise a dominant mood among veterans and the British public about the war in general, and the Somme in particular, during the twenties and

---

43 Paul Fussell, *The Great War and Modern Memory* (Oxford: Oxford University Press, 1975), pp. 75-113.
44 Sidney Rogerson, *Twelve Days: The Somme November 1916* (London: Arthur Barker, 1930), p. 96.
45 John Harris, *A Covenant With Death* (London: Hutchinson, 1961), p. 448.

thirties. This is reinforced in Major-General Sir Hereward Wake's foreword which described the text as a "thrilling adventure" revealing the "peculiar characteristics… which make our nation so formidable once roused to action in defence of the things that really seem to us to matter".[46]

Also told from the perspective of the common soldier, but in the form of fiction, is Fredric Manning's *Her Privates We* (1930). Originally published for private circulation under the title *The Middle Parts of Fortune* in 1929, but reprinted in 1930 after extensive cuts were made due to its obscene and blasphemous language, Manning's novel is an excoriating account of life at the sharp end of the Somme fighting, although the specific geographical location is largely unimportant. Depicting the survival of men in the most brutal of conditions, Manning never reduces his subjects to caricatures nor strips them totally of agency. His soldiers may be overtaken by the bloodlust of battle, they may face shattering bombardments in a seemingly powerless and abject condition, but they never become utterly pitiful victims of war. Instead, they somehow trudge on, enduring it all whilst trying not to think too hard about their circumstances. This was realism about the nature of modern war, but with the meanings left deeply implicit for the reader to deduce for his or herself.

In terms of literary explorations of the Somme battle itself, one of the finest is David Jones's remarkable epic poem, *In Parenthesis* (1937). Although it was awarded the highly prestigious Hawthornden Prize for literature in 1938, it is easy to see why Jones's great work has never achieved wide public knowledge, for it is a challenging read. What perhaps makes it seem even harder to grasp is the inability to make the work fit the dominant interpretation of British Great War poetry as an expression of protest. Instead, Jones, after much reflection and meditation, self-consciously set out to memorialise and mythologise. For Jones, the Western Front and Somme campaign (Part 7), became the new landscape of the Arthurian legends and the search for the Holy Grail. The poem is inspired throughout by medieval literature. Thus, far from representing an aberration or watershed in history, Jones found deep continuities in the life of the soldier, his experiences of environment and motivations for battle. Jones's remarkable literary odyssey was the last great literary interpretation of the battle of the interwar years. During the Second World War, the Somme was still perceptible in popular culture but as a fleeting reminder of the earlier conflict in press coverage of the BEF's battles in the same region during 1940 and 1944.[47] In the immediate aftermath of the second great conflict of the twentieth century the British people,

---

46   Giles E.M. Eyre, *Somme Harvest: Memories of a P.B.I. in the Summer of 1918* (London: Jarrolds, 1938), p. 9.
47   For examples see *Daily Mail*, 27 May 1940; *Sunday Express*, 26 May 1940; *The Times*, 25 May 1940; *Daily Express*, 5, 8 September 1944; *Daily Mirror*, 2 September 1944; *Daily Mail*, 2 September 1944. See also G.D. Sheffield, 'The Shadow of the Somme: The Influence of the First World War on British Soldiers' Perceptions and Behaviour in the Second World War' in Paul Addison & Angus Calder (eds.), *Time to Kill: The Soldier's Experience of the War in the West 1939-1945* (London: Pimlico, 1997), pp. 29-39.

unsurprisingly, relived that recent experience, particularly through cinema, rather than the Great War. However, by the late 1950s the first signs of a rekindling of interest were present and this refocusing accelerated massively with the fiftieth anniversary cycle.

Given the overwhelming profile of Ypres in the British imagination in the interwar period, the emergence of the Somme since the 1960s, and particularly since its fiftieth anniversary year, is a fascinating phenomenon. Flanders poppies may blow in the elegiac final sequence of *Blackadder Goes Forth*, but they are in a Picardy landscape; the birds that sing in Sebastian Faulks's battlefield do so over the chalky rolling hills of the Somme front; when the author and journalist, Geoff Dyer, put his insightful reflections about the contemporary meanings of the conflict into print, he titled them, *The Missing of the Somme*.[48] Explaining this rise in significance definitively is impossible, but a few speculative ideas can be offered. First, for many people the Somme has actually come to mean 1 July 1916 and not the entire battle. In turn, this throws up a number of permutations in the British cultural pattern emerging from the 1960s. Notably, by that stage Britain had clearly moved a long way from being an imperial power with an imperial outlook. This made 1 July much easier to fit into a national narrative containing as it did only two imperial elements in the Newfoundlanders and the entirely peripheral Indian cavalry units.

A second important element is the way the Somme landscape could be made to fit the narrative of innocence to experience. This theme had been given eloquent expression in Philip Larkin's *MCMXIV* in which his powerful threnody had declared "never such innocence again". To generations growing up in the shadow of atomic and nuclear weapons and the sense of sudden and total destruction descending on utterly unsuspecting people, the concept of instantaneous and irrevocably lost innocence was potent. And, in effect, the Somme landscape could be read in this way. Unlike the imperial battlefield of Ypres which was smashed to a pulp through a series of huge battles, with even the lulls hardly quiet, the Somme could be perceived as almost virginal until the bombardment commenced in late June. It then became desecrated in an unbelievably short time, the destruction emphasized by the existence of massive craters, which could still be visited.

David Jones.

---

48 Geoff Dyer, *The Missing of the Somme* (London: Hamish Hamilton, 1994).

Two other themes came together. With the British education system placing more emphasis on Great War poetry, the Somme was the converging point for the most important voices. At the same time, the battle marked the debut in action of the ordinary men who would never claim to have an artful urge in their bodies, and in the 1960s world of giving the common person their voice against that of the establishment, the fate of the Kitchener divisions on the Somme held a fascination. In short, the Somme was reinvented because it had so many elements that appeared to overlap with contemporary concerns.

The unwitting curtain-raiser for much of this new interpretation of the Somme was the sixth novel (of fifteen) in Henry Williamson's *A Chronicle of Ancient Sunlight* series. Titled with deliberate poignancy, *The Golden Virgin*, it follows the story of Lieutenant Phillip Maddison and was first published in September 1957. A remarkable aspect of the novel is the extreme attention given to the recounting of orders and identification of places in the run-up to 1 July. Maddison's unit is set to advance across Mash Valley over the ground actually fought over by the 2nd Middlesex. Having set the scene with such care, Williamson was then remarkably spare about the denouement as Maddison is wounded on the first day and finds himself evacuated home via the Casualty Clearing Station at Heilly. It leaves the reader with the impression that Williamson was actually writing for his fellow veterans who could fill in the rest of the picture for themselves. It remains a haunting novel of the Somme for those willing to broach it and wrestle with its contours.

Then came a new generation of books to explore the military history of the battle in which Brian Gardner's 1961 work, *The Big Push*, can be utilised as the starting point. Driven by vivid vignettes drawn from a variety of veteran publications, and relying extensively on the official history, Gardner's work contained flashes of the sardonic irony used by Leon Wolff in his *In Flanders Fields* (1959). Although just as stinging as Wolff, Gardner did, at least, use the official history far more judiciously. Three years later, Anthony Farrar-Hockley's *The Somme* was published. The polar opposite of Gardner's anecdote-rich approach, Farrar-Hockley brought his commanding officer's eye to a detailed discussion of the higher and intermediary decision-making and actions during the course of the battle. Whilst refusing to condemn British commanders, their culture and systems as anachronistic by 1916, he did not paint them as a set of misunderstood military visionaries, either. Rather, they were products of their time dealing with an extremely complicated set of events.

Despite the rush of books about the conflict, and the specific studies of the Somme itself, that occurred in the 1960s, the true publishing phenomenon was about to occur. Inspired to investigate the battle further after a visit in 1967, the Lincolnshire poultry farmer, Martin Middlebrook started contacting veterans of the 1 July. Within a short space of time he had gained a huge number of replies leading to an exhaustive schedule of interviews which were cross-referenced against the recently opened official files. Initially, publishers were resistant believing the market was already saturated, and expert reviews of the sample chapters saw in the text a disastrous re-statement of the 'lions led by donkeys' approach. Nonetheless, Middlebrook persisted; adding more veteran testimony including that of German soldiers, and Penguin eventually accepted and published the book on 1 July 1971. Although it was not an instant and soaring success, the book gradually hit a wider and wider readership partly through Penguin striking a deal with many book club selling schemes, and in 1984 it went into paperback as the Great War renaissance matured.[49]

Whether consciously or not, Middlebrook had tapped into a number of interlocking elements which were to dominate popular interpretations of, and approaches to, the conflict for much of the following thirty-forty years. First, as with the phenomenally successful *The Great War* series, broadcast by the BBC during 1964-65, the major voices were those of frontline officers and men. Second, this necessarily meant a focus on life at the sharp end of the war with relatively little in terms of broader context. Such balances allowed Middlebrook to engage the casual reader quickly and many became hooked by his approach, including the present writer who owes much of his interest in the conflict to reading the book as a teenager.

A new standard had been set, driven by eye-witness testimony which was quickly emulated by other writers, most notably Lyn Macdonald. Having already achieved a success with a vivid account of Third Ypres, *They Called It Passchendaele* (1978), her *Somme* was published in 1983. Macdonald consciously played upon the sense that the British Commonwealth reader understood the war as a literary phenomenon giving her works a highly polished prose style in which the novelist's eye for detail, particularly of landscape, was given much attention.

Significant improvements in transport links in the form of increased car-ownership, the roll-on, roll-off ferry and the spread of the motorway network across Europe then made Picardy itself much more accessible. Pioneered by Rose Coombs's magisterial overview, *Before Endeavours Fade*, first published in August 1976 and now in its thirteenth, fully-revised, edition, a whole new generation of guidebooks appeared with the Somme featuring as fully as Ypres had done in the twenties and thirties. A new rush of pilgrims and visitors commenced, which shows no sign of tailing off, and since the 1980s a new wave of memorialisation has occurred along the old battle fronts of the Somme which almost exceeds the original activity in terms of number and aesthetic diversity.

As the memorials people visited came strongly back into public focus it also meant their significance as political landscape re-emerged. For Northern Ireland, Newfoundland and South Africa all three memorials have left a long term legacy making the commemoration of the Somme, and everything that it symbolises, an on-going political debate. In Northern Ireland the Somme Association took over the running of the Ulster Tower in 1989 and has worked tirelessly since to detach the memorial from any sectarian connection. For Newfoundland, Beaumont-Hamel is an important symbol of its special status within the Canadian confederation,

---

49 For Middlebrook's own summary of the writing process see <http://www.hellfirecorner.co.uk/middlebrook2.htm> (Accessed 23 March 2016).

which it was forced to join through economic necessity in 1949, but it has seen its hallowed site rebadged with the Canadian flag and renamed the Beaumont-Hamel Newfoundland Memorial. South Africa is also still trying to come to terms with the origins of Delville Wood and find ways of incorporating it into a more inclusive narrative of its history.[50]

Through books such as Coombs's iconic guide, the image of these memorials was re-established in popular culture. Arguably even more potent was television's interest in the war. In July 1976, a month before the first edition of *Before Endeavours Fade* was published, Malcolm Brown's documentary, *The Battle of the Somme*, was first broadcast on BBC 1 as part of its observations of the sixtieth anniversary of the battle. Rather than turn to the John Terraine – Correlli Barnett team behind, *The Great War*, Brown brought in Middlebrook as historical adviser and in effect made a documentary summarising his book. The title of the programme was therefore something of a misnomer, as a disproportionate amount of its running time was dedicated to the 1 July. Nonetheless, it was a wonderful piece of television driven by Leo McKern's verve as presenter and accompanied by the haunting trumpet call imitating the Last Post in the second movement of Vaughan Williams's third symphony. Heard over lingering shots of the Somme landscape bathed in late winter sunlight, the combination of music, commentary and image was exceptionally powerful. And its effect was, of course, the complete antithesis of everything Terraine and Barnett had tried to impart in both their printed and televised works. However, when compared with Channel 4's 1985 documentary, *Lions Led by Donkeys*, the BBC 1 documentary was a production of quiet understatement. Established as a deliberate alternative to the mainstream independent television companies, Channel 4's mandate to produce challenging and controversial outputs was certainly revealed in this particular example. Featuring a large number of veterans, many of whom were taken back to the Somme and filmed recounting their memories on the spots where they had actually fought, the documentary also made deliberate comparisons with the Britain of the 1980s using a left-wing political perspective to judge both the past and present. Thus, the Britain of 1914 was presented as similar to that of the mid-80s being disfigured by unemployment, social tensions and a sense of disillusionment among its youth; the number of casualties suffered on 1 July was visualised by saying it was equal to the size of the crowd at Wembley for the Live Aid concert; shots of the Accrington War Memorial were accompanied by a narrative implying the futility of the sacrifice before the camera panned down to the panel containing the name of the town's Falklands Conflict casualty. Such a heavy-handed approach may have been appreciated by the

---

50   See Nasson, 'Delville Wood', *English Historical Review*, Vol. 119, No. 480, 2004, pp. 57-86; Paul Gough, 'Contested commemorations: Newfoundland and its unique heritage on the Western Front', *The Round Table*, Vol. 96, No. 393, 2007, pp. 693-705; Catherine Switzer, *Ulster, Ireland and the Somme. War Memorials and Battlefield Pilgrimages* (Dublin: The History Press Ireland, 2013), pp. 188-208.

channel's core audience, but must have seemed an odd set of juxtapositions to others, and worse still detracted from the power of the veteran testimony.

More recently, Channel 4 returned to the battle with its powerful drama-documentary, *The Somme* (2007) which told the story of the first day through the letters and diaries of those that took part. A year earlier the BBC had deliberately juxtaposed the disaster of much of 1 July with the triumph of the capture of Thiepval in September in a drama-documentary entitled *The Somme: From Defeat to Victory*. Here the impact of the so-called 'revisionist' school of military historians was much in evidence with the influence of John Bourne and Peter Simkins obvious in the shaping of the programme. The BBC contributed a further drama in 2014 as part of its centenary observations. *Pals* formed an episode in the *Our World War* series broadcast on BBC4. Consciously deploying a visual style drawing on *Saving Private Ryan*, *Band of Brothers* and Quentin Tarantino, this series of films was part of a deliberate attempt to make the conflict relevant to younger people and thus reflected a wider cultural shift in representations of the past which is to privilege this particular demographic above many others. A similar shift in emphasis can be seen in the government's plan to commemorate the centenary of the battle. At the same time as the more formal observations at Thiepval, there will be a form of 'living history' event at Heaton Park, Manchester, built around the experience of the war at home and for those not in the combat services on the front line. In this can be seen a very deliberate attempt to create what is perceived to be a more inclusive and broader interpretation of the battle capable of speaking to a wider

The Somme: From Defeat to Victory (2006) production still. (Taff Gillingham)

section of society. Whether this belief is accurate or not is largely immaterial. What is fascinating is the fact that so many with responsibility for the official centenary commemorations perceive this to be the case. Arguably, the Somme as a historical phenomenon does not exist in this context: it has thus become a tool for making a statement about contemporary Britain, with history translated into heritage 'edutainment', underpinned by a message of social and cultural inclusion.

The image and profile of the Somme has therefore undergone a transformation since it was fought one hundred years ago. In the twenties and thirties it always had to play second fiddle to Ypres, *the* imperial battleground, and the palimpsest on to which so many narratives could so easily be written. The sheer physical inaccessibility of much of the Somme battle front combined with the drawn-out process of erecting a central memorial also meant it could never quite compete with the focus that Ypres provided for the Empire and its metropolis. Nonetheless, the Somme was still part of the wider British narrative of the war. It was a narrative that never denied the horror and bloodiness of the battle, but used them as proof of the qualities of British-Imperial soldiers and challenged the living to be worthy of their sacrifices. After the Second World War, and in particular during the 1960s, new socio-cultural forces came into play that made the Somme a metaphor for British twentieth century history. It is that legacy of the Somme we have inherited. We are stuck in the shimmering heat of Picardy's summer poppy daze.

20

The Somme: War Memoirs and Personal Memories

Brian Bond

In retrospect it seems strange that I did not visit any Western Front battlefields until May 1988, especially in view of the fact that several years earlier my wife and I had made a tiring journey to Gallipoli because I felt I must be familiar with the terrain before offering an undergraduate special subject on the campaign. I can only reflect that there were far fewer organised tours to the Western Front then, and my teaching options did not seem to require such specialised knowledge.

The weather for this first tour was cold and wet, and my wife complained that we visited too many cemeteries. But we were comfortably quartered at the Hotel de la Basilique in Albert, and Martin Middlebrook was the ideal guide for 'The First Day on the Somme'. Martin inculcated two main lessons. First, that it was essential to learn precisely where the front line was located at the outset. This would impress on us the enemy's advantage in holding the commanding ground, which he had strongly fortified, and later help us to trace the painfully slow advances made in the coming months.

Second, although the ubiquitous war cemeteries were first and foremost beautifully maintained memorials for solemn remembrance of the known and unknown dead, they were also invaluable assets to military historians since much of the formerly devastated countryside now bore little signs of the fighting which had ravaged it. Martin pointed out that the location, the informative operational plaques near the entrance, the dates and regimental affiliations on the graves could all provide starting points for what had happened in the vicinity. Military historians could profit from this information while still experiencing the shock and sadness of witnessing so many young lives cut short.

After this first, belated visit I made up for lost time by returning regularly. In several successive years I took my small MA Special Subject class on three day visits at the start of their course in early October and again near the end the following spring. These visits proved admirable not only for group bonding and gaining a general knowledge of the terrain, but also in encouraging study of memoirs of survivors who had written so vividly about particular battles. In their weekly class the graduates focused on memoirs and war literature more generally so we all read and discussed a variety of texts, some by well-known authors such as Robert Graves, Siegfried Sassoon and Edmund Blunden, but also less familiar authors such as Frederic Manning, Guy Chapman and Alf Pollard. I also encouraged the study of foreign writers, including Ernst Junger, E.M. Remarque and Ludwig Renn. I too benefitted from these seminars which combined my interest in literature and history, later using them as the basis for my book *Survivors of a Kind* (2008), recently re-published (2018) by Helion & Company.[1]

It is not difficult to understand why my enthusiasm for repeated visits to the Somme is widely shared. The area of the fighting in 1916 is compact and mostly accessible by car and on foot, and can be explored in sectors over two or three days; the Albert – Bapaume Road making a natural division. More importantly, the battle area has changed remarkably little, the trench lines and fortifications have mostly disappeared, though a rusty harvest of shell cases and unexploded bombs is still in evidence, and the woods have re-grown in the same positions. Most of the obliterated villages were re-built in the early 1920s in a basic, unappealing style and have changed very little since, creating a strange sense of being frozen in time. Only recently has there been some urban sprawl around Albert and some other towns. The Somme countryside is not spectacular, but in good weather the uplands provide wonderful wide vistas to the south.

The battlefield visitor now has a wide choice of excellent guidebooks. Rose Coombs' seminal *Before Endeavours Fade* (1976) set a high standard, but has been joined by Martin and Mary Middlebrooks' *The Somme Battlefields* (1991) and Major and Mrs Holt's *Battlefield Guide to the Somme* (1996) amongst others. Consequently, even after many visits there still remains many unfamiliar places and points of interest to explore: new memorials are being unveiled every year, and previously neglected battle sites, Thiepval Wood for example, have been renovated. In the last fifteen years or so a few popular battle sites, notably Newfoundland Park, the Ulster Tower, Lochnagar Crater, Thiepval and Delville Wood have been made more appealing to coach tourists, but more enterprising explorers can easily find remote, lonely places where the cemetery visitors' book contains few recent signatures.

A selection of war writers' memoirs will be drawn upon to illustrate particular episodes of the campaign, moving chronologically from 1 July to 13 November and roughly from north to south-east. Some of these necessarily brief accounts can be studied further in my book mentioned above but the others are referenced. Well-informed readers will doubtless think of additional sources I might have used, but I hope they will be indulgent towards what is avowedly a personal selection.

---

[1] I have not duplicated references to authors and books here because they can be explored further in the relevant chapters of Brian Bond, *Survivors of a Kind: Memoirs of the First World War* (Solihull: Helion & Company, 2018).

Charles Carrington was a subaltern in the 1/5th Warwicks of 48th (South Midland) Division. Carrington was still lacking in combat experience when he witnessed 56th (London) Division's diversionary attack south of Gommecourt village on 1 July. After ferocious bombardments from both sides, he saw a battalion of the London Scottish running forward into the smoke. There were several thousand troops within his range of vision, but not one living soldier could be seen, and this remained the case even after the smoke had cleared. After noon the enemy launched a fierce counter-attack all along the British line before an eerie silence prevailed. In the evening Carrington heard that the survivors had all returned to their trenches but No Man's Land echoed with pitiful cries from the wounded. The 56th Division had lost over 100 officers and more than 3,000 other ranks out of a total strength of some 5,000. Both divisions had suffered horrendous losses without achieving any diversion of enemy reserves. This was as terrible a disaster as any that occurred on this fateful day. The Gommecourt Salient was never captured during the whole campaign.

In mid-July, 48th Division was given the daunting task of capturing the hill top village of Ovillers, defended by a regiment of the Prussian Guards. En route to the attack near La Boisselle, Carrington saw a grassy slope strewn with corpses, but only discovered later that these were men he had helped to train with the 9th Yorks & Lancs.

On the night of 15-16 July, Carrington was in the leading wave of a daring surprise attack which crossed one thousand yards of open ground to occupy trenches behind the Ovillers garrison. In conditions of fierce heat and acute shortage of water, the Warwicks held their position until the enemy surrendered. This was an encouraging minor victory, but Carrington's part in it was far from heroic. In the initial advance he had led bravely, experiencing a spirit of exaltation, but when the enemy counter-attacked he lost his nerve and was about to order a retreat when he was firmly rebuked by his sergeant. Ordered by his captain to organise a counter-attack he collapsed in the trench and replied "I'm damned if I will. I'm done for!" He also lost his revolver (a serious offence), but meekly followed his captain and regained his nerve. By his own account, Carrington continued to show further signs of loss of nerve until the battalion had stumbled back to the start line, and rest. Even under the pseudonym of "Charles Edmonds" it is remarkable that Carrington chose to publish these serious personal failings in *A Subaltern's War* (1929) when former colleagues could easily recognise the author.

In the weeks before the Somme offensive began Siegfied Sassoon was serving with the 1st Battalion, Royal Welch Fusiliers near Bois Francais on the high ground south of Fricourt. On 23 May 1916 he was awarded a Military Cross for heroic, though vain, attempts to rescue soldiers trapped in a crater after a failed night attack. This was only one episode in which he deliberately tried to show that poets could also be warriors. In his diary he had frequently used phrases like "great fun" to describe his experience, but in March the death of a young officer, David Thomas, whom he loved transformed him into an avowed "Hun hater" determined to exact personal vengeance. His voluntary night patrols, armed with bombs or a *knobkerrie* earned him the nickname "Mad Jack". His battalion commander wanted prisoners, but Sassoon's aim was to smash skulls.

Sassoon's company was in reserve for the first three days of the Somme offensive, but on 4th July, in an act of reckless gallantry, he charged part of the enemy-occupied Quadrangle Trench on the approach to Mametz Wood, scattering the defenders by bombing and uttering fierce hunting cries. Since enemy fire prevented reinforcements from reaching him he remained alone in the trench for several hours, refusing an order to pull out. This was a more obvious, if foolhardy, heroic action than the one that had earned him the Military Cross, but if he anticipated a further decoration he was to be bitterly disappointed. Instead he was severely reprimanded for not withdrawing with the bombing party and for refusing an order to abandon the trench, thereby delaying a bombardment of the front line for several hours. His ardour for further daring exploits and personal awards remained undiminished.

The one disappointing aspect of Middlebrook's tour was that we did not visit Mametz Wood because the fighting there did not occur on the first day. I quickly remedied this on my next visit and returned many times, sometimes posing with friends and students on the steps of the Welsh Dragon monument.

Only a brief discussion of the 38th (Welsh) Division's ultimately successful, but costly clearance of the naturally formidable and powerfully defended wood is necessary here.[2] The first attack on 7 July was a hastily improvised affair which could serve as a model of how not to plan and conduct a battle. The front of the attack was too narrow and too close to the northern end of the wood, raked by enfilade machine gun fire from Flatiron Copse and Sabot Copse; artillery support was poor and there was no co-ordination with 17th (Northern) Division attacking from the south. Staff work and orders were confused, resulting in several senior officers being removed. Three days later a second attack was launched much further down the valley, on a broader front and with much better support. Attacking up a steep slope without cover against strongly fortified enemy defences on the edge of the wood was still a hazardous undertaking, but by the evening of 10 July the leading Welsh battalions had penetrated the forward defence lines and, with reserves, would clear the wood over the next three days. In doing so they created a "charnel house" of devastation and mangled bodies.

Poet and artist Private David Jones, 15th Battalion (London Welsh) Royal Welch Fusiliers, constituted the original inspiration for my long-held fascination with Mametz Wood. He took part in the second successful attack, though not in the first wave, and experienced the full horror of close combat in the dense undergrowth where it was nearly impossible to distinguish friend from foe. Jones was badly wounded in the legs late in the day; after some hours he crawled out of the trees, abandoning his rifle. He was eventually carried to safety and took no further part in the campaign.

---

2   Colin Hughes *Mametz: Lloyd George's 'Welsh Army' at the Battle of the Somme* (Gerrards Cross: Orion Press, 1982).

MA group at the Welsh Dragon Memorial, Mametz Wood, 1 November 1996. Rear row: Brian Bond, Simon Doughty, Mark Williams. Front row: Sam Clark, Ryan Walsh and Alan Jeffreys. Photograph taken by Michael Piercy. (Author)

Thousands of other ordinary soldiers shared Jones's ordeal, or even worse, but only this frail and eccentric genius could elevate this relatively minor battle into the status of an epic through his remarkable poem *In Parenthesis*, first published in 1937.

It is now established that the poem was closely based on Jones's personal experience.[3] Though richly embellished by Celtic myths and extravagant poetic language, Jones was deeply concerned to present historical truth. Where he had not directly experienced or witnessed scenes himself he was careful to use the evidence of colleagues, and others closely involved in the battalion or the division. There is no dodging the

3   Colin Hughes, *David Jones. The Man Who Was on the Field: In Parenthesis as Straight Reporting* (Manchester: David Jones Society, 1979).

fact that this is a dense and difficult poem requiring numerous explanatory endnotes so that unsurprisingly it is more praised by literary specialists than widely read.

In my own case, however, help was at hand in the form of a wonderful recording of a third programme version of the epic on CD. Douglas Cleverdon produced the initial radio presentation in 1948 and it was repeated several times in the 1950s and 1960s with a few changes to the impressive cast. Richard Burton played Private John Ball (i.e. David Jones), Carleton Hobbs was Bill Grower, Leonard Sachs was Lieutenant Jenkins and the recorded voice of Dylan Thomas proclaimed the "boast of Dai". Elizabeth Poston's music perfectly suited the generally sombre but sometimes ecstatic or heroic moods of the poem. The CD proved a stimulating teaching aid when played as we approached Mametz Wood and other nearby battles. Some listeners, including my friend John Lee, who heard the CD most times as a driver, memorised some of the most striking episodes such as Sergeant Quilter's grim roll call of Welsh casualties, the death of Mr. Jenkins, Private Ball's wounding and the garlands bestowed on the dead of both sides. David Jones had brilliantly captured the voices and behaviour of real soldiers on both sides and, more widely, in "the disciplines of war" throughout the centuries. His dedication characteristically concludes, "to the enemy front fighters against whom we found ourselves by misadventure".

A week after David Jones's wounding and escape from combat, Lieutenant Basil Hart also became a casualty in the ravaged charnel house of Mametz Wood.[4] In temporary command of a company of 9th KOYLI, Hart was withdrawing his troops in darkness when he became aware of enemy shells plopping rather exploding around him. He carried on, apparently unharmed apart from a superficial wound in the hand, but some hours later became seriously ill with throat and chest pains and difficulty in breathing. He had been badly gassed by phosgene shells, a new development in the method of delivery after the earlier use of canisters. After an uncertain period of delay he was stretchered from the wood, treated in field hospitals and eventually sent to England to recuperate.

This was his third, and as it turned out, final experience of front-line combat and hence, in retrospect, a critical moment in his career. The account in his *Memoirs* is succinct and clear, but leaves the impression that it has been carefully rehearsed and does not give the full story. Basil must have been aware of this because he had made several previous attempts to describe this crucial incident more fully. He clearly wanted to know the whole truth but the lack of eye witnesses made this impossible.

Basil's biographer, the late Alex Danchev, was willing to speculate boldly, believing that the psychological aspect, providing a key to his later career, had been insufficiently explored.[5] He had more than once quoted the obsessive fear of another infantry officer

---

4 Following the First World War, he restyled himself as "Captain B.H. Liddell Hart" and in 1965 became "Sir Basil".
5 Alex Danchev, *Alchemist of War: The Life of Basil Liddell Hart* (London: Weidenfeld & Nicolson, 1998).

and survivor of the Somme, Sidney Rogerson, that he would be wounded, abandoned, and left to die alone in some dark place. Danchev suggests that in the early hours of 18th July, Basil was already in a state of shock, even before he was shelled, panicked and gassed in that ghastly wood.

In a reflective note written in April 1939 – a time of another impending personal crisis – Basil presented the 1916 incident in a positive light. He had stayed in the front line for two days after his wound had given him a reason for pulling out, and he had stayed in the wood longer than necessary to warn other platoons of the danger of gas. But he added: "All that sounds quite noble. But it is not all the facts – as I am aware of them. It does not record the extent to which they were due to a fear of being afraid, nor the extent to which I yielded to fear."[6]

Danchev concludes, persuasively in my opinion, that Basil had discovered that he was not physically brave; that he lacked "intestinal fortitude; the liver had been searched, painfully, and found wanting." For Basil the "real war" of front-line soldiering was over. Henceforth he would build an international reputation as a military critic, historian and theorist of war; a world in which moral integrity, original thinking and a talent for polemical journalism would count for more than physical courage.

I suspect that most keen visitors to the Somme want to penetrate the dominant woods which so influenced the campaign, but in nearly all cases – Delville Wood being an exception – there are two obstacles: the undergrowth is dense and forbidding; and the woods are leased to local shooting or hunting associations who do all they can to deter intruders. Nevertheless I was determined to find out if any trenches or other evidence of combat could be found in Mametz Wood. Accordingly on 28 February 1990, a very wet and windy day, I led our small group of MA candidates right through the wood from Strip Trench to the Bazentin road. Our scramble through briars and branches yielded only a few rusty shell cases and nothing collectable, but still it was an achievement. When we reached the road, wet and hungry, Peter Robinson – a Welshman particularly interested in this battle – remarked that all we needed now was snow, and as he spoke the first flakes began to fall. We were glad to find refuge in the Burma Star café at Poziéres where a prized photograph shows us in good spirits.

Robert Graves, serving with the 2nd Royal Welch Fusiliers, survived the ordeal of Mametz Wood unscathed, but then endured a curious life-threatening experience near Bazentin-le-Petit when his unit was in reserve for the attack on High Wood. A heavy shell landed just behind him, filling his body with metal splinters. He seemed unlikely to survive these terrible wounds and his commanding officer, seeing him that evening, decided he was "a goner" and said so in an official report. His mother was informed that he had "died of wounds" yet a few days later she received a letter from Robert saying he was wounded but alive. The letter was dated 24 July – his 21st birthday. He remained close to death for several days, suffering terribly from the heat,

---

6   Ibid., p. 63.

MA group at the Burma Star café, Poziéres, 28 February 1990. John Lee is second from the left and Brian Bond third from the left respectively; Peter Robinson is third from the right. Standing: Café proprietor Madame Brihier. Notebooks on table; shell cases and rum jar in window. (Author)

the bumpy roads, and railways, and the suppuration of his lesser wounds, but eventually returned to England.

Only whilst convalescing in a Highgate hospital did Graves learn of his official death which greatly amused him. His mother received some effusive letters of condolence from people he could not stand, while *The Times* published a retraction in the "Court Circular" section, graciously withholding their charge.

Graves's misreported death later provided him with the perfect metaphor for his celebrated memoir *Goodbye to All That* (1929); he had decisively ended one period of his life, by dying, only to "rise again" to start afresh. But, unlike some other successful authors of war memoirs, Graves never completely succeeded in putting the war out of his mind. True, in his poetry and novels he embraced new experiences and a new life in Majorca, but he remained intensely proud of his service with the Royal Welch Fusiliers, and would have served again in 1939 had age not condemned him to a desk job which he declined.

The battles fought near Ginchy are worthy of more attention than visitors and historians have given them. I confess that I also neglected these battles when taking groups of students to the Somme. We regularly visited Delville Wood for its cosy cafe and splendid South African memorial but all to the east was, so to speak, off the map. I only became interested in retirement when writing about the Guards Division which had played such an important part in these battles.

The triangle Ginchy – Lesboeufs – Morval seems less appealing to British visitors than other sectors of the 1916 Somme campaign. The eastward thrust has more to do with assisting the French advance than the Allied push northwards towards Bapaume. No spectacular events occurred there in September compared with the much-publicised tank attack against Flers. Above all, the battle area east of Ginchy is now bare and desolate. All traces of the Quadrilateral and Triangle defensive strong points and surrounding German trench lines have disappeared. The beautiful and extensive Guards cemetery lies in Lesboeufs rather than on the battlefield. The visitor must therefore rely on a few roadside memorials to units and individuals.

The attack on 15 September, part of the broad general offensive, with the first use of tanks, was a very costly failure the causes of which are plain to see. Enemy machine-gun posts were still active on the flanks of the start line; tanks and artillery were ineffectual; and the divisions attacking on either side of the Guards made little progress.

Soon after the advance began, the two leading Coldstream battalions which were ahead of the Grenadier Guards veered so far to the left that contact was lost. Consequently the latter found the enemy front line still intact and when the barrage moved on they were isolated. Such confusion reigned that the neatly coloured successive enemy lines on the map quickly lost all significance: leading units believed they were attacking the enemy second or even third lines when they were still fighting to clear his front line.

All battalions suffered heavy fatalities on this chaotic day, the most famous individual loss being the Prime Minister's son, Raymond Asquith. Also killed early in the day was Earl Stanhope's younger brother Dick, serving with 3rd Grenadier Guards. When he was wounded his orderly, Giles, stayed with him in a shell hole, but he insisted on climbing out and was killed by a sniper. Giles, also wounded, covered him with a waterproof sheet, but no trace of his body was ever found. Dick's child arrived, stillborn, on the day after he was killed.[7]

Perhaps the most positive feature of this disastrous day was that the Guards attacked with their customary determination and in this case, ferocity. Oliver Lyttelton (later Lord Chandos) who distinguished himself and was immediately awarded a D.S.O, recounts how his men, seeing a group of Germans just in front of them uttered "a hoarse blood cry", rushed the line "and before we could stop them bayoneted or shot most of the defenders ... After that, nothing would have stopped the Grenadiers – nothing."[8] He admits that he too, for a few minutes, was fighting mad. With only a

---

7   Brian Bond (ed.), *War Memoirs of Earl Stanhope of Chevening: General Staff Officer in France 1914-1918* (Brighton: Tom Donovan, 2006), pp. xii, 94.
8   Oliver Lyttleton Chandos, *The War Memoirs of Lord Chandos* (London: Bodley Head, 1962), pp. 60-64.

dozen or so mixed Guardsmen, he cleared a trench and captured about one hundred prisoners. Lyttelton's assorted company advanced so far ahead of the main body that they could even see into the outlying gardens of Lesboeufs. They held out for several hours, expecting reinforcements, but none arrived and they were eventually forced to retreat. Lyttelton's nonchalant account clearly understates the confusion and horror of this day's fighting, though he does mention some of his close friends who were killed.

Harold Macmillan, 4th Grenadier Guards, experienced a traumatic day and nightmarish aftermath, which left wounds that troubled him for the rest of his life. Stuck by a shell fragment below his right kneecap, he stayed with his men until the enemy front trench had been taken. He was then hit at close range by machine gun bullets which penetrated his left thigh while others lodged in his pelvis. He rolled into a deep shell hole and dosed himself with morphine. His position was desperate because he lay between disputed trench lines; shells fell around him; and German soldiers ran around the lip of his shell-hole. An astonishing revelation, which I find credible in such an avid reader, was that he happened to have a copy of Aeschylus' *Prometheus* in Greek in his pocket and read it "intermittently". He lay there alone for more than twelve hours without water and fearing that he might have been wounded in a vital place. At last, after dark, he was found by a search party and carried back to the captured trench. His ordeal was far from over. Determined to reach the first aid station without stretcher bearers he became separated from another wounded officer in the darkness, and found himself alone and in great pain. He admitted that fear, and even panic, seized him. He was eventually picked up by another battalion's transport but remembered nothing more until, days later, he reached a French military hospital at Abbeville.

The second attack on 25 September was much better organised and started from a stronger position against a weakened enemy. The Allied forward line was pushed beyond Lesboeufs nearly to Le Transloy where it remained for the rest of this campaign. Failure to press on with the advance in the autumn of 1916 was largely determined by the terrible mud which presented almost insurmountable logistic problems. These are vividly described by an unusual officer whose book *A Subaltern on the Somme* (1927) deserves to be better-known. Max Plowman, writing under the pseudonym 'Mark VII', was deeply religious, pacifistic man who, after an initial delay, decided he must "do his bit". As an idealist, already concerned to play a post-war role in securing world peace, he was disgusted by many aspects of Army life, while retaining profound admiration for the ordinary soldiers' cheerfulness and stoic endurance.

In November 1916, Plowman's company experienced heavy rain and appalling muddy conditions in the featureless morass east of Ginchy. In charge of the nightly rations party he recorded that a journey of 3,000 yards took seven hours. His men had reached the very limits of their endurance and suffered badly from frostbite. When they were at last relieved half the men had to be carried off in wagons because they were unable to walk. Plowman did not receive the MC for which he was recommended because the higher command were simply ignorant of the conditions at the front.

This decoration would have greatly helped Plowman in his later conflict with the authorities, as it did the more colourful and famous protester Siegfried Sassoon. In the event, though now thoroughly disillusioned about the war, Plowman carried on until badly concussed and sent home in January 1917. When convalescing Plowman reached the difficult decision that all taking of human life was immoral and he could not be party to it. This raised acute difficulties for the tribunals at home which would probably have been kindly disposed towards his elaborate philosophical justifications had he been willing to make even a token gesture towards supporting the war effort. This he adamantly refused to do, and consequently suffered great hardships (including the desperate plight of his family), and would surely have gone to prison had the war not ended in November 1918.

Plowman was a brooding, difficult man always wrestling with moral issues. He lacked Sassoon's social prestige, literary reputation and glamour, but his protest against the war was more deeply principled and adamantine. Curiously, however, he could not abandon his old soldier's viewpoint that only men who had served at the front were fully deserving of respect, which set him at odds with fellow pacifists. Plowman continued to work for peace in the inter-war decades but was devastated by the failure of his hopes with the outbreak of war in September 1939. The effort to combine writing, administration and hard work in the fields of a co-operative farm proved too much for a man already in poor health. Sick and exhausted, he died in 1941. He surely deserves a biography.

Some of the most bleak and dispiriting conditions of the Somme campaign were experienced at Le Sars and its ironically termed "rest area" around Contalmaison. Even Graham Greenwell's incredibly frank yet also jolly letters to his mother could not conceal the harsh reality of this godforsaken sector. On 2nd November he wrote from bivouacs near Contalmaison, "just a hurried line written amidst the filthiest surroundings; the mud is perfectly ghastly, never have I seen anything like it: men and horses are caked in it from head to foot. It takes ten horses to get the smallest guns about." Two days later he wrote from trenches near Le Sars: "We are living like dogs or rats far from any sign of civilisation … the trenches are absolutely impassable, sometimes waist-deep in liquid mud. Everything has to be carried for miles across country and at night … such food as we can get is gritty with mud, our clothes are caked with it; we think mud, dream mud, and eat mud. Last winter I thought was bad, but this winter … is quite unimaginable."[9] Yet he ended, "Please don't think from this letter that I am at all depressed". On 6th November, he wrote in the dark to say "'Fit as a Flea' but fagged out and absolutely filthy." Two questions must strike us: how did these letters get past the censor, and what effect did they have on his mother?

Charles Carrington has similar descriptions of winter conditions in support at Contalmaison and in the front line at Le Sars. Not a single house or barn remained

---

9   Graham H. Greenwell, *An Infant in Arms: War Letters of a Company Officer 1914-1918* (London: Allen Lane, 1972 reprint of 1932 edition), pp. 145-49.

standing. The stench of rotting corpses was always with them. Some 200,000 men had been killed in the area since 1st July and many them remained unburied or had been hastily buried and then blown out of their shallow graves. At Le Sars the British entered a new "valley of humiliation" in which movement was impossible during daylight. Even without a battle the battalion lost a third of its strength because of sickness and stray shelling on the approach routes. Carrington admits that his morale sunk to its lowest ebb. Exhausted and dispirited, he wrote to his mother that he was "heartily sick of the whole affair", which was the nearest he ever came to an expression of defeatism.

Frederic Manning was a most unusual scholar and soldier. A classical scholar in a prosperous Australian family he moved to England as a young man where he lived a sheltered life with an elderly tutor and guardian, Francis Gaitan. He enlisted, presumably, for patriotic reasons, in 1915 and served for a few months as a private with 7th King's Shropshire Light Infantry. He moved at least a dozen times in this short but hectic tour in which uncertainty, boredom and being "mucked about" were the daily round. He was eventually commissioned but was allowed to resign honourably when unable to perform his duties through bouts of heavy drinking. After the war, when his editor, Peter Davies pressed him to write about his war experiences Manning rapidly produced a masterpiece which is hard to categorise. He wrote eloquently about soldiers and soldiering rather than strategy or battles. His keen ear for the soldiers' slang, gossip and perpetual swearing was skilfully orchestrated to avoid monotony, but even so was deemed too shocking for the general public. As a result, his memoir was published in two editions: an expensive limited edition of *The Middle Parts of Fortune* was published in 1929, and a bowdlerized version as *Her Privates We* in 1930. The author's identity was not revealed in his lifetime (he was simply 'Private 19022') and the original, unexpurgated text was not fully published until 1977.

There was too little dramatic structure in the book for it to be termed a novel, and the author's character was too indirectly portrayed in the central figure of 'Bourne' (no Christian name) for it to be counted a personal memoir. What distinguished the book was its eloquent style; accurate reporting of ordinary soldiers' daily routine and foul language; yet also showing a profound, humane empathy with the stress and hardship of their lives. These crude and simple characters exemplify the underlying theme of the book; namely the vital necessity of 'sticking it out' and not breaking. This permits Manning to cast his former companions in an almost heroic light.

In the culmination of the narrative on 13th November 'Bourne' dies as one of the 214 other ranks lost in the battalion's failed attack in 3rd Division's offensive at Serre. When Bourne dies the perspective is necessarily changed and we see him briefly through his comrades' eyes. His special ally, Sergeant Tozer, quietly accepts the loss "He was sorry about Bourne, he thought, more sorry than he could say … there was a bit of a mystery about him; but then, when you come to think of it, there's a bit of a mystery about all of us."

The Middle Parts of Fortune is so beautifully written that it is easy to read, but also stimulates profound thoughts and emotions. It remains one of my favourite books about soldiering in the First World War and I believe the majority of my graduate students would endorse this opinion.

Although desperate fighting in appalling conditions in the Somme campaign continued to the end of the year, and even into January 1917, the Battle of the Ancre, which began on 13 November, is usually regarded as the final act.

2nd Lieutenant Edmund Blunden, 11th Royal Sussex Regiment, was also engaged in action on that day, but on the north side of the Ancre near Thiepval. There, on 21 October, he had sheltered in a foul shell hole containing two German corpses, and on the next night had led a relief party to reach Sussex survivors stranded in Stuff Trench. On 13 November, with a runner, he was sent on a reconnaissance mission in preparation for an attack on Grandcourt. When caught in a heavy German bombardment he took the bold decision to press on right up to the German front line. This show of bravery, following his admirable conduct in the earlier operation at the Schwaben Redoubt, earned him the Military Cross, a distinction which he does not mention in his memoirs.

Finally, in the early weeks of 1917 Alfred Pollard, a noted 'fire-eater' and recently commissioned into the Honourable Artillery Company, commanded a series of small reconnaissance and bombing parties across the flooded Ancre. After several days of intense fighting, for which he won the Military Cross, he wrote to his mother, "I was the first man over the Hun parapet and landed right on top of two Huns who tried to do me in, but fortunately I managed to finish them off with my jolly old revolver. Hand to hand fighting was rather fun, but we soon cleared them out." Soon afterwards he won a Bar to his MC, writing home "By the way I have killed another Hun. Hurrah." The ultimate distinction of the VC was won by this remarkable killing machine the following year at Gavrelle. The gulf in attitudes towards war and killing between Max Plowman and Alfred Pollard shows how unwise it is to generalise about officers' memoirs of the First World War.

I had not re-read many of the books discussed here since I finished teaching the MA course on war literature and later published *Survivors of a Kind* (2008) which drew on this experience combined with numerous battlefield visits. It has been a great pleasure to re-acquaint myself with the likes of Charles Carrington, Robert Graves, Max Plowman and Frederic Manning – fine, stimulating writers as well as interesting scholars. Whether I shall visit their battlefields again may be doubtful, but the Somme will continue to haunt my imagination and exercise its magnetic attraction.

Index

Index of People

Asquith, Prime Minister Herbert v, 38, 42-43, 45-48, 50, 52, 55-56, 58, 61-62, 68, 505

Balfourier, General Maurice vii, 285-286, 292, 301-302, 304-306, 314, 317, 323
Below, General Fritz von viii, 157-158, 181, 198, 200-201, 214, 216, 218, 241, 266, 276, 307, 365, 383, 420, 460-461, 506
Bernard, Lieutenant-Colonel H.C. 96, 198, 211, 261, 434, 449
Birch, Major General Noel vi, xx, 161-163, 253, 358, 484
Birdwood, Lieutenant-General Sir William vii, 268, 355, 357-362, 366-368
Boening, Lieutenant 208, 223, 226
Byng, Lieutenant-General Julian vii, 268, 370-372, 384, 391-392

Callwell, Charles 56-57, 59, 63
Carrington, Lieutenant Charles 346, 393, 435, 499, 507-509
Charrington, Major Sidney Herbert 440-443, 446-447
Charteris, John 60, 65, 93, 100-105, 107-110
Churchill, Sir Winston xxxi, 42, 46, 48, 55-56, 110, 155, 218, 264, 395, 397-400, 480
Clayton, Sir Frederick 130-132, 135, 202
Congreve, Lieutenant-General Walter vii, xxix, 161, 165, 253, 257, 259, 273-282, 284-286, 288
Cotton, Lieutenant-Colonel 342, 344, 445
Currie, Major-General Arthur vii, xx, 370, 372-373, 375, 381, 384, 391, 393

des Vallières, General Pierre 99, 104, 106-108, 110, 114

Dumas, Lieutenant 208, 223, 225-226, 228, 231, 250

Edmonds, Brigadier-General Sir James xxv-xxvi, 35, 55, 98, 102, 109, 119-121, 137, 139, 142, 148, 151, 154, 165-168, 172, 194-198, 202, 206, 212-213, 220, 249, 254-258, 260-261, 263-264, 266-267, 275, 287, 334-342, 344, 346, 350-351, 372, 374, 376, 380, 382, 435, 451, 475-476, 499
Elles, Major-General Hugh 120, 395, 399, 413

Falkenhayn, General Erich von 35-36, 83, 93-95, 97-98, 104, 112-113, 116, 227, 453, 462
Fayolle, General Émile vii, 121, 142-143, 153, 158, 293, 295-297, 301-302, 316
ffrench-Mullen, Captain Ernest 214, 217, 237, 243-244, 250-251
Foch, General Ferdinand xxii, 35, 90, 142-146, 152-155, 160, 163, 293-295, 300, 311, 317, 487
French, Field Marshal Sir John iv-vi, ix-x, xiii, xix-xxii, xxvii-xxx, 33-36, 38-42, 45-46, 48, 50-51, 53-57, 59, 61-65, 69, 74, 76, 78-79, 82-83, 88-89, 93-95, 97-125, 127, 129, 131, 133-134, 137, 142-148, 150-160, 162-164, 166-167, 172, 174, 193, 196, 199, 201-202, 205-206, 231, 246, 255, 265, 270-272, 285-287, 291-293, 297-301, 304, 306, 310-312, 314-316, 323, 329, 332, 351-352, 359, 391-393, 396-398, 400, 414, 453-455, 460-462, 464, 466, 471, 478, 480, 482, 487, 505-506

Index   511

Frizzell, Lieutenant-Colonel Charles William 440-441, 445, 447

Geddes, Sir Eric v, xxi, 117, 122, 128-130, 132-134, 137-138
George V, King v, 56-57, 61, 68
Goodman, Lieutenant-Colonel G.D. viii, 435-437, 443, 449
Gough, General Sir Herbert vii, 51, 83, 89, 91, 268, 324, 326, 350-352, 354-357, 359-361, 365-368, 371, 373-374, 383-385, 390-391, 405, 494
Graves, Captain Robert x, 182, 251, 372, 392, 452, 480, 483, 485, 497-498, 503-504, 508-509

Haig, General Sir Douglas iii, v, xii, xiv, xvi, xx, xxvi, xxix, 37-38, 43, 45-48, 50-53, 57, 60, 63-68, 71-114, 116, 118, 123, 127-131, 133-137, 144-146, 151, 155-162, 166-168, 192-193, 245, 252-253, 255, 257-258, 260, 262-266, 268, 271, 273, 277-278, 327-328, 351, 358-359, 367, 385, 391, 399-400, 410, 412, 420-421, 423, 433, 451, 464-465, 468, 484
Haldane, Major-General J.A.L. 54, 248, 259, 265, 414-417
Headlam, Major General Sir John 162, 192, 253, 256
Hentig, Captain Hans von 451-452, 464-465, 472
Hindenburg, Field Marshal Paul von 36, 453, 457, 461, 468
Horne, Lieutenant-General Henry Sinclair iv, vi, xiii-xiv, xxix, 161, 252-263, 265-269, 277
Hudson, Major-General Havelock vi, 196-197, 235, 237-239, 242
Hughes, Brigadier-General Garnett vii, 290, 373, 376-377, 380, 382, 384-385, 389-390, 500-501

Irwin, Major Alfred P.B. 440-441, 443-444, 447-449

Jardine, Brigadier-General James 338-340, 342, 344
Joffre, General Joseph v, 33, 39, 61, 64, 68, 74-75, 79-80, 88, 94, 99, 102, 104-110, 113-114, 118, 123, 127, 145-146, 153, 166-167, 292, 302, 412

Kiggell, Lieutenant-General Sir Launcelot 65-67, 120, 127, 155, 162, 257, 262, 351, 400, 405-406
Kitchener, Field Marshal Lord v, xix, 42, 46-51, 55-58, 60-61, 66-67, 69, 73, 80, 106-107, 114, 127, 175, 265, 325, 339, 399, 415, 417, 419, 427-428, 492

Lake, Second Lieutenant W.V.C. 214-215, 243, 250
Liddell Hart, Basil xii, 53, 93, 120, 253, 259, 278, 394, 399-400, 407-409, 413, 476, 502
Lloyd George, David 33, 36, 42, 48, 50, 52, 56-58, 64, 66-70, 85, 122, 127-134, 159, 264, 411, 476, 500
Lucas, Major C. C. 59, 257, 371
Ludendorff, General Erich von 36, 90, 453, 457, 468, 473

Macdonogh, Major-General Sir George 46, 60, 98, 107-108
Mahon, Captain J. H. 64-65, 187-188, 192
Maxse, Major-General Ivor vii, xxix-xxx, 272-274, 278-283, 289, 291, 327, 339, 439-441, 443-444, 446, 448
Mayne, Major E.C. 214, 220, 235-239, 250
Middlebrook, Martin 284, 492-494, 497, 500
Montgomery, Brigadier-General Archibald xxx, 75, 257, 267, 272, 281-283, 291
Morland, Lieutenant-General Sir Thomas 161, 203, 206, 242, 341

Pétain, General Philippe 142, 145-146, 153, 163
Plowman, Max viii, 488, 506-507, 509
Pollard, Brigadier-General J.H.W. vi, 199, 213, 215, 236-238, 242, 246, 498, 509
Price, Captain H. xxix, 121, 156, 174, 178, 183, 272, 327, 369, 440-442, 446-448, 477
Pulteney, Lieutenant-General Sir William vi, 161, 195-197, 218, 233, 239, 243, 246-247

Rawlinson, General Sir Henry vii, xxiii, 37-38, 51, 72, 74-85, 87-91, 118-119, 121, 127, 139, 145, 154-155, 158-162,

179, 196, 218, 232-234, 239-240, 243, 245-246, 253, 255, 257-259, 262, 265, 268, 277-278, 284, 324, 334, 338-339, 346, 350, 352, 405
Robertson, General Sir William iii, v, xv, xxix, 37-38, 46-48, 50, 52-70, 93, 98, 103, 105-110, 113-114, 127, 131-132, 167, 252-253, 257, 259, 265, 268, 278, 360, 365
Rupprecht, Crown Prince viii, 35, 457-458, 463, 466-471
Rycroft, Major-General W.H. vii, 334-336, 338, 340-341, 344-345, 349-352

Sassoon, Second Lieutenant Siegfried 191, 498-500, 507
Sawyer, Major G.H 236, 238, 240, 433
Scott, Lieutenant A.B. 331-332, 379-380, 440-441, 443, 447
Shea, Major-General John vii, xxix, 165, 273-274, 279-280, 283
Stradtmann, Lieutenant 208, 211, 222-226, 250
Swinton, Colonel E. D. vii, 84-85, 395-407, 410-413, 483

Thring, Edward 421, 423, 425
Turner, Major-General Richard 249, 372, 374, 376
Tuxford, Brigadier-General George S. vii, 373, 376, 382

Vaughan, Brigadier-General Sir LouisR. 253-255, 259, 360, 494
Vietinghoff, *Oberst Freiherr* von 206, 218-220, 227-228, 230-231, 246
Vuillemot, General Eugene 304-305, 317, 321

Wagener, Captain Otto 208, 211, 219-227, 229, 246, 249, 251
Watts, Major-General H.E. vi, 259, 263, 265-266, 380
Whigham, Major-General Robert 59-60, 252, 406
Whitfield, Lieutenant W.H.P. 214-215, 217-220, 240, 242, 247-248, 250
Wilson, Field Marshal Sir Henry xv, 36, 48, 63, 70, 121, 268, 277-278, 285, 396
Wisser, Assistant-Surgeon 208, 219, 226
Woodroffe, Colonel C.R. 120, 122, 129, 133-134

Index of Places

Africa xiv, xix, 49, 144, 196, 213-214, 371, 440, 485-486, 493-494
Aisne 148, 273, 278
Albert vii, 78, 119, 122, 124, 144, 155, 178, 197, 214, 219, 227, 249, 267, 270, 324, 326, 356, 398-399, 477-479, 482, 484, 487, 497-498
Amiens xiii, 85, 118-119, 122, 124, 131, 136, 196, 260, 281, 477
Ancre River viii-ix, 88-89, 227, 255, 335, 337, 351, 373, 469, 487, 509
Arras 101, 109, 118-119, 146, 190, 263, 271, 393, 466
Artois xxvii, 144-145, 202, 271, 292-293, 297, 310, 329
Aubers 57, 139, 150-154, 166, 196
Austria-Hungary xxix, 35-38, 40, 64, 453, 463
Authuille 197, 335, 344-345, 434, 449
Avoca Valley 197, 212, 251

Bapaume 78, 80, 144, 146, 155, 162, 197, 249, 270, 356, 479, 482, 487, 498, 505

Beaumont Hamel xiv, 75, 89, 160, 245, 434
Bécourt vi, 197, 207, 212-214, 227, 250-251
Belgium xix, xxv, 33, 35, 37, 39-40, 95, 98-100, 104, 109, 116, 119, 123, 139, 165, 194-198, 202, 206, 208, 212-213, 220, 249, 255-257, 259-261, 267, 275, 339, 356-357, 372, 374, 398, 451, 475
Berlin 90, 96, 114, 233, 452-454, 466-467
Besenhecke 203, 209, 220, 223, 227
Birmingham xiii-xv, xxii-xxiii, xxvii, 122, 196, 263, 328, 482

Cambrai xiii, 85, 195, 457
Canada xv, 370-372, 374, 377, 379-381, 390
Carnoy 129, 172, 234, 245, 283, 288-290
Champagne 95, 99-101, 104, 107-109, 144-145, 150, 293, 307-308, 437, 489
Chantilly v, 33-35, 37-38, 41, 46, 51, 75, 118, 146, 166
Chatham 121, 135, 163, 409
Combles viii, 76, 465
Contalmaison 198, 200, 205, 507

Corbie 120, 244, 321
Courcelette vii, ix, 83, 373-374, 376, 385, 487
Curlu vii, 196, 313-314, 320, 323

Dardanelles 40, 46-47, 56-58, 61-62, 64, 372
Delville Wood 80, 83, 188, 259, 443-444, 449, 483, 485-486, 494, 498, 503, 505
Dernacourt 214, 240, 243
Dublin xix, 44-45, 195, 217, 232, 432, 483, 494

Egypt xix, 44-45, 47, 64-65, 196, 206, 213, 250, 253, 354-355

Festubert 57, 153-154, 166, 253, 354, 388
Flanders 53, 62-63, 66, 74, 95, 98-99, 118, 180, 196, 199, 395, 485, 491-492
Flers ix, 80, 83, 87, 261, 267, 373, 413, 455, 505
Fricourt 75, 78, 121-122, 145, 200, 245, 253, 255-256, 262, 434, 499
Frise vii, 144, 202, 295, 313, 319

Gallipoli xiv, 40, 42, 45, 48-49, 51, 57, 63-64, 66, 206, 247, 355, 497
Givenchy 153, 182, 383
Gommecourt 160, 435, 499
Greece 35, 40, 64, 485

High Wood 82-83, 259, 503
Holland 97, 122, 132, 484
Hooge 273, 275, 280, 284-286

India 45, 196, 264, 268
Ireland v-vi, 43-44, 232, 239, 248, 479, 483, 493-494
Italy xix, 40-41, 45, 49, 166-167, 453

La Boisselle iii, vi, viii-ix, xxix, 134, 145, 169, 175, 179, 194-195, 197-201, 203-204, 206-228, 230, 237, 240-242, 245, 247, 249, 251, 288, 478, 499
Leipzig Redoubt 145, 340, 342, 345, 348
Leipzig Salient vii, 340-341, 350
Lens xxviii, 152, 352, 393, 474, 486
Liverpool vi, 165, 172, 174, 187, 189, 191, 289
Loos xxv, xxvii, 57, 74, 98, 118, 153-154, 166, 185, 189-190, 260, 268, 272, 284, 354

Mametz viii, 78, 129, 145, 253, 256-257, 262-263, 266, 270, 340, 488-489, 500-503
Maricourt v, 123, 125, 172, 270, 279, 288, 304, 306, 311, 315, 320-322
Marne River 38, 148, 292, 299
Mash Valley 197, 207, 212, 492
Mesopotamia xix, 44-45, 62-63
Meuse 95, 104-105, 108, 110, 113, 156
Middle East xix, 45, 64, 68, 250
Montauban iv, vii, 78, 144-146, 155, 158, 257, 270, 277, 287-289, 319, 339, 436-437, 449
Morval 35, 267, 469, 482, 505

Neuve Chapelle 57, 74, 77-78, 146, 150-152, 154, 162, 196, 273, 350
New Zealand xix, 44, 267, 372
Newfoundland viii, 44, 431-432, 482-487, 493-494, 498

Ovillers 145, 197-200, 207, 212-213, 219, 226-227, 237, 249, 434-435, 482, 487, 499

Paris v, 33, 47, 95-96, 98, 100, 109, 119, 152, 292-293, 297, 300-301, 303, 314, 316, 319, 451, 454
Passchendaele xiv, xvi, 72, 91, 118, 191, 391, 476, 478, 493
Picardy xx, 118, 136, 199, 261, 477-478, 491, 493, 496
Pozières iv, vi-vii, ix, xiii, xxviii, xxx, 76, 80, 229, 354-361, 364-366, 368-369, 435, 455, 479

Romania xix, 36-37, 40, 52, 68, 453, 459
Russia xix, 38-41, 45, 48, 50, 64, 97, 102, 166-167, 453

Salonika xix, 35, 41, 62-65, 68
Sausage Valley 134, 198, 212, 249, 251
Schwaben Redoubt 162, 445-446, 509
Serbia 40-41, 64, 98-99
Serre 146, 155, 160, 204, 482, 508
Somerset 180-181, 419, 424-425, 434
Somme River/Region iii-vi, viii-ix, xiii-xv, xix-xxi, xxiii, xxv-xxxi, 33-38, 43-44, 48-52, 66, 68, 71-85, 87-92, 94, 104, 107, 111, 113-115, 117-123, 125-128, 131, 133-134, 136-137, 139, 141-142, 144, 146, 150, 153-155, 157-159, 161-168,

172, 175, 191-192, 194-202, 205, 211, 214, 227, 245-247, 249-253, 255-257, 259-262, 267-274, 276, 279, 281, 283-284, 286-288, 290-293, 295-299, 302, 304-305, 307-308, 310-312, 314, 316, 318-322, 325, 329, 333-335, 340, 348-349, 351-352, 354-361, 364, 366-369, 371-372, 379-385, 389-394, 398, 406, 410, 413, 415, 430-431, 435, 437-440, 443-445, 447-448, 450-455, 457-468, 470-480, 482-500, 503, 505-507, 509
South Africa 196, 213-214, 440, 485-486, 493-494
Suez Canal 39, 45, 252
Suzanne 303-305, 321-322

Thiepval vii-ix, 75, 79-80, 145, 162, 174, 179, 205, 242, 245, 285, 324, 334-335, 340-344, 347, 349, 360-361, 365, 367, 373-374, 445-446, 448-449, 478-481, 483-484, 495, 498, 509

Uppingham School xiii, 420-421, 423-425, 427

Verdun iii, v, xix-xxi, xxix, 34, 36-37, 50, 74-75, 79, 82, 88, 93-116, 120, 122, 145-146, 155-158, 162-163, 202, 206, 227, 231, 233, 292, 298, 308, 370-371, 391-393, 453-455, 458-463, 467, 470, 472
Vimy 150, 152-154, 202, 372, 392-393

Woolwich 267, 411, 425

Ypres 35, 48, 76, 91, 98, 119, 137, 202, 247, 271, 372-373, 390, 474-479, 481, 491, 493, 496

Index of Military Formations & Units

Armies:
British Expeditionary Force (BEF) iii, x, xix-xxii, xxvi, xxviii-xxx, 37, 43, 45-46, 48, 51, 53-54, 56-57, 59-60, 69, 71-77, 79, 81-82, 84, 87-89, 91-93, 98, 102, 106, 108, 116-140, 143-145, 148, 150, 153-154, 158-159, 163-169, 172, 184, 192-193, 195-196, 202, 248, 260, 262-263, 265, 271-274, 280-281, 284, 291, 324-326, 332-333, 338, 344, 346, 348, 352-353, 383, 391-393, 397, 399-400, 431, 438-439, 490
First Army 46-47, 146, 150-151, 153-154, 196, 215, 252, 261, 268, 273, 393
Second Army 77, 170, 180, 265
Third Army 186, 196, 246, 430
Fourth Army xiii, 37, 51, 74, 76, 81, 83, 118-124, 127, 139, 143-146, 154-155, 157-159, 161-162, 168, 196-197, 199, 202, 208, 218, 233-235, 238-240, 242, 245-246, 253, 257-258, 262-263, 265, 267, 272, 274, 285, 302, 334, 339, 346, 360-361, 365-367, 371, 373, 376, 405, 477
Fifth Army/Reserve Army xx, 51, 83, 89, 98, 202, 268, 324, 350-351, 354, 356-357, 359-362, 365-368, 371, 373, 376, 382-384, 386, 390, 405, 453

Indian Army 44-45, 264, 279, 430, 432, 439-440
New Army xix, xxvi, xxxi, 33, 51, 73, 83, 164, 175, 179, 192, 199, 206, 262, 265, 272, 274, 291, 324, 408, 415, 417, 419-420, 427-428, 430-433, 439, 450, 476, 488
Territorial Force (TF) xi, 248, 416-417, 430-433, 435, 439, 450

French
French Army x, xiii, xx, xxii, xxvii-xxviii, 33, 36, 48, 64, 76, 93, 107-108, 114, 122, 129, 133, 137, 152, 157-158, 205, 255, 271-272, 285-286, 292-293, 299, 306, 316, 329
First Army 35
Sixth Army 93, 98, 119, 133-134, 202, 352
Tenth Army 102-104, 106, 108

German
German Army iv, viii, xii, xxvii, xxx-xxxi, 36-37, 60, 72, 84, 90, 93, 97, 111, 113, 115, 150, 193, 197, 200, 202, 204-205, 227, 245, 288, 314, 329, 332, 380, 451-452, 454, 456, 460, 462-465, 467-468, 471-473

Index   515

First Army 467-468
Second Army 200, 202, 205-206, 227, 457, 460, 467-468

Corps:
I Corps 151, 161, 354
II Corps 360, 363, 365, 367, 370, 374, 376
III Corps vi, 100-101, 112, 120, 144-145, 158, 160, 194, 196-199, 205-206, 208, 215-216, 218, 220-222, 224, 226-227, 231-233, 235-236, 238-240, 242-243, 246, 249, 277, 383, 386
IV Corps 36, 150-151
VII Corps 142, 160, 275
VIII Corps xiv, 145, 158, 160, 168, 174, 196, 213, 243, 247, 360
X Corps 145, 158, 162, 196, 199, 205, 242, 333-334, 341, 350, 360
XIII Corps iv, ix, xxix, 78-79, 82, 144-145, 158, 165, 196, 198, 234, 253, 257-258, 261, 270-279, 281-291, 293, 307
XIV Corps 88, 204-205, 267
XV Corps ix, 78, 100-101, 145, 158, 161, 197, 252-261, 267-268, 277
I Anzac Corps vi, 229, 354-357, 359-362, 364-369, 373
Canadian Corps xv, xxviii, 280, 370-374, 376-378, 382, 384-385, 387, 389, 391, 393
Indian Corps 150-151, 196

French
I Colonial Corps 286, 293, 307, 312
XX Corps iv, vii, ix, xxix, 145, 285-286, 292-294, 296-297, 299, 301-308, 310-315, 317-318

German
XIV Reserve Corps xxviii, 194, 200-203, 206, 245, 250, 473

Divisions:
1st Australian Division 356-357, 365-366
1st Canadian Division 370, 372-374, 376, 381-385, 387, 391-392
2nd Division 265
2nd Australian Division 360
2nd Canadian Division 372-374, 376
3rd Division xxi, 258-259, 265, 391, 508
3rd Canadian Division 372-373, 374, 376, 382
4th Division 160

4th Australian Division 360, 365
4th Canadian Division 383
6th Division 273, 275-276, 279
7th Division 256-259, 263, 265, 354
8th Division vi, 172, 191, 196-197, 199, 201, 207, 211-221, 224, 226-227, 232, 234-236, 238-239, 243-244, 246, 248-249
9th (Scottish) Division 272, 284
17th (Northern) Division 262-263, 265-266
18th (Eastern) Division 234, 271, 273, 278-279, 281-283, 286, 288-291, 325, 339, 436, 439, 441-444, 446-448
23rd Division 179, 199, 262, 386
29th Division 160, 174-175, 213, 227, 247
30th Division 165, 172, 174, 272-273, 279-281, 283, 286, 288, 291, 304
32nd Division iv, xxvii, xxx, 199, 203-204, 206, 242, 324, 328, 330-336, 338, 340, 342, 344-346, 348-352
34th Division 175-180, 194, 196, 249
36th (Ulster) Division 166, 339, 342, 483
48th (South Midland) Division 160, 363, 499

French
11th Division 298, 303-308, 311, 314, 317
39th Division 286, 304-307, 311, 315, 317

German
5th Ersatz Division 470-471
6th Infantry Division 470
15th Division 457
26th Reserve Division vi, 200, 204, 213
28th Reserve Division 200
29th Infantry Division 470-471
39th Bavarian Reserve Division 453-454, 459
53rd Reserve Division 460
206th Infantry Division 470
211th Infantry Division 470
Guard Reserve Division 451-452

Brigades:
1st Canadian Brigade 371, 373, 376, 379-386, 389
2nd Canadian Brigade 374,
3rd Canadian Brigade 373, 376, 379-380, 382, 390
7th Brigade 171, 373, 376-377, 389
14th Brigade 324, 340, 345, 349
21st Brigade 172, 303, 311, 317

22nd Brigade 311, 314, 317
25th Brigade vi, 199, 213-215, 221, 235-236, 238, 243-244, 246
55th Brigade 436-437, 441, 444-445
70th Brigade 199, 212-213, 215, 217, 243
87th Brigade 174, 213, 227, 247
89th Brigade 165, 172, 174, 276, 279, 281-282, 286, 288
96th Brigade 204, 206, 324, 340
97th Brigade 324, 338-340, 342, 344-345, 348-349
164th Brigade 186, 188, 332

Regiments/Battalions:
7th Bedfordshire Regiment 283, 288-290, 440-441, 446, 448
11th Border Regiment 335, 344, 348, 434
7th Buffs (East Kent Regiment) 436, 441, 446-447
1st Dorsetshire Regiment 198, 201
8th East Surrey Regiment 436-437, 440-441, 444, 448
10th Essex Regiment 203, 246-247, 281-282, 440-441, 443-445
17th Highland Light Infantry vi, 173, 242, 324, 340
18th King's Liverpool Regiment 172, 174, 289
15th Lancashire Fusiliers 332, 340-341, 349
16th Lancashire Fusiliers 324, 341, 348
19th Lancashire Fusiliers 324, 335, 345
12th Middlesex Regiment 234, 440-442, 445, 448
2nd Rifle Brigade 199, 213, 240
2nd Royal Berkshire Regiment 199, 213-217, 219-221, 226, 232, 236, 433
Royal Irish Fusiliers 214, 440, 449
1st Royal Irish Rifles 214-217, 219-222, 224, 226, 228, 232, 235, 237-238, 240, 242-244, 247, 249, 251

2nd Royal Welsh Fusiliers 166, 182, 183-184
15th Royal Welch Fusiliers 185, 340
7th Royal West Kent Regiment 437, 441, 446
Scottish Rifles 169, 182-183, 199
Sherwood Foresters 199, 427-428, 434-436
South Wales Borderers 174, 213, 408
Suffolk Regiment 362, 445, 447
West Yorkshire Regiment 214, 419, 440

Canadian
1st Battalion 386
2nd Battalion 380, 384, 384-389
3rd Battalion 380-381, 382, 384, 386-388
4th Battalion 380-381, 383, 385-388
5th Battalion 382
8th Battalion 381
13th Battalion 382, 386
15th Battalion 382
22nd Battalion 375
24th Battalion 375-376
25th Battalion 375-376
42nd Battalion 377
43rd Battalion 377-379
49th Battalion 377-378, 389
58th Battalion 378
72nd Battalion 380
Royal Canadian Regiment (RCR) 377

Newfoundland Regiment 44, 431-432, 483

Machine Gun Corps 399, 404, 406
Royal Artillery ii, xi, xv, 152, 161-162, 257, 259-261, 267, 288, 338, 349, 355, 383, 385, 403, 415, 425, 462
Royal Engineers x-xi, 121-123, 126, 181, 192, 198, 215, 335, 415

Index of General & Miscellaneous Terms

Armistice 118, 191, 438, 447

Battles:
  Ancre ix, 89, 335, 351, 487, 509
  Loos xxv, 154, 260, 272, 284, 354
  Pozières Ridge xiii, xxviii, 354-356, 359
  Second Battle of Artois xxvii, 144, 271, 292, 329
  Somme iii, ix, xiv-xv, xxv-xxxi, 33-38, 43-44, 48-49, 51-52, 68, 74, 76, 79, 88-89, 117-119, 125, 127, 164-165, 168, 175, 192, 202, 247, 250, 252, 256, 262, 269-273, 276, 279, 284, 292-293, 299, 310, 316, 325, 334, 355, 398, 415, 439, 451, 453, 460-462, 465-467, 471, 473, 487, 494, 500
  Verdun iii, 34, 93-95, 109, 111, 115, 162
Boer War xiv, 39, 54, 65, 121, 273, 275, 279, 286, 327-328, 416-417, 423
Brusilov Offensive xix, 35-37, 112, 453-454, 459

Central Powers xix, 33, 35, 37, 39, 41, 49, 52, 62, 64, 68, 118, 146, 283, 453
Chantilly Conference 33, 38, 41, 51, 118

Distinguished Service Order x, 185, 203, 380, 387, 423, 440, 444

Entente xiii, 38, 62, 64, 329

Liberal Party xiv, 50, 52, 56, 416

Military Cross 174, 178, 191, 243, 250, 375, 506, 509

Russo-Japanese War 140, 148, 163, 339

Second World War 249, 351, 428, 490, 496

Victoria Cross vi, viii, xi, xxix, 121, 164-165, 185-188, 191, 253, 261, 273, 276, 380, 442, 509

Wolverhampton Military Studies
www.helion.co.uk/wolverhamptonmilitarystudies

Editorial board

Professor Stephen Badsey
Wolverhampton University

Professor Michael Bechthold
Wilfred Laurier University

Professor John Buckley
Wolverhampton University

Major General (Retired) John Drewienkiewicz

Ashley Ekins
Australian War Memorial

Dr Howard Fuller
Wolverhampton University

Dr Spencer Jones
Wolverhampton University

Nigel de Lee
Norwegian War Academy

Major General (Retired) Mungo Melvin President of the British Commission for Military History

Dr Michael Neiberg
US Army War College

Dr Eamonn O'Kane
Wolverhampton University

Professor Fransjohan Pretorius
University of Pretoria

Dr Simon Robbins
Imperial War Museum

Professor Gary Sheffield
Wolverhampton University

Commander Steve Tatham PhD
Royal Navy
The Influence Advisory Panel

Professor Malcolm Wanklyn
Wolverhampton University

Professor Andrew Wiest University of Southern Mississippi

Submissions

The publishers would be pleased to receive submissions for this series. Please contact us via email (info@helion.co.uk), or in writing to Helion & Company Limited, 26 Willow Road, Solihull, West Midlands, B91 1UE.

Titles

No.1 *Stemming the Tide. Officers and Leadership in the British Expeditionary Force 1914* Edited by Spencer Jones (ISBN 978-1-909384-45-3)

No.2 *'Theirs Not To Reason Why'. Horsing the British Army 1875–1925* Graham Winton (ISBN 978-1-909384-48-4)

No.3 *A Military Transformed? Adaptation and Innovation in the British Military, 1792–1945* Edited by Michael LoCicero, Ross Mahoney and Stuart Mitchell (ISBN 978-1-909384-46-0)

No.4 *Get Tough Stay Tough. Shaping the Canadian Corps, 1914–1918* Kenneth Radley (ISBN 978-1-909982-86-4)

No.5 *A Moonlight Massacre: The Night Operation on the Passchendaele Ridge, 2 December 1917. The Forgotten Last Act of the Third Battle of Ypres* Michael LoCicero (ISBN 978-1-909982-92-5)

No.6 *Shellshocked Prophets. Former Anglican Army Chaplains in Interwar Britain* Linda Parker (ISBN 978-1-909982-25-3)

No.7 *Flight Plan Africa: Portuguese Airpower in Counterinsurgency, 1961–1974* John P. Cann (ISBN 978-1-909982-06-2)

No.8 *Mud, Blood and Determination. The History of the 46th (North Midland) Division in the Great War* Simon Peaple (ISBN 978 1 910294 66 6)

No.9 *Commanding Far Eastern Skies. A Critical Analysis of the Royal Air Force Superiority Campaign in India, Burma and Malaya 1941–1945* Peter Preston-Hough (ISBN 978 1 910294 44 4)

No.10 *Courage Without Glory. The British Army on the Western Front 1915* Edited by Spencer Jones (ISBN 978 1 910777 18 3)

No.11 *The Airborne Forces Experimental Establishment: The Development of British Airborne Technology 1940–1950* Tim Jenkins (ISBN 978-1-910777-06-0)

No.12 *'Allies are a Tiresome Lot' – The British Army in Italy in the First World War* John Dillon (ISBN 978 1 910777 32 9)

No.13 *Monty's Functional Doctrine: Combined Arms Doctrine in British 21st Army Group in Northwest Europe, 1944–45* Charles Forrester (ISBN 978-1-910777-26-8)

No.14 *Early Modern Systems of Command: Queen Anne's Generals, Staff Officers and the Direction of Allied Warfare in the Low Countries and Germany, 1702–11* Stewart Stansfield (ISBN 978 1 910294 47 5)

No.15 *They Didn't Want To Die Virgins: Sex and Morale in the British Army on the Western Front 1914–1918* Bruce Cherry (ISBN 978-1-910777-70-1)

No.16 *From Tobruk to Tunis: The Impact of Terrain on British Operations and Doctrine in North Africa, 1940–1943* Neal Dando (ISBN 978-1-910294-00-0)

No.17 *Crossing No Man's Land: Experience and Learning with the Northumberland Fusiliers in the Great War* Tony Ball (ISBN 978-1-910777-73-2)

No.18 *"Everything worked like clockwork": The Mechanization of the British Cavalry between the Two World Wars* Roger E Salmon (ISBN 978-1-910777-96-1)

No.19 *Attack on the Somme: 1st Anzac Corps and the Battle of Pozières Ridge, 1916* Meleah Hampton (ISBN 978-1-910777-65-7)

No.20 *Operation Market Garden: The Campaign for the Low Countries, Autumn 1944: Seventy Years On* Edited by John Buckley & Peter Preston Hough (ISBN 978 1 910777 15 2)

No.21 *Enduring the Whirlwind: The German Army and the Russo-German War 1941-1943* Gregory Liedtke (ISBN 978-1-910777-75-6)

No.22 *'Glum Heroes': Hardship, fear and death – Resilience and Coping in the British Army on the Western Front 1914-1918* Peter E. Hodgkinson (ISBN 978-1-910777-78-7)

No.23 *Much Embarrassed: Civil War Intelligence and the Gettysburg Campaign* George Donne (ISBN 978-1-910777-86-2)

No.24 *They Called It Shell Shock: Combat Stress in the First World War* Stefanie Linden (ISBN 978-1-911096-35-1)

No. 25 *New Approaches to the Military History of the English Civil War. Proceedings of the First Helion & Company 'Century of the Soldier' Conference* Ismini Pells (editor) (ISBN 978-1-911096-44-3)

No.26 *Reconographers: Intelligence and Reconnaissance in British Tank Operations on the Western Front 1916-18* Colin Hardy (ISBN: 978-1-911096-28-3)

No.27 *Britain's Quest for Oil: The First World War and the Peace Conferences* Martin Gibson (ISBN: 978-1-911512-07-3)

No.28 *Unfailing Gallantry: 8th (Regular) Division in the Great War 1914-1919* Alun Thomas (ISBN: 978-1-910777-61-9)

No.29 *An Army of Brigadiers: British Brigade Commanders at the Battle of Arras 1917* Trevor Harvey (ISBN: 978-1-911512-00-4)

No.30 *At All Costs: The British Army on the Western Front 1916* Edited by Spencer Jones (ISBN 978-1-912174-88-1)